Changing Women,
Changing History

71025

Changing Women, Changing History

A Bibliography of the History of Women in Canada
Second edition

Women's Experience Series #9

Diana Pedersen

CARLETON UNIVERSITY PRESS

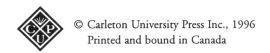 © Carleton University Press Inc., 1996
Printed and bound in Canada

Canadian Cataloguing in Publication Data

Pedersen, Diana L. (Diana Lynn)
    Changing women, changing history : a
bibliography of the history of women in Canada

2nd ed.
(Women's experience series ; 9)
ISBN 0-88629-280-8

    1. Women—Canada—History—Bibliography
I. Title. II. Series

Z7964.C3P44 1996   016.3054'0971'09   C96-900409-5

Cover design: Barbara Cumming, Carleton University Press.

Cover photograph: "The mail carrier at Point au Baril on Georgian Bay," by
Edith S. Watson. Source: Frances Rooney, *Working Light: The Wandering Life of
Photographer Edith S. Watson.* Ottawa: Carleton University Press, 1996. Used by
permission of Frances Rooney.

Carleton University Press gratefully acknowledges the support extended to its
publishing program by the Canada Council and the financial assistance of the
Ontario Arts Council. The Press would also like to thank the Department of
Canadian Heritage, Government of Canada, and the Government of Ontario
through the Ministry of Culture, Tourism and Recreation for their
assistance.

For Deborah Gorham, mentor and friend, and for my students,
in hopes that I may be for them what she has been for me

CONTENTS

HOW TO USE THIS BIBLIOGRAPHY

IF YOU HAVE A GENERAL AREA of interest such as Education or Religion, begin by examining the Table of Contents to locate the appropriate section of the bibliography. Note that the larger sections have been divided into sub-sections to facilitate your search. Each section is introduced by a mini-essay that will introduce you to the scholarship in this area and highlight some of its most important features.

If you have in mind a specific individual, organization, place or event, turn to the Subject Index for a more detailed list of entries which supplement but do not duplicate the entries in the Table of Contents. An entry in the subject index may direct you to citations in several different sections of the bibliography.

If you are interested in the work of a particular author, consult the Author Index for a listing of all the citations in this bibliography by that particular author. Again, these may appear in several different sections.

Note: Make full use of the Table of Contents, the Subject Index, and the Author Index. They are designed to be used together, so do not attempt to rely on only one of them. For example, studies of First Nations women will be found throughout this bibliography. You should begin your search by locating the First Nations section in the Table of Contents. After perusing this section, turn to the Subject Index where the more detailed entries for Inuit women, the Indian Act, Molly Brant, and the Native Women's Association of Canada, among others, will direct you to many more citations in other sections of the bibliography. Remember that if you find something useful by a particular author, you can use the Author Index to locate additional related citations by the same author that may appear in other sections of the bibliography.

INTRODUCTION

NOT SO LONG AGO, Canadian women's history presented a much less daunting challenge to the prospective bibliographer. The astonishing growth of this vibrant field in little more than two decades has been documented over the years in a series of review articles that began with Veronica Strong-Boag's "Cousin Cinderella," its title a commentary on the marginal status of Canadian women's history in 1973. In 1994, by contrast, Wendy Mitchinson's update constituted a chapter in the major bibliographic guide to post-Confederation Canadian historical scholarship.[1] Since its founding in 1975, the Canadian Committee on Women's History (CCWH) has become one of the largest and most active subgroups of the Canadian Historical Association, (CHA) publishing a newsletter and directory, organizing meetings and conferences, and facilitating electronic networking among scholars in the field.[2] This vitality derives both from a substantial influx of women into the discipline of history and from the feminist impulse underlying so much of the scholarship in the field, which emerged during the upheavals of the 1960s and 1970s and continues to engage with issues of direct concern to the contemporary women's movement. For more than two decades, feminist scholars have worked to reclaim the diverse pasts of Canadian women and to change the practice of history. This bibliography presents the products of their labours.

The launching of Canadian women's history as a scholarly enterprise initially depended on the existence of several supportive women's studies journals, notably *Atlantis* and the *Canadian Newsletter of Research on Women*, which published some of the most important early articles as well as bibliographies and guides to archival resources.[3] In 1996, by contrast, virtually all of the major Canadian historical journals regularly publish articles on women, and theme issues devoted to women's history are becoming a frequent occurrence.[4] The Hilda Neatby Prize, presented annually by the CCWH for the best scholarly articles on women's history in both English and French, has added to the visibility and credibility of the field, as has the awarding of some of the CHA's major prizes in recent years to monographs on women's history.[5] Within the last five years, the number of monograph studies in Canadian women's history has increased dramatically, although it is still

the case that most of the scholarship appears in article form.[6] In the past decade, anthologies on women's history have proliferated, many reflecting the vigorous growth of regional scholarship.[7] While collections of published primary documents appear less frequently than in the 1970s and early 1980s, some excellent resources of this kind continue to be produced.[8] The publication of several book-length guides to archival resources on women demonstrates a significant demand on the part of researchers and a growing commitment to women's history within the archival community in Canada.[9]

Students and teachers in search of the latest scholarship on Canadian women's history must now range far beyond the standard historical publications to monitor periodicals in a wide range of disciplines. The interdisciplinary tendency of women's history has been encouraged by the growing interest of Canadian historians in the post-1945 era, leading to stronger links with disciplines such as sociology, law, political science, and Canadian Studies.[10] The increasing sophistication of this emerging scholarship is evident in the fact that it is now making its appearance in international publications.[11] New international journals devoted specifically to women's history, gender history and the history of sexuality are serving as a forum to introduce Canadian scholarship to historians in other countries.[12] This impressive productivity on the part of Canadian women's historians, however, has made it much more difficult for those knowledgeable in the field, let alone those making their first acquaintance with it, to keep abreast of new developments, or even to learn of the existence of many significant new publications.

The advent of gender history and the adoption of post-structuralist approaches by historians in recent years has considerably complicated the task of the bibliographer by raising questions about the definition of "women's history." Since the 1970s, women's historians have insisted that femininity is a social construction rather than a biological given and is thus an appropriate subject for historical study. Many historians are now arguing that masculinity, too, is a social construction and that men, as well as women, must be studied as gendered subjects. Thus, women's historians have been responsible for introducing the category of gender into Canadian historical analysis, for insisting that it be recognized as an analytical tool equal in importance to class and race, and for demonstrating that gender studies are not synonymous with women's studies. Since gender is now understood to be relational, femininity is often studied in relation to masculinity, and gender is regularly explored in relation to class, race, ethnicity, religion and sexual orientation.[13] Some of the most important new work in gender history does not focus on the "lived experience" of actual people at all, but examines the gendered processes of policy and state formation, or the construction of gender and sexuality through educational, legal, and medical discourses.[14] For students, teachers, scholars, and bibliographers alike, it is no longer a straightforward matter to identify scholarly titles that are or are not about "women," a term that will yield inadequate results at best for novice researchers embarking on a standard library search.

This project was initiated in 1990 as a modest measure to assist my undergraduate students when I began teaching Canadian women's history at the University of Western Ontario. At that time, no comprehensive bibliographic reference tool in this field had been published since the appearance of Veronica Strong-Boag and Beth Light's annotated bibliography, *True Daughters of the North*, in 1980.[15] In 1996, it is not only undergraduate students who find themselves in need of bibliographic assistance. Graduate students preparing fields in women's history or Canadian history, librarians besieged by student researchers, novice teachers facing their first introductory survey course, experienced teachers directing advanced students on unfamiliar topics, and leading scholars preparing textbooks, grant proposals or reviews of the historiography all report difficulties coping with the sheer volume of the scholarship that is now appearing in increasingly disparate locations. The challenge of keeping abreast of new developments is compounded by the barriers of geography, language and culture that isolate women's historians, and other Canadian historians, from one another, slowing the progress of the field and discouraging comparative studies. So long as the substantial and impressive new scholarship on Canadian women's history remains relatively inaccessible, it may also continue to be overlooked by international scholars engaged in comparative research on women's history, and by those scholars in Canada

who have not yet acknowledged the centrality of women or gender to Canadian history.[16]

In this second much expanded and revised edition, I have tried to be as responsive as possible to the needs of a varied group of users. In keeping with its emphasis on ease of use and accessibility to student researchers, this bibliography avoids abbreviations, lists individual articles published in anthologies as well as in periodicals, and provides multiple locations of reprinted articles. To be as comprehensive as possible, it includes scholarship in both English and French, while keeping the book to a manageable size by excluding unpublished materials and by listing each item only once. It also reflects the interdisciplinarity of women's history by incorporating much material from other disciplines, particularly where such studies pertain to the post-1945 era or where the relevant historiography is undeveloped. The table of contents is supplemented by author and subject indices so that citations can be accessed in several different ways, and the citations are now individually numbered to enhance the precision of the references. Finally, a historiographical mini-essay at the beginning of each section of the bibliography highlights important scholarly debates and developments.

Over the course of the last six years, this project has incurred a number of debts. Peter Neary and George Emery, my former colleagues at the University of Western Ontario, first encouraged me to consider publication, and the Office of the Dean of Social Sciences at Western provided assistance with basic research expenses. I have also received two grants from Concordia University's General Research Fund which allowed me the luxury of research assistance, in addition to covering the costs of printing and photocopying more drafts of the manuscript than I care to remember. I am indebted to my research assistants, Carrie Hamilton, Nancy Renwick, and Andrea Winlo, the latter for her efficiency in compiling the author index, and the former for many expeditions to the library in search of citations. My colleague, Rosemarie Schade, and her research assistant, Keith Lowther, granted me access to their bibliography project on gender-balancing history when it was still in manuscript form. Pat Staton at Green Dragon Press took on this project when it was much smaller and made possible the publication of the first edition, for which I remain grateful.

On numerous occasions, I have benefitted from letters of support and verbal and written feedback graciously provided by many individuals. My thanks to Marilyn Barber, Gail Cuthbert Brandt, Margaret Conrad, Odette Vincent, Andrée Lévesque, Alison Prentice, Mary Vipond and Keith Walden for their advice and encouragement. I owe particular debts to Bettina Bradbury for a detailed and thoughtful commentary on the organization of the manuscript, and to Suzanne Morton for reading several drafts and for enduring dinner conversations and telephone calls about subject categories. Thanks to Judy Appleby for providing me with a librarian's perspective on bibliographies and her thoughts on the pitfalls of subject indexes. My association with Carleton University Press has been a pleasure. I am grateful to John Flood for agreeing to add this volume to the Women's Experience Series, despite his doubts about whether a bibliography would ever be a best seller, and for

insisting on the historiographical mini-essays which I would otherwise never have written. Jennie Strickland has been a source of much encouragement and useful advice from the beginning, and Barbara Cumming's stunning cover design inspired me to believe that one day the manuscript might actually exist as a real book. I have been thoroughly indulged by Diane Dupuis, another expatriate British Columbian, who consulted me about all aspects of the production of this book, just so that I would like it, and who has been its most enthusiastic supporter at the moments when I never wanted to see it again. Our wide-ranging telephone conversations about book design, publishing, feminism, politics, and life in Central Canada helped me survive a summer of endless indexing, editing, and proofreading. And in the background was Deborah Gorham to whom I am grateful, as always, for her unflagging support and for being an inspiration.

NOTES

1 Veronica Strong-Boag, "Cousin Cinderella: A Guide to Historical Literature Pertaining to Canadian Women," in *Women in Canada*, ed. Marylee Stephenson (Toronto: New Press, 1973); and Wendy Mitchinson, "Women's History," in *Canadian History: A Reader's Guide, Volume 2: Confederation to the Present*, ed. Doug Owram (Toronto: University of Toronto Press, 1994), 202-27. See also Eliane Leslau Silverman, "Writing Canadian Women's History, 1970-1982: An Historiographical Analysis," *Canadian Historical Review* 63, 4 (December 1982): 513-33; Margaret Conrad, "The Re-Birth of Canada's Past: A Decade of Women's History," *Acadiensis* 12 (Spring 1983): 140-62; Rosemary R. Gagan, "Putting Humpty Together Again: The Challenge of Canadian Women's History," *British Journal of Canadian Studies* 4, 2 (1989): 276-95; Gail Cuthbert Brandt, "Postmodern Patchwork: Some Recent Trends in the Writing of Women's History in Canada," *Canadian Historical Review* 72, 4 (December 1991): 441-70; and Bettina Bradbury, "Women and the History of Their Work in Canada: Some Recent Books," *Journal of Canadian Studies* 28, 3 (Fall 1993): 159-78.

2 Veronica Strong-Boag, *Work to Be Done: The Canadian Committee on Women's History/ Comité canadien de l'histoire des femmes: Du travail en perspective* ([Montréal]: Canadian Committee on Women's History/Comité

canadien de l'histoire des femmes, 1995). A 1993 conference held under the auspices of the CCWH has resulted in the recent publication of a landmark collection of papers on teaching women's history in the academy. See Bettina Bradbury, Ruby Heap, Franca Iacovetta, Bina Mehta, Cecilia Morgan, and Joan Sangster, eds. *Teaching Women's History: Challenges and Solutions* (Athabasca, AB: Athabasca University, 1996).

3 Both *Atlantis* and the *CNRW*, which later became *Resources for Feminist Research/Documentation sur la recherche féministe*, continue to serve as important outlets for Canadian women's historians although historical scholarship is certainly less dominant in their pages today than it was in the early years. In the 1980s they were joined by *Canadian Woman Studies/les cahiers de la femme* and *Recherches féministes*. These interdisciplinary publications feature historical scholarship on an ongoing basis and, from time to time, produce special issues on women's history. See especially, *Canadian Woman Studies* 7, 3 (Fall 1986) and 7, 4 (Winter 1986); and *Recherches féministes* 6, 1 (1993).

4 See especially, the *Canadian Historical Review*, *Acadiensis*, *Histoire sociale/Social History*, *Labour/Le Travail*, *Revue d'histoire de l'Amérique française*, *Journal of Canadian Studies*, *Historical Studies in Education* and the *Canadian Bulletin of Medical History*. For special issues on women, see *Manitoba History* 11 (Spring

1986); *Urban History Review* 17, 3 (February 1989); *Cap-aux-Diamants* 21 (printemps 1990); *Canadian Historical Review* 72, 4 (December 1991); *Ontario History* 84, 4 (December 1992); *Canadian Bulletin of Medical History* 11, 1 (1994); *Journal of Canadian Studies* 29, 4 (Winter 1994/95); *Journal of the Canadian Church Historical Society* 37, 1 (April 1995); *International Journal of Canadian Studies* 11 (Spring 1995); *BC Studies* 105/106 (Spring/Summer 1995).

5 The Sir John A. Macdonald Prize, presented annually by the Canadian Historical Association for the best scholarly monograph on the history of Canada, has been awarded in recent years to Veronica Strong-Boag for *The New Day Recalled: Lives of Girls and Women in English Canada, 1919-1939* (Toronto: Copp Clark Pitman, 1988); to Joy Parr for *The Gender of Breadwinners: Women, Men and Change in Two Industrial Towns, 1880-1950* (Toronto: University of Toronto Press, 1990); to Julie Cruikshank for *Life Lived Like a Story: Life Stories of Three Yukon Elders* (Vancouver: University of British Columbia Press, 1991); and to Bettina Bradbury for *Working Families: Age, Gender, and Daily Survival in Industrializing Montreal* (Toronto: McClelland and Stewart, 1993).

6 Boding well for the future development of the field, a record number of monograph studies were published in 1995, with highlights including Janine Brodie, *Politics on the Margins: Restructuring and the Canadian Women's Movement* (Halifax: Fernwood Publishing); Louise I. Carbert, *Agrarian Feminism: The Politics of Ontario Farm Women* (Toronto: University of Toronto Press); Johanne Collin, *Changement d'ordonnance: mutations professionnelles, identité sociale et féminisation de la profession pharmaceutique au Québec, 1940-1980* (Montréal: Boréal); Sharon Anne Cook, *"Through Sunshine and Shadow": The Woman's Christian Temperance Union, Evangelicalism, and Reform in Ontario, 1874-1930* (Montreal and Kingston: McGill-Queen's University Press); Micheline Dumont, *Les religieuses sont-elles féministes?* (Montréal: Bellarmin) Elizabeth Jane Errington, *Wives and Mothers, School Mistresses and Scullery Maids: Working Women in Upper Canada, 1790-1840* (Montreal and Kingston: McGill-Queen's University Press); Kirsten K. Johnson, *Undressing the Canadian State: The Politics of Pornography from Hicklin to Butler* (Halifax: Fernwood Publishing); Mary Kinnear, *In Subordination: Professional Women, 1870-1970* (Montreal and Kingston: McGill-Queen's University Press); Andrée

Lévesque, *Résistance et transgression: Etudes en histoire des femmes au Québec* (Montréal: Les éditions du remue-ménage); Suzanne Morton, *Ideal Surroundings: Domestic Life in a Working-Class Suburb in the 1920s* (Toronto: University of Toronto Press); Janice Newton, *The Feminist Challenge to the Canadian Left, 1900-1918* (Montreal and Kingston: McGill-Queen's University Press); Margaret Prang, *A Heart at Leisure from Itself: Caroline Macdonald of Japan* (Vancouver: University of British Columbia Press); Becki Ross, *The House That Jill Built: A Lesbian Nation in Formation* (Toronto: University of Toronto Press); Joan Sangster, *Earning Respect: The Lives of Working Women in Small-Town Ontario, 1920-1960* (Toronto: University of Toronto Press); Carolyn Strange, *Toronto's Girl Problem: The Perils and Pleasures of the City, 1880-1930* (Toronto: University of Toronto Press).

7 See especially, Veronica Strong-Boag and Anita Clair Fellman, eds., *Rethinking Canada: The Promise of Women's History,* 2nd edition (Toronto: Copp Clark Pitman Ltd., 1991); Franca Iacovetta and Mariana Valverde, eds., *Gender Conflicts: New Essays in Women's History* (Toronto: University of Toronto Press, 1992); Bettina Bradbury, ed., *Canadian Family History: Selected Readings* (Toronto: Copp Clark Pitman, 1992); Dianne Dodd and Deborah Gorham, eds., *Caring and Curing: Historical Perspectives on Women and Healing in Canada* (Ottawa: University of Ottawa Press, 1994); Elizabeth Gillan Muir and Marilyn Färdig Whiteley, eds., *Changing Roles of Women within the Christian Church in Canada* (Toronto: University of Toronto Press, 1995); and Wendy Mitchinson, et al, eds., *Canadian Women: A Reader* (Toronto: Harcourt Brace Canada, 1996). Regional collections include Nadia Fahmy-Eid and Micheline Dumont, eds., *Maîtresses de maison, maîtresses d'école: Femmes, famille et éducation dans l'histoire du Québec* (Montreal: Boréal Express, 1983); Marie Lavigne and Yolande Pinard, eds., *Travailleuses et féministes: Les femmes dans la société québécoise* (Montreal: Boréal Express, 1983); Mary Kinnear, ed., *First Days, Fighting Days: Women in Manitoba History* (Regina: Canadian Plains Research Center, University of Regina, 1987); Ruby Heap and Alison Prentice, eds., *Gender and Education in Ontario: An Historical Reader* (Toronto: Canadian Scholars' Press, 1991); Gillian Creese and Veronica Strong-Boag, eds., *British Columbia Reconsidered: Essays on Women* (Vancouver: Press Gang Publishers, 1992); Catherine A. Cavanaugh and Randi R. Warne, eds., *Standing on*

New Ground: Women in Alberta (Edmonton: University of Alberta Press, 1993); Linda Kealey, ed., *Pursuing Equality: Historical Perspectives on Women in Newfoundland and Labrador* (St. John's: Memorial University of Newfoundland, Institute of Social and Economic Research, 1993); Janet Guildford and Suzanne Morton, eds., *Separate Spheres: Women's Worlds in the 19th Century Maritimes* (Fredericton: Acadiensis Press, 1994); David de Brou and Aileen Moffatt, eds., *"Other" Voices: Historical Essays on Saskatchewan Women* (Regina: Canadian Plains Research Center, 1995); and Joy Parr, ed., *A Diversity of Women: Ontario, 1945-1980* (Toronto: University of Toronto Press, 1995).

8 The most influential early collections were Ramsay Cook and Wendy Mitchinson, eds., *The Proper Sphere: Woman's Place in Canadian Society* (Toronto: Oxford University Press, 1976); Beth Light and Alison Prentice, eds., *Pioneer and Gentlewomen of British North America, 1713-1867* (Toronto: New Hogtown Press, 1980); and Beth Light and Joy Parr, eds., *Canadian Women on the Move, 1867-1920* (Toronto: New Hogtown Press and the Ontario Institute for Studies in Education, 1983). More recent additions to this genre include Margaret Conrad, Toni Laidlaw and Donna Smyth, eds., *No Place Like Home: Diaries and Letters of Nova Scotia Women, 1771-1938* (Halifax: Formac Publishing Company Limited, 1988); Beth Light and Ruth Roach Pierson, eds., *No Easy Road: Women in Canada, 1920s-1960s* (Toronto: New Hogtown Press, 1990); Ruth Roach Pierson, Marjorie Griffin Cohen, Paula Bourne and Philanda Masters, *Canadian Women's Issues, Volume I: Strong Voices* (Toronto: James Lorimer and Company, 1994); and Ruth Roach Pierson and Marjorie Griffin Cohen, *Canadian Women's Issues, Volume II: Bold Visions* (Toronto: James Lorimer and Company, 1995).

9 See especially, Mary Kinnear and Vera Fast, *Planting the Garden: An Annotated Archival Bibliography of the History of Women in Manitoba* (Winnipeg: University of Manitoba Press, 1987); Madeleine Lamothe, Ghislaine Fecteau and Pierrette Lalancette, *Les archives des femmes au Québec: Guide sommaire* (Québec: Gouvernement du Québec, Ministère des affaires culturelles, 1990); Joanna Dean and David Fraser, *Women's Archives Guide: Manuscript Sources for the History of Women* (Ottawa: National Archives of Canada, 1991); Margaret Fulford, *The Canadian Women's Movement, 1960-1990: A Guide to Archival Resources* (Toronto: ECW Press, 1992).

10 Articles on Canadian women's history appear regularly in the *Journal of Canadian Studies, Canadian Review of Sociology and Anthropology, Canadian Journal of Sociology, Recherches sociographiques, Canadian Journal of Political Science, Canadian Journal of Law and Society*, and *Studies in Political Economy*.

11 For example, Ruth Roach Pierson, "Experience, Difference, Dominance and Voice in the Writing of Canadian Women's History," in *Writing Women's History: International Perspectives*, eds. Karen Offen, Ruth Roach Pierson and Jane Rendall (Bloomington: Indiana University Press, 1991), 79-106; Line Chamberland, "Remembering Lesbian Bars: Montreal, 1955-1975," *Journal of Homosexuality* 25, 3 (1993): 231-69; Franca Iacovetta, "Writing Women into Immigration History: The Italian Canadian Case," *Altreitalie: International Journal of Studies of Peoples of Italian Origin in the World* (Turin, Italy) 9 (January-June 1993): 5-47; Andrée Lévesque, "Les Québécoises et leur citoyenneté: la citoyenneté selon Eva Circé-Côté," in *La politique des droits: Citoyenneté et construction des genres aux 19e et 20e siècles*, eds. Hans Ulrich Jost, Monique Pavillon and François Valloton (Paris: Editions Kimé, 1994), 89-104; Dominique Marshall, "Nationalisme et politiques sociales au Québec depuis 1867: un siècle de rendez-vous manqués entre l'Etat, l'Eglise et les familles," *British Journal of Canadian Studies* 9, 2 (1994): 301-47.

12 For example, Denyse Baillargeon, "'If You Had No Money, You Had No Trouble, Did You?': Montreal Working-class Housewives during the Great Depression," *Women's History Review* 1, 2 (1992): 217-37; Angus McLaren, "Sex Radicalism in the Canadian Pacific Northwest, 1890-1920," *Journal of the History of Sexuality* 2, 4 (April 1992): 527-46; Margaret Hobbs, "Rethinking Antifeminism in the 1930s: Gender Crisis or Workplace Justice? A Response to Alice Kessler-Harris," *Gender and History* 5, 1 (Spring 1993): 4-15; Joan Sangster, "Telling Our Stories: Feminist Debates and the Use of Oral History," *Women's History Review* 3, 1 (1994): 5-28; Mary Louise Adams, "Youth, Corruptibility, and English-Canadian Postwar Campaigns against Indecency, 1948-1955," *Journal of the History of Sexuality* 6, 1 (July 1995): 89-117.

13 For assessments of the impact of gender history on Canadian historical scholarship, see Joy Parr, "Gender History and Historical Practice," *Canadian Historical Review* 76, 3 (September 1995): 354-76; Joy Parr and

Mark Rosenfeld, eds., *Gender and History in Canada* (Toronto: Copp Clark Ltd., 1996); and Joan Sangster, "Beyond Dichotomies: Re-Assessing Gender History and Women's History in Canada," *left history* 3, 1 (Spring/Summer 1995): 109-21.

14 For example, Margaret Hobbs and Ruth Roach Pierson, "'A Kitchen That Wastes No Steps...': Gender, Class and the Home Improvement Plan, 1936-40," *Histoire sociale/Social History* XXI (May 1988): 9-37; Ruth Roach Pierson, "Gender and the Unemployment Insurance Debates in Canada, 1934-1940," *Labour/Le Travail* 25 (Spring 1990): 77-103; Lykke de la Cour, Cecilia Morgan and Mariana Valverde, "Gender Regulation and State Formation in Nineteenth-Century Canada," in *Colonial Leviathan: State Formation in Mid-Nineteenth-Century Canada*, eds. Allan Greer and Ian Radforth (Toronto: University of Toronto Press, 1992), 163-91; Cynthia Wright, "'Feminine Trifles of Vast Importance': Writing Gender into the History of Consumption," in *Gender Conflicts: New Essays in Women's History*, eds. Franca Iacovetta and Mariana Valverde (Toronto: University of Toronto Press, 1992), 229-60; Mary Louise Adams, "Almost Anything Can Happen: A Search for Sexual Discourse in the Urban Spaces of 1940s Toronto,"

Canadian Journal of Sociology 19, 2 (1994): 217-32; Karen Dubinsky, "'The Pleasure is Exquisite but Violent': The Imaginary Geography of Niagara Falls in the Nineteenth Century," *Journal of Canadian Studies* 29, 2 (Summer 1994): 64-88.

15 *True Daughters of the North: Canadian Women's History, An Annotated Bibliography* (Toronto: OISE Press, 1980) remains an indispensible resource for the pre-1980 period.

16 On the opposition to the growing strength of women's history in Canada, see Ruth Roach Pierson, "Colonization and Canadian Women's History," *Journal of Women's History* 4, 2 (Fall 1992): 134-56; Linda Kealey, Ruth Roach Pierson, Joan Sangster and Veronica Strong-Boag, "Teaching Canadian History in the 1990s: Whose 'National' History Are We Lamenting?" *Journal of Canadian Studies* 27, 2 (Summer 1992): 129-31; Bryan D. Palmer, "Canadian Controversies," *History Today* 44, 11 (November 1994): 44-49; Veronica Strong-Boag, "Contested Space: The Politics of Canadian Memory," *Journal of the Canadian Historical Association*, NS 5 (1994): 3-17.

Changing Women,
Changing History

ARTS

SCHOLARS AND CRITICS have often noted the prominence of women in Canadian arts and letters. Many writers have left behind a rich legacy for historians, including the correspondence of Susanna Moodie and Gabrielle Roy, and the diaries of Lucy Maud Montgomery and Elizabeth Smart, which have recently been edited and made available to a wider readership. Reflecting the current revival of interest in biography, Canadian scholars have produced well-merited biographical treatments of Sara Jeannette Duncan, Anna Jameson, Lucy Maud Montgomery, Pauline Johnson, Frances Brook, Mazo de la Roche, Alice Munro, and others. Most studies have focused on individual writers, but scholars such as Carole Gerson have helped to stimulate interest in women's autobiography as a distinct genre. The nineteenth century produced many women writers, given that middle-class women had few other respectable options for earning money, resulting in invaluable accounts of the pioneer experience of British emigrant gentlewomen, outstanding among whom were Susanna Moodie and Catharine Parr Traill. Little attention has yet been paid to regional patterns in Canadian women's writing, with the exception of the Maritime region, thanks largely to the efforts of Gwendolyn Davies, and Quebec, where a substantial body of scholarship by Patricia Smart and others traces the development of women's writing "in the father's house."

The achievements of Canadian women in the performing arts have been much less studied in comparison with the literary and visual arts, perhaps because so many women seeking stardom had to leave the country to find it. Only a few who won international renown, such as nineteenth-century opera singer, Emma Albani, have so far been reclaimed by Canadian women's historians. Public performance, especially acting, was also considered unseemly for women, making it less accessible than writing or painting, a situation that was aggravated by outright discrimination. The fascinating story of the Montreal Women's Symphony, for example, reminds us of how recently highly trained female musicians were denied outlets for their talents. Somewhat better documented than the careers of individual artists is the crucial role played by Canadian women in the establishment of theatre and dance companies as part of a long tradition of voluntary association and community building. Carol Budnick's examination of the activities of Winnipeg women in the field of the performing arts is a model for future studies.

To find Canadian women in the visual arts, Maria Tippett's recent survey of three hundred years of art by Canadian women is an excellent starting point. No female artist has received more attention from Canadian art historians than Emily Carr who has been the subject of several full-length biographies. Some notice has also been paid to war artists commissioned by the Canadian government, especially World War One painter, Mary Riter Hamilton, and sculptors Frances Loring and Florence Wyle, and World War Two painter, Molly Lamb Bobak. Despite the importance of painting among Canadian middle-class women in British North America, we know far less about early artists like Elizabeth Amherst Hale and Frances Anne Hopkins, than about their "scribbling sisters," who employed pen rather than brush. Women eagerly embraced the new technology of photography during the nineteenth and early twentieth centuries, as demonstrated by recent studies of Hannah Maynard, Mattie Gunterman, and Edith Watson. The art of First Nations women, especially the sculpture and graphic designs of Inuit artists, is also generating much interest among Canadian scholars and art historians.

GENERAL

1   BEALE, Alison and Annette Van Den Bosch, eds. *Ghosts in the Machine: Women and Cultural Policy in Canada and Australia.* Toronto: Garamond Press, 1995.

2   GWYN, Sandra. *Women in the Arts in Canada.* Royal Commission on the Status of Women in Canada, Study No. 7. Ottawa: Information Canada, 1971.

LITERARY

3   AHMANSSON, Gabriella. *A Life and Its Mirrors: A Feminist Reading of the Work of L.M. Montgomery.* Uppsala, Sweden: University of Uppsala Press, 1991.

4   AITKEN, Johan Lyall. *Masques of Morality: Females in Fiction.* Toronto: Women's Press, 1987.

5   ATLANTIC WORK GROUP. *Women in Canadian Literature.* Toronto: Writers Development Trust, n.d.

6   ATWOOD, Margaret. *Survival: A Thematic Guide to Canadian Literature.* Toronto: Anansi, 1972.

7   BALLSTADT, Carl. "Susanna Moodie and the English Sketch." *Canadian Literature* 51 (Winter 1972): 32-37.

8   BALLSTADT, Carl. "Catharine Parr Traill." In *Canadian Writers and Their Works,* eds., Robert Lecker, *et al.* Toronto: ECW Press, 1983.

9   BALLSTADT, Carl. "'The Embryo Blossom': Susanna Moodie's Letters to Her Husband in Relation to *Roughing It in the Bush.*" In *Re(Dis)covering Our Foremothers: Nineteenth Century Canadian Women Writers,* ed. Lorraine McMullen, 137-45. Ottawa: University of Ottawa Press, 1989.

10   BALLSTADT, Carl, Elizabeth Hopkins and Michael Peterman, eds. *Susanna Moodie: Letters of a Lifetime.* Toronto: University of Toronto Press, 1985.

11   BALLSTADT, Carl, Elizabeth Hopkins and Michael Peterman, eds. *Letters of Love and Duty: The Correspondence of Susanna and John Moodie.* Toronto: University of Toronto Press, 1993.

12   BARNARD, Ann. "A North American Connection: Women in Prairie Novels." *Great Plains Quarterly* 14, 1 (Winter 1994): 21-28.

13   BARRY, Sandra. "The Art of Remembering: The Influence of Great Village, Nova Scotia, on the Life and Works of Elizabeth Bishop." *Nova Scotia Historical Review* 11, 1 (1991): 2-38.

14   BARRY, Sandra. "Elizabeth Bishop: The Autobiography of a Poet." *Dalhousie Review* 71 (Winter 1991/92): 489-93.

15   BEYEA, Marion. "Archival Sources for Research on Nineteenth-Century Women Writers." In *Re(Dis)covering Our Foremothers: Nineteenth Century Canadian Women Writers,* ed. Lorraine McMullen, 23-29. Ottawa: University of Ottawa Press, 1989.

16   BIRBALSINGH, Frank. "Ethel Wilson: Innocent Traveller." *Canadian Literature* (Summer 1971): 35-46.

17   BOLGER, Francis W.P., ed. *Spirit of Place: Lucy Maud Montgomery and Prince Edward Island.* With photography by Wayne Barrett and Anne Mackay. Toronto: Oxford University Press, 1982.

18   BOLGER, Francis. *The Years Before Anne.* Charlottetown: PEI Heritage Foundation, 1974; Halifax: Nimbus Publishing, 1991. [Lucy Maud Montgomery]

19   BOLGER, Francis W.P. and Elizabeth Epperly, eds. *My Dear Mr. M: Letters to G.B. MacMillan from L.M. Montgomery.* Toronto: McGraw-Hill Ryerson, 1980.

20   BOUTELLE, Ann Edwards. "Frances Brooke's *Emily Montague* (1769): Canada and Woman's Rights." *Women's Studies* 12 (1986): 7-16. Reprinted in *Rethinking Canada: The Promise of Women's History,* 2nd edition, eds. Veronica Strong-Boag and Anita Clair Fellman, 51-58. Toronto: Copp Clark Pitman Ltd. 1991.

21   BOUTELLE, Ann Edwards. "Margaret Atwood, Margaret Laurence and Their Nineteenth Century Forerunners." In *Faith of a (Woman) Writer,* eds. Alice Kessler-Harris and William McBrien, 41-48. Westport, CT: Greenwood Press, 1988.

22   BRADY, Elizabeth. "Voices from the Periphery: First-generation Lesbian Fiction in Canada." *Resources for Feminist Research* 12, 1 (March 1983): 22-26.

23   BRANT, Beth, ed. *A Gathering of Spirit: A Collection by North American Indian Women.* Toronto: The Women's Press, 1988.

24   BROWN, Anne. "Brèves réflexions sur le roman féminin québécois à l'heure de la Révolution tranquille." *Québec Studies* 12 (Spring 1991): 127-37.

25   BROWN, Anne. "Unhiding the Hidden: Writing during the Quiet Revolution." In *The Anatomy of Gender: Women's Struggle for the Body,* eds. Dawn H. Currie and Valerie Raoul, 222-31. Ottawa: Carleton University Press, 1992.

26   BROYNARD-FROT, Janine. *Un matriarcat sans procès: Analyse systématique de romans canadiens-français, 1860-1960.* Montréal: Presse de l'Université de Montréal, 1982.

27   BRUCE, Harry. *Maud: The Life of L.M. Montgomery.* New York: Bantam-Seal, 1992.

28   BRUNET, Manon. "Les femmes dans la production de la littérature francophone du début du XIXe siècle québécois." In *Livre et lecture au Québec, 1800-1850,* eds. Claude Galarneau and Maurice Lemire, 167-80. Québec: Institut québécois de recherche sur la culture, 1988.

29   BURNS, Jane. "Anne and Emily: L.M. Montgomery's Children." *Room of One's Own* 3, 3 (1977): 37-48.

30   BURNS, Robert Alan. "The Poet in Her Time: Isabella Valancy Crawford's Social, Economic, and Political Views." *Studies in Canadian Literature* 14, 1 (1989): 30-53.

31   BURSEY, Maureen. "Maria Campbell: Putting the Pieces Together." *Branching Out* 7, 1 (1980): 6-7.

32 BUSS, Helen M. "Canadian Women's Autobiography: Some Critical Directions." In *A Mazing Space: Writing Canadian Women Writing*, eds. Shirley Neuman and Smaro Kamboureli, 154-66. Edmonton: Longspoon-NeWest Press, 1986.

33 BUSS, Helen M. "'The Dear Domestic Circle': Frameworks for the Literary Study of Women's Personal Narratives in Archival Collections." *Studies in Canadian Literature* 14, 1 (1989): 1-17.

34 BUSS, Helen M. "Women and the Garrison Mentality: Pioneer Women Autobiographers and their Relation to the Land." In *Re(Dis)covering Our Foremothers: Nineteenth Century Canadian Women Writers,* ed. Lorraine McMullen, 123-36. Ottawa: University of Ottawa Press, 1989.

35 BUSS, Helen M. *Canadian Women's Autobiography: An Introductory Guide for Researchers and Teachers.* Ottawa: Canadian Research Institute for the Advancement of Women, 1991.

36 BUSS, Helen M. "Anna Jameson's *Winter Studies and Summer Rambles in Canada* as Epistolatory Dijournal." In *Essays on Life Writing: From Genre to Critical Practice,* ed. Marlene Kadar. Toronto: University of Toronto Press, 1992.

37 BUSS, Helen M. *Mapping Our Selves: Canadian Women's Autobiography.* Montreal and Kingston: McGill-Queen's University Press, 1993.

38 BUSS, Helen M. "Decoding L.M. Montgomery's Journals/Encoding a Critical Practice for Women's Private Literature." *Essays on Canadian Writing* 54 (Winter 1994): 80-100.

39 CAMERON, Anne. *Daughters of Copper Woman.* Vancouver: Press Gang Publishers, 1981.

40 CAMPBELL, Sandra and Lorraine McMullen, eds. *New Women: Short Stories by Canadian Women, 1900-1920.* Ottawa: University of Ottawa Press, 1991.

41 CARPENTIER, Louise E. and Lucie Lequin. "Bibliographie des écrits des femmes de Québec de 1945 à 1960." *Resources for Feminist Research* 17, 4 (1988): 49-61.

42 CHALMERS, John W. "Tekahionwake." *Alberta Historical Review* (Summer 1974): 24-25. [Pauline Johnson]

43 CHARNLEY, Kerrie. "Concepts of Anger, Identity, Power and Vision in the Writings and Voices of First Nations Women." *Fireweed* 32 (Spring 1991): 32-43.

44 COLDWELL, Joan, ed. *The Tightrope Walker: Autobiographical Writings of Anne Wilkinson.* Toronto: University of Toronto Press, 1992.

45 COLDWELL, Joyce-Ione Harrington. "Folklore as Fiction: The Writings of L.M. Montgomery." In *Folklore Studies in Honour of Herbert Halpert: A Festschrift,* 125-36. St. John's: Memorial University of Newfoundland, 1980.

46 COLLET, Pauline. "Les romancières québécoise des années 60 face à la maternité." *Atlantis* 5, 2 (Spring 1980): 131-41.

47 COWAN, Ann S. "Canadian Writers: Lucy Maud and Emily Byrd." *Canadian Children's Literature* 3 (1975): 42-49.

48 DAGG, Anne Innis. "Canadian Voices of Authority: Non-Fiction and Early Women Writers." *Journal of Canadian Studies* 27, 2 (Summer 1992): 107-22.

49 DAHL, Edward H. *"Mid-Forests Wild": A Study of the Concept of Wilderness in the Writings of Susanna Moodie, J.W.D. Moodie, Catharine Parr Traill and Samuel Strickland.* Ottawa: National Museums of Canada, 1973.

50 DAVIES, Gwendolyn. "'Dearer Than His Dog': Literary Women in Pre-Confederation Nova Scotia." In *Gynocritics/La Gynocritique,* ed. Barbara Godard. Toronto: ECW Press, 1987. Reprinted in *Studies in Maritime Literary History, 1760-1930,* ed. Gwendolyn Davies, 71-87. Fredericton: Acadiensis Press, 1991.

51 DAVIES, Gwendolyn. "The Literary 'New Woman' and Social Activism in Maritime Literature, 1880-1920." In *Separate Spheres: Women's Worlds in the 19th Century Maritimes,* eds. Janet Guildford and Suzanne Morton, 233-50. Fredericton: Acadiensis Press, 1994.

52 DAVIS, Marilyn. "Fiction of a Feminist: Nellie McClung's Work for Children." *Canadian Children's Literature* 62 (1991): 37-51.

53 DEAN, Misao. "The Process of Definition: Nationality in Sara Jeannette Duncan's Early International Novels." *Journal of Canadian Studies* 20, 2 (1985): 132-49.

54 DEAN, Misao. "'You may imagine my feelings': Reading Sara Jeannette Duncan's Challenge to Narrative." In *Re(Dis)covering Our Foremothers: Nineteenth Century Canadian Women Writers,* ed. Lorraine McMullen, 187-97. Ottawa: University of Ottawa Press, 1989.

55 DEAN, Misao. "Voicing the Voiceless: Language and Genre in Nellie McClung's Fiction and Her Autobiography." *Atlantis* 15, 1 (Fall 1989): 65-75.

56 DEAN, Misao. *A Different Point of View: Sara Jeannette Duncan.* Montreal and Kingston: McGill-Queen's University Press, 1991.

57 DE LA ROCHE, Mazo. *Ringing the Changes: An Autobiography.* Toronto: Macmillan, 1957.

58 DI BIASE, Linda Popp. "The Alberta Years of Winnifred Eaton." *Alberta History* 39, 2 (Spring 1991): 1-8.

59 DORNEY, Lindsay, Gerald Noonan, and Paul Tiessen, eds. *A Public and Private Voice: Essays on the Life and Work of Dorothy Livesay.* Waterloo: University of Waterloo Press, 1986.

60 DOYLE, James. *Annie Howells and Achille Fréchette.* Toronto: University of Toronto Press, 1979. [a couple at the centre of cultural and literary life in late-19th-century Ottawa]

61 DOYLE, James. "Canadian Women Writers and the American Literary Milieu of the 1890s." In *Re(Dis)covering Our Foremothers: Nineteenth Century Canadian Women Writers,* ed. Lorraine McMullen, 30-36. Ottawa: University of Ottawa Press, 1989.

62 DUVERT, Sylvia. *Theosophic Thoughts Concerning L.M. Montgomery.* Toronto: University of Toronto Press, 1988.

63 EDWARDS, Caterina and Kay Stewart, eds. *Eating Apples: Knowing Women's Lives.* Edmonton: NeWest Press, 1994.

64 EGGLETON, Wilfrid, ed. *The Green Gables Letters: From L.M. Montgomery to Ephraim Weber, 1905-1909.* Toronto: Ryerson Press, 1960.

65 EGOFF, Sheila. *The Republic of Childhood: A Critical Guide to Children's Literature in English.* Toronto: Oxford University Press, 1967.

66 EPPERLY, Elizabeth R. "L.M. Montgomery and the Changing Times." *Acadiensis* 17, 2 (Spring 1988): 177-85.

67 EPPERLY, Elizabeth R. "The Restraints of Romance: L.M. Montgomery's Limiting and Liberating Fictions." In *The more we get together: Women and Dis/ability,* eds. Houston Stewart, Beth Percival and Elizabeth R. Epperly, 215-22. Charlottetown: Gynergy Books, 1992.

68 EPPERLY, Elizabeth Rollins. *The Fragrance Of Sweet-Grass: L.M. Montgomery's Heroines and the Pursuit of Romance.* Toronto: University of Toronto Press, 1992.

69 EPPERLY, Elizabeth R. "Chivalry and Romance: L.M. Montgomery's Re-vision of the Great War in Rainbow Valley." In *Myth and Milieu: Atlantic Literature and Culture, 1918-1939,* ed. Gwendolyn Davies, 87-94. Fredericton: Acadiensis Press, 1993.

70 FAIRBANKS, Carol. *Prairie Women: Images in American and Canadian Fiction.* New Haven: Yale University Press, 1986.

71 FEDER, Alison. *Margaret Duley: Newfoundland Novelist.* St. John's: Harry Cuff Publications, 1983.

72 FIELD, Clara C. "Literary Landmarks of Several Countries." *Ontario History* 25 (1928): 220-25.

73 FIFE, Connie, ed. *The Colour of Resistance: A Contemporary Collection of Writing by Aboriginal Women.* Toronto: Sister Vision Press, 1993.

74 FITZPATRICK, Helen. "Anne's First Sixty Years." *Canadian Author and Bookman* 44, 3 (Spring 1969): 5-13. [Lucy Maud Montgomery]

75 FOWLER, Marian. *Redney: A Life of Sara Jeannette Duncan.* Toronto: House of Anansi, 1980.

76 FRASER, Wayne. *The Dominion of Women: The Personal and the Political in Canadian Women's Literature.* Westport, CT: Greenwood Press, 1991.

77 FREIWALD, Bina. "'Femininely Speaking': Anna Jameson's *Winter Studies and Summer Rambles in Canada.*" In *A Mazing Space: Writing Canadian Women Writing,* eds. Shirley Neuman and Smaro Kamboureli, 61-73. Edmonton: Longspoon-NeWest Press, 1986.

78 FREIWALD, Bina. "'The tongue of woman': The Language of the Self in Moodie's *Roughing It in the Bush.*" In *Re(Dis)covering Our Foremothers: Nineteenth Century Canadian Women Writers,* ed. Lorraine McMullen, 155-72. Ottawa: University of Ottawa Press, 1989.

79 GABRIEL, Barbara and Lorraine M. York, eds. "The Gender Issue." A special issue of *Essays in Canadian Writing* 54 (Winter 1994).

80 GAIRDNER, W.D. "Traill and Moodie: The Two Realities." *Journal of Canadian Fiction* 1, 2 (Spring 1972): 35-42.

81 GALVIN, Elizabeth McNeill. *Isabella Valancy Crawford: We Scarcely Knew Her.* Toronto: Natural Heritage/Natural History, 1994.

82 GENUIST, Monique. *La création romanesque chez Gabrielle Roy.* Montréal: Cercle du livre des femmes, 1966.

83 GÉRIN, Pierre. "Une écrivaine acadienne à la fin du XIXe siècle: Marichette." *Atlantis* 10, 1 (Fall 1984): 38-45.

84 GÉRIN, Pierre M. and Pierre Gérin. "Qui êtes vous Marichette?" *Cahiers de la société acadienne* 8, 4 (décembre 1977): 165-72.

85 GÉRIN, Pierre M. and Pierre Gérin. "Une femme à la recherche et la défense de l'identité acadienne à la fin du XIXe siècle, Marichette." *Revue de l'Université de Moncton* 11, 2 (mai 1978): 17-26.

86 GERRY, Thomas M.F. "'I Am Translated': Anna Jameson's Sketches and *Winter Studies and Summer Rambles in Canada.*" *Journal of Canadian Studies* 25, 4 (Winter 1990/91): 34-49.

87 GERSON, Carole. "Anthologies and the Canon of Early Canadian Women Writers." In *Re(Dis)covering Our Foremothers: Nineteenth Century Canadian Women Writers,* ed. Lorraine McMullen, 55-76. Ottawa: University of Ottawa Press, 1989.

88 GERSON, Carole. *A Purer Taste: The Writing and Reading of Fiction in English in Nineteenth-Century Canada.* Toronto: University of Toronto Press, 1989.

89 GERSON, Carole. "Marie Joussaye Fotheringham: Canada's First Woman Labour Poet." *Canadian Notes & Queries* 44 (Spring 1991): 21-23.

90 GERSON, Carole. "The Canon Between the Wars: Field-notes of a Feminist Literary Archaeologist." In *Canadian Canons: Essays in Literary Value,* ed. Robert Lecker, 46-56. Toronto: University of Toronto Press, 1991.

91 GERSON, Carole. "The Literary Culture of Atlantic Women Between the Wars." In *Myth and Milieu: Atlantic Literature and Culture, 1918-1939*, ed. Gwendolyn Davies, 62-70. Fredericton: Acadiensis Press, 1993.

92 GERSON, Carole. *Canada's Early Women Writers: Texts in English to 1859*. CRIAW Papers No. 33. Ottawa: Canadian Research Institute for the Advancement of Women, 1994.

93 GERSON, Carole. "Roughing It in the Library: Some Personal Research Experiences." Canadian Institute for Historical Microreproductions. *Facsimile* 12 (November 1994): 2-4.

94 GILLEN, Mollie. *The Wheel of Things: A Biography of L.M. Montgomery*. Don Mills: Fitzhenry & Whiteside, 1975.

95 GILLEN, Mollie. *Lucy Maud Montgomery*. Don Mills: Fitzhenry & Whiteside, 1978.

96 GINGRAS, Marcelle. "Laure Conan." *Vie française* 10 (1956): 363-67.

97 GIVNER, Joan. *Mazo de la Roche: The Hidden Life*. Toronto: Oxford University Press, 1989.

98 GODARD, Barbara. "A Portrait With Three Faces: The New Woman in Fiction by Canadian Women 1880-1920." *The Literary Criterion* 19, 3/4 (1984).

99 GODARD, Barbara. *Talking About Ourselves: The Literary Productions of Native Women of Canada*. CRIAW Papers No. 11. Ottawa: Canadian Research Institute for the Advancement of Women, 1985.

100 GODARD, Barbara. "Voicing Difference: The Literary Production of Native Women." In *A Mazing Space: Writing Canadian Women Writing*, eds. Shirley Neuman and Smaro Kamboureli, 87-107. Edmonton: Longspoon-NeWest Press, 1986.

101 GODARD, Barbara, ed. *Gynocritics/Gynocritiques: Feminist Approaches to Canadian and Quebec Women's Writing*. Toronto: ECW Press, 1986.

102 GODARD, Barbara, ed. *Collaboration in the Feminine: Writings on Women and Culture from Tessera*. Toronto: Second Story Press, 1995.

103 GOTTLIEB, Lois C. and Wendy Keitner. "Bird at the Window: An Annotated Bibliography of Canadian Fiction Written by Women, 1970-1975." *American Review of Canadian Studies* 9, 2 (Autumn 1979): 3-56.

104 GRANT, Agnes. "The Politics of Representation: Some Canadian Women Writers." *Canadian Literature* 124/125 (1990): 183-228.

105 GRANT, Agnes, ed. *Our Bit of Truth: An Anthology of Canadian Native Literature*. Winnipeg: Pemmican Publications, 1990.

106 GREEN, Mary Jean. "The 'Literary Feminists' and the Fight for Women's Writing in Quebec." *Journal of Canadian Studies* 21, 1 (1986): 128-43.

107 GREEN, Mary Jean, Paula Gilbert Lewis and Karen Gould. "Inscriptions of the Feminine: A Century of Women Writing in Quebec." *American Review of Canadian Studies* 15 (Winter 1985): 361-88.

108 GROSSKURTH, Phyllis. "Gabrielle Roy and the Silken Noose." *Canadian Literature* 42 (Autumn 1969): 6-13.

109 GUNNARS, Kristjana, ed. *Crossing the River: Essays in Honour of Margaret Laurence*. Winnipeg: Turnstone Press, 1988.

110 HALPENNY, Frances G. "Problems and Solutions in the Dictionary of Canadian Biography, 1800-1900." In *Re(Dis)covering Our Foremothers: Nineteenth Century Canadian Women Writers*, ed. Lorraine McMullen, 37-48. Ottawa: University of Ottawa Press, 1989.

111 HAMBLETON, Ronald. *Mazo de la Roche of Jalna*. New York: Hawthorn Books, 1966.

112 HAMEL, Reginald. *Bibliographie sommaire sur l'histoire de l'écriture féminine au Canada 1791-1961*. Montréal: Université de Montréal, 1974.

113 HART, Julia Catherine Beckwith. *St. Ursula's Convent, or The Nun of Canada Containing Scenes from Real Life* [1824]. Edited and introduced by Douglas G. Lochhead. Ottawa: Carleton University Press, 1991.

114 HESSE, M. G. *Women in Canadian Literature*. Ottawa: Borealis Press, 1976.

115 HOWELLS, Carol A. "Canadian Women Novelists of the 1970s and 1980s." *London Journal of Canadian Studies* 32 (1986).

116 HOWELLS, Carol A. *Private and Fictional Words: Canadian Women Novelists of the 1970s and 1980s*. Toronto: Methuen, 1987.

117 HYAM, Grace. "Pauline Johnson ('Tekahionwake')." *The Archivist* 20, 1 (1993): 21-22.

118 IRVINE, Lorna. "Surfacing, Surviving, Surpassing: Canada's Women Writers." *Journal of Popular Culture* 15 (Winter 1981): 70-77.

119 IRVINE, Lorna M. *Critical Spaces: Margaret Laurence and Janet Frame*. Columbia, SC: Camden House, 1995.

120 JACKEL, Susan. "Canadian Women's Autobiography: A Problem of Criticism." In *Gynocritics/Gynocritiques: Feminist Approaches to Canadian and Quebec Women's Writing*, ed. Barbara Godard, 95-110. Toronto: ECW Press, 1986.

121 JAQUES, Edna. *Uphill All the Way: The Autobiography of Edna Jaques*. Saskatoon: Western Producer Prairie Books, 1977.

122 JOHNSTON, Sheila. *Buckskin and Broadcloth: A Documentary Biography of E. Pauline Johnson-Tekhionawake*. Kingston: Quarry Press, 1994.

123 KADAR, Marlene, ed. *Essays on Life Writing: From Genre to Critical Practice*. Toronto: University of Toronto Press, 1992.

124 KELLER, Betty. *Pauline: A Biography of Pauline Johnson*. Halifax: Goodread Biographies, 1981.

125 KELLER, Betty C. "On Tour with Pauline Johnson." *The Beaver* 66, 6 (Dec. 1986/Jan. 1987): 19-25.

126 KIZUK, Alexander. "Molly Beresford and the Song Fishermen of Halifax: Cultural Production, Canon and Desire in 1920s Canadian Poetry." In *Myth and Milieu: Atlantic Literature and Culture, 1918-1939*, ed. Gwendolyn Davies, 175-94. Fredericton: Acadiensis Press, 1993.

127 LANGER, Beryl Donaldson. "Women and Literary Production: Canada and Australia." *Australian Canadian Studies* 2 (1984): 70-83. Reprinted in *Australian/Canadian Literatures in English: Comparative Perspectives*, eds. Russell McDougall and Gillian Whitlock, 133-50. Melbourne: Methuen Australia, 1984.

128 LAURENCE, Margaret. *Dance on the Earth: A Memoir*. Toronto: McClelland and Stewart, 1989.

129 LENNOX, John, ed. *Margaret Laurence–Al Purdy: A Friendship in Letters*. Toronto: McClelland and Stewart, 1993.

130 LIM, Shirley Geok-lin. "Japanese American Women's Life Stories: Maternality in Monica Sone's *Nisei Daughter* and Joy Kogawa's *Obasan*." *Feminist Studies* 16, 2 (Summer 1990): 289-312.

131 LISCHE-MCNAB, Ute and David McNab. "Petition from the Backwoods." *The Beaver* 308 (Summer 1977): 52-57. [Catharine Parr Traill]

132 LITT, Paul. "The Cultivation of Progress: Sara Jeannette Duncan's Social Thought." *Ontario History* 80, 2 (June 1988): 97-119.

133 LIVESAY, Dorothy. *Right Hand, Left Hand: A True Life of the Thirties*. Erin, ON: Press Porcepic Ltd., 1977.

134 LIVESAY, Dorothy. *Journey With My Selves: A Memoir, 1909-1963*. Vancouver: Douglas & McIntyre, 1991.

135 LUCAS, Alec. "The Function of the Sketches in Susanna Moodie's *Roughing It in the Bush*." In *Re(Dis)covering Our Foremothers: Nineteenth Century Canadian Women Writers*, ed. Lorraine McMullen, 146-54. Ottawa: University of Ottawa Press, 1989.

136 LYON, George W. "Pauline Johnson: A Reconsideration." *Studies in Canadian Literature* 15, 2 (1990): 136-59.

137 MacDONALD, R.D. "Design and Purpose." *Canadian Literature* 51 (Winter 1972): 20-31. [Susanna Moodie]

138 MacMILLAN, Carrie. "Research in Nineteenth Century Canadian Women Writers: An Exercise in Literary Detection." In *Re(Dis)covering Our Foremothers: Nineteenth Century Canadian Women Writers*, ed. Lorraine McMullen, 49-53. Ottawa: University of Ottawa Press, 1989.

139 MacMILLAN, Carrie, Lorraine McMullen and Elizabeth Waterson. *Silenced Sextet: Six Nineteenth-Century Canadian Women Novelists*. Montreal and Kingston: McGill-Queen's University Press, 1993. [Rosanna Leprohon, May Agnes Fleming, Margaret Murray Robertson, Susan Frances Harrison, Margaret Marshall Saunders, Joanna E. Wood]

140 MARANDA, Jeanne and Mair Verthuy. "Quebec Feminist Writing." *Emergency Librarian* 5, 1 (September/October 1977): 2-11 (English), 12-20 (French).

141 MARTIN, Mary F. "The Short Life of Isabella Valancy Crawford." *Dalhousie Review* 52, 3 (Autumn 1972): 390-400.

142 MAGUIÈRE, Bénédicte. "Idéologies et écriture des femmes au Québec (1970-1980): la quête d'une identité." *Présence francophone* 39 (1991): 111-25.

143 MAXWELL, Lilian. "The First Canadian Born Novelist." *Dalhousie Review* 31, 1 (Spring 1951): 59-64. [Julia Beckwith (Hart)]

144 McCOMBS, Judith. "Country, Politics and Gender in Canadian Studies: A Report from Twenty Years of Atwood Criticism." *Canadian Issues* 10, 5 (1988): 27-48.

145 McEWAN, Gil and Ruth McEwan. "Two Sisters in the Backwoods." In *Women Unite!: An Anthology of the Canadian Women's Movement*, 16-20. Toronto: Canadian Women's Educational Press, 1972.

146 McGAHAN, Elizabeth, ed. *Whispers from the Past: Selections from the Writings of New Brunswick Women*. Fredericton: Gooselane Editions, 1986.

147 McKENNA, Isobel. "Women in Canadian Literature." *Canadian Literature* 62 (August 1974): 69-78.

148 McCLUNG, M. G. *Literature*. Women in Canadian Life Series. Toronto: Fitzhenry and Whiteside, 1977.

149 McMULLEN, Lorraine. *An Odd Attempt in a Woman: The Literary Life of Frances Brooke*. Vancouver: University of British Columbia Press, 1983.

150 McMULLEN, Lorraine, ed. *Re(Dis)covering Our Foremothers: Nineteenth Century Canadian Women Writers*. Ottawa: University of Ottawa Press, 1989.

151 McMULLEN, Lorraine and Sandra Campbell, eds. *Aspiring Women: Short Stories by Canadian Women, 1880-1900*. Ottawa: University of Ottawa Press, 1993.

152 McMULLEN, Lorraine and Sandra Campbell, eds. *Pioneering Women: Short Stories by Canadian Women, Beginnings to 1880*. Ottawa: University of Ottawa Press, 1993.

153 MONTGOMERY, Lucy Maud. *The Alpine Path: The Story of My Career* (1917). Don Mills: Fitzhenry & Whiteside, 1974.

154 MORGAN, Bernice, Helen Porter and Geraldine Rubio, eds. *From This Place: A Selection of Writing by Women of Newfoundland and Labrador*. St. John's: Jesperson, 1977.

155 NARDOCCHIO, E.F. "Antonine Maillet et la naissance de l'Acadie moderne: de La Sagouine à Pélagie-la-Charrette." *Études canadiennes/Canadian Studies* 21, 1 (1986): 209-15.

156 NEUMAN, Shirley. "(Re)reading Nineteenth Century Women Authors: Critical Approaches." *Australian-Canadian Studies* 8, 1 (1990): 5-20.

157 NEUMAN, Shirley and Smaro Kamboureli, eds. *A Mazing Space: Writing Canadian Women Writing.* Edmonton: Longspoon-NeWest Press, 1986.

158 O'FLAHERTY, Patrick. "Margaret Duley and Newfoundland." *Dalhousie Review* 58, 4 (Winter 1977/78): 634-44.

159 O'NEILL, Patrick. "The Playwrights' Studio Group: An Interview with Two Women Playwrights of the 1930s." *Atlantis* 8, 1 (Fall 1982): 89-96.

160 O'REILLY, Magessa. "Une écriture qui célèbre la tradition orale: Pélagie-La-Charette d'Antonine Maillet." *Studies in Canadian Literature* 18, 1 (1993): 118-27.

161 PANOFSKY, Ruth. "Eclectic Views." *Journal of Canadian Studies* 29, 2 (Summer 1994): 189-94. [review essay on studies of women writers]

162 PANOFSKY, Ruth. "'Don't let me do it!': Mazo de la Roche and Her Publishers." *International Journal of Canadian Studies* 11 (Spring 1995): 171-84.

163 PARADIS, Suzanne. *Femme fictive, femme réelle: le personage féminin dans le roman féminin canadien-français, 1884-1966.* Québec: Garneau, 1966.

164 PASCAL, Gabrielle, ed. *Le roman québécois au féminin, 1980-1995.* Montréal: Triptyque, 1995.

165 PERCIVAL, W.L. *Leading Canadian Poets.* Toronto: Ryerson Press, 1948.

166 PERREAULT, Jeanne and Sylvia Vance, eds. *Writing the Circle: Native Women of Western Canada, An Anthology.* Edmonton: NeWest Press, 1990.

167 PETERMAN, Michael A. "Susanna Moodie." In *Canadian Writers and Their Works,* eds. Robert Lecker, *et al.* Downsview: ECW Press, 1983.

168 PETERMAN, Michael. "*Roughing It in the Bush* as Autobiography." In *Reflections: Autobiography and Canadian Literature,* ed. K.P. Stich, 35-43. Ottawa: University of Ottawa Press, 1988.

169 PETERMAN, Michael A. and Carl Ballstadt, eds. *Forest and Other Gleanings: The Fugitive Writings of Catharine Parr Traill.* Ottawa: University of Ottawa Press, 1994.

170 PETERONE, Penny, ed. *Northern Voices: Inuit Writing in English.* Toronto: University of Toronto Press, 1988.

171 PIERCE, Lorne Albert. *Marjorie Pickthall: A Book of Remembrance.* Toronto: Ryerson Press, 1925.

172 RASPORICH, Beverly. "Vera Lysenko's Fictions: Engendering Prairie Spaces." *Prairie Forum* 16, 2 (Fall 1991): 249-63.

173 REANEY, James. "Isabella Valancy Crawford." In *Our Living Tradition,* ed. Robert L. McDougall. Toronto: University of Toronto Press, 1959.

174 RELKE, Diana M.A. "Myths of Nature and the Poetry of Canadian Women: An Alternative Reading of Literary History." *New Literatures Review* 23 (Summer 1992): 31-49.

175 RIDLEY, Hilda M. *The Story of L.M. Montgomery.* Toronto: McGraw-Hill Ryerson, 1956.

176 ROBERTSON, Margaret M. *Shenac's Work at Home* (1866). With an introduction by Gwendolyn Guth. Early Canadian Women Writers Series. Ottawa: The Tecumseh Press, 1993.

177 ROSS, Becki. "Tracking Lesbian Speech: The Social Organization of Lesbian Periodical Publishing in English Canada, 1973-1988." In *Women's Writing and the Literary Institution,* eds. C. Potvin, J. Williamson and S. Tötösy de Zepetnek, 173-87. Edmonton: Research Institute for Comparative Literature, University of Alberta, 1992.

178 ROSS, Catherine Sheldrick. *Alice Munro: A Double Life.* Toronto: ECW Press, 1992.

179 ROY, Gabrielle. *The Road Past Altamont.* Translated by Joyce Marshall. Toronto: McClelland and Stewart, 1966.

180 ROY, Gabrielle. *Enchantment and Sorrow: The Autobiography of Gabrielle Roy.* Translated by Patricia Claxton. Toronto: Lester & Orpen Dennys, 1987.

181 ROY, Gabrielle. *Ma chère petite soeur.* Montréal: Les éditions du Boréal Express, 1988.

182 ROY, Gabrielle. *Letters to Bernadette.* Translated by Patricia Claxton. With an introduction by François Ricard. Toronto: Lester & Orpen Dennys Limited, 1990.

183 RUBIO, Mary. "Subverting the trite: L.M. Montgomery's 'room of her own.'" *Canadian Children's Literature* 65 (1992): 6-39.

184 RUBIO, Mary and Elizabeth Waterston, eds. *The Selected Journals of L.M. Montgomery, Vol. I: 1889-1910.* Toronto: Oxford University Press, 1985.

185 RUBIO, Mary and Elizabeth Waterston, eds. *The Selected Journals of L.M. Montgomery, Volume II: 1910-1921.* Toronto: Oxford University Press, 1987.

186 RUBIO, Mary and Elizabeth Waterston, eds. *The Selected Journals of L.M. Montgomery: Vol. III, 1921-1929.* Toronto: Oxford University Press, 1992.

187 RUBIO, Mary and Elizabeth Waterston. *Writing a Life: L.M. Montgomery.* Toronto: ECW Press, 1995.

188 RUSSELL, D.W. "L.M. Montgomery: la vie et l'oeuvre d'un écrivain populaire." *Etudes canadiennes/Canadian Studies* 20 (1986): 101-13.

189 RUSSELL, Ruth Weber, D.W. Russell and Rea Wilmshurst. *Lucy Maud Montgomery: A Preliminary Bibliography.* Waterloo: University of Waterloo Library, 1986.

190 SAINTE-MARIE-ÉLEUTHÈRE, Soeur. *La Mère dans le roman canadien-français.* Québec: Presses de l'Université Laval, 1964.

191 SAINT-MARTIN, Lori. "Gabrielle Roy: The Mother's Voice, The Daughter's Text." *American Review of Canadian Studies* 20, 3 (Autumn 1990): 303-26.

192 ST. PETER, Christine. "'Woman's Truth' and the Native Tradition: Anne Cameron's *Daughters of Copper Woman.*" *Feminist Studies* 15, 3 (Fall 1989): 499-523.

193 SCHEIER, L., S. Sheard, and E. Wachtel, eds. *Language in Her Eye: Views on Writing and Gender by Canadian Women Writing in English*. Toronto: Coach House Press, 1990.

194 SHIELDS, Carol. *Susanna Moodie: Voice and Vision*. Ottawa: Borealis Press, 1977.

195 SHIELDS, Carol. "Three Canadian Women: Fiction or Autobiography?" *Atlantis* 4, 1 (Fall 1978): 49-54. [Susanna Moodie, Jane Ellice, Susan Moir Allison]

196 SILVERA, Makeda, ed. *Piece of My Heart: A Lesbian of Colour Anthology*. Toronto: Sister Vision Press, 1992.

197 SILVERA, Makeda, ed. *The Other Woman: Women of Colour in Contemporary Canadian Literature*. Toronto: Sister Vision Press, 1995.

198 SIMARD, Louise. "Les romancières de l'histoire: Le Québec en fiction." *Recherches féministes* 6, 1 (1993): 69-83.

199 SMART, Patricia. *Writing in the Father's House: The Emergence of the Feminine in the Quebec Literary Tradition*. Toronto: University of Toronto Press, 1990.

200 SMART, Patricia. "The (In?)Compatibility of Gender and Nation in Canadian and Québécois Feminist Writing." *Essays on Canadian Writing* 54 (Winter 1994): 12-22.

201 SMART, Patricia. "Writing in the Father's House: the Emergence of the Feminine in the Québec Literary Tradition." *Journal of Canadian Studies* 29, 2 (Summer 1994): 189-94.

202 SMITH, Erin. "Gender and National Identity in *The Journals of Susanna Moodie* and *Tamsen Donner: A Woman's Journey*." *Frontiers* 13, 2 (1993): 75-88.

203 SRIVASTAVA, Aruna. "Imag(in)ing Racism: South Asian Canadian Women Writers." In *ReImagining Women: Representations of Women in Culture*, eds. Shirley Neuman and Glennis Stephenson, 299-314. Toronto: University of Toronto Press, 1993.

204 STANZEL, Franz K. "Innocent Eyes? Canadian Landscape as Seen by Frances Brooke, Susanna Moodie and Others." *International Journal of Canadian Studies* 4 (Fall 1991): 97-110.

205 STEVENS, Peter. *Dorothy Livesay: Patterns in a Poetic Life*. Toronto: ECW Press, 1992.

206 STOUCK, D. "'Secrets of the Prison House': Mrs. Moodie and the Canadian Imagination." *Dalhousie Review* 54, 3 (Autumn 1974): 463-72.

207 STOUCK, David, ed. *Ethel Wilson: Stories, Essays, Letters*. Vancouver: University of British Columbia Press, 1987.

208 STRATFORD, Philip. *Marie-Claire Blais*. Toronto: Forum House, 1971.

209 SULLIVAN, Rosemary. *Shadow Maker: The Life of Gwendolyn MacEwen*. Toronto: HarperCollins, 1995.

210 TAUSKY, Thomas E. *Sara Jeannette Duncan: Novelist of Empire*. Port Credit, ON: P.D. Meany Co., 1979.

211 TAUSKY, Thomas E. "In Search of a Canadian Liberal: The Case of Sara Jeannette Duncan." *Ontario History* 83, 2 (June 1991): 85-108.

212 THÉRY, Chantal. "Ecrivaines de la Nouvelle France: entre le mal du pays et prendre pays." *Québec Studies* 12 (Spring/Summer 1991): 11-19.

213 THOMAS, Clara. "Happily Ever After: Canadian Women in Fiction and Fact." *Canadian Literature* 34 (Autumn 1967): 45-53.

214 THOMAS, Clara. *Love and Work Enough: The Life of Anna Jameson*. Toronto: University of Toronto Press, 1967.

215 THOMAS, Clara. *Margaret Laurence*. Toronto: McClelland and Stewart, 1969.

216 THOMAS, Clara. "Proud Lineage: Willa Cather and Margaret Laurence." *Canadian Review of American Studies* (Spring 1971): 1-12.

217 THOMAS, Clara. "Journeys to Freedom." *Canadian Literature* 51 (Winter 1972): 11-19. [Anna Jameson, Catharine Parr Traill, Susanna Moodie]

218 THOMAS, Clara. "Traill's Canadian Settlers." *Canadian Children's Literature* 5/6 (1976): 31-39.

219 THOMAS, Clara. "Canadian Social Mythologies in Sara Jeannette Duncan's *The Imperialist*." *Journal of Canadian Studies* 12, 2 (Spring 1977): 38-49.

220 THOMAS, Clara. "Women Writers and the New Land." In *The New Land: Studies in a Literary Theme*, eds. Richard Chadbourne and Hallvard Dahlie. Waterloo: Wilfrid Laurier University Press, 1978.

221 THOMAS, Clara, Carol Shields and Donna E. Smyth. "'Thinking Back Through Our Mothers': Tradition in Canadian Women's Writing." In *Re(Dis)covering Our Foremothers: Nineteenth Century Canadian Women Writers*, ed. Lorraine McMullen, 5-21. Ottawa: University of Ottawa Press, 1989.

222 THOMPSON, Elizabeth. *The Pioneer Woman: A Canadian Character Type*. Montreal and Kingston: McGill-Queen's University Press, 1991.

223 THURSTON, John. "Rewriting *Roughing It*." In *Future Indicative: Literary Theory and Canadian Literature*, ed. John Moss. Ottawa: University of Ottawa Press, 1987.

224 THURSTON, John, ed. *Voyages: Short Narratives of Susanna Moodie*. Ottawa: University of Ottawa Press, 1991.

225 TIERNEY, Frank M., ed. *The Isabella Valancy Crawford Symposium*. Ottawa: University of Ottawa Press, 1979.

226 TOUGAS, Gérard. *Histoire de la littérature canadienne-française*. Paris: Presses Universitaires de France, 1960.

227 TYE, Diane. "Women's Oral Narrative Traditions as Depicted in Lucy Maud Montgomery's Fiction, 1918-1939." In *Myth and Milieu: Atlantic Literature and Culture, 1918-1939*, ed. Gwendolyn Davies, 123-35. Fredericton: Acadiensis Press, 1993.

228 VAN HERK, Aritha. "Women Writers and the Prairie: Spies in an Indifferent Landscape." In *A Passion for Identity: An Introduction to Canadian Studies*, 2nd edition, eds. David Taras, Beverly Rasporich and Eli Mandel, 471-79. Nelson Canada, 1993.

229 VAN STEEN, Marcus. *Pauline Johnson: Her Life and Work*. Toronto: Hodder and Stoughton, 1965; 2nd edition, 1973.

230 VAN WART, Alice, ed. *Necessary Secrets: The Journal of Elizabeth Smart*. Ottawa: Deneau, 1986.

231 VAN WART, Alice. "'Life Out of Art': Elizabeth Smart's Early Journals." In *Essays on Life Writing: From Genre to Critical Practice*, ed. Marlene Kadar. Toronto: University of Toronto Press, 1992.

232 VERDUYN, Christl. "Between the Lines: Marian Engel's *Cahiers* and Notebooks." In *Essays on Life Writing: From Genre to Critical Practice*, ed. Marlene Kadar. Toronto: University of Toronto Press, 1992.

233 VERDUYN, Christl, ed. *Dear Marian, Dear Hugh: The MacLennan-Engel Correspondence*. Ottawa: University of Ottawa Press, 1995.

234 VERDUYN, Christl. *Marian Engel's Writings*. Montreal and Kingston: McGill-Queen's University Press, 1995.

235 VINCENT, Thomas. "The Image and Function of Women in the Poetry of Affection in Eighteenth Century Maritime Canada." In *Making Adjustments: Change and Continuity in Planter Nova Scotia, 1759-1800*, ed. Margaret Conrad, 234-46. Fredericton, Acadiensis Press, 1991.

236 WALDIE, Jean H. "The Iroquois Poetess, Pauline Johnson." *Ontario History* 60 (1948): 65-76.

237 WATERSTON, Elizabeth. "Lucy Maud Montgomery, 1874-1942." In *The Clear Spirit: Twenty Canadian Women and Their Times*, ed. Mary Quayle Innis. Toronto: University of Toronto Press, 1966.

238 WEAVER, John. "Society and Culture in Rural and Small-Town Ontario: Alice Munro's Testimony on the Last Forty Years." In *Patterns of the Past: Interpreting Ontario's History*, eds. Roger Hall, William Westfall and Laurel Sefton MacDowell, 381-402. Toronto and Oxford: Dundurn Press, 1988.

239 WHITRIDGE, Margaret Coulby. "The Distaff Side of the Confederation Group: Women's Contribution to Early Nationalist Canadian Literature." *Atlantis* 4, 1 (Fall 1978): 30-39.

240 WILKINSON, Shelagh. "By and About Women." In *Changing Patterns: Women in Canada*, eds. Sandra Burt, Lorraine Code and Lindsay Dorney, 204-36. Toronto: McClelland & Stewart, 1988; revised in 2nd edition, 338-90, 1993.

241 WILLIAMSON, Janice. *Sounding Differences: Conversations with Seventeen Canadian Women Writers*. Toronto: University of Toronto Press, 1993.

242 WOOD, Susan. "God's Doormats: Women in Canadian Prairie Fiction." *Journal of Popular Culture* 14, 2 (1980): 350-59.

243 YOUNG, Alan R. "L.M. Montgomery's *Rilla of Ingleside* (1920): Romance and the Experience of War." In *Myth and Milieu: Atlantic Literature and Culture, 1918-1939*, ed. Gwendolyn Davies, 95-122. Fredericton: Acadiensis Press, 1993.

244 ZELMANOVITS, Judith. "Louisa Murray, Writing Woman." *Canadian Woman Studies* 7, 3 (Fall 1986): 39-42.

245 ZIMMERMAN, Cynthia. *Playwrighting Women: Female Voices in English Canada*. Edited by Christopher Innes. Toronto: Simon & Pierre Publishing, 1994.

PERFORMING

246 ALBANI, Emma. *Forty Years of Song*. London: Mills and Boon, 1911; New York: Arno Press, 1977.

247 BASZCZYNSKI, Marilyn. "Laure Conan: Un théâtre au féminin au 19e siècle." *Theatre History in Canada* 14, 1 (Spring 1993): 20-30.

248 BEAUCAGE, Christian. "La 'divine' scandaleuse: Sarah Bernhardt au Québec." *Cap-aux-Diamants* 35 (automne 1993): 38-41.

249 BROTMAN, Ruth C. *Pauline Donalda: The Life and Career of a Canadian Prima Donna*. Montreal: Eagle Publishing Co., 1975.

250 BUDNICK, Carol. "The Performing Arts as a Field of Endeavour for Winnipeg Women, 1870-1930." *Manitoba History* 11 (Spring 1986): 15-21.

251 CHERNIAVSKY, Felix Benjamin. *The Salome Dancer: The Life and Times of Maud Allan*. Toronto: McClelland & Stewart, 1991.

252 DARLINGTON, Esther Hope. "The Fabulous Fanny Faucault." *British Columbia Historical News* 28, 4 (Fall 1995): 6-14.

253 DAY, Moira and Marilyn Potts. "Elizabeth Sterling Haynes: Initiator of Alberta Theatre." *Theatre History in Canada* 8 (Spring 1987): 8-35.

254 DYBA, Kenneth. *Betty Mitchell*. Calgary: Detselig, 1986. [theatre in Calgary]

255 FLYNN, Anne. "Prairie Pioneers: Canadian Women in Dance." In *Women as Artist: Papers in Honour of Marsha Hanen*, eds. Christine Mason Sutherland and Beverly Matson Rasporich. Calgary: University of Calgary Press, 1993.

256 FOWKE, Edith with Jay Rahn. *A Family Heritage: LaRena Clark's Story and Songs*. Calgary: University of Calgary Press, 1993.

257 FOWLER, Marian. "High Priestess of 'It.'" *The Beaver* 74, 5 (October/November 1994): 18-25. [Elinor Sutherland Glyn]

258 FRENCH, Maida Parlow. *Kathleen Parlow, A Portrait*. Toronto: Ryerson Press, 1967.

259 GOLD, Muriel. "A Missionary of the French Language Through Drama: Madame Jean-Louis Audet (1890-1970)." *Theatre History in Canada* 12, 1 (Spring 1991): 79-94.

260 GRIFFITHS, Linda and Maria Campbell. *The Book of Jessica: A Theatrical Transformation.* Toronto: Coach House Press, 1989.

261 KELLER, Betty C. "The Chastely Voluptuous Weblings." *The Beaver* 66, 2 (April/May 1986): 13-18.

262 KIVI, K. Linda. *Canadian Women Making Music.* Toronto: Green Dragon Press, 1992.

263 LAMB, Kathryn. "Kitchener Ladies' Band." *Waterloo Historical Society* 63 (1975): 4-10. [1920s and 1930s]

264 LAWRENCE, R. "Lillie Langtry in Canada and the USA, 1882-1917." *Theatre History in Canada* 10 (Spring 1989): 30-42.

265 LEFÈBVRE, Marie-Thérèse. *La création musicale des femmes au Québec.* Montréal: Éditions du remue-ménage, 1991.

266 LE VAY, John. *Margaret Anglin, A Stage Life.* Toronto: Simon & Pierre, 1989.

267 MacDONALD, Cheryl. *Emma Albani: Victorian Diva.* Toronto: Dundurn Press, 1984.

268 MacDONALD, Cheryl. "Canada's Queen of Song." *The Beaver* 66, 6 (Dec. 1986/Jan. 1987): 19-25. [Emma Albani]

269 MacDONALD, Cheryl. "The Star from Hamilton." *The Beaver* 69, 6 (Dec. 1989/Jan. 1990): 23-29. [Julia Arthur]

270 MacLENNAN, Joss. "Canadian Film Stars." *Fireweed* 8 (Fall 1980): 75-79.

271 MAYES, Hubert G. "Kathleen Parlow: A Life in Music." *The Beaver* 74, 4 (Aug./Sept. 1994): 30-36.

272 MEW, Diane, ed. *Life Before Stratford: The Memoirs of Amelia Hall.* Toronto: Dundurn Press, 1989.

273 MOSS, Jane. "Filial (Im)pieties: Mothers and Daughters in Quebec Women's Theatre." *American Review of Canadian Studies* 19, 2 (1989): 177-86.

274 MUCH, Rita, ed. *Women on the Canadian Stage: The Legacy of Hrotsvit.* Winnipeg: Blizzard Publishing, 1992.

275 O'NEILL, P.B. "Regina's Golden Age of Theatre: Her Playhouses and Players." *Saskatchewan History* 28, 1 (Winter 1975): 29-37.

276 PELLETIER, Pol. "Petite histoire du théâtre des femmes au Québec." *Canadian Women's Studies* 2, 2 (1980): 58-87.

277 POTVIN, Gilles, trans. and ed. *Mémoires d'Emma Albani.* Montréal: Éditions du Jour, 1972.

278 ROBERTSON, William. *k.d. lang: Carrying the Torch.* Toronto: ECW Press, 1992.

279 ROONEY, Frances. "The Montreal Women's Symphony." *Atlantis* 5, 1 (Fall 1979): 70-82.

280 SCHWARTZ, Ellen. *Born a Woman: Seven Canadian Women Singer-Songwriters.* Winlaw, BC: Polestar, 1988.

281 SHORTT, Mary. "Victorian Temptations." *The Beaver* 68 (December 1988/January 1989): 4-13.

282 SPERDAKOS, Paula. *Dora Mavor Moore: Pioneer of the Canadian Theatre.* Toronto: ECW Press, 1995.

283 STARR, Victoria. *All You Get is Me: The Real Story of k.d. lang.* Toronto: Random House, 1994.

284 VOGAN, Nancy. "The Musical Traditions of the Planters and 'Mary Miller her book.'" In *Making Adjustments: Change and Continuity in Planter Nova Scotia, 1759-1800,* ed. Margaret Conrad, 247-52. Fredericton, Acadiensis Press, 1991.

285 WAGNER, Anton. "Elsie Park Gowan: 'Distinctively Canadian.'" *Theatre History in Canada* 8 (Spring 1987): 68-82.

286 WARNER, Mary Jane. "Anne Fairbrother Hill: 'A Chaste and Elegant Dancer.'" *Theatre History in Canada* 12, 2 (Fall 1992): 169-91.

VISUAL

287 ADAMS, Annmarie. "Les représentations des femmes dans la revue de l'Institut royal d'architecture du Canada, de 1924 à 1973." *Recherches féministes* 7, 2 (1994): 7-36.

288 ADAMS, Annmarie. "Building Barriers: Images of Women in Canada's Architectural Press, 1924-73." *Resources for Feminist Research* 23, 3 (Fall 1994): 11-23.

289 ADAMS, Timothy Dow. "'Painting Above Paint': Telling Li(v)es in Emily Carr's Literary Self-Portraits." *Journal of Canadian Studies* 27, 2 (Summer 1992): 37-48.

290 BERLO, Janet. "Inuit Women and Graphic Arts: Female Creativity and its Cultural Context." *Canadian Journal of Native Studies* 9, 2 (1989): 293-315.

291 BERLO, Janet Catherine. "Dreaming of Double Woman: The Ambivalent Role of the Female Artist in North American Indian Myth." *American Indian Quarterly* 17, 1 (Winter 1993): 31-44.

292 BLANCHARD, Paula. *The Life of Emily Carr.* Vancouver: Douglas & McIntyre, 1987.

293 CARDINAL-SCHUBERT, Joane. "Surviving as a Native Woman Artist." *Canadian Woman Studies* 11, 1 (Spring 1990): 50-51. Reprinted in *Racism in Canada,* ed. Ormond McKague, 7-10. Saskatoon: Fifth House Publishers, 1991.

294 CARR, Emily. *The Book of Small.* Toronto: Clarke Irwin, 1971.

295 CARR, Emily. *The House of All Sorts.* Toronto: Clarke Irwin, 1971.

296 CARR, Emily. *Growing Pains.* Toronto: Clarke Irwin, 1971.

297 CARR, Emily. *Hundreds and Thousands.* Toronto: Clarke Irwin, 1971.

298 COATES, Colin M. "Like 'The Thames towards Putney': The Appropriation of Landscape in Lower Canada." *Canadian Historical Review* 74, 3 (Sept. 1993): 317-43.[Elizabeth Amherst Hale]

299 COBB, Myrna and Sher Morgan. *Eight Women Photographers of British Columbia*. Victoria: Applied Communication Program, Camosun College, 1979. [100-year photographic anthology]

300 COLLINS, Alice Roger. *Katherine E. Wallis: Canadian Sculptor*. Fort Erie, ON: Review Company, 1949.

301 COLMAN, M.E. "Emily Carr and Her Sisters." *Dalhousie Review* 27 (April 1947): 29-32.

302 DAVIS, Angela E. "Mary Riter Hamilton: Manitoba Artist, 1873-1954." *Manitoba History* 11 (Spring 1986): 22-27.

303 DAVIS, Angela E. *No Man's Land: The Battlefield Paintings of Mary Riter Hamilton, 1919-1922*. Winnipeg: University of Winnipeg, 1989; 2nd edition, 1992.

304 DAVIS, Angela. "An Artist in No-Man's Land." *The Beaver* 69, 5 (Oct./Nov. 1989): 6-16. [Mary Riter Hamilton]

305 DODD, Kerry Mason, ed. *Sunlight in the Shadows: The Landscape of Emily Carr*. With photography by Michael Breuer. Toronto: Oxford University Press, 1984.

306 DOUGLAS, R. Alan. "Paintings of Catherine Reynolds." *University of Windsor Review* 2, 1 (Fall 1966): 57-66. [Upper Canada]

307 DRISCOLL-ENGELSTAD, Bernadette. "A Woman's Vision, A Woman's Voice: Inuit Textile Art from Arctic Canada." *Inuit Art Quarterly* 9, 2 (Summer 1994): 4-13.

308 "Ella Hartt: Pioneer Photographer." *Alberta History* 27, 1 (Winter 1979): 17-24.

309 FARR, Dorothy and Natalie Luckyj, eds. *From Women's Eyes: Women Painters in Canada*. Kingston: Agnes Etherington Art Centre, 1975.

310 FULFORD, Robert. "The Trouble with Emily." *Canadian Art* 10, 4 (Winter 1993): 33-39. Reprinted in *Coming of Age: Readings in Canadian History Since World War II*, eds. Donald Avery and Roger Hall, 24-31. Toronto: Harcourt Brace & Company Canada, 1996. [Emily Carr]

311 GOSSAGE, Carolyn, ed. *Double Duty: Sketches and Diaries of Molly Lamb Bobak—Canadian War Artist*. Toronto: Dundurn Press, 1992.

312 HALL, Constance. "Women Artists in Canada: A History of Our Own." *Canadian Review of Art Education–Research and Issues* 20, 1 (1993): 24-29.

313 HAYMAN, Sasha McInnes, Marguerite Andersen, Joyce Scane and Anneke Steenbeck, eds. "Women's Art." A special issue of *Resources for Feminist Research* 13, 4 (Dec. 1984/Jan. 1985).

314 HAYWARD, Victoria and Edith S. Watson. *Romantic Canada*. Toronto: Macmillan, 1920.

315 HEMBROFF-SCHLEICHER, Edythe. *M. E.: A Portrayal of Emily Carr*. Toronto: Clarke Irwin, 1969.

316 HEMBROFF-SCHLEICHER, Edythe. *Emily Carr: The Untold Story*. Saanichton, BC: Hancock House, 1978.

317 HOPKINS, Elisabeth Margaret. "Grandmama." *The Beaver* (Winter 1976): 25-29. [Frances Anne Hopkins]

318 HUNEAULT, Kristina. "Heroes of a Different Sort: Gender and Patriotism in the War Workers of Frances Loring and Florence Wyle." *Journal of Canadian Art History* 15, 2 (1993): 26-49.

319 INGLIS, D. Grace. "Hortense Gordon, ARCA." *Journal of Canadian Studies* 29, 3 (Fall 1994): 108-30.

320 JOHNSON, A.M. "Edward and Frances Hopkins of Montreal." *The Beaver* (Autumn 1971): 4-19.

321 JOHNSON, Ellen H. *Fragments: Recalled at 80: The Art Memoirs of Ellen Johnson*. North Vancouver: Gallerie Publications, 1993.

322 JONES, Laura. "Hannah Maynard: Pioneer Photographer." *This Magazine* 10, 1 (February 1976).

323 JONES, Laura. "Canadian Woman Photographers, 1841-1910." *Resources for Feminist Research* 13, 4 (Dec. 1984/Jan. 1985): 13-17.

324 JONES, Laura and Monique Brunet, eds. "Canadian Women Photographers." A special issue of *Canadian Women's Studies* 2, 3 (1980).

325 JOYCE-JONES, Susanna. "A Stitch Here...A Stitch There." *Resources for Feminist Research* 13, 4 (Dec. 1984/Jan. 1985): 11-13. [Canadian women artists, pre-1930]

326 LAMBTON, Gunda. "A Collaboration in Ottawa: The Saint-Vincent Hospital Mural." *Woman's Art Journal* 13 (Spring/Summer 1992): 19-22.

327 LAMBTON, Gunda. *Stealing the Show: Seven Women Artists in Canadian Public Art*. Montreal and Kingston: McGill-Queen's University Press, 1994.

328 LEFEBVRE, Florent. "Emily Carr 1871-1945." *Québec-Histoire* 2, 1 (automne 1972): 9-11.

329 LEROUX, Odette, Marion E. Jackson and Minnie Aodla Freeman, eds. *Inuit Women Artists: Voices from Cape Dorset*. Vancouver/Seattle/Hull: Douglas & MacIntyre/University of Washington Press/Canadian Museum of Civilization, 1994.

330 "Letters from Emily Carr." *University of Toronto Quarterly* 41, 2 (Winter 1971): 93-150.

331 LUCKYJ, Natalie. *Visions and Victories: Ten Canadian Women Artists, 1914-1945*. London, ON: London Regional Art Gallery, 1983.

332 MAJZELS, Claudine. "Constructing the Woman Artist: Marie Hewson Guest in Winnipeg." *Manitoba History* 29 (Spring 1995): 2-10.

333 MARSH, Winifred. "A Woman and Her Art: Winifred Marsh's Northern Encounter." *The Review* 62, 5 (1978): 20-25.

334 McCARTHY, Doris. *A Fool in Paradise: An Artist's Early Life*. Toronto: Macfarlane Walter & Ross, 1990.

335 McCARTHY, Doris. *The Good Wine: An Artist Comes of Age*. Toronto: Macfarlane Walter & Ross, 1991.

336 McDOUGALL, Anne. *Anne Savage: The Story of a Canadian Painter.* Montreal: Harvest House, 1977.

337 MEADOWCROFT, Barbara. "A Feminist Methodology for a Biography of the Beaver Hall Group." Simone de Beauvoir Institute. *Newsletter* 12, 2 (1992): 8-17.

338 MILLAR, Joyce. "The Beaver Hall Group: Painting in Montreal, 1920-1940." *Woman's Art Journal* 13 (Spring/Summer 1992): 3-9.

339 MURRAY, Joan. "Daffodils in Winter: Pegi Nicol MacLeod in Canadian Art." *Resources for Feminist Research* 13, 4 (Dec. 1984/Jan. 1985): 26-28.

340 MURRAY, Joan. "Isabel McLaughlin." *Resources for Feminist Research* 13, 4 (Dec. 1984/Jan.1985): 17-20.

341 MURRAY, Joan. "The Passion of Emily Carr." *Journal of Canadian Studies* 25, 3 (Fall 1990): 167-70.

342 NASH, Joanna. "Montreal's Powerhouse Gallery: The Evolution of a Woman's Art Space." *Fireweed* 3/4 (Summer 1979): 22-27.

343 PAZDRO, Roberta J. "Mildred Valley Thornton (1890-1967): painter of the native people." *Canadian Women's Studies* 1 (Spring 1979): 103-4.

344 PAZDRO, Roberta J. "From Pastels to Chisel: The Changing Role of BC Women Artists." In *Not Just Pin Money: Selected Essays on the History of Women's Work in British Columbia,* eds. Barbara K. Latham and Roberta J. Pazdro, 119-40. Victoria: Camosun College, 1984.

345 PEARSON, Carol. *Emily Carr as I Knew Her.* Toronto: Clarke, Irwin, 1954.

346 PEDERSEN, Diana and Martha Phemister. "Women and Photography in Ontario, 1839-1929: A Case Study of the Interaction of Gender and Technology." *Scientia Canadensis* 9, 1 (June 1985): 27-52. Reprinted in *Despite the Odds: Essays on Canadian Women and Science,* ed. Marianne Gosztonyi Ainley, 88-111. Montreal: Véhicule Press, 1990.

347 ROBIDEAU, Henri. "Mattie Gunterman: Photographer." *This Magazine* 12, 3 (July/August 1978): 19-20.

348 ROBIDEAU, Henri. *Flapjacks and Photographs: A History of Mattie Gunterman, Camp Cook and Photographer.* Vancouver: Polestar Press, 1995.

349 ROONEY, Frances. "Finding Edith S. Watson." *Blatant Image* 1 (1981): 86.

350 ROONEY, Frances. "Edith S. Watson, Photographer, and Victoria Hayward, Writer." *Fireweed* 13 (Summer 1982): 60-68.

351 ROONEY, Frances. "Finding Edith S. Watson." *Resources for Feminist Research* 12, 1 (March 1983): 26-28.

352 ROONEY, Frances. "Loring and Wyle, Sculptors." *Pink Ink* (July 1983): 18-20.

353 ROONEY, Frances. "Frances Loring and Florence Wyle, Sculptors." *Resources for Feminist Research,* 13, 4 (Dec. 1984/Jan. 1985): 21-23.

354 ROONEY, Frances. "Edith S. Watson: A Photoessay." *Canadian Woman Studies* 7, 3 (Fall 1986): 48-49.

355 ROONEY, Frances. *Edith S. Watson: Rural Canadians at Work, 1890-1920.* Sackville, NB: Owens Art Gallery, Mount Allison University, 1991.

356 ROONEY, Frances. *My Dear, Dear Edith.* Galiano Island, BC: Nuse Gallery, 1994.

357 ROONEY, Frances. "Edith S. Watson: Photographing Women in Rural Canada." *International Journal of Canadian Studies* 11 (Spring 1995): 185-94.

358 ROONEY, Frances. *Working Light: The Wandering Life of Photographer Edith S. Watson.* Ottawa: Carleton University Press, 1996.

359 SHADBOLT, Doris. "Emily Carr: Legend and Reality." *Artscanada* 156/7 (June/July 1971): 17-21.

360 SHADBOLT, Doris. *Emily Carr.* Vancouver: J.J. Douglas, 1975.

361 SHADBOLT, Doris. *The Art of Emily Carr.* Vancouver: Douglas & McIntyre, 1979.

362 SHRIVE, Norman. "What Happened to Pauline?" *Canadian Literature* 12 (Summer 1962): 25-38. [Pauline Johnson]

363 SISLER, Rebecca. *The Girls: A Biography of Frances Loring and Florence Wyle.* Toronto: Clarke, Irwin, 1972.

364 SMITH, Peter L. "Emily Carr: A Review Article." *BC Studies* 45 (Spring 1980): 128-34.

365 SPARLING, Mary. "'The lighter auxiliaries': Women artists in Nova Scotia in the early nineteenth century." *Atlantis* 5, 1 (Fall 1979): 83-106.

366 SUTHERLAND, Christine and Beverly Rasporich, eds. *Woman as Artist: Essays in Honour of Marsha Hanen.* Calgary: University of Calgary Press, 1994.

367 TAYLOR, Charles. "Emily Carr." In his *Six Journeys: A Canadian Pattern,* 153-88. Toronto: Anansi, 1977.

368 TIPPETT, Maria. "'A Paste Solitaire in a Steel Claw Setting': Emily Carr and Her Public." *BC Studies* 20 (Winter 1973/74): 265-81.

369 TIPPETT, Maria. *Emily Carr: A Biography.* Markham, ON: Penguin Books, 1979.

370 TIPPETT, Maria. *By A Lady: Celebrating Three Centuries of Art by Canadian Women.* Toronto: Penguin Books Canada, 1992.

371 WALKER, Doreen, ed. *"Dear Nan": Letters of Emily Carr, Nan Cheney, and Humphrey Toms.* Vancouver: University of British Columbia Press, 1990.

372 WHITEHEAD, Ruth Holmes. "Christina Morris: Micmac Artist and Artist's Model." *Material History Bulletin* 3 (Spring 1977): 1-14.

373 WILKS, Claire Weissman. *The Magic Box: The Eccentric Genius of Hannah Maynard.* Toronto: Exile Editions, 1980. [photographer]

374 WILKS, Claire Weissman. "The Eccentric Genius of Hannah Maynard." *Saturday Night* 95 (November 1980): 35-40.

EDUCATION

IN CANADA, as in other countries, feminist scholars in the 1970s developed an intense interest in the study of women's education, recognizing its importance in their own lives and believing it to be a critical determinant of the status of women in society. One of the first topics to attract scholarly attention was the struggle of nineteenth-century women to gain access to higher education and professional training. Female enclaves within the university, particularly schools of nursing and home economics, have generated a good deal of interest, and several scholars are now examining paramedical education in Quebec universities. The status of women faculty from the nineteenth century to the present decade of "chilly climate" reports has been, not surprisingly, an ongoing preoccupation of feminist scholars. More recently, historians of higher education have turned their attention to curriculum, female student culture, and the relations between female and male students in co-educational institutions.

In many studies of the public and private schooling of girls, feminist scholars have noted the prevalence throughout Canada's past of the view that the aim of girls' education should be the preparation of ideal wives and mothers. Campaigns to introduce domestic science, or home economics, into the schools of Ontario, Quebec and British Columbia in the early twentieth century have been examined by several scholars, with special attention paid to the prominent role of Adelaide Hoodless. The introduction of commercial and vocational education for girls is just beginning to attract the notice of historians. The support of women's organizations, especially the WCTU and the IODE, for educational reform at the turn of the century has been documented in several studies, as has the role of women in the Home and School Movement. Quebec historians have paid particular attention to the influence of religious nationalism on girls' education, and to the dominant role of female teaching orders from New France until the mid-twentieth century.

Since the publication of Alison Prentice's pioneering 1975 study of the feminization of the teaching profession in the nineteenth century, teachers have received more attention from Canadian women's historians than any other occupational group, with the possible exception of nurses. Continuing interest in the gendering of educational structures and institutions has led historians to document the processes by which the ranks of teachers came to be dominated by women, and the nature of their relationships with male teachers, school trustees, principals and school inspectors. Many recent studies have examined both the difficult working conditions faced by female teachers, especially in rural schools, and the formation of teachers' associations, with particular attention to the separate associations that addressed the special concerns of women teachers.

GENERAL

375 BOURNE, Paula, *et al*, eds. *Feminism and Education: A Canadian Perspective, Volume 2.* Toronto: Centre for Women's Studies in Education, Ontario Institute for Studies in Education, 1994.

376 BRODRIBB, Somer. "Special Topic Annotated Bibliographies: Women's Education." *Resources for Feminist Research* 13, 1 (March 1984): 38-76.

377 BRODRIBB, Somer and Mary O'Brien, eds. "Women and Education." A two-part special issue of *Resources for Feminist Research* 12, 3 (1983) and 13, 1 (1984).

378 CANADIAN CONGRESS FOR LEARNING OPPORTUNITIES FOR WOMEN. *Decade of Promise: An Assessment of Canadian Women's Status in Education, Training and Employment, 1976-1985.* Toronto: Avebury Research and Consulting, 1986.

379 FAHMY-EID, Nadia and Micheline Dumont, eds. *Maîtresses de maison, maîtresses d'école: Femmes, famille et éducation dans l'histoire du Québec.* Montréal: Boréal Express, 1983.

380 FORMAN, Frieda, *et al*, eds. *Feminism and Education: A Canadian Perspective.* Toronto: Centre for Women's Studies in Education, Ontario Institute for Studies in Education, 1990.

381 GASKELL, Jane and Arlene McLaren, eds. *Women and Education: A Canadian Perspective.* Calgary: Detselig, 1987; 2nd edition, 1991.

382 GASKELL, Jane, Arlene McLaren and Myra Novogrodsky. *Claiming an Education: Feminism and Canadian Schools.* Toronto: Our Schools/Our Selves Education Foundation and Garamond Press, 1989.

383 HEAP, Ruby and Alison Prentice, eds. *Gender and Education in Ontario: An Historical Reader.* Toronto: Canadian Scholars' Press, 1991.

384 PIERSON, Ruth Roach. "Education and Training." In *Canadian Women's Issues, Volume II: Bold Visions,* Ruth Roach Pierson and Marjorie Griffin Cohen, 162-262. Toronto: James Lorimer and Company, 1995.

385 PRENTICE, Alison. "Towards a Feminist History of Women and Education." In *Approaches to Educational History,* eds. David C. Jones, Nancy M. Sheehan, Robert M. Stamp and Neil G. McDonald. Winnipeg: University of Manitoba Press, 1981.

386 REYNOLDS, Cecilia and Beth Young, eds. *Women and Leadership in Canadian Education.* Calgary: Temeron Books Inc., 1995.

HIGHER EDUCATION/ PROFESSIONAL EDUCATION

387 AINLEY, Marianne Gosztonyi. "A Woman of Integrity: Kathleen Gough's 'Career' in Canada, 1967-1990." *Anthropologica* 35, 2 (June 1993): 235-43.

388 ANDERSON, R.O. "A Study of the Leisure Time Interests and Activities of First Year Women at the University of Alberta." *Alberta Journal of Educational Research* 7 (1961): 65-73.

389 ARMOUR, Margaret-Ann. "WISEST: An Initiative at the University of Alberta to Encourage Women into the Sciences and Engineering." In *Standing on New Ground: Women in Alberta,* eds. Catherine A. Cavanaugh and Randi R. Warne, 145-53. Edmonton: University of Alberta Press, 1993.

390 AXELROD, Paul. "Moulding the middle class: Student life at Dalhousie University in the 1930s." *Acadiensis* 15, 1 (Autumn 1985): 84-122.

391 AXELROD, Paul. *Making a Middle Class: Student Life in Canada During the Thirties.* Montreal and Kingston: McGill-Queen's University Press, 1990.

392 BACKHOUSE, Constance. "Women Faculty at the University of Western Ontario: Reflections on the Employment Equity Award." *Canadian Journal of Women and the Law* 4, 1 (1990): 36-65.

393 BANNERJI, Himani, Linda Carty, Kari Dehli, Susan Heald and Kate McKenna. *Unsettling Relations: The University as a Site of Feminist Struggles.* Toronto: Women's Press, 1991.

394 BRAMADAT, I.J. and K.I. Chalmers. "Nursing Education in Canada: Historical 'Progress' — Contemporary Issues." *Journal of Advanced Nursing* 14 (1989): 719-26.

395 BURKE, Sara Z. "Science and Sentiment: Social Service and Gender at the University of Toronto, 1888-1910." *Journal of the Canadian Historical Association* NS 4 (1993): 75-93.

396 CAOUETTE, Marie. "Première à l'Université Laval: une femme enseignante." *Cap-aux-Diamants* 21 (printemps 1990): 51-53.

397 CAPLAN, Paula J. *Lifting a Ton of Feathers: A Woman's Guide to Surviving in the Academic World.* Toronto: University of Toronto Press, 1993.

398 CARTY, Linda. "Women's Studies in Canada: A Discourse and Praxis of Education." *Resources for Feminist Research* 20, 3/4 (Fall/Winter 1991): 12-18.

399 CHALUS, Elaine H. "From Friedan to Feminism: Gender and Change at the University of Alberta, 1960-1970." In *Standing on New Ground: Women in Alberta,* eds. Catherine A. Cavanaugh and Randi R. Warne, 119-44. Edmonton: University of Alberta Press, 1993.

400 CHILLY COLLECTIVE, eds. *Breaking Anonymity: The Chilly Climate for Women Faculty.* Waterloo: Wilfrid Laurier University Press, 1995.

401 COLLIN, Johanne. "La dynamique des rapports de sexes à l'université 1940-1980: une étude de cas." *Histoire sociale/Social History* XIX, 38 (November 1986): 365-85.

402 CONWAY, Jill Ker. *True North: A Memoir.* Toronto: Knopf Canada, 1994.

403 DAGG, Anne Innis and Patricia J. Thompson. *MisEducation: Women and Canadian Universities.* Toronto: OISE Press, 1988.

404 DE LA COUR, Lykke and Rose Sheinin. "The Ontario Medical College for Women, 1883 to 1906: Lessons from Gender-separatism in Medical Education." *Canadian Woman Studies* 7, 3 (Fall 1986): 73-77. Reprinted in *Despite the Odds: Essays on Canadian Women and Science,* ed. Marianne Gosztonyi Ainley, 112-20. Montreal: Véhicule Press, 1990; and in *Rethinking Canada: The Promise of Women's History,* 2nd edition, eds. Veronica Strong-Boag and Anita Clair Fellman, 206-14. Toronto: Copp Clark Pitman Ltd., 1991.

405 DEMBSKI, Peter Paul. "Jenny Kidd Trout and the Founding of the Women's Medical Colleges at Kingston and Toronto." *Ontario History* 77, 3 (1985): 183-206.

406 DEN BOGGENDE, Bert. "'The Vassar of the Dominions': The Wesleyan Female College and the Project of a Women's University, 1861-97." *Ontario History* 85, 2 (June 1993): 95-117.

407 DEN BOGGENDE, Bert. "The Female Department of Cobourg's Upper Canada Academy, 1836-42: 'A Monument of Wisdom, Piety, Loyalty and Patriotism.'" *Ontario History* 87, 3 (September 1995): 271-91.

408 DIXON, Marlene. *Things Which Are Done in Secret.* Montreal: Black Rose Books, 1976. [academic purges at McGill]

409 DRAKICH, Janice and Eleanor Maticka-Tyndale. "Feminist Organizing in the Academic Disciplines: The Canadian Sociology and Anthropology Association." In *Women and Social Change: Feminist Activism in Canada,* eds. Jeri Dawn Wine and Janice L. Ristock, 283-98. Toronto: James Lorimer and Company, 1991.

410 DUMONT, Micheline. "Un certificat en Études sur les femmes à Sherbrooke." *Resources for Feminist Research* 20, 3/4 (Fall/Winter 1991): 37-38.

411 FAHMY-EID, Nadia and Aline Charles. "Savoir contrôlé ou pouvoir confisqué? La formation des filles en technologie médicale, réhabilitation et diététique à l'Université de Montréal (1940-1970)." *Recherches féministes* 1, 1 (1988): 5-29.

412 FAHMY-EID, Nadia and Johanne Collin. "Savoir et pouvoir dans l'univers des disciplines paramédicales: la formation en physiothérapie et en diététique à l'Université McGill, 1940-1970." *Histoire sociale/Social History* XXII, 43 (May 1989): 35-63.

413 FINGARD, Judith. "Gender and Inequality at Dalhousie: Faculty Women Before 1950." *Dalhousie Review* 64 (Winter 1984/85): 687-703.

414 FINGARD, Judith. "College, Career and Community: Dalhousie Coeds, 1881-1921." In *Youth, University and Canadian Society: Essays in the Social History of Higher Education,* eds. Paul Axelrod and John G. Reid, 26-50. Montreal and Kingston: McGill-Queen's University Press, 1989.

415 FORD, Anne Rochon. *A Path Not Strewn with Roses: One Hundred Years of Women at the University of Toronto, 1884-1984.* Toronto: University of Toronto Press, 1985.

416 FOSTER, Margaret. *The First Fifty Years: A History of the University Women's Club of Toronto, 1903-1953.* Toronto: University Women's Club of Toronto, 1953.

417 FULTON, Keith Louise and Michele Pujol. "One Step Forward, Two Steps Back: Twenty Years of Women's Studies at the University of Manitoba." *Resources for Feminist Research* 20, 3/4 (Fall/Winter 1991): 31-36.

418 FULTON, Margaret E. "Status of Women in Canadian Universities." *Peace Research* 24, 3 (August 1992): 59-75.

419 GAMMON, Carolyn. "Lesbian Studies Emerging in Canada." In *The More we get Together: Women and Dis/ability,* eds. Houston Stewart, Beth Percival and Elizabeth R. Epperly, 95-111. Charlottetown: Gynergy Books, 1992.

420 GILLETT, Margaret. "Sexism in Higher Education." *Atlantis* 1 (1975/76): 68-81.

421 GILLETT, Margaret. *We Walked Very Warily: A History of Women at McGill.* Montreal: Eden Press, 1982.

422 GILLETT, Margaret. "Carrie Derick (1862-1941) and the Chair of Botany at McGill." In *Despite the Odds: Essays on Canadian Women and Science,* ed. Marianne Gosztonyi Ainley, 74-87. Montreal: Véhicule Press, 1990.

423 GILLETT, Margaret and Kay Sibbald, eds. *A Fair Shake: Autobiographical Essays by McGill Women.* Montreal: Eden Press, 1984.

424 GIROUARD, Guylaine. *L'admission des femmes à l'Université Laval, 1901-1945: un compromis entre des objectifs féministes et des objections cléricales.* Québec: Université Laval, Groupe de recherche multidisciplinaire féministe, 1993.

425 GLEASON, Mona. "'A Separate and "Different" Education': Women and Coeducation at the University of Windsor's Assumption College, 1950-1957." *Ontario History* 84, 2 (June 1992): 119-31.

426 GODFREY, C.M. "The Origins of Medical Education of Women in Ontario." *Medical History* XVII (January 1973): 89-94.

427 GOYDER, John. "Gender Inequalities in Academic Rank." *Canadian Journal of Sociology* 17, 3 (1992): 333-44.

428 GUPPY, N. and K. Pendakur. "The Effects of Gender and Parental Education on Participation within Post-Secondary Education in the 1970s and 1980s." *Canadian Journal of Higher Education* 19, 1 (1989): 49-62.

429 HAYDEN, Michael. "Women and the University of Saskatchewan: Patterns of a problem." *Saskatchewan History* 40, 2 (Spring 1987): 72-82.

430 HEAP, Ruby and Gabriella Logan. "'Contribue à la gloire de Dieu et au bonheur de la patrie': les filles à l'école normale de l'Université d'Ottawa, 1923-1940." *Éducation et francophonie* 19, 3 (1991): 14-22.

431 HOECKER-DRYSDALE, Susan. "Women Sociologists in Canada: The Careers of Helen MacGill Hughes, Aileen Dansken Ross and Jean Robertson Burnet." In *Despite the Odds: Essays on Canadian Women and Science,* ed. Marianne Gosztonyi Ainley, 152-76. Montreal: Véhicule Press, 1990.

432 INNIS, Mary Quayle, ed. *Nursing Education in a Changing Society.* Toronto: University of Toronto Press, 1970. [50th anniversary history of University of Toronto School of Nursing]

433 JACKEL, Susan, ed. *Reaching Out: Canadian Studies, Women's Studies and Adult Education.* Ottawa: Canadian Studies Association, 1984.

434 JEAN, Michèle. "L'enseignement supérieur des filles et son ambigüité: Le collège Marie-Anne, 1932-1958." In *Maîtresses de maison, maîtresses d'école: Femmes, famille et éducation dans l'histoire du Québec,* eds. Nadia Fahmy-Eid and Micheline Dumont, 143-70. Montréal: Boréal Express, 1983.

435 KENNEDY, Dolly Sinclair. "U.B.C.'s Deans of Women." *British Columbia Historical News* 26, 2 (Spring 1993): 19-21.

436 KINNEAR, Mary. "Disappointment in Discourse: Women University Professors at the University of Manitoba Before 1970." *Historical Studies in Education* 4, 2 (Fall 1992): 269-87.

437 KINNEAR, Mary. "How Difference Made a Difference: Women Medical Students at the University of Manitoba in the 1940s." *Manitoba Medicine* 63, 4 (1993): 135-36.

438 KIRKWOOD, Rondalynn. "Discipline Discrimination and Gender Discrimination: The Case of Nursing in Canadian Universities, 1920-1950." *Atlantis* 16, 2 (Spring 1991): 52-63.

439 KIRKWOOD, Rondalynn. "Blending Vigorous Leadership and Womanly Virtues: Edith Kathleen Russell at the University of Toronto, 1920-52." *Canadian Bulletin of Medical History* 11, 1 (1994): 175-205. [nursing education]

440 KIRKWOOD, Rondalynn and Jeannette Bouchard. *"Take Counsel with One Another": A Beginning History of the Canadian Association of University Schools of Nursing.* Ottawa: Canadian Association of University Schools of Nursing, 1992.

441 LAPIERRE, Jo. "The Academic Life of Canadian Coeds, 1880-1900." *Historical Studies in Education* 2, 2 (Fall 1990): 225-45. Reprinted in *Gender and Education in Ontario: An Historical Reader,* eds. Ruby Heap and Alison Prentice, 307-32. Toronto: Canadian Scholars' Press, 1991.

442 LAUZON, Lyne. "Et un jour, elles furent admises à l'Université." *Interface* 15, 1 (janvier-février 1994): 46-47.

443 LEDUC, Constance. "Les orientations des femmes à l'Université de Montréal en 1949/50 et en 1974/75." *Canadian and International Education* 7 (June 1978): 51-58.

444 LENTON, Rhonda L. "Academic Feminists and the Women's Movement in Canada: Continuity or Discontinuity." *Atlantis* 16, 1 (Fall 1990): 57-68.

445 LOOKER, E. Diane. *The Marginal Majority: A Report to the President on the Status of Women at Acadia.* Wolfville, NS: Acadia University, 1990.

446 MacKINNON, Alison. "Interfering With Nature's Mandate: Women, Higher Education and Demographic Change." *Historical Studies in Education* 1, 2 (Fall 1989): 219-37.

447 MacLEOD, Enid Johnson. *Petticoat Doctors: The First Forty Years of Women in Medicine at Dalhousie University.* Lawrencetown Beach, NS: Pottersfield Press, 1990.

448 MANDAL-GIRI, Nilima. "Canadian Women Academics of South Asian Origin in Montreal: Work in Progress." Simone de Beauvoir Institute. *Newsletter* 12, 2 (1992): 18-42.

449 MANN, Marion and Janet Berton. "The Canadian Co-ed." *The Chronicle* 40 (1967/68): 41-43. [achievement of co-education in the late 19th century]

450 MARKS, Lynne and Chad Gaffield. "Women at Queen's University, 1895-1905: A 'Little Sphere' All Their Own?" *Ontario History* 78, 4 (December 1986): 331-49.

451 McFADDEN, Eileen. "Coeducation in the Rural West: Brandon College, 1880-1920." In *Learning Women: A Collection of Essays,* eds. Agnes Grant, *et al,* 11-23. Brandon: Brandon University, Status of Women Organization, 1990.

452 McMULLEN, L. "Educational Retrenchment and Feminist Scholarship." In *Hitting the Books: The Politics of Educational Retrenchment,* ed. T. Wotherspoon. Toronto: Garamond, 1990.

453 MONTGOMERY, Lucy Maud. "A Girl's Place at Dalhousie College, 1896." *Atlantis* 5, 1 (Fall 1979): 146-53.

454 MORLEY, Mary. "The History of Home Economics Education." *Insight* 8, 1 (Fall 1978): 30-36.

455 NEATBY, Nicole. "Preparing for the Working World: Women at Queen's During the 1920s." *Historical Studies in Education* 1, 1 (Spring 1989): 53-72. Reprinted in *Gender and Education in Ontario: An Historical Reader,* eds. Ruby Heap and Alison Prentice, 333-56. Toronto: Canadian Scholars' Press, 1991.

456 NETT, Emily M. "Gender and the Canadian Introductory Sociology Textbook." *Atlantis* 7, 1 (Fall 1981): 127-33.

457 OSBORNE, Rachel L. "Sexual Harrassment in Universities: A Critical View of the Institutional Response." *Canadian Woman Studies* 12, 3 (Spring 1993): 72-75.

458 OVERDUN, Hendrick. *People and Ideas: Nursing at Western, 1920-1970.* London, ON: Faculty of Nursing, University of Western Ontario, 1973.

459 PARR, Joy, ed. *Still Running...: Personal stories by Queen's women celebrating the fiftieth anniversary of the Marty Scholarship.* Kingston: Queen's University Alumnae Association, 1987.

460 PEDERSEN, Diana. "'The Call to Service': The YWCA and the Canadian College Woman, 1886-1920." In *Youth, University and Canadian Society: Essays in the Social History of Higher Education,* eds. Paul Axelrod and John G. Reid, 187-215. Montreal and Kingston: McGill-Queen's University Press, 1989.

461 PEDERSEN, Diana. "Are You a Woman or an Historian? A Feminist's Guide to Surviving the Academic Job Interview." *Atlantis* 18, 1/2 (Fall/Winter 1992–Spring/Summer 1993): 168-76.

462 PIERSON, Ruth Roach. "Women Have Nothing to Gain from a Harvard of the North." *Journal of Canadian Studies* 20, 1 (Spring 1985): 154-61.

463 PRENTICE, Alison. "'Friendly Atoms in Chemistry': Women and Men at Normal School in Mid-Nineteenth-Century Ontario." In *Old Ontario: Papers in Honour of J.M.S. Careless,* eds. David Keane and Colin Read, 285-317. Toronto: Dundurn Press, 1990.

464 PRENTICE, Alison. "Bluestockings, Feminists, or Women Workers? A Preliminary Look at Women's Early Employment at the University of Toronto." *Journal of the Canadian Historical Association,* NS 2 (1991): 231-61.

465 REID, John G. "The Education of Women at Mount Allison, 1854-1914." *Acadiensis* 12 (Spring 1983): 3-33. Reprinted in *Atlantic Canada After Confederation,* eds. Phillip A. Buckner and David Frank, 261-83. Fredericton: Acadiensis Press, 1985.

466 RICHER, Stephen and Lorna Weir, eds. *Beyond Political Correctness: Toward the Inclusive University.* Toronto: University of Toronto Press, 1995.

467 RONISH, Donna. "The Montreal Ladies' Educational Association, 1871-1885." *McGill Journal of Education* 6, 1 (Spring 1971): 78-83.

468 ROWLES, Edith Child. *Home Economics in Canada: The Early History of Six College Programmes.* Saskatoon: Modern Press, 1966.

469 SAIDAK, Patricia. "Home Economics as an Academic Science." *Resources for Feminist Research* 15 (November 1986): 49-51.

470 SELLES-RONEY, Johanna. "'Manners and Morals'? or 'Men in Petticoats'? Education at Alma College, 1871-1898." In *Gender and Education in Ontario: An Historical Reader,* eds. Ruby Heap and Alison Prentice, 249-71. Toronto: Canadian Scholars' Press, 1991.

471 SELLES-RONEY, Johanna. "A Canadian Girl at Cheltenham: The Diary as an Historical Source." *Historical Studies in Education* 3, 1 (Spring 1991): 93-104.

472 SHEEHAN, Nancy M. "Collegiate Women in Canada." *History of Education Quarterly* 24, 1 (1984): 143-51.

473 SHEPPARD, Colleen and Sarah Westphal. "Equity and the University: Learning from Women's Experience." *Canadian Journal of Women and the Law* 5, 1 (1992): 5-36.

474 SMYTH, Elizabeth. "'A Noble Proof of Excellence': The Culture and Curriculum of a Nineteenth Century Ontario Convent Academy." In *Gender and Education in Ontario: An Historical Reader,* eds. Ruby Heap and Alison Prentice, 273-93. Toronto: Canadian Scholars' Press, 1991.

475 SMYTH, Elizabeth. "Educating Girls and Young Women in a Nineteenth-Century Convent School: The St. Joseph's Academy Experience." In *Dimensions of Childhood: Essays in the History of Children and Youth in Canada,* eds. Russell Smandych, Gordon Dodds and Alvin Esau, 85-106. Winnipeg: University of Manitoba, Legal Research Institute, 1991.

476 SMYTH, Elizabeth. "'Developing the Powers of the Youthful Mind': The Evolution of Education for Young Women at St. Joseph's Academy, Toronto, 1845-1911." *Canadian Catholic Historical Studies* 690 (1993/94): 103-25.

477 SONSER, Anna. "'A Respectable English Education': Innovation and Tradition in Literary Studies at Wesleyan Ladies' College (1861-1897)." *English Studies in Canada* 19, 1 (March 1993): 87-104.

478 SQUAIR, John. "Admission of Women to the University of Toronto." *University of Toronto Monthly* (February-May 1924).

479 STATON, Pat. "A Decade of Women's Studies." *Canadian Women's Studies* 2, 2 (1980): 58-59.

480 STEWART, Lee. "Women on Campus in British Columbia: Strategies for Survival, Years of War and Peace, 1906-1920." in *Not Just Pin Money: Selected Essays on the History of Women's Work in British Columbia,* eds. Barbara K. Latham and Roberta J. Pazdro, 185-93. Victoria: Camosun College, 1984,

481 STEWART, Lee. "The Politics of Women's Education: Establishing Home Economics at the University of British Columbia, 1914-1949." *Historical Studies in Education* 1, 2 (Fall 1989): 261-81.

482 STEWART, Lee. *"It's Up to You": Women at UBC in the Early Years.* Vancouver: University of British Columbia Press, 1990.

483 STRONG-BOAG, Veronica, ed. *A Woman With a Purpose: The Diaries of Elizabeth Smith.* Toronto: University of Toronto Press, 1980.

484 SUTTON, Barbara, ed. *Sanctum Hildam Canimus: A Collection of Reminiscences.* Toronto: St. Hilda's College, 1988.

485 TRAVILL, A.A. "Early Medical Co-Education and Women's Medical College, Kingston, Ontario 1880-1894." *Historic Kingston* 30 (January 1982): 68-89.

486 VICKERS, Jill McCalla and June Adam. *But Can You Type?: Canadian Universities and the Status of Women.* Toronto: Canadian Association of University Teachers and Clarke Irwin, 1977.

487 WINE, Jeri Dawn. "On Prejudice and Possibility: Lesbians in Canadian Academe." *Atlantis* 14 (Fall 1988): 44-55.

488 WINE, Jeri Dawn. "Outsiders on the Inside: Lesbians in Canadian Academe." In *Lesbians in Canada,* ed. Sharon Dale Stone, 157-70. Toronto: Between the Lines, 1990.

489 WINTER, Brian, ed. *Vox collegi: Centennial Education, 1874-1974.* Whitby, ON: Ontario Ladies College, 1974.

490 *Women at Acadia University: The First Fifty Years, 1884-1934.* Wolfville, NS: Acadia University, 1984.

491 ZILM, Glennis and Ethel Warbinek. *Legacy: History of Nursing Education at the University of British Columbia, 1919-94.* Vancouver: University of British Columbia Press, 1994.

SCHOOLING/VOCATIONALISM

492 ANISEF, Paul and Paul Axelrod, eds. *Transitions: Schooling and Employment in Canada.* Toronto: Thompson Educational Publishing, 1993.

493 BARMAN, Jean. "Separate and Unequal: Indian and White Girls at All Hallows School, 1884-1920." In *Indian Education in Canada, Vol I: The Legacy,* eds. Jean Barman, Yvonne Hébert and Don McCaskill, 110-31. Vancouver: University of British Columbia Press, 1986. Reprinted in *Rethinking Canada: The Promise of Women's History,* 2nd edition, eds. Veronica Strong-Boag and Anita Clair Fellman, 215-33. Toronto: Copp Clark Pitman Ltd., 1991.

494 BARMAN, Jean, Neil Sutherland and J. Donald Wilson, eds. *Children, Teachers and Schools in the History of British Columbia.* Calgary: Detselig, 1995.

495 BELL, Walter. *The Development of the Ontario High School.* Toronto: University of Toronto Press, 1918. [Ch. 9, "The Admission of Girls"]

496 BREDIN, Thomas F. "The Red River Academy." *The Beaver* (1974): 10-17.

497 CHAMPAGNE, Lucie and Micheline Dumont. "Le financement des pensionnats de jeunes filles au Québec: le modèle de la congrégation des Soeurs de Sainte-Anne, 1850-1950." Société canadienne d'histoire de l'Église catholique. *Sessions d'étude* 53 (1986): 63-91.

498 CHAMPAGNE, Lucie and Micheline Dumont. "Le financement d'un séminaire diocésain: le Séminaire de Sherbrooke, 1915-1950: Comparaison avec le financement des pensionnats de religieuses." *Historical Studies in Education* 2, 2 (Fall 1990): 339-51.

499 CHAPMAN, Ethel. "Adelaide Hoodless" In *Pioneers in Adult Education,* ed. Harriet Rouillard, 14-20. Toronto: Thomas Nelson and Sons, 1953.

500 COOK, Sharon Anne. "Educating for Temperance: The Woman's Christian Temperance Union and Ontario Children, 1880-1916." *Historical Studies in Education* 5, 2 (Fall 1993): 251-77.

501 COULTER, Rebecca Priegert and Ivor F. Goodson, eds. *Rethinking Vocationalism: Whose Work/Life is It?* Toronto: James Lorimer & Company, 1995.

502 CROWLEY, Terry. "Ada Mary Brown Courtice: Pacifist, Feminist and Educational Reformer in Early Twentieth Century Canada." *Studies in History and Politics* (1980): 76-114.

503 CROWLEY, Terry. "Adelaide Hoodless: Women's Education and Guelph." *Historic Guelph* 25 (1985/86): 26-49.

504 CROWLEY, Terry. "Madonnas Before Magdalens: Adelaide Hoodless and the Making of the Canadian Gibson Girl." *Canadian Historical Review* 67, 4 (1986): 520-47.

505 CROWLEY, Terry. "Parents in a Hurry: The Early Home and School Movement in Ontario." *Histoire sociale/Social History* XIX, 38 (November 1986): 323-42.

506 CURTIS, Bruce. "'Illicit' Sexuality and Public Education in Ontario, 1840-1907." *Historical Studies in Education* 1, 1 (Spring 1989): 73-94.

507 DANYLEWYCZ, Marta. "Domestic Science Education in Ontario, 1900-1940." In *Gender and Education in Ontario: An Historical Reader,* eds. Ruby Heap and Alison Prentice, 129-47. Toronto: Canadian Scholars' Press, 1991.

508 DANYLEWYCZ, Marta, Nadia Fahmy-Eid and Nicole Thivierge. "L'enseignement ménager et les 'home economics' au Québec et en Ontario au début du 20e siècle: une analyse comparée." In *An Imperfect Past: Education and Society in Canadian History,* ed. J. Donald Wilson, 67-119. Vancouver: Centre for the Study of Curriculum and Instruction, University of British Columbia, 1984.

509 DAVEY, Ian E. "Trends in Female School Attendance in Mid-Nineteenth-Century Ontario." *Histoire sociale/Social History* VIII (November 1975): 238-54. Reprinted in *Gender and Education in Ontario: An Historical Reader,* eds. Ruby Heap and Alison Prentice, 1-23. Toronto: Canadian Scholars' Press, 1991.

510 DAVISON, James Doyle. "Alice Shaw and her Grand Pré Seminary: A story of female education." In *Repent and Believe: The Baptist Experience in Maritime Canada,* ed. Barry M. Moody, 124-37. Hantsport, NS: Lancelot Press, 1980.

511 DAVISON, James Doyle. *Alice of Grand Pré. Alice T. Shaw and her Grand Pré seminary: Female Education in Nova Scotia and New Brunswick.* Wolfville, NS: Acadia University, 1981.

512 DEHLI, Kari. "Women in the Community: Reform of Schooling and Motherhood in Toronto." In *Community Organization and the Canadian State,* eds. Roxana Ng, Gillian Walker and Jacob Muller, 47-64. Toronto: Garamond Press, 1990.

513 DEHLI, Kari. "For Intelligent Motherhood and National Efficiency: The Toronto Home and School Council, 1916-1930." In *Gender and Education in Ontario: An Historical Reader,* eds. Ruby Heap and Alison Prentice, 149-65. Toronto: Canadian Scholars' Press, 1991.

514 DEWAR, Kenneth C. "Hilda Neatby and the Ends of Education." *Queen's Quarterly* 97, 1 (Spring 1990): 36-51.

515 DUMONT, Micheline. "L'instruction des filles avant 1960." *Interface: la revue des chercheurs* 7, 3 (mai/juin 1986): 22-29.

516 DUMONT, Micheline. "L'éducation des filles au Québec: Structures institutionelles et conjoncture économique (1900-1960)." *Resources for Feminist Research* 15, 4 (December 1986/January 1987): 52-53.

517 DUMONT, Micheline. *Girls' Schooling in Quebec, 1639-1960.* Historical Booklet No. 49. Ottawa: Canadian Historical Association, 1990.

518 DUMONT, Micheline. "Des filles à l'école." *Cap-aux-Diamants* 21 (printemps 1991): 11-14.

519 DUMONT, Micheline and Nadia Fahmy-Eid. "Histoire de l'éducation des filles au Québec: le cadre scolaire de 1840 à 1960." *Resources for Feminist Research* 13 (March 1984): 77-88.

520 DUMONT, Micheline and Nadia Fahmy-Eid. "La pointe de l'iceberg: l'histoire de l'éducation et l'histoire de l'éducation des filles au Québec." *Historical Studies in Education* 3, 2 (Fall 1991): 211-36.

521 DUMONT, Micheline, Nadia Fahmy-Eid and Lucie Dufour. "Bibliographie de l'histoire de l'éducation des filles au Québec et au Canada." *Resources for Feminist Research* 14, 2 (July 1985): 45-70.

522 DUNNIGAN, Lise. *Analyse des stéréotypes masculins et féminins dans les manuels scolaires au Québec.* Québec: Conseil du statut de la femme, 1976.

523 ELLIS, Dormer. "The Schooling of Girls." In *The House That Ryerson Built: Essays in Education to Mark Ontario's Bicentennial,* H. Oliver *et al,* 89-101. Toronto: OISE Press, 1984.

524 FAHMY-EID, Nadia. "L'éducation des filles chez les Ursulines de Québec sous le Régime français." In *Maîtresses de maison, maîtresses d'école: Femmes, famille et éducation dans l'histoire du Québec,* eds. Nadia Fahmy-Eid and Micheline Dumont, 49-76. Montréal: Boréal Express, 1983.

525 FAHMY-EID, Nadia. "Le sexe du savoir: perspectives historiques sur l'éducation des filles au Québec (19e-20e siècles)." In *Encrages féministes,* ed. Isabelle Lasvergnas, 51-67. Montréal: Université du Québec à Montréal, Centre de recherche féministe, Group interdisciplinaire d'enseignement et de recherche féministes, 1989.

526 FAHMY-EID, Nadia. "The Education of Girls by the Ursulines of Quebec during the French Regime." In *Canadian Women: A Reader,* eds. Wendy Mitchinson, *et al,* 33-49. Toronto: Harcourt Brace Canada, 1996.

527 FAHMY-EID, Nadia and Micheline Dumont. "Les rapports femmes/famille/éducation au Québec: bilan de la recherche." In *Maîtresses de maison, maîtresses d'école: Femmes, famille et éducation dans l'histoire du Québec,* eds. Nadia Fahmy-Eid and Micheline Dumont, 5-46. Montréal: Boréal Express, 1983.

528 FAHMY-EID, Nadia and Nicole Laurin-Frenette. "Théories de la famille et rapports famille/pouvoir dans le secteur éducatif au Québec et en France, 1850-1960." *Revue d'histoire de l'Amérique française* 34, 2 (septembre 1980): 197-222. Reprinted in *Maîtresses de maison, maîtresses d'cole: Femmes, famille et éduca-tion dans l'histoire du Québec,* eds. Nadia Fahmy-Eid and Micheline Dumont, 339-61. Montréal: Boréal Express, 1983.

529 FAHMY-EID, Nadia and Nicole Laurin-Frenette. "Theories of the Family and Family/Authority Relationships in the Educational Sector in Québec and France, 1850-1960." In *The Politics of Diversity: Feminism, Marxism and Nationalism,* eds. Roberta Hamilton and Michèle Barrett, 287-302. Montreal: Book Centre, 1986.

530 FAHMY-EID, Nadia and Nicole Thivièrge. "L'éducation des filles au Québec et en France (1880-1930): une analyse comparée." In *Maîtresses de maison, maîtresses d'école: Femmes, famille et éduca-tion dans l'histoire du Québec,* eds. Nadia Fahmy-Eid and Micheline Dumont, 191-220. Montréal: Boréal Express, 1983.

531 GAFFIELD, Chad. "Children, Schooling, and Family Reproduction in Nineteenth-Century Ontario." *Canadian Historical Review* 72, 2 (June 1991): 157-91. Reprinted in *The Invention of Canada: Readings in Pre-Confederation History,* ed. Chad Gaffield, 502-31. Toronto: Copp Clark Longman Ltd., 1994.

532 GAGNON, Anne. "The Pensionnat Assomption: Religious Nationalism in a Franco-Albertan Boarding School for Girls, 1926-1960." *Historical Studies in Education* 1, 1 (Spring 1989): 95-117.

533 GASKELL, Jane S. "Course Enrollment in the High School: The Perspective of Working-Class Females." *Sociology of Education* 58 (January 1985): 48-59. Reprinted in *British Columbia Reconsidered: Essays on Women,* eds. Gillian Creese and Veronica Strong-Boag, 244-66. Vancouver: Press Gang Publishers, 1992.

534 GASKELL, Jane S. *Gender Matters From School to Work.* Toronto: OISE Press, 1991.

535 GOSSAGE, Carolyn A. *A Question of Privilege.* Toronto: Peter Martin, 1977. [private schools]

536 GREER, Allan. "The Pattern of Literacy in Quebec, 1745-1899." *Histoire sociale/Social History* (November 1978): 295-335.

537 GUAY, Hélène. "L'établissement des études classiques chez les religieuses de Jésus-Marie à Sillery, d'après un texte de soeur Léa Drolet." *Recherches féministes,* 3(2) 1990: 179-94.

538 HARRIGAN, Patrick J. "The Schooling of Boys and Girls in Canada." *Journal of Social History* 23, 4 (Summer 1990): 803-16.

539 HARRIGAN, Patrick J. "Patterns of Enrolment and Attendance in Canadian Public Schools since Confederation." *Journal of International and Comparative Education* X (June 1991).

540 HAYDEN, Michael, ed. *So Much to Do, So Little Time: The Writings of Hilda Neatby.* Vancouver: University of British Columbia Press, 1983.

541 HEAP, Ruby. "Les femmes laïques au service de l'enseignement primaire public catholique à Montréal: les écoles des 'dames et demoiselles,' fin 19e-début 20e siècle." *Canadian Woman Studies* 7, 3 (Fall 1986): 55-60.

542 HEAP, Ruby. "Schooling Women for Home or for Work? Vocational Education for Women in Ontario in the Early Twentieth Century: The Case of the Toronto Technical High School, 1892-1920." In *Gender and Education in Ontario: An Historical Reader,* eds. Ruby Heap and Alison Prentice, 197-245. Toronto: Canadian Scholars' Press, 1991.

543 HOSIE, Inez B. "Little White School House." *Alberta Historical Review* 15, 4 (Autumn 1967): 26-28.

544 HOUSTON, Susan and Alison Prentice. *Schooling and Scholars in Nineteenth-Century Ontario.* Toronto: University of Toronto Press, 1988.

545 INKSTER, Anne Ellen. "To School in London." *The Beaver* (Summer 1979): 42-49. [two young Fort Churchill girls are sent to school in England, 1890s]

546 JACKSON, Nancy S. and Jane S. Gaskell. "White Collar Vocationalism: The Rise of Commercial Education in Ontario and British Columbia, 1870-1920." *Curriculum Inquiry* 17, 2 (Summer 1987): 177-201. Reprinted in *Gender and Education in Ontario: An Historical Reader,* eds. Ruby Heap and Alison Prentice, 167-96. Toronto: Canadian Scholars' Press, 1991.

547 JOHNSTON, A.J.B. "Education and Female Literacy at Eighteenth-Century Louisbourg: The Work of the Soeurs de la Congrégation de Notre Dame." In *An Imperfect Past: Education and Society in Canadian History,* ed. J. Donald Wilson, 48-66. Vancouver: Centre for the Study of Curriculum and Instruction, University of British Columbia, 1984.

548 LASERRE, Claudette. "L'église et l'éducation des filles au Québec de 1850 à 1950." *Canadian Woman Studies,* 2 (Winter 1983): 21-23.

549 LASERRE, Claudette. "Du masculin au féminin." *Canadian Woman Studies* (Fall 1986): 61-64.

550 LEBRUN, Josée. "Des charmantes petites perruches...Les étudiantes de sciences-lettres 1916-1960." *Canadian Woman Studies* 7, 3 (Fall 1986): 65-67.

551 LEMIEUX, Lucien. "La Fondation de l'École Ménagère St. Pascal, 1905-1909." *Revue d'histoire de l'Amérique française* 25, 4 (mai 1972): 552-57.

552 LETOURNEAU, Jeanette. *Les écoles normales de jeunes filles au Québec, 1836-1974.* Montréal: Les Éditions Fidès, 1981.

553 MacDONALD, Cheryl. "Angel in the House." *The Beaver* 66, 4 (August/September 1986): 22-29. [Adelaide Hoodless]

554 MacDONALD, Cheryl. *Adelaide Hoodless: Domestic Crusader.* Toronto and Reading: Dundurn Press, 1986.

555 MAGNUSON, Roger. *Education in New France.* Montreal and Kingston: McGill-Queen's University Press, 1992.

556 MALOUIN, Marie-Paule. "Les rapports entre l'école privée et l'école publique: l'académie Marie-Rose au 19e siècle." In *Maîtresses de maison, maîtresses d'école: Femmes, famille et éducation dans l'histoire du Québec,* eds. Nadia Fahmy-Eid and Micheline Dumont, 77-91. Montréal: Boréal Express, 1983.

557 MALOUIN, Marie-Paule. *Ma soeur, à quelle école allez-vous? deux écoles de filles à la fin du XIXe siècle.* Montréal: Fides, 1985.

558 MALOUIN, Marie-Paule. "Idéologie et pratiques scolaires." *Canadian Woman Studies* 7, 3 (Fall 1986): 68-72.

559 MALOUIN, Marie-Paule. *Que sont devenues les soeurs de nos écoles? Recherche sur les orientations actuelles des religieuses enseignantes du Québec.* Montréal: Fides, 1989.

560 MALOUIN, Marie-Paule. "La laïcisation de l'école publique Québécoise entre 1939 et 1969: Un processus de masculinisation." *Historical Studies in Education* 4, 1 (Spring 1992): 1-29.

561 MARKS, Lynne. "Kale Meydelach or Shulamith Girls: Cultural Change and Continuity Among Jewish Parents and Daughters—a Case Study of Toronto's Harbord Collegiate in the 1920s." *Canadian Woman Studies* 7, 3 (Fall 1986): 85-89. Reprinted in *Gender and Education in Ontario: An Historical Reader*, eds. Ruby Heap and Alison Prentice, 295-305. Toronto: Canadian Scholars' Press, 1991.

562 MATTINGLY, Paul H. and Michael B. Katz. *Education and Social Change: Themes From Ontario's Past*. New York: New York University Press, 1975.

563 MAXWELL, Mary P. and James D. Maxwell. "Women and the Elite: Educational and Occupational Aspirations of Private School Females, 1966-76." *Canadian Review of Sociology and Anthropology* 21, 4 (November 1984): 371-94.

564 MAXWELL, Mary Percival and James D. Maxwell. "Three decades of private school females' ambitions: Implications for Canadian elites." *Canadian Review of Sociology and Anthropology* 31, 2 (1994): 139-67.

565 McKENZIE, Mrs. M.I. "School Memories." *Alberta Historical Review* 7, 1 (Winter 1959): 14-17.

566 MORISON, C.K. "Helen Gordon Stewart." In *Pioneers in Adult Education*, ed. Harriet Rouillard, 48-54. Toronto: Thomas Nelson and Sons, 1953.

567 MORISSETTE, Brigitte. "Cent ans d'éducation des jeunes filles de bonne famille." *Perspectives (La Presse)*, 30 July 1977: 14-17.

568 PEDERSEN, Diana. "'The Scientific Training of Mothers': The Campaign for Domestic Science in Ontario Schools, 1890-1913." In *Critical Issues in the History of Canadian Science, Technology and Medicine*, eds. Richard A. Jarrell and Arnold E. Roos, 178-94. Ottawa and Thornhill: HSTC Publications, 1983.

569 PHILLIPS, Charles Edward. *The Development of Education in Canada*. Toronto: W.J. Gage, 1957.

570 PRENTICE, Alison and Susan E. Houston, eds. *Family, School and Society in Nineteenth-Century Canada*. Toronto: Oxford University Press, 1975.

571 RAPLEY, Elizabeth. "Fenelon Revisited: A Review of Girls' Education in Seventeenth-Century France." *Histoire sociale/Social History* (November 1987): 299-318.

572 RAZACK-BROOKWELL, Sherene. "Les instituts familiaux: Nationalisme religieux et préparation des filles à la vie familiale, 1937-1940." In *Idéologies au Canada français 1940-1976. Tome III: Les Partis politiques—L'Eglise*, ed. Fernand Dumond, 325-54. Québec: Les Presses de l'Université Laval, 1981.

573 RAZACK, Sherene. "Schools for Happiness: *Instituts Familiaux* and the Education of Ideal Wives and Mothers." In *Delivering Motherhood: Maternal Ideologies and Practices in the 19th and 20th Centuries*, eds. Katherine Arnup, Andrée Lévesque and Ruth Roach Pierson, 211-37. London and New York: Routledge, 1990. Abridged in *Rethinking Canada: The Promise of Women's History*, 2nd edition, eds. Veronica Strong-Boag and Anita Clair Fellman, 356-75. Toronto: Copp Clark Pitman Ltd., 1991.

574 RICHER, S. "Schooling and the Gendered Subject: An Exercise in Planned Social Change." *Canadian Review of Sociology and Anthropology* 25, 2 (February 1987): 1-22.

575 RILEY, Barbara. "Six Saucepans to One: Domestic Science vs. the Home in British Columbia, 1900-1930." In *Not Just Pin Money: Selected Essays on the History of Women's Work in British Columbia*, eds. Barbara K. Latham and Roberta J. Pazdro, 159-81. Victoria: Camosun College, 1984. Reprinted in *British Columbia Reconsidered: Essays on Women*, eds. Gillian Creese and Veronica Strong-Boag, 119-42. Vancouver: Press Gang Publishers, 1992.

576 ROBENSTINE, Clark. "French Colonial Policy and the Education of Women and Minorities: Louisiana in the Early Eighteenth Century." *History of Education Quarterly* 32, 2 (Summer 1992): 193-212.

577 ROYCE, Marion V. "A Landmark in Victorian Education for Young Ladies." *Improving College and University Teaching* 22 (Winter 1975): 9-11.

578 ROYCE, Marion V. "Arguments Over the Education of Girls—Their Admission to Grammar Schools in This Province." *Ontario History* 67 (March 1975): 1-13.

579 ROYCE, Marion V. "Education of Girls in Quaker Schools in Ontario." *Atlantis* 3, 1 (Fall 1977): 181-92.

580 ROYCE, Marion V. "Methodism and the Education of Women in Nineteenth Century Ontario." *Atlantis* 3, 2, Part I (Spring 1978): 131-43.

581 ROYCE, Marion V. "Notes on Schooling for Girls in Upper Canada from the Pre-Conquest Period until the Mid-Nineteenth Century." *Canadian Women's History Series No. 10*. Toronto: Women in Canadian History Project, Ontario Institute for Studies in Education, 1978.

582 SHEEHAN, Nancy M. "Temperance, Education and the WCTU in Alberta, 1905-1930." *Journal of Educational Thought* 14, 2 (August 1980): 108-24.

583 SHEEHAN, Nancy M. "The WCTU and Educational Strategies on the Canadian Prairie." *History of Education Quarterly* 24, 1 (1984): 101-19.

584 SHEEHAN, Nancy M. "The IODE, the Schools and World War I." *History of Education Review* 3, 1 (1984): 29-44.

585 SHEEHAN, Nancy M. "Women's Organizations and Educational Issues, 1900-1930." *Canadian Woman Studies* 7, 3 (Fall 1986): 90-94.

586 SHEEHAN, Nancy M. "National Issues and Curricula Issues: Women and Educational Reform, 1900-1930." In *Women and Education: A Canadian Perspective,* eds. Jane Gaskell and Arlene McLaren, 223-40. Calgary: Detselig, 1987.

587 SHEEHAN, Nancy M. "Philosophy, Pedagogy, and Practice: The IODE and the Schools in Canada, 1900-1945." *Historical Studies in Education* 2, 2 (Fall 1990): 307-21.

588 STAMP, Robert M. "Adelaide Hoodless, Champion of Women's Rights." In *Profiles of Canadian Educators,* eds. Robert S. Patterson *et al,* 213-32. Toronto: D.C. Heath, 1974,

589 STAMP, Robert M. "Teaching Girls Their 'God-Given Place in Life': The Introduction of Home Economics in the Schools." *Atlantis* 2, 2, Part 1 (Spring 1977): 18-34.

590 STEELE, Catherine. "Frances Ridley Havergal and Havergal College." *York Pioneer* (1973): 36-45.

591 SUTHERLAND, Neil and Jean Barman. "Out of the Shadows: Retrieving the History of Urban Education and Urban Childhood in Canada." In *The City and Education in Four Nations,* eds. Ronald K. Goodenow and William E. Marsden, 87-108. New York: Cambridge University Press, 1992.

592 THIVIÈRGE, Nicole. *Écoles ménagères et instituts familiaux: un modèle féminin traditionnel.* Québec: Institut québécois de recherche sur la culture, 1982.

593 THIVIÈRGE, Nicole. *Histoire de l'enseignement ménager-familial au Québec, 1882-1970.* Québec: Institut québécois de recherche sur la culture, 1982.

594 THIVIÈRGE, Nicole. *L'enseignement ménager au Québec 1880-1910.* Québec: Institut québécois de recherche sur la culture, 1982.

595 THIVIERGE, Nicole. "L'enseignement ménager, 1880-1970." In *Maîtresses de maison, maîtresses d'école: Femmes, famille et éducation dans l'histoire du Québec,* eds. Nadia Fahmy-Eid and Micheline Dumont, 119-42. Montréal: Boréal Express, 1983.

596 WEISS, Gillian. "An Essential Year For the Child: The Kindergarten in British Columbia." In *Schooling and Society in 20th Century British Columbia,* eds. J.D. Wilson and D.C. Jones. Calgary: Detselig, 1980.

TEACHERS/TEACHING

597 ABBOTT, John. "Accomplishing a Man's Task: Rural Women Teachers, Male Culture and the School Inspectorate in Turn-of-the-Century Ontario." *Ontario History* 78, 4 (Dec. 1986): 313-30. Reprinted in *Gender and Education in Ontario: An Historical Reader,* eds. Ruby Heap and Alison Prentice, 51-72. Toronto: Canadian Scholars' Press, 1991.

598 ALBISETTI, J.C. "The Feminization of Teaching in the Nineteenth Century: A Comparative Perspective." *History of Education* 22, 3 (September 1993): 253-64.

599 ALPHONSUS, Sister Mary. "Life on Baccalieu: The Reminiscences of the Last Teacher There, Miss Margaret Noonan." *Newfoundland Quarterly* 75, 3 (Christmas 1979): 10-12.

600 ARBUS, Judith. "Grateful to Be Working: Women Teachers During the Great Depression" In *Feminism and Education: A Canadian Perspective,* eds. Frieda Forman, *et al,* 169-90. Toronto: Centre for Women's Studies in Education, Ontario Institute for Studies in Education, 1990.

601 BARBER, Marilyn. "The Fellowship of the Maple Leaf Teachers." In *The Anglican Church and the World of Western Canada, 1820-1970,* ed. Barry Ferguson, 154-66. Regina: Canadian Plains Research Center, University of Regina, 1991.

602 BARMAN, Jean. "Birds of Passage or Early Professionals? Teachers in Late Nineteenth-Century British Columbia." *Historical Studies in Education* 2, 1 (Spring 1990): 17-36.

603 BARMAN, Jean. "Pioneer Teachers of British Columbia." *British Columbia Historical News* 25, 1 (Winter 1991/92): 15-18.

604 BAUDOUX, Claudine. "Effets de la laïcisation et de la mixité sur le nombre de femmes responsables d'établissements scolaires du Québec de 1958 à 1985." *Revue des sciences de l'éducation* 17, 1 (1991): 1-24.

605 BOWMAN, Henry B. "Miss Alma Crawforth and the Continuation School in Elmira." *Waterloo Historical Society* 61 (1973): 24-28.

606 BROWN, Helen. "Gender and Space: Constructing the Public School Teaching Staff in Nanaimo, 1891-1914." *BC Studies* 105/106 (Spring/Summer 1995): 59-79.

607 CAMPBELL, Helen Richards. *From Chalkdust to Hayseed.* Belleville, ON: Mika Publishers, 1975.

608 CHAPUT, Donald. "The 'Misses Nolin' of Red River." *The Beaver* (Winter 1975): 14-17. [Métis]

609 CHAPUT, Donald. "Charlotte de Rocheblave: Métisse Teacher of the Teachers." *The Beaver* (Autumn 1977): 55-58.

610 COOK, Maisie Emery. *Memories of a Pioneer Schoolteacher.* [n.p.], 1968. [Alberta and Northwest Territories]

611 COOPER, Afua. "The Search for Mary Bibb, Black Woman Teacher in Nineteenth-Century Canada West." *Ontario History* 83, 1 (March 1991): 39-54.

612 COOPER, Afua. "Black Women and Work in Nineteenth-Century Canada West: Black Woman Teacher Mary Bibb." In *"We're Rooted Here and They Can't Pull Us Up": Essays in African Canadian Women's History,* Peggy Bristow, *et al.,* 143-70. Toronto: University of Toronto Press, 1994.

613 CROSS, Carolyn. "Adelaide Bailey: Exemplary Teacher, 1857-1949." *British Columbia Historical News* 27, 4 (Fall 1994): 19-22.

614 DANYLEWYCZ, Marta. "Sexes et classes sociales dans l'enseignement: le cas de Montréal à la fin du 19e siècle." In *Maîtresses de maison, maîtresses d'école: Femmes, famille et éducation dans l'histoire du Québec*, eds. Nadia Fahmy-Eid and Micheline Dumont, 93-118. Montréal: Boréal Express, 1983.

615 DANYLEWYCZ, Marta, Beth Light and Alison Prentice. "The Evolution of the Sexual Division of Labour in Teaching: A Nineteenth Century Ontario and Quebec Case Study." *Histoire sociale/Social History* XVI, 31 (May 1983), 81-109. Reprinted in *Women and Education: A Canadian Perspective*, eds. Jane Gaskell and Arlene McLaren, 33-60. Calgary: Detselig, 1987.

616 DANYLEWYCZ, Marta and Alison Prentice. "Teachers, Gender and Bureaucratizing School Systems in 19th Century Montreal and Toronto." *History of Education Quarterly* 24 (Spring 1984): 75-100.

617 DANYLEWYCZ, Marta and Alison Prentice. "Revising the History of Teachers: A Canadian Perspective." *Interchange* 17, 2 (1986): 135-46.

618 DANYLEWYCZ, Marta and Alison Prentice. "Teachers' Work: Changing Patterns and Perceptions in the Emerging School Systems of Nineteenth and Early Twentieth Century Central Canada." *Labour/Le Travail* 17 (Spring 1986): 59-80. Reprinted in *Women Who Taught: Perspectives on the History of Women and Teaching*, eds. Alison Prentice and Marjorie Theobald, 136-59. Toronto: University of Toronto Press, 1991; and in *Interpreting Canada's Past: Volume Two, Post-Confederation*, 2nd edition, ed. J.M. Bumsted, 254-74. Toronto: Oxford University Press, 1993.

619 DEL C. BRUNO-JOFRÉ, Rosa. "The Oblate Sisters, A Manitoban Order: Reconstructing Early Years, 1904-1915." In *Issues in the History of Education in Manitoba: From the Construction of the Common School to the Politics of Voices*, ed. Rosa del C. Bruno-Jofré, 511-67. Lewiston, NY and Queenston, ON: The Edwin Mellen Press, 1993.

620 DEL C. BRUNO-JOFRÉ, Rosa and Colleen Ross. "Decoding the Subjective Image of Women Teachers in Rural Towns and Surrounding Areas in Southern Manitoba: 1947-1960." In *Issues in the History of Education in Manitoba: From the Construction of the Common School to the Politics of Voices*, ed. Rosa del C. Bruno-Jofré, 569-93. Lewiston, NY and Queenston, ON: The Edwin Mellen Press, 1993.

621 DORION, Jacques. "Mathilde Millette, Eusebe Morin, Lénaide Lemay, Dame Pinault: Coupables ou non-coupables?" *Culture et tradition* 2 (1977): 51-64.

622 DRUMMOND, Anne. "Gender, Profession, and Principals: The Teachers of Quebec Protestant Academies, 1875-1900." *Historical Studies in Education* 2, 1 (Spring 1990): 59-71.

623 DUFOUR, Andrée. "Un commentaire sur une prétendue suprématie masculine écrasante chez enseignants bas-canadiens du premier tiers du XIXe siècle." *Histoire sociale/Social History* XXIII, 45 (mai 1990): 114-16.

624 DUMONT, Micheline. "Le défi des religieuses enseignantes d'aujourd'hui." *Canadian Woman Studies* 7, 3 (Fall 1986): 51-54.

625 DUMONT, Micheline. "La gestion financière des religieuses enseignantes: Hypothèses provisoires," In *Féminisation et masculinisation de la gestion*, ed. Claudine Baudoux, 107-42. Québec: L'université Laval, Groupe de recherche multidisciplinaire féministe, 1989.

626 ERRINGTON, Jane. "Ladies and Schoolmistresses: Educating Women in Early Nineteenth-Century Upper Canada." *Historical Studies in Education* 6, 1 (Spring 1994): 71-96.

627 FAIR, Myrtle. *I Remember the One-Room School.* Cheltenham, ON: Boston Mills Press, 1979. [Ontario, 1890-1960]

628 FLEMING, Thomas and Carol Smyly. "Beyond Hope, Past Redemption: The Lottie Bowron Story." *The Beaver* 71, 2 (April/May 1991): 33-41. [teaching in the BC hinterland, 1928-1933]

629 FRENCH, Doris. *High Button Boot Straps: Federation of Women Teachers' Association of Ontario, 1918-1968.* Toronto: Ryerson Press, 1968.

630 GELMAN, Susan. "'The "Feminization" of the High Schools'? Women Secondary School Teachers in Toronto, 1871-1930." *Historical Studies in Education* 2, 1 (Spring 1990): 119-48. Reprinted in *Gender and Education in Ontario: An Historical Reader*, eds. Ruby Heap and Alison Prentice, 73-104. Toronto: Canadian Scholars' Press, 1991.

631 GELMAN, Susan. "Selected Bibliography." In *Women Who Taught: Perspectives on the History of Women and Teaching*, eds. Alison Prentice and Marjorie Theobald, 285-301. Toronto: University of Toronto Press, 1991.

632 GELMAN, Susan and Alison Prentice, eds. *The History of Gender and Teaching: A Selected Bibliography of English Language Published Sources.* Critical Perspectives Papers. Toronto: Centre for Women's Studies in Education, 1990.

633 GOODWIN, Theresa. "Recollections and Reminiscences: An English School Marm in Saskatchewan." *Saskatchewan History* 27, 3 (Autumn 1974): 103-7.

634 GRAHAM, Elizabeth. "Schoolmarms and Early Teaching in Ontario." In *Women at Work: Ontario, 1850-1930*, eds. Janice Acton, *et al*, 165-209. Toronto: Canadian Women's Educational Press, 1974.

635 GRATTON, P. *La résistance tranquille: bilan et perspective de la lutte des femmes à la CEQ.* Québec: Centrale l'enseignement du Québec, 1991.

636 GRAY, Rachel. "Teaching: A Career...or a Little Hat Money? An Oral History with Alice Gray." *Ontario History* 84, 4 (Dec. 1992): 315-27.

637 GRIFFIS, Edith May. "The Lady of the Bay." *The Beaver* (Winter 1960): 46-50. [teaching in northern Manitoba, 1912]

638 GUILDFORD, Janet. "'Separate Spheres': The Feminization of Public School Teaching in Nova Scotia, 1838-1880." *Acadiensis* 22, 1 (Autumn 1992): 44-64. Reprinted in *Separate Spheres: Women's Worlds in the 19th Century Maritimes*, eds. Janet Guildford and Suzanne Morton, 119-43. Fredericton: Acadiensis Press, 1994.

639 GUILLET, Edwin Clarence. *In the Cause of Education: The Centennial History of the Ontario Educational Association, 1861-1960.* Toronto: University of Toronto Press, 1960.

640 HALLMAN, Dianne M. "'A Thing of the Past': Teaching in One-Room Schools in Rural Nova Scotia, 1936-1941." *Historical Studies in Education* 4, 1 (Spring 1992): 113-32. Reprinted in *Feminism and Education: A Canadian Perspective, Volume 2*, eds. Paula Bourne, *et al*, 175-202. Toronto: Centre for Women's Studies in Education, Ontario Institute for Studies in Education, 1994; and in *Canadian Women: A Reader*, eds. Wendy Mitchinson, *et al*, 233-50. Toronto: Harcourt Brace Canada, 1996.

641 HAMEL, Thérèse. "L'enseignement d'hier à aujourd'hui: Les transformations d'un métier 'féminin' au Québec." *Questions de Culture, No 9: Identités féminines: mémoire et création*, 51-70. Québec, Institut québécois de recherche sur la culture, 1986.

642 HARRIGAN, Patrick J. "The Development of a Corps of Public School Teachers in Canada, 1870-1980." *History of Education Quarterly* 32, 4 (Winter 1992): 483-521.

643 HEAP, Ruby and Alison Prentice. "'The Outlook for Old Age is Not Hopeful': The Struggle of Female Teachers over Pensions in Quebec, 1880-1914." *Histoire sociale/Social History* XXVI, 51 (May 1993): 67-94.

644 HEBERT, Monique. "Telle était la lutte: les institutrices du Manitoba." *Éducation et francophonie* 19, 3 (1991): 9-13.

645 HINDS, Margery. *School-House in the Arctic.* London: Geoffrey Bles, 1958. [teaching Inuit children, 1940s and 1950s]

646 HOLT, Miss C.E. *An Autobiographical Sketch of a Teacher's Life.* Quebec: Carrel, 1875.

647 KINNEAR, Mary. "'Mostly for the Male Members': Teaching in Winnipeg, 1933-1966." *Historical Studies in Education* 6, 1 (Spring 1994): 1-20.

648 KOJDER, Apolonja Maria. "The Saskatoon Women Teachers' Association: A Demand for Recognition." *Saskatchewan History* (Spring 1977): 63-74. Reprinted in *Shaping the Schools of the Canadian West*, eds. David C. Jones, *et al.*, 177-91. Calgary: Detselig, 1979.

649 KOJDER, Apolonja Maria. "In Union There is Strength: The Saskatoon Women Teachers' Association." *Canadian Woman Studies* 7, 3 (Fall 1986): 82-84.

650 LASKIN, Susan, Beth Light and Alison Prentice. "Studying the History of Occupation: Quantitative Sources on Canadian Teachers in the Nineteenth Century." *Archivaria* 14 (Summer 1982): 75-92.

651 LATHAM, Barbara and Roberta Pazdro. "A Simple Matter of Justice: Agnes Deans Cameron and the British Columbia Department of Education, 1906-8." *Atlantis* 10, 1 (Fall 1984): 111-15.

652 LAVOIE, Rita. "Olivine Tremblay: Une femme qui a contribué au développement du Québec." *Saguenayensia* 18, 5/6 (Sept./déc. 1976): 110-11.

653 MACK, Hughena. "Wanderlust of Eastern School Ma'ams." *Alberta History* 42, 2 (Spring 1994): 16-26. [reprinted from *Calgary Albertan*, 1912]

654 MacLEOD, Linda. *Progress as Paradox: A Profile of Women Teachers.* Ottawa: Canadian Teachers' Federation, 1988.

655 MAYRAND-GAGNON, Cécile. *Les péripéties de la vie d'une maîtresse d'école.* Val-d'Or, D'ici et d'ailleurs, coll. "Confidences et témoignages", no 48, 1994.

656 McKEE-ALLAIN, Isabelle. "La place des communautés religieuses de femmes dans le système d'éducation du Nouveau-Brunswick: un bilan socio-historique." *Education et francophonie* 19, 3 (1991): 3-8.

657 MORRIS, Miggs. "Wilderness Teacher." *North* 14, 2 (1967): 4-6. [Fort Franklin, Great Bear Lake, 1965-1967]

658 NIXON, Mary. "Few Women in School Administration: Some Explanations." *Journal of Educational Thought* 21, 2 (August 1987): 63-70.

659 PATTERSON, Robert S. "Voices From the Past: The Personal and Professional Struggle of Rural School Teachers." In *Schools in the West: Essays in Canadian Educational History*, eds. Nancy M. Sheehan, J. Donald Wilson and David C. Jones, 99-111. Calgary: Detselig, 1986.

660 PENNER, Ida. "A Teacher at Beautiful Meadow." *The Beaver* 73, 5 (Oct./Nov. 1993): 43-45. [Manitoba, 1920s]

661 POELZER, Irene. "Unprincipaled Women: The Saskatchewan Case." *Atlantis* 1, 1 (Fall 1975): 113-18. [1970s]

662 POELZER, Irene. *Saskatchewan Women Teachers 1905-1920: Their Contributions.* Saskatoon: Lindenblatt & Hamonic, 1990.

663 POMEROY, Elsie. "Mary Electa Adams: A Pioneer Educator." *Ontario History* 41, 3 (1949): 106-17.

664 PRENTICE, Alison. "The Feminization of Teaching in British North America and Canada, 1845-1875." *Histoire sociale/Social History* VIII (May 1975): 5-20. Reprinted in *The Neglected Majority: Essays in Canadian Women's History,* eds. Susan Mann Trofimenkoff and Alison Prentice, 49-65. Toronto: McClelland and Stewart, 1977; and in *Interpreting Canada's Past: Volume 1, Before Confederation,* ed. J.M Bumsted, 374-88. Toronto: Oxford University Press, 1986.

665 PRENTICE, Alison. "From Household to School House: The Emergence of the Teacher as Servant of the State." *Material History Bulletin* (Fall 1984): 19-29. Reprinted in *Gender and Education in Ontario: An Historical Reader,* eds. Ruby Heap and Alison Prentice, 25-48. Toronto: Canadian Scholars' Press, 1991.

666 PRENTICE, Alison. "Themes in the Early History of the Women Teachers' Association of Toronto." In *Women's Paid and Unpaid Work: Historical and Contemporary Perspectives,* ed. Paula Bourne, 97-121. Toronto: New Hogtown Press, 1985.

667 PRENTICE, Alison. "Scholarly Passion: Two Persons Who Caught It." *Historical Studies in Education* 1, 1 (Spring 1989): 7-27. Reprinted in *Women Who Taught: Perspectives on the History of Women and Teaching,* eds. Alison Prentice and Marjorie Theobald, 258-83. Toronto: University of Toronto Press, 1991.

668 PRENTICE, Alison. "Multiple Realities: The History of Women Teachers in Canada." In *Feminism and Education: A Canadian Perspective,* eds. Frieda Forman, *et al.* Toronto: Centre for Women's Studies in Education, Ontario Institute for Studies in Education, 1990.

669 PRENTICE, Alison and Marjorie Theobald. "The Historiography of Women Teachers: A Retrospect." In *Women Who Taught: Perspectives on the History of Women and Teaching,* eds. Alison Prentice and Marjorie Theobald, 3-33. Toronto: University of Toronto Press, 1991.

670 REYNOLDS, Cecilia. "Hegemony and Hierarchy: Becoming a Teacher in Toronto, 1930-1980." *Historical Studies in Education* 2, 1 (Spring 1990): 95-118.

671 REYNOLDS, Cecilia. "Too Limiting a Liberation: Discourse and Actuality in the Case of Married Women Teachers." In *Feminism and Education: A Canadian Perspective,* eds. Frieda Forman, *et al,* 145-68. Toronto: Centre for Women's Studies in Education, Ontario Institute for Studies in Education, 1990.

672 REYNOLDS, Cecilia and Harry Smaller. "Ontario School Teachers: A Gendered View of the 1930s." *Historical Studies in Education* 6, 3 (1994): 151-69.

673 ROBERTSON, Heather-Jane. *Progress Revisited: The Quality of (Work) Life of Women Teachers.* Ottawa: Canadian Teachers' Federation, 1993.

674 SCANLON, Kathleen O'Reilly. *Tales Out of School.* Carp, ON: Creative Bound Inc., 1992. [former students recount their memories of teachers]

675 SHACK, Sybil. "The Making of a Teacher, 1917-1935: One Woman's Perspective." In *Issues in the History of Education in Manitoba: From the Construction of the Common School to the Politics of Voices,* ed. Rosa del C. Bruno-Jofré, 431-69. Lewiston, NY and Queenston, ON: The Edwin Mellen Press, 1993.

676 SHACK, Sybil. "Teaching as Growth, 1935-1976: One Woman's Perspective." In *Issues in the History of Education in Manitoba: From the Construction of the Common School to the Politics of Voices,* ed. Rosa del C. Bruno-Jofré, 471-509. Lewiston, NY and Queenston, ON: The Edwin Mellen Press, 1993.

677 SHAW, Bertha M.C. *Broken Threads: Memories of a Northern Ontario Schoolteacher.* New York: Exposition Press, 1955.

678 SHAW, Bertha M.C. *Laughter and Tears.* New York: Exposition Press, 1957.

679 SHAW, Bertha M.C. *Born to Grow Old.* Timmins, ON: Northern Stationery and Printing Co., 1960.

680 SMALLER, Harry. "'A Room of One's Own': The Early Years of the Toronto Women Teachers' Association." In *Gender and Education in Ontario: An Historical Reader,* eds. Ruby Heap and Alison Prentice, 105-26. Toronto: Canadian Scholars' Press, 1991.

681 SMALLER, Harry. "Gender and Status: The Founding Meeting of the Teachers' Association of Canada West, January 25, 1861." *Historical Studies in Education* 6, 2 (Fall 1994): 201-18.

682 SMITH, Vivian Martin. *Faces Along My Way.* Winnipeg: Prairie Publishing, 1970. [teaching in rural Manitoba, 1920 to mid-century]

683 STATON, Pat and Beth Light. *Speak With Their Own Voices: A Documentary History of the Federation of Women Teachers' Associations of Ontario and the Elementary Public School Teachers of Ontario.* Toronto: Federation of Women Teachers' Associations of Ontario, 1987.

684 STORTZ, Paul J. and J. Donald Wilson. "Schools, Teachers and Community Influence in North-Central British Columbia." *Histoire sociale/Social History* XXVI, 52 (November 1993): 265-90.

685 TAYLOR, Phyllis Mary. *Buckskin and Blackboard.* London: Darwen Finlayson, 1955. [Bar Creek, British Columbia, 1940s]

686 TAYLOR, Phyllis Mary. *Dog-Team and School-Desk.* London: Herbert Jenkins, 1960. [All Saints Anglican Residential School, post-World War II Aklavik]

687 THIVIÈRGE, Marise. "La syndicalisation des institutrices catholiques, 1900-1959." In *Maîtresses de maison, maîtresses d'école: Femmes, famille et éducation dans l'histoire du Québec,* eds. Nadia Fahmy-Eid and Micheline Dumont, 171-89. Montréal: Boréal Express, 1983.

688 WHITELEY, Marilyn Färdig. "Annie Leake's Occupation: Development of a Teaching Career, 1858-1886." *Historical Studies in Education* 4, 1 (Spring 1992): 97-112.

689 WILSON, J. Donald. "'I Am Here to Help You if You Need Me': British Columbia's Rural Teachers' Welfare Officer, 1928-1934." *Journal of Canadian Studies* 25, 2 (Summer 1990). Abridged in *British Columbia Reconsidered: Essays on Women,* eds. Gillian Creese and Veronica Strong-Boag, 340-63. Vancouver: Press Gang Publishers, 1992.

690 WILSON, J. Donald. "'I am ready to be of assistance when I can': Lottie Bowron and Rural Women Teachers in British Columbia." In *Women Who Taught: Perspectives on the History of Women and Teaching,* eds. Alison Prentice and Marjorie Theobald, 202-29. Toronto: University of Toronto Press, 1991.

691 WILSON, J. Donald and Paul J. Stortz. "'May the Lord Have Mercy on You': The Rural School Problem in British Columbia in the 1920s." *BC Studies* 79 (Autumn 1988): 24-58.

692 WOODMAN, May. "Reminiscences of a Pioneer Teacher." In *Nanaimo Retrospective: The First Century,* ed. E. Blanche Norcross, 47-48. Nanaimo, BC: Nanaimo Historical Society, 1979.

693 WOTHERSPOON, Terry. "From Subordinate Partners to Dependent Employees: State Regulation of Public School Teachers in Nineteenth-Century British Columbia." *Labour/Le Travail* 31 (Spring 1993): 75-110.

694 WOTHERSPOON, Terry. "The Incorporation of Public School Teachers into the Industrial Order: British Columbia in the First Half of the Twentieth Century." *Studies in Political Economy* 46 (Spring 1995): 119-52.

695 WRIGHT, Robert. "The Plight of Rural Women Teachers in the 1920s." *British Columbia Historical News* 28, 1 (Winter 1994/95): 26-29.

ETHNICITY/IMMIGRATION

TODAY MOST SCHOLARS in the field understand ethnic/racial categories as socially constructed rather than biologically determined. The terms "white" and "black," for example, have been defined in dramatically different ways in various cultural and historical contexts. To some extent, any attempt to categorize women along ethnic and racial lines is both artificial and problematic, yet scholars study these categories because they are powerful constructs, embodied in law, policy, and popular prejudices where they influence many aspects of women's lives and identities. The past decade has witnessed the rapid growth of a sophisticated new scholarship examining the construction of ethnic/racial categories and theorizing their relationship to gender in Canadian history. Interest in this field has been stimulated by Canada's policy of official multiculturalism, which has helped to fund research on ethnic and cultural communities, by the changing ethnic/racial profile of the Canadian population and a growing public awareness of racism, and by the changing composition of the historical profession itself. Particularly among the younger cohorts of Canadian historians, scholars of diverse backgrounds are bringing both language skills and insider perspectives to bear on studies of race, ethnicity and gender in Canadian history.

Closely connected to the study of ethnicity and race is the field of immigration history where scholars study the migration, reception and resettlement of immigrant populations in Canada's past. Since the early 1980s, feminist scholars have challenged the tendency of historians to equate immigration with male immigration, and to ignore the distinctive experiences of women both as immigrants and as refugees. Those distinctive experiences were due in no small measure to sexist and racist provisions of Canadian immigration policies that sometimes refused entry to women, denied them assistance offered to male immigrants, or enforced women's dependence on male sponsors. There is now a substantial literature, much of it produced by sociologists, on the social construction of the "immigrant woman" in Canadian immigration policy and on the concentration of immigrant women in the lower echelons of the Canadian labour force, with particular attention to the situation of migrant domestic workers.

Reflecting the relatively recent scholarly recognition of race and ethnicity as categories that shape the lives of all women, not only those belonging to visible minority populations, women of Anglo-Celtic origin are now being studied as members of a distinct ethnic/racial category. At the same time, scholars are increasingly sensitive to the inadequacy of "British" as a descriptive label and are examining the diverse experiences of English, Irish and Scottish women. Prominent in nineteenth and early twentieth-century migrations to Canada, many highly literate British women left letters and memoirs documenting their experiences. The study of twentieth-century immigrants from European countries, including Italian, Ukrainian, Armenian, Polish and Finnish women, has been facilitated by historians' growing interest in oral history and use of the ethnic press, and reveals the diversity of immigrant experiences in urban and rural contexts. The richness of surviving records and new computer-based methodologies have encouraged a flourishing scholarship on French immigrants and the colonization of New France, with special emphasis on the *filles du roi.*

The growing literature on Canadian women of African or Caribbean origin clearly demonstrates that Black women in Canada do not constitute a homogeneous group. Several historians and sociologists have documented the experiences of twentieth-century immigrants from the Caribbean in the context of Canadian immigration policy and the recruitment of domestic workers. Another body of scholarship, however, traces the much longer history of women in Black communities in southern Ontario and Nova Scotia. Most of these studies address questions pertaining to Black women's experiences in the paid labour force, their roles in family and community life, and the impact of racism and discrimination. There is also an emerging body of scholarship on Canadian women of Chinese, Japanese and South Asian extraction. Most of the work on South Asian women has been undertaken by sociologists and focuses on the post-1945 period of immigration and settlement. Historical scholarship on Chinese women in Canada examines the issues of paid work and immigration policy in the early twentieth century, while a very small body of literature on Japanese women in Canada has begun to examine the experiences of the picture brides during the early twentieth century and internees during the Second World War.

AFRICAN/CARIBBEAN

696 BAKAN, A.B. "The International Market for Female Labour and Individual Deskilling: West Indian Female Workers in Toronto." *Canadian Journal of Latin American and Caribbean Studies* 12, 24 (1987): 69-85.

697 BEARDEN, Jim and Linda Jean Butler. *Shadd: The Life and Times of Mary Shadd Cary.* Toronto: NC Press, 1977.

698 BERNARD, Wanda Thomas, Lydia Lucas-White and Dorothy E. Moore. "Triple Jeopardy: Assessing Life Experiences of Black Nova Scotian Women from a Social Work and Historical Perspective." *Canadian Social Work Review* 10, 2 (Summer 1993): 256-74. Reprinted in *Coming of Age: Readings in Canadian History Since World War II*, eds. Donald Avery and Roger Hall, 186-203. Toronto: Harcourt Brace & Company Canada, 1996.

699 BEST, Carrie M. *That Lonesome Road: The Autobiography of Carrie M. Best.* New Glasgow, NS: Clarion Publishing Co., 1977.

700 BRAITHWAITE, Rella and Tessa Benn-Ireland. *Some Black Women: Profiles of Black Women in Canada.* Toronto: Sister Vision Press, 1993.

701 BRAND, Dionne. "A Working Paper on Black Women in Toronto: Gender, Race and Class." *Fireweed* 19 (Summer/Fall 1984): 26-43.

702 BRAND, Dionne. "Black Women and Work: The Impact of Racially Constructed Gender Roles on the Sexual Division of Labour." *Fireweed* 25 (Fall 1987): 28-37 and 26 (Winter/Spring 1988): 87-92.

703 BRAND, Dionne, ed. *No Burden to Carry: Narratives of Black Working Women in Ontario, 1920s to 1950s.* Toronto: Women's Press, 1991.

704 BRAND, Dionne. *Bread Out of Stone.* Toronto: Coach House Press, 1994.

705 BRISTOW, Peggy. "'Whatever you raise in the ground you can sell it in Chatham': Black Women in Buxton and Chatham, 1850-1865." In *"We're Rooted Here and They Can't Pull Us Up": Essays in African Canadian Women's History*, Peggy Bristow, *et al.* 69-142. Toronto: University of Toronto Press, 1994.

706 BRISTOW, Peggy, *et al.* *"We're Rooted Here and They Can't Pull Us Up": Essays in African Canadian Women's History.* Toronto: University of Toronto Press, 1994.

707 CALLISTE, Agnes. "Canada's Immigration Policy and Domestics from the Caribbean: The Second Domestic Scheme." In *Race, Class and Gender: Bonds and Barriers*, ed. Jessie Vorst, 133-65. Toronto: Between the Lines, 1989. Reprinted in *Canadian Women: A Reader*, eds. Wendy Mitchinson, *et al*, 380-405. Toronto: Harcourt Brace Canada, 1996.

708 CALLISTE, Agnes. "Women of 'Exceptional Merit': Immigration of Caribbean Nurses to Canada." *Canadian Journal of Women and the Law* 6, 1 (1993): 85-102.

709 CALLISTE, Agnes. "Race, Gender and Canadian Immigration Policy: Blacks from the Caribbean, 1900-1932." *Journal of Canadian Studies* 28, 4 (Winter 1993/94): 131-48.

710 CARTY, Linda. "African Canadian Women and the State: 'Labour only, please.'" In *"We're Rooted Here and They Can't Pull Us Up": Essays in African Canadian Women's History*, Peggy Bristow, *et al*, 193-229. Toronto: University of Toronto Press, 1994. [immigrant domestics]

711 DUCHEINE, Vivien. "Les femmes haïtiennes au Québec." *Resources for Feminist Research* 15, 4 (December 1986/January 1987): 10-12.

712 GAYLE, Noga A. "Black Women's Reality and Feminism: An Exploration of Race and Gender." In *The Anatomy of Gender: Women's Struggle for the Body*, eds. Dawn H. Currie and Valerie Raoul, 232-42. Ottawa: Carleton University Press, 1992.

713 HAMILTON, Sylvia. "Our Mothers Grand and Great: Black Women of Nova Scotia." *Canadian Woman Studies* 4, 2 (Winter 1982): 33-37.

714 HAMILTON, Sylvia. "A Glimpse of Edith Clayton." *Fireweed* 18 (Spring 1984): 18-20. [Afro-Nova Scotian basket weaver]

715 HAMILTON, Sylvia. "Naming Names, Naming Ourselves: A Survey of Early Black Women in Nova Scotia." In *"We're Rooted Here and They Can't Pull Us Up": Essays in African Canadian Women's History*, Peggy Bristow, *et al.* 13-40. Toronto: University of Toronto Press, 1994.

716 HAMILTON, Sylvia and Marie Hamilton. "Mothers and Daughters: A Delicate Partnership." *Fireweed* 18 (Spring 1984): 64-68. [personal histories of two Afro-Nova Scotian women]

717 HERBERT, Jacinth. "'Otherness' and the Black Woman." *Canadian Journal of Women and the Law* 3, 1 (1989): 269-79.

718 LEAH, Ronnie and Gwen Morgan. "Immigrant Women Fight Back: The Case of Seven Jamaican Women." *Resources for Feminist Research* 8, 3, Part 2 (November 1979): 23-24.

719 MacDONALD, Cheryl. "Last Stop on the Underground Railway." *The Beaver* 70, 1 (Feb./Mar. 1990): 32-38. [Mary Ann Shadd]

720 MERLETT, Miriam. "Black Women Immigrants." In *Women: Isolation and Bonding: The Ecology of Gender*, ed. Kathleen Storrie. Toronto: Methuen, 1988.

721 MORTON, Suzanne. "Separate Spheres in a Separate World: African-Nova Scotian Women in Late-19th-Century Halifax County." *Acadiensis* 22, 2 (Spring 1993): 61-83. Reprinted in *Separate Spheres: Women's Worlds in the 19th Century Maritimes*, eds. Janet Guildford and Suzanne Morton, 185-210. Fredericton: Acadiensis Press, 1994; and in *Canadian Women: A Reader*, eds. Wendy Mitchinson, *et al*, 172-94. Toronto: Harcourt Brace Canada, 1996.

722 NATIONAL FILM BOARD OF CANADA. *Black on Screen: Images of Black Canadians, 1950's-1990's*. Montreal: National Film Board of Canada, 1992.

723 SADLIER, Rosemary. *Leading the Way: Black Women in Canada*. Toronto: Umbrella Press, 1994.

724 SADLIER, Rosemary. *Harriet Tubman: Her Life in Canada and the United States*. Toronto: Umbrella Press, 1995.

725 SHADD, Adrienne. "Three Hundred Years of Black Women in Canadian History: Circa 1700 to 1980." *Tiger Lily* 1, 2 (1987).

726 SHADD, Adrienne. "Institutionalized Racism and Canadian History: Notes of a Black Canadian." In *Seeing Ourselves: Exploring Race, Ethnicity and Culture*, ed. Carl E. James, 151-55. Oakville, ON: Sheridan College, 1989. Reprinted in *Racism in Canada*, ed. Ormond McKague, 1-5. Saskatoon Fifth House Publishers, 1991.

727 SHADD, Adrienne. "'The Lord seemed to say "Go"': Women and the Underground Railroad Movement." In *"We're Rooted Here and They Can't Pull Us Up": Essays in African Canadian Women's History*, Peggy Bristow, *et al.* 41-68. Toronto: University of Toronto Press, 1994.

728 SILVERA, Makeda. "Immigrant Domestic Workers: Whose Dirty Laundry?" *Fireweed* 9 (Winter 1981): 53-59.

729 SILVERA, Makeda. "Silenced." *Fireweed* 16 (Spring 1983): 53-62.

730 SILVERA, Makeda. *Silenced: Talks With Working Class West Indian Women About Their Lives and Struggles as Domestic Workers in Canada*. Toronto: Sister Vision Press, 1983.

731 SILVERA, Makeda. *Silenced: Caribbean Domestic Workers Talk with Makeda Silvera*. Toronto: Sister Vision Press, 1992.

732 TALBOT, Carol. *Growing Up Black in Canada*. Toronto: Williams-Wallace Publishers, 1984.

733 THORNHILL, Esmeralda. "Black Women's Studies in Teaching Related to Women: Help or Hindrance to Universal Sisterhood?" *Fireweed* (Spring 1983): 77-83.

734 THORNHILL, Esmeralda. "Focus on Black Women." *Canadian Journal of Women and the Law* 1, 1 (1985): 153-62.

735 YEE, Shirley J. "Gender Ideology and Black Women as Community-Builders in Ontario, 1850-70." *Canadian Historical Review* 75, 1 (March 1994): 53-73.

ANGLO-CELTIC

736 ALLAN, Iris. *Mother and Her Family*. Cobalt, ON: Highway Book Shop, 1977. [Scottish immigrants in Transcona, Manitoba]

737 ALLODI, Mary. "Two Gentlewomen of Upper Canada." *Rotunda* 10 (Summer 1977): 2-3.

738 ANDREWS, Elizabeth. *Ellen Elliot, A Pioneer*. Toronto: Ginn, 1972. [Upper Canada]

739 ANGUS, Margaret. "A Gentlewoman in Early Kingston." *Historic Kingston* 24 (1976): 73-95.

740 ARMYTAGE, W.H.G., ed. "A Pioneer's Letter Home." *Queen's Quarterly* 58, 4 (Winter 1951/52): 515-18.

741 BAILEY, Mary C. "Reminiscences of a Pioneer." *Alberta Historical Review* 15, 4 (Autumn 1967): 17-25.

742 BARBER, Marilyn. "The Women Ontario Welcomed: Immigrant Domestics for Ontario Homes, 1870-1930." *Ontario History* 72, 3 (September 1980): 148-72. Reprinted in *The Neglected Majority: Essays in Canadian Women's History, Vol. 2*, eds. Alison Prentice and Susan Mann Trofimenkoff, 102-21. Toronto: McClelland and Stewart, 1985; in *A History of Ontario: Selected Readings*, ed. Michael J. Piva, 301-15. Toronto: Copp Clark Pittman, 1988; and in *Immigration in Canada: Historical Perspectives*, ed. Gerald Tulchinsky, Mississauga: Copp Clark Longman, 1994.

743 BARBER, Marilyn. "In Search of a Better Life: A Scottish Domestic in Rural Ontario." *Polyphony* 8 (1986): 13-16.

744 BARBER, Marilyn. "Sunny Ontario for British Girls, 1900-30." In *Looking into My Sister's Eyes: An Exploration in Women's History*, ed. Jean Burnet, 55-73. Toronto: Multicultural History Society of Ontario, 1986.

745 BARBER, Marilyn. "Immigrant Domestics, 1900-1930: The Use of the Tape Collection of the Multicultural History Society of Ontario." *Polyphony* 9, 1 (Fall/Winter 1987): 83-84.

746 BEATTIE, Susan, ed. *A New Life in Canada: The Letters of Sophia Eastwood, 1843-1870*. Toronto: Canadian Scholars' Press, 1989.

747 BENTLEY, D.M.R. "Breaking the 'Cake of Custom': The Atlantic Crossing as a Rubicon for Female Emigrants to Canada?" In *Re(Dis)covering Our Foremothers: Nineteenth Century Canadian Women Writers*, ed. Lorraine McMullen, 91-122. Ottawa: University of Ottawa Press, 1989.

748 BIRD, Isabella Lucy. *The Englishwoman in America*. Forward by A.H. Clark. Toronto: University of Toronto Press, 1967.

749 BLOM, Margaret Howard and Thomas Blom, eds. *Canada Home: Juliana Horatia Ewing's Fredericton Letters, 1867-1869*. Vancouver: University of British Columbia Press, 1983.

750 BUCKLEY, Suzann. "British Female Emigration and Imperial Development: Experiments in Canada, 1885-1931." *Hecate* 3, 2 (1977): 26-40.

751 BUSH, Julia. "'The Right Sort of Woman': Female Emigrators and Emigration to the British Empire, 1890-1910." *Women's History Review* 3, 3 (1994): 385-410.

752 CONWAY, Sheelagh. *The Faraway Hills are Green: Voices of Irish Women in Canada.* Toronto: Women's Press, 1992.

753 CRAN, Mrs. George. *A Woman in Canada.* London: W.J. Ham-Smith, 1911.

754 CURRIE, Emma Augusta. "Reminiscences of Niagara and St. David's." *Niagara Historical Society* 20 (1911): 23-34. [Upper Canada]

755 CURTIN, Emma. "Two British Gentlewomen." *Alberta History* 38, 4 (Autumn 1990): 10-16. [Barbara Alice Slater and Helen Maria Shaw]

756 DE VRIES, Pieter J. and Georgina MacNab-de Vries. "Work and Gender in a Scottish Community on Cape Breton Island." In *Work, Ethnicity and Oral History*, eds. Dorothy E. Moore and James H. Morrison, 107-19. Halifax: International Education Centre, St. Mary's University, 1988.

757 EARLE, Maria Theresa. *Memoirs and Memories.* London: Smith, Elder and Co., 1911.

758 EATON, Sara. *Lady of the Backwoods.* Toronto: McClelland and Stewart, 1969. [Catharine Parr Traill]

759 EMBLEM, Edith (Lawrence). "In Her Own Words." In *Nanaimo Retrospective: The First Century*, ed. E. Blanche Norcross, 147-51. Nanaimo, BC: Nanaimo Historical Society, 1979. [reminiscences of a young woman immigrant under an informal service contract]

760 ERRINGTON, Jane. "Single Pioneering Women in Upper Canada." *Families* 31, 1 (February 1992): 5-19.

761 FIELD, Edith Coventry. *The Good Old Days: A True Record of Pioneer Life on the North American Continent.* Detroit: Duo-Art Press, 1938. [Scottish immigrants in Ontario]

762 FINLAYSON, Isobel. "York Boat Journal." *The Beaver* (September 1951): 32-35 and (December 1951): 32-37. [Red River District, 1840]

763 FOWLER, Marian. "Portrait of Susan Sibbald: Writer and Pioneer." *Ontario History* 66 (March 1974).

764 FOWLER, Marian. *The Embroidered Tent: Five Gentlewomen in Early Canada.* Toronto: Anansi, 1982. [Elizabeth Simcoe, Catharine Parr Traill, Susanna Moodie, Anna Jameson, Lady Dufferin]

765 GERRARD, Elizabeth. *We Came to Canada.* Toronto: Longmans, 1967.

766 GILTROW, Janet. "'Painful Experience in a Distant Land': Mrs. Moodie in Canada and Mrs. Trollope in America." *Mosaic* 14, 2 (Spring 1981): 131-44.

767 GLENN, Eleanor Margaret. "Pioneer Women of Upper Canada: heroines of hearsay history." *Families* 31, 3 (August 1992):133-40.

768 GREENHILL, Pauline. *Ethnicity in the Mainstream: Three Studies of English Canadian Culture in Ontario.* Montreal and Kingston: McGill-Queen's University Press, 1994.

769 GRESKO, Jacqueline. "Mrs. Moodie's First Impressions of British Columbia." *British Columbia Historical News* 11, 3/4 (April/June 1978): 6-9. [Mary Susannah Moodie, 1859]

770 HAMMERTON, A. James. *Emigrant Gentlewomen: Genteel Poverty and Female Emigration, 1830-1914.* London: Croom Helm, 1979.

771 HARRIS, R. Cole and Elizabeth Phillips, eds. *Letters from Windermere, 1912-1914.* Vancouver: University of British Columbia Press, 1984.

772 HARRISON, Marjorie. *Go West, Go Wise.* London: Edward Arnold and Co., 1930. [prospects for female emigrants described by an English journalist]

773 HARRISON, Phyllis. *The Home Children: Their Personal Stories.* Winnipeg: Watson and Dwyer Publishing, 1979.

774 HATHAWAY, Ann. *Muskoka Memories.* Toronto: William Briggs, 1904.

775 HETT, Francis P., ed. *Memoirs of Susan Sibbald.* London: John Lane the Bodley Head, 1925. [Canada West, 1850s and 1860s]

776 HEWARD, S.A. and W.S. Wallace. "An American Lady in Old Toronto: The Letters of Julia Lambert, 1821-1854." *Transactions of the Royal Society of Canada* (1946), Section II: 101.

777 HIEMSTRA, Mary. *Gully Farm.* Toronto: McClelland and Stewart, 1955. [Barr colonists, 1903]

778 HIGGINSON, T.B. "Moira O'Neill in Alberta." *Alberta Historical Review* 5 (Spring 1957): 22-25.

779 HOPKINS, Elizabeth. "A Prison-House for Prosperity: the Immigrant Experience of the Nineteenth Century Upper-Class British Woman." In *Looking into My Sister's Eyes: An Exploration in Women's History*, ed. Jean Burnet, 7-19. Toronto: Multicultural History Society of Ontario, 1986. Reprinted in *Interpreting Canada's Past: Volume One, Pre-Confederation*, 2nd edition, ed. J.M. Bumsted, 340-51. Toronto: Oxford University Press, 1993.

780 JACKEL, Susan, ed. *A Flannel Shirt and Liberty: British Emigrant Gentlewomen in the Canadian West, 1880-1914.* Vancouver and London: University of British Columbia Press, 1982.

781 JACKSON, Pauline. "Women in 19th Century Irish Emigration." *International Migration Review* 18, 4 (Winter 1984): 1004-20.

782 JAMESON, Anna Brownell. *Winter Studies and Summer Rambles* (1838). Introduction by Clara Thomas. Toronto: McClelland and Stewart, 1965.

783 KORTE, Barbara. "Ladies in der Wildnis." *Zeitschrift der Gesellschaft für Kanada-Studien* 12, 2 (1992): 7-28. [nineteenth-century female settlers]

784 LANGTON, H.H., ed. *A Gentlewoman in Upper Canada: The Journals of Anne Langton.* Toronto: Clarke, Irwin and Company, 1950.

785 LAY, Jackie. "To Columbia on the Tynemouth: The Emigration of Single Women and Girls in 1862." In *In Her Own Right: Selected Essays on Women's History in BC,* eds. Barbara Latham and Cathy Kess, 19-41. Victoria: Camosun College, 1980.

786 LEFROY, Catherine F. "Recollections of Mary Warren Breckenridge, of Clarke Township." *Ontario History* 3 (1901): 110-13. [Upper Canada]

787 LOW, Florence B. *Women out West: Life and Work in Canada.* London: W.T. Cranfield, 1924.

788 MAAS, Barbara. *Helpmates of Man: Middle-Class Women and Gender Ideology in Nineteenth-Century Ontario.* Bochum: Universitätsverlag Dr. N. Brockmeyer 1990.

789 MAAS, Barbara. "Immigration, Household Structure and Sex Roles in the Nineteenth Century: A Case Study from the Maritimes." *Zeitschrift der Gesellschaft für Kanada-Studien.* 12, 2 (1992): 29-36.

790 MacDONALD, Charlotte J. "Ellen Silk and her sisters: female emigration to the New World." In *The Sexual Dynamics of History: Men's power, women's resistance,* eds. London Feminist History Group, 66-86. London: Pluto Press, 1983.

791 MacLEOD, M.A., ed. *The Letters of Letitia Hargrave.* Toronto: Champlain Society, 1947. [York Factory, 1840s]

792 MAY, Mrs. Ernest G. "A British Bride-to-Be Comes to Calgary." *Alberta Historical Review* 6, 1 (Winter 1958): 19-22.

793 McALLISTER, Clare. "The Immigrant Children." *Canadian Welfare* 39, 1 (January/February 1963): 22-26.

794 McDONALD, Donna. *Illustrated News: Juliana Horatia Ewing's Canadian Pictures, 1867-1869.* Saint John/Toronto: New Brunswick Museum/Dundurn Press, 1985.

795 McINTOSH, Dave. "Go West Young Woman." *The Beaver* 72, 6 (Dec. 1992/Jan. 1993): 38-39. [1886 CPR pamphlet]

796 McLEOD, Evelyn J., ed. *One Woman's Charlottetown: Diaries of Margaret Gray Lord, 1863, 1876, 1890.* Hull: Canadian Museum of Civilization, 1988.

797 McLEOD, Evelyn Slater. "Restless Pioneers." *The Beaver* (Summer 1976): 34-41. [homesteading in Alberta, 1909-1915]

798 METCALF, Vicky. *Journey Fantastic: With the Overlanders to the Cariboo.* Toronto: McGraw-Hill Ryerson, 1970. [Catherine Schubert]

799 METCALF, Vicky. *Catherine Schubert.* Toronto: Fitzhenry and Whiteside, 1978. [juvenile]

800 MILLER, Audrey Saunders, ed. *The Journals of Mary O'Brien.* Toronto: Macmillan Co., 1968. [Upper Canada, 1820s and 1830s]

801 MITCHELL, Elizabeth B. *In Western Canada Before the War.* Introduction by Susan Jackel. Saskatoon: Western Producer Prairie Books, 1981.

802 MOODIE, Susanna. *Roughing It In the Bush.* Afterword by Susan Glickman. Toronto: McClelland and Stewart, 1989.

803 MOODIE, Susanna. *Life in the Clearings versus the Bush.* Afterword by Carol Shields. Toronto: McClelland and Stewart, 1989.

804 MORRIS, Audrey Y. *The Gentle Pioneers: Five Nineteenth Century Canadians.* Toronto: Hodder and Stoughton, 1968. [Susanna Moodie and Catharine Parr Traill]

805 MORRIS, Elizabeth Keith. *An Englishwoman in the Canadian West.* Bristol: J.W. Arrowsmith, 1913.

806 MURRAY, Hon. Amelia. *Letters from the United States, Cuba and Canada (1856).* New York: Negro Universities Press, 1969.

807 NEEDLER, G.H. *The Otonabee Pioneers: The Story of the Stewarts, the Stricklands, the Traills and the Moodies.* Toronto: Burns and MacEachern, 1953.

808 NESBITT, J.K., ed. "The Diary of Martha Cheney Ella, 1853-1856." *British Columbia Historical Quarterly,* 13, 2/4 (April-October 1949): 91-112, 257-70.

809 ORMSBY, Margaret A., ed. *A Pioneer Gentlewoman in British Columbia: The Recollections of Susan Allison.* Vancouver: University of British Columbia Press, 1976.

810 "Pages from a Pioneer Diary: The Diary of Ellen McFadden Lowes, 1882-1886." *Manitoba Pageant,* Part 1 (Autumn 1976): 21-25 and Part 2 (Winter 1977): 12-17.

811 PARR, Joy. "'Transplanting from Dens of Iniquity': Theology and Child Emigration." In *A Not Unreasonable Claim: Women and Reform in Canada, 1880s-1920s,* ed. Linda Kealey, 169-83. Toronto: The Women's Press, 1979.

812 PARR, Joy. *Labouring Children: British Immigrant Apprentices to Canada, 1869-1924.* London/Montreal: Croom Helm/McGill-Queen's University Press, 1980; Toronto: University of Toronto Press, 1994.

813 PARR, Joy. "The Skilled Emigrant and Her Kin: Gender, Culture and Labour Recruitment." *Canadian Historical Review* 68 (December 1987): 529-51. Reprinted in *Rethinking Canada: The Promise of Women's History,* 2nd edition, eds. Veronica Strong-Boag and Anita Clair Fellman, 337-55. Toronto: Copp Clark Pitman Ltd., 1991; in *The Challenge of Modernity: A Reader on Post-Confederation Canada,* ed. Ian McKay, 204-24. Toronto: McGraw-Hill Ryerson, 1992; and in *Immigration in Canada: Historical Perspectives,* ed. Gerald Tulchinsky, Mississauga: Copp Clark Longman, 1994.

814 PERRY, Adele. "'Oh I'm Just Sick of the Faces of Men': Gender Imbalance, Race, Sexuality, and Sociability in Nineteenth-Century British Columbia." *BC Studies* 105/106 (Spring/Summer 1995): 27-44.

815 PINKHAM, Mrs. W.C. "Selections from the Unpublished Recollections of Mrs. W.C. Pinkham, an Early Manitoban." *Manitoba Pageant* 19/20 (1974/75).

816 "A Pioneer Woman's Advice to Immigrant Women." *Canadian Women's Studies* 1, 1 (1978): 29-30.

817 REID, Ida May. "Good Hope Days." *Alberta Historical Review* 9, 2 (Spring 1961): 22-24.

818 "Reminiscence of Mrs. White, of White's Mills, Near Cobourg, Upper Canada, Formerly Miss Catherine Chrysler of Sydney, Near Belleville, Aged 79." *Ontario History* 7 (1906): 153-57.

819 RENDELL, Alice. "Letters of a Barr Colonist." *Alberta Historical Review* 11, 1 (Winter 1963): 12-27.

820 ROBERTS, Barbara. "'A Work of Empire': Canadian Reformers and British Female Immigration." In *A Not Unreasonable Claim: Women and Reform in Canada, 1880s-1920s,* ed. Linda Kealey, 185-201. Toronto: The Women's Press, 1979.

821 ROURKE, Louise. *The Land of the Frozen Tide.* London: Hutchinson and Co., 1928. [an English bride at Fort Chipewyan, Northern Alberta, 1924-1926]

822 ROUSLIN, Virgina Watson. "The Intelligent Woman's Guide to Pioneering in Canada." *Dalhousie Review* 56, 2 (Summer 1976): 319-35. [Upper Canada]

823 ST. JOHN, Seward T. "Diary of Mrs. S.T. St. John." *Saskatchewan History* 2 (May 1949): 25-29 and (Autumn 1949): 25-30. [1902-1904]

824 SCOTT, Irene G. *The Trek of the Overlanders.* Don Mills: Burns and MacEachern, 1968. [Catherine Schubert]

825 SIMPSON, Frances. "Journey for Frances." *The Beaver* (December 1953): 50-54, (March 1954): 12-16, (Summer 1954): 12-18. [Frances Ramsay Simpson, canoe trip from Montreal to York Factory, 1830]

826 SKELTON, Isabel. *The Backwoodswoman: A Chronicle of Pioneer Home Life in Upper Canada.* Toronto: Ryerson, 1924.

827 SMITH, Helen E.H. and Lisa M. Sullivan. "'Now that I know how to manage': Work and Identity in the Journals of Anne Langton." *Ontario History* 87, 3 (September 1995): 253-69.

828 STEELE, Millicent Pollock and Ellen Frances Steele. "Diary of a Voyage from London to Upper Canada in 1833." *Ontario History* 23 (1926): 483-510.

829 STEWART, Frances. *Our Forest Home.* Compiled and edited by E.S. Dunlop. Toronto: Presbyterian Publishing Co., 1889. [Upper Canada]

830 SYKES, Ella Constance. *A Home-Help in Canada.* London: Smith, Elder, 1915.

831 TEGELBERG, Laurie. "Catherine Sutherland of Point Douglas: Woman of Head and Heart." *Manitoba Pageant* (Autumn 1957): 19-24.

832 TIVY, Louis, ed. *Your Loving Anna: Letters from the Ontario Frontier.* Toronto: University of Toronto Press, 1972. [Anna Leveridge, 1883-1891]

833 TRAILL, Catharine Parr. *The Canadian Settler's Guide.* Toronto: McClelland and Stewart, 1969.

834 TRAILL, Catharine Parr. *The Backwoods of Canada.* Afterword by D.M.R. Bentley. Toronto: McClelland and Stewart, 1989.

835 TURNER, Wesley B. "80 Stout and Healthy Looking Girls." *Canada: An Historical Magazine* 3, 2 (December 1975): 36-49. [Irish immigrant domestics]

836 TURNER, Wesley B. "Miss Rye's Children and the Ontario Press, 1875." *Ontario History* 68, 3 (September 1976): 169-203.

837 WILLIAMS, Barbara. *Anne Langton: Pioneer Woman and Artist.* Peterborough, 1986.

ASIAN

838 ADILMAN, Tamara. "A Preliminary Sketch of Chinese Women and Work in British Columbia, 1858-1950." In *Not Just Pin Money: Selected Essays on the History of Women's Work in British Columbia,* eds. Barbara K. Latham and Roberta J. Pazdro, 53-78. Victoria: Camosun College, 1984. Reprinted in *British Columbia Reconsidered: Essays on Women,* eds. Gillian Creese and Veronica Strong-Boag, 309-39. Vancouver: Press Gang Publishers, 1992.

839 AYUKAWA, Midge. "Good Wives and Wise Mothers: Japanese Picture Brides in Early Twentieth-Century British Columbia." *BC Studies* 105/106 (Spring/Summer 1995): 103-18.

840 CHAN, Kwok B. "Coping with Aging and Managing Self-Identity: The Social World of the Elderly Chinese Woman." *Canadian Ethnic Studies* 15, 3 (1983): 36-50.

841 CHINESE CANADIAN NATIONAL COUNCIL, WOMEN'S BOOK COMMITTEE. *Jin Guo: Voices of Chinese Canadian Women.* Toronto: Women's Press, 1992.

842 COOMARASAMY, Sudha. "SriLankan Tamil Women: Resettlement in Montreal." *Canadian Woman Studies* 10, 1 (Spring 1989): 69-72.

843 DAS GUPTA, Tania. "Political Economy of Gender, Race and Class: Looking at South Asian Immigrant Women in Canada." *Canadian Ethnic Studies* 26, 1 (1994): 59-73.

844 FERNANDEZ, Sharon, *et al,* eds. "Asian Canadian Women." A special issue of *Fireweed* 30 (Winter 1990).

845 GHOSH, Ratna. "Minority Within a Minority—On Being South Asian and Female in Canada." In *Women in the Family and the Economy: An International Comparative Study,* eds. George Kurian and Ratna Ghosh, 413-26. Westport, CT: Greenwood Press, 1981.

846 GHOSH, Ratna. "Social and Economic Integration of South Asian Women in Montreal, Canada." In *Women in the Family and the Economy: An International Comparative Study*, eds. George Kurian and Ratna Ghosh, 59-71. Westport, CT: Greenwood Press, 1981.

847 GHOSH, Ratna. "Sarees and the Maple Leaf: Indian Women in Canada." In *Overseas Indians: A Study in Adaptation*, eds. G. Kurian and R.P. Srivastava, 90-99. New Dehli: Vikas Publishing House, 1983.

848 GHOSH, Ratna. "South Asian Women in Canada: Adaptation." In *South Asians in the Canadian Mosaic*, ed. S.N. Kanungo, 145-56. Montreal: Kala Bharati Foundation, 1984.

849 GHOSH, Ratna. "Multicultural Policy and Social Integration: South Asian Canadian Women." *Indian Journal of Gender Studies* 1, 1 (1994): 49-68.

850 GO, Amy. "Chinese Canadian Women and the Effects of the Exclusion Act and Head Tax." *Fireweed* 30 (Winter 1990): 20-22.

851 HUANG, Evelyn and Lawrence Jeffrey. *Chinese Canadians: Voices from a Community.* Vancouver: Douglas & McIntyre, 1992.

852 KHOSLA, Prabha. "Profiles of Working Class East Indian Women." *Fireweed* 16 (Spring 1983): 43-48.

853 KITIGAWA, Muriel. *This is My Own: Letters to Wes and Other Writings on Japanese Canadians, 1941-1948.* Edited by Roy Miki. Vancouver: Talonbooks, 1985.

854 KOBAYASHI, Audrey. "For the Sake of the Children: Japanese/Canadian/Workers/Mothers." In *Women, Work and Place*, ed. Audrey Kobayashi, 45-72. Montreal and Kingston: McGill-Queen's University Press, 1994.

855 KORETCHUK, Pat as told by Lorine Wong Chu. "Lorine's Legacy." *British Columbia Historical News* 27, 1 (Winter 1993/94): 5-9.

856 MAKABE, Tomoko. *Picture Brides: Japanese Women in Canada.* Translated by Kathleen Merken. Toronto: University of Toronto Press, 1995.

857 NAIDOO, Josephine C. "Women of South Asian and Anglo-Saxon Origins in the Canadian Context: Self Perceptions, Socialization, Achievement Aspirations." In *Sex Roles*, ed. C.S. Adams, Montreal: Eden Press, 1979.

858 NAIDOO, Josephine C. "Contemporary South Asian Women in the Canadian Mosaic." *International Journal of Women's Studies* 8 (September/October 1985): 338-50.

859 NAIDOO, Josephine C. "Cultural Perspectives on the Adjustment of South Asian Women in Canada." In *From a Different Perspective: Studies of Behaviour Across Cultures*, eds. I.R. Lacqunes and Y.H. Poortinga, 76-92. Lisse, The Netherlands: Swets and Zeitlinger, 1985.

860 NAIDOO, Josephine C. "Women of South Asian Origins: Status of Research, Problems, Future Issues." In *The South Asian Diaspora in Canada: Six Essays*, ed. Milton Israel, 37-58. Toronto: Multicultural History Society of Ontario, 1987.

861 NAIDOO, Josephine C. and J. Campbell Davis. "South Asian and Anglo Saxon Women in Canada: Attitudes Toward Multiculturalism." In *Asian Canadians: Contemporary Issues*, eds. Victor Ujimoto and Josephine Naidoo, 73-103. Guelph: University of Guelph, 1986.

862 NAIDOO, Josephine C. and J. Campbell Davis. "Canadian South Asian Women in Transition: A Dualistic View of Life." *Journal of Comparative Family Studies* 19, 2 (Summer 1988): 311-27.

863 NIPP, Dora. "'But Women Did Come': Working Chinese Women in the Interwar Years." In *Looking into My Sister's Eyes: An Exploration in Women's History*, ed. Jean Burnet, 179-94. Toronto: Multicultural History Society of Ontario, 1986.

864 "Note on Asian Indian Women in British Columbia, 1900-1935." In *Not Just Pin Money: Selected Essays on the History of Women's Work in British Columbia*, eds. Barbara K. Latham and Roberta J. Pazdro, 99-104. Victoria: Camosun College, 1984.

865 RALSTON, Helen. "Ethnicity, Class and Gender Among South Asian Women in Metro Halifax: An Exploratory Study." *Canadian Ethnic Studies* 20, 3 (1988): 63-83.

866 RALSTON, Helen. "Race, Class, Gender and Work Experience of South Asian Immigrant Women in Atlantic Canada." *Canadian Ethnic Studies* 33, 2 (1991): 129-39. Reprinted in *Canadian Women: A Reader*, eds. Wendy Mitchinson, *et al*, 405-16. Toronto: Harcourt Brace Canada, 1996.

867 RALSTON, Helen. "Immigration Policies and Practices: Their Impact on South Asian Women in Canada and Australia." *Australian-Canadian Studies* 12, 1 (1994): 1-48.

868 RALSTON, Helen. "Organizational Empowerment Among South Asian Immigrant Women in Canada." *International Journal of Canadian Studies* 11 (Spring 1995): 121-46.

869 TAKASHIMA, Shizue. *A Child in Prison Camp.* Montreal: Tundra Books, 1971.

870 YEE, May. "Chinese Canadian Women: Our Common Struggle." *Canadian Ethnic Studies* 19, 3 (1987): 174-84. Reprinted in *British Columbia Reconsidered: Essays on Women*, eds. Gillian Creese and Veronica Strong-Boag, 233-43. Vancouver: Press Gang Publishers, 1992.

871 YEE, May. "Out of the Silence: 'Voices of Chinese Canadian Women.'" *Resources for Feminist Research* 16, 1 (March 1987): 15-16.

872 YEE, May. "Out of a Silent History—'Voices of Chinese-Canadian Women.'" *Polyphony* 9, 1 (Fall/Winter 1987): 85-87.

873 YOUNG, Charles and Helen Y. Reid. *The Japanese Canadians: With a Second Paper on Oriental Standards of Living by W.A. Carrothers.* Toronto: University of Toronto Press, 1938.

EUROPEAN

874 BACKSTROM, Elvira. "Pioneer Parents." *Alberta Historical Review* 9, 4 (Autumn 1961): 14-21.

875 BEAUDOIN, Marie-Louise. *Les Premières et les filles du roi à Ville-Marie.* Montréal: Soeurs de la Congrégation de Notre-Dame, 1971.

876 BEAUREGARD, Yves, *et al.* "Famille, parenté et colonisation en Nouvelle-France." *Revue d'histoire de l'Amérique française* 39, 3 (hiver 1986): 391-406.

877 BLAIN, Jean. "La moralité en Nouvelle-France: les phases de la thèse et de l'antithèse." *Revue d'histoire de l'Amérique française* 27, 3 (décembre 1973): 408-16. [les filles du roi]

878 BOHACHEVSKY-CHOMIAK, Martha. *Feminists Despite Themselves: Women in Ukranian Community Life, 1884-1939.* Edmonton: Canadian Institute of Ukranian Studies, 1988.

879 BRADY, Elizabeth and Shelagh Wilkinson, eds. "Mediterranean Women in Canada." A special issue of *Canadian Woman Studies* 8, 2 (Summer 1987).

880 CAROLI, Betty Boyd, Robert F. Harney and Lydio F. Tomasi, eds. *The Italian Immigrant Woman in North America.* Toronto: Multicultural History Society of Ontario, 1978.

881 CHARBONNEAU, Hubert, Bertrand Desjardins, André Guillemette, Yves Landry, Jacques Legaré and François Nault. *Birth of a Population: The French who Settled in the St. Lawrence Valley in the XVIIth Century.* Newark: University of Delaware Press, 1991.

882 DAWSON, Nelson M. "Les filles du roi: des pollueuses? La France du XVIIe siècle." *Historical Reflections* 12, 1 (1985): 9-38.

883 DAWSON, Nelson M. "The *Filles du Roy* Sent to New France: Protestant, Prostitute, or Both?" *Historical Reflections* 16, 1 (Spring 1989): 55-78.

884 DEROY-PINEAU, Françoise. *Madeleine de la Peltrie: Amazone du Nouveau Monde, Alençon 1603-Québec 1671.* Montréal: Bellarmin, 1992.

885 DUMAS, Silvio. *Les Filles du roi en Nouvelle-France. Étude historique avec répertoire biographique.* Québec: Société historique de Québec, 1972.

886 FEILBERG, Julie. "Christmas Letter from Nokomis." *Canadian Ethnic Studies* 8, 2 (1976): 93-95. [1912 letter from Saskatchewan to Denmark]

887 FOULCHÉ-DELBOSC, Isabel. "Women of Three Rivers: 1651-63." In *The Neglected Majority: Essays in Canadian Women's History*, eds. Susan Mann Trofimenkoff and Alison Prentice, 14-26. Toronto: McClelland and Stewart, 1977.

888 FREUND, Alexander and Laura Quilici. "Exploring Myths in Women's Narratives: Italian and German Immigrant Women in Vancouver, 1947-1961." *BC Studies* 105/106 (Spring/Summer 1995): 159-82.

889 GLYNN, Alexandra Kruchka. "Vera Lysenko: Growing Up in North Winnipeg." *Canadian Society for Ukrainian Labour Research: Selected Papers Presented at the National Centenary Conference Marking the 100th Anniversary of Ukrainian Immigration to Canada, Sponsored by the CSULR, Toronto, June 9-10, 1990,* 44-52. Toronto: Canadian Society for Ukrainian Labour Research, 1994.

890 IACOVETTA, Franca. "'Primitive Villagers and Uneducated Girls': Canada Recruits Domestics from Italy, 1951-52." *Canadian Woman Studies* 7, 4 (Winter 1986): 14-18.

891 IACOVETTA, Franca. "From *Contadina* to Worker: Southern Italian Immigrant Working Women in Toronto, 1947-62." In *Looking into My Sister's Eyes: An Exploration in Women's History*, ed. Jean Burnet, 195-222. Toronto: Multicultural History Society of Ontario, 1986. Reprinted in *Canadian Family History: Selected Readings,* ed. Bettina Bradbury, 281-303. Toronto: Copp Clark Pitman, 1992; in *Canadian Working Class History: Selected Readings,* eds. Laurel Sefton-MacDowell and Ian Radforth. Toronto: Canadian Scholars Press, 1992; and in *Immigration in Canada: Historical Perspectives,* ed. Gerald Tulchinsky. Mississauga: Copp Clark Longman, 1994. Abridged in *Rethinking Canada: The Promise of Women's History,* 2nd edition, eds. Veronica Strong-Boag and Anita Clair Fellman, 376-95. Toronto: Copp Clark Pitman Ltd., 1991.

892 IACOVETTA, Franca. "Trying to Make Ends Meet: An Historical Look at Italian Immigrant Women, the State and Family Survival Strategies in Post-War Toronto." *Canadian Woman Studies* 8, 2 (Summer 1987): 6-11.

893 IACOVETTA, Franca. *Such Hardworking People: Italian Immigrants in Postwar Toronto.* Montreal and Kingston: McGill-Queen's University Press, 1992.

894 IACOVETTA, Franca. "Writing Women into Immigration History: The Italian Canadian Case." *Altreitalie: International Journal of Studies of Peoples of Italian Origin in the World* (Turin, Italy) 9 (January-June 1993): 5-47.

895 KAPRIELIAN, Isabel. "Women and Work: The Case of Finnish Domestics and Armenian Boarding-House Operators." *Resources for Feminist Research* 12, 4 (December 1983/January 1984): 51-54.

896 KAPRIELIAN, Isabel. "Creating and Sustaining an Ethnocultural Heritage in Ontario: the Case of Armenian Women Refugees." In *Looking into My Sister's Eyes: An Exploration in Women's History,* ed. Jean Burnet, 139-53. Toronto: Multicultural History Society of Ontario, 1986.

897 KAPRIELIAN, Isabel. "The Saved: Armenian Refugee Women." *Canadian Woman Studies* 7, 4 (Winter 1986): 6-9.

898 KAPRIELIAN, Isabel. "Refugee Women as Domestics: A Documentary Account." *Canadian Woman Studies* 10, 1 (Spring 1989): 75-79.

899 KAPRIELIAN, Isabel. "Armenian Refugee Women: The Picture Brides, 1920-30." *Journal of American Ethnic History* 12, 3 (Spring 1993): 3-29.

900 KEYWAN, Zonia. "Women Who Won the West." *Branching Out* (November/December 1975): 17-19. [Ukrainian]

901 KOJDER, Apolonja. "Slavic Immigrant Women in Northwestern Saskatchewan During the Depression." *Canadian Woman Studies* 4, 2 (Winter 1982): 82-85.

902 KOJDER, Apolonja. "Women and the Polish Alliance of Canada." In *A Community in Transition: The Polish Group in Canada,* ed. Benedykt Heydenkorn, 119-204. Toronto: Canadian Polish Research Institute, 1985.

903 KOJDER, Apolonja. "Women and the Polish Alliance of Canada." In *Looking into My Sister's Eyes: An Exploration in Women's History,* ed. Jean Burnet, 91-105. Toronto: Multicultural History Society of Ontario, 1986.

904 KOJDER, Apolonja Maria and Barbara Glogowska. *Marynia, Don't Cry: Memoirs of Two Polish Canadian Families.* Toronto: University of Toronto Press, 1995.

905 KRAWCHUK, Peter. *Reminiscences of Courage and Hope: Stories of Ukrainian Canadian Women Pioneers.* Toronto: Kobzar Publishing, 1991.

906 LANCTOT, Gustave. *Filles de joie ou filles du roi: Étude sur l'émigration féminine en Nouvelle-France.* Montréal: Éditions du Jour, 1964.

907 LANDRY, Yves. "De France à Nouvelle-France: les filles du roi au XVIIe siècle." In *Famille, économie et société rurale en contexte d'urbanisation, 17e - 20e siècle,* eds. G. Bouchard and J. Goy, 349-58. Chicoutimi: Centre universitaire SOREP/Paris: Ecole des hautes études en sciences sociales, 1990.

908 LANDRY, Yves. "Migrations internationales et comportement démographique: la canadianisation des filles du roi au XVIIe siècle." *Annales de démographie historique* (1990): 337-44.

909 LANDRY, Yves. "La moralité des filles du roi: bilan de travaux récents sur un vieux problème." *Mémoires de la Société généalogique canadienne-française* 42, 4 (hiver 1991): 285-97.

910 LANDRY, Yves. *Orphelines en France, pionnières au Canada: les filles du roi au XVIIe siècle.* Montréal: Leméac Éditeur, 1992.

911 LANDRY, Yves. "Les filles du roi et les soldats du régiment de Carignan-Salières." *Cap-aux-Diamants* 34 (été 1993): 24-27.

912 LINDSTRÖM-BEST, Varpu. "'Going to Work in America': Finnish Maids, 1911-30." *Polyphony* 8 (1986): 17-20.

913 LINDSTRÖM-BEST, Varpu. "'I Won't Be a Slave!'—Finnish Domestics in Canada, 1911-30." In *Looking into My Sister's Eyes: An Exploration in Women's History,* ed. Jean Burnet, 33-53. Toronto: Multicultural History Society of Ontario, 1986.

914 LINDSTRÖM-BEST, Varpu. "Hide and Seek: Interviewing Immigrant Women." *Polyphony* 9, 1 (Fall/Winter 1987): 88-89.

915 LINDSTRÖM-BEST, Varpu, ed. "Nordic Women." A special issue of *Canadian Woman Studies* 9, 2 (Summer 1988).

916 LINDSTRÖM-BEST, Varpu. "Finnish Immigrant Women in Canada, 1890-1935: A Photo Essay." *Canadian Woman Studies* 9, 2 (Summer 1988): 34-40.

917 LINDSTRÖM-BEST, Varpu. *Defiant Sisters: A Social History of Finnish Immigrant Women in Canada.* Toronto: Multicultural History Society of Ontario, 1988.

918 LINDSTRÖM-BEST, Varpu and Allen Seager. "*Toveritar* and Finnish Canadian Women, 1900-1930." In *The Press of Labour Migrants in Europe and North America, 1880s to 1930s,* eds. Christiane Harzig and Dick Hoerder, 243-264. Bremen: Publications of the Labour Newspaper Preservation Project, 1985.

919 LUCAS, Daisy. "A Pioneer Norwegian Family." *Alberta History* 41, 4 (Autumn 1993): 16-19.

920 LUCAS, H. "Growing Up Greek." *Canadian Woman Studies* 4, 2 (Winter 1982): 74-76.

921 MARTEL, Suzanne. *Jeanne, fille du roi.* Montréal: Éditions Fides, 1974.

922 MAZZONE, Perry A. "An Immigrant Family in Saskatchewan, 1903-1943." *Canadian Ethnic Studies* 12, 3 (1980): 131-39. [Austro-Hungarian]

923 NILSEN, Kirsti. *The Baker's Daughters: Memoirs of a Finnish Immigrant Family in Timmins.* Toronto: Multicultural History Society of Ontario, 1985.

924 PATRIAS, Carmela. "Passages from the Life: An Italian Woman in Welland, Ontario." *Canadian Woman Studies* 8 (Summer 1987): 69-73.

925 PETROFF, Lillian. "Contributors to Ethnic Cohesion: Macedonian Women in Toronto to 1940." In *Looking into My Sister's Eyes: An Exploration in Women's History,* ed. Jean Burnet, 125-38. Toronto: Multicultural History Society of Ontario, 1986.

926 PETRYSHYN, Marusia K. "The Changing Status of Ukrainian Women in Canada, 1921-1971." In *Changing Realities: Social Trends Among Ukrainian Canadians,* ed. W. Roman Petryshyn, 189-209. Edmonton: Canadian Institute of Ukrainian Studies, 1980.

927 PIVATO, Joseph. "Italian-Canadian Women Writers Recall History." *Canadian Ethnic Studies* 18, 1 (1986): 79-88.

928 POHLE, Adella. *Pioneering in Two Worlds: The Life of Carl and Adella Pohle.* Vancouver: Evergreen Press, 1974. [Austrian immigrants to British Columbia]

929 POLOWY, Hannah. "The Role of Pioneer Women in Family Life." *Ukrainian Canadian* (March 1972): 20-21.

930 POLYZOI, Eleoussa. "Greek Immigrant Women from Asia Minor in Prewar Toronto: the Formative Years." In *Looking into My Sister's Eyes: An Exploration in Women's History,* ed. Jean Burnet, 107-24. Toronto: Multicultural History Society of Ontario, 1986.

931 POLYZOI, Eleoussa. "Greek Immigrant Women from Asia Minor: Philoptoho and Language Schools." *Polyphony* 11 (1989): 28-36.

932 POTREBENKO, Helen. *No Streets of Gold: A Social History of the Ukrainians in Alberta.* Vancouver: New Star Press, 1977.

933 PROCHAZKA, Marta. "An Absurd Way of Life, 'A Very Unusual Feeling.'" *Canadian Ethnic Studies* 25, 2 (1993): 119-35. [memoir of a Czech refugee]

934 "Recollections of a Pioneer Woman." *Ukrainian Canadian* (March 1972): 22-24.

935 ROMANYSHYN, O. "The Canadian League for the Liberation of Ukraine and Its Women's Association." *Polyphony* 10 (1988): 153-67.

936 ROMERO-CACHINERO, M. Carmen. "Hispanic Women in Canada: A Framework for Analysis." *Resources for Feminist Research* 16, 1 (March 1987): 19-20.

937 SALVERSON, Laura. *Confessions of an Immigrant's Daughter.* London: Faber and Faber, 1939; Toronto: University of Toronto Press, 1981.

938 SANGSTER, Joan. "Finnish Women in Ontario, 1890-1930." *Polyphony* 3, 2 (Fall 1981): 46-54.

939 SCHNEIDER, Aili Granlund. *The Finnish Baker's Daughters.* Toronto: Multicultural History Society of Ontario, 1986.

940 SIGURDSON, Helen. "Pioneer Mother." *Icelandic Canadian* 50, 4 (Summer 1992): 223-28.

941 STONE, Sharon D. "Emilia's Story: A Ukranian Grandmother." *Canadian Woman Studies* 7, 4 (Winter 1986): 10-12.

942 STURINO, Franc. "The Role of Women in Italian Immigration to the New World." In *Looking into My Sister's Eyes: An Exploration in Women's History,* ed. Jean Burnet, 21-32. Toronto: Multicultural History Society of Ontario, 1986.

943 SWYRIPA, Frances. "Outside the Bloc Settlement: Ukrainian Women in Ontario during the Formative Years of Community Consciousness." In *Looking into My Sister's Eyes: An Exploration in Women's History,* ed. Jean Burnet, 155-78. Toronto: Multicultural History Society of Ontario, 1986.

944 SWYRIPA, Frances. "Nation-Building into the 1920s: Conflicting Claims on Ukrainian Immigrant Women." In *Continuity and Change: The Cultural Life of Alberta's First Ukrainians,* ed. Manoly R. Lupul, 125-51. Edmonton: Canadian Institute of Ukrainian Studies, 1988.

945 SWYRIPA, Frances. "Baba and the Community Heroine: The Two Images of Ukrainian Pioneer Women." *Alberta: Studies in the Arts and Sciences* 2, 1 (1989): 59-80.

946 SWYRIPA, Frances. *Wedded to the Cause: Ukrainian Canadian Women and Ethnic Identity, 1891-1991.* Toronto: University of Toronto Press, 1993.

947 THOMAS, Geraldine. "Women in the Greek Community of Nova Scotia." *Canadian Ethnic Studies* 20, 3 (1988): 84-93.

948 UKAS, Michael. "Ukrainian Canadian Women Pioneers: Their Contribution to the Building of Canada." *Canadian Society for Ukrainian Labour Research: Selected Papers Presented at the National Centenary Conference Marking the 100th Anniversary of Ukrainian Immigration to Canada, Sponsored by the CSULR, Toronto, June 9-10, 1990,* 11-22. Toronto: Canadian Society for Ukrainian Labour Research, 1994.

949 WELCH, David. "The Dionne Quintuplets: More Than an Ontario Showpiece—Five Franco-Ontarian Children." *Journal of Canadian Studies* 29, 4 (Winter 1994/95): 36-64.

950 WOYWITKA, Anna B. "A Roumanian Pioneer." *Alberta Historical Review* (Autumn 1973): 20-27.

951 WOYWITKA, Anna B. "Homesteader's Woman." *Alberta History* 24, 2 (Spring 1976): 20-24. [Ukrainian]

952 WYNNYCKYJ, Iroida. "Oral History: Ukrainian Women's Voices." *Polyphony* 10 (1988): 251-55.

IMMIGRANTS/IMMIGRATION

953 ANDERSON, Joan M. "Migration and Health: Perspectives on Immigrant Women." *Sociology of Health and Illness* 9, 4 (1987): 410-38. Reprinted in *British Columbia Reconsidered: Essays on Women,* eds. Gillian Creese and Veronica Strong-Boag, 267-89. Vancouver: Press Gang Publishers, 1992.

954 ANDERSON, Joan M. and M. Judith Lynam. "The Meaning of Work for Immigrant Women in the Lower Echelons of the Canadian Labour Force." *Canadian Ethnic Studies* 19, 2 (1987): 67-90.

955 ARAT-KOC, Sedef. "Immigration Policies, Migrant Domestic Workers and the Definition of Citizenship in Canada." In *Deconstructing a Nation: Immigration, Multiculturalism and Racism in '90s Canada,* ed. Victor Satzewich, 229-42. Halifax: Fernwood Publishing, 1992.

956 ARAT-KOC, Sedef. "In the Privacy of Our Own Home: Foreign Domestic Workers as Solution to the Crisis in the Domestic Sphere in Canada." *Studies in Political Economy* 28 (Spring 1989): 33-58. Reprinted in *Feminism in Action: Studies in Political Economy,* eds. M. Patricia Connelly and Pat Armstrong. Toronto: Canadian Scholars' Press, 1993.

957 ARNOPOLOUS, Sheila McLeod. *Problems of Immigrant Women in the Canadian Labour Force.* Ottawa: Canadian Advisory Council on the Status of Women, 1979.

958 ASHWORTH, Mary. *Children of the Canadian Mosaic: A Brief History to 1950.* Toronto: OISE Press, 1993.

959 BARBER, Marilyn. *Immigrant Domestic Servants in Canada.* Canada's Ethnic Groups, Booklet No. 16. Ottawa: Canadian Historical Association, 1991.

960 BARNDT, Deborah, Ferne Cristall and Dian Marino. *Getting There: Producing Photostories with Immigrant Women.* Toronto: Between the Lines, 1982.

961 BASAVARAJAPPA, K.G. and Ravi B.P. Verma. "Occupational Composition of Immigrant Women." In *Ethnic Demography: Canadian Immigrant, Racial and Cultural Variations,* eds. Shiva S. Halli, *et al,* 297-313. Ottawa: Carleton University Press, 1990.

962 BEACH, Charles M. and Christopher Worswick. "Is There a Double Effect on the Earnings of Immigrant Women?" *Canadian Public Policy* 19, 1 (March 1993): 36-53.

963 BOYD, Monica. "At a Disadvantage: The Occupational Attainments of Foreign-Born Women in Canada." *International Migration Review* 18, 4 (1984): 1091-1119.

964 BOYD, Monica. "Immigrant Women in Canada." In *International Migration: The Female Experience,* eds. Rita James Simon and Caroline B. Brettell, 45-61. Totowa, NJ: Rowman & Allanheld, 1986. Reprinted in *Gender and Society: Creating A Canadian Woman's Sociology,* ed. Arlene Tigar McLaren, 316-36. Toronto: Copp Clark Pitman, 1988.

965 BOYD, Monica. "Immigrant Women: Language and Socioeconomic Inequalities and Policy Issues." In *Ethnic Demography: Canadian Immigrant, Racial and Cultural Variations,* eds. Shiva S. Halli, *et al,* 275-95. Ottawa: Carleton University Press, 1990.

966 BOYD, Monica. "Immigration and Living Arrangements: Elderly Women in Canada." *International Migration Review* 25, 1 (Spring 1991): 4-27.

967 BOYD, Monica. *Adding Gender: Immigration Trends and Language Fluency Issues in Canada and the United States.* Ottawa: Carleton University, Department of Sociology and Anthropology, 1991.

968 BOYD, Monica. "Gender, Visible Minority and Immigrant Earnings Inequality: Reassessing an Employment Equity Premise." In *Deconstructing a Nation: Immigration, Multiculturalism and Racism in '90s Canada,* ed. Vic Satzewich, 279-322. Halifax: Fernwood, 1992.

969 BOYD, Monica and Chris Taylor. "The Feminization of Temporary Workers: The Canadian Case." *International Migration* 24, 4 (December 1986): 717-34.

970 BOYD, Monica, Chris Taylor and Paul Delaney. "Temporary Workers in Canada: A Multifaceted Program." *International Migration Review* 20, 4 (Winter 1986): 929-50.

971 BURNET, Jean with Howard Palmer. *"Coming Canadians": An Introduction to a History of Canada's Peoples.* Toronto: McClelland & Stewart, 1988.

972 CARTY, Linda and Dionne Brand. "'Visible Minority' Women—A Creation of the Canadian State." *Resources for Feminist Research* 17, 3 (1988).

973 CORDASCO, Francesco. *The Immigrant Woman in North America: An Annotated Bibliography.* Metuchen, NJ: Scarecrow Press, 1985.

974 DAENZER, Patricia M. *Regulating Class Privilege: Immigrant Servants in Canada, 1940s-1990s.* Toronto: Canadian Scholars' Press, 1993.

975 DAS GUPTA, Tania. "Unravelling the Web of History." *Resources for Feminist Research* 16, 1 (March 1987): 13-14. [immigrant women's organizing in Ontario]

976 DJAO, Angela W. and Roxanna Ng. "Structured Isolation: Immigrant Women in Saskatchewan." In *Women: Isolation and Bonding: The Ecology of Gender,* ed. Kathleen Storrie, Toronto: Methuen, 1988.

977 ESTABLE, Alma. *Immigrant Women in Canada: Current Issues.* Ottawa: Canadian Advisory Council on the Status of Women, 1986.

978 GRINDSTAFF, Carl F. *The Economic Status of Immigrant Women at Age 30, Canada, 1981.* Edmonton: University of Alberta, Department of Sociology, 1985.

979 GULBINOWICZ, Eva. *Problems of Immigrant Women, Past and Present: A Bibliography.* Toronto: Ontario Ministry of Labour, 1979.

980 IACOVETTA, Franca. "Making 'New Canadians': Social Workers, Women, and the Reshaping of Immigrant Families." In *Gender Conflicts: New Essays in Women's History,* eds. Franca Iacovetta and Mariana Valverde, 261-303. Toronto: University of Toronto Press, 1992.

981 IACOVETTA, Franca. "Remaking Their Lives: Women, Immigrants, Survivors, and Refugees." In *A Diversity of Women: Ontario, 1945-1980,* ed. Joy Parr, 135-67. Toronto: University of Toronto Press, 1995.

982 IACOVETTA, Franca. "Manly Militants, Cohesive Communities, and Defiant Domestics: Writing About Immigrants in Canadian Historical Scholarship." *Labour/Le Travail* 36 (Fall 1995): 217-52.

983 KUTZ-HARDER, Helga. "Breaking the Barriers: Refugee Women in Canada." *Canadian Woman Studies* 10, 1 (Spring 1989): 26-28.

984 LABELLE, Micheline and Marianne Kempineers. "Multiples visages: les femmes immigrées au Québec." In *Encrages féministes: Un moment de reflexion dans la recherche féministe,* ed. Isabelle Lasvergnas, 93-110. Montréal: Université du Québec à Montréal, Centre de recherche féministe, Group interdisciplinaire d'enseignement et de recherche féministes, 1989.

985 LABELLE, Micheline, Deirdre Meintel, Geneviève Turcotte and Marianne Kempineers. "Étude comparée de la condition des ouvrières immigrées à Montréal. Présentation d'une recherche menée à l'UQAM (1981-1985)." *Resources for Feminist Research* 16, 1 (March 1987): 34-35.

986 LABELLE, Micheline, Geneviève Turcotte, Marianne Kempineers and Deirdre Meintel. *Histoire d'immigrées: Itinéraires d'ouvrières Colombiennes, Grecques, Haïtiennes et Portugaises de Montréal.* Montréal: Les Éditions de Boréal Express, 1987.

987 MACKLIN, A. "Foreign Domestic Worker: Surrogate Housewife or Mail Order Servant?" *McGill Law Journal* 37 (1992): 681-760.

988 McLUHAN, Elizabeth, ed. *Safe Haven: The Refugee Experience of Five Families.* Toronto: University of Toronto Press, 1995.

989 MEINTEL, Deirdre, Micheline Labelle, Geneviève Turcotte and Marianne Kempineers. "Migration, Wage Labor and Domestic Relationships: Immigrant Women Workers in Montreal." *Anthropologica* 26, 2 (1984): 135-69.

990 MEINTEL, Deirdre, Micheline Labelle, Geneviève Turcotte and Marianne Kempineers. "The New Double Workday of Immigrant Women Workers in Quebec." *Women's Studies* 13, 3 (1987): 273-93.

991 MIEDEMA, Baukje and Nancy Nason-Clark. "Second Class Status: An Analysis of the Lived Experience of Immigrant Women in Fredericton." *Canadian Ethnic Studies* 21, 2 (1989): 63-73.

992 MONTERO, Gloria. *The Immigrants.* Toronto: James Lorimer, 1977.

993 NG, Roxana. "The Social Construction of 'Immigrant Women' in Canada." In *The Politics of Diversity: Feminism, Marxism and Nationalism,* eds. Roberta Hamilton and Michèle Barrett, 269-86. Montreal: The Book Centre, Inc., 1986.

994 NG, Roxana. "Immigrant Women in Canada: A Socially Constructed Category." *Resources for Feminist Research* 15, 1 (March 1986): 13-15.

995 NG, Roxana. *The Politics of Community Services: A Study of an Employment Agency for Immigrant Women.* Toronto: Garamond Press, 1988; 2nd edition, 1996.

996 NG, Roxana. "Immigrant Women: The Construction of a Labour Market Category." *Canadian Journal of Women and the Law* 4, 1 (1990): 96-112.

997 NG, Roxana. "Managing Female Immigration: A Case of Institutional Sexism and Racism." *Canadian Woman Studies* 12, 3 (Spring 1993): 20-23.

998 NG, Roxana, Himani Bannerji, Joyce Scane, Didi Khayatt and Makeda Silvera, eds. "Immigrant Women." A special issue of *Resources for Feminist Research* 16, 1 (March 1987).

999 NG, Roxana and Alma Estable. "Immigrant Women in the Labour Force: An Overview of Present Knowledge and Research Gaps." *Resources for Feminist Research* 16, 1 (March 1987): 29-33.

1000 NG, Roxana and Judith Ramirez. *Immigrant Housewives in Canada.* Toronto: Immigrant Women's Centre, 1981.

1001 POIRIER, Marie. *Les femmes immigrées au Québec: bibliographie annotée.* Québec: Ministère des communautés culturelles et de l'immigration, 1985.

1002 SCANE, Joyce. "Selected Bibliography of Community Papers Concerning Immigrant Women in Canada: 1975-1986." *Resources for Feminist Research* 16, 1 (March 1987): 47-53.

1003 SCANE, Joyce and Marjatta Holt. *Immigrant Women: Their Untold History.* Toronto: OISE Press, 1988.

1004 TROVATO, Frank and Carl F. Grindstaff. "Economic Status: A Census Analysis of Thirty Year Old Immigrant Women in Canada." *Canadian Review of Sociology and Anthropology* 23, 4 (November 1986): 569-87.

1005 WARREN, Catherine E. *Vignettes of Life: Experiences and Self-Perceptions of New Canadian Women.* Calgary: Detselig Enterprises, 1986.

1006 ZIEBA, Mietka and Nancy Hohn. "Socio-Demographic Profile of Immigrant Women in Alberta." *Resources for Feminist Research* 16, 1 (March 1987): 21-22.

RACE/ETHNICITY

1007 BACKHOUSE, Constance. "White Female Help and Chinese-Canadian Employers: Race, Class, Gender and Law in the Case of Yee Clun, 1924." *Canadian Ethnic Studies* 26, 3 (1994): 34-52. Reprinted in *Canadian Women: A Reader,* eds. Wendy Mitchinson, *et al,* 280-99. Toronto: Harcourt Brace Canada, 1996.

1008 BANNERJI, Himani, ed. *Re: Turning the Gaze: Essays on Racism, Feminism and Politics.* Toronto: Sister Vision Press, 1993.

1009 BILLSON, Janet M. "Interlocking Identities: Gender, Ethnicity and Power in the Canadian Context." *International Journal of Canadian Studies* 3 (Spring 1991): 49-67.

1010 BIZZARRI, Aoura. *Je ne suis pas raciste, mais...* Montréal: Collectif des femmes immigrantes du Québec, 1994.

1011 BRAND, Dionne and Krisantha Sri Bhaggiyadatta. *Rivers Have Sources, Trees Have Roots: Speaking of Racism.* Toronto: Cross Cultural Communications Centre, 1986.

1012 BRINKERHOFF, Merlin and Marlene Mackie. "Ethnicity's Impact Upon Familial/Gender Attitudes and Behaviors: Social 'Reality' or Social 'Fiction'?" *Canadian Ethnic Studies* 14, 2 (1982): 99-113.

1013 BROWN, Rosemary. "Overcoming Sexism and Racism—How." In *Racism in Canada*, ed. Ormond McKague, 163-77. Saskatoon: Fifth House Publishers, 1991.

1014 BURNET, Jean, ed. "Women and Ethnicity." A special issue of *Polyphony* 8, 1/2 (1986).

1015 BURNET, Jean, ed. *Looking into My Sister's Eyes: An Exploration in Women's History.* Toronto: Multicultural History Society of Ontario, 1986.

1016 BYSTYDZIENSKI, Jill. "Minority Women of North America: A Comparison of French-Canadian and Afro-American Women." *American Review of Canadian Studies* 15, 4 (Winter 1985): 465-80.

1017 CAIRNS, Alan and Cynthia Williams, eds. *The Politics of Gender, Ethnicity and Language in Canada.* Toronto: University of Toronto Press, 1986.

1018 CAMPER, Carol, ed. *Miscegenation Blues: Voices of Mixed Race Women.* Toronto: Sister Vision Press, 1994.

1019 DENIS, Ann B. "Femmes: ethnie et occupation au Québec et en Ontario, 1931-1971." *Canadian Ethnic Studies* 13, 1 (1981): 75-90.

1020 DHRUVARAJAN, Vanaja. "The Multiple Oppression of Women of Colour." *Briarpatch* 20, 2 (March 1991): 18-19. Reprinted in *Racism in Canada*, ed. Ormond McKague, 101-4. Saskatoon: Fifth House Publishers, 1991.

1021 "Ethnicity and Femininity." A special issue of *Canadian Ethnic Studies* 13, 1 (1981).

1022 FINGARD, Judith. "Race and Respectability in Victorian Halifax." *Journal of Imperial and Commonwealth History* 20, 2 (May 1992): 169-95. Reprinted in *Interpreting Canada's Past: Volume Two, Post-Confederation,* 2nd edition, ed. J.M. Bumsted, 107-34. Toronto: Oxford University Press, 1993.

1023 GUPTA, Nila, Makeda Silvera, *et al.*, eds. "Women of Colour." A special issue of *Fireweed* 16 (Spring 1983).

1024 INDRA, Doreen Marie. "The Invisible Mosaic: Women, Ethnicity and the Vancouver Press, 1905-1976." *Canadian Ethnic Studies* 13, 1 (1981): 63-74.

1025 JUTEAU-LEE, Danielle and Barbara Roberts. "Ethnicity and Feminism." *Canadian Ethnic Studies* 13, 1 (1981): 1-23.

1026 KHAYATT, Didi. "The Boundaries of Identity at the Intersection of Race, Class and Gender." *Canadian Woman Studies* 14, 2 (Spring 1994): 6-12. Reprinted in *Coming of Age: Readings in Canadian History Since World War II,* eds. Donald Avery and Roger Hall, 31-42. Toronto: Harcourt Brace & Company Canada, 1996.

1027 KOSTASH, Myrna. "Coming Home to Work: Between the Lines of Ethnic History." *Resources for Feminist Research* 8, 3, Part 2 (November 1979): 12-16.

1028 LAMBERT, Ronald D. and James E. Curtis. "Québécois and English Canadian Opposition to Racial and Religious Intermarriage, 1968-1983." *Canadian Ethnic Studies* 16, 2 (1984): 30-46.

1029 MUSZYNSKI, Alicja. "Deconstructing the Categorical Reality of Race and Gender." *Canadian Ethnic Studies* 26, 3 (1994): 18-33.

1030 NG, Roxana. "Immigrant Women and Institutionalized Racism." In *Changing Patterns: Women in Canada,* eds. Sandra Burt, Lorraine Code and Lindsay Dorney, 184-203. Toronto: McClelland & Stewart, 1988. Revised and retitled as "Racism, Sexism, and Immigrant Women," 279-308, 2nd edition, 1993.

1031 NG, Roxana. "Racism, Sexism and Visible Minority Immigrant Women in Canada." *Zeitschrift der Gesellschaft für Kanada-Studien* 10, 2 (1990): 21-34.

1032 NG, Roxana. "Sexism, Racism and Canadian Nationalism." In *Race, Class and Gender: Bonds and Barriers,* ed. Jessie Vorst, 10-25. Winnipeg: Society for Socialist Studies, 1991.

1033 QADIR, Reem Abdul, *et al,* eds. "Racism and Gender." A special issue of *Canadian Woman Studies* 14, 2 (Spring 1994).

1034 RAMIREZ-CASSALI, Lucy. *Les modalités d'insertion des femmes chiliennes à Montréal: une décade d'immigration.* Montreal: Université de Montréal, Département de sociologie, 1986.

1035 RICHARD, Madeline A. *Ethnic Groups and Marital Choices: Ethnic History and Marital Assimilation, Canada 1871 and 1971.* Vancouver: University of British Columbia Press, 1991.

1036 SCANE, Joyce and Pat Staton with Roxana Ng. *Multicultural, Intercultural Education and Race Relations: An Annotated Bibliography.* Toronto: Green Dragon Press, 1992.

1037 SILVERA, Makeda. *The Issue is 'ISM': Women of Colour Speak Out.* Toronto: Sister Vision, 1989.

1038 SIMMS, Glenda P. "Racism as a Barrier to Canadian Citizenship." In *Belonging: The Meaning and Future of Canadian Citizenship,* ed. William Kaplan, 333-48. Montreal and Kingston: McGill-Queen's University Press, 1993.

1039 STASIULIS, Daiva. "Theorizing Connections: Gender, Race, Ethnicity and Class." In *Race and Ethnic Relations in Canada,* ed. Peter S. Li, 269-305. Toronto: Oxford University Press, 1990.

1040 TAYLOR, Donald M. *The Integration of Visible Minority Women to Quebec Society.* Québec: Conseil québécois de la recherche sociale, 1988.

1041 WALLIS, M., W. Giles and C. Hernandy. "Defining the Issues on Our Terms: Gender, Race and State—Interviews with Racial Minority Women." *Resources for Feminist Research* 3 (September 1988).

FAMILIES/LIFE STAGES

FAMILY HISTORY PRE-DATED women's history as a legitimate field of study, and its emphasis on quantitative approaches reflects the strong influence of the social sciences. In recent years, historians have largely abandoned attempts to trace the function and characteristics of "the family" in history in favour of exploring the diversity of "families," a significant shift reflected in the titles of several recent textbooks. A growing interest in "life course" approaches is producing new understandings of the experience of women in the past at various biologically defined and socially constructed stages of their lives from childhood to old age.

Demographic studies of family size, household structure, fertility and nuptiality can tell historians a great deal about family life as experienced by the masses of women who left no written records, as demonstrated in recent scholarship on nineteenth-century Ontario and the Maritime colonies. The majority of such studies, however, have been produced by Quebec historians and sociologists. This interest derives partly from the legacy of rich parish records produced by the Roman Catholic church that have no counterpart elsewhere in Canada, from the attraction of Quebec scholars to the quantitative approaches pioneered by the Annales school of French historians, and from the stimulus provided by contemporary debates about the declining birthrate among the francophone population of Quebec.

Diaries and letters, some of which are now available in published form, have provided much of the raw material for qualitative studies of Canadian family life in contexts that include New France, the western fur trade, the Maritime colonies in British North America, the elite society of Upper Canada, and modern suburban Ontario. Studies of marriage patterns and practices, especially numerous in the case of the *filles du roi* of New France and the mixed-blood women of the western fur trade, have drawn upon both quantitative and qualitative sources. Some attention has also been paid to attitudes toward marriage in a variety of contexts, and to the rituals of courtship and marriage, especially the charivari.

Despite the paucity of written records produced by children, with outstanding exceptions such as the adolescent diary of Henriette Dessaulles, Canadian historians are taking a growing interest in the study of childhood, although the scholarship on the distinctive experience of girlhood remains very small. The study of the female experience of old age has also been neglected by historians, but a small body of scholarship is emerging which focuses on the care of the aged within the family and the circumstances of widows. Given the prominence of motherhood in the lives of most Canadian women in the past, maternal practices and ideologies have attracted much more notice, with special attention being paid to the single mothers who violated the convention that motherhood should occur within the framework of heterosexual marriage.

Family history has intersected with both women's history and working-class history to produce an exceptionally rich body of literature, pioneered by Bettina Bradbury, on the impact of industrialization on urban working-class family life. Examining the family as a working unit, these studies have emphasized the importance of the unpaid domestic labour of married women to the "family economy" on which all members depended for their survival and material well-being, and to which all but infants contributed, and to the development of "family survival strategies" as a response to grossly inadequate wages.

AGING/WIDOWHOOD

1042 AUGER, Jeanette A. "Living in the Margins: Lesbian Aging." *Canadian Woman Studies* 12, 2 (Winter 1992): 80-84.

1043 BRADBURY, Bettina. "Surviving as a Widow in Nineteenth-Century Montreal." *Urban History Review* 17, 3 (February 1989): 148-60. Reprinted in *Rethinking Canada: The Promise of Women's History,* 2nd edition, eds. Veronica Strong-Boag and Anita Clair Fellman, 113-33. Toronto: Copp Clark Pitman Ltd., 1991.

1044 CHARLES, Aline. "Travail et vieillesse féminine: une histoire à suivre...mais possible." *Recherches féministes* 6, 1 (1993): 105-11. [volunteer work of older women in Montreal hospitals, 1940-1980]

1045 COHEN, Leah. *Small Expectations: Society's Betrayal of Older Women.* Toronto: McClelland and Stewart, 1984.

1046 CONRAD, Margaret. "'No Discharge in This War': A Note on the History of Women and Aging." *Resources for Feminist Research* 11 (July 1982): 216-18.

1047 DULUDE, Louise. *Women and Aging: A Report on the Rest of Our Lives.* Ottawa: Advisory Council on the Status of Women, 1978.

1048 DUNN, Brenda. "L'inventaire de la veuve Plemarais, 1705." La société historique acadienne. *Les cahiers* 25, 1 (janvier/mars 1994): 27-37. [Marguerite de Saint-Étienne de La Tour]

1049 GEE, Ellen M. and Meredith M. Kimball. *Women and Aging.* Toronto and Vancouver: Butterworths, 1987.

1050 HAWLEY, Donna Lea. *Women and Aging: A Comprehensive Bibliography.* Burnaby, BC: Simon Fraser University, 1985.

1051 HOLBROOK, J.H. and M.H. Farmer, eds. "Diary of Hannah Aikman (Hammill) Kern of Dundas and Ancaster, Wentworth County, Ontario, 9 April 1870—1 January 1885." *Western Ontario Historical Notes* 26 (1958): 1-29.

1052 MATTHEWS, Anne M. "Women and Widowhood." In *Aging in Canada: Social Perspectives,* ed. Victor W. Marshall, 145-53. Toronto: Fitzhenry and Whiteside, 1980.

1053 McLEAN, Lorna. "Single Again: Widow's Work in the Urban Family Economy, Ottawa, 1871." *Ontario History* 83, 2 (June 1991): 127-50.

1054 MONTIGNY, Edgar-André. "The Decline in Family Care for the Aged in Nineteenth-Century Ontario." *Canadian Bulletin of Medical History* 11, 2 (1994): 357-74.

1055 NETT, Emily M., ed. "Women as Elders." A special issue of *Resources for Feminist Research* 11, 2 (July 1982).

1056 NETT, Emily M. "The Family and Aging." In *Families: Changing Trends in Canada,* Maureen Baker, *et al,* 241-71. Toronto: McGraw-Hill Ryerson, 1990.

1057 NORTHCOTT, Herbert C. "Widowhood and Remarriage Trends in Canada, 1956 to 1981." *Canadian Journal on Aging* 3, 2 (Summer 1984): 63-78.

1058 SYNGE, Jane. "Work and Family Support Patterns of the Aged in the Early Twentieth Century." In *Aging in Canada: Social Perspectives,* ed. Victor W. Marshall. Toronto: Fitzhenry and Whiteside, 1980.

DEMOGRAPHY/FAMILY SIZE

1059 BALAKRISHNAR, T.R., Evelyne Lapierre-Adamczyk and Karol K. Krotki. *Family and Childbearing in Canada: A Demographic Analysis.* Toronto: University of Toronto Press, 1993.

1060 BASAVARAJAPPA, K.G. and S.S. Halli. "Ethnic Fertility Differences in Canada, 1926-71: An examination of assimilation hypotheses." *Journal of Biosocial Science* 16 (January 1984): 45-54.

1061 BEAUJOT, Roderic. *Population Change in Canada: The Challenges of Policy Adaptation.* Toronto: McClelland and Stewart, 1992.

1062 BEAUJOT, Roderic P. and Kevin McQuillan. "The Social Effects of Demographic Change: Canada, 1851-1981." *Journal of Canadian Studies* 21 (Spring 1986): 57-69.

1063 BEAUREGARD, Yves, *et al.* "La famille à la croisée des chemins [au Québec]: entrevue avec Serge Gagnon." *Cap-aux-Diamants* 39 (automne 1994): 36-40.

1064 BOUCHARD, Gérard. "La reproduction familiale en terroirs neufs, comparaisons sur des données québécoises et françaises." *Annales: Economies, Sociétés, Civilisations* 48, 2 (1993): 421-51.

1065 BOUCHARD, Gérard and Isabelle de Pourbaix. "Individual and Family Life Courses in the Saguenay Region, Quebec, 1842-1911." *Journal of Family History* 12, 1/3 (1987): 225-42.

1066 BOUCHARD, Gérard and Richard Lalou. "La surfécondité des couples québécois depuis le XVIIe siècle, essai de mesure d'interprétation." *Recherches sociographiques* 34, 1 (janvier-avril 1993): 9-43.

1067 BOUCHARD, Gérard and Raymond Roy. "Fécondité et alphabétisation au Saguenay et au Québec (XIXe - XXe siècles)." *Annales de démographie historique* (1991): 173-201.

1068 BOUVIER, Léon F. "Genealogical Approach to the Study of French-Canadian Fertility." *Sociological Analysis* 26 (Fall 1965): 148-56.

1069 BOUVIER, Léon F. "The Spacing of Births among French Canadian Families: An Historical Approach." *Canadian Review of Sociology and Anthropology* 1 (February 1968): 17-26.

1070 BROWN, Jennifer S.H. "A Demographic Transition in the Fur Trade Country: Family Sizes and Fertility of Company Officers and Country Wives, ca. 1759-1850." *Western Canadian Journal of Anthropology* 6, 1 (1976): 61-71.

1071 BURCH, Thomas K. "Age-Sex Roles and Demographic Change: An Overview." *Canadian Studies in Population* 14, 2 (1987): 129-46.

1072 CALDWELL, Gary. "La baisse de la fécondité au Québec à la lumière de la sociologie québécoise." *Recherches sociographiques* (1976): 7-22.

1073 CALDWELL, Gary, *et al.* "L'évolution récente de la fécondité au Québec: facteurs démographiques, économiques et sociaux." *Cahiers québécois de démographie* 22, 1 (printemps 1993): 93-132. [1960-1990]

1074 "Changing Age and Sex Composition of the Canadian Population." *Canadian Statistical Review* 39 (January 1964): 1-4.

1075 CHARBONNEAU, Hubert. *Vie et Mort de nos ancêtres.* Collection "Démographie canadienne" no. 3. Montréal: Les Presses de l'Université de Montréal, 1975.

1076 CHARBONNEAU, Hubert and Bertrand Desjardins. "Les familles nombreuses en Nouvelle-France." *Mémoires de la Société généalogique canadienne-française* 44, 4 (hiver 1993): 293-305.

1077 CHARLES, Enid. *The Changing Size of the Family in Canada.* Ottawa: King's Printer, 1948.

1078 CONSEIL DU STATUT DE LA FEMME. *Femmes et questions démographiques, un nouveau regard.* Québec: Publications du Québec, 1991.

1079 DANDURAND, Renée Brien. "La famille au Québec: un brusque virage dans la modernité?" *Canadian Woman Studies* 7, 4 (Winter 1986): 64-67.

1080 DAVIDS, Leo. "Marital Status and Fertility Among Sub-Groups within Canadian Jews." In *The Jews in Canada,* eds. Robert Brym, William Shaffir and Morton Weinfeld. Toronto: Oxford University Press, 1993.

1081 EMERY, George. "Incomplete Registration of Births in Civil Systems: The Example of Ontario, Canada, 1900-1960." *Historical Methods* 23, 1 (Winter 1990): 5-21.

1082 EMERY, George. *Facts of Life: The Social Construction of Vital Statistics, Ontario, 1869-1952.* Montreal and Kingston: McGill-Queen's University Press, 1993.

1083 GEE, Ellen. "Early Canadian Fertility Transition: A Comparative Analysis of Census Data." *Canadian Studies in Population* 6 (1979): 23-32.

1084 GEE, Ellen M. "The Life Course of Canadian Women: An Historical and Demographic Analysis." *Social Indicators Research* (1986): 263-83. Reprinted in *Gender and Society: Creating a Canadian Women's Sociology,* ed. Arlene Tigar McLaren, 187-204. Toronto: Copp Clark Pitman, 1988.

1085 GRINDSTAFF, Carl. "A Vanishing Breed: Women with Large Families: Canada in the 1980s." *Canadian Studies in Population* 19, 2 (1992): 145-62.

1086 HALLI, Shiva S. "Minority Group Status and Fertility of Chinese and Japanese in Canada." *Canadian Ethnic Studies* 19, 2 (1987): 44-66.

1087 HAMEL, Martine. "De Charlevoix au Saguenay: caractéristiques des familles émigrantes au XIX siècle." *Revue d'histoire de l'Amérique française* 47, 1 (été 1993): 5-25.

1088 HENRIPIN, Jacques. *La population canadienne au début du XVIIIe siècle: nuptialité, fécondité, mortalité infantile.* Travaux et Documents, cahier no. 22. Paris: Institut national d'études démographiques, 1954.

1089 HENRIPIN, Jacques. *Tendances et facteurs de la fécondité au Canada.* Census monograph. Ottawa: Federal Census Bureau, 1968.

1090 HENRIPIN, Jacques. *Trends and Factors of Fertility in Canada.* Ottawa: Federal Census Bureau, 1972.

1091 HENRIPIN, Jacques. "From Acceptance of Nature to Control: The Demography of French Canadians Since the 17th Century." In *Studies in Canadian Social History,* eds. M. Horn and R. Sabourin, 74-84. Toronto: McClelland and Stewart, 1974.

1092 HENRIPIN, Jacques. "Trois siècles de 'grosses familles.'" *Cap-aux-Diamants* 39 (automne 1994): 30-35.

1093 HENRIPIN, Jacques and Evelyne LaPierre-Adamczyk. *La fin de la revanche des berceaux: qu'en pensent les Québécoises?* Montréal: Presses de l'Université de Montréal, 1974.

1094 HERRING, D.A., Paul Driben and L.A. Sawchuk. "Historical Fertility in a Northern Ontario Ojibwa Community: The Fort Hope Band." *Anthropologica* 25, 2 (1983): 147-61.

1095 HOGG, Robert S. "Evaluating Historic Fertility Change in Small Reserve Populations." *BC Studies* 101 (Spring 1994): 79-95.

1096 HURD, Burton W. "The Decline in the Canadian Birthrate." *Canadian Journal of Economics and Political Science* 3, 1 (February 1937): 40-57.

1097 KATZ, Michael B. "Age, Ethnicity and Sex." *First Research Report, Working Paper no. 6, York Social History Project.* Downsview, ON: York Social History Project, York University, 1975. [Canada West, 1851-1871]

1098 LAMONTAGNE, M. and J.C. Faladeau. "The Life-Cycle of French-Canadian Urban Families." *Canadian Journal of Economics and Political Science* 13, 2 (May 1947): 233-47.

1099 LANDRY, Yves. "Fécondité et habitat des immigrantes françaises en Nouvelle-France." *Annales de démographie historique* (1988): 259-76.

1100 LANDRY, Yves. "La descendance des couples en France et en Nouvelle-France: une reproduction inégale." In *Transmettre, hériter, succéder: la reproduction familiale en milieu rural, France-Québec, XVIIIe-XXe siècles,* eds. Rolande Bonnain, *et al,* 15-26. Lyon: Presses Universitaires de Lyon, 1992.

1101 LANDRY, Yves. "Fertility in France and New France: The Distinguishing Characteristics of Canadian Behavior in the Seventeenth and Eighteenth Centuries." *Social Science History* 17, 4 (1993): 577-92.

1102 LANDRY, Yves and Réal Bates. "Population et reproduction sociale à l'île d'Orléans aux XVIIe et XVIIIe
siècles." *Revue d'histoire de l'Amérique française* 45, 3
(hiver 1992): 403-13.

1103 LANDRY, Yves and Jacques Légaré. "Le cycle de vie
familiale en Nouvelle-France: méthodologie et application à un échantillon." *Histoire sociale/Social
History* XVII (May 1984): 7-20.

1104 LANDRY, Yves and Jacques Légaré. "The Life
Course of Seventeenth-Century Immigrants to
Canada." *Journal of Family History* 21, 1/3 (1987):
210-12.

1105 LANGLOIS, Simon, *et al. Recent Social Trends in
Quebec, 1960-1990.* Montreal and Kingston:
McGill-Queen's University Press, 1992.

1106 LAPIERRE-ADAMCZYK, Evelyne, *et al.* "Le cycle de la
vie familiale au Québec: vues comparatives, XVII-
XX siècle." *Cahiers québécois de démographie* 13, 1
(avril 1984): 59-76.

1107 LAVIGNE, Marie. "Réflexions féministes autour de
la fertilité des Québécoises." In *Maîtresses de maison, maîtresses d'école: Femmes, famille et éducation
dans l'histoire du Québec,* eds. Nadia Fahmy-Eid
and Micheline Dumont, 319-38. Montréal: Boréal
Express, 1983.

1108 LEBOURG, Eric, *et al.* "Reproductive Life of French
Canadians in the 17-18th Centuries: A Search for a
Trade-Off Between Early Fecundity and Longevity."
Experimental Gerontology 28, 3 (1993): 217-32.

1109 LI, Peter, S. "Labour Reproduction and the Family
Under Advanced Capitalism: Female Labour Force
Participation and Fertility in Twentieth Century
Canada." *Journal of Comparative Family Studies* 24,
3 (Autumn 1993): 367-85.

1110 LONG, Harry H. "Fertility Patterns among Religious
Groups in Canada." *Demography* 8, 2 (May 1970):
135-50.

1111 MAISONNEUVE, Daniel. "Structure familiale et
exode rural: le cas de Saint-Damase, 1852-1861."
Cahiers québécois de démographie 14, 2 (octobre
1986): 231-40.

1112 MARR, William L. *Fertility Rates Among Married
Couples in Rural Canada West, 1851: Some First
Estimates.* Waterloo: Wilfrid Laurier University,
1986.

1113 MARR, William L. "Family-Size Limitation in
Canada West, 1851: Some Historical Evidence." In
Canadian Papers in Rural History, vol. VII, ed.
Donald H. Akenson, 273-91. Gananoque, ON:
Langdale Press, 1990.

1114 MATHEWS, Georges. *Le choc démographique: le déclin
du Québec est-il inévitable?* Montréal: Boréal Express,
1984.

1115 McCONACHIE, Kathleen. "A Note on Fertility Rates
Among Married Women in Toronto, 1871."
Ontario History 75 (March 1983): 87-97.

1116 MEDJUCK, Sheva. "Family and Household
Composition in the Nineteenth Century: The Case
of Moncton, New Brunswick, 1851 to 1871."
Canadian Journal of Sociology 4, 3 (Summer 1979):
275-86. Reprinted in *The Canadian City: Essays in
Urban and Social History,* 2nd edition, eds. Gilbert
A. Stelter and Alan F.J. Artibise, 249-61. Toronto:
McClelland and Stewart, 1984.

1117 MEDJUCK, Sheva. "Women's Response to Economic
and Social Change in the Nineteenth Century:
Moncton Parish, 1851 to 1891." *Atlantis* 11, 1 (Fall
1985): 7-21.

1118 MOORE, Eric G. and Brian S. Osborne. "Marital
Fertility in Kingston, 1861-1881: A Study of Socio-
Economic Differentials." *Histoire sociale/Social
History* XX, 39 (May 1987): 9-27.

1119 OLSON, Sherry and Patricia Thornton. "Familles
montréalaises du XIXe siècle: trois cultures, trois trajectoires." *Cahiers québécois de démographie* 21, 2
(automne 1992): 51-75.

1120 PAGE, H.G. "Changes in the Fertility Pattern in
Quebec." *Canadian Journal of Public Health* 58
(1967): 197-203.

1121 RICHARD, Madeline A. *Ethnic Groups and Marital
Choices: Ethnic History and Marital Assimilation,
Canada 1871 and 1971.* Vancouver: University of
British Columbia Press, 1991.

1122 ROCHON, M. "La vie réproductive des femmes
aujourd'hui: le cas du Québec." *Cahiers québécois de
démographie* 18, 1 (1989): 15-61.

1123 RODGERS, Roy H. and Gail Witney. "The Family
Cycle in Twentieth Century Canada." *Journal of
Marriage and the Family* 43, 3 (August 1981): 727-40.

1124 ROMANIUC, A. *Fertility in Canada: From Baby-Boom
to Baby-Bust.* Ottawa: Statistics Canada, 1984.

1125 ROTH, E.A. "Historic Fertility Differentials in a
Northern Athapaskan Community." *Culture* 2, 2
(1982): 63-76.

1126 ROY, Raymond and Hubert Charbonneau. "La nuptialité en situation de déséquilibre des sexes: le
Canada du XVIIe siècle." *Annales de démographie historique* (1978): 285-94.

1127 SABAGH, Georges. "The Fertility of French-
Canadian Women during the Seventeenth
Century." *American Journal of Sociology* 47 (March
1942): 680-89.

1128 SHARMA, Raghubar D. "Pre-marital and Ex-nuptial
Fertility (Illegitimacy) in Canada, 1921-1972."
Canadian Studies in Population 9 (1982): 1-15.

1129 STODDART, Jennifer. "L'histoire des femmes et la
démographie." *Cahiers québécois de démographie* 13,
1 (avril 1984): 79-85.

1130 TASCHEREAU, Sylvie. *Pays et Patrie: Mariages et lieux
d'origine des Italiens de Montréal, 1906-1930.*
Montréal: Université de Montréal, 1987.

1131 TEPPERMAN, Lorne. "Ethnic Variations in Marriage and Fertility: Canada, 1871." *Canadian Review of Sociology and Anthropology* 11, 4 (November 1974): 324-43.

1132 THORNTON, Patricia A. and Sherry Olson. "Family Contexts of Fertility and Infant Survival in Nineteenth-Century Montreal." *Journal of Family History* 16, 4 (1991): 401-18.

1133 TROVATO, Frank and Gloria Lauris. "Marital Status and Mortality in Canada, 1951-1981." *Journal of Marriage and the Family* 51, 4 (November 1989): 907-22.

1134 TROVATO, Frank and Dave Odynak. "The Seasonality of Births in Canada and the Provinces, 1881-1989: Theory and Analysis." *Canadian Studies in Population* 20, 1 (1993): 1-41.

1135 WARGON, Sylvia. "Women in Demography in Canada: The 1940s to the Late 1960s." *Canadian Studies in Population* 19, 2 (1992): 181-216.

1136 WRIGHT, Robert E. and Paul S. Maxim. "Canadian Fertility Trends: A further test of the Easterlin Hypothesis." *Canadian Review of Sociology and Anthropology* 24, 3 (August 1987): 339-57.

FAMILY LIFE

1137 ARNUP, Katherine, ed. *Lesbian Parenting: Living with Pride and Prejudice.* Charlottetown: Gynergy Books, 1995.

1138 BAILEY, Alfred G., ed. *The Letters of James and Ellen Robb: Portrait of a Fredericton Family in Early Victorian Times.* Fredericton: Acadiensis Press, 1983.

1139 BAKER, Maureen. "The Future of Family Life." In *Families: Changing Trends in Canada,* Maureen Baker, *et al.* 330-45. Toronto: McGraw-Hill Ryerson, 1990.

1140 BARRY, Francine. "Familles et domesticité féminine au milieu du 18e siècle." In *Maîtresses de maison, maîtresses d'école: Femmes, famille et éducation dans l'histoire du Québec,* eds. Nadia Fahmy-Eid and Micheline Dumont, 223-35. Montréal: Boréal Express, 1983.

1141 BEAUDREAU, Sylvie and Yves Frenette. "Les stratégies familiales des francophones de la Nouvelle-Angleterre: Perspective diachronique." *Sociologie et sociétés* 26, 1 (printemps 1994): 167-78.

1142 BELAND, Mario. "Éclatée et recomposée: Image de la famille dans les arts." *Cap-aux-Diamants* 39 (automne 1994): 22-28.

1143 BONNAIN, Rolande, Gérard Bouchard and Joseph Goy, eds. *Transmettre, hériter, succéder: la reproduction familiale en milieu rural, France-Québec, XVIIIe-XXe siècles.* Paris, Lyon et Villeurbanne: École des hautes études en sciences sociales, Presses universitaires de Lyon, et Programme Rhône-Alpes Recherches en sciences humaines, 1992.

1144 BOSHER, John F. "The Family in New France." In *In Search of the Visible Past,* ed. Barry Gough, 1-13. Waterloo: Wilfrid Laurier University Press, 1975. Reprinted in *An Introduction to Canadian History,* ed. A.I. Silver. Toronto: Canadian Scholars Press, 1991.

1145 BOUCHARD, Gérard. "Transmission of Family Property and the Cycle of Quebec Rural Society From the Seventeenth to the Twentieth Century." In *Canadian Family History: Selected Readings,* ed. Bettina Bradbury, 112-34. Toronto: Copp Clark Pitman, 1992.

1146 BROWN, Jennifer S.H. *Strangers in Blood: Fur Trade Company Families in Indian Country.* Vancouver: University of British Columbia Press, 1980.

1147 BROWN, Jennifer S.H. "A Cree Nurse in a Cradle of Methodism: Little Mary and the Egerton R. Young Family at Norway House and Berens River." In *First Days, Fighting Days: Women in Manitoba History,* ed. Mary Kinnear, 18-40. Regina: Canadian Plains Research Center, University of Regina, 1987. Reprinted in *Canadian Family History: Selected Readings,* ed. Bettina Bradbury, 93-110. Toronto: Copp Clark Pitman, 1992.

1148 BROWN, Jennifer. "Fur Trade as Centrifuge: Familial Dispersal and Offspring Identity in Two Company Contexts." In *North American Indian Anthropology: Essays on Society and Culture,* eds. Raymond DeMallie and Alfonso Ortiz, 197-219. Norman: University of Oklahoma Press, 1994.

1149 BUCK, Ruth Matheson. "The Mathesons of Saskatchewan Diocese." *Saskatchewan History* 13, 2 (Spring 1960): 41-62.

1150 BUMSTED, J.M. and Wendy Owen. "The Victorian Family in Canada in Historical Perspective: The Ross Family of Red River and the Jarvis Family of Prince Edward Island." *Manitoba History* 13 (Spring 1987): 12-18. Reprinted in *Reappraisals in Canadian History: Pre-Confederation,* eds. A.D. Gilbert, C.M. Wallace and R.M. Bray, 477-87. Scarborough: Prentice Hall Canada Inc., 1993; and in *Interpreting Canada's Past: Volume One, Pre-Confederation,* 2nd edition, ed. J.M. Bumsted, 502-14. Toronto: Oxford University Press, 1993.

1151 BYERS, Mary and Margaret McBurney. *Atlantic Hearth: Early Homes and Families of Nova Scotia.* Toronto: University of Toronto Press, 1994.

1152 CARRISSE, C. and J. Dumazedier. "Valeurs familiales de sujets féminins novateurs." *Sociologie et Sociétés* 2, 2 (1970): 265-81.

1153 DANDURAND, Renée. "Transformation et diversification de la vie familiale au Québec entre 1940 et 1990." *Intervention* 88 (mars 1991): 26-35.

1154 DARROCH, A. Gordon and Michael Ornstein. "Family and Household in Nineteenth-Century Canada: Regional Patterns and Regional Economies." *Journal of Family History* 9, 2 (Summer 1984): 158-77.

1155 DAVIS, Dona. "The Family and Social Change in the Newfoundland Outport." *Culture* 3, 1 (1983): 19-32.

1156 DELANEY, Paul. "The Husbands and Children of Agathe de la Tour." *Les Cahiers de la Société historique acadienne* 25, 4 (oct.-déc. 1994): 263-84.

1157 DONNELLY, F.K., ed. *Family and Household in Mid-nineteenth-century New Brunswick.* Saint John: Division of Social Science, University of New Brunswick at Saint John, 1986.

1158 DONOVAN, Kenneth. "Communities and Families: Family Life and Living Conditions in Eighteenth-Century Louisbourg." *Material History Bulletin* 15 (1982): 33-47.

1159 DOUGLAS, Althea. "From Mother to Daughter: Some Maritime Planter Family Links." *Nova Scotia Historical Review* 13, 1 (1993): 139-56.

1160 FIREWEED COLLECTIVE. "Blood Relations." A special issue of *Fireweed* 12 (Spring 1982). [personal narratives/photo stories on family history]

1161 GAFFIELD, Chad M. "Canadian Families in Cultural Context: Hypotheses from the Mid-Nineteenth Century." Canadian Historical Association. *Historical Papers* (1979): 49-70. Reprinted in *Canadian Family History: Selected Readings*, ed. Bettina Bradbury, 135-57. Toronto: Copp Clark Pitman, 1992.

1162 GARIQUE, Philippe. *La vie familiale des Canadiens français.* Montréal: Les Presses de l'Université de Montréal, 1962.

1163 GELLER, Peter. "Family Memory, Photography and the Fur Trade: The Sinclairs at Norway House, 1902-1911." *Manitoba History* 28 (Autumn 1994): 2-11.

1164 HAGGERTY, Joan. *The Invitation: A Memoir of Family Love and Reconciliation.* Vancouver: Douglas & McIntyre, 1994.

1165 HALIBURTON, Gordon M. "Haliburton Family Letters, 1789-1839." *Nova Scotia Historical Review* 13, 1 (1993): 109-38.

1166 HUMPHREYS, Ruth. "Early Days in the Shiny House." *The Beaver* (Summer 1977): 20-28. [Saskatchewan, 1888-1903]

1167 JOHNSON, J.K., ed. *Affectionately Yours: The Letters of Sir John A. Macdonald and His Family.* Toronto: Macmillan, 1969.

1168 JUDGE, Gail D. "The Tremaine Family of Nova Scotia, 1764-1994, Part I." *Nova Scotia Historical Review* 14, 1 (1994): 169-92.

1169 LITTLE, J.I., ed. *The Child Letters: Public and Private Life in a Canadian Merchant-Politician's Family, 1841-1845.* Montreal and Kingston: McGill-Queen's University Press, 1995.

1170 McKAY, F. "Family Life at a Northern Post Circa Nineteen Hundred." *North* 15, 2 (1968): 8-12.

1171 McKENNA, Katherine M.J. "Options for Elite Women in Early Upper Canadian Society: The Case of the Powell Family." In *Historical Essays on Upper Canada: New Perspectives*, eds. J.K. Johnson and Bruce G. Wilson, 401-23. Ottawa: Carleton University Press, 1989.

1172 McKENNA, Katherine M.J. *A Life of Propriety: Anne Murray Powell and Her Family, 1755-1849.* Montreal and Kingston: McGill-Queen's University Press, 1994.

1173 NICHOLSON, Murray W. "Women in the Irish-Canadian Catholic Family." *Polyphony* 8,1/2 (1986): 9-12.

1174 PECK, Mary Biggar, ed. *A Full House and Fine Singing: Diaries and Letters of Sadie Harper Allen.* Fredericton: Goose Lane Editions, 1992.

1175 PETERS, John. "Cultural Variations: Past and Present." In *Families: Changing Trends in Canada*, Maureen Baker, *et al.* 166-91. Toronto: McGraw-Hill Ryerson, 1990.

1176 POWELL, Barbara. "The Diaries of the Crease Family Women." *BC Studies* 105/106 (Spring/Summer 1995): 45-58.

1177 RICHARDSON, Evelyn May. *We Keep a Light.* Toronto: Ryerson Press, 1945. [a pre-World War II lighthouse-keeping family in Nova Scotia]

1178 SEELEY, John R., *et al.* *Crestwood Heights: A Study of the Culture of Suburban Life.* New York: Basic Books, 1956. [middle-class family life in a mid-20th-century Canadian suburb]

1179 SILVERMAN, Eliane Leslau. "In Their Own Words: Mothers and Daughters on the Alberta Frontier, 1890-1929." *Frontiers* 2, 2 (Summer 1977): 37-44.

1180 SIMARD, Mme. Johnny. "Mémoires d'une ancienne." *Saguenayensia* 18, 1 (janvier/février 1976): 19-23.

1181 SISSONS, C.B., ed. *My Dearest Sophie: Letters from Egerton Ryerson to His Daughter.* Toronto: University of Toronto Press, 1955.

1182 STANLEY, Della, ed. *A Victorian Lady's Album: Kate Shannon's Halifax and Boston Diary of 1892.* Halifax: Formac Publishing, 1993.

1183 STRONG-BOAG, Veronica. "'Their Side of the Story': Women's Voices from Ontario Suburbs, 1945-60." In *A Diversity of Women: Ontario, 1945-1980*, ed. Joy Parr, 46-74. Toronto: University of Toronto Press, 1995.

1184 WETHERELL, Alice, ed. "The Diary of Augusta Silverthorn." *Ontario History* 45, 2 (1953): 75-81. [Peel County, 1878-79]

GENERAL

1185 ANDERSON, Karen L., *et al.* *Family Matters: Sociology and Contemporary Canadian Families.* Scarborough: Nelson Canada, 1988.

1186 ARMSTRONG, Pat. "Economic Conditions and Family Structures." In *Families: Changing Trends in Canada*, Maureen Baker, *et al.* 67-92. Toronto: McGraw-Hill Ryerson, 1990.

1187 BAKER, Maureen, *et al. The Family: Changing Trends in Canada*. Toronto: McGraw-Hill Ryerson, 1984.

1188 BAKER, Maureen, *et al. Families: Changing Trends in Canada*. Toronto: McGraw-Hill Ryerson, 1990.

1189 BRADBURY, Bettina. "Commentaires sur l'histoire des travailleurs des femmes et de la famille." *Bulletin du Regroupement des chercheurs en histoire des travailleurs du Québec* 11, 2/3 (été-automne 1985): 77-84.

1190 BRADBURY, Bettina. "Femmes et Familles." In *Guide d'histoire du Québec du Régime français à nos jours: Bibliographie commentée*, ed. Jacques Rouillard, 233-50. Montréal: Editions du Méridien, 1991.

1191 BRADBURY, Bettina, ed. *Canadian Family History: Selected Readings*. Toronto: Copp Clark Pitman, 1992.

1192 CANADIAN YOUTH COMMISSION. *Youth, Marriage and the Family.* Toronto: Ryerson Press, 1948.

1193 COMACCHIO, Cynthia R. "Beneath the 'Sentimental Veil': Families and Family History in Canada." *Labour/Le Travail* 33 (Spring 1994): 279-302.

1194 CONWAY, John F. *The Canadian Family in Crisis*, 2nd edition. Toronto: James Lorimer & Company, 1993.

1195 DOUCETTE, Laurel. "Family Studies as an Approach to Oral History." Canadian Oral History Association. *Journal* 2 1976-1977.

1196 EICHLER, Margrit. "Families: Evolving Structures." In *Understanding Canadian Society*, eds. James Curtis and Lorne Tepperman, 371-92. Toronto: McGraw-Hill Ryerson, 1988.

1197 FOX, Bonnie, ed. *Family Bonds and Gender Divisions: Readings in the Sociology of the Family* . Toronto: Canadian Scholars' Press, 1988.

1198 GAFFIELD, Chad. "The Social and Economic Origins of Contemporary Families." In *Families: Changing Trends in Canada*, Maureen Baker, *et al.* 23-40. Toronto: McGraw-Hill Ryerson, 1990.

1199 ISHWARAN, K., ed. *The Canadian Family.* Toronto: Holt, Rinehart and Winston, 1971.

1200 LARSON, Lyle E. *The Family in Alberta.* Edmonton: Human Resources Council of Alberta, 1971.

1201 LEMIEUX, Denise and Lucie Mercier. "Familles et destins féminins: le prisme de la mémoire, 1880-1940." *Recherches sociographiques* 28, 2/3 (1987): 255-71.

1202 MANDELL, Nancy and Ann Duffy, eds. *Reconstructing the Canadian Family: Feminist Perspectives.* Toronto: Butterworths, 1988.

1203 MANDELL, Nancy and Ann Duffy, eds. *Canadian Families: Diversity, Conflict and Change.* Toronto: Harcourt Brace Canada, 1995.

1204 McDANIEL, Susan A. "The Changing Canadian Family: Women's Roles and the Impact of Feminism." In *Changing Patterns: Women in Canada*, eds. Sandra Burt, Lorraine Code and Lindsay Dorney, 103-28. Toronto: McClelland & Stewart, 1988. Revised in 2nd edition, 422-51, 1993.

1205 McDANIEL, Susan A. and Wendy Mitchinson. "Canadian Family Fictions and Realities: Past and Present." *The New Quarterly* (May 1987).

1206 McKIE, Craig and Keith Thompson, eds. *Canadian Social Trends, Volume 1.* Toronto: Thompson Educational Publishing, 1990. [Unit 2: Women, Marriage and the Family]

1207 McKIE, Craig and Keith Thompson, eds. *Canadian Social Trends, Volume 2.* Toronto: Thompson Educational Publishing, 1994. [Unit 2: Women, Marriage and the Family]

1208 NETT, Emily M. "Canadian Families in Social-Historical Perspective." *Canadian Journal of Sociology* 6, 3 (1981): 239-60.

1209 NETT, Emily M. *Canadian Families: Past and Present.* Toronto and Vancouver: Butterworths, 1988.

1210 POULIN, Gonzalve. *Brève histoire de la famille canadienne.* Montréal: Les Éditions de la famille, 1940.

1211 *Profiling Canada's Families.* Ottawa: Vanier Institute of the Family, 1994.

1212 RIBODY, Geneviève. "La famille en Nouvelle-France: bilan historiographique." *Cahiers d'histoire* 12, 2 (été 1992): 24-50.

1213 SCHLESINGER, Benjamin. *The One Parent Family in the 1980s: Perspectives and Annotated Bibliography, 1978-1984.* Toronto: University of Toronto Press, 1985.

1214 SCHLESINGER, Rachel Aber and Benjamin Schlesinger. *Canadian Families in Transition.* Toronto: Canadian Scholars' Press, 1992.

GIRLHOOD/CHILDHOOD

1215 AITKEN, Kate. *Never A Day So Bright.* Toronto: Longman, 1956. [reminiscences of turn-of-the-century Beeton, Ontario]

1216 ALLAN, Gladys Lamb. *Dew Upon the Grass.* Saskatoon: Modern Press, 1963. [reminiscences of a fur trader's daughter, northern Manitoba]

1217 ANDERSON, L. "Young Women in the Labour Market: Age, Gender and Unemployment." *Atkinson Review of Canadian Studies* 3, 2 (Spring/Summer) 1986: 20-26.

1218 BARMAN, Jean. "Accounting for Gender and Class in Retrieving the History of Canadian Childhood." *Canadian History of Education Association Bulletin* 5, 2 (May 1988): 5-29.

1219 BEATTIE, Jessie L. *A Season Past: Reminiscences of a Rural Canadian Childhood.* Toronto: McClelland and Stewart, 1968.

1220 BECKER, E.A. "Little Girl in the Klondike Gold Fields." *Alaska Sportsman* 28, 11 (1962): 22-24.

1221 BRADBURY, Bettina. "Gender at Work at Home: Family Decisions, the Labour Market and Girls' Contributions to the Family Economy." In *Canadian and Australian Labour History: Towards a Comparative Perspective*, eds. Gregory S. Kealey and Greg Patmore, 119-40. Sydney: Australian-Canadian Studies, 1990. Reprinted in *Canadian Family History: Selected Readings,* ed. Bettina Bradbury, 177-98. Toronto: Copp Clark Pitman, 1992; and in *Readings in Canadian History: Post Confederation,* 4th edition, eds. R. Douglas Francis and Donald B. Smith, 217-37. Toronto: Harcourt Brace, 1993.

1222 BROWN, Jennifer. "Ultimate Respectability: Fur Trade Children in the 'Civilized World.'" *The Beaver* (Winter 1977): 4-10 and (Spring 1978): 48-55.

1223 BROWN, Jennifer S.H. "Children of the Early Fur Trades." In *Childhood and Family in Canadian History,* ed. Joy Parr, 44-68. Toronto: McClelland and Stewart, 1982.

1224 BROWNRIDGE, Violet. *My Heritage, or, Jottings.* Halton Hills, ON: Esquesing Historical Society, 1979. [20th-century rural childhood]

1225 BULLEN, John. "Hidden Workers: Child Labour and the Family Economy in Late Nineteenth Century Urban Ontario." *Labour/Le Travail* XVIII (Fall 1986): 163-88. Reprinted in *Canadian Family History: Selected Readings,* ed. Bettina Bradbury, 199-219. Toronto: Copp Clark Pitman, 1992; and in *Canadian Working Class History: Selected Readings,* eds. Laurel Sefton-MacDowell and Ian Radforth. Toronto: Canadian Scholars Press, 1992. Abridged in *The Challenge of Modernity: A Reader on Post-Confederation Canada,* ed. Ian McKay, 92-98. Toronto: McGraw-Hill Ryerson, 1992.

1226 CAMPBELL, G.G. "Susan Dunlap: Her Diary." *Dalhousie Review* 46, 2 (Summer 1966): 215-22. [Stewiake, Nova Scotia, 1850s]

1227 CARMICHAEL, May. *Child of the Pioneers.* Cobalt, ON: Highway Book Shop, 1977.

1228 CARTER, Charles Ambrose and Thomas Melville Bailey, eds. *The Diary of Sophia MacNab* (1846). Hamilton: W.L. Griffin, 1968; revised edition, 1974.

1229 CASWELL, Mary Anne. *Pioneer Girl.* Toronto: McGraw-Hill of Canada, 1964. [Saskatchewan, 1887-1888]

1230 COCHRANE, Jean. "Children of the Farm: At Work and Play on the Canadian Frontier." *The Beaver* 72, 4 (Aug./Sept. 1992): 12-18.

1231 COOK, Mary. *View From the West Hill.* Carleton Place, ON: Wallace Enterprises, 1987. [Ottawa Valley girlhood, 1930s]

1232 COULTER, Rebecca Priegert. "The Working Young of Edmonton, 1921-1931." In *Childhood and Family in Canadian History,* ed. Joy Parr, 143-59. Toronto: McClelland and Stewart, 1982.

1233 COULTER, Rebecca Priegert. "Between School and Marriage: A Case Study Approach to Young Women's Work in Early 20th Century Canada." *History of Education Review* 18, 2 (1989): 21-31.

1234 CREGHEUR, Alain and Mary Sue Devereaux. "Les enfants au Canada." *Tendances sociales canadiennes* 21 (été 1991): 2-10.

1235 DECHÊNE, Louise, ed. *Journal d'Henriette Dessaulles, 1874-1880.* Montréal: Hurtubise HMH, 1971.

1236 GAFFIELD, Chad and David Levine. "Dependency and Adolescence on the Canadian Frontier: Orillia, Ontario in the Mid-Nineteenth Century." *History of Education Quarterly* 18, 1 (Spring 1978): 35-48.

1237 GAGNON, Anne. "'Our Parents Did Not Raise Us to be Independent': The Work and Schooling of Young Franco-Albertan Women, 1890-1940." *Prairie Forum* 19, 2 (Fall 1994): 169-88.

1238 GALLOWAY, Margaret A. *I Lived in Paradise.* Winnipeg: Bulman Brothers, 1941. [childhood in small-town Manitoba]

1239 GRAY, James. *The Boy From Winnipeg.* Toronto: Macmillan, 1970.

1240 HAWKE, Liedewy, trans. *Hopes and Dreams: The Diary of Henriette Dessaulles, 1874-1881.* With an introduction by Louise Saint-Jacques Dechêne. Willowdale: Hounslow Press, 1986.

1241 HURL, Lorna F. "Overcoming the Inevitable: Restricting Child Factory Labour in Late Nineteenth Century Ontario." *Labour/Le Travail* 21 (Spring 1988): 87-121.

1242 INKSTER, Anne Ellen. "Memoirs of Fort Churchill (1885-1893)." *Manitoba Pageant* (Winter 1975): 2-5.

1243 IREDALE, Jennifer. "Flowers from Martha's Diary." *British Columbia Historical News* 27, 2 (Spring 1994): 30-31 [Martha Douglas, 1866-1869]

1244 JABLONSKI, Eugenie. *When I was a little girl living in Nova Scotia.* Toronto: Parkdale People's Press, 1990.

1245 KITZ, Janet F. *The Survivors: Children Who Lived Through the Halifax Explosion.* Halifax: Nimbus, 1992.

1246 KOESTER, Mavis Addie. "Childhood Recollections of Lundbreck." *Alberta History* 26, 4 (Autumn 1978): 23-30.

1247 LAMB, W. Kaye. "Letters to Martha." *British Columbia Historical Quarterly* 1, 1 (January 1937): 33-44 [Sir James Douglas to his daughter at school in England, 1872-1874]

1248 LEMIEUX, Denise. "La socialisation des filles dans la famille." In *Maîtresses de maison, maîtresses d'école: Femmes, famille et éducation dans l'histoire du Québec,* eds. Nadia Fahmy-Eid and Micheline Dumont, 237-60. Montréal: Boréal Express, 1983.

1249 LEMIEUX, Denise. *Les Petits innocents: l'enfance en Nouvelle-France.* Québec: Institut québécois de recherche sur la culture, 1985.

1250 LEMIEUX, Denise. "L'enfance en Nouvelle-France: une rencontre des cultures." *Cap-aux-Diamants* 32 (1993): 10-13.

1251 LEMIEUX, Denise. "Les enfants perdus et retrouvés: la recherche sur les enfants au Québec." *Recherches sociographiques* 45, 2 (1995): 327-52.

1252 LE NORMAND, Michelle. *Autour de la Maison.* Trois Rivières: Éditions le Bien Public, 1939.

1253 LIVESAY, Dorothy. *Beginnings: A Winnipeg Childhood.* Toronto: New Press, 1975.

1254 MACKIE, Marlene. "Socialization: Changing Views of Child Rearing and Adolescence." In *Families: Changing Trends in Canada,* Maureen Baker, *et al,* 115-48. Toronto: McGraw-Hill Ryerson, 1990.

1255 McCRACKEN, Melinda. *Memories are Made of This: What It Was Like To Grow Up in the Fifties.* Toronto: James Lorimer and Co., 1975. [Winnipeg]

1256 MOOGK, Peter N. "Les Petits Sauvages: The Children of Eighteenth-Century New France." In *Childhood and Family in Canadian History,* ed. Joy Parr, 17-43. Toronto: McClelland and Stewart, 1982. Reprinted in *Interpreting Canada's Past: Volume One, Pre-Confederation,* 2nd edition, ed. J.M. Bumsted, 122-46. Toronto: Oxford University Press, 1993.

1257 MUNRO, Alice. *Lives of Girls and Women.* Markham: New American Library of Canada, 1974.

1258 NEY, Elizabeth Aikins as told to Adele Rose Wickett. "A Girlhood in Government House." *The Beaver* 70, 2 (April/May 1990): 14-21. [Winnipeg, 1910s]

1259 NOLAN, Shelagh. "A Young Girl in the Old West." *The Beaver* 66, 4 (August/September 1986): 49-55.

1260 PARR, Joy. "For Men and Girls: The Politics and Experience of Gendered Wagework." In *Constructing Modern Canada: Readings in Post-Confederation History,* ed. Chad Gaffield, 311-28. Toronto: Copp Clark Longman Ltd., 1994. [excerpted from *The Gender of Breadwinners*]

1261 PARRY, Caroline. *Eleanora's Diary: The Journals of a Canadian Pioneer Girl.* Richmond Hill, ON: Scholastic Canada Ltd., 1994 [juvenile]

1262 PERRY, Beulah Gullison. "Remembering Growing Up as a Sea Captain's Daughter." *Nova Scotia Historical Review* 7, 2 (1987): 31-44.

1263 RABER, Jessie Brown. *Pioneering in Alberta.* New York: Exposition Press, 1951. [memories of childhood on a homestead, 1895-1905]

1264 RICHARDSON, Evelyn May. *My Other Islands.* Toronto: Ryerson Press, 1960. [growing up in coastal Nova Scotia]

1265 ROHR, Joan Michener with Terrence Heath. *Memories of a Governor-General's Daughter.* Toronto: Bedford House Publishing, 1990.

1266 STEWART, Mrs. E.C. "Pioneer Days in the Graytown District." *Saskatchewan History* 10, 2 (Spring 1957): 71-76.

1267 STRONG-BOAG, Veronica. "Growing Up Female." In *Readings in Canadian History: Post-Confederation,* 3rd edition, eds. R. Douglas Francis and Donald B. Smith, 290-322. Toronto: Holt, Rinehart and Winston of Canada, 1990. [excerpted from *The New Day Recalled*]

1268 SUTHERLAND, Neil. "'We always had things to do': The Paid and Unpaid Work of Anglophone Children Between the 1920s and the 1960s." *Labour/Le Travail* 25 (Spring 1990): 105-41.

1269 SUTHERLAND, Neil. "'I Can't Recall When I Didn't Help': The Working Lives of Children in Twentieth-Century British Columbia." *Histoire sociale/Social History* XXIV, 48 (November 1991): 263-88.

1270 SUTHERLAND, Neil. "When You Listen to the Winds of Childhood, How Much Can You Believe?" *Curriculum Inquiry* 22, 3 (1992): 235-56.

1271 SUTHERLAND, Neil, Jean Barman and Linda Hale, comps. *Contemporary Canadian Childhood and Youth: A Bibliography.* Westport, CT: Greenwood Press, 1992.

1272 SUTHERLAND, Neil, Jean Barman and Linda Hale, comps. *History of Canadian Childhood and Youth: A Bibliography.* Westport, CT: Greenwood Press, 1992.

1273 SYNGE, Jane. "Young Working-Class Women in Early Twentieth-Century Hamilton: Their Work and Family Lives." In *Proceedings, Workshop Conference on Blue Collar Workers and their Communities, York University, 10-11 April 1975,* ed. A.H. Turritin.

1274 SYNGE, Jane. "The Transition from School to Work: Growing Up Working Class in Early 20th Century Hamilton, Ontario." In *Childhood and Adolescence in Canada,* ed. K. Ishwaran, 249-69. Toronto: McGraw-Hill Ryerson, 1979.

1275 VINCENT-DOMEY, Odette. *Filles et familles au milieu ouvier: Hull à la fin du XXe siècle.* Montréal: RCHTQ, Coll. Études et Documents no. 4, 1991.

1276 WILSON, Helen Dacey. *Tales from Barrett's Landing.* Toronto: McClelland and Stewart, 1965. [childhood in Nova Scotia]

1277 WILSON, Helen Dacey. *More Tales from Barrett's Landing.* Toronto: McClelland and Stewart, 1967.

MARRIAGE/COURTSHIP/COUPLES

1278 BROWN, Jennifer S.H. "Changing Views of Fur Trade Marriage and Domesticity: James Hargrave, His Colleagues and 'the Sex.'" *Western Canadian Journal of Anthropology* 6, 3 (1976): 92-105.

1279 BYSTYDZIENSKI, Jill M. "Marriage and Family in the United States and Canada: A Comparison." *American Review of Canadian Studies* 23, 4 (Winter 1993): 565-82.

1280 CAZA, Margaret A. *Walk Alone Together: Portrait of a French-English Marriage.* Don Mills: Stoddart, 1990.

1281 CHAPMAN, Terry L. "Women, Sex and Marriage in Western Canada, 1890-1920." *Alberta History* 33, 4 (1985): 1-12.

1282 COULTER, John, ed. *Prelude to A Marriage: Letters and Diaries of John Coulter and Olive Clare Primrose.* Montreal: Oberon Press, 1979.

1283 DANDURAND, Renée. *Le mariage en question. Essai sociohistorique.* Québec: Institut québécois de recherche sur la culture, 1988.

1284 DEMPSEY, Hugh A. "Dorothy and the Bachelors." *Alberta History* 24, 1 (Winter 1976): 12-14. [scarcity of marriageable women on the prairies, 1895]

1285 DUMAS, Jean and Yves Péron. *Mariage et vie conjugale au Canada—Marriage and Conjugal Life in Canada.* Ottawa: Statistique Canada, 1992.

1286 DUNCAN, Joy, ed. *Red Serge Wives.* Edmonton: Coop Press, 1974.

1287 FERRETTI, Lucia. "Mariage et cadre de vie familiale dans une paroisse ouvrière montréalaise: Sainte Brigide, 1900-1914." *Revue d'histoire de l'Amérique française* 39, 2 (automne 1985): 233-51.

1288 FROST, S.B. "A Transatlantic Wooing." *Dalhousie Review* 58, 3 (Autumn 1978): 458-70. [1840s]

1289 GAGNON, Serge. "Amours interdites et misères conjugales dans le Québec rural de la fin du XVIIIe siècle jusque vers 1830 (l'arbitrage des prêtres)." In *Sociétés villageoises et rapports villes-campagnes au Québec et dans la France de l'ouest, XVIIe-XXe siècles,* eds. François Lebrun and Norman Séguin. Trois-Rivières: Université du Québec à Trois-Rivières/Presses universitaires de Rennes, 1987.

1290 GAGNON, Serge. *Mariage et famille au temps de Papineau.* Sainte-Foy: Presses de l'Université Laval, 1993.

1291 GAUVREAU, Danielle. "Nuptialité et catégories professionelles à Québec pendant le régime français." *Sociologie et sociétés* 19, 1 (avril 1987): 25-35.

1292 GAVREAU, Danielle. "Nuptialité et industrialisation: éléments de comparaison entre l'Ancien et le Nouveau Monde." In *Transmettre, hériter, succéder: la reproduction familiale en milieu rural, France-Québec, XVIIIe-XXe siècles,* eds., Rolande Bonnain, *et al,* 27-41. Lyon: Presses Universitaires de Lyon, 1992.

1293 GAUVREAU, Danielle and Mario Bourque. "Jusqu'à ce que la mort nous sépare: Le destin des femmes et des hommes mariés au Saguenay avant 1930." *Canadian Historical Review* 71, 4 (December 1990): 441-61.

1294 GEE, Ellen. "Female Marriage Patterns in Canada: Changes and Differentials." *Journal of Comparative Family Studies* 11, 4 (1980): 457-73.

1295 GEE, Ellen. "Marriage in Nineteenth Century Canada." *Canadian Review of Sociology and Anthropology* 19, 3 (1982): 311-25.

1296 GILLETT, Margaret, ed. *Dear Grace: A Romance of History.* Montreal: Eden Press, 1986.

1297 GOSSAGE, Peter. "Family Formation and Age at Marriage in Saint-Hyacinthe, Quebec, 1854-1891." *Histoire sociale/Social History* XXIV, 47 (May 1991): 61-84.

1298 GRINDSTAFF, Carl. "Adolescent Marriage and Childbearing: The Long-Term Economic Outcome, Canada in the 1980s." *Adolescence* 23, 89 (1988): 45-58.

1299 HUTCHINSON, Lorna. "'God Help Me for No One Else Can': The Diary of Annie Waltham, 1869-1881." *Acadiensis* 21, 2 (Spring 1992): 72-89. [wife abuse]

1300 KERMAGHAN, Lois D. "A Man and His Mistress: J.F.W. DesBarres and Mary Cannon." *Acadiensis* 11, 1 (Autumn 1981): 23-42.

1301 KEYES, Jane. "Marriage Patterns Among Early Quakers." *Nova Scotia Historical Quarterly* 8, 4 (December 1978): 299-307.

1302 LACHANCE, Paul. "L'effet du déséquilibre des sexes sur le comportement matrimonial: comparaison entre la Nouvelle-France, Saint-Domingue et la Nouvelle-Orléans." *Revue d'histoire de l'Amérique française* 39, 2 (automne 1985): 211-32.

1303 LANDRY, Yves. "Les filles du roi émigrées au Canada au XVIIe siècle, ou un exemple de choix du conjoint en situation de déséquilibre des sexes." *Histoire, économie et société* 2 (1992): 197-216.

1304 LANDRY, Yves. "Gender Imbalance, Les Filles du Roi, and Choice of Spouse in New France." In *Canadian Family History: Selected Readings,* ed. Bettina Bradbury, 14-32. Toronto: Copp Clark Pitman, 1992.

1305 LAPP, Eula C. "When Ontario Girls Were Going West." *Ontario History* 60, 2 (June 1968): 71-80.

1306 LECLERC, P.A. "Le mariage sous le régime français." *Revue d'histoire de l'Amérique française* 13/14 (1959/60): 230-46, 374-401, 525-43.

1307 MARSHALL, Stephan D.E. "Courtship and Marriage in Nineteenth Century Ontario." *Families* 29, 4 (November 1990): 197-208.

1308 MASSICOTTE, E.Z. "Le Charivari au Canada." *Bulletin des recherches historiques* 32 (November 1926): 712-25.

1309 MATHIEU, Jacques, *et al.* "Les alliances matrimonial exogames dans le gouvernement de Québec, 1700-1760." *Revue d'histoire de l'Amérique française* 35, 1 (juin 1981): 3-32.

1310 MERTENS, Walter. "Canadian Nuptiality Patterns: 1911-1961." *Canadian Studies in Population* 3 (1976): 57-71.

1311 MOLLOY, Maureen. "Considered Affinity: Kinship, Marriage, and Social Class in New France, 1640-1729." *Social Science History* 14, 1 (Spring 1990): 1-26.

1312 MORRISON, Monica. "Wedding Night Pranks in Western New Brunswick." *Southern Folklore Quarterly* 38, 4 (December 1974): 285-97.

1313 MORRISON, N.F. "A Wedding Trip of 1854." *Ontario History* 49 (1957): 195-97.

1314 MORTON, Suzanne. "The June Bride as the Working-Class Bride: Getting Married in a Halifax Working-Class Neighbourhood in the 1920s." In *Canadian Family History: Selected Readings*, ed. Bettina Bradbury, 360-79. Toronto: Copp Clark Pitman, 1992.

1315 NOËL, Françoise. "'My Dear Eliza': The Letters of Robert Hoyle (1831-1844)." *Histoire sociale/Social History* XXVI, 51 (May 1993):115-30.

1316 ODERKIRK, Jillian. "Le mariage au Canada: évolution des croyances et des comportements, 1600-1900." *Tendances sociales canadiennes* 33 (été 1994): 2-7.

1317 PALMER, Bryan D. "Discordant Music: Charivaris and Whitecapping in Nineteenth Century North America." *Labour/Le Travailleur* 3 (1978): 5-62.

1318 PETERKIN, Audrey and Margaret Shaw. *Mrs. Doctor: Reminiscences of Manitoba Doctors' Wives*. Winnipeg: Prairie Publishing Company, 1976.

1319 RAIBLE, Chris. "All for Love: A Tragedy of the Heart in Old Upper Canada." *The Beaver* 72, 6 (December 1992/January 1993): 32-37. [Anne Powell and John Beverley Robinson]

1320 RAMU, G.N., ed. *Marriage and the Family in Canada Today*. Scarborough: Prentice-Hall Canada, Inc., 1989.

1321 RIDDELL, W.R. "The 'Shivaree' and the Original." *Ontario History* 27 (1931): 522-24.

1322 RIOUX, Hélène. "Les amours québécoises au XVIIIe siècle." *Histoire* 11 (avril 1979).

1323 RUBINGER, Catherine. "Marriage and the Women of Louisbourg." *Dalhousie Review* 60 (Autumn 1980): 445-61.

1324 SHIPLEY, Nan. "Anne and Alexander (Hunter) Murray." *The Beaver* (Winter 1967): 33-37. [Hudson Bay territory]

1325 SILVERMAN, Eliane Leslau. "Women's Perceptions of Marriage on the Alberta Frontier." In *Building Beyond the Homestead: Rural History on the Prairies*, eds. D. Jones and I. MacPherson, 49-64. Calgary: University of Calgary Press, 1985.

1326 SMITH, Donald B. "The Transatlantic Courtship of the Reverend Peter Jones." *The Beaver* (Summer 1977): 4-13. [marriage of an Englishwoman to an Indian minister]

1327 SMITH, Donald B. "Eliza and the Reverend Peter Jones." *The Beaver* (Autumn 1977): 40-46.

1328 SMITH, Donald B. "Peter and Eliza Jones: Their Last Years." *The Beaver* (Winter 1977): 16-23.

1329 SNELL, James G. "Marriage Humour and Its Social Functions, 1900-1939." *Atlantis* 11, 2 (Spring 1986): 70-85.

1330 SNELL, James G. "The Gendered Construction of Elderly Marriage, 1900-1950." *Canadian Journal on Aging* 12, 4 (1993): 509-23.

1331 SPEIGHT, Anne M. "The Chivaree." *Alberta History* 26, 3 (Summer 1978): 34-35.

1332 TROVATO, Frank. "A Macrosocial Analysis of Change in the Marriage Rate: Canadian Women, 1921-25 and 1981-85." *Journal of Marriage and the Family* 50 (1988): 507-21.

1333 VAN KIRK, Sylvia. "'The Custom of the Country': An Examination of Fur Trade Marriage Practices." In *Essays on Western History*, ed. L.H. Thomas, 49-68. Edmonton: University of Alberta Press, 1976. Reprinted in *Canadian Family History: Selected Readings*, ed. Bettina Bradbury, 67-92. Toronto: Copp Clark Pitman, 1992.

1334 WAITE, P.B. "Late Harvest: Mackenzie King and the Italian Lady." *The Beaver* 75, 6 (Dec. 95/Jan. 96): 4-10.

1335 WARD, W. Peter. "Courtship and Social Space in Nineteenth-Century English Canada." *Canadian Historical Review* 68, 1 (1987): 35-62.

1336 WARD, W. Peter. *Courtship, Love and Marriage in Nineteenth-Century English Canada*. Montreal and Kingston: McGill-Queen's University Press, 1990.

1337 WOOD-HOLT, B. *Early Marriage Records of New Brunswick: Saint John City and County from the British Conquest to 1839*. Saint John: Holland House, 1987.

MOTHERHOOD/ILLEGITIMACY

1338 ARNUP, Katherine. "'We Are Family': Lesbian Mothers in Canada." *Resources for Feminist Research* 20, 3/4 (Fall/Winter 1991): 101-7.

1339 ARNUP, Katherine, Andrée Lévesque and Ruth Roach Pierson, eds. *Delivering Motherhood: Maternal Ideologies and Practices in the 19th and 20th Centuries*. London and New York: Routledge, 1990.

1340 BATES, Réal. "Les conceptions prénuptiales dans la vallée du Saint-Laurent avant 1725." *Revue d'histoire de l'Amérique française* 40, 2 (automne 1986): 253-72.

1341 BENOIT, Cecilia. "Mothering in a Newfoundland Community: 1900-1940." In *Delivering Motherhood: Maternal Ideologies and Practices in the 19th and 20th Centuries*, eds. Katherine Arnup, Andrée Lévesque and Ruth Roach Pierson, 173-89. London and New York: Routledge, 1990. Reprinted in *Canadian Women: A Reader*, eds. Wendy Mitchinson, *et al*, 268-80. Toronto: Harcourt Brace Canada, 1996.

1342 BOUCHARD, Gérard. "L'évolution des conceptions prénuptiales comme indicateur de changement culturel." *Annales de démographie historique* (1993): 25-49. [la région du Saguenay entre 1842 et 1971]

1343 CAHILL, Bette L. *Butterbox Babies: Baby Sales, Baby Deaths. The Scandalous Story of the Ideal Maternity Home*. Toronto: Seal Books, 1992. [Nova Scotia 1930s-1940s]

1344 CLICHE, Marie-Aimée. "Morale chrétienne et 'double standard sexuel': Les filles-mères à l'hôpital de la Miséricorde à Québec, 1874-1972." *Histoire sociale/Social History* XXIV, 47 (mai 1991): 85-125.

1345 CLICHE, Marie-Aimée. "Unwed Mothers, Families, and Society During the French Regime." In *Canadian Family History: Selected Readings,* ed. Bettina Bradbury, 33-65. Toronto: Copp Clark Pitman, 1992.

1346 DUMAS, Monique. "La mère dans la société québécoise: Étude éthique d'un modèle à partir de deux journaux féministes: *La Bonne Parole* (1913-1958) et *Les Têtes de Pioche* (1966-1979)." CRIAW Papers No. 5. Ottawa: Canadian Research Institute for the Advancement of Women, 1983.

1347 GAUVREAU, Danielle. "Destins des femmes, destins des mères: Images et réalités historiques de la maternité au Québec." *Recherches sociographiques* 32, 3 (1991): 321-46.

1348 GOSSAGE, Peter. "Foundlings and the Institution: The Case of the Grey Nuns of Montreal." Canadian Historical Association. *Historical Papers* (1986).

1349 GOSSAGE, Peter. "Les enfants abandonnés à Montréal au 19è siècle: la creche d'Youville des Soeurs Grises, 1829-1871." *Revue d'histoire de l'Amérique française* 40, 4 (printemps 1987): 537-59.

1350 LEMIEUX, Denise. "Des mythes de la mère à la parole des mères." *Questions de Culture* 9 (1986).

1351 LÉVESQUE, Andrée. "Deviant Anonymous: Single Mothers at the Hôpital de la Miséricorde in Montreal, 1929-1939." Canadian Historical Association. *Historical Papers* (1984): 168-84. Reprinted in *Delivering Motherhood: Maternal Ideologies and Practices in the 19th and 20th Centuries,* eds. Katherine Arnup, Andrée Lévesque and Ruth Roach Pierson, 108-25. London and New York: Routledge, 1990; in *Rethinking Canada: The Promise of Women's History,* 2nd edition, eds. Veronica Strong-Boag and Anita Clair Fellman, 322-36. Toronto: Copp Clark Pitman Ltd., 1991; and in *The Challenge of Modernity: A Reader on Post-Confederation Canada,* ed. Ian McKay, 289-304. Toronto: McGraw-Hill Ryerson, 1992.

1352 LEWIS, Jane. "'Motherhood Issues' in the Late Nineteenth and Twentieth Centuries." In *Delivering Motherhood: Maternal Ideologies and Practices in the 19th and 20th Centuries,* eds. Katherine Arnup, Andrée Lévesque and Ruth Roach Pierson, 1-19. London and New York: Routledge, 1990.

1353 LIGHT, Beth. "Mothers and Children in Canadian History." *Canadian Women's Studies* 2, 1 (1980): 102.

1354 LITTLE, Margaret. "Manhunts and Bingo Blabs: The Moral Regulation of Ontario Single Mothers." *Canadian Journal of Sociology* 19, 2 (1994): 233-48.

1355 McQUILLAN, Kevin. "Falling Behind: The Income of Lone-Mother Families, 1970-1985." *Canadian Review of Sociology and Anthropology* 29, 4 (November 1992): 511-23.

1356 ORKIN, Mark M. *The Great Stork Derby.* Toronto: General Publishing, 1981.

1357 MORTON, Suzanne. "Women on Their Own: Single Mothers in Working-Class Halifax in the 1920s." *Acadiensis* 21, 2 (Spring 1992): 90-107.

1358 PAQUETTE, Lyne and Réal Bates. "Les naissances illégitimes sur les rives du Saint-Laurent avant 1730." *Revue d'histoire de l'Amérique française* 40, 2 (automne 1986): 239-52.

1359 ROBERGE, Andrée. "Entre maternités et maternage, condition des femmes au Québec." In *Encrages féministes: Un moment de reflexion dans la recherche féministe,* ed. Isabelle Lasvergnas, 21-32. Montréal: Université du Québec à Montréal, Centre de recherche féministe, Group interdisciplinaire d'enseignement et de recherche féministes, 1989.

1360 SAVAGE, Leslie. "Perspectives on Illegitimacy: The Changing Role of the Sisters of Misericordia in Edmonton, 1900-1906." In *Studies in Childhood History: A Canadian Perspective,* eds. Patricia T. Rooke and R.L. Schnell, 105-33. Calgary: Detselig Enterprises, 1982.

1361 WARD, W. Peter. "Unwed Motherhood in Nineteenth Century English Canada." Canadian Historical Association. *Historical Papers* (1981): 34-56.

WORK/FAMILY ECONOMIES

1362 AMES, Herbert B. *The City Below the Hill: A Sociological Study of a Portion of the City of Montreal, Canada* (1897). With an introduction by P.F.W. Rutherford. Toronto: University of Toronto Press, 1972.

1363 ARMSTRONG, Pat. "Work and Family Life: Changing Patterns." In *Marriage and the Family in Canada Today,* ed. G.N. Ramu, 121-41. Scarborough: Prentice-Hall, 1989.

1364 BAILLARGEON, Denyse. "Maîtresses de maison dépareillées? L'apprentissage du travail domestique à Montréal au début du siècle." *Bulletin du Regroupement des chercheurs-chercheures en histoire des travailleurs et travailleuses du Québec* 17, 2 (été 1991): 7-22.

1365 BAILLARGEON, Denyse. *Ménagères au temps de la Crise.* Montréal: Les Éditions du remue-ménage, 1991.

1366 BAILLARGEON, Denyse. "'If You Had No Money, You Had No Trouble, Did You?': Montreal Working-class Housewives during the Great Depression." *Women's History Review* 1, 2 (1992): 217-37. Reprinted in *Canadian Women: A Reader,* eds. Wendy Mitchinson, *et al,* 251-68. Toronto: Harcourt Brace Canada, 1996.

1367 BAILLARGEON, Denyse. "La Crise ordinaire: Les ménagères montréalaises et la crise des années trente." *Labour/Le Travail* 30 (Fall 1992): 135-62.

1368 BRADBURY, Bettina. "The Family Economy and Work in an Industrializing City, Montreal, 1871." Canadian Historical Association. *Historical Papers* (1979): 71-96. Reprinted in *Interpreting Canada's Past: Volume II, After Confederation,* ed. J.M. Bumsted, 92-115. Toronto: Oxford University Press, 1986; 2nd edition, 136-65, 1993.

1369 BRADBURY, Bettina. "The Fragmented Family: Family Strategies in the Face of Death, Illness and Poverty, Montreal, 1860-1885." In *Childhood and Family in Canadian History,* ed. Joy Parr, 109-28. Toronto: McClelland and Stewart, 1982. Reprinted in *Family Bonds and Gender Divisions: Readings in the Sociology of the Family,* ed. Bonnie Fox, 155-75. Toronto: Canadian Scholars' Press Inc., 1988; and in *An Introduction to Canadian History,* ed. A.I. Silver. Toronto: Canadian Scholars' Press, 1991.

1370 BRADBURY, Bettina. "Pigs, Cows, and Boarders: Non-Wage Forms of Survival Among Montreal Families, 1861-91." *Labour/Le Travail* 14 (1984): 9-46. Reprinted in *The Challenge of Modernity: A Reader on Post-Confederation Canada,* ed. Ian McKay, 65-91. Toronto: McGraw-Hill Ryerson, 1992.

1371 BRADBURY, Bettina. *Working Families: Age, Gender, and Daily Survival in Industrializing Montreal.* Toronto: McClelland and Stewart, 1993.

1372 BUREAU DE LA STATISTIQUE DU QUÉBEC. *L'évolution du revenu des familles au Québec, 1971-1986.* Québec: Les Publications du Québec, 1991.

1373 EARLY, Frances. "The French Canadian Family Economy and Standard of Living in Lowell, Massachusetts." *Journal of Family History* 7 (Summer 1982).

1374 GAFFIELD, Chad. "Wage Labour, Industrialization, and the Origins of the Modern Family." In *The Family: Changing Trends in Canada,* ed. Maureen Baker. Toronto: McGraw-Hill Ryerson, 1984.

1375 KATZ, Michael B. *The People of Hamilton, Canada West: Family and Class in the Mid-Nineteenth Century.* Cambridge, MA: Harvard University Press, 1975.

1376 LIVINGSTONE, D.W. and Meg Luxton. "Gender Consciousness at Work: Modification of the Male Breadwinner Norm among Steelworkers and their Spouses." *Canadian Review of Sociology and Anthropology* 26, 2 (May 1989): 240-75.

1377 LUXTON, Meg and Harriet Rosenberg. *Through the Kitchen Window: The Politics of Home and Family.* Toronto: Garamond Press, 1986.

1378 LUXTON, Meg, Harriet Rosenberg and Sedef Arat Koç. *Through the Kitchen Window: The Politics of Home and Family,* 2nd edition. Toronto: Garamond Press, 1990.

1379 MacBRIDE-KING, Judith and Hélène Paris. "Balancing Work and Family Responsibilities." *Canadian Business Review* 16, 3 (Autumn 1989): 17-21. Reprinted in *Work in Canada: Readings in the Sociology of Work and Industry,* eds. Graham S. Lowe and Harvey J. Krahn, 380-88. Scarborough: Nelson Canada, 1993.

1380 McINNIS, R. Marvin. "Women, Work and Childbearing: Ontario in the Second Half of the Nineteenth Century." *Histoire sociale/Social History* XXIV, 48 (November 1991): 237-62. Reprinted in *Perspectives on Canadian Economic History,* 2nd edition, eds. Douglas McCalla and Michael Huberman. Mississauga: Copp Clark Longman, 1994.

1381 MORTON, Suzanne. *Ideal Surroundings: Domestic Life in a Working-Class Suburb in the 1920s.* Toronto: University of Toronto Press, 1995.

1382 ROSENFELD, Mark. "'It was a hard life': Class and Gender in the Work and Family Rhythms of a Railway Town 1920-1950." Canadian Historical Association. *Historical Papers* (1988): 237-79. Reprinted in *Canadian Family History: Selected Readings,* ed. Bettina Bradbury, 241-80. Toronto: Copp Clark Pitman, 1992; and in *Constructing Modern Canada: Readings in Post-Confederation History,* ed. Chad Gaffield, 329-69. Toronto: Copp Clark Longman Ltd., 1994.

FEMINISM/WOMEN'S MOVEMENTS

NO OTHER TOPIC in Canadian women's history, with the exception of women's work, has attracted as much attention as feminism and women's movements. With a mixture of admiration and condescension, feminists in the early 1970s sought to document the accomplishments of their predecessors and learn from their mistakes. The early scholarship focussed on what some scholars christened the "first-wave" of feminist organizing from the 1880s to the 1920s, and on the most prominent organizations, such as the National Council of Women of Canada, Women's Christian Temperance Union, and the Fédération nationale Saint-Jean-Baptiste, whose activities were conveniently documented in well-preserved and accessible record collections. While interest in these early national and umbrella organizations continues unabated, more recent studies have tended to focus on activities at the provincial and community levels. Studies of "second-wave" feminism since 1960 have also focussed on major national organizations such as the Voice of Women and the Women's Legal and Education Action Fund (LEAF). Thanks largely to the efforts of the Canadian Women's Movement Archives, which set out to preserve the records of the ephemeral grassroots feminist organizations so characteristic of the 1970s and 1980s, studies of the women's liberation movement and community-based feminist activism are now making an appearance.

Early scholarship on the history of first-wave feminism in Canada investigated the social standing and objectives of feminists, changing definitions of feminism, organizational strategies and accomplishments, the perception and treatment of feminists by others, and feminist links with socialism and a variety of social reform movements. To date, most studies have focussed on urban middle-class white women, although the perception of this group by feminist scholars has altered considerably over two decades. While the dominant "maternal" strand of turn-of-the-century feminism was initially dismissed as more conservative than "equal rights" feminism, this dichotomous interpretation has lost ground to a less judgmental assessment of maternal feminism as a strategic adaptation to the ideology of separate spheres. This shift has been most obvious in the growing literature on the suffrage movement, which is receiving renewed attention at the provincial level.

A dramatic development in recent scholarship on early feminism in Canada has been a new sensitivity to the importance of religion. While Quebec scholars have long been interested in the relationship of feminism to religious nationalism, and to the relationship of Catholic feminists with the church hierarchy and the women religious, it is only recently that anglophone scholars have begun to acknowledge the centrality of evangelical Protestantism to feminist organizing in other parts of Canada. Also clearly evident is a flowering of scholarship on the relationship of rural women to Canadian feminism, leading to reassessments of the ostensibly conservative roles played by organizations such as the Women's Institutes and the Cercles de Fermières. That the interests of early feminists ranged far beyond the demand for suffrage is evident in many studies linking feminism to support for Prohibition, immigration reform, eugenics, anti-prostitution and venereal disease campaigns, dower rights, equal guardianship laws, child welfare, mothers' pensions, minimum wage laws, and protective legislation. A vigorous debate is in progress over the relative importance of class, race, and gender-based concerns in turn-of-the-century feminism, especially in recent studies linking feminism to moral panics over issues such as "white slavery" and "race suicide."

More than twenty-five years have now passed since the *Report of the Royal Commission on the Status of Women*, and historians are turning their attention to the study of the more recent feminist past, including the Royal Commission itself. The rapidly growing scholarship in this area, much of it produced by sociologists, includes studies of lesbian feminist organizing, the First Nations women's movement and campaigns to change the Indian Act, immigrant women and community organizing, women's peace activism, disabled women's organizing, campaigns against pornography and violence against women, the struggle for pay equity, rural women's fight to save the family farm, Quebec feminism since the Quiet Revolution, racism in the women's movement, and the relationship of feminism to the state. The very small body of scholarship on the critically important subject of anti-feminism in Canada has recently been amplified by studies of the "pro-family" movement of the 1980s and the role of REAL Women.

In recent studies, historians are moving beyond the problematic "first-wave" and "second-wave" model because of its strong implication of discontinuity in the history of twentieth-century Canadian feminism. Early organizations such as the YWCA remained active during the "trough" from the 1920s to the 1960s, and new organizations such as the Canadian Federation of Business and Professional Women's Clubs came to prominence over the issue of married women's right to work. Autobiographical and biographical accounts of the lives of individual feminists such as Kay McPherson, Simonne Monet-Chartrand, Margaret McWilliams, and Charlotte Whitton are already providing an important window into this period.

ANTI-FEMINISM

1383 BOURASSA, Henri. *Femmes-Hommes ou Hommes et Femmes?* Montréal: Le Devoir, 1925.

1384 DUBINSKY, Karen. *Lament for a 'Patriarchy Lost'? Anti-feminism, Anti-abortion and R.E.A.L. Women in Canada.* Feminist Perspectives No. 1. Ottawa: Canadian Research Institute for the Advancement of Women, 1985.

1385 DUBINSKY, Karen. "Really Dangerous: The Challenge of R.E.A.L. Women." *Canadian Dimension* 21, 6 (October 1987): 4-7.

1386 EICHLER, Margrit. *The Pro-Family Movement: Are They For or Against Families?* Feminist Frameworks. Ottawa: Canadian Research Institute for the Advancement of Women, 1985.

1387 ERWIN, Lorna. "Researching Anti-Feminism." *Resources for Feminist Research* 17, 2 (1988): 3-5.

1388 ERWIN, Lorna. "REAL Women, Anti-Feminism, and the Welfare State." *Resources for Feminist Research* 17, 3 (1988): 147-49.

1389 ERWIN, Lorna. "Neoconservatism and the Canadian pro-family movement." *Canadian Review of Sociology and Anthropology* 30, 3 (1993): 401-20.

1390 GILL, Donna. "REAL Women and the Press: An Ideological Alliance of Convenience." *Canadian Journal of Communication* 14, 3 (Sept. 1989): 1-16.

1391 HOBBS, Margaret. "Rethinking Antifeminism in the 1930s: Gender Crisis or Workplace Justice? A Response to Alice Kessler-Harris." *Gender and History* 5, 1 (Spring 1993): 4-15.

1392 STEELE, Betty. *The Feminist Take Over: Patriarchy to Matriarchy in Two Decades.* Toronto: Simon & Pierre, 1991.

1393 STEUTER, Erin. "Women Against Feminism: An Examination of Feminist Social Movements and Anti-Feminist Countermovements." *Canadian Review of Sociology and Anthropology* 29, 3 (1992): 288-306.

1394 STORRIE, Kathleen. "The Modern Movement for the Submission of Women." *Canadian Woman Studies* 5, 2 (Winter 1983): 9-10.

1395 STRONG-BOAG, Veronica. *Independent Women, Problematic Men: First and Second-Wave Anti-Feminism in Canada from Goldwin Smith to Betty Steele.* Occasional Working Papers 2, 2. Vancouver: Centre for Research in Women's Studies and Gender Relations, University of British Columbia, 1993.

1396 TROFIMENKOFF, Susan Mann. "Henri Bourassa and 'the Woman Question.'" *Journal of Canadian Studies* 10, 4 (November 1975): 3-11. Reprinted in *The Neglected Majority: Essays in Canadian Women's History,* eds. Susan Mann Trofimenkoff and Alison Prentice, 104-15. Toronto: McClelland and Stewart, 1977.

1397 TROFIMENKOFF, Susan Mann. "Les femmes dans l'oeuvre de Groulx." *Revue d'histoire de l'Amérique française* 32, 3 (décembre 1978): 385-98.

1398 TROFIMENKOFF, Susan. "Feminism, Nationalism and the Clerical Defensive." In *Rethinking Canada: The Promise of Women's History,* eds. Veronica Strong-Boag and Anita Clair Fellman, 123-36. Toronto: Copp Clark Pitman Ltd., 1986. [excerpted from *The Dream of Nation*]

BIOGRAPHIES/MEMOIRS

1399 ADILMAN, Tami. "Evlyn Farris and the University Women's Club." In *In Her Own Right: Selected Essays on Women's History in BC,* eds. Barbara Latham and Cathy Kess, 147-66. Victoria: Camosun College, 1980.

1400 ANDERSON, Doris. *To Change the World: A Biography of Pauline Jewett.* Richmond Hill: Irwin Pub., 1987.

1401 BERTRAND, Réal. *Thérèse Casgrain.* Montréal: Lidec, 1981.

1402 BRIGDEN, Beatrice. "One Woman's Campaign for Social Purity and Social Reform." In *The Social Gospel in Canada,* ed. Richard Allen, 36-62. Ottawa: National Museums of Canada, 1975.

1403 BROUWER, Ruth Compton. "Moral Nationalism in Victorian Canada: The Case of Agnes Machar." *Journal of Canadian Studies* 20, 1 (1985): 90-108.

1404 BURTON, Betty. "Nellie McClung." *Manitoba Pageant* 20, 4 (Summer 1975): 1-10.

1405 COOK, Sharon Anne. "Letitia Youmans: Ontario's Nineteenth-Century Temperance Educator." *Ontario History* 84, 4 (Dec. 1992): 329-42.

1406 DAVIS, Angela. "A Life of Service." *The Beaver* 74, 5 (October/November 1994): 35-39. [Mary Barrett Speechly]

1407 DEMBSKI, Peter E. Paul. "An English, Protestant, Upper-Class Feminist on the Grand Tour: Elizabeth Smith Shortt in Great Britain and Europe, 1911." *Journal of Canadian Studies* 28, 4 (Winter 1993/94): 72-87.

1408 FORBES, Ernest. "Battles in another war: Edith Archibald and the Halifax feminist movement." In his *Challenging the Regional Stereotype,* 67-89. Fredericton: Acadiensis Press, 1989.

1409 FRENCH, Doris. *Ishbel and the Empire: A Biography of Lady Aberdeen.* Toronto: Dundurn Press, 1988.

1410 GORHAM, Deborah. "Flora MacDonald Denison: Canadian Feminist." In *A Not Unreasonable Claim: Women and Reform in Canada, 1880s-1920s,* ed. Linda Kealey, 47-70. Toronto: The Women's Press, 1979.

1411 GORHAM, Deborah. "Vera Brittain, Flora MacDonald Denison and the Great War: The Failure of Non-Violence." In *Women and Peace: Theoretical, Historical and Practical Perspectives,* ed. Ruth Roach Pierson, 192-221. London: Croom Helm, 1987.

1412 GRAHAM, Frank W. *Ahead of Her Time: A Biography of Ellen Carbery.* St. John's: Creative Publishers, 1987.

1413 HACKER, Carlotta. *E. Cora Hind.* Toronto: Fitzhenry and Whiteside, 1979.

1414 HALLETT, Mary and Marilyn Davis. *Firing the Heather: The Life and Times of Nellie McClung.* Saskatoon: Fifth House, 1993.

1415 HALLETT, Mary E. and Marilyn I. Davis. "Votes for Women." *The Beaver* 73, 5 (Oct./Nov. 1993): 17-22. [Nellie McClung]

1416 HAM, Mary C. "Grandmother Kaufman: Mary Ratz Kaufman, December 14, 1856–December 24, 1943." *Waterloo Historical Society* 78 (1990): 62-68.

1417 HANCOCK, Carol L. *No Small Legacy: Canada's Nellie McClung.* Winfield, BC: Woodlake Books, Inc., 1986.

1418 HARVEY, Dr. Robert. "McClung of Manitou." In *Pioneers of Manitoba,* 41-44. Winnipeg: Prairie Publishing Co., 1970.

1419 HICKS, Anne. "Francis Beynon and *The Guide.*" In *First Days, Fighting Days: Women in Manitoba History,* ed. Mary Kinnear, 41-52. Regina: Canadian Plains Research Centre, University of Regina, 1987.

1420 HOWARD, Irene. *The Struggle for Social Justice in British Columbia: Helena Gutteridge, the Unknown Reformer.* Vancouver: University of British Columbia Press, 1992.

1421 JAMES, Donna. *Emily Murphy.* Toronto: Fitzhenry and Whiteside, 1977.

1422 KINNEAR, Mary. "Margaret McWilliams and *Her* Social Gospel: The Formation of an Interwar Feminist." *Manitoba History* 22 (Autumn 1991): 30-34.

1423 KINNEAR, Mary. *Margaret McWilliams: An Interwar Feminist.* Montreal and Kingston: McGill-Queen's University Press, 1991.

1424 LAMOUREUX, Diane. "Idola Saint-Jean et le radical-isme féministe de l'entre-deux-guerres." *Recherches féministes* 4, 2 (1991): 45-60.

1425 LESTER, Tanya. "Rebel with a Cause: Irene Parlby and the Persons Case." *Herizons* 3, 7 (October/November 1985): 18-19.

1426 MacGILL, Elsie. *My Mother the Judge: A Biography of Judge Helen Gregory MacGill.* Toronto: Ryerson Press, 1955.

1427 MacKENZIE, Jean. "Nellie Was a Lady." *United Church Observer* 37 (October 1973): 18-19.

1428 MacPHERSON, Kay. *When in Doubt, Do Both: The Times of My Life.* Toronto: University of Toronto Press, 1994.

1429 MARR, Lucille. "'If you want peace, prepare for peace': Hanna Newcombe, Peace Researcher and Peace Activist." *Ontario History* 84, 4 (December 1992): 263-81.

1430 MATHESON, Gwen. "Nellie McClung." *Canadian Dimension* 10, 8 (June 1975): 42-48.

1431 MATHESON, Gwen and V.E. Lang. "Nellie McClung: 'Not a Nice Woman.'" In *Women in the Canadian Mosaic,* ed. Gwen Matheson, 1-20. Toronto: Peter Martin Associates, 1976.

1432 McCLUNG, Nellie. *Clearing in the West.* Toronto: Thomas Allen, 1935; reprint edition, 1976.

1433 McCLUNG, Nellie. *The Stream Runs Fast.* Toronto: Thomas Allen, 1945.

1434 McMANUS, Brie. "Francis Marion Beynon: The Forgotten Suffragist." *Manitoba History* 28 (Autumn 1994): 22-30.

1435 MITCHELL, Penni. "A Monumental Tribute to Nellie McClung." *Herizons* 1, 4 (June 1983): 31-34.

1436 MONET-CHARTRAND, Simonne. *Ma vie comme riv-ière: Récit autobiographique, 1963-1992, tome 4.* Montréal: Éditions du remue-ménage, 1992.

1437 NOELL, Marilyn. *Another Path to My Garden: My Life as a Quadriplegic.* Toronto: Dundurn Press, 1992.

1438 PELLETIER-BAILLARGEON, Hélène. *Marie Gérin-Lajoie: De mère en fille, la cause des femmes.* Montréal: Boréal, 1985.

1439 PELLETIER-BAILLARGEON, Hélène, *et al. Simonne Monet-Chartrand: Un héritage et des projets.* Montréal: Éditions Fides/Éditions du remue-ménage, 1993.

1440 RAY, Janet. *Emily Stowe.* Toronto: Fitzhenry and Whiteside, 1978.

1441 ROBERTS, Barbara. "Women Against War, 1914-1918: Francis Beynon and Laura Hughes." In *Up and Doing: Canadian Women and Peace,* eds. Janice Williamson and Deborah Gorham, 48-65. Toronto: The Women's Press, 1989.

1442 ROOKE, Patricia T. "Public Figure, Private Woman: Same-sex Support Structures in the Life of Charlotte Whitton." *International Journal of Women's Studies* 6, 5 (1983): 412-28.

1443 ROOKE, Patricia T. and R.L. Schnell. "'An Idiot's Flowerbed'—A Study of Charlotte Whitton's Feminist Thought, 1941-50." *International Journal of Women's Studies* 5, 1 (January/February 1982): 29-46. Reprinted in *Rethinking Canada: The Promise of Women's History,* eds. Veronica Strong-Boag and Anita Clair Fellman, 208-25. Toronto: Copp Clark Pitman Ltd., 1986.

1444 ROOKE, Patricia T. and R.L. Schnell. "Chastity as Power: Charlotte Whitton and the Ascetic Ideal." *American Review of Canadian Studies* 15, 4 (1985): 389-403.

1445 ROOKE, Patricia T. and R.L. Schnell. *No Bleeding Heart: Charlotte Whitton, A Feminist on the Right.* Vancouver: University of British Columbia Press, 1987.

1446 SANDERS, Byrne Hope. *Emily Murphy, Crusader.* Toronto: Macmillan, 1945.

1447 SAVAGE, Candace. *Our Nell: A Scrapbook Biography of Nellie L. McClung.* Saskatoon: Western Producer Prairie Books, 1979.

1448 SHEEHAN, Nancy M. "Achieving Personhood: Louise McKinney and the WCTU in Alberta, 1905-30." Women as Persons, Special Publication No. 8. *Resources for Feminist Research* (Fall 1980): 105-8.

1449 SPERDAKOS, Sophia. "'For the joy of the working': Laura Elizabeth McCully, First-Wave Feminist." *Ontario History* 84, 4 (December 1992): 283-314.

1450 STRONG-BOAG, Veronica. "Canadian Feminism in the 1920s: The Case of Nellie McClung." *Journal of Canadian Studies* 12, 4 (Summer 1977): 58-68. Reprinted in *The Prairie West: Historical Readings,* eds. R. Douglas Francis and Howard Palmer, 466-80. Edmonton: Pica Pica Press, 1985.

1451 STRONG-BOAG, Veronica. "'Ever a Crusader': Nellie McClung, First-Wave Feminist." In *Rethinking Canada: The Promise of Women's History,* eds. Veronica Strong-Boag and Anita Clair Fellman, 178-90. Toronto: Copp Clark Pitman Ltd., 1986; 2nd edition, 308-21, 1991.

1452 TAYLOR, Georgina M. "Grace Fletcher, Temperance, Women's Rights and 'British Fair Play' in Saskatoon, 1885-1907." *Saskatchewan History* 46, 1 (Spring 1994): 3-21.

1453 THOMPSON, Joanne Emily. "The Influence of Dr. Emily Howard Stowe on the Woman Suffrage Movement in Canada." *Ontario History* 54, 4 (December 1962): 253-66.

1454 WADE, Susan. "Joan Kennedy and the British Columbia Women's Service Corps." In *Not Just Pin Money: Selected Essays on the History of Women's Work in British Columbia,* eds. Barbara K. Latham and Roberta J. Pazdro, 407-28. Victoria: Camosun College, 1984.

1455 WARNE, R.R. "Nellie McClung and Peace." In *Up and Doing: Canadian Women and Peace,* eds. Janice Williamson and Deborah Gorham, 35-47. Toronto: The Women's Press, 1989.

1456 WARNE, Randi R. "Looking Forward Through the Past: Recalling Nellie McClung." *Women's Education des femmes* 7, 2 (1989): 27-29.

1457 WARNE, Randi R. *Literature as Pulpit: The Christian Social Activism of Nellie L. McClung.* Waterloo: Wilfrid Laurier University Press, 1993.

1458 WRIGHT, Helen K. *Nellie McClung and Women's Rights.* Agincourt, ON: The Book Society of Canada, 1980.

1459 YOUMANS, Letitia. *Campaign Echoes.* Toronto: William Briggs, 1893.

1460 ZEILIG, Martin. "Emma Goldman in Winnipeg." *Manitoba History* 25 (Spring 1993): 23-27.

ISSUES/CAMPAIGNS

1461 ABELLA, Rosalie. *Equality in Employment.* Ottawa: Minister of Supply and Services, 1984.

1462 ADAMSON, Nancy. "Feminists, Libbers, Lefties, and Radicals: The Emergence of the Women's Liberation Movement." In *A Diversity of Women: Ontario, 1945-1980,* ed. Joy Parr, 252-80. Toronto: University of Toronto Press, 1995.

1463 ADAMSON, Nancy, Linda Briskin and Margaret McPhail. *Feminist Organizing for Change: The Contemporary Women's Movement in Canada.* Toronto: Oxford University Press, 1988.

1464 AGNEW, Vijay. "Canadian Feminism and Women of Colour." *Women's Studies International Forum* 16, 3 (1993).

1465 AIRHART, Phyllis D. "'Sweeter Manners, Purer Laws': Women as Temperance Reformers in Late-Victorian Canada." *Touchstone* 9, 3 (Sept. 1991): 21-31.

1466 AJZENSTADT, Mimi. "Cycles of Control: Alcohol Regulation and the Construction of Gender Role, British Columbia 1870-1925." *International Journal of Canadian Studies* 11 (Spring 1995): 101-20.

1467 ANDERSEN, Margret, ed. *Mother Was Not a Person.* Montreal: Content Publishing and Black Rose Books, 1972.

1468 ANDERSEN, Marguerite. "Le Québec: féminisme contemporain et écrits de femmes (1970-1983): Une bibliographie pilote." *Resources for Feminist Research* 12, 4 (December 1983/January 1984): 18-28.

1469 ANDERSEN, Marguerite, Melanie Randall and Anita Sheth, eds. "Transforming Knowledge and Politics." A 20th anniversary double issue of *Resources for Feminist Research* 20, (3/4) (Fall/Winter 1991).

1470 ARSCOTT, Jane. "Twenty-Five Years and Sixty-Five Minutes After the Royal Commission on the Status of Women." *International Journal of Canadian Studies* 11 (Spring 1995): 33-58.

1471 ASSHETON-SMITH, Marilyn and Barbara Spronk, eds. *Women and Social Location: Our Lives, Our Research.* Charlottetown: Gynergy Books, 1993.

1472 BACCHI, Carol. "Liberation Deferred: The Ideas of the English Canadian Suffragists, 1877-1918." *Histoire sociale/Social History* X, 2 (November 1977): 433-34.

1473 BACCHI, Carol. "Race Regeneration and Social Purity: A Study of the Social Attitudes of Canada's English-Speaking Suffragists." *Histoire sociale/Social History* XI, 22 (November 1978): 460-74. Reprinted in *Interpreting Canada's Past: Volume II, After Confederation,* ed. J.M. Bumsted, 192-205. Toronto: Oxford University Press, 1986; 2nd edition, 237-53, 1993.

1474 BACCHI, Carol. "Divided Allegiances: The Response of Farm and Labour Women to Suffrage." In *A Not Unreasonable Claim: Women and Reform in Canada, 1880s-1920s,* ed. Linda Kealey, 89-107. Toronto: The Women's Press, 1979.

1475 BACCHI, Carol. "'First Wave' Feminism in Canada: The Ideas of the English-Canadian Suffragists, 1877-1918." *Women's Studies International Forum* 5, 6 (1982): 575-83.

1476 BACCHI, Carol. *Liberation Deferred? The Ideas of the English Canadian Suffragists, 1877-1918.* Toronto: University of Toronto Press, 1982.

1477 BACKHOUSE, Constance and David H. Flaherty, eds. *Challenging Times: The Women's Movement in Canada and the United States.* Montreal and Kingston: McGill-Queen's University Press, 1992.

1478 BAINES, Carol. *Women's Reform Organizations in Canada, 1870-1930.* Toronto: Faculty of Social Work, University of Toronto, 1988.

1479 BAINES, Carol, Patricia Evans and Sheila Neysmith, eds. *Women's Caring: Feminist Perspectives on Social Welfare.* Toronto: McClelland and Stewart, 1991.

1480 BANNERJI, Himani, *et al.* "Organizing Exclusion: Race, Class, Community and the White Women's Movement." *Fireweed* 17 (Summer/Fall 1983): 57-65.

1481 BASHEVKIN, Sylvia. "Confronting Neo-conservatism: Anglo-American Women's Movements under Thatcher, Reagan and Mulroney." *International Political Science Review* 15, 3 (July 1994): 275-96.

1482 BASILETTI, Mari, Donna Greenwood and Beverly Mills Stretson, eds. *Changing Times: Essays by Island Women.* Charlottetown: The Women's Legal Project of PEI, 1977.

1483 BASSETT, Isabel. *The Parlour Rebellion: Profiles in the struggle for women's rights.* Toronto: McClelland and Stewart, 1975.

1484 BATCHER, Elaine. "Language and the New Woman." *Resources for Feminist Research* 13, 3 (November 1984): 49-51.

1485 BAXTER, Sheila. *No Way to Live: Poor Women Speak Out.* Vancouver: New Star Books, 1988; 2nd edition, 1994.

1486 BAXTER, Sheila. "No Way to Live: Poor Women Speak Out." In *British Columbia Reconsidered: Essays on Women,* eds. Gillian Creese and Veronica Strong-Boag, 416-27. Vancouver: Press Gang Publishers, 1992.

1487 BEAR, Shirley with the Tobique Women's Group. "You Can't Change the Indian Act?" In *Women and Social Change: Feminist Activism in Canada,* eds. Jeri Dawn Wine and Janice L. Ristock, 198-220. Toronto: James Lorimer and Company, 1991.

1488 BEAUDRY, Lucille. "Intervention de la question des femmes dans les groupes de la gauche au Québec (1972-1982): État d'un rapport subversif." In *Reaching Out: Canadian Studies, Women's Studies and Adult Education,* ed. Susan Jackel, 50-68. Ottawa: Canadian Studies Association, 1984.

1489 BEAUDRY, Lucille. "Le féminisme radical au Québec (1969-1985), une réflexion politique en évolution." *Resources for Feminist Research* 15, 1 (March 1986): 44-46.

1490 BÉGIN, Monique. "The Royal Commission on the Status of Women in Canada: Twenty Years Later." In *Challenging Times: The Women's Movement in Canada and the United States,* eds. Constance Backhouse and David H. Flaherty, 21-38. Montreal and Kingston: McGill-Queen's University Press, 1992.

1491 BEHIEL, Janet. *Finding Our Way: Rethinking Eco-Feminist Politics.* Montreal: Black Rose Books, 1990.

1492 BELL, Laurie, ed. *Good Girls/Bad Girls: Sex Trade Workers and Feminists Face to Face.* Toronto: The Women's Press, 1987.

1493 BENNETT, Paul. "The Canadian Women's Movement, 1880-1920s: A Struggle for Political Rights or Social Reform?" In *Emerging Identities: Selected Problems and Interpretations in Canadian History,* eds. Paul W. Bennett and Cornelius J. Jaenen, 376-405. Scarborough: Prentice-Hall Canada, 1986.

1494 BENSTON, Margaret. "The Political Economy of Women's Liberation." *Monthly Review* 21 (September 1969).

1495 BEYNON, Francis Marion. *Aleta Day.* With an introduction by Anne Hicks. London: Virago Press, 1988.

1496 BILLSON, Janet Mancini. "Scottish Ancestry Women of Rice Point, PEI: Feminism and Shifting Roles in a Rural Context." In *The more we get together: Women and Dis/ability,* eds. Houston Stewart, Beth Percival and Elizabeth R. Epperly, 125-37. Charlottetown: Gynergy Books, 1992.

1497 BLACK, Dawn. *Twenty Years Later: An Assessment of the Implementation of the Recommendations of the Royal Commission on the Status of Women.* Ottawa: 1990.

1498 BLACK, Naomi. "The Canadian Women's Movement: The Second Wave." In *Changing Patterns: Women in Canada,* eds. Sandra Burt, Lorraine Code and Lindsay Dorney, 80-102 Toronto: McClelland & Stewart, 1988; revised in 2nd edition, 151-76, 1993.

1499 BLACK, Naomi. "Ripples in the Second Wave: Comparing the Contemporary Women's Movement in Canada and the United States." In *Challenging Times: The Women's Movement in Canada and the United States,* eds. Constance Backhouse and David H. Flaherty, 94-109. Montreal and Kingston: McGill-Queen's University Press, 1992.

1500 BLACK, Naomi and Gail Cuthbert Brandt. "'Il en faut un peu': Farm Women and Feminism in Québec and France Since 1945." *Journal of the Canadian Historical Association,* NS 1 (1990): 73-96.

1501 BLACK, Naomi and Gail Cuthbert Brandt. "Alcohol and the First Canadian Women's Movement." *Études canadiennes/Canadian Studies* 35 (1993): 95-106.

1502 BLUE, J. "Women's Organizations and Activities." In *Alberta Past and Present,* J. Blue. Chicago: Pioneer Historical Publishing, 1924.

1503 BOYD, Monica. "English-Canadian and French-Canadian Attitudes Toward Women: Results of the Canadian Gallup Polls." *Journal of Comparative Family Studies* 6, 2 (Autumn 1975): 153-69.

1504 BOYD, Monica. *Canadian Attitudes Towards Women: Thirty Years of Change.* Ottawa: Labour Canada, Women's Bureau, 1984.

1505 BRANDT, Gail Cuthbert. "Organizations in Canada: The English Protestant Tradition." In *Women's Paid and Unpaid Work: Historical and Contemporary Perspectives,* ed. Paula Bourne, 79-95. Toronto: New Hogtown Press, 1985.

1506 BRODEUR, Violette, *et al. Le mouvement des femmes au Québec, étude des groupes montréalais et nationaux.* Montréal: Ed. Centre de formation populaire, 1982.

1507 BRODIE, Janine. *Politics on the Margins: Restructuring and the Canadian Women's Movement.* Halifax: Fernwood Publishing, 1995.

1508 BRODRIBB, Somer and Diane Lamoureux, eds. "Feminist Practice in Quebec." A special issue of *Resources for Feminist Research* 15, 4 (Dec. 1986/Jan. 1987).

1509 BRUNERS, Daina. "The Influence of the Women's Liberation Movement on the Lives of Canadian Farm Women." *Resources for Feminist Research* 14, 3 (1985): 18-19.

1510 BRYM, Robert J. with Bonnie J. Fox. *From Culture to Power: The Sociology of English Canada.* Toronto: Oxford University Press, 1989.

1511 BURSTYN, Varda, ed. *Women Against Censorship.* Vancouver: Douglas and McIntyre, 1985.

1512 BURSTYN, Varda. "Political Precedents and Moral Crusades: Women, Sex and the State." In *Women Against Censorship,* ed. Varda Burtsyn, 4-31. Vancouver: Douglas and McIntyre, 1985.

1513 BURT, Sandra. "Women's Issues and the Women's Movement in Canada Since 1970." In *The Politics of Gender, Ethnicity and Language in Canada,* eds. Alan Cairns and Cynthia Williams, 111-69. Toronto: University of Toronto Press, 1986.

1514 BURT, Sandra. "Canadian Women's Groups in the 1980s: Organizational Development and Policy Influence." *Canadian Public Policy* 16, 1 (March 1990): 17-28.

1515 BURT, Sandra. "Variations on an Earlier Theme: The Second Wave of the Canadian Women's Movement." In *Canadian Politics: An Introduction to the Discipline,* eds. Alain G. Gagnon and James Bickerton. Peterborough: Broadview Press, 1990.

1516 CANADIAN ADVISORY COUNCIL ON THE STATUS OF WOMEN. *As Things Stand: Ten Years of Recommendations.* Ottawa: Canadian Advisory Council on the Status of Women, 1983.

1517 CARBERT, Louise I. *Agrarian Feminism: The Politics of Ontario Farm Women.* Toronto: University of Toronto Press, 1995.

1518 CARDINAL, Linda. "La recherche sur les femmes francophones vivant en milieu minoritaire: un questionnement sur le féminisme." *Recherches féministes* 5, 1 (1992): 5-29.

1519 CARDINAL, Linda. "Making a Difference: The Theory and Practice of Francophone Women's Groups, 1969-82." In *A Diversity of Women: Ontario, 1945-1980,* ed. Joy Parr, 281-316. Toronto: University of Toronto Press, 1995.

1520 CARDINAL, Linda and Cécile Coderre. "Éducation et identité: l'expérience des femmes francophones vivant en milieu minoritaire." *Éducation et francophonie* 19, 3 (1991): 23-26.

1521 CARNIOU, Juliette. "Les fonctions sociales de l'enseignement agricole féminin." *Études rurales* 92 (oct.-déc. 1983): 41-56.

1522 CARTY, Linda, ed. *And Still We Rise: Feminist Political Mobilizing in Contemporary Canada.* Toronto: Women's Press, 1993.

1523 CASTELLANO, Marlene Brant and Janice Hill. "First Nations Women: Reclaiming Our Responsibilities." In *A Diversity of Women: Ontario, 1945-1980,* ed. Joy Parr, 232-51. Toronto: University of Toronto Press, 1995.

1524 CASTLEMAN, Lana. "Self, Sex and Moral Reform in English Canada." *blurred Genres: A Journal of Writing by Students in the University of Victoria Department of History* 2 (Winter/Spring 1994): 35-49.

1525 CEBOTAREV, E.A. (Nora). "From Domesticity to the Public Sphere: Farm Women, 1945-86." In *A Diversity of Women: Ontario, 1945-1980,* ed. Joy Parr, 200-31. Toronto: University of Toronto Press, 1995.

1526 CHATER, Nancy. "Unexamined History Repeats Itself: Race and Class in the Canadian Reproductive Rights Movement." *Fireweed* 33 (Summer 1991): 44-60.

1527 CHOWN, Alice A. *The Stairway.* With an introduction by Diana Chown. Toronto: University of Toronto Press, 1988.

1528 CLARK, Lorenne and Debra Lewis. *Rape: The Price of Coercive Sexuality.* Toronto: The Women's Press, 1977.

1529 CLEVERDON, Catherine Lyle. *The Woman Suffrage Movement in Canada,* 2nd edition. With an introduction by Ramsay Cook. Toronto: University of Toronto Press, 1970.

1530 CLICHE, Marie-Aimée. "Droits égaux ou influence accrue? Nature et role de la femme d'après les féministes chrétiennes et les antiféministes au Québec 1896-1930." *Recherches féministes* 2, 2 (1989): 101-20.

1531 CODERRE, Cécile. "Les luttes de femmes contre la pornographie: bref historique Québécois." *Resources for Feminist Research* 15, 4 (December 1986/January 1987): 7-9.

1532 COHEN, Marjorie Griffin. "The Canadian Women's Movement and Its Efforts to Influence the Canadian Economy." In *Challenging Times: The Women's Movement in Canada and the United States*, eds. Constance Backhouse and David H. Flaherty, 215-24. Montreal and Kingston: McGill-Queen's University Press, 1992.

1533 COHEN, Marjorie Griffin. "The Canadian Women's Movement." In *Canadian Women's Issues, Volume I: Strong Voices*, Ruth Roach Pierson, Marjorie Griffin Cohen, Paula Bourne and Philanda Masters, 1-97. Toronto: James Lorimer and Company, 1994.

1534 COHEN, Yolande, ed. *Femmes et politique*. Montréal: Le Jour, 1981.

1535 COHEN, Yolande. "Pouvoirs et contre-pouvoirs: la place des femmes." *Possibles* 9, 2 (hiver 1985): 75-86.

1536 COHEN, Yolande, ed. *Femmes et Contre-pouvoir*. Montréal: Boréal Express, 1987.

1537 COHEN, Yolande. "La journée des femmes: fermières et sociabilité rurale." In *La radicalité du quotidien*, eds. M.-B. Tahon and A. Cohen, 145-55. Montréal: VLB, 1987.

1538 COHEN, Yolande. "Pour ou contre un espace politique aux femmes?" In *Encrages féministes: Un moment de reflexion dans la recherche féministe*, ed. Isabelle Lasvergnas, 33-50. Montréal: Université du Québec à Montréal, Centre de recherche féministe, Group interdisciplinaire d'enseignement et de recherche féministes, 1989.

1539 COHEN, Yolande, ed. *Women and Counter-Power*. Montreal: Black Rose Books, 1989.

1540 COHEN, Yolande. "La participation des femmes à la modernisation du monde rural." In *Le Québec rural dans tous ses états*, ed. B. Vachon, 167-83. Montréal: Boréal, 1991.

1541 COHEN, Yolande. "Du féminin au féminisme: l'exemple québécois." In *Histoire des Femmes, Tome 5: Le vingtième siècle*, eds. Georges Duby and Michelle Perrot, 521-38. Paris: Plon, 1992.

1542 COHEN, Yolande. "From Feminine to Feminism in Quebec." In *A History of Women in the West, v. 5 Toward a Cultural Identity in the Twentieth Century*, eds. Georges Duby and Michelle Perrot, 548-66. London and Cambridge, MA: Belknap Press of Harvard University Press, 1994.

1543 COHEN, Yolande. "Femmes, citoyenneté et politique dans les années 1920 et 1930 au Québec." *Cahiers du GEDISST: Travail, politique et genre. Politique internationale* 9/10, IRESCO/CNRS (Paris) 1994: 121-32.

1544 COHEN, Yolande. "Le rôle des mouvements de femmes dans l'élargissement de la citoyenneté au Québec." In *Québec: Etat et société*, ed. Alain G. Gagnon, 173-94. Montréal: Québec/Amérique, 1994.

1545 COLE, Susan G. *Pornography and the Sex Crisis*. Toronto: Amanita, 1989.

1546 CONCORDIA UNIVERSITY, OFFICE OF THE STATUS OF WOMEN. *Fifty Years of Women's Right to Vote in Quebec: Viewpoints of Women From Different Minority Groups*. Montreal: Concordia University, Office of the Status of Women, 1993.

1547 CONNELLY, M. Patricia and Pat Armstrong, eds. *Feminism in Action: Studies in Political Economy*. Toronto: Canadian Scholars' Press, 1993.

1548 CORBEIL, Carol. *Femmes, féminisme et maternité: une bibliographie sélective*. Montréal: Centre de recherche féministe, Université du Québec à Montréal, 1989.

1549 CORBET, Elise A. "Women's Canadian Club of Calgary." *Alberta History* 25, 3 (Summer 1977): 29-36.

1550 COUILLARD, Marie-Andrée. "Le pouvoir dans les groupes de femmes de la région de Québec." *Recherches sociographiques* 35, 1 (1994): 39-65.

1551 CRAMER, Michael H. "Public and Political: Documents of the Woman's Suffrage Campaign in British Columbia, 1871-1917: The View from Victoria." In *In Her Own Right: Selected Essays on Women's History in BC*, eds. Barbara Latham and Cathy Kess, 79-100. Victoria: Camosun College, 1980. Reprinted in *British Columbia Reconsidered: Essays on Women*, eds. Gillian Creese and Veronica Strong-Boag, 55-72. Vancouver: Press Gang Publishers, 1992.

1552 CURRIE, Dawn H. "Representation and Resistance: Feminist Struggles Against Pornography." In *The Anatomy of Gender: Women's Struggle for the Body*, eds. Dawn H. Currie and Valerie Raoul, 191-208. Ottawa: Carleton University Press, 1992.

1553 D'AUGEROT-AREND, Sylvie. "Les concepts d'égalité et de spécificité dans les arguments en faveur du suffrage féminin au Canada anglais et États-Unis." *Atlantis* 13, 1 (Fall 1987): 1-12.

1554 D'AUGEROT-AREND, Sylvie. "Why So Late? Cultural and Institutional Factors in the Granting of Quebec and French Women's Political Rights." *Journal of Canadian Studies* 26, 1 (Spring 1991): 138-65.

1555 DAGG, Anne Innis. *The 50% Solution: Why Should Women Pay for Men's Culture?* Waterloo: Otter Press, 1986.

1556 DAS GUPTA, Tania. *Learning From Our History: Community Development by Immigrant Women in Ontario, 1958-1986: A Tool for Action*. Toronto: Cross Cultural Communication Centre, 1986.

1557 DEMERS, Jeanne and Line McMurray, eds. *Femmes scandales, 1965-1985*. Outremont, QC: La nouvelle barre du jour, 1987.

1558 DÉPATIE, F. "La femme dans la vie économique et sociale du Québec." *Forces* 27 (1974): 15-23.

1559 DE SÈVE, Micheline. *Pour un féminisme libertaire*. Montréal: Boréal Express, 1985.

1560 DE SÈVE, Micheline. "The Perspectives of Quebec Feminists." In *Challenging Times: The Women's Movement in Canada and the United States,* eds. Constance Backhouse and David H. Flaherty, 110-16. Montreal and Kingston: McGill-Queen's University Press, 1992.

1561 DESJARDINS, Marc. "Les lièvres et les tortues? Les mouvements féministes et le droit à l'égalité aux États-Unis et au Canada." *Études canadiennes/Canadian Studies* 33 (1992): 235-48.

1562 DESROCHERS, Lucie. *Femmes et pouvoir, la Révolution tranquille.* Québec: Conseil du statut de la femme, 1993.

1563 DODDS, Michelle. "Vote Without Victory: The Paradoxical Situation of the Prairie Farm Woman, 1910-1930." *Manitoba History* 22 (autumn 1991): 19-22.

1564 DOERR, Audrey. "Women's Rights in Canada: Social and Economic Realities." *Atlantis* 9, 2 (Spring 1984): 35-47.

1565 DULEY, Margot Iris. "'The Radius of Her Influence for Good': The Rise and Triumph of the Women's Suffrage Movement in Newfoundland, 1909-1925." In *Pursuing Equality: Historical Perspectives on Women in Newfoundland and Labrador,* ed. Linda Kealey, 14-65. St. John's: Memorial University of Newfoundland, Institute of Social and Economic Research, 1993.

1566 DULEY, Margot Iris. *Where Once Our Mothers Stood We Stand: Women's Suffrage in Newfoundland, 1890-1925.* Charlottetown: Gynergy Books, 1993.

1567 DULUDE, Louise. "The Status of Women Under the Mulroney Government." In *Canada Under Mulroney: An End-of-Term Report,* eds. Andrew B. Gollner and Daniel Salée. Montreal: Véhicule Press, 1988.

1568 DUMONT, Micheline. *Le mouvement des femmes, hier et aujourd'hui.* Ottawa: Institut canadien de recherches sur les femmes, 1986.

1569 DUMONT, Micheline. "The Origins of the Women's Movement in Quebec." In *Challenging Times: The Women's Movement in Canada and the United States,* eds. Constance Backhouse and David H. Flaherty, 72-89. Montreal and Kingston: McGill-Queen's University Press, 1992.

1570 DUMONT, Micheline. "Le mouvement des femmes à Sherbrooke." *Possibles* 18, 4 (automne 1994): 51-63.

1571 DUMONT, Micheline, *et al.* "The Turbulent Years: Feminism Ignites." In *The Challenge of Modernity: A Reader on Post-Confederation Canada,* ed. Ian McKay, 387-93. Toronto: McGraw-Hill Ryerson, 1992.[excerpted from *Quebec Women: A History*]

1572 EARLY, Frances H. "The Historic Roots of the Women's Peace Movement in North America." *Canadian Woman Studies* 7, 4 (Winter 1986): 43-48.

1573 EGAN, Carolyn, *et al.* "The Politics of Transformation: Struggles with Race, Class and Sexuality in the March 8th Coalition." In *Social Movements/Social Change: The Politics and Practice of Organizing,* eds. Frank Cunningham, *et al,* 20 47. Toronto: Between the Lines, 1988.

1574 EICHLER, Margrit. "Sociology of Feminist Research in Canada." *Signs* 3, 2 (Winter 1977): 409-22.

1575 ERRINGTON, Jane. "Pioneers and Suffragists." In *Changing Patterns: Women in Canada,* eds. Sandra Burt, Lorraine Code and Lindsay Dorney, 51-79. Toronto: McClelland & Stewart, 1988; revised in 2nd edition, 59-91, 1993.

1576 FAITH, Karlene, Mary Gottfriedson, Cherry Joe, Wendy Leonard and Sharon McIvor. "Native Women in Canada: A Quest for Justice." *Social Justice* 17, 3 (1990): 167-88.

1577 FALLDING, Helen. "A Decade of Lesbian Organizing." *Canadian Woman Studies* 14, 4 (Fall 1994): 24-26.

1578 FEMMES EN TÊTE. *De travail et d'espoir. Des groupes de femmes racontent le féminisme.* Montréal: Éditions du remue-ménage, 1990.

1579 FERGIE, Lynne, *et al.,* eds. "Lesbiantics." A special issue of *Fireweed* 13 (Summer 1982).

1580 FINDLAY, Sue. "Facing the State: The Politics of the Women's Movement Reconsidered." In *Feminism and Political Economy: Women's Work, Women's Struggles,* eds. Heather Jon Maroney and Meg Luxton, 31-50. Toronto: Methuen, 1987.

1581 FINDLAY, Sue. "Feminist Struggles with the Canadian State: 1966-1988." *Resources for Feminist Research* 17, 3 (September 1988).

1582 FINDLAY, Sue and Melanie Randall, eds. "Feminist Perspectives on the Canadian State." A special issue of *Resources for Feminist Research* 17, 3 (September 1988).

1583 FINN, Geraldine, ed. *Limited Edition: Voices of Women, Voices of Feminism.* Halifax: Fernwood Publishing Ltd., 1993.

1584 FITZGERALD, Maureen, Connie Guberman and Margie Wolfe, eds. *Still Ain't Satisfied: Canadian Feminism Today.* Toronto: The Women's Press, 1982.

1585 FLANAGAN, Thomas. "Equal Pay for Work of Equal Value: An Historical Note." *Journal of Canadian Studies* 22, 3 (Fall 1987): 5-19.

1586 FORBES, Ernest. "The Ideas of Carol Bacchi and the Suffragists of Halifax: A Review Essay on *Liberation Deferred? The Ideas of the English Canadian Suffragists, 1877-1918.*" *Atlantis* 10, 2 (Spring 1985): 119-26. Reprinted in his *Challenging the Regional Stereotype,* 90-99. Fredericton: Acadiensis Press, 1989.

1587 FUDGE, Judy and Patricia McDermott, eds. *Just Wages: A Feminist Assessment of Pay Equity.* Toronto: University of Toronto Press, 1991.

1588 GAGNON, Mona-Josée. *Les femmes vues par le Québec des hommes: 30 ans d'histoire des idéologies, 1940-1970.* Montréal: Éditions du jour, 1974.

1589 GALANA, L. and G. Covina. *The New Lesbians: Interviews with Women Across the U.S. and Canada.* New York: Random House, 1977.

1590 GARIGUE, Philippe. "La participation des femmes au développement du Québec." *La Canadienne* 18 (Oct. 1965): 6-9.

1591 GELLER, Gloria. "The Wartime Elections Act of 1917 and the Canadian Women's Movement." *Atlantis* 2, 1 (Fall 1976): 88-106.

1592 GERMAIN, Annick. "L'émergence d'une scène politique: mouvement ouvrier et mouvements de réforme urbaine à Montréal au tournant du siècle—Essai d'interpretation." *Revue d'histoire de l'Amérique française* 37, 2 (septembre 1983): 185-200.

1593 GILROY, Joan. "Social Work and the Women's Movement." In *Social Work and Social Change in Canada,* ed. Brian Wharf. Toronto: McClelland and Stewart, 1990.

1594 GIROUX, Nicole. "Des femmes et des coopératives: une histoire à écrire." *Canadian Woman Studies* 7, 4 (Winter 1986): 39-42.

1595 GORHAM, Deborah. "English Militancy and the Canadian Suffrage Movement." *Atlantis* 1, 1 (Fall 1975): 83-112.

1596 GORHAM, Deborah. "Singing Up the Hill." *Canadian Dimension* 10, 8 (June 1975): 26-38. Reprinted in *Readings in Canadian History: Post-Confederation,* 3rd edition, eds. R. Douglas Francis and Donald B. Smith, 267-86. Toronto: Holt, Rinehart and Winston, 1990; 4th edition, 267-85, Harcourt Brace Canada, 1994.

1597 GORHAM, Deborah. "The Canadian Suffragists." In *Women in the Canadian Mosaic,* ed. Gwen Matheson, 23-56. Toronto: Peter Martin Associates, 1976.

1598 GOTELL, Lise. "Employment Equity for Women: A Bibliography." *Resources for Feminist Research* 16, 4 (1987): 48-49.

1599 GOULD, K. "Spatial Poetics, Spatial Politics: Quebec Feminists on the City and the Countryside." *American Review of Canadian Studies* 12, 2 (Spring 1982): 1-9.

1600 GRAVELINE, M. Jean, Katherine A.Fitzpatrick, and Barbara E. Mark. "Networking in Northern Manitoba." In *Women and Social Change: Feminist Activism in Canada,* eds. Jeri Dawn Wine and Janice L. Ristock, 134-47. Toronto: James Lorimer and Company, 1991.

1601 GUBERMAN, Connie and Margie Wolfe, eds. *No Safe Place: Violence Against Women and Children.* Toronto: The Women's Press, 1985.

1602 GUETTEL, Charnie. *Marxism and Feminism.* Toronto: Women's Press, 1974.

1603 GUNDERSON, Morley. "Equal Pay in Canada: History, Progress and Problems." In *Equal Pay for Women,* ed. Barrie Pettman, 129-46. Washington: Hemisphere, 1977.

1604 HALE, Linda Louise. "Votes for Women: Profiles of Prominent British Columbia Suffragists and Social Reformers." In *In Her Own Right: Selected Essays on Women's History in BC,* eds. Barbara Latham and Cathy Kess, 287-302. Victoria: Camosun College, 1980.

1605 HAMILTON, Roberta. "Feminism and Motherhood, 1970-1990: Reinventing the Wheel?" *Resources for Feminist Research* 19, 3/4 (September/December 1990): 23-32.

1606 HAMILTON, Roberta. "Feminist Theories." *left history* 1, 1 (Spring 1993): 9-33.

1607 HAMILTON, Roberta and Michèle Barrett, eds. *The Politics of Diversity: Feminism, Marxism and Nationalism.* Montreal: Book Centre Inc., 1986.

1608 HEATH, T.C. "Protest Songs of Saskatchewan." *Saskatchewan History* 25, 3 (Autumn 1972): 81-91. [includes song by the Wiseton Women Grain Growers' Association]

1609 HERNANDEZ, Carmencita R. "The Coalition of Visible Minority Women." In *Social Movements/Social Change: The Politics and Practice of Organizing,* eds. Frank Cunningham, *et al,* Toronto: Between the Lines, 1988.

1610 HOBBS, Margaret. "Equality and Difference: Feminism and the Defence of Women Workers During the Great Depression." *Labour/Le Travail* 32 (Fall 1993): 201-23. Reprinted in *Canadian Women: A Reader,* eds. Wendy Mitchinson, *et al,* 212-33. Toronto: Harcourt Brace Canada, 1996.

1611 HOLT, Faye Reinberg. "Women's Suffrage in Alberta." *Alberta History* 39, 4 (Autumn 1991): 25-31.

1612 HOUDEBINE-GRAVAUD, Anne-Marie. "Sur la féminisation des noms de métiers en français contemporain." *Recherches féministes* 5, 1 (1992): 153-59.

1613 HUGHES, Nym, Yvonne Johnson and Yvette Perrault. *Stepping Out of Line: A Workbook on Lesbianism and Feminism.* Vancouver: Press Gang, 1984.

1614 HYNES, Maureen. "A History of the Rise of Women's Consciousness in Canada and Quebec." In *The Hidden History of the Female,* ed. M. Atkins, Toronto: New Hogtown Press, 1971.

1615 JACKEL, Susan. "First Days, Fighting Days: Prairie Presswomen and Suffrage Activism, 1906-1916." In *First Days, Fighting Days: Women in Manitoba History,* ed. Mary Kinnear, 53-75. Regina: Canadian Plains Research Center, University of Regina, 1987.

1616 JACOBSON, Helga E. and Naida D. Hyde. "Still Kissing the Rod: Women and Violence in British Columbia." In *British Columbia Reconsidered: Essays on Women,* eds. Gillian Creese and Veronica Strong-Boag, 217-29. Vancouver: Press Gang Publishers, 1992.

1617 JAMESON, Sheilagh S. "Give Your Other Vote to the Sister." *Alberta Historical Review* 15, 4 (Autumn 1967): 10-16.

1618 JAMIESON, Kathleen. "Multiple Jeopardy: The Evolution of a Native Women's Movement." *Atlantis* 4, 2 (1979): 157-78.

1619 JEAN, Michèle. "La femme au passé." *Forum* 7, 22 (February 1973): 4-5.

1620 JEAN, Michèle. "Condition féminine et féminisme au Québec: Où en-sommes nous?" *Communauté chrétienne* 16, 95 (septembre/octobre 1977): 441-49.

1621 JEAN, Michèle. "Histoire des luttes féministes au Québec." *Possibles* 4, 1 (automne 1979): 17-32.

1622 JEAN, Michèle. "Two Decades of Feminism in Quebec, 1960-1979." *Fireweed* 5/6 (Winter 1979/80-Spring 1980): 189-93.

1623 JOHNSON, Kirsten K. *Undressing the Canadian State: The Politics of Pornography from Hicklin to Butler.* Halifax: Fernwood Publishing, 1995.

1624 KALMAKOFF, Elizabeth. "Naturally Divided: Women in Saskatchewan Politics, 1916-1919." *Saskatchewan History* 46, 2 (Fall 1994): 3-18.

1625 KEALEY, Linda, ed. *A Not Unreasonable Claim: Women and Reform in Canada, 1880s-1920s.* Toronto: The Women's Press, 1979.

1626 KINNEAR, Mary. "The Icelandic Connection: *Freyja* and the Manitoba Woman Suffrage Movement." *Canadian Woman Studies* 7, 4 (Winter 1986): 25-28.

1627 KIRKNESS, Verna. "Emerging Native Woman." *Canadian Journal of Women and the Law* 2, 2 (1987/88): 408-15.

1628 KROKER, Marilouise, *et al.,* eds. *Feminism Now: Theory and Practice.* Montreal: New World Perspectives, 1985. Co-published as *Canadian Journal of Political and Social Theory* 9, 1/2 (1985).

1629 KRONBERG, Mona. "Brief Summary of a Decade of Affirmative Action in Canada." *Canadian Women's Studies* 6, 4 (1984/85): 17-19.

1630 LACHAPELLE, Caroline. "Beyond Barriers: Native Women and the Women's Movement." In *Still Ain't Satisfied! Canadian Feminism Today,* eds. Maureen Fitzgerald, Connie Guberman and Margie Wolfe, 257-64. Toronto: The Women's Press, 1982.

1631 LACOMBE, Dany. *Blue Politics: Pornography and the Law in the Age of Feminism.* Toronto: University of Toronto Press, 1994.

1632 LAMONT, Michèle. "Les rapports politiques au sein du mouvement des femmes au Québec." *Politiques* 5 (hiver 1984): 75-106.

1633 LAMOTHE, Jacqueline and Celine Labrosse. "Un fragment du féminisme québécois des années 80: la féminisation linguistique." *Recherches féministes* 5, 1 (1992): 143-51.

1634 LAMOUREUX, Diane. *Fragments et collages: Essai sur le féminisme québécois des années 70.* Montréal: Éditions du remue-ménage, 1986.

1635 LAMOUREUX, Diane. "Nationalism and Feminism in Quebec: An Impossible Attraction." In *Feminism and Political Economy: Women's Work, Women's Struggles,* eds. Heather Jon Maroney and Meg Luxton, 51-68. Toronto: Methuen, 1987.

1636 LAMOUREUX, Diane. *Entre le féminin et le féminisme.* Québec: Laboratoire d'études politiques et administratives, Département de science politique, Faculté des sciences sociales, Université Laval, 1991.

1637 LAMOUREUX, Diane and Jacinthe Michaud. "Les parlementaires canadiens et le suffrage féminin: un aperçu des débats." *Canadian Journal of Political Science* 21, 2 (June 1988): 319-29.

1638 LANDSBERG, Michèle. *Women and Children First.* Toronto: McClelland and Stewart, 1982.

1639 LANGFORD, Jan. "First Nations Women: Leaders in Community Development." *Canadian Woman Studies* 14, 4 (Fall 1994): 34-36.

1640 LAURIN-FRENETTE, Nicole. "La libération des femmes." In *Les femmes dans la société québécoise: Aspects historiques,* eds. Marie Lavigne and Yolande Pinard. Montréal: Boréal Express, 1977. Reprinted in *Travailleuses et féministes: Les femmes dans la société québécoise,* eds. Marie Lavigne and Yolande Pinard, 359-87. Montréal: Boréal Express, 1983.

1641 LAVIGNE, Marie and Michèle Jean. "40 ans de vote...et après." *La Gazette des Femmes* 2, 1 (avril 1980): 8-10.

1642 LEAH, Ronnie and Cydney Ruecker. "Saskatchewan Women Respond to Cutbacks: The Founding of a Provincial Women's Coalition." In *Women and Social Change: Feminist Activism in Canada,* eds. Jeri Dawn Wine and Janice L. Ristock, 117-33. Toronto: James Lorimer and Company, 1991.

1643 LEMIEUX, Denise. "Mouvements sociaux et culture: Le mouvement féministe au Québec." *Journal of Canadian Studies* 30, 1 (Spring 1995): 75-89.

1644 LENSKYJ, Helen Jefferson. "What's Sport Got to Do with It?" *Canadian Woman Studies* 15, 4 (Fall 1995): 6-10.

1645 LESBIANS MAKING HISTORY COLLECTIVE. "People Think This Didn't Happen in Canada—But It Did." *Fireweed* 28 (Spring 1989): 81-86, 142.

1646 LESTER, Tanya. "A Bevy of Firsts." *Herizons* 1, 4 (June 1983): 28-29. [accomplishments of Manitoba women in former male bastions]

1647 LOCKHERST, Augusta and Raymonde Lincourt. "Bilan du Centre d'Aide du viol." *Canadian Women's Studies* 2, 2 (1980): 95-96.

1648 LORTIE, Monique. "Women's Suffrage in Canada – A Brief Look." *Contact* 20 (February 1977): 3-16.

1649 MacDONALD, Christine. "How Saskatchewan Women Got the Vote." *Saskatchewan History* 1, 3 (October 1948): 1-9.

1650 MacDONALD, Flora. "The Status and Economic Prospects of Women in Canada." *Queen's Quarterly* 90, 3 (1983): 655-62.

1651 MacLAREN, Sherrill. *Invisible Power: Behind the Scenes with Canadian Women of Influence.* Toronto: Seal Books, 1991.

1652 MacLEAN, Una. "The Famous Five." *Alberta Historical Review* 10, 2 (Spring 1962): 1-4. [Persons Case]

1653 MacPHEE, Susan C. *Talking Peace: The Women's International Peace Conference.* Charlottetown: Ragweed Press, 1990.

1654 MacPHERSON, Kay. "The Seeds of the Seventies." *Canadian Dimension* 10, 8 (June 1975): 39-41.

1655 MAHOOD, Sally. "The Women's Suffrage Movement in Canada and Saskatchewan." In *Women Unite!: An Anthology of the Canadian Women's Movement*, 21-30. Toronto: Canadian Women's Educational Press, 1972.

1656 MALENFANT, Romaine with Madeleine Blanchet. "Le droit au retrait préventif de la travailleuse enceinte ou qui allaite: à la recherche d'un consensus." *Sociologie et sociétés* 25, 1 (printemps 1993): 61-76.

1657 MANION, Eileen. "We Objects Object: Pornography and the Women's Movement." *Canadian Journal of Political and Social Theory* 9, 1/2 1985): 65-80.

1658 MARCHAK, Patricia. "A Critical Review of the Status of Women Report." *Canadian Review of Sociology and Anthropology* 9 (1972): 73-85.

1659 MARION, Donna. "Raising a Feminist Voice: Interview with Deborah Holmberg-Schwartz and Penni Mitchell." *Women's Education des femmes* 7, 1 (1989): 13-16. [*Herizons* magazine]

1660 MARSHALL, Barbara L. "Studying the Second Wave: Recent Work on the Canadian Women's Movement." *Journal of Canadian Studies* 29, 4 (Winter 1994/95): 162-70.

1661 MASSON, Dominique and Pierre-André Tremblay. "Mouvement des femmes et développement local." *Canadian Journal of Regional Science* 16, 2 (Summer 1993): 165-83.

1662 McCLUNG, Nellie. *In Times Like These.* With an introduction by Veronica Strong-Boag. Toronto: University of Toronto Press, 1972.

1663 McCLUNG, Nellie. *Purple Springs.* With an introduction by Randi R. Warne. Toronto: University of Toronto Press, 1992.

1664 MENZIES, June. "Votes for Saskatchewan Women." In *Politics in Saskatchewan*, eds. Norman Ward and Duff Spafford, 78-92. Toronto: Longmans, 1968.

1665 MILES, Angela and Geraldine Finn, eds. *Feminism: From Pressure to Politics.* Montreal: Black Rose Books, 1988.

1666 MILROY, Beth Moore and Susan Wismer. "Communities, Work and Public/Private Sphere Models." *Gender, Place and Culture* 1, 1 (1994): 71-90. [women's community work in Kitchener-Waterloo, 1900-1980]

1667 MITCHELL, Penni. "Linking Past and Present." *Herizons* 1, 4 (June 1983): 17-26. [photo essay on Manitoba women's movement]

1668 MITCHINSON, Wendy. "Early Women's Organizations and Social Reform: Prelude to the Welfare State." In *The 'Benevolent' State: The Growth of Welfare in Canada*, eds. Allan Moscovitch and Jim Albert, 77-92. Toronto: Garamond Press, 1987.

1669 MONTONEN, Susan, Beth Moore Milroy and Susan Wismer. "Community-Building in Berlin: Mary Ratz Kaufman, 1856-1943." *Waterloo Historical Society* 78 (1990): 54-61.

1670 MORRIS, Cerise. "'Determination and Thoroughness': The Movement for a Royal Commission on the Status of Women in Canada." *Atlantis* 5, 2 (Spring 1980): 1-21.

1671 MORRISON, T.R. "'Their Proper Sphere': Feminism, the Family and Child-centered Social Reform in Ontario, 1875-1900." *Ontario History* 68, 1 (March 1976) and 68, 2 (June 1976).

1672 NATIONAL COUNCIL OF WOMEN OF CANADA. *Women of Canada: Their Life and Work* (1900). Toronto: National Council of Women of Canada, 1975.

1673 NEMIROFF, Greta Hofman. *Interesting Times: Women in Canada, 1970-1990.* Ottawa: Canadian Advisory Council on the Status of Women, 1991.

1674 NG, Roxana. "Finding Our Voices: Reflections on Immigrant Women's Organizing." In *Women and Social Change: Feminist Activism in Canada*, eds. Jeri Dawn Wine and Janice L. Ristock, 184-97. Toronto: James Lorimer and Company, 1991.

1675 NG, Winnie. "Immigrant Women: The Silent Partners of the Women's Movement." In *Still Ain't Satisfied: Canadian Feminism Today*, eds. M. Fitzgerald, *et al*, 249-56. Toronto: Women's Press, 1982.

1676 NIELSEN, Sharon Froese and Patricia Froese, eds. "Women Working for Peace." A special issue of *Canadian Woman Studies* 9, 1 (Spring 1988).

1677 NORELL, Donna. "'The most humane institution in all the village': The Women's Rest Room in Rural Manitoba." *Manitoba History* 11 (Spring 1986): 38-50.

1678 NUNES, Maxine and Deanna White. *The Lace Ghetto.* Toronto: New Press, 1973.

1679 OGG, Kathryn. "'Especially When No One Agrees': An Interview with May Campbell." In *Not Just Pin Money: Selected Essays on the History of Women's Work in British Columbia*, eds. Barbara K. Latham and Roberta J. Pazdro, 237-47. Victoria: Camosun College, 1984. [credit union activist]

1680 OLSON, Sherry. "Paternalism and Urban Reform: An Introduction." *Urban History Review* 17, 3 (February 1989): 143-47.

1681 OUELLETTE, Françoise-Romaine. *Les groupes de femmes du Québec, en 1985: champs d'intervention, structures et moyens d'action.* Québec: Conseil du statut de la femme, 1986.

1682 PAGE, Donald. "The Development of a Western Canadian Peace Movement." In *The Twenties in Canada,* ed. Susan Mann Trofimenkoff, 75-106. Ottawa: National Museum of Man, 1972.

1683 PAL, Leslie A. *Interests of State: The Politics of Language, Multiculturalism, and Feminism in Canada.* Montreal and Kingston: McGill-Queen's University Press, 1993.

1684 PAQUETTE, Carmen. "Personal Reflections on Lesbian Organizing in Ottawa." In *Lesbians in Canada,* ed. Sharon Dale Stone, 221-29. Toronto: Between the Lines, 1990.

1685 PAQUETTE, Louise. *La situation socio-économique des femmes: fait et chiffres.* Québec: Publications de Québec, 1989.

1686 PAZDRO, Roberta J. "Of British Columbia Suffragists and Barristers." *Canadian Journal of Women and the Law* 1, 1 (1985): 15-17.

1687 PESTIEAU, Caroline. "Women in Quebec." In *Women in the Canadian Mosaic,* ed. Gwen Matheson, 57-69. Toronto: Peter Martin Associates, 1976.

1688 PIERSON, Ruth Roach, ed. *Women and Peace: Theoretical, Historical and Practical Perspectives.* London: Croom Helm, 1987.

1689 PIERSON, Ruth Roach. "The Politics of the Body." In *Canadian Women's Issues, Volume I: Strong Voices,* Ruth Roach Pierson, Marjorie Griffin Cohen, Paula Bourne and Philanda Masters, 98-185. Toronto: James Lorimer and Company, 1994.

1690 PIERSON, Ruth Roach. "The Mainstream Women's Movement and the Politics of Difference." In *Canadian Women's Issues, Volume I: Strong Voices,* Ruth Roach Pierson, Marjorie Griffin Cohen, Paula Bourne and Philanda Masters, 186-263. Toronto: James Lorimer and Company, 1994.

1691 PIERSON, Ruth Roach. "Global Issues." In *Canadian Women's Issues, Volume II: Bold Visions,* Ruth Roach Pierson and Marjorie Griffin Cohen, 360-465. Toronto: James Lorimer and Company, 1995.

1692 PIERSON, Ruth Roach and Marjorie Griffin Cohen. *Canadian Women's Issues, Volume II: Bold Visions.* Toronto: James Lorimer and Company, 1995.

1693 PIERSON, Ruth Roach, Marjorie Griffin Cohen, Paula Bourne and Philanda Masters. *Canadian Women's Issues, Volume I: Strong Voices.* Toronto: James Lorimer and Company, 1994.

1694 PINARD, Yolande. "Les débuts du mouvement des femmes." In *Les femmes dans la société québécoise: Aspects historiques,* eds. Marie Lavigne and Yolande Pinard, 89-108. Montréal: Boréal Express, 1977.

1695 PINARD, Yolande. "Les débuts du mouvement des femmes à Montréal, 1893-1902." In *Travailleuses et féministes: Les femmes dans la société québécoise,* eds. Marie Lavigne and Yolande Pinard, 177-98. Montréal: Boréal Express, 1983.

1696 POELZER, Dolores T. and Irene A Poelzer. *In Our Words: Northern Saskatchewan Metis Women Speak Out.* Saskatoon: Lindenblatt and Hamonic, 1986.

1697 POPE, Sharon Gray and Jane Burnham. "Change Within and Without: The Modern Women's Movement in Newfoundland and Labrador." In *Pursuing Equality: Historical Perspectives on Women in Newfoundland and Labrador,* ed. Linda Kealey, 163-256. St. John's: Memorial University of Newfoundland, Institute of Social and Economic Research, 1993.

1698 RANDALL, Melanie. "Feminist Theory, Political Philosophy and the Politics of Reproduction: An Annotated Bibliography." *Resources for Feminist Research* 18, 3 (1989): 111-22.

1699 REDDIN, J. Estelle. "Organizing in a Small Community—Prince Edward Island." In *Women and Social Change: Feminist Activism in Canada,* eds. Jeri Dawn Wine and Janice L. Ristock, 148-68. Toronto: James Lorimer and Company, 1991.

1700 RISTOCK, Janice L. "Canadian Feminist Social Service Collectives: Caring and Contradictions." In *Bridges of Power: Multicultural Women's Alliances,* eds. Lisa Albrecht and Rose M. Brewer, 172-81. Philadelphia: New Society Publishers, 1990.

1701 RISTOCK, Janice and Jeri Dawn Wine, eds. *Feminist Community Organizing in Canada: From Activism to Academe.* Toronto: University of Toronto Press, 1990.

1702 ROBERTS, Barbara. "Sex, Politics and Religion: Controversies in Female Immigration Reform Work in Montreal, 1881-1919." *Atlantis* 6, 1 (1980): 25-38.

1703 ROBERTS, Barbara. "Women's Peace Activism in Canada." In *Beyond the Vote: Canadian Women and Politics,* eds. Linda Kealey and Joan Sangster, 276-308. Toronto: University of Toronto Press, 1989.

1704 ROBERTS, Barbara. "Ladies, Women and the State: Managing Female Immigration, 1880-1920." In *Community Organization and the Canadian State,* eds. Roxana Ng, Gillian Walker and Jacob Muller, 108-30. Toronto: Garamond Press, 1990.

1705 ROBERTS, Julian V. and Renate M. Mohr, eds. *Confronting Sexual Assault in Canada: A Decade of Legal and Social Change.* Toronto: University of Toronto Press, 1994.

1706 ROBERTS, Wayne. "Six New Women: A Guide to the Mental Map of Women Reformers in Toronto." *Atlantis* 3, 1 (Fall 1977): 145-64.

1707 ROBERTS, Wayne. "'Rocking the Cradle for the World': The New Woman and Maternal Feminism, Toronto, 1877-1914." In *A Not Unreasonable Claim: Women and Reform in Canada, 1880s-1920s,* ed. Linda Kealey, 15-45. Toronto: The Women's Press, 1979.

1708 ROONEY, Frances and Marguerite Andersen, eds. "Women and Language." A special issue of *Resources for Feminist Research* 13, 3 (November 1984).

1709 ROONEY, Frances and Pat Israel, eds. "Women and Disability." A special issue of *Resources for Feminist Research* 14, 1 (March 1985).

1710 ROSS, Aileen D. "Control and Leadership in Women's Groups: An Analysis of Philanthropic Money-Raising Activity." *Social Forces* 37, 2 (1958): 124-31.

1711 ROSS, Becki. "The House That Jill Built: Lesbian Feminist Organizing in Toronto, 1976-1980." *Feminist Review* 35 (Summer 1990): 75-91.

1712 ROSS, Becki. "Whatever Happened to 'A is for Amazon'?: The High-Wire Performance of Lesbian Subjectivity in the 1990s." *Resources for Feminist Research* 20, 3/4 (Fall/Winter 1991): 124-29.

1713 ROSS, Becki. "'Wanna His Fantasies': The State/d Indefensibility of Lesbian Smut." *Fireweed* 38 (Spring 1993): 38-47. [1992 Bad Attitude trial]

1714 ROSS, Becki. "Like Apples and Oranges: Lesbian Feminist Responses to the Politics of *The Body Politic.*" *Fuse* 26, 4 (May/June 1993).

1715 ROSS, Becki. *The House That Jill Built: A Lesbian Nation in Formation.* Toronto: University of Toronto Press, 1995.

1716 ROY, C. *Les lesbiennes et le féminisme.* Montréal: Éditions Saint-Martin, 1985.

1717 SAINT-JEAN, Armande. *Pour en finir avec le patriarcat.* Montréal: Ed. Primeur, 1983.

1718 SAWER, Marian. "Feminism and the State: Theory and Practice in Australia and Canada." *Australian-Canadian Studies* 12, 1 (1994): 49-68.

1719 SCHNEIDER, Ruth. "Someone's Got to Do It." *Fireweed* 18 (Spring 1984): 10-16. [Nova Scotia women's struggle against pesticides]

1720 SCHREADER, Alicia. "The State-Funded Women's Movement: A Case of Two Political Agendas." In *Community Organization and the Canadian State,* eds. Roxana Ng, Gillian Walker and Jacob Muller, 184-99. Toronto: Garamond Press, 1990.

1721 SEBIRE, Dawn. "'To Shield From Temptation': The Business Girl and the City." *Urban History Review* 17, 3 (February 1989): 203-8.

1722 HAVER, Frances M. "A Critique of the Feminist Charges Against Prostitution." *Atlantis* 14, 1 (Fall 1988): 82-89.

1723 SILMAN, Janet (as told to). *Enough is Enough: Aboriginal Women Speak Out.* Toronto: The Women's Press, 1987.

1724 SILVERMAN, Eliane Leslau. "Women in the First Person: Women Changing and Changing Society." In *A Passion for Identity: An Introduction to Canadian Studies,* 2nd edition, eds. David Taras, Beverly Rasporich and Eli Mandel, 175-88. Toronto: Nelson Canada, 1993.

1725 SKULASON, Hrund. "The Battle of the Sexes." *Icelandic Canadian* 33, 2 (Winter 1975): 42-45. [women's rights in Iceland and Manitoba, 1880s-1890s]

1726 SNEIDER, Alison. "The Impact of Empire on the North American Woman Suffrage Movement: Suffrage Racism in an Imperial Context." *UCLA Historical Journal* 14 (1995).

1727 SOCKNATT, Thomas P. "For Peace and Freedom: Canadian Feminists and the Interwar Peace Campaign." In *Up and Doing: Canadian Women and Peace,* eds. Janice Williamson and Deborah Gorham, 66-88. Toronto: The Women's Press, 1989.

1728 STACEY-MOORE, Gail. "In Our Own Voice: Aboriginal Women Demand Justice." *Herizons* 6, 4 (Winter 1993): 21-23.

1729 STASIULIS, Daiva. "Rainbow Feminism: Perspectives on Minority Women in Canada." *Resources for Feminist Research* 16, 1 (1987): 5-9.

1730 STEWART, Houston, Beth Percival and Elizabeth R. Epperly, eds. *The more we get together: Women and Dis/ability.* Charlottetown: Gynergy Books, 1992.

1731 STODDART, Jennifer. "The Woman Suffrage Bill in Quebec." In *Women in Canada,* 2nd edition, ed. Marylee Stephenson, 90-106. Don Mills: General Publishing Co. Ltd., 1977.

1732 STONE, Sharon Dale. "Lesbian Mothers Organizing." In *Lesbians in Canada,* ed. Sharon Dale Stone, 198-208. Toronto: Between the Lines, 1990.

1733 STONE, Sharon Dale. "Lesbians Against the Right." In *Women and Social Change: Feminist Activism in Canada,* eds. Jeri Dawn Wine and Janice L. Ristock, 236-51. Toronto: James Lorimer and Company, 1991.

1734 STONE, Sharon D. "Getting the Message Out: Feminists, the press and violence against women." *Canadian Review of Sociology and Anthropology* 30, 3 (1993): 377-400. [Toronto, 1988]

1735 STRONG-BOAG, Veronica. "'Setting the Stage': National Organization and the Women's Movement in the Late 19th Century." In *The Neglected Majority: Essays in Canadian Women's History,* eds. Susan Mann Trofimenkoff and Alison Prentice, 87-103. Toronto: McClelland and Stewart, 1977.

1736 STRONG-BOAG, Veronica. "Pulling in Double Harness or Hauling a Double Load: Women, Work and Feminism on the Canadian Prairie." *Journal of Canadian Studies* 21, 3 (1986): 32-52. Reprinted in *The Prairie West: Historical Readings,* 2nd edition, eds. R. Douglas Francis and Howard Palmer, 401-23. Edmonton: Pica Pica Press, 1992.

1737 STRONG-BOAG, Veronica. "Peace-making Women: Canada, 1919-1939." In *Women and Peace: Theoretical, Historical and Practical Perspectives,* ed. Ruth Roach Pierson, 170-91. London: Croom Helm, 1987.

1738 STUART, M. and G. Ellerington. "Unequal Access: Disabled Women's Exclusion from the Mainstream Women's Movement in Canada." *Women and Environment* 12 (May/June 1990): 16-19.

1739 TARDY, Évelyne, *et al. Sexes et militantisme.* Montréal: Éditions du Cidihca, 1989.

1740 *Ten Years Later: An Assessment of the Federal Government's Implementation of the Recommendations Made by the Royal Commission on the Status of Women.* Ottawa: Canadian Advisory Council on the Status of Women, 1979.

1741 TENNYSON, Brian D. "Premier Hearst, the War, and Votes for Women." *Ontario History* 57, 3 (1965): 115-21.

1742 TOUPIN, Louise. "Une histoire du féminisme est-elle possible?" *Recherches féministes* 6, 1 (1993): 25-51.

1743 TREGEBOV, Rhea, ed. *Work in Progress: Building Feminist Culture.* Toronto: The Women's Press, 1987.

1744 TRIFIRO, Luigi. "Une intervention à Rome dans la lutte pour le suffrage féminin au Québec (1922)." *Revue d'histoire de l'Amérique française* 32, 1 (juin 1978): 3-18.

1745 TURNER, Joan, ed. *Living the Changes.* Winnipeg: University of Manitoba Press, 1990.

1746 TURNER, Joan and Lois Emery, eds. *Perspectives on Women in the 1980s.* Winnipeg: University of Manitoba Press, 1983.

1747 VACHON-L'HEUREUX, Pierrette. "Quinze ans de féminisation au Québec: de 1976 à 1991." *Recherches féministes* 5, 1 (1992): 139-42. [Office de la Langue française]

1748 VALVERDE, Mariana. *The Age of Light, Soap and Water: Moral Reform in English Canada, 1885-1925.* Toronto: McClelland and Stewart, 1991.

1749 VALVERDE, Mariana. "'When the Mother of the Race is Free': Race, Reproduction, and Sexuality in First-Wave Feminism." In *Gender Conflicts: New Essays in Women's History,* eds. Franca Iacovetta and Mariana Valverde, 3-26. Toronto: University of Toronto Press, 1992.

1750 VALVERDE, Mariana and Lorna Weir. "The Struggles of the Immoral: Preliminary Remarks on Moral Regulation." *Resources for Feminist Research* 17, 3 (September 1988): 31-34.

1751 VICKERS, Jill. "Bending the Iron Law of Oligarchy: Debates on the Feminization of Organization and Political Process in the English Canadian Women's Movement, 1970-1988." In *Women and Social Change: Feminist Activism in Canada,* eds. Jeri Dawn Wine and Janice L. Ristock, 75-94. Toronto: James Lorimer and Company, 1991.

1752 VICKERS, Jill. "The Intellectual Origins of the Women's Movement in Canada." In *Challenging Times: The Women's Movement in Canada and the United States,* eds. Constance Backhouse and David H. Flaherty, 39-60. Montreal and Kingston: McGill-Queen's University Press, 1992.

1753 VOISEY, Paul. "The 'Votes for Women' Movement." *Alberta History* 23, 3 (Summer 1975): 10-23. Reprinted in *The Best from Alberta History,* ed. Hugh Dempsey, 166-201. Saskatoon: Western Producer Prairie Books, 1981.

1754 VON HEYKING, Amy. "Red Deer Women and the Roots of Feminism." *Alberta History* 42, 1 (Winter 1994): 14-26.

1755 WALKER, Gillian A. *Family Violence and the Women's Movement: The Conceptual Politics of Struggle.* Toronto: University of Toronto Press, 1990.

1756 WALKER, Gillian. "The Conceptual Politics of Struggle: Wife Battering, the Women's Movement and the State." In *Feminism in Action: Studies in Political Economy,* eds. M. Patricia Connelly and Pat Armstrong. Toronto: Canadian Scholars' Press, 1993.

1757 WARING, Wendy, ed. *by, for & about: Feminist Cultural Politics.* Toronto: Women's Press, 1994.

1758 WEISS, Gillian. "Women and Reform in British Columbia: Some Preliminary Suggestions." In *In Her Own Right: Selected Essays on Women's History in BC,* eds. Barbara Latham and Cathy Kess, 279-84. Victoria: Camosun College, 1980.

1759 WEISS, Gillian. "The Brightest Women of Our Land: Vancouver Clubwomen, 1910-1928." In *Not Just Pin Money: Selected Essays on the History of Women's Work in British Columbia,* eds. Barbara K. Latham and Roberta J. Pazdro, 199-209. Victoria: Camosun College, 1984.

1760 WHITE, Charles A. "Winning the Vote: The Quiet Revolution." *Canada and the World* (December 1974): 12-13. [Canadian suffrage movement]

1761 WILLLIAMS, Carol. "A Working Chronology of Feminist Cultural Activities and Events in Vancouver: 1970-1990." In *The Vancouver Anthology: The Institutional Politics of Art,* ed. Stan Douglas, 171-207. Vancouver: Talonbooks, 1991.

1762 WILLIAMS, Toni. "Re-forming 'Women's' Truth: A Critique of the Report of the Royal Commission on the Status of Women in Canada." *Ottawa Law Review* 22 (1990).

1763 WILLIAMSON, Janice and Deborah Gorham, eds. *Up and Doing: Canadian Women and Peace.* Toronto: The Women's Press, 1989.

1764 WINE, Jeri Dawn and Janice L. Ristock, eds. *Women and Social Change: Feminist Activism in Canada.* Toronto: James Lorimer and Company, 1991.

1765 WINE, Jeri Dawn and Janice L. Ristock. "Feminist Activism in Canada." In *Women and Social Change: Feminist Activism in Canada*, eds. Jeri Dawn Wine and Janice L. Ristock, 1-18. Toronto: James Lorimer and Company, 1991.

1766 WINZER, Margaret. "Talking deaf mutes: the special role of women in the methodological conflict regarding the deaf, 1867-1900." *Atlantis* 6, 2 1981: 123-33.

1767 "Women's Place: How It Was, Examples of Early Canadian Feminism." In *Mother Was Not A Person*, ed. M. Anderson. Montreal: Black Rose Books, 1972.

1768 *Women Unite!: An Anthology of the Canadian Women's Movement.* Toronto: Canadian Women's Educational Press, 1972.

ORGANIZATIONS

1769 AIRHART, Phyllis. "Sobriety, Sentimentality and Science: The WCTU and the Reconstruction of Christian Womanhood." Canadian Methodist Historical Society. *Papers* (1990): 117-36.

1770 AMBROSE, Linda M. "'What Are the Good of Those Meetings Anyway?': Early Popularity of the Ontario Women's Institutes." *Ontario History* 87, 1 (Spring 1995): 1-19.

1771 BAMMAN, Haley P. "The Ladies Benevolent Society of Hamilton, Ontario: Form and Function in Mid-Nineteenth Century Urban Philanthropy." In *Education and Social Change: Themes from Ontario's Past*, eds. Michael B. Katz and Paul H. Mattingly. New York: New York University Press, 1975.

1772 BARBER, Marilyn. "The Gentlewomen of Queen Mary's Coronation Hostel." In *Not Just Pin Money: Selected Essays on the History of Women's Work in British Columbia*, eds. Barbara K. Latham and Roberta J. Pazdro, 141-58. Victoria: Camosun College, 1984.

1773 BELL, Lily M. and Kathleen E. Bray. *Women of Action, 1876-1976.* St. Catharines, ON: Local Council of Women, 1976.

1774 BLISS, Michael. "Neglected Radicals: A Sober Second Look." *Canadian Forum* (April/May 1970): 16-17. [Women's Christian Temperance Union]

1775 BRISTOW, Peggy. "The Hour-a-Day Study Club." In *And Still We Rise: Feminist Political Mobilizing in Contemporary Canada*, ed. Linda Carty, 145-72. Toronto: Women's Press, 1993. [Black mothers' club, Windsor]

1776 BRUNET, Lucie and Chantal P. Cholette. "D'un siècle à l'autre: la Fédération nationale des femmes canadiennes-françaises." *Canadian Woman Studies* 7, 4 (Winter 1986): 52-53.

1777 CARTER, Eva. *The History of Organized Farm Women of Alberta.* Edmonton: Farm Women's Union of Alberta, 1954.

1778 CHRISTIANSEN-RUFFMAN, Linda. "Bridging the Gap Between Feminist Activism and Academe: The Canadian Research Institute for the Advancement of Women." In *Women and Social Change: Feminist Activism in Canada*, eds. Jeri Dawn Wine and Janice L. Ristock, 258-82. Toronto: James Lorimer and Company, 1991.

1779 COHEN, Yolande. "Des paysannes aux fermières: l'Association des Cercles des fermières canadiennes-françaises." *Pénélope* (Paris) 7 (automne 1982): 87-93.

1780 COHEN, Yolande. "L'association des Cercles de fermières au Québec: sociabilité et influence sociale." In *Femmes et Contre-pouvoir*, ed. Yolande Cohen, 135-54. Montreal: Boréal Express, 1987.

1781 COHEN, Yolande. "Les Cercles de fermières: une contribution à la survie du monde rural." *Recherches sociographiques* 29, 2/3 1988: 311-27.

1782 COHEN, Yolande. "L'Association des Cercles de fermières in Québec: Sociability and Social Influence." In *Women and Counter-Power*, ed. Yolande Cohen, 124-41. Montreal: Black Rose Books, 1989.

1783 COHEN, Yolande. "Le déploiement géographique des Cercles de fermières au Québec, 1915-1949." *Espaces, Population et Sociétés* (Paris) 1 (1989): 87-98.

1784 COHEN, Yolande. *Femmes de Parole: l'histoire des Cercles de fermières du Québec, 1915-1990.* Montréal: Le Jour, 1990.

1785 COHEN, Yolande and Pierre Van Den Dungen. "À l'origine des Cercles des fermières: étude comparée Belgique-Québec." *Revue d'histoire de l'Amérique française* 48, 1 (été 1994): 29-56.

1786 COLE, Catherine C. and Ann Milovic. "Education, Community Service, and Social Life: The Alberta Women's Institutes and Rural Families, 1909-1945." In *Standing on New Ground: Women in Alberta*, eds. Catherine A. Cavanaugh and Randi R. Warne, 19-31. Edmonton: University of Alberta Press, 1993.

1787 COOK, Sharon Anne. "'Earnest Christian Women, Bent on Saving Our Canadian Youth': The Ontario Woman's Christian Temperance Union and Scientific Temperance Instruction, 1881-1930." *Ontario History* 86, 3 (1994): 249-67.

1788 COOK, Sharon Anne. "'Sowing Seeds for the Master': The Ontario WCTU and Evangelical Feminism, 1874-1930." *Journal of Canadian Studies* 30, 3 (Fall 1995): 175-94.

1789 CORBET, Elise. "The Woman's Canadian Club of Calgary." *Alberta History* 24, 3 (Summer 1977): 29-36.

1790 CREET, M. Julia. "A Test of Unity: Lesbian Visibility in the British Columbia Federation of Women." In *Lesbians in Canada*, ed. Sharon Dale Stone, 183-97. Toronto: Between the Lines, 1990.

1791 CROWLEY, Terry. "The Origins of Continuing Education for Women: The Ontario Women's Institutes." *Canadian Woman Studies* 7, 3 (Fall 1986): 78-81.

1792 CUMMING, Judi. "The Canadian Federation of Business and Professional Women's Clubs." *The Archivist* 14, 1 (January-February 1987).

1793 DENNISON, Carol J. "They Also Served: The British Columbia Women's Institutes in Two World Wars." In *Not Just Pin Money: Selected Essays on the History of Women's Work in British Columbia*, eds. Barbara K. Latham and Roberta J. Pazdro, 211-19. Victoria: Camosun College, 1984.

1794 DENNISON, Carol J. "'Housekeepers of the Community': The British Columbia Women's Institutes, 1909-46." In *Knowledge for the People: The Struggle for Adult Learning in English-Speaking Canada, 1828-1973*, ed. Michael R. Welton, 52-72. Toronto: OISE Press, 1987.

1795 DESJARDINS, Ghislaine. "Les Cercles de fermières et l'action féminine en milieu rural, 1915-1944." In *Travailleuses et féministes: Les femmes dans la société québécoise*, eds. Marie Lavigne and Yolande Pinard, 217-43. Montréal: Boréal Express, 1983.

1796 DESJARDINS, Micheline. *Les femmes de la diaspora canadienne-française: Brève histoire de la FNFCF de 1914 à 1991*. Ottawa: Fédération nationale des femmes canadiennes-françaises, 1991.

1797 DOUCETTE, Joanne. "The DisAbled Women's Network: A Fragile Success." In *Women and Social Change: Feminist Activism in Canada*, eds. Jeri Dawn Wine and Janice L. Ristock, 221-35. Toronto: James Lorimer and Company, 1991.

1798 ENNS, Helga M. and Bev Le François. *Story of a Woman's Centre*. Port Coquitlam, BC: Port Coquitlam Area Women's Centre, 1979.

1799 FLETCHER, E. *History of the Manitoba Women's Institute, 1919-1975*. Winnipeg: Manitoba Women's Institute, 1976.

1800 FORBES, Elizabeth. *With Enthusiasm and Faith: History of the Canadian Federation of Business and Professional Women's Clubs, 1930-1972*. Ottawa: Canadian Federation of Business and Professional Women, 1974.

1801 FRIDERES, James S. with Lilianne Ernestine Krosenbrink-Gelissen. *Native Peoples in Canada: Contemporary Conflicts*, 4th edition, 335-64. Scarborough: Prentice Hall, 1993. [Chapter 9, The Native Women's Association of Canada]

1802 GIARDINI, Anne Shields. "Rural Women United." *This Country Canada* 6 (Summer 1994): 48-55. [Kamloops Women's Institute]

1803 GOGAN, Tanya. "The WCTU's Contribution to the Woman's Suffrage Movement in Nova Scotia." *Dalhousie Undergraduate History Society Academic Journal* 3 (1992): 55-64.

1804 GORHAM, Deborah and Florence Kellner Andrews. "The La Leche League: A Feminist Perspective." In *Delivering Motherhood: Maternal Ideologies and Practices in the 19th and 20th Centuries*, eds.

Katherine Arnup, Andrée Lévesque and Ruth Roach Pierson, 238-69. London and New York: Routledge, 1990.

1805 GOUGH, Lyn. *As Wise as Serpents: Five Women and an Organization That Changed British Columbia, 1883-1939*. Victoria: Swan Lake Publishing, 1988. [Women's Christian Temperance Union]

1806 GRAVEL, Pauline. "Les cercles des fermières à l'origine du mouvement féministe." *Interface* 12, 3 (mai-juin 1991): 53-55.

1807 GREAVES, Lorraine. "Reorganizing the National Action Committee on the Status of Women, 1986-1988." In *Women and Social Change: Feminist Activism in Canada*, eds. Jeri Dawn Wine and Janice L. Ristock, 101-16. Toronto: James Lorimer and Company, 1991.

1808 GRIFFITHS, N.E.S. *The Splendid Vision: Centennial History of the National Council of Women of Canada, 1893-1993*. Ottawa: Carleton University Press, 1993.

1809 HALEY, Ella. "Getting Our Act Together: The Ontario Farm Women's Movement." In *Women and Social Change: Feminist Activism in Canada*, eds. Jeri Dawn Wine and Janice L. Ristock, 169-83. Toronto: James Lorimer and Company, 1991.

1810 HARKIN, D. *A Summary of the New Farm Women's Movement, 1975-1990*. Ottawa: Agriculture Canada, 1991.

1811 HARSHAW, Josephine P. *When Women Work Together: A History of the Young Women's Christian Association in Canada, 1870-1966*. Toronto: Ryerson Press, 1966.

1812 HATHAWAY, Debbie. "The Political Equality League of Manitoba." *Manitoba History* 3 (1982): 8-10.

1813 HEWITT, Molly. *Sixty Years of CGIT, 1915-1975*. Toronto: Anniversary Task Force of the National CGIT Committee, 1975. [Canadian Girls in Training]

1814 HUTCHINS, Nancy Bowden. *Guides, All Guides: A History of Girl Guiding in Nova Scotia, 1911-1977*. Halifax: McCurty Printing, 1977.

1815 INNIS, Mary Quayle. *Unfold the Years: A History of the Young Women's Christian Association in Canada*. Toronto: McClelland and Stewart, 1949.

1816 INTERNATIONAL COUNCIL OF WOMEN. *Women in a Changing World: The Dynamic Story of the International Council of Women Since 1888*. London: Routledge and Kegan Paul, 1966.

1817 IRELAND, Giselle. *The Farmer Takes a Wife: A Study of Concerned Farm Women*. Chesley, ON: Concerned Farm Women, 1983.

1818 JAHN, Cheryle. "Class, Gender and Agrarian Socialism: The United Farm Women of Saskatchewan, 1926-1931." *Prairie Forum* 19, 2 (Fall 1994): 189-206.

1819 JARVIS, Julia. "The Founding of the Girl Guide Movement in Canada, 1910." *Ontario History* 62, 4 (December 1970): 213-20.

1820 KECHNIE, Margaret. "The United Farm Women of Ontario: Developing a Political Consciousness." *Ontario History* 77, 4 (1985): 267-80.

1821 KENNEY, Leslie and Warren Magnusson. "In Transition: The Women's House Saving Action." *Canadian Review of Sociology and Anthropology* 30, 3 (1993): 359-76. [Transition House, Vancouver, 1985-86]

1822 KERR, Vivian. *A Flame of Compassion: A History of the Provincial Council of Women of Ontario.* Toronto: T.H. Best Printing Co., 1967.

1823 KERTLAND, May G. *IODE: The Third Twenty-Five Years, 1950-1975.* Don Mills: T.H. Best Printing Co., 1975.

1824 LACROIX, Marie-Josée. "Les cercles de fermières ont 80 ans!" *Le Bel âge* 7, 9 (juillet-août 1994): 114-15.

1825 LAMOUREUX, Jocelyne, Michèle Gélinas and Katy Tari. *Femmes en mouvement: Trajectoires de l'Association féminine d'éducation et d'action sociale, AFÉAS, 1966-1991.* Québec: Éditions du Boréal, 1993.

1826 LAVIGNE, Marie, Yolande Pinard and Jennifer Stoddart. "La Fédération nationale Saint-Jean-Baptiste et les revendications féministes au début du 20e siècle." *Revue d'histoire de l'Amérique française* 29 (décembre 1975): 353-73. Revised and reprinted in *Travailleuses et féministes: Les femmes dans la société québécoise,* eds. Marie Lavigne and Yolande Pinard, 199-216. Montréal: Boréal Express, 1983.

1827 LAVIGNE, Marie, Yolande Pinard and Jennifer Stoddart. "The Fédération Nationale Saint-Jean-Baptiste and the Women's Movement in Quebec." In *A Not Unreasonable Claim: Women and Reform in Canada, 1880s-1920s,* ed. Linda Kealey, 71-87. Toronto: The Women's Press, 1979.

1828 LAVOIE, Stella. "Les cercles de fermières de la province de Québec dans la région." *Revue d'histoire du Bas St-Laurent* 5 (décembre 1978): 24-26.

1829 LEFURGY, Estelle. "British Columbia Women's Institute: A Brief History." *British Columbia Historical News* 27, 4 (Fall 1994): 31-32.

1830 LOEWEN, Candace. "Mike Hears Voices: Voice of Women and Lester Pearson, 1960-1963." *Atlantis* 12, 2 (Spring 1987): 24-30.

1831 MacPHERSON, Kay. "Persistent Voices: Twenty-Five Years with the Voice of Women." *Atlantis* 12, 2 (Spring 1987): 60-72.

1832 MacPHERSON, Kay and Meg Sears. "The Voice of Women: A History." In *Women in the Canadian Mosaic,* ed. Gwen Matheson, 71-89. Toronto: Peter Martin Associates, 1976.

1833 MacQUEEN, Bonnie. "Domesticity and Discipline: The Girl Guides in British Columbia, 1910-1943." In *Not Just Pin Money: Selected Essays on the History of Women's Work in British Columbia,* eds. Barbara K. Latham and Roberta J. Pazdro, 221-35. Victoria: Camosun College, 1984.

1834 MARCHESSAULT-LUSSIER, Lucie. "Une agent d'éducation populaire pas comme les autres (AFÉAS)." *Canadian Women's Studies* 3 (Summer 1982): 88-89.

1835 MARCHILDON, R.G. "Improving the Quality of Rural Life in Saskatchewan: Some Activities of the Women's Section of the Saskatchewan Grain Growers, 1913-1920." In *Building Beyond the Homestead: Rural History on the Prairies,* eds. D.C. Jones and I. MacPherson, 89-109. Calgary: University of Calgary Press, 1985.

1836 MARCOTTE, Jacinthe. "La Bonne Fermière 1920-1933." *Bulletin de la bibliothèque nationale de Québec* 14, 1 (mars 1980). [Cercles de fermières]

1837 MARSDEN, Lorna R. "The Role of the National Action Committee on the Status of Women in Facilitating Equal Pay Policy in Canada." In *Equal Employment Policy for Women: Strategies for Implementation in the United States, Canada, and Western Europe,* ed. Ronnie Steinberg Ratner, 242-60. Philadelphia: Temple University Press, 1980.

1838 McMANUS, Sheila. "...these women realized the power of union...": Mutuality as Empowerment in the United Farm Women of Alberta." *blurred Genres: A Journal of Writing by Students in the University of Victoria Department of History* 2 (Winter/Spring 1994): 114-28.

1839 MEIKLEJOHN, Heather. "The Women's Institute's Loan Collection of Handicrafts Finds a Home." *Manitoba History* 23 (Spring 1992): 21-22.

1840 MITCHINSON, Wendy. "The WCTU: 'For God, Home and Native Land': A Study in Nineteenth-Century Feminism." In *A Not Unreasonable Claim: Women and Reform in Canada, 1880s-1920s,* ed. Linda Kealey, 151-67. Toronto: The Women's Press, 1979. Reprinted in *Canada's Age of Industry, 1849-1896,* eds. Michael S. Cross and Gregory S. Kealey, 190-209. Toronto: McClelland and Stewart Limited, 1982; and in *An Introduction to Canadian History,* ed. A.I. Silver. Toronto: Canadian Scholars' Press, 1991.

1841 MITCHINSON, Wendy. "The YWCA and Reform in the 19th Century." *Histoire sociale/Social History* XII, 24 (November 1979): 368-84.

1842 MITCHINSON, Wendy. "The Woman's Christian Temperance Union: A Study in Organization." *International Journal of Women's Studies* 4, 2 (1981): 143-56.

1843 MONCTON COUNCIL OF WOMEN. *Sharing Responsibility, 1920-1980: Diamond Jubilee History.* Moncton, NB: Moncton Council of Women, 1980.

1844 MONTONEN, Susan, Beth Moore Milroy and Susan Wismer. "Siting the Berlin YWCA." *Waterloo Historical Society* 78 (1990): 39-53.

1845 MORISSETTE, Yvonne Rialland. *Le passé conjugué au présent: Cercles de fermières du Québec, historique, 1915-1980.* Montréal: Pénélope, 1980.

1846 MURISON, Blanche E.H. "Women of the West in Clubland: The Athenaeum Club, Vancouver, BC." *BC Studies* 7, 3 (1991).

1847 NADEAU, Aurella. *Soixante-quinze ans de l'Institut féminin francophone de Saint-François-de-Madawaska, Nouveau-Brunswick*. [S.l.: s.n. 1992].

1848 O'LEARY, Véronique and Louise Toupin. *Québécoises deboutte! Tome 1, Une anthologie de textes du Front de libération des femmes (1969-1971) et du Centre des femmes (1972-1975)*. Montréal: Les éditions du remue-ménage, 1982.

1849 O'LEARY, Véronique and Louise Toupin. *Québécoises deboutte! Tome 2, Collection complète suivie de deux tables rondes avec des femmes du Front de libération des femmes (1969-1971) et du Centre des femmes (1972-1975)*. Montréal: Les éditions du remue-ménage, 1983.

1850 OSBORNE, Ken. "An Early Example of the Analysis of History Textbooks in Canada." *Canadian Social Studies* 29, 1 (Fall 1994): 21-25. [Women's International League for Peace and Freedom, 1933]

1851 OTTY, Marianne G. *Fifty Years of Women's Institutes in New Brunswick, Canada, 1911-1961: A History*. New Brunswick: Women's Institutes, c. 1961.

1852 PANABAKER, Katherine. *The Story of the Girl Guides in Ontario*. Toronto: Ryerson Press, 1966.

1853 PEARSON, Nelda K. "Women's Leadership Styles and Empowerment: A Case Study of a Canadian Farm Women's Movement." *International Journal of Canadian Studies* 11 (Spring 1995): 83-100. [Women for the Survival of Agriculture]

1854 PEDERSEN, Diana. "'Keeping Our Good Girls Good': The YWCA and the 'Girl Problem', 1870-1930." *Canadian Woman Studies* 7, 4 (Winter 1986): 20-24.

1855 PEDERSEN, Diana. "'Building Today for the Womanhood of Tomorrow': Businessmen, Boosters and the YWCA, 1890-1930." *Urban History Review* 15, 3 (1987): 225-42.

1856 PEDERSEN, Diana. "The Photographic Record of the Canadian YWCA, 1890-1930: A Visual Source for Women's History." *Archivaria* 24 (Summer 1987): 10-35.

1857 POWELL, Mary Patricia. "A Response to the Depression: The Local Council of Women of Vancouver." In *In Her Own Right: Selected Essays on Women's History in BC*, eds. Barbara Latham and Cathy Kess, 255-78. Victoria: Camosun College, 1980.

1858 PROKOP, Mary. "Looking Back on Fifty Years." *Ukrainian Canadian* (March 1972): 7-14. [Women's Branches of the Association of United Ukrainian Canadians]

1859 RANKIN, Pauline. "The Politicization of Ontario Farm Women." In *Beyond the Vote: Canadian Women and Politics*, eds. Linda Kealey and Joan Sangster, 309-32. Toronto: University of Toronto Press, 1989.

1860 RASMUSSEN, Pat. "Telling Our Story: Women's Program and Resource Centre, 1981-1991." In *Standing on New Ground: Women in Alberta*, eds. Catherine A. Cavanaugh and Randi R. Warne, 155-70. Edmonton: University of Alberta Press, 1993.

1861 REID, Diane, *et al. A Bridge to the Future: A History of the Council of Women of Ottawa and Area*. Ottawa: Regional Municipality of Ottawa-Carleton, 1976.

1862 "Report on the Home for Young Women Seeking Employment, Halifax, 1870." *Atlantis* 5, 2 (Spring 1980): 196-200.

1863 ROBERTSON, Sheila. "The Life and Times of CAAWS." *Canadian Woman Studies* 15, 4 (Fall 1995): 16-21. [Canadian Association for the Advancement of Women and Sport and Physical Activity]

1864 ROBINSON, Helen Caister. *Decades of Caring: The Big Sister Story*. Toronto: Dundurn Press, 1979.

1865 SAINT-PIERRE, Chantal. "Une forme d'éducation populaire: l'expérience du groupe Entre-femmes." *Éducation et francophonie* 19, 3 (1991): 37-40.

1866 SCHNEIDER, Elise. "Addressing the Issues: Two Women's Groups in Edmonton, 1905-16." *Alberta History* 36, 3 (Summer 1988): 15-22. [Local Council of Women and Imperial Order Daughters of the Empire]

1867 [SEBIRE, Dawn]. *A Woman's Place: The History of the Hamilton Young Women's Christian Association*. [Hamilton: Hamilton YWCA, 1990]

1868 SHAW, Rosa L. *Proud Heritage: A History of the National Council of Women of Canada*. Toronto: The Ryerson Press, 1957.

1869 SHEEHAN, Nancy M. "The WCTU on the Prairies, 1886-1930: An Alberta-Saskatchewan Comparison." *Prairie Forum* 6, 1 (Spring 1981): 17-33.

1870 SHEEHAN, Nancy M. "'Women Helping Women': The WCTU and the Foreign Population in the West, 1905-1930." *International Journal of Women's Studies* 6, 5 (1983): 395-411.

1871 SHEEHAN, Nancy M. "The Red Cross and Relief in Alberta, 1920s-1930s." *Prairie Forum* 12, 2 (Fall 1987): 277-94.

1872 SILVERMAN, Eliane Leslau. "The National Council of Jewish Women: Private Lives, Public People." *Canadian Woman Studies* 7, 4 (Winter 1986): 49-51.

1873 SIMMONS, Christina. "'Helping the Poorer Sisters': The Women of the Jost Mission, Halifax, 1905-1945." *Acadiensis* 14, 1 (1984): 3-27. Reprinted in *Rethinking Canada: The Promise of Women's History*, eds. Veronica Strong-Boag and Anita Clair Fellman, 157-77. Toronto: Copp Clark Pitman Ltd., 1986; 2nd edition, 286-307, 1991.

1874 STRONG-BOAG, Veronica. "The Roots of Modern Canadian Feminism: The National Council of Women of Canada, 1893-1929." *Canada: An Historical Magazine* 3, 2 (December 1975): 22-33. Reprinted in *Canadian History Since Confederation*, eds. Bruce Hodgins and Robert Page, Georgetown, ON: Irwin-Dorsey Ltd., 1979.

1875 STRONG-BOAG, Veronica. *The Parliament of Women: The National Council of Women of Canada, 1893-1929*. History Division Paper No. 18. Ottawa: National Museums of Canada, 1976.

1876 SWYRIPA, Frances. "The Ideas of the Ukrainian Women's Organization of Canada, 1930-1945." In *Beyond the Vote: Canadian Women and Politics,* eds. Linda Kealey and Joan Sangster, 239-57. Toronto: University of Toronto Press, 1989.

1877 THOMPSON, Retha L.B. *Synoptic View of the WCTU of Saskatchewan, Canada, 1913-1973*. Saskatoon: Early Mailing Service, 1975. [60th anniversary of the Women's Christian Temperance Union in Saskatchewan]

1878 VARPALOTAI, Aniko. "A 'Safe Place' for Leisure and Learning—The Girl Guides of Canada." *Loisir et Société/Society and Leisure* 15, 1 (Spring 1992): 115-34.

1879 VARPALOTAI, Aniko. "'Women Only and Proud of It!': The Politicization of the Girl Guides of Canada." *Resources for Feminist Research* 23, 1/2 (Spring/Summer 1994): 14-23.

1880 VEER, Joanne. "The Attack of the Maternal Feminists of the Maritime Woman's Christian Temperance Union on the Victorian Double Sexual Standard, 1875-1900." In *The more we get together: Women and Dis/ability,* eds. Houston Stewart, Beth Percival and Elizabeth R. Epperly, 113-24. Charlottetown: Gynergy Books, 1992.

1881 VICKERS, Jill, Christine Appelle and Pauline Rankin. *Politics as if Women Mattered: A Political Analysis of the National Action Committee on the Status of Women.* Toronto: University of Toronto Press, 1993.

1882 VINEBERG, Ethel. *The History of the National Council of Jewish Women of Canada.* Montreal: National Council of Jewish Women of Canada, 1967.

1883 WILSON, L.J. "Educational Role of the United Farm Women of Alberta." *Alberta History* 25, 2 (Spring 1977): 28-36. Reprinted in *Shaping the Schools of the Canadian West,* eds. David C. Jones, Nancy M. Sheehan and Robert Stamp, 124-35. Calgary: Detselig, 1979.

1884 WOLFE, Jeanne M. and Grace Strachan. "Practical Idealism: Women in Urban Reform, Julia Drummond and the Montreal Parks and Playgrounds Association." In *Life Spaces: Gender, Household, Employment,* eds. Caroline Andrew and Beth Moore Milroy, 65-80. Vancouver: University of British Columbia Press, 1988.

1885 "WSPU Deputation to Prime Minister Borden, 1912." *Atlantis* 5, 2 (Spring 1980): 188-95. [Women's Social and Political Union]

1886 ZACHARIAS, Alexandra. "British Columbia Women's Institute in the Early Years: Time to Remember." In *In Her Own Right: Selected Essays on Women's History in BC,* eds. Barbara Latham and Cathy Kess, 55-78. Victoria: Camosun College, 1980.

FIRST NATIONS

GIVEN THE TRADITIONAL reliance of historians on written texts, the writing of the history of First Nations women has posed a special challenge for Canadian women's historians. Until very recently, First Nations women produced no written accounts of their own lives, and the surviving documents, authored mostly by white men, are riddled with gender, class and cultural biases. To overcome this difficulty, women's historians have adopted methodologies both from ethnohistory—learning to read between the lines of problematic texts by contextualizing them and directly confronting the biases of their authors—and from anthropology—using oral interviews to construct life histories in collaboration with contemporary First Nations women.

In the 1970s and early 1980s, Canadian feminist scholars were preoccupied with the question of the historical origins of women's oppression and, more specifically, of the female job ghettos that marginalized women workers in the Canadian labour force. For this reason, both historians and anthropologists were drawn to study the political economy of traditional native societies, hoping to find answers to their questions about the origins of the sexual division of labour. A vigorous debate took place among scholars such as Judith Brown, Eleanor Leacock and Karen Anderson about the sources of women's power in pre-Contact Iroquois and Montaignais-Nascapi societies, and about the impact of colonization on women, particularly the introduction of the concept of private property.

The wealth of records produced by the Jesuits and Ursulines, who established missions to convert the First Nations to Christianity in seventeenth-century New France, have been mined by women's historians to produce a rich body of scholarship dominated by Karen Anderson and Carol Devens, with exciting new contributions from Natalie Zemon Davis. These scholars have been particularly interested in missionary perspectives on the social organization of native societies, the role of Iroquois and Montaignais women in resisting colonization, the implications of conversion to Christianity for the status of women, and the centrality of European constructs of gender and the patriarchal family to the objectives of the French colonial enterprise.

In an imaginative rereading of the massive body of records left by the Hudson's Bay Company, Sylvia Van Kirk was the first historian to draw attention to the important role played by Native and mixed-blood women in the fur-trade society of the North West from the seventeenth to the nineteenth centuries. Country marriages, she demonstrated convincingly, were not merely the sexual dalliances that lightened the pages of popular histories, but were economic and diplomatic alliances that produced benefits for both fur traders and their country wives, until the arrival of white women in the North West heralded a dramatic loss of status for First Nations women.

In some recent studies of the history of First Nations women, scholars are turning their attention to the Maritime fur trade and the complex hierarchical societies of the Northwest Coast, challenging some of the earlier generalizations made by scholars studying the more egalitarian societies of the St. Lawrence Valley. Northern native women are beginning to receive attention from anthropologists, who are also displaying a lively interest in constructs of gender in traditional Inuit societies. Studies of the impact of residential schools on First Nations women are only now making their appearance. Some important new work by historian Sarah Carter on the construction of the Indian woman applies discourse analysis to nineteenth-century captivity narratives, and is suggestive of future trends in the scholarship.

BIOGRAPHIES/LIFE STORIES

1887 AHENAKEW, Freda and H.C. Wolfart, eds. *Kôhkominawak Otâcimowiniwâwa/Our Grandmothers' Lives: As Told in Their Own Words.* Saskatoon: Fifth House Publishers, 1992.

1888 ANAHEREO. *My Life with Grey Owl.* London: Peter Davies, 1940.

1889 ANDERSON, Margaret Seguin and Tammy Anderson Blumhagen. "Memories and Moments: Conversations and Re-Collections." *BC Studies* 104 (Winter 1994/95): 85-102.[Tsimshian women]

1890 BERGMANN, Linda S. "Women Against a Background of White: The Representation of Self and Nature in Women's Arctic Narratives." *American Studies* 34, 2 (Fall 1993): 53-68.

1891 BLACKMAN, Margaret B. *During My Time: Florence Edensaw Davidson, a Haida Woman.* Vancouver: Douglas and MacIntyre/Seattle: University of Washington Press, 1982.

1892 BLACKMAN, Margaret B. *Sadie Bower Neakok: An Inupiag Woman.* Vancouver: Douglas and McIntyre, 1989.

1893 BRAND, Johanna. *The Life and Death of Anna Mae Aquash.* Toronto: James Lorimer & Company, 1978; 2nd edition, 1993.

1894 CAMPBELL, Maria. *Halfbreed.* Toronto: McClelland and Stewart, 1973.

1895 CARMEN, L. and Nootura, with K. Colwell. "Three Inuit Women Speak: Surviving is What Counts." *Canadian Woman Studies* 10, 2/3 (Summer/Fall 1989): 58-61.

1896 CARPENTER, Jock. *Fifty Dollar Bride: Mary Rose Smith: A Chronicle of Métis Life in the 19th Century.* Sidney, BC: Gray's Publishing, 1977.

1897 CLUTTON-BROCK, Elizabeth. *Woman of the Paddle Song.* Toronto: Copp Clark, 1972. [novel depicting native wife of explorer David Thompson]

1898 CRNKOVICH, Mary, ed. *"Gossip": A Spoken History of Women in the North.* Ottawa: Canadian Arctic Resources Committee, 1990.

1899 CRUIKSHANK, Julie. *Athapaskan Women: Lives and Legends.* Canadian Ethnology Service Paper No. 57. Ottawa: National Museum of Man, 1979.

1900 CRUIKSHANK, Julie. *The Stolen Woman: Female Journeys in Tagish and Tutchone Narrative.* Ottawa: National Museums of Canada, 1983.

1901 CRUIKSHANK, Julie in collaboration with Angela Sidney, Kitty Smith and Annie Ned. *Life Lived Like a Story: Life Stories of Three Yukon Elders.* Vancouver: University of British Columbia Press, 1991.

1902 FLANNERY, Regina. *Ellen Smallboy: Glimpses of a Cree Woman's Life.* Montreal and Kingston: McGill-Queen's University Press, 1995.

1903 FRENCH, Alice. "My Name Is Masak." *The Beaver* (Autumn 1976): 28-31.

1904 FRENCH, Alice. *My Name is Masak.* Winnipeg: Peguis Publishers, 1977.

1905 FRENCH, Alice. *The Restless Nomad.* Winnipeg: Pemmican Books, 1991. [an Inuit girl who had to relearn her culture and language after years in an Anglican boarding school]

1906 GREENE, Alma. *Forbidden Voice: Reflections of a Mohawk Indian.* Don Mills: Hamlyn, 1971.

1907 HOLLOWAY, Josephine. "Three Yukon First Nations Elders Share Their Knowledge." *Canadian Woman Studies* 14, 4 (Fall 1994): 62-70.

1908 IREDALE, Jennifer. "Cecilia Douglas Helmcken." *British Columbia Historical News* 28, 4 (Fall 1995): 26-30.

1909 JENSEN, Marilyn. "How We Were: Growing Up as a Yukon First Nations Girl." *Canadian Woman Studies* 14, 4 (Fall 1994): 87-89.

1910 KEGGE, Maude. *Portage Lake: Memories of an Ojibwe Childhood.* Edited and transcribed by John D. Nichols. Edmonton: University of Alberta Press, 1991.

1911 KLUGIE, Garry. "The Poverty and the Poetry: A Native Woman's Life History." *Canadian Woman Studies* 4, 2 (Winter 1982): 39-41.

1912 MARACLE, Lee. *Bobbi Lee: Indian Rebel.* Toronto: Women's Press, 1990.

1913 McKENNA, M. Olga. *Micmac By Choice: Elsie Sark, An Island Legend.* Halifax: Formac Publishing, 1990. [English bride of war hero John J. Sark, son of Micmac chief]

1914 MEILI, Dianne. *Those Who Know: Profiles of Alberta's Native Elders.* Edmonton: NeWest Press, 1991.

1915 MINOR, Kathleen. "Elizabeth: An Elder Inuk Woman's Story of Traditional Infanticide." *Canadian Woman Studies* 14, 4 (Fall 1994): 55-57.

1916 MONTURE-ANGUS, Patricia. *Thunder in My Soul: A Mohawk Woman Speaks.* Halifax: Fernwood Publishing, 1995.

1917 MORAN, Bridget. *Stoney Creek Woman: The Story of Mary John.* Vancouver: Tillacum Library, 1988.

1918 PARADIS, Roger. "Lisa—La jeune esclave indienne/A Young Indian Slave." *Canadian Folklore* 14, 2 (1992): 95-112.

1919 SAUNDERS, Doris. "A Daughter of Labrador." *Canadian Women's Studies* 2, 1980.

1920 SAUNDERS, Doris. "Women in Labrador: A Personal Viewpoint." *Atlantis* 8, 1 (Fall 1982): 84-88.

1921 SPEARE, Jean E., ed. *The Days of Augusta.* Vancouver: J.J. Douglas, 1973.

1922 THERIAULT, Madeline. *Moose to Moccasins: The Story of Ka Kita Wa Pa No Kwe.* Toronto: Natural Heritage/Natural History, 1992.

1923 VANDERBURGH, R.M. *I Am Nokomis, Too: The Biography of Verna Patronella Johnston.* Don Mills: General Publishing, 1977.

1924 VAN KIRK, Sylvia. "Thanadelthur." *The Beaver* (Spring 1974): 40-45.

1925 WINTER, Keith. *Shananditti: The Last of the Beothucks.* North Vancouver: J.J. Douglas, 1975.

GENERAL

1926 BATAILLE, Gretchen M. and Kathleen M. Sands. *American Indian Women: A Research Guide.* New York: Garland, 1991.

1927 DROLET, Gaeten and Marie-France Labrecque. *Les femmes amérindiennes au Québec: Guide annotée des sources d'information.* Québec: Université Laval, 1986.

1928 GREEN, R. *Native American Women: A Contextual Bibliography.* Bloomington: Indiana University Press, 1983.

1929 JAMIESON, Kathleen. *Native Women in Canada: A Selected Bibliography.* Ottawa: Social Sciences and Humanities Research Council of Canada, 1983.

1930 KOCHLER, L. "Native Women of the Americas: A Bibliography." *Frontiers* 6, 3 (1981): 73-101.

1931 LEGARE, Evelyn and Richard A. Barazzuoi. *Native Women of BC and the Yukon: A Selected Bibliography.* Vancouver: Department of Sociology and Anthropology, University of British Columbia, 1982.

1932 VAN KIRK, Sylvia. *Towards a Feminist Perspective in Native History.* Occasional Paper No. 14. Toronto: Centre for Women's Studies, Ontario Institute for Studies in Education, 1987.

1933 WHITE, Pamela Margaret. *Native Women: A Statistical Overview.* Ottawa: Secretary of State, 1987.

WORK/ROLES/COLONIZATION

1934 ACKERMAN, Lillian. "Gender Status in Yup'ik Society." *Études Inuit Studies* 14, 1/2 (1990): 209-22.

1935 ACOOSE, Janice. *Iskwekwak-kah'ki yaw ni wahko-makanak: Neither Indian Princesses nor Squaw Drudges.* Toronto: Women's Press, 1995.

1936 ALBERS, Patricia. "New Perspectives on Plains Indian Women." In *The Hidden Half: Studies of Plains Indian Women,* eds. Patricia Albers and Beatrice Medicine. New York: University Press of America, 1983.

1937 ALBERS, Patricia and Beatrice Medicine, eds. *The Hidden Half: Studies of Plains Indian Women.* New York: University Press of America, 1983.

1938 ANDERSON, Karen. *Commodity Exchange and Subordination: A Comparison of Montagnais-Naskapi Women circa 1600-1650.* Toronto: Department of Sociology, University of Toronto, 1983.

1939 ANDERSON, Karen. "Commodity Exchange and Subordination: Montagnais-Nascapi and Huron Women, 1600-1650." *Signs* 11, 1 (Autumn 1985): 48-62.

1940 ANDERSON, Karen. "Shrews and Lambs: Images of Montaignais-Naskapi and Huron Women in the Writings of the 17th Century Jesuits." In *Women, Images, Role Models,* ed. E. Trady, 84-90. Ottawa: Canadian Research Institute for the Advancement of Women, 1985.

1941 ANDERSON, Karen. "A Gendered World: Women, Men, and the Political Economy of the Seventeenth Century Huron." In *Feminism and Political Economy: Women's Work, Women's Struggles,* eds. Heather Jon Maroney and Meg Luxton. Toronto: Methuen, 1987.

1942 ANDERSON, Karen. "As Gentle as Little Lambs: Images of Huron and Montaignais-Naskapi Women in the Writings of the 17th Century Jesuits." *Canadian Review of Sociology and Anthropology* 25, 4 (November 1988): 560-76.

1943 ANDERSON, Karen. *Chain Her By One Foot: The Subjugation of Native Women in Seventeenth-Century New France.* London and New York: Routledge, 1991.

1944 ARMSTRONG, Jeannette J. "Across the Cultural Gap." In *British Columbia Reconsidered: Essays on Women,* eds. Gillian Creese and Veronica Strong-Boag, 290-95. Vancouver: Press Gang Publishers, 1992.

1945 BAIRD, Irene. "The Eskimo Woman: Her Changing World." *The Beaver* (Spring 1959): 48-55.

1946 BASKIN, Cyndy. "Women in Iroquois Society." *Canadian Woman Studies* 4, 2 (Winter 1982): 42-46.

1947 BEAUDET, Christianne. "Mes mocassins, ton canot, nos raquettes: la division sexuelle du travail et la transmission des connaissances chez les Montagnais de la Romaine." *Recherches amérindiennes au Québec* 14, 3 (1984): 37-44.

1948 BLACKMAN, Margaret B. "The Changing Status of Haida Women: An Ethnohistorical and Life History Approach." In *The World is as Sharp as a Knife: Essays in Honour of Wilson Duff,* ed. Donald N. Abbott, 65-77. Victoria: Provincial Museum of British Columbia, 1981.

1949 BLACKWOOD, Evelyn. "Sexuality and Gender in Certain Native American Tribes: The Case of Cross-Gender Females." *Signs* 10, 1 (Autumn 1984): 27-42.

1950 BODENHORN, Barbara. "'I'm not the Great Hunter, My Wife is': Inupiat and Anthropological Models of Gender." *Études Inuit Studies* 14, 1/2 (1990): 55-74.

1951 BONVILLAIN, Nancy. "Gender Relations in Native North America." *American Indian Culture and Research Journal* 13, 2 (1989): 1-28.

1952 BOURGEAULT, Ron. "The Development of Capitalism and the Subjugation of Women in Northern Canada." *Alternate Routes* 6 (1983): 109-40.

1953 BOURGEAULT, Ron. "The Indians, the Métis and the Fur Trade: Class, Sexism and Racism in the Transition from Communism to Capitalism." *Studies in Political Economy* 12 (Autumn 1983): 45-80.

1954 BOURGEAULT, Ron. "Race, Class, and Gender: Colonial Domination of Indian Women." In *Race, Class and Gender: Bonds and Barriers,* ed. Jessie Vorst, 87-115. Toronto: Between the Lines, 1989. Reprinted in *Racism in Canada,* ed. Ormond McKague, 129-50. Saskatoon: Fifth House Publishers, 1991.

1955 BRODRIBB, Somer. "The Traditional Roles of Native Women in Canada and the Impact of Colonization." *Canadian Journal of Native Studies* 4, 1 (1984): 85-103.

1956 BROWN, Jennifer. "A Colony of Very Useful Hands." *The Beaver* (Spring 1977): 39-45.

1957 BROWN, Jennifer S.H. "Woman as Centre and Symbol in the Emergence of Métis Communities." *Canadian Journal of Native Studies* 3, 1 (1983): 39-46.

1958 BROWN, Judith K. "Economic Organization and the Position of Women Among the Iroquois." *Ethnohistory* 17, 3/4 (Summer 1970): 151-67. Reprinted in *Iroquois Women: An Anthology,* ed. W.G. Spittal, 182-98. Ohsweken, ON: Iroqrafts Ltd., 1990.

1959 BROWN, Judith K. "Iroquois Women: An Ethnohistoric Note." In *Family Bonds and Gender Divisions: Readings in the Sociology of the Family,* ed. Bonnie Fox, 83-98. Toronto: Canadian Scholars' Press Inc., 1988.

1960 BUFFALOHEAD, Priscilla. "Farmers, Warriors and Traders: A Fresh Look at Ojibwa Women." *Minnesota History* 48, 3 (1983): 236-44.

1961 CAMPBELL, Marjorie Wilkins. "Her Ladyship, My Squaw." *The Beaver* (September 1954): 14-17.[role of native women in fur trade society]

1962 CARTER, Sarah. "'A Fate Worse Than Death': Indian Captivity Stories Thrilled Victorian Readers, But Were They True?" *The Beaver* 68, 2 (April/May 1988): 21-28.

1963 CARTER, Sarah. "Categories and Terrains of Exclusion: Constructing the 'Indian Woman' in the Early Settlement Era in Western Canada." *Great Plains Quarterly* 13, 3 (Summer 1993): 147-61.

1964 CASTELLANO, Marlene Brant. "Women in Huron and Ojibwa Societies." *Canadian Woman Studies* 10, 2/3 (Summer/Fall 1989): 45-48.

1965 CHASKE, Ivy, *et al,* eds. "Native Women." A special issue of *Fireweed* 22 (Winter 1986).

1966 CHEDA, Sherrill. "Indian Women: An historical example and a contemporary view." In *Women in Canada,* 2nd edition, ed. Marylee Stephenson, 195-208. Don Mills: General Publishing Co. Ltd., 1977.

1967 CLERMONT, Norman. "La place de la femme dans les sociétés iroquoiennes de la période du contacte." *Recherches amérindiennes au Québec* 13, 4 (1983): 286-90.

1968 COLLIN, Dominique. "La discrète émancipation de Talasia: Identité féminine et vision du monde d'une jeune Inuk du Québec nordique." *Recherches amérindiennes au Québec* 13, 4 (1983): 255-64.

1969 COOPER, Carol. "Native Women of the Northern Pacific Coast: An Historical Perspective, 1830-1900." *Journal of Canadian Studies* 27, 4 (Winter 1992/93): 44-75. Reprinted in *Canadian Women: A Reader,* eds. Wendy Mitchinson, *et al,* 89-119. Toronto: Harcourt Brace Canada, 1996.

1970 CROSBY, Marcia. "Construction of the Imaginary Indian." In *The Vancouver Anthology: The Institutional Politics of Art,* ed. Stan Douglas, 267-95. Vancouver: Talonbooks, 1991. Reprinted in *by, for & about: Feminist Cultural Politics,* ed. Wendy Waring, 85-114. Toronto: Women's Press, 1994.

1971 CRUIKSHANK, Julie. "Becoming A Woman in Athapaskan Society: Changing Traditions on the Upper Yukon River." *Western Canadian Journal of Anthropology* 5, 2 (1975): 1-14.

1972 CRUIKSHANK, Julie. "Claiming Legitimacy: Prophecy Narratives from Northern Aboriginal Women." *American Indian Quarterly* 18, 2 (Spring 1994): 147-67.

1973 DAGENAIS, Huguette and Denise Piché, eds. *Women, Feminism and Development.* Montreal and Kingston: McGill-Queen's University Press, 1994.

1974 DAVIS, Natalie Zemon. "Iroquois Women, European Women." In *Women, "Race," and Writing in the Early Modern Period,* eds. Margo Hendricks and Patricia Parker, 243-58. London and New York: Routledge, 1994.

1975 DEMOS, John. *The Unredeemed Captive: A Family Story from Early America.* New York: Vintage Books, 1995.

1976 DESMARAIS, Danielle, Carole Lévesque and Dominque Raby. "La contribution des femmes naskapies aux travaux de la vie quotidienne à l'époque de Fort McKenzie." *Recherches féministes* 7, 1 (1994): 23-42.

1977 DEVENS, Carol. "Separate Confrontations: Gender as a Factor in Indian Adaptation to European Colonization in New France." *American Quarterly* 38, 3 (1986): 461-80.

1978 DEVENS, Carol. *Countering Colonization: Native American Women and Great Lakes Missions, 1630-1900.* Berkeley: University of California Press, 1992.

1979 DEVENS, Carol. "'If We Get the Girls, We Get the Race': Missionary Education of Native American Girls." *Journal of World History* 3, 2 (Fall 1992): 219-38.[19th century, Ojibwa and Dakota]

1980 DRAPEAU, Lynn. "L'émancipation des femmes dans le vocabulaire montagnais." *Recherches amérindiennes au Québec* 14, 3 (1984): 45-54.

1981   DRIBEN, Paul. "A Death in the Family: The Strategic Importance of Women in Contemporary Northern Ojibwa Society." *Native Studies Review* 6, 1 (1990): 83-110.

1982   DUFOUR, Rose. *Femme et enfantement: Sagesse dans la culture Inuit.* Québec: Éditions Papyrus, 1988.

1983   FALCONER, Patrick. "The Overlooked of the Neglected: Native Single Mothers in Major Cities on the Prairies." In *The Political Economy of Manitoba,* eds. Jim Silver and Jeremy Hull, 188-210. Regina: Canadian Plains Research Centre, 1990.

1984   FIENUP-RIORDAN, Ann. "The Real People: The Concept of Personhood Among the Yup'ik Eskimos of Western Alaska." *Études Inuit Studies* 10, 1/2 (1986): 9-24.

1985   FISKE, Jo-Anne. "Fishing is Women's Business: Changing Economic Roles of Carrier Women and Men." In *Native People/Native Lands: Canadian Indians, Inuit and Metis,* ed. Bruce Alden Cox, 186-98. Ottawa: Carleton University Press, 1988.

1986   FISKE, Jo-Anne. "Colonization and the Decline of Women's Status: The Tsimshian Case." *Feminist Studies* 17, 3 (Fall 1991): 509-35.

1987   FISKE, Jo-Anne. "Carrier Women and the Politics of Mothering." In *British Columbia Reconsidered: Essays on Women,* eds. Gillian Creese and Veronica Strong-Boag, 198-216. Vancouver: Press Gang Publishers, 1992.

1988   FISKE, Jo-Anne. "Child of the State, Mother of the Nation: Aboriginal Women and the Ideology of Motherhood." *Culture* 13, 1 (1993): 17-35.

1989   FISKE, Jo-Anne. "The Supreme Law and the Grand Law: Changing Significance of Customary Law for Aboriginal Women of British Columbia." *BC Studies* 105/106 (Spring/Summer 1995): 183-200.

1990   FRIDERES, James S. *Native People in Canada: Contemporary Conflicts.* Scarborough: Prentice-Hall, 1983.

1991   GERBER, Linda. "Multiple Jeopardy: A Socio-Economic Comparison of Men and Women Among the Indian, Metis and Inuit Peoples of Canada." *Canadian Ethnic Studies* 22, 3 (1990): 69-84.

1992   GONZALES, Ellice B. *Changing Economic Roles for Micmac Men and Women: An Ethnohistorical Analysis.* Ottawa: National Museums of Canada, 1981.

1993   GONZALES, Ellice B. "An Ethnohistorical Analysis of Micmac Male and Female Economic Roles." *Ethnohistory* 29, 2 (1982): 117-29.

1994   GREEN, Gretchen. "Molly Brant, Catharine Brant, and Their Daughters: A Study in Colonial Acculturation." *Ontario History* 81, 3 (Sept. 1989): 235-50.

1995   GUEMPLE, Lee. "Men and Women, Husbands and Wives: The Role of Gender in Traditional Inuit Society." *Études Inuit Studies* 10, 1/2 (1986): 9-24.

1996   GUÉRIN, Yvonne. "La femme Inuit dominée: création mythique alloctone?" *Anthropologie et Sociétés* 6, 3 (1982): 129-54.

1997   HAIG-BROWN, Celia. *Resistance and Renewal: Surviving the Indian Residential School.* Vancouver: Tillacum Library, 1988.

1998   HOUSTON, C. Stuart and Robert H. Buhr. "Swaddling of Indian Infants in Northern Saskatchewan." *Musk-Ox* 36 (1988): 5-14.

1999   ING, N. Rosalyn. "The Effects of Residential Schools on Native Child-Rearing Practices." *Canadian Journal of Native Education* 18 (Supplement 1991): 65-118.

2000   JAENEN, Cornelius J. "Education for Francization: The Case of New France in the Seventeenth Century." *Canadian Journal of Native Studies* 11, 1 (1983): 1-19.

2001   JAENEN, Cornelius J. "Miscegenation in Eighteenth-Century New France." In *New Dimensions in Ethnohistory: Papers of the Second Laurier Conference on Ethnohistory and Ethnology,* eds. Barry Gough and Laird Christie, 79-115. Hull: Canadian Museum of Civilization, 1991.

2002   JOLLES, Carol Zane and Kaningok. "Qayuutat and Angyapiget: Gender Relations and Subsistence Activities in Sivuqaq (Gambell, St. Lawrence Island, Alaska)." *Études Inuit Studies* 15, 2 (1991): 23-53.

2003   "Journals of Helen Anne English, Field Matron on the Little Pine Reserve, 1913-1917." *Saskatchewan History* 45, 2 (Fall 1993): 37-42.

2004   KAPLAN, Sidney. "Historical Efforts to Encourage White-Indian Intermarriage in the United States and Canada." *International Social Sciences Review* 65, 3 (Summer 1990): 126-32.

2005   KEHOE, Alice. "Old Women Had Great Power." *Western Canadian Journal of Anthropology* 6, 3 (1976): 68-78. [Blackfoot]

2006   KEHOE, Alice. "The Shackles of Tradition." In *The Hidden Half: Studies of Plains Indian Women,* eds. Patricia Albers and Beatrice Medicine. New York: University Press of America, 1983.

2007   KIDWELL, Clara S. "Indian Women as Cultural Mediators." *Ethnohistory* 39, 2 (Spring 1992): 97-107.

2008   KLEIN, Alan. "The Political Economy of Gender: A 19th Century Plains Indian Case Study." In *The Hidden Half: Studies of Plains Indian Women,* eds. Patricia Albers and Beatrice Medicine. New York: University Press of America, 1983.

2009   KLEIN, Laura. "'She's one of us you know': The Public Life of Tlingit Women: Traditional, Historical and Contemporary Perspectives." *Western Canadian Journal of Anthropology* 6 (1976).

2010   LABRECQUE, Marie-France. "Des femmes de Weymontachie." *Recherches amérindiennes au Québec* 14, 3 (1984): 3-16.

2011 LABRECQUE, Marie-France. "Développement du capitalisme dans la région de Weymontachie (Haute-Maurice): incidences sur la condition des femmes attikamèques." *Recherches amérindiennes au Québec* 14, 3 (1984): 75-87.

2012 LEACOCK, Eleanor. "Montagnais Women and the Jesuit Program for Colonization." In *Women and Colonization: Anthropological Perspectives,* eds. Mona Etienne and Eleanor Leacock, 25-41. New York: Praeger, 1980. Reprinted in *Rethinking Canada: The Promise of Women's History,* eds. Veronica Strong-Boag and Anita Clair Fellman, 7-22. Toronto: Copp Clark Pitman Ltd., 1986; 2nd edition, 11-27, 1991.

2013 LEACOCK, Eleanor B. "Women in an Egalitarian Society: The Montagnais-Naskapi of Canada." In her *Myths of Male Dominance: Collected Articles on Woman Cross-Culturally,* 31-81. New York: Monthly Review Press, 1981.

2014 LEACOCK, Eleanor. "Women in Egalitarian Societies." In *Becoming Visible: Women in European History,* eds. Renate Bridenthal, Claudia Koonz and Susan Stuard, 11-35. Boston: Houghton Mifflin, 1977; 2nd edition, 1987.

2015 LEACOCK, Eleanor and Jacqueline Goodman. "Montagnais Marriage and the Jesuits in the Seventeenth Century: Incidents from the *Relations* of Paul Le Jeune." *Western Canadian Journal of Anthropology* 6, 3 (1976): 77-91.

2016 LÉVEILLÉ, Danielle. *L'androcentrisme et anthropologie: un example: les femmes inuit.* Québec: Groupe de recherche multidisciplinaire féministe, Université Laval, 1989.

2017 LITTLEFIELD, Loraine. "Women Traders in the Maritime Fur Trade." In *Native People/Native Lands: Canadian Indians, Inuit and Metis,* ed. Bruce Alden Cox, 173-85. Ottawa: Carleton University Press, 1988. Reprinted in *Canadian Women: A Reader,* eds. Wendy Mitchinson, *et al,* 6-19. Toronto: Harcourt Brace Canada, 1996. [Northwest Coast]

2018 MATTIASSON, John S. "Northern Baffin Island Women in Three Cultural Periods." *Western Canadian Journal of Anthropology* 6, 3 (1976): 201-12.

2019 McELROY, Ann. "Canadian Arctic Modernization and Change in Female Inuit Role Identification." *American Ethnologist* 2 (1975): 662-86.

2020 McELROY, Ann. "The Negotiation of Sex-Role Identity in Eastern Arctic Culture Change." In *Sex Roles in Changing Cultures: Occasional Papers in Anthropology,* eds. Ann McElroy and C. Matthiasson, 49-60. Buffalo: Dept. of Anthropology, 1979.

2021 MEDICINE, Beatrice. "'Women Warriors'—Sex Role Alternatives for Plains Indian Women." In *The Hidden Half: Studies of Plains Indian Women,* eds. Patricia Albers and Beatrice Medicine. New York: University Press of America, 1983.

2022 MIKKELSEN, Glen. "Games Indians Played." *Alberta History* 41, 3 (Summer 1993): 2-7.

2023 MILLWARD, Marilyn. "Clean Behind the Ears?: Micmac Parents, Micmac Children and the Shubenacadie Residential School." *New Maritimes* 10 (March/April 1992): 6-15.

2024 MITCHELL, Marjorie. "The Indian Act: Social and Cultural Consequences for Native Women on a British Columbia Reserve." *Atlantis* 4, 2 (1979): 179-88.

2025 MITCHELL, Marjorie and Anna Franklin. "When You Don't Know the Language, Listen to the Silence: An Historical Overview of Native Indian Women in BC." In *Not Just Pin Money: Selected Essays on the History of Women's Work in British Columbia,* eds. Barbara K. Latham and Roberta J. Pazdro, 17-35. Victoria: Camosun College, 1984. Reprinted in *A History of British Columbia: Selected Readings,* ed. Patricia E. Roy, 49-68. Mississauga: Copp Clark, 1989.

2026 MOHAWK WOMEN OF CAUGHNAWAGA. "The Least Members of Our Society." *Canadian Women's Studies* 2, 2 (1980): 64-66.

2027 NATIVE WOMEN'S ASSOCIATION OF CANADA. *Native Women—Labour Force Development.* Ottawa: Employment and Immigration Canada, 1981.

2028 NICHOLSON, J. Phillip. *Economic Issues Facing Native Women in Ontario.* Toronto: Ontario Women's Directory, 1987.

2029 OLSEN, Karen. "Native Women and the Fur Industry." *Canadian Woman Studies* 10, 2/3 (Summer/Fall 1989): 55-56.

2030 O'MEARA, Walter. *Daughters of the Country: The Women of the Fur Traders and Manitoba Men.* New York: Harcourt, Brace and World, 1968.

2031 OOSTEN, Jaarich G. "Male and Female in Inuit Shamanism." *Études Inuit Studies* 10, 1/2 (1986): 115-31.

2032 PAPER, Jordan. "The Forgotten Grandmothers: Amerindian Women and Religion in Colonized North America." *Canadian Woman Studies* 5, 2 (Winter 1983): 48-51.

2033 PETERSON, Jacqueline. "Women Dreaming: The Religiopsychology of Indian White Marriages and the Rise of Metis Culture." In *Western Women: Their Land, Their Lives,* eds. Lillian Schlissel, Vicki Ruiz and Janice Monk, 49-68. Albuquerque: University of New Mexico Press, 1988.

2034 RAVICZ, Marilyn, Diane Battung, and Laura Baker. "Rainbow Women of the Fraser Valley: Lifesongs Through the Generations." In *Not Just Pin Money: Selected Essays on the History of Women's Work in British Columbia,* eds. Barbara K. Latham and Roberta J. Pazdro, 37-52. Victoria: Camosun College, 1984.

2035 REMIE, Cornelius. "Towards a New Perspective on Netjilik Female Infanticide." *Études Inuit Studies* 9, 1 (1985): 67-76.

2036 RIDINGTON, Robin. "Stories of the Vision Quest Among Dunne-Za Women." *Atlantis* 9, 1 (1983): 68-78.

2037 ROARK-CALNEK, Sue N. "Un mariage dans les bois: continuité et changement dans le mariage algonquin." *Recherches amérindiennes au Québec* 23, 2/3 (automne 1993): 87-107.

2038 ROUTHIER, Marie-Josée. "Que sont devenues les sages-femmes d'antan? L'accouchement chez les femmes attikamèques de Manouan." *Recherches amérindiennes au Québec* 14, 3 (1984): 26-36.

2039 AUNDERS, Douglas. "Indian Women: A Brief History of Their Roles and Rights." *McGill Law Journal* 21, 4 (1975): 656-72.

2040 SCHNEIDER, Mary Jane. "Women's Work: An Examination of Women's Roles in Plains Indian Arts and Crafts." In *The Hidden Half: Studies of Plains Indian Women*, eds. Patricia Albers and Beatrice Medicine, New York: University Press of America, 1983.

2041 SÉGUIN, Claire. "Essai sur la condition de la femme indienne au Canada." *Recherches amérindiennes au Québec* 10, 4 (1981): 251-60.

2042 *Speaking Together: Canada's Native Women*. Ottawa: Secretary of State/Toronto: Hunter Rose, 1975.

2043 SPITTAL, W.G., ed. *Iroquois Women: An Anthology.* Ohsweken, Ontario: Iroqrafts, 1990.

2044 SWAMPY, Grace Marie. "The Role of the Native Woman in a Native Society." *Canadian Journal of Native Education* 9, 2 (Winter 1982): 2-20.

2045 THOMPSON, Virginia. "How Residential School Affected Indian Women." In *Learning Women: A Collection of Essays*, eds. Agnes Grant, *et al.* Brandon: Brandon University, Status of Women Organization, 1990.

2046 TOOKER, Elisabeth. "Women in Iroquois Society." In *Extending the Rafters: Interdisciplinary Approaches to Iroquoian Studies*, ed. Michael K. Foster, 109-23. Albany: State University of New York Press, 1984. Reprinted in *Canadian Women: A Reader*, eds. Wendy Mitchinson, *et al*, 19-32. Toronto: Harcourt Brace Canada, 1996.

2047 VANAST, Walter J. "The Death of Jennie Kanajuq: Tuberculosis, Religious Competition and Cultural Conflict in Coppermine, 1929-1931." *Études Inuit Studies* 15, 1 (1991): 75-104.

2048 VAN KIRK, Sylvia. "The Impact of White Women on Fur Trade Society." *The Beaver* (Winter 1972): 4-21. Reprinted in *The Neglected Majority: Essays in Canadian Women's History*, eds. Susan Mann Trofimenkoff and Alison Prentice, 27-48. Toronto: McClelland and Stewart, 1977; and in *Sweet Promises: A Reader on Indian-White Relations in Canada*, ed. J.R. Miller, 180-204. Toronto: University of Toronto Press, 1991.

2049 VAN KIRK, Sylvia. "'Destined to Raise Her Caste': Sarah Ballenden and the Foss-Pelly Scandal." *Historical and Scientific Society of Manitoba. Series III*, 31 (1974-75): 41-52.

2050 VAN KIRK, Sylvia. "'Women in Between': Indian Women in Fur Trade Society in Western Canada." Canadian Historical Association. *Historical Papers* (1977): 30-47. Reprinted in *Pre-Industrial Canada, 1760-1849*, eds. Michael S. Cross and Gregory S. Kealey, 191-211. Toronto: McClelland and Stewart, 1982; in *Interpreting Canada's Past: Volume 1, Before Confederation*, ed. J.M Bumsted, 168-83. Toronto: Oxford University Press, 1986; in *An Introduction to Canadian History*, ed. A.I. Silver, Toronto: Canadian Scholars' Press, 1991; and in *A Passion for Identity: An Introduction to Canadian Studies*, 2nd edition, eds. David Taras, Beverly Rasporich and Eli Mandel, 53-68. Scarboroough: Nelson Canada, 1993.

2051 VAN KIRK, Sylvia. *"Many Tender Ties": Women in Fur-Trade Society, 1670-1870.* Winnipeg: Watson & Dwyer Publishing, 1980.

2052 VAN KIRK, Sylvia. "'What If Mama is an Indian?': The Cultural Ambivalence of the Alexander Ross Family." In *The Developing West: Essays on Canadian History in Honor of Lewis H. Thomas*, ed. John E. Foster, 123-36. Edmonton: University of Alberta Press, 1983. Reprinted in *The New Peoples: Being and Becoming Métis in North America*, eds. Jacqueline Peterson and Jennifer S.H. Brown, 207-17. Winnipeg: University of Manitoba Press, 1985; and in *The Invention of Canada: Readings in Pre-Confederation History*, ed. Chad Gaffield, 402-12. Toronto: Copp Clark Longman Ltd., 1994.

2053 VAN KIRK, Sylvia. "The Role of Native Women in the Fur Trade Society of Western Canada, 1670-1830." *Frontiers* 7, 3 (1984): 9-13. Reprinted in *Rethinking Canada: The Promise of Women's History*, eds. Veronica Strong-Boag and Anita Clair Fellman, 59-66. Toronto: Copp Clark Pitman Ltd., 1986; 2nd edition, 73-80, 1991. Also reprinted in *The Women's West*, eds. Susan Armitage and Elizabeth Jameson. Norman: University of Oklahoma Press, 1987; and in *Perspectives on Canadian Economic Development: Class, Staples, Gender, and Elites*, ed. Gordon Laxer, 353-61. Toronto: Oxford University Press, 1991.

2054 VAN KIRK, Sylvia. "'The Reputation of a Lady': Sarah Ballenden and the Foss-Pelly Scandal." *Manitoba History* 11 (Spring 1986): 4-11. Reprinted in *Unequal Sisters: A Multicultural Reader in U.S. Women's History*, 2nd edition, eds. Ellen Carol DuBois and Vicki L. Ruiz, 128-38. New York: Routledge, 1994.

2055 WEAVER, Sally. "The Status of Indian Women." In *Two Nations, Many Cultures: Ethnic Groups in Canada*, 2nd edition, ed. Jean L. Elliott, 56-79. Scarborough: Prentice-Hall, 1983.

2056 WEIST, Kathleen M. "Beasts of Burden and Menial
      Slaves: Nineteenth Century Observations of
      Northern Plains Indian Women." In *The Hidden
      Half: Studies of Plains Indian Women,* eds. Patricia
      Albers and Beatrice Medicine, 29-52. Lanham,
      MD: University Press of America, 1983.

2057 WELSH, Christine. "Voices of the Grandmothers:
      Reclaiming a Métis Heritage." *Canadian Literature*
      131 (Winter 1991): 15-24.

2058 WILLIAMS, Shirley. "Woman's Role in Ojibway
      Spirituality." *Journal of Canadian Studies* 27, 3 (Fall
      1992): 100-4.

2059 WRIGHT, Mary C. "Economic Development and
      Native American Women in the Early Nineteenth
      Century." *American Quarterly* 33, 5 (Winter 1981):
      525-36.

GENERAL

IN THIS SECTION, readers will find items of general interest that do not fit neatly into one of the other subject categories or that contain materials pertaining to several subject categories. Archival guides, bibliographies, historiographical articles or collections dealing with specific topics such as Education or Work will be found in the relevant sections of this bibliography.

Since the 1970s, the publication of bibliographies and guides to archival holdings has been crucial to the development of Canadian women's history as a distinct field of study. Strong support for women's history in the archival community has recently resulted in several book-length archival bibliographies, as well as articles in *Archiva*, the journal of the Association of Canadian Archivists. As the scholarship has expanded since the early 1980s, bibliographies on Canadian women's history have become more specialized, being increasingly devoted to particular topics or to individual provinces or regions of the country. Beth Light and Veronica Strong-Boag's *True Daughters of the North*, with its detailed annotations, remains an essential guide to the scholarship on Canadian women's history produced prior to 1980.

The many collections of articles and primary documents listed in this section contain materials pertaining to every subject category in this bibliography. The most significant development in recent years has been the appearance of a number of strong collections of articles with a provincial or regional focus.

Rethinking Canada, the standard reader for introductory survey courses, has recently been joined by *Canadian Women: A Reader*. The major survey text, *Canadian Women: A History*, has just appeared in a second revised edition incorporating new developments in the scholarship since 1988. Also encouraging is the appearance of several national and provincial survey texts in Canadian history which integrate women and gender into their analyses. Compilations of profiles of individual women deemed "outstanding" in some way were a mainstay of publishing in Canadian women's history in the 1970s but interesting variations on this genre still appear from time to time. Most recently, *Ces femmes qui ont bâti Montréal* may provide a model for other cities to emulate. Other memoirs and profiles will be found throughout this bibliography.

Since the 1970s, a number of historians have produced excellent historiographical review articles tracing the major trends and developments in Canadian women's history from the 1940s to the 1990s. Some recent contributions have focused on the "colonization" of Canadian women's history, the debate over women's history and gender history, women in the historical profession, the use of oral history and the writing of biography in women's history. The teaching of women's history has also been a concern of scholars since the 1970s with discussions focussing on feminist pedagogy and strategies for integrating women's history into the traditional history curriculum.

ARCHIVES

2060 ANDERSON, Ann Leger and Patricia Marie Chuchryk. "Archival Holdings in Saskatchewan Women's History: preliminary survey." *Resources for Feminist Research* 8 (July 1979): 44-55.

2061 *Archives des femmes au Québec: Guide sommaire.* Québec: Archives nationales du Québec, 1990.

2062 AUBREY, Merrily K. *Sources for Women's History at the Provincial Archives of Alberta*, revised edition. Provincial Archives of Alberta. Occasional Paper No. 2. Alberta Culture and Multiculturalism, Historical Resources Division, 1989.

2063 BEATTIE, Diane L. "An Archival User Study: Researchers in the Field of Women's History." *Archivaria* 29 (Winter 1989-90): 33-50.

2064 BELLINGHAM, Susan. "Special Collections: University of Waterloo Library Special Collection Related to women." *Canadian Women's Studies* 2, 2 (1980): 18-20.

2065 BELLINGHAM, Susan. "Women's Studies Collection in the University of Waterloo Library." *Atlantis* 10, 2 (Spring 1985): 148-61.

2066 BROWN, Catherine. *Sources on Women in the Toronto City Hall Archives.* Toronto: Women in Canadian History Project, Ontario Institute for Studies in Education, 1977.

2067 CONRAD, Margaret. "Report on the archival resources of the Atlantic provinces on the subject of women's history." *Canadian Newsletter of Research on Women* 7 (July 1978): 103-12.

2068 DEAN, Joanna and David Fraser. *Women's Archives Guide: Manuscript Sources for the History of Women.* Ottawa: National Archives of Canada, 1991.

2069 DRYDEN, Jean. *Some sources for women's history at the Provincial Archives of Alberta.* Edmonton: Alberta Culture, Historical Resources Division, 1980.

2070 DUBINSKY, Karen. "Looking Forward, Reaching Backward: The Canadian Women's Movement Archives." *Fireweed* 29 (Summer 1989): 117-20.

2071 FULFORD, Margaret, ed. *The Canadian Women's Movement, 1960-1990: A Guide to Archival Resources.* Toronto: ECW Press, 1992.

2072 HALE, Linda Louise. *Selected Bibliography of Manuscripts and Pamphlets Pertaining to Women Held by Archives, Museums and Associations in British Columbia.* Toronto: Women in Canadian History Project, Ontario Institute for Studies in Education, 1978.

2073 KINNEAR, Mary and Vera Fast. *Planting the Garden: An Annotated Archival Bibliography of the History of Women in Manitoba.* Winnipeg: University of Manitoba Press, 1987.

2074 LAMOTHE, Madeleine, Ghislaine Fecteau and Pierrette Lalancette. *Les archives des femmes au Québec: Guide sommaire.* Québec: Gouvernement du Québec, Ministère des affaires culturelles, 1990.

2075 LARADE, Sharon P. and Johanne M. Pelletier. "Mediating in a Neutral Environment: Gender-Inclusive or Neutral Language in Archival Description." *Archivaria* 35 (Spring 1993): 99-109.

2076 LAVIGNE, Marie and Jennifer Stoddart. "Rapport sur les Archives du Quebec." *Canadian Newsletter of Research on Women* 5, 3 (October 1976): 87-89.

2077 LEBLANC, T. *Les femmes: guide des ressources documentaires à Montréal.* Montréal: Éditions François Hunt, 1987.

2078 LIGHT, Beth. "An inventory of sources on women in the personal papers, family papers and manuscript collection in the Archives of Ontario." *Canadian Newsletter of Research on Women* 6 (1977): 171-95.

2079 LIGHT, Beth. *Sources in Women's History at the Public Archives of Ontario.* Toronto: Women in Canadian History Project, Ontario Institute for Studies in Education, 1977.

2080 LOEWEN, Candace. "'Liberating the Canadian Clio': Some Recent Archival Resources on Women." *Resources for Feminist Research* 23, 1/2 (Spring/Summer 1994): 31-34.

2081 MELNYK, Olenka. *What's Cooking in Women's History: An Introductory Guide to Preserving Archival Records About Women.* Edmonton: Northern Alberta Women's Archives Association, 1993.

2082 NESMITH, Tom. "Sources for the history of women at the Public Archives of Canada." *Canadian Women's Studies* 3, 1 (1981): 113.

2083 PELLETIER, Johanne M. "Declaring a Scotch Verdict: Common Elements in Women's History." *Archivaria* 39 (Spring 1995): 132-36.

2084 PINARD, Yolande. "Des archives des femmes pour le début du siècle." *Bulletin du regroupement des chercheurs en histoire des travailleurs québécois* 3, 2 (juin/juillet 1976): 24-39.

2085 PRENTICE, Alison, Beth Light and Marion Royce. "Archival Material on Canadian Women." *Canadian Newsletter of Research on Women* 6, 1 (February 1977): 169-214.

2086 REILLY, Heather and Marilyn Hindmarch. *Some Sources for Women's History in the Public Archives of Canada.* Ottawa: National Museum of Man, 1974.

2087 ROYCE, Marion. "An inventory of manuscript holdings in the Baldwin Room of the Metropolitan Toronto Public Library." *Canadian Newsletter of Research on Women* 6 (February 1977): 197-214.

2088 SILVERMAN, Eliane Leslau and Anne Muir Rodney. "Archival holdings in Canadian Women's History: Alberta, Manitoba and Saskatchewan." *Canadian Newsletter of Research on Women* 6 (Feb. 1977): 127-30.

2089 "Sources on Women at the York University Archives." *Canadian Newsletter of Research on Women* 7 (July 1978): 112-16.

2090 STRONG-BOAG, Veronica. "Raising Clio's Consciousness: Women's History and Archives in Canada." *Archivaria* 6 (Summer 1978): 70-82.

2091 STRONG-BOAG, Veronica and Jean Dryden. "Archival Holdings on Canadian Women's History: Ontario." *Canadian Newsletter of Research on Women* 5, 1 (February 1976): 40-47.

2092 THOMPSON, Aisla. "Interview: The Canadian Women's Movement Archives Collective." *Women's Education des femmes* 5, 2 (Winter 1986): 18-23.

2093 WALLIS, Faith and Robert Michel, comps. *Sources for the Study of Women in the McGill University Archives, Fact Sheet No. 18.* Montreal: McGill University Archives, 1978.

BIBLIOGRAPHIES/RESOURCE GUIDES

2094 ATNIKOV, P., *et al. Out From the Shadows: A Bibliography of the History of Women in Manitoba.* Winnipeg: Manitoba Human Rights Commission, 1975.

2095 CANADA. DEPARTMENT OF SECRETARY OF STATE, WOMEN'S PROGRAM. *Women's Resource Catalogue,* 3rd edition. Ottawa: Secretary of State, Women's Program, 1984.

2096 CANADIAN WOMEN'S INDEXING GROUP (CWIG). *Canadian Feminist Thesaurus.* Toronto: OISE Press, 1990.

2097 CANADIAN WOMEN'S INDEXING GROUP. *Canadian Feminist Periodical Index, 1972-1985.* Toronto: OISE Press, 1991.

2098 CLARK, Marlene-Russell. "Women and the Island Heritage." In *Exploring Island History: A Guide to the Historical Resources of Prince Edward Island,* ed. Harry Baglole, 119-24. Belfast, PEI: Ragweed Press, 1977.

2099 COHEN, Yolande. "La recherche universitaire sur les femmes au Québec 1929-1980. Répertoire de thèses de maîtrise et de doctorat déposées dans les universités du Québec: présentation thématique." *Resources for Feminist Research* 10, 4 (December 1981/January 1982): 5-24.

2100 COHEN, Yolande. *Les thèses québécoises sur les femmes.* Collection Instruments de travail, no. 7. Québec: Institut québécois de recherche sur la culture, 1983.

2101 EICHLER, Margrit, Jennifer Newton and Lynne Primrose, comps. "A Bibliography of Social Science Materials on Canadian Women, Published Between 1950-1975." In *Women in Canada,* 2nd edition, ed. Marylee Stevenson. Don Mills: General Publishing, 1977.

2102 FISCHER, Gayle V., comp. *Journal of Women's History: Guide to Periodical Literature.* Bloomington: Indiana University Press, 1992.

2103 GWYN, Sandra. "Women." In *Read Canadian: A Book About Canadian Books,* eds. R. Fulford, *et al,* 144-53. Toronto: James, Lewis and Samuel, 1972.

2104 HAUCK, Philomena, comp. *Sourcebook on Canadian Women.* Ottawa: Canadian Library Association, 1979.

2105 HEALEY, Theresa. "Finding Women in British Columbia: A Select Bibliography." In *British Columbia Reconsidered: Essays on Women,* eds. Gillian Creese and Veronica Strong-Boag, 431-49. Vancouver: Press Gang Publishers, 1992.

2106 HOULE, Ghislaine, comp. *La femme et la société québécoise.* Bibliographies québécoises no. 1. Montréal: Bibliothèque nationale du Québec, Ministère des affaires culturelles, 1975.

2107 HOULE, Ghislaine. *La femme au Québec.* Québec: Bibliothèque nationale du Québec, 1975.

2108 JACKEL, Susan. *Canadian Prairie Women's History: A Bibliographic Survey,* 1-22. The CRIAW Papers, No. 14. Ottawa: Canadian Research Institute for the Advancement of Women, 1987.

2109 LEMIEUX, Denise and Lucie Mercier. *La recherche sur les femmes au Québec: bilan et bibliographie.* Collection Instruments de travail, no. 5. Montréal: Institut québécois de recherche sur la culture, 1982.

2110 LIGHT, Beth, comp. "Recent Publications in Canadian Women's History." *Canadian Women's Studies* 3, 1 (1981): 114-17.

2111 MAZUR, Carol, and Sheila Pepper, comps. *Women in Canada, 1965 to 1975: A Bibliography.* Hamilton: McMaster University Library Press, 1976.

2112 MAZUR, Carol and Sheila Pepper, comps. *Women in Canada—A Bibliography 1965 to 1982.* Toronto: OISE Press, 1984.

2113 MOORE, Catherine. "A checklist of some audio visual materials in Canadian women's history." *Resources for Feminist Research* 8 (July 1979): 39-41.

2114 NATIONAL FILM BOARD OF CANADA. *Women Breaking Through: A Cross-curriculum Resource Guide for Secondary School.* Montreal: National Film Board of Canada, 1988.

2115 NATIONAL FILM BOARD OF CANADA. *Beyond the Image: Films and Videos About Women's Culture, Politics and Values.* Montreal: National Film Board of Canada, 1991.

2116 ROBERTS, Barbara. "Seeing is Believing: audio-visual aids in Canadian women's history." *Resources for Feminist Research* 8 (July 1979): 37-38.

2117 SCHADE, Rosemarie and Keith J. Lowther, eds. *Gender Balancing History: Towards an Inclusive Curriculum, v. 4, A Bibliography for Canadian History, 1982-1993.* Keith Lowther, comp. Montreal: Concordia University, Simone de Beauvoir Institute, 1993.

2118 STRONG-BOAG, Veronica. "Cousin Cinderella: A Guide to Historical Literature Pertaining to Canadian Women." In *Women in Canada,* ed. Marylee Stephenson. Toronto: New Press, 1973; 2nd edition, 245-74, 1977.

2119 STRONG-BOAG, Veronica. "The Fugitive Female: An Introduction to the Bibliography of Canadian Women's Studies." In *Bibliography for Canadian Studies: Present Trends and Future Needs,* ed. Anne B. Piternick, 48-57. Association for Canadian Studies, 1983.

2120 STRONG-BOAG, Veronica and Beth Light. *True Daughters of the North: Canadian Women's History, An Annotated Bibliography.* Toronto: OISE Press, 1980.

2121 WALSH, Susan. "Studying Women at Home and Abroad: A Bibliographic Guide to English-Language Sources, 1970-1982." *Journal of Educational Thought* 17, 2 (August 1983): 187-200.

2122 WEITZ, Margaret Collins. "An Introduction to 'les Québécoises.'" *Contemporary French Civilization* 5, 1 (Fall 1980): 105-29.

COLLECTIONS

2123 BOURNE, Paula, Gail Brandt and Jacinthe Fraser, eds. "Canadian Women's History." A special double issue of *Canadian Woman Studies* 7, 3 (Fall 1986) and 7, 4 (Winter 1986).

2124 BURT, Sandra, Lorraine Code and Lindsay Dorney, eds. *Changing Patterns: Women in Canada.* Toronto: McClelland & Stewart, 1988; revised 2nd edition, 1993.

2125 CAVANAUGH, Catherine A. and Randi R. Warne, eds. *Standing on New Ground: Women in Alberta.* Edmonton: University of Alberta Press, 1993.

2126 CONRAD, Margaret, Toni Laidlaw and Donna Smyth, eds. *No Place Like Home: Diaries and Letters of Nova Scotia Women, 1771-1938.* Halifax: Formac Publishing Company Limited, 1988.

2127 COOK, Ramsay and Wendy Mitchinson, eds. *The Proper Sphere: Woman's Place in Canadian Society.* Toronto: Oxford University Press, 1976.

2128 CREESE, Gillian and Veronica Strong-Boag, eds. *British Columbia Reconsidered: Essays on Women.* Vancouver: Press Gang Publishers, 1992.

2129 CURRIE, Dawn H. and Valerie Raoul, eds. *The Anatomy of Gender: Women's Struggle for the Body.* Ottawa: Carleton University Press, 1992.

2130 DE BROU, David and Aileen Moffatt, eds. *"Other" Voices: Historical Essays on Saskatchewan Women.* Regina: Canadian Plains Research Center, 1995.

2131 FIREWEED COLLECTIVE. "Atlantic Women." A special issue of *Fireweed* 18 (Spring 1984).

2132 GEDDES, Carol, *et al,* eds. "Women of the North." A special issue of *Canadian Woman Studies* 14, 4 (Fall 1994).

2133 GENOVA, Judith, ed. *Power, Gender, Values.* Edmonton: Academic Printing and Publishing, 1987.

2134 GÖLZ, Annalee and Lynne Marks, eds. "Women's History and Gender Studies." A special issue of *BC Studies* 105/106 (Spring/Summer 1995).

2135 GREENGLASS, Esther. *A World of Difference: Gender Roles in Perspective.* Toronto: John Wiley, 1982.

2136 GUILDFORD, Janet and Suzanne Morton, eds. *Separate Spheres: Women's Worlds in the 19th Century Maritimes.* Fredericton: Acadiensis Press, 1994.

2137 HORN, Michiel, ed. *The Dirty Thirties: Canadians in the Great Depression.* Toronto: Copp Clark, 1972.

2138 IACOVETTA, Franca and Mariana Valverde, eds. *Gender Conflicts: New Essays in Women's History.* Toronto: University of Toronto Press, 1992.

2139 JEAN, Michèle, ed. *Québécoises du 20e siècle.* Montréal: Éditions du jour, 1974.

2140 KEALEY, Linda, ed. *Pursuing Equality: Historical Perspectives on Women in Newfoundland and Labrador.* St. John's: Memorial University of Newfoundland, Institute of Social and Economic Research, 1993.

2141 KINNEAR, Mary, ed. *First Days, Fighting Days: Women in Manitoba History.* Regina: Canadian Plains Research Center, University of Regina, 1987.

2142 LASVERGNAS, Isabelle, ed. *Encrages féministes: Un moment de reflexion dans la recherche féministe.* Montréal: Université du Québec à Montréal, Centre de recherche féministe, Group interdisciplinaire d'enseignement et de recherche féministes, 1989.

2143 LATHAM, Barbara and Cathy Kess, eds. *In Her Own Right: Selected Essays on Women's History in BC.* Victoria: Camosun College, 1980.

2144 LATHAM, Barbara K. and Roberta J. Pazdro, eds. *Not Just Pin Money: Selected Essays on the History of Women's Work in British Columbia.* Victoria: Camosun College, 1984.

2145 LAVIGNE, Marie and Yolande Pinard, eds. *Les femmes dans la société québécoise: Aspects historiques.* Montréal: Boréal Express, 1977.

2146 LAVIGNE, Marie and Yolande Pinard, eds. *Travailleuses et féministes: Les femmes dans la société québécoise.* Montréal: Boréal Express, 1983.

2147 LIGHT, Beth and Joy Parr, eds. *Canadian Women on the Move, 1867-1920.* Toronto: New Hogtown Press and the Ontario Institute for Studies in Education, 1983.

2148 LIGHT, Beth and Ruth Roach Pierson, eds. *No Easy Road: Women in Canada, 1920s-1960s.* Toronto: New Hogtown Press, 1990.

2149 LIGHT, Beth and Alison Prentice, eds. *Pioneer and Gentlewomen of British North America, 1713-1867.* Toronto: New Hogtown Press, 1980.

2150 LINDO, Millicent A., ed. *Making History: An Anthology of British Columbia.* Victoria: Millicent A. Lindo, 1974.

2151 MACKIE, Marlene. *Exploring Gender Relations: A Canadian Perspective.* Toronto: Butterworths, 1983.

2152 MACKIE, Marlene. *Constructing Women and Men: Gender Socialization.* Toronto: Holt, Rinehart and Winston, 1987.

2153 MARONEY, Heather Jon and Meg Luxton, eds. *Feminism and Political Economy: Women's Work, Women's Struggles.* Toronto: Methuen, 1987.

2154 MATHESON, Gwen, ed. *Women in the Canadian Mosaic.* Toronto: Peter Martin Associates, 1976.

2155 McLAREN, Arlene Tigar, ed. *Gender and Society: Creating a Canadian Women's Sociology.* Toronto: Copp Clark Pitman, 1988.

2156 MITCHINSON, Wendy, Paula Bourne, Alison Prentice, Gail Cuthbert Brandt, Beth Light and Naomi Black, eds. *Canadian Women: A Reader.* Toronto: Harcourt Brace Canada, 1996.

2157 NEMIROFF, Greta Hofmann, ed. *Women and Men: Interdisciplinary Readings on Gender.* Toronto: Fitzhenry and Whiteside, 1987.

2158 PARR, Joy, ed. *A Diversity of Women: Ontario, 1945-1980.* Toronto: University of Toronto Press, 1995.

2159 PRENTICE, Alison and Susan Mann Trofimenkoff, eds. *The Neglected Majority: Essays in Canadian Women's History, Vol. 2.* Toronto: McClelland and Stewart, 1985.

2160 SMITH, Margot and Carol Pasternak, eds. *Pioneer Women of Western Canada.* Toronto: Ontario Institute for Studies in Education, 1978.

2161 STEPHENSON, Marylee, ed. *Women in Canada.* Toronto: New Press, 1973; 2nd edition, Don Mills: General Publishing Co. Ltd., 1977.

2162 STORRIE, Kathleen, ed. *Women, Isolation and Bonding: The Ecology of Gender.* Toronto: Methuen, 1987.

2163 STRONG-BOAG, Veronica and Anita Clair Fellman, eds. *Rethinking Canada: The Promise of Women's History.* Toronto: Copp Clark Pitman Ltd., 1986; 2nd edition, 1991.

2164 TROFIMENKOFF, Susan Mann and Alison Prentice, eds. *The Neglected Majority: Essays in Canadian Women's History.* Toronto: McClelland and Stewart, 1977.

2165 VORST, Jessie, ed. *Race, Class and Gender: Bonds and Barriers.* Winnipeg: Society for Socialist Studies, 1991.

2166 "Women in Canadian Society." A special issue of *International Journal of Canadian Studies* 11 Spring 1995.

2167 ZAREMBA, Eve, ed. *Privilege of Sex: A Century of Canadian Women.* Toronto: Anansi, 1974.

HISTORIOGRAPHY/METHODOLOGY

2168 ANDERSON, Ann Leger. "Saskatchewan Women, 1880-1920: A Field for Study." In *The New Provinces: Alberta and Saskatchewan, 1905-1980,* eds. Howard Palmer and Donald Smith, 65-90. Vancouver: Tantalus Research Limited, 1980.

2169 ANDREW, Caroline, ed. *Getting the Word Out: Communicating Feminist Research.* Ottawa: University of Ottawa Press, 1989.

2170 ANDREWS, Margaret W. "Review Article: Attitudes in Canadian Women's History, 1945-1975." *Journal of Canadian Studies* 12, 4 (1977): 69-78.

2171 BAILLARGEON, Denyse. "Histoire: mot féminin?" *Canadian Woman Studies* 7, 3 (Fall 1986): 13-14.

2172 BAILLARGEON, Denyse. "Histoire orale et histoire des femmes: itinéraire et points de rencontre." *Recherches féministes* 6, 1 (1993): 53-68.

2173 BLACK, Naomi. "Women in Canadian Political Science." *Resources for Feminist Research* 8, 1 (March 1979): 36-38.

2174 BLACK, Naomi. "'The Child is Father to the Man': The Impact of Feminism on Canadian Political Science." In *The Effects of Feminist Approaches on Research Methodologies,* ed. Winnifred Tomm, 225-43. Waterloo: Wilfrid Laurier University Press, 1989.

2175 BRANDT, Gail Cuthbert. "Postmodern Patchwork: Some Recent Trends in the Writing of Women's History in Canada." *Canadian Historical Review* 72, 4 (December 1991): 441-70.

2176 BUCKLEY, Suzann. "Review Essay: Women's Experiences and the Tapestries of History and Sociology." *American Review of Canadian Studies* 20, 4 (Winter 1990): 467-72.

2177 CAMPBELL, Gail G. "Canadian Women's History: A View from Atlantic Canada." *Acadiensis* 20, 1 (Autumn 1990): 184-99.

2178 COHEN, Yolande. "L'histoire des femmes au Québec 1900-1950." *Recherches sociographiques* 21, 3 (septembre-décembre 1980): 339-45.

2179 COHEN, Yolande. "La recherche universitaire sur les femmes au Québec, 1929-1980." *Resources for Feminist Research* 10, 4 (Dec. 1981/Jan. 1982): 5-24.

2180 COHEN, Yolande. "Femmes et histoire." *Recherches sociographiques* 25 (1984): 467-77.

2181 COLLIN, Françoise. "Histoire et mémoire ou la marque et la trace." *Recherches féministes* 6, 1 (1993): 13-23.

2182 CONRAD, Margaret. "The Re-Birth of Canada's Past: A Decade of Women's History." *Acadiensis* 12 (Spring 1983): 140-62. Reprinted in *Contemporary Approaches to Canadian History,* ed. Carl Berger, 181-200. Toronto: Copp Clark Pitman, 1987.

2183 CONRAD, Margaret. "'Sundays Always Make Me Think of Home': Time and Place in Canadian Women's History." In *Not Just Pin Money: Selected Essays on the History of Women's Work in British Columbia,* eds. Barbara K. Latham and Roberta J. Pazdro, 1-16. Victoria: Camosun College, 1984. Reprinted in *Rethinking Canada: The Promise of Women's History,* eds. Veronica Strong-Boag and Anita Clair Fellman, 67-81. Toronto: Copp Clark Pitman Ltd., 1986; 2nd edition, 97-112, 1991.

2184 CONRAD, Margaret. "Recording Angels: The Private Chronicles of Women from the Maritime Provinces of Canada, 1750-1950." In *The Neglected Majority: Essays in Canadian Women's History, Vol. 2*, eds. Alison Prentice and Susan Mann Trofimenkoff, 41-60. Toronto: McClelland and Stewart, 1985.

2185 CONRAD, Margaret. "Out of the kitchen and into the curriculum: Women's Studies in Maritime Canada." In *Teaching Maritime Studies*, ed. Phillip Buckner, 108-18. Fredericton: Acadiensis Press, 1986.

2186 CREESE, Gillian and Veronica Strong-Boag. "Introduction: Taking Gender into Account in British Columbia." In *British Columbia Reconsidered: Essays on Women*, eds. Gillian Creese and Veronica Strong-Boag, 1-17. Vancouver: Press Gang Publishers, 1992.

2187 CREESE, Gillian and Veronica Strong-Boag. "Taking Gender into Account in British Columbia: More Than Just Women's Studies." *BC Studies* 105/106 (Spring/Summer 1995): 9-26.

2188 DAIGLE, Johanne. "Femmes et histoires: l'autopsie du genre d'une science de l'homme." In *Les théories scientifiques ont-elles un sexe?*, ed. Anne Decerf, 249-66. Moncton: Éditions d'Acadie, 1991.

2189 DE LA COUR, Lykke, Karen Dubinsky, Nancy Forestell, Mary Ellen Kelm, Lynne Marks and Cecilia Morgan. "Highlights of the Preliminary Report on the Status of Women as Graduate Students in History in Canada." Canadian Historical Association. *Bulletin* 17, 1 (Winter 1991): 1, 8.

2190 DRIEDGER, Diane. "Discovering Disabled Women's History." In *The more we get together: Women and Dis/ability*, eds. Houston Stewart, Beth Percival and Elizabeth R. Epperly, 81-93. Charlottetown: Gynergy Books, 1992. Reprinted in *And Still We Rise: Feminist Political Mobilizing in Contemporary Canada*, ed. Linda Carty, 173-87. Toronto: Women's Press, 1993.

2191 DUMONT-JOHNSON, Micheline. "Peut-on faire l'histoire de la femme?" *Revue d'histoire de l'Amérique française* 29, 3 (décembre 1975): 421-28.

2192 DUMONT, Micheline. "Découvrir la mémoire des femmes." *Devenirs de femmes*, 51-65. Montréal: Fides, 1980. Reprinted in *Maîtresses de maison, maîtresses d'école: Femmes, famille et éducation dans l'histoire du Québec*, eds. Nadia Fahmy-Eid and Micheline Dumont, 363-76. Montréal: Boréal Express, 1983.

2193 DUMONT, Micheline. "Histoire: mot féminin." *Liberté* 147 (juin 1983): 27-33.

2194 DUMONT, Micheline. "Historienne et sujet de l'histoire." *Questions de culture no. 7*, 21-34. Institut Québécois de recherche sur la culture, 1985.

2195 DUMONT, Micheline. *"Les pièges de l'histoire:" Différentes mais égales. Actes du colloque international de philosophie de l'Université de Montréal*, 65-82. Montréal: Presses de l'université de Montréal, 1985.

2196 DUMONT, Micheline. "The Influence of Feminist Perspectives on Historical Research Methodology." In *The Effects of Feminist Approaches on Research Methodologies*, ed. Winnifred Tomm, 111-29. Waterloo: Wilfrid Laurier University Press, 1989.

2197 DUMONT, Micheline. "L'histoire des femmes." *Histoire sociale/Social History* XXIII, 45 (May 1990): 117-28.

2198 DUMONT, Micheline. "L'alphabétisation masculine." *Histoire sociale/Social History* XXIII, 45 (May 1990): 129-31.

2199 DUMONT, Micheline. "L'histoire des femmes à quinze ans." *Traces* 29, 1 (janvier/février 1991).

2200 DUMONT, Micheline. "L'histoire à la barre." *Recherches féministes* 4, 2 (1991): 131-38. [1987 Quebec court case in which a historian is called to serve as expert witness]

2201 DUMONT, Micheline and Nadia Fahmy-Eid. "Temps et mémoire." *Recherches féministes* 6, 1 (1993): 1-12.

2202 EICHLER, Margrit. *The Double Standard: A Feminist Critique of Feminist Social Science*. London: Croom Helm, 1980.

2203 EICHLER, Margrit. "Sexism in Research and Its Policy Implications." In *Taking Sex Into Account: The Policy Consequences of Sexist Research*, ed. Jill McCalla Vickers, 17-39. Ottawa: Carleton University Press, 1984.

2204 EICHLER, Margrit and Jeanne Lapointe. *On the Treatment of the Sexes in Research*. Ottawa: Social Science and Humanities Research Council of Canada, 1985.

2205 FAHMY-EID, Nadia. "Histoire, objectivité et scientificité: Jalons pour une reprise du débat épistémologique." *Histoire sociale/Social History* XXIV, 47 (May 1991): 9-34.

2206 FELLMAN, Anita Clair. "Please May I Have Some More? Requests for Further Research Work in Canadian Women's History." *Resources for Feminist Research* 8, 2 (July 1979): 11-13.

2207 FISKE, Jo-Anne. "Ask My Wife: A Feminist Interpretation of Fieldwork Where the Women are Strong But the Men are Tough." *Atlantis* 11, 2 (Spring 1986).

2208 FRANKLIN, Ursula Martius, *et al. Knowledge Reconsidered: A Feminist Overview*. Ottawa: Canadian Research Institute for the Advancement of Women, 1984.

2209 GAGAN, Rosemary R. "Putting Humpty Together Again: The Challenge of Canadian Women's History." *British Journal of Canadian Studies* 4, 2 (1989): 276-95.

2210 GÖLZ, Annalee and Lynne Marks. "Introduction," *BC Studies* 105/106 (Spring/Summer 1995): 3-8.

2211 GRANT, Gail. "'That Was a Woman's Satisfaction': The Significance of Life History for Woman-Centred Research." Canadian Oral History Association. *Journal* 11 (1991): 29-38.

2212 HALE, Linda and Melanie Houlden. "The Study of BC Women: A Quarter-Century Review, 1960-1984." *Resources for Feminist Research* 15, 2 (July 1986): 58-68.

2213 HALLMAN, Dianne M. "Introduction." *Ontario History* 84, 4 (December 1992): 257-61. [special issue on biographies of women]

2214 KAY, Jeanne. "Landscapes of Women and Men: Rethinking the Regional Historical Geography of the United States and Canada." *Journal of Historical Geography* 17, 4 (October 1991): 435-52.

2215 KEALEY, Linda. "The Status of Women in the Historical Profession in Canada, 1989 Survey." *Canadian Historical Review* 72, 3 (September 1991): 370-88.

2216 KEALEY, Linda. "Crossing Borders: The Influence of American Women's History on the Writing of Canadian Women's History." *Canadian Review of American Studies*, Special Issue, Part II (1992): 279-300.

2217 KINNEAR, Mary. "'An Aboriginal Past and a Multicultural Future': Margaret McWilliams and Manitoba History." *Manitoba History* 24 (Autumn 1992): 2-7.

2218 LAVIGNE, Marie. "L'histoire de quelles femmes...?" *Sciences sociales au Canada* 4, 4 (1976).

2219 LEMIEUX, Denise. "Women's Studies: Problems of Frontiers from a Quebec Perspective." *Canadian Issues/Thèmes Canadiens* 15 (1993): 85-102.

2220 LÉVESQUE, Andrée. "Historiography: History of Women in Quebec since 1985." *Québec Studies* 12 (Spring-Summer 1991): 83-91.

2221 LUTZ, John. "The Woman Who Wrote the Book on BC History." *BC Historical News* 27, 2 (Spring 1994): 2. [Margaret Ormsby]

2222 MACKENZIE, Suzanne. "Building Women, Building Cities: Toward Gender Sensitive Theory in the Environmental Disciplines." In *Life Spaces: Gender, Household, Employment*, eds. Caroline Andrew and Beth Moore Milroy, 13-30. Vancouver: University of British Columbia Press, 1988.

2223 MARIE, Gillian. "Writing Women into British Columbia's History" In *In Her Own Right: Selected Essays on Women's History in BC*, eds. Barbara Latham and Cathy Kess, 1-18. Victoria: Camosun College, 1980.

2224 McKAY, Ian. "Why Tell This Parable? Some Ethical Reflections on the Dionne Quintuplets." *Journal of Canadian Studies* 29, 4 (Winter 1994/95): 144-52.

2225 MEDJUCK, Sheva. "Discovering Maritime Women: New Developments in the Social Sciences." In *Teaching Maritime Studies*, ed. Phillip Buckner, 130-35. Fredericton: Acadiensis Press, 1986.

2226 MITCHINSON, Wendy. "The Historiography of Canadian Women's History." *Conference Group in Women's History Newsletter* 4, 2 (January 1979): 16-21.

2227 MITCHINSON, Wendy. "Women's History." In *Canadian History: A Reader's Guide, Volume 2: Confederation to the Present*, ed. Doug Owram, 202-27. Toronto: University of Toronto Press, 1994.

2228 MOORE, Christopher. "Lives of Men and Women." *The Beaver* 71, 3 (June/July 1991): 50-53. [interview with historian Joy Parr]

2229 MOORE, Christopher. "The First People of America." *The Beaver* 72, 5 (Oct./Nov. 1992): 53-56. [interview with historian Olive Dickason]

2230 MOORE, Christopher. "A Light on New France." *The Beaver* 74, 3 (June/July 1994): 53-56. [interview with historian Louise Dechêne]

2231 MOORE, Christopher. "The Problem of the Hyphen." *The Beaver* 75, 2 (April/May 1995): 53-55. [interview with historian Franca Iacovetta]

2232 OUELLET, Fernand. "La question sociale au Québec, 1880-1930: la condition féminine et le mouvement des femmes dans l'historiographie." *Histoire sociale/Social History* XXI, 42 (November 1988): 319-45.

2233 PALMER, Bryan D. "Canadian Controversies." *History Today* 44, 1(November 1994): 44-49.

2234 PARR, Joy. "Nature and Hierarchy: Reflections on Writing the History of Women and Children." *Atlantis* 11, 1 (Fall 1985): 39-44.

2235 PARR, Joy. "Gender History and Historical Practice." *Canadian Historical Review* 76, 3 (Sept. 1995): 354-76.

2236 PIERSON, Ruth. "Women's History: The State of the Art in Atlantic Canada." *Acadiensis* 7, 1 (Autumn 1977): 121-31.

2237 PIERSON, Ruth Roach. "Experience, Difference, Dominance and Voice in the Writing of Canadian Women's History." In *Writing Women's History: International Perspectives*, eds. Karen Offen, Ruth Roach Pierson and Jane Rendall, 79-106. Bloomington: Indiana University Press, 1991.

2238 PIERSON, Ruth Roach. "Colonization and Canadian Women's History." *Journal of Women's History* 4, 2 (Fall 1992): 134-56.

2239 PIERSON, Ruth and Beth Light. "Women in the Teaching and Writing of Canadian History." *History and Social Science Teacher* 17, 2 (Winter 1982): 83-95.

2240 PIERSON, Ruth and Alison Prentice. "Feminism and the Writing and Teaching of History." *Atlantis* 7, 2 (Spring 1982): 37-46. Reprinted in *Clio's Craft: A Primer of Historical Methods*, ed. Terry Crowley, 211-24. Toronto: Copp Clark Pitman, 1988.

2241 PORTER, Marilyn. "Peripheral Women: Towards a Feminist Analysis of the Atlantic Region." *Studies in Political Economy* 23 (Summer 1987): 41-72.

2242 RIEGLER, Natalie. "Some Issues to Be Considered in the Writing of Biography." *Canadian Bulletin of Medical History* 11, 1 (1994): 219-27. [Harriet Goldie]

2243 ROOKE, Patricia T. and R. L. Schnell. "The Making of a Feminist Biography: Reflections on a Miniature Passion." *Atlantis* 15, 1 (Fall 1989): 56-64. [Charlotte Whitton]

2244 ROOME, Patricia. "Remembering Together: Reclaiming Alberta Women's Past." In *Standing on New Ground: Women in Alberta,* eds. Catherine A. Cavanaugh and Randi R. Warne, 171-202. Edmonton: University of Alberta Press, 1993.

2245 SANGSTER, Joan. "New Departures in Canadian Women's History." *Journal of Canadian Studies* 23, 1/2 (1988): 234-40.

2246 SANGSTER, Joan. "The Legal and Medical Regulation of Nineteenth Century Women." *Journal of Canadian Studies* 28, 1 (Spring 1993): 199-207.

2247 SANGSTER, Joan. "Telling Our Stories: Feminist Debates and the Use of Oral History." *Women's History Review* 3, 1 (1994): 5-28.

2248 SANGSTER, Joan. "Beyond Dichotomies: Re-Assessing Gender History and Women's History in Canada." *left history* 3, 1 (Spring/Summer 1995): 109-21.

2249 SILVERMAN, Eliane Leslau. "Writing Canadian Women's History, 1970-1982: An Historiographical Analysis." *Canadian Historical Review* 63, 4 (Dec. 1982): 513-33.

2250 SILVERMAN, Eliane, Leslau. "Re-visions of the Past." In *Gender Bias in Scholarship: The Pervasive Prejudice,* eds. Winnifred Tomm and Gordon Hamilton, 117-30. Calgary: Institute for the Humanities, 1988.

2251 STRONG-BOAG, Veronica. "Writing About Women." In *Writing About Canada: A Handbook for Modern Canadian History,* ed. John Schultz, 175-200. Scarborough: Prentice-Hall Canada, 1990.

2252 STRONG-BOAG, Veronica. "Contested Space: The Politics of Canadian Memory." *Journal of the Canadian Historical Association* NS 5 (1994): 3-17.

2253 STRONG-BOAG, Veronica. *Work to Be Done: The Canadian Committee on Women's History/Comité canadien de l'histoire des femmes: Du travail en perspective.* [Montreal]: Canadian Committee on Women's History/Comité canadien de l'histoire des femmes, 1995.

2254 TANCRED-SHERIFF, Peta, ed. *Feminist Research: Prospect and Retrospect.* Montreal and Kingston: McGill-Queen's University Press for the Canadian Research Institute for the Advancement of Women, 1988.

2255 TANCRED, Peta. "Into the Third Decade of Canadian Women's Studies: A Glass Half Empty or Half Full?" *Women's Studies Quarterly* 22, 3/4 (Fall/Winter 1994/95): 12-25.

2256 TOMM, Winnifred, ed. *The Effects of Feminist Approaches on Research Methodologies.* Waterloo: Wilfrid Laurier University Press, 1989.

2257 TOMM, Winnifred and Gordon Hamilton, eds. *Gender Bias in Scholarship: The Pervasive Prejudice.* Calgary: Calgary Institute for the Humanities, 1988.

2258 TROFIMENKOFF, Susan Mann. "Nationalism, Feminism and Canadian Intellectual History." *Canadian Literature* 83 (Winter 1979): 7-20.

2259 TROFIMENKOFF, Susan Mann. "Feminist Biography." *Atlantis* 5 (Spring 1985): 1-10.

2260 VAN KIRK, Sylvia. "What Has the Feminist Perspective Done for Canadian History?" In *Knowledge Reconsidered: A Feminist Overview,* Ursula Martius Franklin, *et al.* 46-58. Ottawa: Canadian Research Institute for the Advancement of Women, 1984.

PEDAGOGY

2261 ANDERSON, Ann Leger. "On Teaching Women's History." *Resources for Feminist Research* 8, 2 (July 1979): 9-10.

2262 BALDWIN, Patricia and Douglas Baldwin. "The Portrayal of Women in Classroom Textbooks." *Canadian Social Studies* 26, 3 (Spring 1992): 110-14.

2263 BRANDT, Gail Cuthbert. "The Teaching of Women's Past in the Present and the Future: Some Comments." *Resources for Feminist Research* 8, 2 (July 1979): 8-9.

2264 BRANDT, Gail Cuthbert. "Teacher Education and the Teacher of Women's History." *History and Social Science Teacher* 25 1 (Fall 1989): 9-10.

2265 COOMBER, Jan and Rosemary Evans. "Redressing the Balance: Practical Strategies for Integrating Women into 20th Century Canadian History." *History and Social Science Teacher* 25, 1 (Fall 1989): 11-12.

2266 COULTER, Rebecca Priegert. "To Know Themselves: The Transformative Possibilities of History for Young Women's Lives." *History and Social Science Teacher* 25, 1 (Fall 1989): 25-28.

2267 FLAHERTY, Peter. "HIStory and/or HERstory: One Man's Thoughts on Learning and Teaching Women's History in High School." *History and Social Science Teacher* 25, 1 (Fall 1989): 14-17.

2268 KEALEY, Linda, Ruth Pierson, Joan Sangster and Veronica Strong-Boag. "Teaching Canadian History in the 1990s: Whose 'National' History Are We Lamenting?" *Journal of Canadian Studies* 27, 2 (Summer 1992): 129-31.

2269 LIGHT, Beth, Pat Staton and Paula Bourne. "Sex Equity Content in History Textbooks." *History and Social Science Teacher* 25, 1 (Fall 1989): 18-20.

2270 MCKENNA, Katherine. "An Examination of Sex Equity in the 1986 Ontario Curriculum Guideline for History and Contemporary Studies." *History and Social Science Teacher* 25, 1 (Fall 1989): 21-24.

2271 MOORE, Catherine, Sylvia Van Kirk and Susan Bazilli. "Courses on Canadian Women's History/Histoire des Femmes au Québec et Canada—Études Féminines." *Resources for Feminist Research* 8, 2 (July 1979): 15-19.

2272 SCHADE, Rosemarie. "Introducing Gender into the History Curriculum: A Progress Report From Concordia University." In *Feminism and Education: A Canadian Perspective, Volume 2,* eds. Paula Bourne, *et al,* 243-56. Toronto: Centre for Women's Studies in Education, Ontario Institute for Studies in Education, 1994.

2273 STATON, Pat with Paula Bourne. *Claiming Women's Lives: History and Contemporary Studies, Grade 7-12/OAC.* Toronto: Green Dragon Press, 1994.

2274 STEVENS, Alta Mae and Linda McDowell. "Filling in the Picture: Resources for Teaching all About Women in Canada." *History and Social Science Teacher* 14, 1 (Fall 1978): 7-14.

2275 STRONG-BOAG, Veronica. "Graduating into Women's History." *Resources for Feminist Research* 8, 2 (July 1979): 10-11.

2276 *Teaching Women's History: Sources and Resources.* Toronto: Green Dragon Press, 1993.

2277 VAN KIRK, Sylvia, ed. "Canadian Women's History: Teaching and Research." A special issue of *Resources for Feminist Research* 7, 2 (July 1979).

PROFILES/MEMOIRS

2278 ALLAIRE, Emilia. *Profils féminins.* Québec: Éditions Garneau, 1967.

2279 ALLAIRE, Emilia. *Têtes de femmes: essais biographiques.* Québec: Éditions de l'Équinoxe, 1971.

2280 ALLISON, Susan L. "Allison Pass Memoirs." *Canada West Magazine* 1, 1/2 (Winter 1969) and (Spring/Winter 1970).

2281 ANDERSON, George W. and Robert N. Anderson, eds. *Two White Oxen: A Perspective of Early Saskatoon, 1874-1905, from the Memoirs of Barbara (Hunter) Anderson.* Lethbridge: G.W. Anderson, 1974.

2282 ANDERSON, Marnie. *Women of the West Coast, Then and Now.* Sidney, BC: Sand Dollar Press, 1993.

2283 ANDERSON, William Ashley. *Angel of Hudson Bay: The True Story of Maud Watt.* Toronto: Clarke Irwin, 1974.

2284 ANGIER, Bradford and Vena Angier. *Wilderness Wife.* Radnor, PA.: Chilton Book Co., 1976. [pioneering in Peace River region, mid-20th century]

2285 ASSOCIATION FÉMININE D'ÉDUCATION ET D'ACTION SOCIALE. *Pendant que les hommes travaillaient les femmes elles....* Montréal: Guérrin, 1978.

2286 BALL, Jean. *Remarkable Women of Newfoundland and Labrador.* St. John's: Valhalla, 1976.

2287 BANNERMAN, Jean. *Leading Ladies: Canada, 1639-1967.* Dundas, ON: Carrswood, 1967; Belleville, ON: Mika Publishing, 1978.

2288 BARTLETT, Anne Sinclair. *Along Life's Way: A Book of Reminiscences and Travels.* Beamsville, ON: Rannie Publications, 1966.

2289 BÉGON, Élisabeth. *Lettres au cher fils: Correspondance d'Élisabeth Bégon avec son gendre, 1748-1753.* Montréal: Éditions Hurtubise HMH, 1972.

2290 BELLIVEAU, John Edward. *The Splendid Life of Albert Smith and the Women He Left Behind.* Windsor, NS: Lancelot Press, 1976.

2291 BENHAM, Leslie and Lois Benham. *The Heroine of Long Point.* Toronto: Macmillan, 1963.

2292 BENNETT, Ethel M.G. "Madame de La Tour." In *The Clear Spirit: Twenty Canadian Women and Their Times.* ed. Mary Quayle Innis, 3-4. Toronto: University of Toronto Press, 1966.

2293 BUBLITZ, Dorothea, E. *Life on the Dotted Line.* New York: Vantage Press, 1960.

2294 BURNFORD, Sheila. *One Woman's Arctic.* Toronto: McClelland and Stewart, 1973.

2295 CAKE, Sharon, ed. *Eminent Women of Grey County.* Owen Sound, ON: Grey County Historical Society, 1977.

2296 CALLBECK, Lorne. "Eliza and the Argonauts." *Atlantic Advocate* 65, 1 (September 1974): 22-25. [Eliza Ann Clark, Prince Edward Island]

2297 CAMERON, Charlotte. *A Cheechako in Alaska and Yukon.* London: T.W. Unwin, 1920.

2298 *Canadian Encyclopedia,* 2nd edition. Edmonton: Hurtig Publishers, 1988.

2299 CHAPIN, Mrs. Adele de Bourgeois. *Their Trackless Way.* London: Constable and Co., 1931.

2300 COBURN, Kathleen. *The Grandmothers.* Toronto: Oxford University Press, 1949.

2301 CONRAD, Margaret, ed. "Mary Bradley's Reminiscences: A Domestic Life in Colonial New Brunswick." *Atlantis* 7, 1 (Autumn 1981): 92-101.

2302 CORBETT, Gail, ed. *Portraits: Peterborough Area Women Past and Present.* Peterborough: Portraits' Group, 1975.

2303 COUSINS, Leone Banks. "Woman of the Year—1842: The Life of Eliza Ruggles." *Nova Scotia Historical Quarterly* 6, 4 (December 1976): 349-76.

2304 CURRIE, Emma A. *The Story of Laura Secord and Canadian Reminiscences.* Toronto: William Briggs, 1900.

2305 DARSIGNY, Maryse, Francine Descarries, Lyne Kurtzman and Evelyne Tardy, eds. *Ces femmes qui ont bâti Montréal.* Montréal: Éditions du remue-ménage, 1994.

2306 DUGAS, G. *La première Canadienne au Nord-Ouest.* Saint-Dizier, France: J. Thevenot, 1907. Translated as *The First Canadian Woman in the Northwest,* Historical and Scientific Society of Manitoba, Transactions no. 62, 1901. [Marie-Ann Gaboury]

2307 DUPRÉ, Céline. *Élisabeth Bégon.* Collection Classiques Canadiens. Montreal and Paris: Fides, 1961.

2308 DYER, Brenda, *et al. Outstanding Women of Oxford County*. Woodstock, ON: Oxford County Board of Education, 1979.

2309 EATON, Flora McCrea. *Memory's Wall: The Autobiography of Flora McCrae Eaton*. Toronto: Clarke Irwin, 1956.

2310 FITZGERALD, Emily. *An Army Doctor's Wife on the Frontier: Letters from Alaska and the Far West 1874-1878*. Pittsburgh: University of Pittsburgh Press, 1962.

2311 FITZGIBBON, Mary Agnes. *A Trip To Manitoba*. Toronto: Rose-Belford Publishing, 1880.

2312 FORBES, Elizabeth. *Wild Roses at Their Feet: Pioneer Women of Vancouver Island*. Vancouver: British Columbia Centennial Committee, 1971.

2313 FOSTER, Pat. "Grandmother and Granddaughter: The Pioneer Spirit." *British Columbia Historical News* 28, 2 (Spring 1995): 2-4.

2314 FROMENT, Marie B. *Les Trois courageuses québécoises: un aventure dans l'Ouest canadien*. Montréal: Éditions Parti Pris, 1974. [1926 resettlement of destitute Quebec women and children in the Okanagan Valley of British Columbia]

2315 GAUTHIER, Thérèse S., ed. *Personnalités féminines*. Ottawa: Les Cahiers de la société d'étude et de conférences, no.1, 1975.

2316 GILEAD, Heather. *The Maple Leaf for Quite a While*. London: J.M. Dent and Sons, 1967.

2317 GILLS, Elsie McCall. *North Pole Boarding House*. Toronto: Ryerson Press, 1951. [life on Baffin Island, 1945-1947]

2318 GOULD, Jan. *Women of British Columbia*. Saanichton, BC: Hancock House Publishers, 1975.

2319 GRANT, Francis W. "A Daughter of Maitland." *Nova Scotia Historical Quarterly* 2, 2 (June 1972): 153-62. [wife of a ship's captain]

2320 HART, Margaret J. *Janet Fisher Archibald*. Victoria: Colonist Printing and Publishing, 1934.

2321 HARVEY, Robert Paton. "When Victor Hugo's Daughter was a Haligonian." *Nova Scotia Historical Quarterly* 7, 3 (September 1977): 243-56. [Adèle Hugo, 1860s]

2322 HEALY, W.J. *Women of Red River* (1923). Winnipeg: Peguis Publishing Co., 1977.

2323 HERIOT, Joan. "Edited Tape Recording of Miss J. Topham Brown's Canadian Journal." *Okanagan Historical Society Report* 37 (1974): 87-92.

2324 HERRINGTON, Walter S. *Heroines of Canadian History*. Toronto: William Briggs, 1909.

2325 HICKS, Myrtle. *The Bridges I Have Crossed: Reminiscences of a Manitoba Farm Girl*. Brandon: Privately printed, n.d.

2326 HILL, Beth. *The Remarkable World of Frances Barkley, 1769-1845*. Sidney, BC: Gray's Publishing, 1978.

2327 HOLLOWAY, Sam. "The Story of Edna Eldorado." *British Columbia Historical News* 28, 1 (Winter 1994/95): 25.

2328 HOPKINS, Ida Scharf. *To the Peace River Country and On*. Richmond, BC: The author, 1973. [pioneer life in the Peace River District, 1930s and 1940s]

2329 HOWEY, Florence R. *Pioneering on the CPR*. Ottawa: n.p., 1938.

2330 INNIS, Mary Quayle, ed. *The Clear Spirit: Twenty Canadian Women and Their Times*. Toronto: University of Toronto Press for the Canadian Federation of University Women, 1966.

2331 JOHNSTON, Jean. *Wilderness Women: Canada's Forgotten History*. Toronto: Peter Martin Associates, 1973.

2332 KILVERT, Barbara. "Pioneer Woman." *The Beaver* (Autumn 1957): 16-20.

2333 KOSTASH, Myrna, *et al. Her Own Woman: Profiles of Ten Canadian Women*. Toronto: Macmillan, 1975.

2334 LAJEUNE, Louise Marie. *Dictionnaire Général de Biographie, Littérature, Agriculture, Commerce, Industrie et des Arts, Sciences, Moeurs, Coutumes, Institutions Politiques et Religieuses du Canada*, 2 vols. Ottawa: Université d'Ottawa, 1931.

2335 LAMB, W. Kaye. "The Mystery of Mrs. Barkley's Diary: Notes on the Voyage of the Imperial Eagle, 1786-1787." *British Columbia Historical Quarterly* 6 (1942): 31-59.

2336 LEIGHTON, Caroline C. *Life at Puget Sound*. Boston: Lee and Shepard Publishers, 1884.

2337 LEMOINE, J. M. "The Heroines of New France." In *Canadian Leaves*, ed. G.M. Fairchild, 107-26. New York: Napoléon Thompson and Co., 1887.

2338 LUGRIN, N. de Bertrand. *The Pioneer Women of Vancouver Island 1843-1866*. Victoria: Women's Canadian Club of Victoria, 1928.

2339 MacEWAN, Grant. *...And Mighty Women Too: Stories of Notable Western Canadian Women*. Saskatoon: Western Producer Prairie Books, 1975. Reprinted and retitled as *Mighty Women: Stories of Western Canadian Pioneers*. Vancouver and Toronto: Douglas & McIntyre, 1995.

2340 McCALLAN, N.J. and Katherine Roback. *An Ordinary Life: Life Histories of Women in the Urban Core of Vancouver*. Ottawa: Canadian Research Institute for the Advancement of Women, 1979.

2341 McKINLEY, Mabel Burns. *Famous Men and Women of Canada*. Toronto: Longman Green and Co., 1938.

2342 McLEOD, Carol. *Legendary Canadian Women*. Hantsport, NS: Lancelot Press, 1983.

2343 McWILLIAMS, Anita. "Annie Ronayne–Pemberton Pioneer, 1885-1966." *British Columbia Historical News* 28, 3 (Summer 1995): 15-17.

2344 MERRITT, Susan E. *Her Story: Women from Canada's Past*. St. Catharine's: Vanwell Publishing Limited, 1993. [juvenile]

2345 MERRITT, Susan. *Her Story II: Women from Canada's Past*. St. Catharine's: Vanwell Publishing Limited, 1995. [juvenile]

2346 MIDDLETON, Clara and J.E. Middleton. *Green Fields Afar*. Toronto: Ryerson Press, 1947.

2347 MIDDLETON, J.E. and W.S. Downs, eds. *National Encyclopedia of Canadian Biography*, 2 vols. Toronto: Dominion Publishing Co., 1935-37.

2348 MONTGOMERY, Lucy M. *et al. Courageous Women.* Toronto: McClelland and Stewart, 1934.

2349 MORGAN, Henry J. *The Canadian Men and Women of the Time: A Handbook of Canadian Biography.* Toronto: William Briggs, 1898.

2350 MORGAN, Henry James, ed. *Types of Canadian Women.* Toronto: William Briggs, 1913.

2351 MUNDAY, Luta. *A Mounty's Wife.* London: Sheldon Press, 1930.

2352 NORCROSS, E. Blanche. *Pioneers Every One: Canadian Women of Achievement.* Toronto: Burns and MacEarchern, 1979.

2353 PEPPER, Mary S. *Maids and Matrons of New France.* Boston: Little Brown and Co., 1901.

2354 PERRY, Hattie A. *Mrs. Mary and Others: Women of Barrington.* Barrington, NS: Spindrift Publishing, 1993.

2355 PRÉVOST, Robert. *Québécoises d'hier et d'aujourd'hui: Profils de 275 femmes hors du commun.* Montréal: Les éditions internationales Alain Stanké, 1985.

2356 PUMPHREY, Marilyn. *Who's Who and Why: Newfoundland Women, 1991.* St. John's: M. Pumphrey, 1990.

2357 PURDY, Harriet and David Gagan, eds. "Pioneering in the North-West Territories: Harriet Johnson Neville." *Canada: An Historical Magazine* 2, 4 (June 1975): 1-64. [1882-1925]

2358 ROSEN, Ruth and Sue Davidson, eds. *The Maimie Papers.* New York: The Feminist Press and Indiana University Press, 1977. [correspondence of Maimie Pinzer, a young Jewish former prostitute, struggling to survive as a working woman in Philadelphia and Montreal, 1910-1922]

2359 ROBERTS, G.D. and Arthur L. Tunnell. *A Standard Dictionary of Canadian Biography,* 2 vols. Toronto: Trans-Canada Press, 1934-38.

2360 ROMPKEY, Ronald. "Mrs. Hester Thrale (Piozzi) and the Pursuit of Her Nova Scotia Fortune." *Dalhousie Review* 58, 3 (Autumn 1978): 434-42.

2361 SANDERS, Byrne Hope. *Famous Women: Carr, Hind, Gullen, Murphy.* Toronto: Clarke, Irwin, 1958.

2362 SILVER, Marietta. "Mrs. Alexander Graham Bell." *Atlantic Advocate* 62, 1 (September 1971): 32.

2363 SMITH, Dorothy Blakely, ed. *Lady Franklin visits the Pacific Northwest.* Victoria: Provincial Archives of British Columbia, 1974.

2364 STEVENSON, A. "Feminine Fortitude." *North* 15, 2 (1968): 34-39 and 15, 3 (1968): 16-21. [Lady Jane Franklin's search for the lost Franklin expedition]

2365 STIRLING, Lilla. *In the Vanguard: Nova Scotia Women, Mid-Twentieth Century.* Windsor, NS: Lancelot Press, 1976.

2366 SUTHERLAND, Ronald. "Indiscrétions montréalaises: Maria Monk, Charlotte Führer." *Études françaises* 27, 3 (hiver 1991): 65-72.

2367 SWEENEY, Lawrence Kent, ed. "The Journal of Helen Sophia Perry, Winter of 1909-1910." *Nova Scotia Historical Quarterly* 4, 4 (December 1974): 345-53.

2368 TARDY, Evelyne, Francine Descarries, Lorraine Archambault, Lyne Kurtzman and Lucie Piché. *Les Bâtisseuses de la Cité.* Montréal, Actes du Colloque Les Bâtisseuses de la Cité, ACFAS 1992. [Cahiers scientifiques de l'ACFAS: 79], 1993.

2369 TESSIER, A. *Canadiennes.* Montréal: Fides, 1962.

2370 THACKER, J. Lindsay. "BC Diary of Beatrice Sprague, 1906." *British Columbia Historical News* 28, 2 (Spring 1995): 20-24.

2371 THOMAS, Lillian Beynon. "Some Manitoba Women Who Did First Things." *Historical and Scientific Society of Manitoba* (1947/48): 13-25.

2372 WOODCOCK, George. *Faces From History: Canadian Profiles and Portraits,* Edmonton: Hurtig, 1978.

2373 ZONTA CLUB OF CHARLOTTETOWN, comps. *A Century of Women.* Charlottetown: Dillon Printing Co., n.d.

SURVEYS/OVERVIEWS

2374 *Agenda 1978, Notes sur l'histoire des femmes au Québec.* Montréal: Éditions du rémue-ménage, 1977.

2375 ARMOUR, Moira and Pat Staton. *Canadian Women in History: A Chronology.* Vancouver: Seacraft, 1990.

2376 BARMAN, Jean. *The West Beyond the West: A History of British Columbia.* Toronto: University of Toronto Press, 1991; revised 2nd edition, 1996.

2377 CANADA. *Royal Commission on the Status of Women in Canada Report.* Ottawa: Information Canada, 1970.

2378 CARISSE, Colette and Joffre Dumazedier. *Les femmes innovatrices: problèmes post-industriels d'une Amérique francophone: le Québec.* Paris: Éditions du Seuil, 1975.

2379 CLOUTIER, Renée, Gabrielle Lachance, Denise Lemieux, Madeleine Préclaire and Luce Ranger-Poisson. *Femmes et Culture au Québec.* Quebec: Institut Québécois de recherche sur la culture, 1982.

2380 CONRAD, Margaret, Alvin Finkel and Cornelius Jaenen. *History of the Canadian Peoples: Volume 1, Beginnings to 1867.* Toronto: Copp Clark Pitman, 1993.

2381 CORRECTIVE COLLECTIVE. *she named it Canada because that's what it was called.* Vancouver: Press Gang, 1972.

2382 CREIGHTON, Luella. *The Elegant Canadians.* Toronto: McClelland and Stewart, 1967.

2383 DECHÊNE, Louise. *Habitants et marchands de Montréal au XVIIe siècle.* Paris and Montréal: Plon, 1974.

2384 DECHÊNE, Louise. *Habitants and Merchants in Seventeenth-Century Montreal.* Montreal and Kingston: McGill-Queen's University Press, 1992.

2385 DOLMENT, Marcelle and Marcel Barthe. *La femme Au Québec*. Montréal: Les Presses Libres, 1973.

2386 DOUGLAS, James. "The Status of Women in New England and New France." *Queen's Quarterly* (1912): 359-74.

2387 DUMONT-JOHNSON, Micheline. "History of the Status of Women in the Province of Quebec." *The Cultural Tradition and Political History of Women in Canada*. Study no. 8 of the Royal Commission on the Status of Women in Canada. Ottawa: Information Canada, 1971.

2388 DUMONT, Micheline. "Les femmes de la Nouvelle-France: étaient-elles favorisées?" *Atlantis* 8, 1 (Fall 1982): 118-24.

2389 DUMONT, Micheline, Michèle Jean, Marie Lavigne and Jennifer Stoddart (COLLECTIF CLIO). *L'Histoire des femmes au Québec depuis quatre siècles*. Montréal: Quinze, 1982; revised 2nd edition, Le Jour, 1992.

2390 DUMONT, Micheline, Michèle Jean, Marie Lavigne and Jennifer Stoddart. *Quebec Women: A History*. Translated by Roger Gannon and Rosalind Gill. Toronto: Women's Press, 1987.

2391 ELLIOTT, Sophy L. *The Women Pioneers of North America*. Gardenvale, QC: Garden City Press, 1941.

2392 FINKEL, Alvin and Margaret Conrad with Veronica Strong-Boag. *History of the Canadian Peoples: Volume 2, 1867 to the Present*. Toronto: Copp Clark Pitman, 1993.

2393 FORBES, Ernest R. and D.A. Muise, eds. *The Atlantic Provinces in Confederation*. Toronto and Fredericton: University of Toronto Press and Acadiensis Press, 1993.

2394 FRYER, Barbara. "The Hand That Rocked the Cradle." In *Loyal She Remains: A Pictorial History of Ontario*, eds. Mary Beacock Fryer and Charles J. Humber, 420-31. Toronto: United Empire Loyalists' Association of Canada, 1984.

2395 GRIFFITHS, N.E.S. *Penelope's Web: Some Perceptions of Women in European and Canadian Society*. Toronto: Oxford University Press, 1976.

2396 GRIFFITHS, N.E.S. "Les femmes en Acadie: un survol historique." In *Les Acadiens: État de la recherche*, eds. Jacques Lapointe and André Leclerc, 7-13. Québec: Conseil de la vie française en Amérique, 1987.

2397 JEAN, Michèle. "Les Québécoises, ont-elles une histoire?" *Forces* 27, 2 (1974): 4-14. Reprinted in *Québécoises du 20e siècle*, ed. Michèle Jean. Montréal: Éditions du Jour, 1974.

2398 KLOPPENBORG, Anne, ed. "Women in Our Past: A Brief History of the Status of Women in British Columbia." *Urban Reader* 3, 4 (May 1975).

2399 KLOPPENBORG, Anne, ed. "The Twenties and the Thirties." *Urban Reader* (July/August 1975). [Vancouver]

2400 KLOPPENBORG, Anne, ed. "The Forties and the Fifties." *Urban Reader* (January/February 1976).

2401 LABARGE, Margaret Wade. "The Cultural Tradition of Canadian Women: The Historical Background." *The Cultural Tradition and Political History of Women in Canada*. Study no. 8 of the Royal Commission on the Status of Women in Canada. Ottawa: Information Canada, 1971.

2402 LACHANCE, André. *La vie urbaine en Nouvelle-France*. Montréal: Boréal Express, 1987.

2403 LEMIEUX, Denise and Lucie Mercier. *Les femmes au tournant du siècle 1880-1940: Ages de la vie, maternité et quotidien*. Québec: Institut québécois de la recherche sur la culture, 1989.

2404 L'ESPÉRANCE, Jeanne. *The Widening Sphere: Women in Canada, 1870-1940*. Ottawa: Public Archives of Canada, 1982.

2405 LÉVESQUE, Andrée. *La norme et les déviantes: les femmes au Québec pendant l'entre-deux-guerres*. Montréal: Les éditions du remue-ménage, 1989.

2406 LÉVESQUE, Andrée. *Making and Breaking the Rules: Women in Quebec, 1919-1939*. Translated by Yvonne M. Klein. Toronto: McClelland and Stewart, 1994.

2407 LÉVESQUE, Andrée. *Résistance et transgression: Études en histoire des femmes au Québec*. Montréal: Les éditions du remue-ménage, 1995.

2408 MacDONALD, I.L. *The Status of Women in the Province of Quebec*. History and Economics Series 6, No. 6. Montreal: McGill University Publications, 1920.

2409 McALLISTER, Clare. "Women of the West Kootenay." *British Columbia Historical Notes* 10, 3 (April 1977): 13-17.

2410 McCARTHY, Michael. "Role of the Woman in Newfoundland History." *Newfoundland Teachers' Association Journal* 65 (Summer 1974): 34-42, 44-47.

2411 McINTOSH, Teresa. "Newfoundland as recorded by women." *The Archivist* 16 (March-April 1989): 20-21.

2412 MONET-CHARTRAND, Simonne. *Pionnières québécoises et regroupements de femmes d'hier à aujourd'hui*. Montréal: Éditions du remue-ménage, 1990.

2413 MONET-CHARTRAND, Simonne. *Pionnières québécoises et regroupements de femmes (tome 2), 1970-1990*. Montréal: Éditions du remue-ménage, 1994.

2414 MURRAY, Hilda Chaulk. *More Than Fifty Percent: Women's Life in a Newfoundland Outport, 1900-1950*. St. John's: Breakwater Books, 1979.

2415 NOEL, Jan. "New France: les femmes favorisées." *Atlantis* 6, 2 (Spring 1981): 80-98. Revised and reprinted in *The Neglected Majority: Essays in Canadian Women's History, Vol. 2*, eds. Alison Prentice and Susan Mann Trofimenkoff, 18-40. Toronto: McClelland and Stewart, 1985; in *Rethinking Canada: The Promise of Women's History*, eds. Veronica Strong-Boag and Anita Clair Fellman, 23-44. Toronto: Copp Clark Pitman Ltd., 1986; 2nd edition, 28-50, 1991; and in *Reappraisals in Canadian History: Pre-Confederation*, eds. A.D. Gilbert, C.M. Wallace and R.M. Bray, 63-90. Scarborough: Prentice Hall Canada Inc., 1993.

2416 NOEL, Jan. "Women in New France: Further Reflections." *Atlantis* 8, 1 (Fall 1982): 125-30.

2417 PARENT, France. *Entre le juridique et le social: le pouvoir des femmes à Québec au XVIIe siècle.* Québec: Groupe de recherche multidisciplinaire féministe, Université Laval [1991].

2418 PHILIP, Catherine. "The Fair Frail Flower of Western Womanhood." In *Frontier Calgary.* eds. A.W. Rasporich and Henry C. Klassen, 114-23. Calgary: University of Calgary, McClelland and Stewart West, 1975.

2419 POLDON, Amelia. "Women in Pioneer Life." Ontario Historical Society. *Papers and Records* 17 (1919): 25-29. [Upper Canada]

2420 PRENTICE, Alison, Paula Bourne, Gail Cuthbert Brandt, Beth Light, Wendy Mitchinson and Naomi Black. *Canadian Women: A History.* Toronto: Harcourt Brace Jovanovich, 1988; revised 2nd edition, Harcourt Brace Canada, 1996.

2421 RASMUSSEN, Linda, *et al. A Harvest Yet to Reap: A History of Prairie Women.* Toronto: Canadian Women's Press, 1976.

2422 ROCHER, Guy. "Pattern and Status of French Canadian Women." *International Social Science Journal* 14, (1962): 131-37.

2423 RUSSELL, Loris. *Everyday Life in Colonial Canada.* Toronto: Copp Clark Publishing, 1973.

2424 SANDERSON, K. *One Hundred Years of Alberta Women.* Calgary: Alberta Historical Resources Foundation, 1982.

2425 SASKATOON WOMEN'S CALENDAR COLLECTIVE. *Herstory: A Canadian Women's History Calendar* Regina: Coteau Books, 1974-1996.

2426 SÉGUIN, Robert-Lionel. "La Canadienne au XVIIe et XVIIIe siècles." *Revue d'histoire de l'Amérique française* 13, 4 (mars 1960): 492-508.

2427 STRONG-BOAG, Veronica. *The New Day Recalled: Lives of Girls and Women in English Canada, 1919-1939.* Toronto: Copp Clark Pitman, 1988.

2428 STRONG-BOAG, Veronica. *"Janey Canuck": Women in Canada, 1919-1939.* Historical Booklet No. 53. Ottawa: Canadian Historical Association, 1994.

2429 STRONG-BOAG, Veronica. "Daughters of the True North, 1900-1995." *The Beaver* 74, 6 (December 1994/January 1995): 29-40.

2430 TROFIMENKOFF, Susan Mann. *The Dream of Nation: A Social and Intellectual History of Quebec.* Toronto: Gage Publishing, 1983.

2431 URQUHART, M.C. and K.A.H. Buckley. *Historical Statistics of Canada.* Cambridge: At the University Press, 1965.

2432 WALKER, Audrie. "Yukon History and Women, 1850-1950." In *Yukon Women,* eds. Jo-Ann Badley *et al.*. Yukon: Yukon Status of Women Council, 1975.

2433 WALLACE, Cecelia. "Women in Canadian History." *Women Speaking* 4, 7 (July/September 1975): 19-21.

HEALTH/MEDICINE

FOR MORE THAN two decades, women's health issues have been a major preoccupation of Canadian women's historians. Much of the early scholarship reflected feminist anger over the treatment of women by the male-dominated medical profession and an eagerness to uncover the historical roots of medical attitudes toward women and the marginalization of women in the medical profession and the healthcare system. Although interest in these topics remains constant, Canadian women's historians are increasingly drawn to examinations of the role of the state in these developments and to the analysis of medical discourses.

Since the 1970s, historians have produced a substantial body of scholarship on birth control and abortion, with particular attention to the abortion struggle in Quebec and to the early twentieth century birth control movements in British Columbia and Ontario. The medical management of childbirth has been an ongoing concern of feminist scholars, with several exploring the medicalization of childbirth, reflected in the shift from home to hospital births, and others raising questions about the implications of the new reproductive technologies and trend toward assisted reproduction in recent decades. Of late, there has been considerable interest in early twentieth century government campaigns to reduce infant and maternal mortality and to promote expert intervention in child health and childrearing.

Historical studies of medical perceptions of female sexuality and the medical treatment of women in Canada were pioneered by Wendy Mitchinson, whose *The Nature of Their Bodies* remains an excellent point of entry into this literature. The treatment of insanity, "feeble-mindedness" and venereal disease, with their links to eugenics, moral regulation and the control of women, have been examined by a number of scholars, as has women's role in the promotion of public health, going as far back as Jeanne Mance and the establishment of the Hôtel-Dieu in New France.

Women's early struggles to gain entry into the medical profession and the marginalization of female physicians in subsequent decades have generated renewed interest in recent years as historians turn their attention to the history of women in the professions. The question of the relationship of women doctors to early feminism and eugenics are ongoing subjects of investigation. Directly related to the "re-emergence of midwifery" in Canada in the past two decades are recent attempts to document the historical significance of midwives in rural frontier regions of the country and a vigorous debate about the role of the medical profession in the decline of midwifery as a respected occupation for women. A rich body of scholarship on the history of nursing has also emerged in recent years, produced by both historians and nurses seeking the origins of the contemporary crisis in the nursing profession. Major themes have included the creation of nursing as a female profession subordinate to doctors, the training of nurses in hospital nursing schools, and the ongoing struggles of nurses to gain increased professional autonomy and improved working conditions.

BIRTH CONTROL/ABORTION

2434 ANNAU, Catherine. "Eager Eugenicists: A Reappraisal of the Birth Control Society of Hamilton." *Histoire sociale/Social History* XXVII, 53 (May 1994): 111-34.

2435 BACKHOUSE, Constance B. "Involuntary Motherhood: Abortion, Birth Control and the Law in 19th Century Canada." *Windsor Yearbook of Access to Justice* 3 (1983): 61-130.

2436 BACKHOUSE, Constance B. "The Celebrated Abortion Trial of Dr. Emily Stowe, Toronto, 1879." *Canadian Bulletin of Medical History* 8, 2 (1991): 159-87.

2437 BACKHOUSE, Constance B. "Physicians, Abortions and the Law in Early Twentieth Century Ontario." *Canadian Bulletin of Medical History* 10 (1993): 229-49.

2438 BISHOP, Mary F. "The Politics of Abortion... Revisited." *Atlantis* 9, 1 (Fall 1983):106 17.

2439 BISHOP, Mary F. "The Early Birth Controllers of BC." *BC Studies* 61 (Spring 1984): 64-84.

2440 BISHOP, Mary F. "Vivian Dowding: Birth Control Activist." In *Not Just Pin Money: Selected Essays on the History of Women's Work in British Columbia*, eds. Barbara K. Latham and Roberta J. Pazdro, 327-35. Victoria: Camosun College, 1984. Reprinted in *Rethinking Canada: The Promise of Women's History*, eds. Veronica Strong-Boag and Anita Clair Fellman, 200-7. Toronto: Copp Clark Pitman Ltd., 1986.

2441 BOUTIN, Raymond. "The History of the Family Planning Movement in Canada." In *Family Planning and Social Work*, ed. Cenovia Addy, 16-29. Ottawa: Health and Welfare Canada, 1976.

2442 BRODIE, Janine, Shelly A.M. Gavigan and Jane Jenson, eds. *The Politics of Abortion: Representations of Women in Canada*. Toronto: Oxford University Press, 1992.

2443 COHEN, May. "Therapeutic Abortion and the Law." *Canadian Women's Studies* 2, 4 (1980): 94-96.

2444 COLLINS, Anne. *The Big Evasion: Abortion, The Issue That Won't Go Away.* Toronto: Lester Orpen and Denis, 1985.

2445 COLLINS, Larry D. "The Politics of Abortion: Trends in Canadian Fertility Policy." *Atlantis* 7, 2 (Spring 1982): 2-20.

2446 DAY, Shelagh and Stan Persky, eds. *The Supreme Court of Canada Decision on Abortion.* Vancouver: New Star Books, 1988.

2447 DODD, Dianne. "The Hamilton Birth Control Clinic of the 1930s." *Ontario History* 75, 1 (March 1983): 71-86. Reprinted in *The Depression in Canada: Responses to Economic Crisis*, ed. Michiel Horn. Toronto: Copp Clark Pitman, 1988.

2448 DODD, Dianne. "The Canadian Birth Control Movement on Trial, 1936-1937." *Histoire sociale/Social History* XVI, 32 (November 1983): 411-28.

2449 DODD, Dianne. "The Canadian Birth Control Movement: Two Approaches to the Dissemination of Contraceptive Technology." *Scientia Canadensis* 9, 1 (June 1985): 53-66. Reprinted in *Science, Technology and Medicine in Canada's Past: Selections from Scientia Canadensis*, eds. Richard A. Jarrell and James P. Hull, 309-22. Thornhill, ON: Scientia Press, 1991.

2450 DODD, Dianne. "Women's Involvement in the Canadian Birth Control Movement of the 1930s: The Hamilton Birth Control Clinic." In *Delivering Motherhood: Maternal Ideologies and Practices in the 19th and 20th Centuries*, eds. Katherine Arnup, Andrée Lévesque and Ruth Roach Pierson, 150-72. London and New York: Routledge, 1990.

2451 EMERY, George. "British Columbia's Criminal Abortion History, 1922-1949: A Critique of the Evidence and Methods in the Work of Angus and Arlene Tigar McLaren." *BC Studies* 82 (Summer 1989): 39-60.

2452 GAVIGAN, Shelley A.M. "On 'Bringing on the Menses': The Criminal Liability of Women and the Therapeutic Exception in Canadian Abortion Law." *Canadian Journal of Women and the Law* 1, 2 (1986): 279-312.

2453 GODARD, Beatrice. *L'avortement entre la loi et la médecine.* Montréal: Liber, 1992.

2454 GOSSAGE, Peter. "Absorbing Junior: The Use of Patent Medicines as Abortifacients in Nineteenth Century Montreal." *The Register* 3, 1 (March 1982).

2455 HALPERN, Sylvie. *Morgentaler, l'obstiné.* Montréal: Éditions du Boréal, 1993.

2456 LAMOUREUX, Diane. "La lutte pour le droit à l'avortement (1969-1981)." *Revue d'histoire de l'Amérique française* 37, 1 (juin 1983): 81-90.

2457 LAMOUREUX, Diane, ed. *Avortement: Pratiques, enjeux, contrôle social.* Montréal: Éditions du remue-ménage, 1993.

2458 LARUE, Caroline and Colette Blais. "The Abortion Struggle in Quebec: Fifteen Years in View." *Resources for Feminist Research* 15, 4 (Dec. 1986/Jan. 1987): 4-5.

2459 MARCIL-GRATTON, Nicole. "Vingt ans de révolution contraceptive au Québec: de l'aléatoire à l'irréversible." In *La population du Québec d'hier à demain*, eds. Jacques Henripin and Yves Martin, 51-61. Montréal: Les Presses de l'Université de Montréal, 1991.

2460 MARTIN, Sheilah. *Women's Reproductive Health, the Canadian Charter of Rights and Freedoms and the Canada Health Act.* Ottawa: Canadian Advisory Council on the Status of Women, 1989.

2461 McCALLUM, Margaret E. "Men, Women, and the Liberal Ideal: An Historian's Reflections on the Morgentaler Case." *Queen's Quarterly* 96, 2 (Summer 1989): 298-313.

2462 McCULLOCH, Michael. "'Dr. Tumblety, the Indian Herb Doctor': Politics, Professionalism, and Abortion in Mid-Nineteenth-Century Montreal." *Canadian Bulletin of Medical History* 10, 1 (1993): 49-66.

2463 McDANIEL, Susan A. "Implementation of Abortion in Canada as a Women's Issue." *Atlantis* 10 (Spring 1985): 74-91.

2464 McDONNELL, Kathleen. *Not An Easy Choice: A Feminist Re-Examines Abortion.* Toronto: Women's Press, 1984.

2465 McLAREN, Angus. "Birth Control and Abortion in Canada, 1870-1920." *Canadian Historical Review* 59, 3 (September 1978): 319-40. Reprinted in *The Neglected Majority: Essays in Canadian Women's History, Vol. 2,* eds. Alison Prentice and Susan Mann Trofimenkoff, 84-101. Toronto: McClelland and Stewart, 1985; and in *Medicine in Canadian Society: Historical Perspectives,* ed. S.E.D. Shortt, 285-313. Montreal: McGill-Queen's University Press, 1981.

2466 McLAREN, Angus. "'What Has This to do With Working Class Women?': Birth Control and the Canadian Left, 1900-1939." *Histoire sociale/Social History* XIV, 28 (Nov. 1981): 435-54.

2467 McLAREN, Angus. "The First Campaigns for Birth Control Clinics in British Columbia." *Journal of Canadian Studies* 19, 3 (Fall 1984): 50-64.

2468 McLAREN, Angus. "A Motherhood Issue." *Horizon Canada* 87 (1986): 2072-77. Reprinted in *Readings in Canadian History: Post Confederation,* 3rd edition, eds. R. Douglas Francis and Donald B. Smith, 286-90. Toronto: Holt, Rinehart and Winston of Canada, 1990.

2469 McLAREN, Angus. "'Keep Your Seats and Face Facts': Western Canadian Women's Discussion of Birth Control in the 1920s." *Canadian Bulletin of Medical History* 8, 2 (1991): 189-201.

2470 McLAREN, Angus. "Illegal Operations: Women, Doctors, and Abortion, 1886-1939." *Journal of Social History* 26, 4 (Summer 1993): 797-816. [Vancouver Island]

2471 McLAREN, Angus and Arlene Tigar McLaren. "Discoveries and Dissimulations: The Impact of Abortion Deaths on Maternal Mortality in British Columbia." *BC Studies* 64 (Winter 1984/85): 3-26. Reprinted in *Delivering Motherhood: Maternal Ideologies and Practices in the 19th and 20th Centuries,* eds. Katherine Arnup, Andrée Lévesque and Ruth Roach Pierson, 126-49. London and New York: Routledge, 1990.

2472 McLAREN, Angus and Arlene Tigar McLaren. *The Bedroom and the State: The Changing Practices and Politics of Contraception and Abortion in Canada, 1880-1980.* Toronto: McClelland & Stewart, 1986.

2473 McLAREN, Angus and Arlene Tigar McLaren. "'The Forest and the Trees': A Response to George Emery." *BC Studies* 82 (Summer 1989): 61-64.

2474 MENZIES, Heather. "Rethinking Abortion: Comprehending the abortion issue in women's own words." *Canadian Forum* (October 1991): 13-18.

2475 MULDOON, Maureen. *The Abortion Debate in the United States and Canada: A Source Book.* New York: Garland, 1991.

2476 PELRINE, Eleanor Wright. *Abortion in Canada.* Toronto: New Press, 1972.

2477 PELRINE, Eleanor Wright. *Morgentaler: The Case That Rocked Canada.* Toronto: Gage Educational Publishing/Signet-New American Library, 1976.

2478 SCHLESINGER, Benjamin. *Family Planning in Canada: A Source Book.* Toronto: University of Toronto Press, 1974.

2479 STORZ, Gerald and Murray Eaton. "Pro Bono Publico: The 1936 Eastview Birth Control Trial." *Atlantis* 8 (1983): 51-60.

2480 VALLÉE, Madeleine. "De la contraception à l'avortement: outrage à l'autonomie des femmes." *Canadian Journal of Women and the Law* 3, 2 (1989): 483-509.

CHILD/MATERNAL HEALTH

2481 ABEELE, Cynthia R. "'The Infant Soldier': The Great War and the Medical Campaign for Child Welfare." *Canadian Bulletin of Medical History* 5, 2 (Winter 1988): 99-119.

2482 ABEELE, Cynthia Comacchio. "'The Mothers of the Land Must Suffer': Child and Maternal Welfare in Rural and Outpost Ontario, 1918-1940." *Ontario History* 80, 3 (Sept. 1988): 183-205.

2483 ARNUP, Katherine. "Educating Mothers: Government Advice for Women in the Inter-War Years." In *Delivering Motherhood: Maternal Ideologies and Practices in the 19th and 20th Centuries,* eds. Katherine Arnup, Andrée Lévesque and Ruth Roach Pierson, 190-210. London and New York: Routledge, 1990.

2484 ARNUP, Katherine. *Education for Motherhood: Advice for Mothers in Twentieth-Century Canada.* Toronto: University of Toronto Press, 1994.

2485 ARNUP, Katherine. "Raising the Dionne Quintuplets: Lessons for Modern Mothers." *Journal of Canadian Studies* 29, 4 (Winter 1994/95): 65-85.

2486 BAILLARGEON, Denyse. "Les gardes de La Métropolitaine, les Gouttes de lait et l'Assistance maternelle: l'encadrement de la maternité au Québec entre les deux guerres." *Bulletin du Regroupement des chercheurs-chercheures en histoire des travailleurs et travailleuses du Québec* 16, 1/2 (été/automne 1990): 19-45.

2487 BAILLARGEON, Denyse. "Care of Mothers and Infants in Montreal Between the Wars: The Visiting Nurses of Metropolitan Life, les Gouttes de lait, and Assistance maternelle." In *Caring and Curing: Historical Perspectives on Women and Healing in Canada,* eds. Dianne Dodd and Deborah Gorham, 163-81. Ottawa: University of Ottawa Press, 1994.

2488 BUCKLEY, Suzann. "Efforts to Reduce Infant and Maternal Mortality in Canada Between the Two World Wars." *Atlantis* 2, 2 Part 2 (Spring 1977): 76-84.

2489 BUCKLEY, Suzann. "Ladies or Midwives? Efforts to Reduce Infant and Maternal Mortality." In *A Not Unreasonable Claim: Women and Reform in Canada, 1880s-1920s*, ed. Linda Kealey, 131-49. Toronto: The Women's Press, 1979.

2490 BUCKLEY, Suzann. "The Search for the Decline of Maternal Mortality: The Place of Hospital Records." In *Essays in the History of Canadian Medicine*, eds. Wendy Mitchinson and Janice Dickin McGinnis, 148-63. Toronto: McClelland & Stewart, 1988.

2491 COMACCHIO, Cynthia R. *"Nations Are Built of Babies": Saving Ontario's Mothers and Children, 1900-1940*. Montreal and Kingston: McGill-Queen's University Press, 1993.

2492 DEHLI, Kari. "Fictions of the Scientific Imagination: Researching the Dionne Quintuplets." *Journal of Canadian Studies* 29, 4 (Winter 1994/95): 86-110.

2493 DODD, Dianne. "Advice to Parents: The Blue Books, Helen MacMurchy, M.D., and the Federal Department of Health, 1920-1934." *Canadian Bulletin of Medical History* 8, 2 (1991): 203-30.

2494 EMERY, George. "Age-Parity and Marital Status Compositional Influences on the Maternal Mortality Rate in Canada, 1930-1969: A Regional Comparison." *Histoire sociale/Social History* XXV, 50 (November 1992): 229-56.

2495 FORTIER, Broquerie. "Les 'gouttes de lait' à Québec, 1905-1970: Au secours des nourrissons." *Cap-aux-Diamants* 28 (hiver 1992): 52-55.

2496 GAUVREAU, Danielle. "A propos de la mise en nourrice à Québec pendant le régime français." *Revue d'histoire de l'Amérique française* 41, 1 (été 1987): 53-61.

2497 GAUVREAU, Danielle. "Donner la vie et en mourir: la mortalité des femmes en couches au Québec avant 1960." In *Population, reproduction, sociétés: perspectives et enjeux de démographie sociale*, Dennis D. Cordell, *et al*, 235-56. Montréal: Les Presses de l'Université de Montréal, 1993.

2498 HAFFEY, Helen. "Six Cots and A Prayer." *York Pioneer* (1975): 15-25. [Toronto Hospital for Sick Children]

2499 LENSKYJ, Helen. "Raising 'Good Vigorous Animals': Medical Interest in Children's Health in Ontario, 1890-1930." *Scientia Canadensis* XII, 2 (Fall/Winter 1988): 129-49.

2500 LÉVESQUE, Andrée. "Mères ou malades: les Québécoises de l'entre-deux-guerres vues par les médecins." *Revue d'histoire de l'Amérique française* 38, 1 (été 1984): 23-37.

2501 LÉVESQUE, Andrée. "La santé des femmes en période de dépression économique: l'exemple des patientes de l'Hôpital de la Miséricorde à Montréal pendant les années trente." *Bulletin du Regroupement des chercheurs-chercheures en histoire des travailleurs et travailleuses du Québec* 47/48 (été/automne 1990): 7-17.

2502 LEWIS, Norah L. "Physical Perfection for Spiritual Welfare: Health Care for the Urban Child, 1900-1939." In *Studies in Childhood History: A Canadian Perspective*, eds. Patricia T. Rooke and R.L. Schnell, 135-66. Calgary: Detselig Enterprises, 1982.

2503 LEWIS, Norah L. "Creating the Little Machine: Child Rearing in British Columbia, 1919 to 1939." *BC Studies* 56 (Winter 1982-83): 44-60.

2504 LEWIS, Norah L. "Reducing Maternal Mortality in British Columbia." In *Not Just Pin Money: Selected Essays on the History of Women's Work in British Columbia*, eds. Barbara K. Latham and Roberta J. Pazdro, 337-55. Victoria: Camosun College, 1984.

2505 SIEGEL, Linda S. "Child Health and Development in English Canada, 1790-1850." In *Health, Disease and Medicine: Essays in Canadian History*, ed. Charles G. Roland, 360-80. Toronto: Clarke Irwin for the Hannah Institute for the History of Medicine, 1984.

2504 STRONG-BOAG, Veronica. "Intruders in the Nursery: Childcare Professionals Reshape the Years One to Five, 1920-1940." In *Childhood and Family in Canadian History*, ed. Joy Parr, 160-78. Toronto: McClelland and Stewart, 1982.

2507 TETREAULT, Martin. "De la difficulté de naître et de survivre dans une ville industrielle de la Nouvelle-Angleterre au XIXe siècle: mortalité infantile, infanticide et avortement à Lowell, Massachusetts, 1870-1900." *Revue d'histoire de l'Amérique française* 47, 1 (été 1993): 53-82.

2508 WARD, W. Peter. *Birth Weight and Economic Growth: Women's Living Standards in the Industrializing West*. Chicago: University of Chicago Press, 1993. [Boston, Dublin, Edinburgh, Montreal, and Vienna, 1850-1930]

2509 WARD, W. Peter and Patricia C. Ward. "Infant Birth Weight and Nutrition in Industrializing Montreal." *American Historical Review* 89, 2 (April 1984): 324-45.

2510 YOUNG, Judith. "A Divine Mission: Elizabeth McMaster and the Hospital for Sick Children, Toronto, 1875-92." *Canadian Bulletin of Medical History* 11, 1 (1994): 71-90.

CHILDBIRTH/REPRODUCTION

2511 ACHILLES, Rona. "Artificial Reproduction: Hope Chest or Pandora's Box?" In *Changing Patterns: Women in Canada*, eds. Sandra Burt, Lorraine Code and Lindsay Dorney, 291-312. Toronto: McClelland & Stewart, 1988. Revised and retitled as "Assisted Reproduction: The Social Issues" in 2nd edition, 488-516, 1993.

2512 ACHILLES, Rona. "Desperately Seeking Babies: New Technologies of Hope and Despair." In *Delivering Motherhood: Maternal Ideologies and Practices in the 19th and 20th Centuries*, eds. Katherine Arnup, Andrée Lévesque and Ruth Roach Pierson, 284-312. London and New York: Routledge, 1990.

2513 ANDREWS, Margaret W. "Medical Attendance in Vancouver, 1886-1920." *BC Studies* 40 (Winter 1978/79): 32-56.

2514 ARNUP, Katherine. "Finding Fathers: Artificial Insemination, Lesbians, and the Law." *Canadian Journal of Women and the Law* 7, 1 (1994): 97-115.

2515 GAUTHIER, Josée. "La naissance au Saguenay et dans Charlevoix (1900-1950): continuités et ruptures culturelles." *Revue d'histoire de l'Amérique française* 48, 3 (hiver 1995): 351-74.

2516 LAFORCE, Hélène and Renald Lessard. "Une césarienne en 1760." *Cap-aux-Diamants* 1, 3 (automne 1985): 41-42.

2517 LAURENDEAU, France. "La médicalisation de l'accouchement." *Recherches sociographiques* 24, 2 (mai/août 1983): 203-34.

2518 MAIR, Kelly E. "Assessing Reproductive Wrongs: A Feminist Social Work Perspective." In *The Anatomy of Gender: Women's Struggle for the Body*, eds. Dawn H. Currie and Valerie Raoul, 147-60. Ottawa: Carleton University Press, 1992.

2519 McDANIEL, Susan A. "Women's Roles and Reproduction: The Changing Picture in Canada in the 1980s." *Atlantis* 14, 1 (Fall 1988): 1-12.

2520 MITCHINSON, Wendy. "Historical Attitudes toward Women and Childbirth." *Atlantis* 4, 2, Part 2, (Spring 1979): 13-34.

2521 O'NEIL, John and Patricia A. Kaufert. "The Politics of Obstetric Care: The Inuit Experience." In *Births and Power: Social Change and the Politics of Reproduction*, ed. W. Penn Handwerker, 53-68. Boulder, CO: Westview Press, 1990. Reprinted in *Canadian Women: A Reader*, eds. Wendy Mitchinson, *et al*, 416-29. Toronto: Harcourt Brace Canada, 1996.

2522 OPPENHEIMER, Jo. "Childbirth in Ontario: The Transition from Home to Hospital in the Early Twentieth Century." *Ontario History* 75, 1 March 1983: 36-60. Reprinted in *Delivering Motherhood: Maternal Ideologies and Practices in the 19th and 20th Centuries*, eds. Katherine Arnup, Andrée Lévesque and Ruth Roach Pierson, 51-74. London and New York: Routledge, 1990.

2523 QUENIART, Anne. "Risky Business: Medical Definitions of Pregnancy." In *The Anatomy of Gender: Women's Struggle for the Body*, eds. Dawn H. Currie and Valerie Raoul, 161-74. Ottawa: Carleton University Press, 1992.

2524 SAILLANT, Francine and Hélène Laforce. "Médecine domestique et pratiques sociales entourant la réproduction chez les Québécoises." *Canadian Folklore* 15, 2 (1993): 31-50. Reprinted in *Avortement: Pratiques, enjeux, contrôle social*, ed. Diane Lamoureux. Montréal: Éditions du remue-ménage, 1993.

2525 STRONG-BOAG, Veronica and Kathryn McPherson. "The Confinement of Women: Childbirth and Hospitalization in Vancouver, 1919-1939." *BC Studies* 69/70 (Spring/Summer 1986): 142-74. Reprinted in *Delivering Motherhood: Maternal Ideologies and Practices in the 19th and 20th Centuries*, eds. Katherine Arnup, Andrée Lévesque and Ruth Roach Pierson, 75-107. London and New York: Routledge, 1990; and in *British Columbia Reconsidered: Essays on Women*, eds. Gillian Creese and Veronica Strong-Boag, 143-71. Vancouver: Press Gang Publishers, 1992.

DOCTORS

2526 ABBOTT, Maude E.S. "Autobiographical Sketch." *McGill Medical Journal* 28 (1959): 127-52.

2527 ANGEL, Barbara and Michael Angel. *Charlotte Whitehead Ross*. Winnipeg: Peguis Publishers, 1982.

2528 BERNIER, Jacques. "Les practiciens de la santé au Québec, 1871-1921: Quelques données statistique." *Recherches sociographiques* 20, 1 (janvier-avril 1979): 41-58.

2529 BLACK, Elinor. "Thinking Back." *Canadian Medical Association Journal* 105, 24 (1971): 143-44.

2530 BLACK, Elinor. "Not So Long Ago." *University of Manitoba Medical Journal* 45, 2 (1975): 54-56.

2531 BUCK, Ruth Matheson. *The Doctor Rode Sidesaddle*. Toronto: McClelland and Stewart, 1974.

2532 DUFFIN, Jacalyn. "The Death of Sarah Lovell and the Constrained Feminism of Emily Stowe." *Canadian Medical Association Journal* 146, 6 (15 March 1992).

2533 EDGE, Fred. *The Iron Rose: The Extraordinary Life of Charlotte Ross, M.D.* Winnipeg: University of Manitoba Press, 1992.

2534 FEDERATION OF MEDICAL WOMEN OF CANADA. *100 Years Of Medicine, 1849-1949*. Federation of Medical Women of Canada, c. 1949.

2535 FRYER, Mary Beacock. *Emily Howard Stowe: Doctor and Suffragist*. Toronto: Dundurn Press, 1990.

2536 GILLETT, Margaret. "The Heart of the Matter: Maude E. Abbott, 1869-1940." In *Despite the Odds: Essays on Canadian Women and Science*, ed. Marianne Gosztonyi Ainley, 179-94. Montreal: Véhicule Press, 1990.

2537 GORHAM, Deborah. "'No Longer an Invisible Minority': Women Physicians and Medical Practice in Late Twentieth-Century North America." In *Caring and Curing: Historical Perspectives on Women and Healing in Canada*, eds. Dianne Dodd and Deborah Gorham, 183-211. Ottawa: University of Ottawa Press, 1994.

2538 HACKER, Carlotta. "Jennie Trout: An Indomitable Lady Doctor Whose History Was Lost for a Half-Century." *Canadian Medical Association Journal* 110 (6 April 1974): 841-43.

2539 HACKER, Carlotta. *The Indomitable Lady Doctors*. Toronto and Vancouver: Clark, Irwin and Co., 1974.

2540 HART, Anne. "Dr. Agnes C. O'Dea, 1911-1993." *Newfoundland Studies* 8, 2 (Fall 1992): 179-81.

2541 HOOPLE, E.L. *Medicine Maid: The Life Story of a Canadian Pioneer*. Belleville, ON: Mika Publishing Co., 1977. [Mary Whitmore]

2542 HOUSTON, C. Stuart. "A Pioneer Woman Doctor, Sigga Christianson Houston." *Manitoba Medicine* 63 (June 1993): 55-58.

2543 JACKSON, Mary Percy. *On the Last Frontier: Pioneering in the Peace River Block*. London: Sheldon Press, 1933.

2544 KERNAGHAN, Lois. "'Someone Wants the Doctor': Maria L. Angwin, M.D. (1849-1898)." *Nova Scotia Historical Society Collections* 43 (1991): 33-48.

2545 KEYWAN, Zonia. "Mary Percy Jackson: Pioneer Doctor." *The Beaver* (Winter 1977): 41-47.

2546 MacDERMOTT, Hugh Ernest. *Maude Abbott: A Memoir*. Toronto: Macmillan Co., 1941.

2547 MacDONALD, Eva M. and Elizabeth Webb. "A Survey of Women Physicians in Canada, 1883-1964." *Canadian Medical Association Journal* 94 (June 1966): 1223-27.

2548 McCONNACHIE, Kathleen. "Methodology in the Study of Women's History: A Case Study of Helen MacMurchy, M.D." *Ontario History* 75 (March 1983).

2549 McGINNIS, Janice Dickin, ed. "'My Life in Keg River' by Mary Percy Jackson." *Canadian Bulletin of Medical History* 12, 1 (1995): 169-86. [Metis health issues]

2550 McGINNIS, Janice Dickin, ed. *Suitable for the Wilds: Letters from Northern Alberta, 1929-1931*. Toronto: University of Toronto Press, 1995. [Dr. Mary Percy Jackson]

2551 PATRIARCHE, M. Elizabeth. "Medical Women: Vive la Différence!" *British Columbia Medical Journal* 27, 1 (1985): 641-43.

2552 ROBINSON, Marion O. *Give My Heart*. New York: Doubleday, 1964. [Marion Hilliard, M.D.]

2553 ROSE, June. *The Perfect Gentleman*. London: Hutchenson and Co., 1977. [Dr. James Miranda Barry who served as a doctor in the British Army, 1813-1859, by disguising her sex]

2554 SHEININ, Rose and Alan Bakes. *Women and Medicine in Toronto Since 1883: A Who's Who*. Toronto: University of Toronto Press, 1987.

2555 SMITH, Helen Pollitt. "Dr. Charlotte W. Ross: Manitoba's Pioneer Woman Doctor." *Manitoba Pageant* (Autumn 1975): 9-13.

2556 STRONG-BOAG, Veronica. "Canada's Women Doctors: Feminism Constrained." In *A Not Unreasonable Claim: Women and Reform in Canada, 1880s-1920s*, ed. Linda Kealey, 109-29. Toronto: The Women's Press, 1979. Reprinted in *Medicine in Canadian Society: Historical Perspectives*, ed. S.E.D. Shortt, 255-83. Montreal and Kingston: McGill-Queen's University Press, 1981.

2557 THOMSON, Kay. "Women in Medicine." *University of Manitoba Medical Journal* 42, 1 (1970): 31-32.

2558 THORSTEINSON, Gerri. "Travelling Prairie Doctor." *Herizons* 1, 4 (June 1983): 35-36. [Dr. Margaret Owens]

2559 VANDERVOORT, Julie. *Tell the Driver: A Biography of Elinor F.E. Black, M.D.* Winnipeg: University of Manitoba Press, 1992. [Canada's first woman obstetrician and gynecologist]

2560 WAUGH, Douglas. *Maudie of McGill: Dr. Maude Abbott and the Foundations of Heart Surgery*. Toronto and Oxford: Hannah Institute and Dundurn Press, 1992.

2561 WAUGH, Douglas. *Maudie: The Life and Work of Maude Abbott*. Toronto: Dundurn Press, 1992.

2562 WAXMAN, Sydell Blossom. "Dr. Emily Stowe: Canada's First Female Practitioner." *Canada West* 10, 1 (Spring 1980): 17-23.

2563 WAXMAN, Sydell. "Emily Stowe: Feminist and Healer." *The Beaver* 72, 2 (April/May 1992): 26-30.

2564 WILD, Marjorie. *Elizabeth Bagshaw*. Toronto: Fitzhenry and Whiteside, 1984.

GENERAL

2565 DODD, Dianne and Deborah Gorham, eds. *Caring and Curing: Historical Perspectives on Women and Healing in Canada*. Ottawa: University of Ottawa Press, 1994.

2566 DRYDEN, Trish, *et al*, eds. "Women and Health." A special issue of *Canadian Woman Studies* 14, 3 (Summer 1994).

2567 DUA, Enakshi, *et al*, eds. *on women healthsharing*. Toronto: Women's Press, 1994.

2568 GAUCHER, Dominique, France Laurendeau and Louise-Hélène Trottier. "Talking About Life: The Contribution of Women to the Sociology of Health." In *Gender and Society: Creating a Canadian Women's Sociology*, ed. Arlene Tigar McLaren, 80-96. Toronto: Copp Clark Pitman, 1988.

2569 GUYON, Louise. *Quand les femmes parlent de leur santé*. Québec: Publications du Québec, 1990.

2570 MITCHINSON, Wendy. "Medical Historiography in English Canada." *Health and Canadian Society* 1, 1 (1993): 205-28.

2571 SAILLANT, Francine. "Savoirs et pratiques des femmes dans l'univers ethnomédical québécois." *Canadian Folklore* 14, 1 (1992): 47-72.

HEALTHCARE/MEDICAL PRACTICE

2572 ADAMS, Mary Louise. "In Sickness and in Health: State Formation, Moral Regulation, and Early VD Initiatives in Ontario." *Journal of Canadian Studies* 28, 4 (Winter 1993/94): 117-31.

2573 ALLARD, Michel, ed. *L'Hôtel-Dieu de Montréal: 1642-1973.* Montréal: Hurtubise HMH, 1973.

2574 BABCOCK, Marguerite and Christine McKay, eds. *Codependency: Feminist Critiques.* Toronto: University of Toronto Press, 1995.

2575 BAEHRE, Rainer. "Victorian Psychiatry and Canadian Motherhood." *Canadian Women's Studies* 2, 1 (1980): 44-46.

2576 BLACKBURN, Mrs. W.D. "Amy Hayhurst Winkles: Matron of Armstrong Hospital." Okanagan Historical Society. *Report* 42 (1978): 105-9.

2577 BUCKLEY, Suzann and Janice Dickin McGinnis. "Venereal Disease and Public Health Reform in Canada." *Canadian Historical Review* 63, 3 (Sept. 1982): 337-54.

2578 CADOTTE, Marcel. "Histoire médicale de l'Hôtel-Dieu de Montréal: Jeanne Mance et les débuts de l'hôpital." *Le médecin du Québec* 27, 6 (juin 1992): 97-105.

2579 CASSEL, Jay. *The Secret Plague: Venereal Disease in Canada, 1838-1939.* Toronto: University of Toronto Press, 1987.

2580 CASSEL, Jay. "Private Acts and Public Actions: The Canadian Response to the Problem of Sexually Transmitted Disease in the Twentieth Century." *Transactions of the Royal Society of Canada* 4 (1989): 305-28.

2581 CELLARD, André. "Folie, norme et rôles sexuels au Québec dans la seconde moitié du XIXe siècle: Quelques observations tirées des archives de la curatelle." *Revue d'histoire de l'Amérique française* 47, 2 (automne 1993): 245-55.

2582 CHAPMAN, Terry L. "Early Eugenics Movement in Western Canada." *Alberta History* 25, 4 (Autumn 1977): 9-17.

2583 CHARLES, Aline. *Travail d'ombre et de lumière: Le bénévolat féminin de l'Hôpital Sainte-Justine, 1907-1960.* Québec: Institut québécois de recherche sur la culture, 1990.

2584 CORMACK, Barbara Villy. *The Red Cross Lady.* Edmonton: Institute of Applied Arts, 1960. [Mary Conquest]

2585 DAVIES, Megan J. "Snapshots: Three Women and Psychiatry, 1920-1935." *Canadian Woman Studies* 8, 4 (Winter 1987): 47-48.

2586 GAGAN, Rosemary. "Mortality Patterns and Public Health in Hamilton, Canada, 1900-1914." *Urban History Review* XVII, 3 (February 1989): 161-76.

2587 GAGNON, Hervé. "Les Hospitalières de Saint-Joseph et les premiers pas de Montréal: Vie quotidienne et soins des malades au XVIIe siècle." *Cahiers d'histoire* 10, 3 (Spring 1990): 5-47.

2588 GALE, Nancy. "The Story of the Women's Auxiliary of the Kelowna Hospital." *Okanagan Historical Society, Report* 34 (1970): 93-100.

2589 GRANT, Dorothy Metie. "We Shall Conquer Yet!" *Nova Scotia Historical Quarterly* 2, 3 (September 1972): 243-51. [Dorothea Lynde Dix and establishment of a hospital for the insane in Nova Scotia, 1856]

2590 "Home Remedies in Pioneering." *Saskatchewan History* 43, 3 (Autumn 1989): 104-5.

2591 HOYT, J. "Great Grandmother's Medicine Ball." New Brunswick Historical Society. *Collections* 17 (1961): 41-43.

2592 KELM, Mary-Ellen. "'The only place likely to do her any good': The Admission of Women to British Columbia's Provincial Hospital for the Insane." *BC Studies* 96 (Winter 1992/93): 66-89.

2593 KELM, Mary-Ellen. "A Life Apart: The Experience of Women and the Asylum Practice of Charles Doherty at British Columbia's Provincial Hospital for the Insane, 1905-15." *Canadian Bulletin of Medical History* 11, 2 (1994): 335-55.

2594 KLEM, Mary-Ellen. "Women, Families, and the Provincial Hospital for the Insane, British Columbia, 1905-1915." *Journal of Family History* 19, 2 (1994): 177-94.

2595 LA PALMA, Loretta. "The Hôtel-Dieu of Quebec: The First Hospital North of the Rio Grande under Its First Two Superiors." Canadian Catholic Historical Association. *Study Sessions* 60 (1974): 53-64.

2596 LEWIS, Norah L. "Goose Grease and Turpentine: Mother Treats the Family's Illnesses." *Prairie Forum* 15, 1 (Spring 1990): 67-84. Abridged in *Rethinking Canada: The Promise of Women's History,* 2nd edition, eds. Veronica Strong-Boag and Anita Clair Fellman, 234-48. Toronto: Copp Clark Pitman Ltd., 1991.

2597 MacDOUGALL, Heather. "Researching Public Health Services in Ontario, 1882-1930." *Archivaria* 10 (Summer 1980): 157-72.

2598 MacDOUGALL, Heather. *Activists and Advocates: Toronto's Health Department, 1883-1983.* Toronto and Oxford: Dundurn Press, 1990.

2599 McDONNELL, Kathleen, ed. *Adverse Effects: Women and the Pharmaceutical Industry.* Toronto: The Women's Press, 1986.

2600 McLAREN, Angus. "The Creation of a Haven for 'Human Thoroughbreds': The Sterilization of the Feeble-Minded and the Mentally Ill in British Columbia." *Canadian Historical Review* 67, 2 (1986): 127-50. Reprinted in *The Challenge of Modernity: A Reader on Post-Confederation Canada,* ed. Ian McKay, 305-30. Toronto: McGraw-Hill Ryerson, 1992.

2601 McLAREN, Angus. *Our Own Master Race: Eugenics in Canada, 1885-1945.* Toronto: McClelland & Stewart, 1990.

2602 MITCHINSON, Wendy. "Thoughts on Research in Progress: Medical Attitudes Towards Women." *Resources for Feminist Research* 8, 2 (July 1979): 13-14.

2603 MITCHINSON, Wendy. "Gynecological Operations on the Insane." *Archivaria* 10 (1980): 125-44.

2604 MITCHINSON, Wendy. "Gynecological Operations on Insane Women: London, Ontario, 1895-1901." *Journal of Social History* 15, 3 (Spring 1982): 467-84.

2605 MITCHINSON, Wendy. "A Medical Debate in Nineteenth-Century English Canada: Ovariotomies." *Histoire sociale/Social History* 17 (May 1984): 133-47.

2606 MITCHINSON, Wendy. "Causes of Disease in Women: The Case of Late 19th Century English Canada." In *Health, Disease and Medicine: Essays in Canadian History,* ed. Charles G. Roland, 381-95. Toronto: Clarke Irwin for the Hannah Institute for the History of Medicine, 1984.

2607 MITCHINSON, Wendy. "Medical Perceptions of Female Sexuality: A Late Nineteenth Century Case." *Scientia Canadensis* 9, 1 (June 1985): 67-81.

2608 MITCHINSON, Wendy. "Hysteria and Insanity in Women: A Nineteenth-Century Perspective." *Journal of Canadian Studies* 21, 3 (1986): 87-105.

2609 MITCHINSON, Wendy. "The Medical View of Women: The Case of Late Nineteenth-Century Canada." *Canadian Bulletin of Medical History* 3, 2 (Winter 1986): 207-24.

2610 MITCHINSON, Wendy. "Gender and Insanity as Characteristics of the Insane: A Nineteenth-Century Case." *Canadian Bulletin of Medical History* 4, 2 (Winter 1987): 99-117.

2611 MITCHINSON, Wendy. "The Medical Treatment of Women." In *Changing Patterns: Women in Canada,* eds. Sandra Burt, Lorraine Code and Lindsay Dorney, 237-63. Toronto: McClelland & Stewart, 1988; revised in 2nd edition, 391-421, 1993.

2612 MITCHINSON, Wendy. *The Nature of Their Bodies: Women and Their Doctors in Victorian Canada.* Toronto: University of Toronto Press, 1991.

2613 MONDOUX, Maria. *L'Hôtel-Dieu: Premier hôpital de Montréal.* Montréal: Joseph Charbonneau, 1941.

2614 MORIN, Soeur. "Annales de l'Hôtel-Dieu de Montréal." *Mémoires de la Société Historique de Montréal* 12 (1921).

2615 MORIN, Marie. *Histoire simple et véritable: les annales de l'Hotel-Dieu de Montréal, 1659-1725.* Edited by Ghislaine Legendre. Montréal: Presses de l'Université de Montréal, 1979.

2616 NOWELL-SMITH, Harriet. "Nineteenth-Century Narrative Case Histories: An Inquiry into Stylistics and History." *Canadian Bulletin of Medical History* 12, 1 (1995): 47-67. [obstetrical and gynaecological case histories]

2617 PENFOLD, P. Susan and Gillian A. Walker. *Women and the Psychiatric Paradox.* Montreal: Eden Press, 1983.

2618 PERRON, Normand. *Un siècle de vie hospitalière au Québec: Les Augustines et l'Hôtel-Dieu de Chicoutimi, 1884-1984.* Sillery: Presses de l'Université du Québec à Chicoutimi/les Augustines de la Miséricorde de Jésus, 1984.

2619 PIERRE-DESCHÊNES, Claudine. "Santé publique et organisation de la profession médicale au Québec, 1870-1918." *Revue d'histoire de l'Amérique française* 35, 3 (décembre 1981): 355-75.

2620 RAVENHILL, Alice. *Memoirs of an Educational Pioneer.* Toronto: J.M. Dent and Sons, 1951.

2621 ROLAND, Charles G. "Health, Disease, and Treatment in Early Upper Canada." In *The Capital Years: Niagara-on-the-Lake, 1792-1796,* eds. Richard Merritt, Nancy Butler and Michael Power, 223-50. Toronto and Oxford: Dundurn Press, 1991.

2622 ROUSSEAU, François. "Hôpital et société en Nouvelle-France: L'Hôtel Dieu de Québec à la fin du XVIIe siècle." *Revue d'histoire de l'Amérique française* 31, 1 (June 1977): 29-48.

2623 SMITH, Dorothy. E. and Sara J. David, eds. *Women Look at Psychiatry.* Vancouver: Press Gang Publishers, 1975.

2624 STOPPARD, Janet M. "A Suitable Case for Treatment? Premenstrual Syndrome and the Medicalization of Women's Bodies." In *The Anatomy of Gender: Women's Struggle for the Body,* eds. Dawn H. Currie and Valerie Raoul, 119-29. Ottawa: Carleton University Press, 1992.

2625 THORNTON, Leon. A. "Grandmother's Pharmacy." New Brunswick Historical Society. *Collections* 18 (1963): 58-63.

2626 WARSH, Cheryl Krasnick. "The First Mrs. Rochester: Wrongful Confinement, Social Redundancy, and Commitment to the Private Asylum, 1883-1923." Canadian Historical Association. *Historical Papers* (1988): 145-67.

2627 WARSH, Cheryl Krasnick. *Moments of Unreason: The Practice of Canadian Psychiatry and the Homewood Retreat, 1883-1923.* Montreal and Kingston: McGill-Queen's University Press, 1990.

2628 WARSH, Cheryl Krasnick. "'Oh, Lord, pour a cordial in her wounded heart': The Drinking Woman in Victorian and Edwardian Canada." In *Drink in Canada: Historical Essays,* ed. Cheryl Krasnick Warsh, 70-91. Montreal and Kingston: McGill-Queen's University Press, 1993.

MIDWIFERY

2629 BELLAMY, Marjory. "Beyond the Call of Duty." *Manitoba Pageant* 20, 4 (Summer 1975): 13-17. Reprinted in *Red Serge Wives,* ed. Joy Duncan. Edmonton: Co-op Press, 1974. [1920s and 1930s]

2630 BENOIT, Cecilia. "Traditional Midwifery Practice: The Limits of Occupational Autonomy." *Canadian Review of Sociology and Anthropology* 26, 4 (August 1989): 633-49.

2631 BENOIT, Cecilia. *Midwives in Passage: The Modernisation of Maternity Care.* St. John's: Institute of Social and Economics Research Books, 1991. [Newfoundland and Labrador]

2632 BIGGS, C. Lesley. "'The Case of the Missing Midwives': A History of Midwifery in Ontario from 1795-1900." *Ontario History* 75, 1 (March 1983): 21-35. Reprinted in *Delivering Motherhood: Maternal Ideologies and Practices in the 19th and 20th Centuries,* eds. Katherine Arnup, Andrée Lévesque and Ruth Roach Pierson, 20-35. London and New York: Routledge, 1990.

2633 BLAKELEY, Phyllis R. "And Having a Love for People." *Nova Scotia Historical Quarterly* 5 (June 1975): 165-76. [Elizabeth Doane, 18th-century midwife]

2634 BURTCH, Brian Eric. "Midwifery and the State: The New Midwifery in Canada." *Contemporary Crises* 10, (1986): 399-420. Revised and reprinted in *Gender and Society: Creating a Canadian Women's Sociology,* ed Arlene Tigar McLaren, 349-71. Toronto: Copp Clark Pitman, 1988.

2635 BURTCH, Brian. *Trials of Labour: The Re-emergence of Midwifery.* Montreal and Kingston: McGill-Queen's University Press, 1994.

2636 CONNOR, J.T.H. "'Larger Fish to Catch Here than Midwives': Midwifery and the Medical Profession in Nineteenth-Century Ontario." In *Caring and Curing: Historical Perspectives on Women and Healing in Canada,* eds. Dianne Dodd and Deborah Gorham, 103-34. Ottawa: University of Ottawa Press, 1994.

2637 DODD, Dianne. "Helen MacMurchy: Popular Midwifery and Maternity Services for Canadian Pioneer Women." In *Caring and Curing: Historical Perspectives on Women and Healing in Canada,* eds. Dianne Dodd and Deborah Gorham, 135-61. Ottawa: University of Ottawa Press, 1994.

2638 FÜHRER, Charlotte. *The Mysteries of Montreal: Memories of a Midwife.* Edited by Peter Ward. Vancouver: University of British Columbia Press, 1984.

2639 GREEN, H. Gordon. *Don't Have Your Baby in the Dory! A Biography of Myra Bennett.* Montreal: Harvest House, 1973.

2640 JACKSON, Elva E. "The True Story of the Legendary Granny Ross." *Nova Scotia Historical Review* 8, 1 (1988): 42-61. [18th-century Acadian pioneer midwife]

2641 KENNEDY, Joan E. "Jane Soley Hamilton, Midwife." *Nova Scotia Historical Review* 2, 1 (1982): 6-29.

2642 LAFORCE, Hélène. "L'univers de la sage-femme aux XVIIe et XVIIIe siècle." *Cap-aux-Diamants* 1, 3 (automne 1985): 3-6.

2643 LAFORCE, Hélène. *Histoire de la sage-femme dans la région de Québec.* Québec: Institut québécois de recherche sur la culture, 1985.

2644 LAFORCE, Hélène. "The Different Stages of the Elimination of Midwives in Quebec." In *Delivering Motherhood: Maternal Ideologies and Practices in the 19th and 20th Centuries,* eds. Katherine Arnup, Andrée Lévesque and Ruth Roach Pierson, 36-50. London and New York: Routledge, 1990.

2645 MASON, Jutta. "A History of Midwifery in Canada." In *Report of the Task Force on the Implementation of Midwifery in Ontario. Appendix I,* Mary Eberts, *et al.* Toronto, 1987.

2646 PARADIS, Roger. "Henriette, La capuche: Portrait of a Frontier Midwife." *Canadian Folklore* 3, 2 (1981): 10-26.

2647 PIERCEY, Rhoda Maude. *"True Tales": Memoirs of an Outport Midwife.* Edited by Janet McNaughton. St. John's: Faculty of Medicine, Memorial University of Newfoundland, 1992.

2648 RUSHING, Beth. "Market Explanations for Occupational Power: The Decline of Midwifery in Canada." *American Review of Canadian Studies* 21, 1 (Spring 1991): 7-27.

NURSING

2649 ADAMS, Annmarie. "Rooms of Their Own: The Nurses' Residences at Montreal's Royal Victoria Hospital." *Material History Review* 40 (Fall 1994): 29-41.

2650 ARMSTRONG, Pat, Jacqueline Choinière and Elaine Day. *Vital Signs: Canadian Nursing in Transition.* Toronto: Garamond Press, 1993.

2651 ARSENAULT, Laurette. "Le nursing, 1926-1976." *Revue d'histoire et de traditions populaires de la Gaspésie* 54/55 (avril/septembre 1976): 171-81.

2652 BANFILL, B.J. *Labrador Nurse.* Toronto: Ryerson Press, 1952. [Grenfell mission]

2653 BANFILL, B.J. *With the Indians of the Pacific.* London: William Kimber, 1966.

2654 BANFILL, B.J. *Pioneer Nurse.* Toronto: Ryerson Press, 1967. [Saskatchewan, 1930s]

2655 BIRTLES, William. "Mary Ellen Birtles: A Tribute to Pioneer Nurses of Manitoba." *Nurscene* (May 1989): 5-6.

2656 BIRTLES, William. "A Pioneer Nurse." *Alberta History* 43, 1(Winter 1995): 2-6.

2657 BOUTILIER, Beverly. "Helpers or Heroines? The National Council of Women, Nursing and 'Woman's Work' in Late Victorian Canada." In *Caring and Curing: Historical Perspectives on Women and Healing in Canada,* eds. Dianne Dodd and Deborah Gorham, 17-47. Ottawa: University of Ottawa Press, 1994.

2658 BRAMADAT, Ina J. and Marion I. Saydak. "Nursing on the Canadian Prairies, 1900-1930: Effects of Immigration." *Nursing History Review* (AAHN) 1 (1993): 105-17.

2659 BRUNT, Pamela N. "Impact of World War II on Nursing in Canada." *Humane Medicine* 7, 4 (October 1991).

2660 BURWELL, Dorothy M. "Changing Attitudes and Images." *Canadian Nurse* 60 (February 1963): 122-25.

2661 CALLBECK, J.A. Claudette, ed. *A History of the Prince Edward Island Hospital School of Nursing, 1891-1971.* Charlottetown: Hospital Nurses Alumnae Association, History Committee, 1974.

2662 CANITZ, Brenda. "Northern Nurses: A Profession in Crisis." *Musk-Ox* 37 (Winter 1989): 175-83.

2663 CARROLL, William K. and Rennie Warburton. "Feminism, Class Consciousness and Household Work Linkages among Registered Nurses in Victoria." *Labour/Le Travail* 24 (1989): 131-45.

2664 CASHMAN, Tony. *Heritage of Service: The History of Nursing in Alberta.* Edmonton: Alberta Association of Registered Nurses, 1966.

2665 COBURN, Judi. "'I See and Am Silent': A Short History of Nursing." In *Women at Work: Ontario, 1850-1930,* eds. Janice Acton, *et al,* 127-63. Toronto: Canadian Women's Educational Press, 1974.

2666 COCKERILL, Art. "Ready Aye Ready: Three Decades of British Women in Newfoundland and Labrador." *North/Nord* (May/June 1976): 22-27. [nursing at the Grenfell Mission, 1947-1976]

2667 COHEN, Yolande and Louise Bienvenue. "Émergence de l'identité professionnelle chez les infirmières québécoises, 1890-1927." *Canadian Bulletin of Medical History* 11, 1 (1994): 119-51.

2668 COHEN, Yolande and Michèle Dagenais. "Le métier d'infirmière: savoirs féminins et reconnaissance professionnelle." *Revue d'histoire de l'Amérique française* 41, 2 (automne 1987): 155-77.

2669 COHEN, Yolande and Michèle Gélinas. "Les infirmières hygiénistes de la ville de Montréal: du service privé au service civique." *Histoire sociale/Social History* XXII, 44 (novembre 1989): 219-46.

2670 COLLEY, Kate Brighty. *While Rivers Flow.* Saskatoon: Western Producer Prairie Books, 1970. [public health nurse, Alberta, 1919-1940]

2671 COPELAND, Donalda McKillop and Eugenie Louise Myles. *Remember, Nurse.* Toronto: Ryerson Press, 1960. [public health nursing among the Inuit of Southampton Island after 1950]

2672 COPELAND, Donalda McKillop and Eugenie Louise Myles. *Nurse Among the Eskimos.* London: Souvenir Press, 1964.

2673 CÔTÉ, Jean. *Jeanne Mance, l'héroïque infirmière.* Outremont: Québecor, coll. "Récit historique," no. 5, 1995.

2674 CRAIG, Barbara L. "Memories and the Memorial: Developing and Managing Nursing Archives for Canada." *Canadian Bulletin of Medical History* 11, 1 (1994): 237-48.

2675 CUTHAND-GOODWILL, Jean. "Indian and Inuit Nurses of Canada." *Saskatchewan Indian Federated College Journal* 4, 1 (1988): 93-104.

2676 DAIGLE, Johanne. "L'éveil syndical des 'religieuses laïques': l'émergence et l'évolution de l'Alliance des infirmières de Montréal, 1946-1966." In *Travailleuses et féministes: Les femmes dans la société québécoise,* eds. Marie Lavigne and Yolande Pinard, 115-38. Montréal: Boréal Express, 1983.

2677 DAIGLE, Johanne. "Devenir infirmière: les modalités d'expression d'une culture soignante au XXe siècle." *Recherches féministes* 4, 1 (1991): 67-86.

2678 DAIGLE, Johanne, Nicole Rousseau and Francine Saillant. "Des traces sur la neige...La contribution des infirmières au développement des régions isolées du Québec au XXe siècle." *Recherches féministes* 6, 1 (1993): 93-103.

2679 DEHLI, Kari. "'Health Scouts' for the State? School and Public Health Nurses in Early Twentieth-Century Toronto." *Historical Studies in Education* 2, 2 (Fall 1990): 247-64.

2680 DESJARDINS, Édouard, Suzanne Giroux and Eileen E. Flanagan. *Histoire de la profession infirmière au Québec.* Montréal: Association des infirmières et infirmiers de la province du Québec, 1970.

2681 DESJARDINS, Édouard, Suzanne Giroux and Eileen E. Flanagan. *Heritage: History of the Nursing Profession from the Augustinians and Jeanne Mance to Medicare.* Montreal: Association of Nurses of the Province of Quebec, 1971.

2682 EMORY, Florence H.M. *Public Health Nursing in Canada.* Toronto: Macmillan of Canada, 1953.

2683 FATCHETT, Anita. *Put Patients before Profits: Politics, Policy and Nursing.* Toronto: W.B. Saunders, 1994.

2684 GIBBON, John Murray. *The Victorian Order of Nurses for Canada, 1897-1947.* Montreal: Southam Press, 1947.

2685 GIBBON, John Murray and Mary S. Mathewson. *Three Centuries of Canadian Nursing.* Toronto: MacMillan, 1947.

2686 GROWE, Sarah Jane. *Who Cares? The Crisis in Canadian Nursing.* Toronto: McClelland and Stewart, 1991.

2687 HART, Christopher. *Behind the Mask: Nurses, Their Unions and Nursing Policy.* Toronto: W.B. Saunders, 1994.

2688 HOPE, Mary E. *Northward My Calling.* Toronto: Ryerson Press, 1954.

2689 HUGHES, Lora Wood. *No Time for Tears.* Boston: Houghton Mifflin, 1946. [nursing in Alberta, 1915]

2690 JARDINE, Pauline O. "An Urban Middle-Class Calling: Women and the Emergence of Modern Nursing Education at the Toronto General Hospital, 1881-1914." *Urban History Review* XVII, 3 (February 1989): 177-90.

2691 JOHNS, Ethel and Beatrice Fines. *The Winnipeg General Hospital and Health Sciences School of Nursing, 1887-1987.* Winnipeg: Alumnae Association of the Winnipeg General Hospital and Health Sciences Centre School of Nursing, 1990.

2692 KEDDY, Barbara A. "Private Duty Nursing Days of the 1920s and 1930s in Canada." *Canadian Woman Studies* 7, 3 (Fall 1986): 99-102.

2693 KEDDY, Barbara. "Nursing in Canada in the 1920s and 1930s: Powerful while Powerless." *History of Nursing* 2, 9 (1989): 1-7.

2694 KEDDY, Barbara. "The Coming of Age of Feminist Research in Canadian Nursing." *Canadian Journal of Nursing Research* 24 (Summer 1993): 5-10.

2695 KEDDY, Barbara, *et al.* "Nurses' Work: Scientific or 'Womanly Ministering'?" *Resources for Feminist Research* 16, 4 (December 1987): 37-39.

2696 KEDDY, Barbara, Judy Glennie, Trudy Larsen, Pat Mallory and Marg Story. "The Personal is Political: A Feminist Analysis of the Social Control of Rank-and-File Nurses in Canada in the 1920s and 1930s." *History of Nursing Society Journal* (RCN) 4 (1992/93): 167-72.

2697 KELLY, Nora. *Quest for a Profession: The History of the Vancouver General Hospital School of Nursing.* Vancouver: General Hospital School of Nursing, 1973.

2698 KERR, Janet C. Ross. "Nursing History at the Graduate Level: State of the Art." *Canadian Bulletin of Medical History* 11, 1 (1994): 229-36.

2699 KINNEAR, Julia L. "The Professionalization of Canadian Nursing, 1924-32: Views in the *CN* and the *CMAJ.*" *Canadian Bulletin of Medical History* 11, 1 (1994): 153-74.

2700 KIRKWOOD, Lynn. "Yesterday, Today and Tomorrow." *The Canadian Nurse* 79, 9 (October 1983): 38-40.

2701 LA SOR, Betsy and M. Ruth Elliott. *Issues in Canadian Nursing.* Scarborough: Prentice-Hall, 1977.

2702 LEE, Betty. *Lutiapik.* Toronto: McClelland and Stewart, 1975. [nursing at Lake Harbour, Baffin Island, 1957-58]

2703 MacDERMOTT, H.E. *History of the School for Nurses of the Montreal General Hospital.* Montreal: The Alumnae Association, 1940.

2704 McPHERSON, Kathryn. "Science and Technique: Nurses' Work in a Canadian Hospital, 1920-1939." In *Caring and Curing: Historical Perspectives on Women and Healing in Canada,* eds. Dianne Dodd and Deborah Gorham, 71-101. Ottawa: University of Ottawa Press, 1994.

2705 McPHERSON, Kathryn. "'The Country is a Stern Nurse': Rural Women, Urban Hospitals and the Creation of a Western Canadian Nursing Work Force, 1920-1940." *Prairie Forum* 20, 2 (Fall 1995): 175-206.

2706 McPHERSON, Kathryn and Meryn Stuart. "Writing Nursing History in Canada: Issues and Approaches." *Canadian Bulletin of Medical History* 11, 1 (1994): 3-22.

2707 MELLOR, Ruth. "The Victorian Order of Nurses: Pioneering Community Health Services in Canada." *Humane Medicine* 5 Autumn 1989: 46-47.

2708 MERRICK, Elliott. *Northern Nurse.* Halifax: Nimbus Publishing, 1994.

2709 MILLS, Thora McIlroy. "Women's Lib in the 1890's...They Didn't Have to Fight For It." *Atlantic Advocate* 63, 4 (December 1972): 51-52. [Victorian Order of Nurses in Dawson]

2710 MILLS, Thora McIlroy. "Gold Rush Nurse." *North/Nord* (Sept./Oct. 1973): 10-13. [Ida May Burkholder, Dawson, 1908-1913]

2711 MONTGOMERY, R. "The Legislative Healthscape in Canada 1867-1975." In *Issues in Canadian Nursing,* eds. Betsy La Sor and M. Ruth Elliott. Scarborough: Prentice-Hall, 1977.

2712 MUSSALLEM, Helen K. "Nurses and Political Action." In *Issues in Canadian Nursing,* eds. Betsy La Sor and M. Ruth Elliott. Scarborough: Prentice-Hall, 1977.

2713 NEVITT, Joyce. *White Caps and Black Bands: Nursing in Newfoundland to 1934.* St. John's: Jesperson Press, 1978.

2714 PAUL, Pauline. "The Contribution of the Grey Nuns to the Development of Nursing in Canada: Historiographical Issues." *Canadian Bulletin of Medical History* 11, 1 (1994): 207-17.

2715 PETITAT, Andre. *Les infirmières: De la vocation à la profession.* Montréal: Boréal, 1989.

2716 ROKEBY-THOMAS, Anna. "Married Under the Midnight Sun." *North* 21, 4 (1974): 14-21. [nurse and wife of an Anglican missionary among the Inuit, 1930s]

2717 ROKEBY-THOMAS, Anna. "Anna's Diary: Arctic Honeymoon." *North* 21, 5 (1974): 26-31.

2718 ROKEBY-THOMAS, Anna. "Christmas 1938." *North* 22, 6 (1975): 52-57.

2719 ROYCE, Marion. *Eunice Dyke: Health Care Pioneer.* Toronto: Dundurn Press, 1983.

2720 SHORE, Helen L. "Emily Susan Patterson: Vancouver's First Nurse." *British Columbia Historical News* 26, 3 (Summer 1993): 20-21.

2721 STREET, Margaret. *Watch-Fires on the Mountains: The Life and Writings of Ethel Johns.* Toronto: University of Toronto Press, 1973.

2722 STRONG-BOAG, Veronica. "Making a Difference: The History of Canada's Nurses." *Canadian Bulletin of Medical History* 8, 2 (1991): 231-48.

2723 STUART, Meryn. "Ideology and Experience: Public Health Nursing and the Ontario Rural Child Welfare Project, 1920-25." *Canadian Bulletin of Medical History* 6, 2 (Winter 1989): 111-31.

2724 STUART, Meryn. "'Half a Loaf is Better than No Bread': Public Health Nurses and Physicians in Ontario, 1920-1925." *Nursing Research* 41, 1 (January/February 1992): 21-27.

2725 STUART, Meryn. "Nursing: The Endangered Profession?" *The Canadian Nurse* (April 1993): 19-21.

2726 STUART, Meryn. "Shifting Professional Boundaries: Gender Conflicts in Public Health, 1920-1925." In *Caring and Curing: Historical Perspectives on Women and Healing in Canada,* eds. Dianne Dodd and Deborah Gorham, 49-70. Ottawa: University of Ottawa Press, 1994.

2727 TURCKE, Katherine Warington. "The Evolution of Accountability in Nursing in Canada." *The Canadian Nurse* 79, 9 (October 1993).

2728 *Victorian Order of Nurses (Truro, N.S.): 1899-1989: Ninety Years of Caring.* Truro: Victorian Order of Nurses, 1989.

2729 VOGEL, Betty. "Nurse Brigid of East Vancouver." *British Columbia Historical News* 26, 1 (Winter 1992): 32.

2730 WARBURTON, Rennie and William K. Carroll. "Ambiguities of Political Consciousness Among Registered Nurses in British Columbia." *BC Studies* 83 (Autumn 1989): 3-28.

2731 WHEELER, Margaret M. "Les infirmières du Québec à la recherche de la sécurité économique." *L'infirmière canadienne* 61 (1965): 231-34.

2732 WHITE, Jerry. "Changing Labour Process and the Nursing Crisis in Canadian Hospitals." *Studies in Political Economy* 40 (Spring 1993): 103-34.

2733 WHITE, Linda. "Who's in Charge Here? The General Hospital School of Nursing, St. John's, Newfoundland, 1903-30." *Canadian Bulletin of Medical History* 11, 1 (1994): 91-118.

2734 WHITTAKER, Jo Ann. "The Search for Legitimacy: Nurses' Registration in British Columbia, 1913-1935." In *Not Just Pin Money: Selected Essays on the History of Women's Work in British Columbia,* eds. Barbara K. Latham and Roberta J. Pazdro, 315-26. Victoria: Camosun College, 1984.

2735 WILSON, Amy V. *No Man Stands Alone.* Sidney, BC: Gray's Publishing, 1966. [public health nursing in Yukon]

LAW/PUBLIC POLICY

SINCE 1976 when Marvin Zuker and June Callwood proclaimed that "The Law is Not for Women!" legal reform has been high on the agenda of Canadian feminists, as it was for earlier generations of feminists. Historians have played a critical role in documenting women's legal status in the past, the operation of discriminatory laws and campaigns for legal reform, the role of the state in enforcing women's subordinate status, and the construction of gender through law and policy. The pioneering work of legal historian, Constance Backhouse, helped to establish the importance of this field, which has since become one of the major growth areas in Canadian women's history.

There is now an extensive literature documenting the evolution of Canadian women's legal rights under British Common Law and under the Civil Code in Quebec. During the past decade, there has been a flurry of activity on affirmative action and pay equity initiatives, the historical relationship of women's rights to human rights legislation, and the impact of the Charter of Rights and Freedoms. Sexual orientation and equality rights, and the status of lesbians under the law, have attracted considerable attention, and there is an abundant literature on the relationship of women's rights to aboriginal rights, focussing on the Indian Act and Bill C-31. The struggle of women to gain admission to the legal profession has also been examined by historians, with special attention to the role of Clara Brett Martin.

Vigorous public debate over the reform of family law in Canada since the 1970s has prompted much scholarly interest in the history of the laws pertaining to marriage, divorce and child custody. There is a growing literature on the legal status of married women, married women's property law, dower rights, farm women and matrimonial property, and the use of marriage contracts in Quebec. The discriminatory operation of divorce laws and the campaigns to broaden the grounds for divorce prior to 1968 have been examined in a number of jurisdictions. Women's struggle to gain equal rights to the guardianship of their children has also been examined by historians, as have the current implications of custody laws for lesbian mothers.

One of the fastest growing bodies of scholarship in Canadian women's history is that pertaining to the criminal justice system, as feminist historians have wrestled with the power of the law to shape and enforce normative constructions of gender and sexuality, and to define and control "deviant" behaviour. An extensive literature now exists documenting the treatment of women under the laws pertaining to rape, seduction, murder, infanticide, and especially prostitution. The literature on female offenders is still relatively undeveloped, but some fascinating work now exists on prostitutes, petty criminals, and a small number of murderers. As violence against women has become a major public issue in the past decade, so have historians sought an historical perspective on the issues of rape and wife assault. The roles of women police, prisons for women and the Elizabeth Fry Society in mediating the female offender's experience of the criminal justice system have also received attention in some recent studies.

Canadian women and their organizations played a crucial role in promoting some of the earliest initiatives that led to the establishment of the welfare state. Yet historians have noted that public policy has often worked against women by supporting the patriarchal family and enforcing conservative definitions of "women's place." Indeed, the welfare state itself has come to be understood as a gendered construct. These themes have been explored in a large and growing literature on daycare and child welfare, mothers' pensions and Family Allowances, the care of the aged, the establishment of family courts, the minimum wage and unemployment insurance, housing and employment policy, and the feminization of poverty.

CRIMINAL JUSTICE/CRIME

2736 ABELL, Jennie and Gloria Geller, eds. "Women and the Criminal Justice System." A special issue of *Resources for Feminist Research* 14, 4 (Dec. 1985/Jan. 1986).

2737 ADELBERG, Ellen and Claudia Currie, eds. *Too Few to Count: Canadian Women in Conflict with the Law.* Vancouver: Press Gang Publishers, 1987.

2738 ADELBERG, Ellen and Claudia Currie, eds. *In Conflict with the Law: Women and the Canadian Justice System.* Vancouver: Press Gang Publishers, 1993.

2739 ARMSTRONG, Frederick H. "Obscenity in Victorian London: The Lotta Davene Poster Trial." In *Simcoe's Choice: Celebrating London's Bicentennial,* ed. Guy St-Denis, 175-92. Toronto and Oxford: Dundurn Press, 1992.

2740 BACKHOUSE, Constance B. "Nineteenth Century Canadian Rape Law, 1800-1892." In *Essays in the History of Canadian Law, Vol. 2,* ed. David Flaherty, 200-47. Toronto: University of Toronto Press for the Osgoode Society, 1983.

2741 BACKHOUSE, Constance B. "Desperate Women and Compassionate Courts: Infanticide in Nineteenth-Century Canada." *University of Toronto Law Journal* 34 (1984): 447-78. Reprinted in *Historical Perspectives on Law and Society in Canada,* eds. Tina Loo and Lorna R. McLean. Mississauga: Copp Clark Longman, 1994.

2742 BACKHOUSE, Constance B. "Nineteenth Century Canadian Prostitution Law: Reflection of a Discriminatory Society." *Histoire sociale/Social History* XVIII, 36 (Nov. 1985): 387-423.

2743 BACKHOUSE, Constance B. "The Tort of Seduction: Fathers and Daughters in Nineteenth Century Canada." *Dalhousie Law Journal* 10, 1 (June 1986): 45-80.

2744 BACKHOUSE, Constance B. "Nineteenth Century Judicial Attitudes Toward Child Custody, Rape and Prostitution." In *Equality and Judicial Neutrality,* eds. Sheilah L. Martin and Kathleen E. Mahoney, 271-81. Calgary: Carswell, 1987.

2745 BAILEY, Martha J. "Servant Girls and Masters: The Tort of Seduction and the Support of Bastards." *Canadian Journal of Family Law* 10 (1991): 137-62.

2746 BAILEY, Martha J. "Servant Girls and Upper Canada's Seduction Act, 1837-1946." In *Dimensions of Childhood: Essays on the History of Children and Youth in Canada,* eds. Russell Smandych, Gordon Dodds and Alvin Esau, 159-82. Winnipeg: University of Manitoba, Legal Research Institute, 1991.

2747 BEDFORD, Judy. "Prostitution in Calgary, 1905-1914." *Alberta History* 29, 2 (1981): 1-11.

2748 BELL, Ernest A. ed. *War on the White Slave Trade* [1911]. Toronto: Coles Publishing, 1980.

2749 BERKINS, Lorraine and Brigid Hayes. "The Diaries of Two Change Agents." In *Too Few to Count: Canadian Women in Conflict with the Law,* eds. Ellen Adelberg and Claudia Currie, 163-79. Vancouver: Press Gang Publishers, 1987. [prison reform]

2750 BERTRAND, Marie-Andrée. "L'augmentation accélérée de la criminalité des femmes." *Atlantis* 3, 2 (Spring 1978): 63-71.

2751 BOISVERT, Raymonde and Maurice Cusson. "L'homicide conjugal à Montréal." *Recherches sociographiques* 35, 2 (1994): 237-54.

2752 BROCKMAN, Joan and Dorothy E. Chunn, eds. *Investigating Gender Bias: Law, Courts and the Legal Profession.* Toronto: Thompson Educational Publishing, 1993.

2753 BURR, Chris. "'Roping in the Wretched, the Reckless, and the Wronged': Narratives of the Late Nineteenth-Century Toronto Police Court." *left history* 3, 1 (Spring/Summer 1995): 83-108.

2754 CALLWOOD, June. *Emma: Canada's Unlikely Spy.* Toronto: Stoddart Publishing, 1984. [Emma Waikin]

2755 CAMPBELL, Deborah A. *The Evolution of Sexual Harassment Case Law in Canada.* Kingston: Industrial Relations Centre, Queen's University, 1992.

2756 CARRIGAN, D. Owen. *Crime and Punishment in Canada: A History.* Toronto: McClelland and Stewart, 1991. [Ch. 6 and 10 on the female offender]

2757 CHAPMAN, Terry L. "The Anti-Drug Crusade in Western Canada, 1885-1925." In *Law and Society in Canada in Historical Perspective,* eds. D.J. Bercuson and L.A. Knafla, 89-115. Calgary: University of Calgary Press 1979.

2758 CHAPMAN, Terry L. "Film Censorship in Lethbridge, 1918-1920." *Alberta History* 33, 1 (1985): 1-9.

2759 CHAPMAN, Terry L. "Sex Crimes in the West, 1890-1920." *Alberta History* 35, 4 (Autumn 1987): 6-21.

2760 CHAPMAN, Terry L. "'Til Death do us Part': Wife Beating in Alberta, 1905-1920." *Alberta History* 36, 4 (Autumn 1988): 13-22.

2761 CHAPMAN, Terry L. "'Inquiring Minds Want to Know': The Handling of Children in Sex Assault Cases in the Canadian West, 1890-1920." In *Dimensions of Childhood: Essays on the History of Children and Youth in Canada,* eds. Russell Smandych, Gordon Dodds and Alvin Esau, 183-204. Winnipeg: University of Manitoba, Legal Research Institute, 1991.

2762 CLICHE, Marie-Aimée. "L'infanticide dans la région de Québec (1660-1969)." *Revue d'histoire de l'Amérique française* 44, 1 (été 1990): 31-59.

2763 CLICHE, Marie-Aimée. "Les filles-mères devant les tribunaux du Québec, 1850-1969." *Recherches sociographiques* 32, 1 (janvier-avril 1991): 9-42.

2764 COOPER, Joy. "Red Lights in Winnipeg." Manitoba Historical and Scientific Society. *Transactions* (16 February 1971): 61-74.

2765 COOPER, Sheelagh (Dunn). "The Evolution of the Federal Women's Prison." In *Too Few to Count: Canadian Women in Conflict with the Law*, eds. Ellen Adelberg and Claudia Currie, 127-44. Vancouver: Press Gang Publishers, 1987.

2766 CROZIER, Alma. "The Canadian Criminal Justice System and Lesbianism: A Research Note on the Relationship Between Systematic Exclusion and Criminal Victimization." *Resources for Feminist Research* 14, 4 (December 1985/January 1986): 18-19.

2767 DEKESEREDY, Walter and Ronald Hinch. *Woman Abuse: Sociological Perspectives*. Toronto: Thompson Educational Publishing, 1991.

2768 DUBINSKY, Karen. "Sex and Shame: Some Thoughts on the Social and Historical Meaning of Rape." *Resources for Feminist Research* 19, 3/4 (September/December 1990): 81-85.

2769 DUBINSKY, Karen. "'Maidenly Girls' or 'Designing Women'? The Crime of Seduction in Turn-of-the-Century Ontario." In *Gender Conflicts: New Essays in Women's History*, eds. Franca Iacovetta and Mariana Valverde, 27-66. Toronto: University of Toronto Press, 1992.

2770 DUBINSKY, Karen. *Improper Advances: Rape and Heterosexual Conflict in Ontario, 1880-1929*. Chicago: University of Chicago Press, 1993.

2771 DUBINSKY, Karen and Franca Iacovetta. "Murder, Womanly Virtue, and Motherhood: The Case of Angelina Napolitano, 1911-1922." *Canadian Historical Review* 72, 4 (December 1991): 505-31. Reprinted in *Historical Perspectives on Law and Society in Canada*, eds. Tina Loo and Lorna R. McLean. Mississauga: Copp Clark Longman, 1994.

2772 ELLIOT, Liz and Ruth Morris. "Behind Prison Doors." In *Too Few to Count: Canadian Women in Conflict with the Law*, eds. Ellen Adelberg and Claudia Currie, 145-62. Vancouver: Press Gang Publishers, 1987.

2773 FINGARD, Judith. *The Dark Side of Life in Victorian Halifax*. Porters Lake, NS: Pottersfield Press, 1989.

2774 GAGNON, Brigitte. "Criminalité féminine dans le Bas-Saint-Laurent durant la grande crise: une affaire de morale féminine ou de justice." *Revue d'histoire du Bas-Saint-Laurent* 14, 1 (décembre 1990): 13-19.

2775 GARTMAN, Rosemary and Bill McCarthy. "The Social Distribution of Femicide in Urban Canada, 1921-1988." *Law and Society Review* 25, 2 (1991): 287-311.

2776 GAVIGAN, Shelley. "Women's Crime: New Perspectives and Old Theories." *Canadian Criminology Forum* 6 (1983): 75-90. Revised and reprinted in *Too Few to Count: Canadian Women in Conflict with the Law*, eds. Ellen Adelberg and Claudia Currie, 47-66. Vancouver: Press Gang Publishers, 1987.

2777 GELLER, Gloria. "Young Women in Conflict with the Law." In *Too Few to Count: Canadian Women in Conflict with the Law*, eds. Ellen Adelberg and Claudia Currie, 113-26. Vancouver: Press Gang Publishers, 1987.

2778 GIBSON, Dale. "A Scandal at Red River." *The Beaver* 70, 5 (Oct./Nov. 1990): 30-38. [lawsuit by a domestic servant against her former employer]

2779 "Girls Cannot Live Morally in Calgary." *Alberta History* 26, 2 (Spring 1978): 30. [Reprinted from the *Regina Leader*, 1913]

2780 GOSSAGE, Peter. "*La marâtre*: Marie-Anne Houde and the Myth of the Wicked Stepmother in Quebec." *Canadian Historical Review* 76, 4 (December 1995): 563-97.

2781 GRANT, Dorothy Metie. "The Tragedy of Catherine Thompson." *Nova Scotia Historical Quarterly*, 6, 1 (March 1976): 49-55.

2782 GRAY, James H. *Red Lights on the Prairies*. Toronto: Macmillan, 1973.

2783 HARVEY, Kathryn. "To Love, Honour and Obey: Wife-Battering in Working Class Montreal, 1869-79." *Urban History Review* XIX, 2 (October 1990): 128-40.

2784 HARVEY, Kathryn. "Amazons and Victims: Resisting Wife Abuse in Working-Class Montréal, 1869-1879." *Journal of the Canadian Historical Association* NS 2, (1991): 131-48.

2785 HAWLEY, Donna Lea, comp. "Prostitution in Canada: A Bibliography." *Resources for Feminist Research* 14, 4 (December 1985/January 1986): 61-63.

2786 HORRALL, S.W. "The (Royal) North-West Mounted Police and Prostitution on the Canadian Prairies." *Prairie Forum* 10, 1 (Spring 1985): 105-27.

2787 HOUSTON, Susan E. "The Role of the Criminal Law in Redefining 'Youth' in Mid-Nineteenth-Century Upper Canada." *Historical Studies in Education* 6, 3 (1994): 39-55.

2788 HUGHES, Patricia. "The Evolving Conceptual Framework of Sexual Harrassment." *Canadian Labour and Employment Law* 3, 1 (December 1994): 1-32.

2789 JOHNSON, Holly. "Getting the Facts Straight: A Statistical Overview." In *Too Few to Count: Canadian Women in Conflict with the Law*, eds. Ellen Adelberg and Claudia Currie, 23-46. Vancouver: Press Gang Publishers, 1987.

2790 JOHNSTON, Susan J. "Twice Slain: Female Sex-Trade Workers and Suicide in British Columbia, 1870-1920." *Journal of the Canadian Historical Association* NS 5 (1994): 147-66.

2791 JONES, Frank. *Murderous Women: True Tales of Women Who Kill.* Toronto: Key Porter Books, 1991.

2792 KENDALL, Kathy. "Sexual Difference and the Law: Premenstrual Syndrome as Legal Defence." In *The Anatomy of Gender: Women's Struggle for the Body,* eds. Dawn H. Currie and Valerie Raoul, 130-46. Ottawa: Carleton University Press, 1992.

2793 KERSHAW, Anne with Mary Lasovich. *Rock a Bye Baby: A Death Behind Bars.* Toronto: McClelland and Stewart, 1991. [Marlene Moore, first woman in Canada declared a dangerous offender]

2794 LABERGE, Danielle and Shirley Roy. "Femmes et criminalité: Le contrôle social est-il sexué? Une analyse des données statistiques québécoises." *Canadian Journal of Women and the Law* 3, 2 (1989): 457-64.

2795 LACASSE, Danielle. *La prostitution féminine à Montréal, 1945-1970.* Montréal: Les Éditions du Boréal, 1994.

2796 LACHANCE, André. "Women and Crime in Canada in the Early Eighteenth Century, 1712-1759." In *Lawful Authority: Readings on the History of Criminal Justice in Canada,* ed. R.C. Macleod. Toronto: Copp Clark, 1988.

2797 LACOURCIÈRE, Luc. "Le triple destin de Marie-Josephte Corriveau (1733-1763)." *Les Cahiers des Dix* 33 (1968): 213-42.

2798 LACOURCIÈRE, Luc. "Le destin posthume de la Corriveau." *Les Cahiers des Dix* 34 (1969): 239-71.

2799 LANGDON, M. Elizabeth. "Female Crime in Calgary, 1914-1941." In *Law and Justice in a New Land: Essays in Western Canadian Legal History,* ed. Louis A. Knafla, 293-312. Toronto: Carswell, 1986.

2800 LAPLANTE, Jacques. "Cent ans de prison: les conditions et les 'privilèges' des détenus hommes, femmes et enfants [au Canada]." *Criminologie* 24, 1 (1991): 11-32.

2801 LAPRAIRIE, Carol Pitcher. "Selected Criminal Justice and Socio-Demographic Data on Native Women." *Canadian Journal of Criminology* 26, 2 (April 1984): 161-70.

2802 LAPRAIRIE, Carol. "Native Women and Crime: A Theoretical Model." *Canadian Journal of Native Studies* 7, 1 (1987): 121-38. Reprinted in *Too Few to Count: Canadian Women in Conflict with the Law,* eds. Ellen Adelberg and Claudia Currie, 103-112. Vancouver: Press Gang Publishers, 1987.

2803 LARSEN, E. Nick. "Canadian Prostitution Controls Between 1914 and 1970: An Exercise in Chauvinistic Reasoning." *Canadian Journal of Law and Society* 7, 2 (1992): 137-56.

2804 LECLERC, Jean-François. "Femmes et violence: quelques réflexions à partir des procès pour voie de fait dans la jurisdiction de Montréal, 1700-1760." *Cahiers d'histoire* 6, 1 (automne 1985): 83-103.

2805 LEMOINE, Réjean. "Maisons malfamées et prostitution: de la tolérance à l'interdiction." *Cap-aux-Diamants* 1, 1 (Spring 1985): 13-18.

2806 LÉVESQUE, Andrée. "Le Bordel: Milieu de Travail Contrôlé." *Labour/Le Travail* 20 (Autumn 1987): 13-37.

2807 LÉVESQUE, Andrée. "Eteindre le 'Red Light': Les réformateurs et la prostitution à Montréal, 1865-1925." *Urban History Review* XVII, 3 (February 1989): 191-201.

2808 MacDONALD, Cheryl. "Was It Murder? The Curious Case of Olive Sternaman." *The Beaver* 71, 5 (Oct./Nov. 1991): 32-38.

2809 MacLEOD, Linda. *Wife Battering in Canada: The Vicious Circle.* Ottawa: Canadian Advisory Council on the Status of Women, 1980.

2810 MacLEOD, Linda. *Battered But Not Beaten.* Ottawa: Canadian Advisory Council on the Status of Women, 1987.

2811 MARTEL, Joane. "Femme battue et mari batteur: une reconstruction médiatique dans *La Presse* au XIXe siècle." *Criminologie* 27, 1 (1994): 117-34.

2812 MARTIN, Sheilah L. and Kathleen E. Mahoney, eds. *Equality and Judicial Neutrality.* Calgary: Carswell, 1987.

2813 MATTERS, Indiana. "Sinners or Sinned Against? Historical Aspects of Female Juvenile Delinquency in British Columbia." In *Not Just Pin Money: Selected Essays on the History of Women's Work in British Columbia,* eds. Barbara K. Latham and Roberta J. Pazdro, 265-77. Victoria: Camosun College, 1984.

2814 MAXIM, Paul S. and Carl Kane. "Gender, Age and the Risk of Violent Death in Canada, 1950-1986." *Canadian Review of Sociology and Anthropology* 29, 3 (1992): 329-45.

2815 McCARTHY, Bill and John Hagan. "Gender, Delinquency, and the Great Depression: A Test of Power-control Theory." *Canadian Review of Sociology and Anthropology* 24, 2 (May 1987): 153-77.

2816 McLAREN, John P.S. "Chasing the Social Evil: Moral Fervour and the Evolution of Canada's Prostitution Laws, 1867-1917." *Canadian Journal of Law and Society* 1 (1986): 125-65.

2817 McLAREN, John P.S. "Twentieth Century Judicial Attitudes Toward Prostitution." In *Equality and Judicial Neutrality,* eds. Sheilah L. Martin and Kathleen E. Mahoney, 282-97. Calgary: Carswell, 1987.

2818 McLAREN, John P.S. "White Slavers: The Reform of Canada's Prostitution Laws and Patterns of Enforcement, 1900-1920." *Criminal Justice History* 8 (1987): 53-119.

2819 McLAREN, John P.S. "The Canadian Magistracy and the Anti-White Slavery Campaign, 1900-1920." In *Canadian Perspectives on Law and Society: Issues in Legal History*, eds. W. Wesley Pue and Barry Wright, 329-53. Ottawa: Carleton University Press, 1988.

2820 McLAREN, John P.S. *Recalculating the Wages of Sin: The Social and Legal Construction of Prostitution in Canada, 1850-1920*. Winnipeg: Canadian Legal History Project, Faculty of Law, University of Manitoba, 1992.

2821 MITCHELL, Tom. "'Blood with the Taint of Cain': Immigrant Labouring Children, Manitoba Politics, and the Execution of Emily Hilda Blake." *Journal of Canadian Studies* 28, 4 (Winter 1993/94): 49-71.

2822 MOREAU, Robert A. "Intempérance et prostitution à Hull, 1896-1914." *Outaouais* 1 (January 1986).

2823 MOREL, A. "Réflexions sur la justice criminelle canadienne au 18e siècle." *Revue d'histoire de l'Amérique française* 29, 2 (septembre 1975): 241-53.

2824 MURPHY, Emily. *The Black Candle*. Toronto: Thomas Allen, 1926. Reprinted with an introduction by Brian Anthony and Robert Soloman. Toronto: Coles Canadiana Collection, 1973. [exposé of drug traffic in Canada]

2825 MYERS, Tamara. "Women Policing Women: A Patrol Woman in Montreal in the 1910s." *Journal of the Canadian Historical Association* NS 4 (1993): 229-45.

2826 NILSEN, Deborah. "The 'Social Evil': Prostitution in Vancouver, 1900-1920." In *In Her Own Right: Selected Essays on Women's History in BC*, eds. Barbara Latham and Cathy Kess, 205-28. Victoria: Camosun College, 1980.

2827 OLSON, Ruth A. "Rape—An 'Un-Victorian' Aspect of Life in Upper Canada." *Ontario History* 68, 2 (June 1976): 75-79.

2828 OSBORNE, Judith A. "The Crime of Infanticide: Throwing Out the Baby With the Bathwater." *Canadian Journal of Family Law* 6, 1 (1987): 47-59.

2829 PARKER, Graham. "The Legal Regulation of Sexual Activity and the Protection of Females." *Osgoode Hall Law Journal* 21, 2 (June 1983): 187-224.

2830 POUTANEN, Mary-Anne. "Reflections of Montreal Prostitution in the Records of the Lower Courts, 1810-1842." In *Class, Gender and the Law in Eighteenth- and Nineteenth-Century Quebec: Sources and Perspective*, eds. Donald Fyson, Colin M. Coates and Kathryn Harvey, 99-125. Montreal: Montreal History Group, 1993.

2831 PRICE, B. Jane. "'Raised in Rockhead. Died in the Poorhouse': Female Petty Criminals in Halifax, 1864-1890." In *Essays in the History of Canadian Law: Volume 3, Nova Scotia*, eds. Philip Girard and Jim Phillips, 200-31. Toronto: University of Toronto Press for the Osgoode Society, 1990.

2832 RECOLLET, Nancy L. "Native Women and the Criminal Justice System: An Increasing Minority." *Resources for Feminist Research* 14, 4 (December 1985/January 1986): 16-18.

2833 REID, Joanne. "Witches, whores and waifs: Judicial treatment of deviant women in pre-Confederation New Brunswick—selected examples." *Canadian Law in History Conference. Papers*. Ottawa: Carleton University, 1987, 108-33.

2834 ROTENBERG, Lori. "The Wayward Worker: Toronto's Prostitute at the Turn of the Century." In *Women at Work: Ontario, 1850-1930*, eds. Janice Acton, *et al*, 33-69. Toronto: Canadian Women's Educational Press, 1974.

2835 SAKOWSKI, Marie H. "Women Guards in Canada: A Study of the First Women to Work in a Federal Penitentiary for Male Offenders." *Resources for Feminist Research* 14, 4 (Dec. 1985/Jan. 1986): 52-53.

2836 SANGSTER, Joan. "'Pardon Tales' from Magistrate's Court: Women, Crime, and the Court in Peterborough County, 1920-50." *Canadian Historical Review* 74, 2 (June 1993): 161-97.

2837 SOMMERS, Evelyn K. *Voices from Within: Women in Conflict with the Law*. Toronto: University of Toronto Press, 1995.

2838 STEWART, Lee. *Women Volunteer to Go to Prison: A History of the Elizabeth Fry Society of BC, 1939-1989*. Victoria: Orca Book Publishers, 1993.

2839 STRANGE, Carolyn. "'The Criminal and Fallen of Their Sex': The Establishment of Canada's First Women's Prison, 1874-1901." *Canadian Journal of Women and the Law* 1, 1 (1985): 79-92.

2840 STRANGE, Carolyn. "Unlocking the Doors on Women's Prison History." *Resources for Feminist Research* 13, 4 (December 1985/January 1986): 13-15.

2841 STRANGE, Carolyn. "Wounded Womanhood and Dead Men: Chivalry and the Trials of Clara Ford and Carrie Davies." In *Gender Conflicts: New Essays in Women's History*, eds. Franca Iacovetta and Mariana Valverde, 149-88. Toronto: University of Toronto Press, 1992.

2842 STRANGE, Carolyn. "Patriarchy Modified: The Criminal Prosecution of Rape in York County, Ontario, 1880-1930." In *Essays in the History of Canadian Law, Volume 5: Crime and Criminal Justice*, eds. Jim Phillips, Tina Loo and Susan Lewthwaite, 207-51. Toronto: University of Toronto Press, 1994.

2843 SWYRIPA, Frances. "Negotiating Sex and Gender in the Ukrainian Bloc Settlement: East-Central Alberta Between the Wars." *Prairie Forum* 20, 2 (Fall 1995): 149-74. [rape and wife assault]

2844 THEORET, Bruno. "Régulation juridique pénale des mineures et discrimination à l'égard des filles—la clause de 1924 amendment de la *Loi sur les jeunes délinquents*." *Canadian Journal of Women and the Law* 4, 2 (1991): 539-55.

2845 WRIGHT, Mary Ellen. "Unnatural Mothers: Infanticide in Halifax, 1850-1875." *Nova Scotia Historical Review* 7, 2 (1987): 13-29.

EQUALITY RIGHTS

2846 ABELLA, Rosalie. "The Critical Century: The Rights of Women and Children from 1882-1982." *Gazette* 18 (1984): 40-53.

2847 ALTSCHUL, Susan and Christine Carron. "Chronology of Some Legal Landmarks in the History of Canadian Women." *McGill Law Journal* 21, 4 (Winter 1975): 476-94.

2848 ATCHESON, Elizabeth, Mary Eberts and Beth Symes with Jennifer Stoddart. *Women and Legal Action: Precedents, Resources and Strategies for the Future.* Ottawa: Canadian Advisory Council on the Status of Women, 1984.

2849 BAINES, Beverley. "Women and the Law." In *Changing Patterns: Women in Canada*, eds. Sandra Burt, Lorraine Code and Lindsay Dorney, 157-83. Toronto: McClelland & Stewart, 1988. Revised and retitled as "Law, Gender, Equality" in 2nd edition, 243-78, 1993.

2850 BAYEFSKY, Anne. "The Human Rights Commission and the Case of Sandra Lovelace." *Canadian Yearbook of International Law* 20 (1982): 244-65.

2851 BAYEFSKY, Anne and Mary Eberts, eds. *Equality Rights and the Canadian Charter of Rights and Freedoms.* Toronto: Carswell, 1985.

2852 BECKTON, C.F. "The Impact on Women of Entrenchment of Property Rights in the Canadian Charter of Rights and Freedoms." *Dalhousie Law Journal* 9 (1985): 288-312.

2853 BÉLAND, François and Micheline de Sève. "L'inégalité et la discrimination sexuelles et linguistiques au Québec." *Canadian Review of Sociology and Anthropology* 23, 3 (August 1986): 309-30.

2854 BLACHE, Pierre. "Les droits politiques de la femme au Québec." In *Le droit dans la vie familiale: Le livre du centenaire du code civil*, eds. Jacques Boucher and André Morel, 233-45. Montréal: Presses de l'Université de Montréal, 1970.

2855 BOHNEN, Linda S. "Women Workers in Ontario: A Socio-Legal History." *University of Toronto Faculty of Law Review* 31 (1973): 45-74.

2856 BOIVIN, Michelle. "L'évolution des droits de la femme au Québec: un survol historique." *Canadian Journal of Women and the Law* 2, 1 (1986): 53-68.

2857 BOUCHER, J. "L'histoire de la condition juridique et sociale de la femme au Canada français." In *Le droit dans la vie familiale: Le livre du centenaire du code civil*, eds. Jacques Boucher and André Morel, 155-68. Montréal: Presses de l'Université de Montréal, 1970.

2858 BOURNE, Paula. *Women in Canadian Society.* Toronto: Ontario Institute for Studies in Education, 1976; revised edition, 1978.

2859 BOURNE, Paula. "Women, Law and the Justice System." In *Canadian Women's Issues, Volume I: Strong Voices*, Ruth Roach Pierson, Marjorie Griffin Cohen, Paula Bourne and Philanda Masters, 321-93. Toronto: James Lorimer and Company, 1994.

2860 BOYLE, Christine, Wayne MacKay, Edward McBride and John Yogis. *Charterwatch: Reflections on Equality.* Toronto: Carswell, 1986.

2861 BRENT, Gail. "The Development of the Law Relating to the Participation of Canadian Women in Public Life." *University of Toronto Law Journal* 25, 4 (1975): 358-70.

2862 BRODSKY, Gwen and Shelagh Day. *Canadian Charter Equality Rights for Women: One Step Forward or Two Steps Back.* Ottawa: Canadian Advisory Council on the Status of Women, 1987.

2863 BRUNER, Arnold. "Sexual Orientation and Equality Rights." In *Equality Rights and the Canadian Charter of Rights and Freedoms*, eds. Anne F. Bayefsky and Mary Eberts, Toronto: Carswell, 1985.

2864 BURT, Sandra. "The Charter of Rights and the Ad Hoc Lobby." *Atlantis* 14, 1 (Fall 1988): 74-81.

2865 CAMPBELL, Elizabeth Bethune. *Where Angels Fear to Tread.* Boston: St. John's Rectory, 1940. [first woman to appear before the Judicial Committee of the Privy Council to support her appeal, 1930]

2866 COLBY, Marion, *et al*, eds. "Affirmative Action." A special issue of *Canadian Woman Studies* 6, 4 (Winter 1985).

2867 COLLECTIF CLIO. "La femme autochtone face à la loi sur les indiens." *Canadian Women's Studies* 2, 4 (1980): 37-41.

2868 CULLUM, Linda and Maeve Baird with Cynthia Penney. "A Woman's Lot: Women and Law in Newfoundland From Early Settlement to the Twentieth Century." In *Pursuing Equality: Historical Perspectives on Women in Newfoundland and Labrador*, ed. Linda Kealey, 66-162. St. John's: Memorial University of Newfoundland, Institute of Social and Economic Research, 1993.

2869 DAWSON, T. Brettel, ed. *Relating to Law: A Chronology of Women and Law in Canada.* North York: Captus, 1990.

2870 DELEURY, Edith. "L'union homosexuelle et le droit de la famille." *Cahiers du Droit* 25 (décembre 1984): 751-75.

2871 DEMERS, Robert. "De la Lex Scantinia au récents amendements du Code Criminal: homosexualité et droit dans une perspective historique." *Cahiers du Droit* 25 (décembre 1984).

2872 DOERR, Audrey and Micheline Carrier. *Women and the Constitution in Canada.* Ottawa: Canadian Advisory Council on the Status of Women, 1981.

2873 DRANOFF, Linda Silver. *Women in Canadian Life: Law.* Toronto: Fitzhenry & Whiteside, 1977.

2874 DUCLOS, Nitya. "Disappearing Women: Racial Minority Women in Human Rights Cases." *Canadian Journal of Women and the Law* 6, 1 (1993): 25-51.

2875 DUPLE, Nicole. "Homosexualité et droits à l'égalité dans les chartes canadienne et québécoise." *Cahiers du Droit* 25 (décembre 1984): 776-800.

2876 DYMOND, M.J. *The Canadian Woman's Legal Guide.* Toronto: Doubleday Canada, 1987.

2877 EATON, Mary. "Lesbians and the Law." In *Lesbians in Canada*, ed. Sharon Dale Stone, 109-32. Toronto: Between the Lines, 1990.

2878 EGRI, C.P. and W.T. Stanbury. "How Pay Equity Legislation Came to Ontario." *Canadian Public Administration* 32 (1989): 274-303.

2879 FINDLAY, Sue. "Representation and Regulation: The Role of State Bureaucracy in Limiting Equal Employment Opportunities for Women." *Canadian Woman Studies* 6, 4 (Winter 1985): 30-33.

2880 FUDGE, Judy. "The Privatization of the Costs of Social Reproduction: Some Recent Charter Cases." *Canadian Journal of Women and the Law* 3, 1 (1989): 246-55.

2881 GARCIA, Veronica Vazquez. "Gender and Land Rights in Mexico and Canada: A Comparative Study." *International Journal of Canadian Studies* 11 (Spring 1995): 147-70. [Indian Act]

2882 GELBER, Sylvia. "Women and Work: The Legislative Base." *Canadian Labour* 20, 2 (June 1975): 7-11, 38.

2883 GIRARD, Philip. "Sexual Orientation as a Human Rights Issue in Canada, 1969-1985." *Dalhousie Law Journal* 10, 2 (October 1986): 267-81.

2884 GIRARD, Philip. "From Subversion to Liberation: Homosexuals and the Immigration Act, 1952-1977." *Canadian Journal of Law and Society* 2 (1987): 1-27.

2885 GOTELL, Lise. *The Canadian Women's Movement, Equality Rights and the Charter.* Feminist Perspectives No. 16. Ottawa: Canadian Research Institute for the Advancement of Women, 1990.

2886 GREEN, J. "Sexual Equality and Indian Government: An Analysis of Bill C-31 Amendments to the Indian Act." *Native Studies Review* 1, 2 (1985): 81-95.

2887 HERMAN, Didi. "Are We Family? Lesbian Rights and Women's Liberation." *Osgoode Hall Law Journal* 28 (1990): 789-815.

2888 HERMAN, Didi. *Rights of Passage: Struggles for Lesbian and Gay Legal Equality.* Toronto: University of Toronto Press, 1994.

2889 HOLMES, Joan. *Bill C-31: equality or disparity? The effects of the new Indian Act on native women.* Ottawa: Canadian Advisory Council on the Status of Women, 1987.

2890 JAMIESON, Kathleen. *Indian Women and the Law in Canada: Citizens Minus.* Hull: Advisory Council on the Status of Women, 1978.

2891 JAMIESON, Kathleen. "Plus ça change, plus c'est pareil? Les femmes autochtones et la question du gouvernement indien autonome et du droit coutumier." *Recherches amérindiennes au Québec* 14, 3 (1984): 65-74.

2892 JAMIESON, Kathleen. "Sex Discrimination and the Indian Act." In *Arduous Journey: Canadian Indians and Decolonization*, ed. J. Rick Ponting, 112-36. Toronto: McClelland and Stewart, 1986. [excerpted from *Indian Women and the Law*]

2893 JOSEPH, Shirley. "Assimilation Tools: Then and Now." In *In Celebration of Our Survival: The First Nations of British Columbia*, eds. Doreen Jensen and Cheryl Brooks, 65-80. Vancouver: University of British Columbia Press, 1991. [Bill C-31]

2894 KHAYATT, D. "Legalized Invisibility—The Effect of Bill 7 on Lesbian Teachers." *Women's Studies International Forum* 13, 3 (1990): 185-93.

2895 KROSENBRINK-GELISSEN, Lilianne E. *Sexual Equality as an Aboriginal Right: The Native Women's Association of Canada and the Constitutional Process on Aboriginal Matters, 1982-1987.* Fort Lauderdale: Verlag Breitenbach Publishers, 1991.

2896 KROSENBRINK-GELISSEN, Lilianne E. "The Canadian Constitution, the Charter, and Aboriginal Women's Rights: Conflicts and Dilemmas." *International Journal of Canadian Studies* 7/8 (Spring/Fall 1993): 207-24.

2897 KROSENBRINK-GELISSEN, Lilianne E. "'Traditional Motherhood' in Defense of Sexual Equality Rights of Canada's Aboriginal Women." *European Review of Native American Studies* 7, 2 (1993): 13-16.

2898 LÉGARÉ, Jocelyne. "La condition juridique des femmes ou l'historique d'une affaire de famille." *Criminologie* 16, 2 (1983): 7-26.

2899 LEOPOLD, Margaret and Wendy King. "Compulsory Heterosexuality, Lesbians and the Law: The Case for Constitutional Protection." *Canadian Journal of Women and the Law* 1, 1 (1985): 163-86.

2900 LÉVESQUE, Carole. "Regards sur les femmes autochtones: les étapes d'une lutte politique et sociale." In *Encrages féministes: Un moment de réflexion dans la recherche féministe*, ed. Isabelle Lasvergnas, 111-25. Montréal: Université du Québec à Montréal, Centre de recherche féministe, Group interdisciplinaire d'enseignement et de recherche féministes, 1989.

2901 MacLELLAN, Margaret E. "History of Women's Rights in Canada." *The Cultural and Political History of Women in Canada.* Study No. 8 of the Royal Commission on the Status of Women in Canada. Ottawa: Information Canada, 1971.

2902 MALARKEY, Robert and John Hagan. "The Socio-Legal Impact of Equal Pay Legislation in Ontario, 1946-1979." *Osgoode Hall Law Journal* 27, 2 (Summer 1989): 295-336.

2903 McIVOR, Sharon D. "Aboriginal Women's Rights as 'Existing Rights.'" *Canadian Woman Studies* 15, 2/3 (Spring/Summer 1995): 34-38.

2904 MOSS, Wendy. "Indigenous Self-Government in Canada and Sexual Equality Under the Indian Act: Resolving Conflict Between Collective and Individual Rights." *Queen's Law Journal* 15 (1990): 279-305.

2905 MOSSMAN, Mary Jane. "Feminism and Legal Method: The Difference It Makes." In *Historical Perspectives on Law and Society in Canada,* eds. Tina Loo and Lorna R. McLean, Mississauga: Copp Clark Longman, 1994.

2906 NATIVE WOMEN'S ASSOCIATION OF CANADA. The Implementation of Bill C-31 (Amendment to the Indian Act)." *Resources for Feminist Research* 3 (September 1988): 125-28.

2907 NATIVE WOMEN'S ASSOCIATION OF CANADA. Aboriginal Women and the Constitutional Debates: Continuing Discrimination." *Canadian Woman Studies* 12, 3 (Spring 1992): 14-17.

2908 O'NEIL, Maureen. "Citizenship and Social Change: Canadian Women's Struggle for Equality." In *Belonging: The Meaning and Future of Canadian Citizenship,* ed. William Kaplan, 314-32. Montreal and Kingston: McGill-Queen's University Press, 1993.

2909 PIERRE-AGGAMAWAY, Marlene. "Native Women and the State." In *Perspectives on Women in the 1980s,* eds. Joan Turner and Lois Emery, 66-73. Winnipeg: University of Manitoba Press, 1983.

2910 RAYSIDE, David. "Gay Rights and Family Values: The Passage of Bill 7 in Ontario." *Studies in Political Economy* 26 (Summer 1988): 109-47.

2911 RAYSIDE, David and Scott Bowler. "Public Opinion and Gay Rights." *Canadian Review of Sociology and Anthropology* 25, 4 (November 1988): 649-60.

2912 RAZACK, Sherene. *Canadian Feminism and the Law: The Women's Legal Education and Action Fund and the Pursuit of Equality.* Toronto: Second Story Press, 1991.

2913 RITCHIE, Marguerite E., QC "Alice Through the Statutes." *McGill Law Journal* 21, 4 (1975): 685-707.

2914 RYDER, Bruce. "Equality Rights and Sexual Orientation: Confronting Heterosexual Privilege." *Canadian Journal of Family Law* 9, 1 (Fall 1990): 40-97.

2915 SANDERS, Douglas. "Constructing Lesbian and Gay Rights." *Canadian Journal of Law and Society* 9, 2 (Fall 1994).

2916 SINEAU, Mariette and Évelyne Tardy. *Droits des femmes en France et au Québec.* Montréal: Éditions du remue-ménage, 1994.

2917 SMITH, Lynn. "Have the Equality Rights Made Any Difference?" In *Protecting Rights and Freedoms: Essays on the Charter's Place in Canada's Political, Legal, and Intellectual Life,* eds. Philip Bryden, Steven Davis and John Russell, 60-89. Toronto: University of Toronto Press, 1994.

2918 SMITH, Lynn, Gisèle Côté-Harper, Robin Elliot and Magda Seydegart. *Righting the Balance: Canada's New Equality Rights.* Saskatoon: The Canadian Human Rights Reporter, 1986.

2919 STODDART, Jennifer. "Quebec's Legal Elite Looks at Women's Rights: The Dorion Commission 1919-1931." In *Essays in the History of Canadian Law, Vol. 1,* ed. D.H. Flaherty, 323-57. Toronto: The Osgoode Society, 1981.

2920 THORNHILL, Esmeralda M.A. "Regard sur le racisme: Perspectives juridiques à partir d'un vécu noir." *Canadian Journal of Women and the Law* 6, 1 (1993): 1-24.

2921 TILLOTSON, Shirley. "Human Rights Law as Prism: Women's Organizations, Unions, and Ontario's Female Employees Fair Remuneration Act, 1951." *Canadian Historical Review* 72, 4 (December 1991): 532-57.

2922 TULLOCH, Elspeth. *We the Undersigned: A Historical Overview of New Brunswick Women's Political and Legal Status, 1784-1984.* Moncton: New Brunswick Advisory Council on the Status of Women, 1985.

2923 TURPEL, Mary Ellen. "Patriarchy and Paternalism: The Legacy of the Canadian State for First Nations Women." *Canadian Journal of Women and the Law* 6, 1 (1993): 174-92.

2924 WEAVER, Sally. "First Nations Women and Government Policy, 1970-92: Discrimination and Conflict." In *Changing Patterns: Women in Canada,* eds. Sandra Burt, Lorraine Code and Lindsay Dorney, 92-150. Toronto: McClelland & Stewart, 1993.

2925 ZUKER, Marvin A. and June Callwood. *The Law is Not for Women!: A Legal Handbook for Women.* Vancouver: Pitman Publishing, 1976.

GENERAL

2926 BACKHOUSE, Constance. *Petticoats and Prejudice: Women and Law in Nineteenth-Century Canada.* Toronto: Women's Press for the Osgoode Society, 1991.

2927 BURSTYN, Varda, Dorothy E. Smith and Roxanna Ng. *Women, Class, Family and the State.* Toronto: Garamond Press, 1985.

2928 MARQUIS, Greg. "Law, Society and History: Whose Frontier?" *Acadiensis* 21, 2 (Spring 1992): 162-74.

2929 RANDALL, Melanie, comp. *The State Bibliography: An Annotated Bibliography on Women and the State in Canada.* Toronto: Resources for Feminist Research, 1989.

2930 SHEEHY, Elizabeth A. and Susan B. Boyd. *Canadian Feminist Perspectives on Law: An Annotated Bibliography of Interdisciplinary Writings.* Toronto: Ontario Institute for Studies in Education, 1989.

LEGAL PROFESSION

2931 ADAM, Barry D. and Douglas E. Baer. "The Social Mobility of Women and Men in the Ontario Legal Profession." *Canadian Review of Sociology and Anthropology* 21 (1984): 21-46.

2932 ANDERSON, Alexandra. "The First Woman Lawyer in Canada: Clara Brett Martin." *Canadian Woman Studies* 2, 4 (1980): 9-11.

2933 BACKHOUSE, Constance B. "'To Open the Way for Others of My Sex': Clara Brett Martin's Career as Canada's First Woman Lawyer." *Canadian Journal of Women and the Law* 1, 1 (1985): 1-41.

2934 BACKHOUSE, Constance B. "Clara Brett Martin: Canadian Heroine or Not?" *Canadian Journal of Women and the Law* 5, 2 (1992): 263-79.

2935 BACKHOUSE, Constance. "Response to Cossman, Kline, and Pearlman." *Canadian Journal of Women and the Law* 5, 2 (1992): 351-54.

2936 BETCHERMAN, Lita-Rose. "Clara Brett Martin's Anti-Semitism." *Canadian Journal of Women and the Law* 5, 2 (1992): 280-97.

2937 BETCHERMAN, Lita-Rose. "Response to Cossman, Kline, and Pearlman." *Canadian Journal of Women and the Law* 5, 2 (1992): 355-56.

2938 CANO, Marlene. "Claire L'Heureux-Dubé et le droit de la famille: Juge innovateur? ... Innovatrice." *Queen's Quarterly* 98, 1 (Spring 1991): 131-59.

2939 CHUNN, Dorothy, E. "Maternal Feminism, Legal Professionalism and Political Pragmatism: The Rise and Fall of Magistrate Margaret Patterson, 1922-1934." In *Canadian Perspectives on Law and Society: Issues in Legal History,* eds. W. Wesley Pue and Barry Wright, 91-117. Ottawa: Carleton University Press, 1988.

2940 COSSMAN, Brenda and Marlee Kline. "'And if not now, when?': Feminism and Anti-Semitism Beyond Clara Brett Martin." *Canadian Journal of Women and the Law* 5, 2 (1992): 298-316.

2941 DRANOFF, Linda Silver. "Women as Lawyers in Toronto." *Osgoode Hall Law Journal* 10 (1972): 177-90.

2942 GORDON, Loraine. "Dr. Margaret Norris Patterson; First Woman Police Magistrate in Eastern Canada, Toronto—January 1922-November 1934." *Atlantis* 10, 1 (Fall 1984): 95-109.

2943 HARVEY, Cameron. "Women in Law in Canada." *Manitoba Law Journal* 4 1 (1970): 9-38.

2944 KASIRER, Nicholas. "*Apostolat Juridique*: Teaching Everyday Law in the Life of Marie Lacoste Gérin-Lajoie (1867-1945)." *Osgoode Hall Law Journal* 30, 2 (1992): 427-70.

2945 KENNEDY, Dolly Sinclair. "Helen Gregory MacGill, First Woman Judge in BC." *British Columbia Historical News* 27, 4 (Fall 1994): 16-18.

2946 KINNEAR, Mary. "'That There Woman Lawyer': Women Lawyers in Manitoba, 1915-1970." *Canadian Journal of Women and the Law* 5, 2 (1992): 411-41.

2947 LESTER, Tanya. "Sissons Called to the Bar." *Herizons* (November 1984): 5.

2948 MACGILL, Elsie G. *My Mother the Judge: A Biography of Helen Gregory MacGill.* With an introduction by Naomi Black. Toronto: Peter Martin, 1981.

2949 MANDER, Christine. *Emily Murphy: First Female Magistrate in the British Empire.* Toronto: Simon & Pierre, 1985.

2950 MOSSMAN, Mary Jane. "Portia's Progress: Women as Lawyers: Reflections on the Past and Future." In *Women in the Legal Profession,* A.1-A.29. Toronto: Law Society of Upper Canada Continuing Legal Education, 1986. Reprinted in *Windsor Yearbook of Access to Justice* (1988).

2951 MOSSMAN, Mary Jane. "'Invisible' Constraints on Lawyering and Leadership: The Case of Women Lawyers." *Ottawa Law Review* 20, 1 (1988): 567-600.

2952 PEARLMAN, Lynne. "Through Jewish Lesbian Eyes: Rethinking Clara Brett Martin." *Canadian Journal of Women and the Law* 5, 2 (1992): 317-50.

2953 ROTH, Theresa. "Clara Brett Martin—Canada's Pioneer Woman Lawyer." *Gazette* 18 (1984): 323-40.

MARRIAGE/DIVORCE/CUSTODY

2954 ALLEN, R.K. "A Survey of Child Custody Law in Ontario." *Canadian Family Law Quarterly* 9 (1992): 11-42.

2955 ARNUP, Katherine. "Lesbian Mothers and Child Custody." *Atkinson Review of Canadian Studies* 1, 2 (Spring 1984): 35-40. Reprinted in *Gender and Society: Creating a Canadian Woman's Sociology,* ed. Arlene Tigar McLaren, 245-56. Toronto: Copp Clark Pitman, 1988.

2956 ARNUP, Katherine. "'Mothers Just Like Others': Lesbians, Divorce and Child Custody in Canada." *Canadian Journal of Women and the Law* 3, 1 (1989): 18-32.

2957 BACKHOUSE, Constance B. "Shifting Patterns in Nineteenth-Century Canadian Custody Law." In *Essays in the History of Canadian Law, Vol. 1,* ed. David H. Flaherty, 212-48. Toronto: University of Toronto Press, 1981.

2958 BACKHOUSE, Constance B. "'Pure Patriarchy': Nineteenth-Century Canadian Marriage." *McGill Law Journal* 31, 2 (March 1986): 264-312.

2959 BACKHOUSE, Constance B. "Married Women's Property Law in Nineteenth-Century Canada." *Law and History Review* 6 (Fall 1988): 211-57. Reprinted in *Canadian Family History: Selected Readings,* ed. Bettina Bradbury, 320-59. Toronto: Copp Clark Pitman, 1992.

2960 BANKS, Margaret A. "Marriage with a Deceased Wife's Sister—Law and Practice in Upper Canada." *Western Ontario Historical Notes* 25, 2 (Spring 1970): 1-6.

2961 BAXTER, Ian F.G. "Family Law Reform: A Historical Perspective of the Ontario Experience." *Canadian Journal of Family Law* 6, 2 (Fall 1987): 247-69.

2962 BEAUPRÉ, Gérard. "L'évolution du droit familial au Québec." *Canadian Bar Association Journal* 2 (October 1971): 1-3.

2963 BOYD, Susan B. "Child Custody Law and the Invisibility of Women's Work." *Queen's Quarterly* 96, 4 (Winter 1989): 831-58.

2964 BOYD, Susan B. "Child Custody, Ideologies and Employment." *Canadian Journal of Women and the Law* 3, 1 (1989): 111-33.

2965 BOYD, Susan B. "From Gender Specificity to Gender Neutrality? Ideologies in Canadian Child Custody Law." In *Child Custody and the Politics of Gender,* eds. Carol Smart and Selma Sevenhuijsen, 126-57. London: Routledge, 1989.

2966 BRADBURY, Bettina, Peter Gossage, Evelyn Kolish and Alan Stewart. "Property and Marriage: The Law and the Practice in Early Nineteenth-Century Montreal." *Histoire sociale/Social History* XXVI, 51 (May 1993): 9-39.

2967 BRIÈRE, Germain. "La réforme de la capacité de la femme mariée dans la province de Québec." *Revue internationale de droit comparé* 18, 1 (janvier-mars 1966): 83-88.

2968 CAVANAUGH, Catherine. "The Limitations of the Pioneering Partnership: The Alberta Campaign for Homestead Dower, 1909-25." *Canadian Historical Review* 74, 2 (June 1993): 198-225.

2969 CLICHE, Marie-Aimee. "Les procès en séparation de corps dans la région de Montréal, 1795-1879." *Revue d'histoire de l'Amérique française* 49, 1 (été 1995): 3-34.

2970 COOMBE, Rosemary J. "'The most disgusting, disgraceful and inequitous proceeding in our law': The action for breach of promise of marriage in nineteenth-century Ontario." *University of Toronto Law Journal* 38, 1 (1988): 64-108.

2971 CREAN, Susan. *In the Name of the Fathers: The Story Behind Child Custody.* Toronto: Amanita Enterprises, 1988.

2972 DANDURAND, Renée Brien. "Les dissolutions matrimoniales, un phénomène latent dans le Québec des années 60." *Anthropologie et sociétés* 9, 3 (1985): 87-115.

2973 DAVIS, Nanciellen. "'Patriarchy from the Grave': Family Relations in 19th Century New Brunswick Wills." *Acadiensis* 13, 2 (1984).

2974 DESROSIERS, Hélène, Céline Lebourdais and Benoit Laplante. "Les dissolutions d'union dans les familles recomposées: l'expérience des femmes canadiennes." *Recherches sociographiques* 36, 1 (janvier-avril 1995): 47-64.

2975 DIONNE, Hélène. *Les contrats de mariage à Québec (1790-1812).* National Museum of Man, History Division, Paper no. 29. Ottawa: National Museums of Canada, 1980.

2976 FINGARD, Judith. "The Prevention of Cruelty, Marriage Breakdown and the Rights of Wives in Nova Scotia, 1880-1990." *Acadiensis* 22, 2 (Spring 1993): 84-101. Reprinted in *Separate Spheres: Women's Worlds in the 19th Century Maritimes,* eds. Janet Guildford and Suzanne Morton 211-31. Fredericton: Acadiensis Press, 1994.

2977 FINNIE, Ross. "Women, Men, and the Economic Consequences of Divorce: Evidence from Canadian Longitudinal Data." *Canadian Review of Sociology and Anthropology* 30, 2 (1993): 205-41.

2978 GIRARD, Philip. "Married Women's Property, Chancery Abolition, and Insolvency Law: Law Reform in Nova Scotia, 1820-1867." In *Essays in the History of Canadian Law: Volume 3, Nova Scotia,* eds. Philip Girard and Jim Phillips, 80-127. Toronto: University of Toronto Press for the Osgoode Society, 1990.

2979 GIRARD, Philip and Rebecca Veinott. "Married Women's Property Law in Nova Scotia, 1850-1910." In *Separate Spheres: Women's Worlds in the 19th Century Maritimes,* eds. Janet Guildford and Suzanne Morton, 67-91. Fredericton: Acadiensis Press, 1994.

2980 GROSS, Wendy L. "Judging the Best Interests of the Child: Child Custody and the Homosexual Parent." *Canadian Journal of Women and the Law* 1, 2 (1986): 505-31.

2981 HOUGH, Janet. "Mistaking Liberalism for Feminism: Spousal Support in Canada." *Journal of Canadian Studies* 29, 2 (Summer 1994): 147-64.

2982 JOHNSON, J.K. "Friends in High Places: Getting Divorced in Upper Canada." *Ontario History* 86, 3 (Sept. 1994): 201-18.

2983 KEET, Jean E. "Matrimonial Property Legislation: Are Farm Women Equal Partners?" In *The Political Economy of Agriculture in Western Canada,* eds. G.S. Basran and David A. Hay, 175-84. Toronto: Garamond Press, 1988.

2984 KEET, J.E. "The Law Reform Process: Matrimonial Property and Farm Women: A Case Study of Saskatchewan, 1980-1986." *Canadian Journal of Women and the Law* 4 (1990): 166-89.

2985 KIERAN, Sheila. *The Family Matters: Two Centuries of Family Law and Life in Ontario.* Toronto: Key Porter Books, 1986.

2986 KOLISH, Evelyn. "Depuis la Conquête: les Canadiens devant deux droits familiaux." *Cap-aux-Diamants* 39 (automne 1994): 14-17.

2987 LAVALLÉE, Louis. "Les Archives notariales et l'histoire sociale de la Nouvelle-France." *Revue d'histoire de l'Amérique française* 28, 3 (décembre 1974): 385-403.

2988 MARSDEN, Lorna R. and Joan E. Busby. "Feminist Influence Through the Senate: The Case of Divorce, 1967." *Atlantis* 14, 2 (Spring 1989): 72-80.

2989 MAYNARD, Kimberley Smith. "Divorce in Nova Scotia, 1750-1890." In *Essays in the History of Canadian Law: Volume 3, Nova Scotia,* eds. Philip Girard and Jim Phillips, 232-72. Toronto: University of Toronto Press for the Osgoode Society, 1990.

2990 McCALLUM, Margaret E. "Prairie Women and the Struggle for a Dower Law, 1905-1920." *Prairie Forum* 18, 1 (Spring 1993): 19-34. Reprinted in *Historical Perspectives on Law and Society in Canada,* eds. Tina Loo and Lorna R. McLean. Mississauga: Copp Clark Longman, 1994.

2991 MORTON, Mary E. "Dividing the Wealth, Sharing the Poverty: The (Re)Formation of 'Family' in Law in Ontario." *Canadian Review of Sociology and Anthropology* 25, 2 (May 1988): 254-75.

2992 MORTON, Mildred. "Controversies within Family Law." In *Families: Changing Trends in Canada,* Maureen Baker, *et al,* 211-40. Toronto: McGraw-Hill Ryerson, 1990.

2993 OWEN, Wendy and J.M. Bumsted. "Divorce in a Small Province: A History of Divorce on Prince Edward Island, 1899-1960." *Acadiensis* 20, 2 (Spring 1991): 86-104.

2994 OWEN, Wendy and J.M. Bumsted. "Canadian Divorce before Reform: The Case of Prince Edward Island, 1946-1967." *Canadian Journal of Law and Society* 8, 1 (Spring 1993): 1-44.

2995 PETERS, John F. "Changing Perspectives on Divorce." In *Family Matters: Sociology and Contemporary Canadian Families,* Karen Anderson, *et al,* 141-62. Scarborough: Nelson Canada, 1988.

2996 PIKE, Robert. "Legal Access and the Incidence of Divorce in Canada: A Sociohistorical Analysis." *Canadian Review of Sociology and Anthropology* 12, 2 (May 1975): 115-33.

2997 POIRIER, Donald. "Les femmes collaboratrices et la loi sur les biens matrimoniaux du Nouveau-Brunswick." *University of New Brunswick Law Journal* 39 (1990): 23-42.

2998 SAVOIE, Sylvie. "La rupture du couple en Nouvelle-France: Les demandes de séparation aux XVIIe et XVIIIe siècles." *Canadian Woman Studies* 7, 4 (Winter 1986): 58-63.

2999 SEV'ER, Aysan. *Women and Divorce in Canada: A Sociological Analysis.* Toronto: Canadian Scholars' Press, 1992.

3000 SISLER, Berenice. *A Partnership of Equals: The Struggle for the Reform of Family Law in Manitoba.* Winnipeg: Watson & Dwyer, 1995.

3001 SNELL, James G. "'The White Life for Two': The Defense of Marriage and Sexual Morality in Canada, 1890-1914." *Histoire sociale/Social History* XVI, 31 (May 1983): 111-28. Reprinted in *Canadian Family History: Selected Readings,* ed. Bettina Bradbury, 381-400. Toronto: Copp Clark Pitman, 1992.

3002 SNELL, James G. "Marital Cruelty: Women and the Nova Scotia Divorce Court, 1900-1939." *Acadiensis* 18, 1 (Autumn 1988): 3-32.

3003 SNELL, James G. "The International Border as a Factor in Marital Behaviour: A Historical Case Study." *Ontario History* 81, 4 (December 1989): 289-302.

3004 SNELL, James G. *In the Shadow of the Law: Divorce in Canada, 1900-1939.* Toronto: University of Toronto Press, 1991.

3005 SNELL, James G. and Cynthia Comacchio Abeele. "Regulating Nuptiality: Restricting Access to Marriage in Early Twentieth-Century English-Speaking Canada." *Canadian Historical Review* 69, 4 (December 1988): 466-89. Reprinted in *Historical Perspectives on Law and Society in Canada,* eds. Tina Loo and Lorna R. McLean. Mississauga: Copp Clark Longman, 1994.

3006 STEWART, Alan M. and Bettina Bradbury. "Marriage Contracts as a Source for Historians." In *Class, Gender and the Law in Eighteenth- and Nineteenth-Century Quebec: Sources and Perspectives,* eds. Donald Fyson, Colin M. Coates and Kathryn Harvey, 29-53. Montreal: Montreal History Group, 1993.

3007 VEINOTT, Rebecca. "Child Custody and Divorce: A Nova Scotia Study, 1866-1910." In *Essays in the History of Canadian Law: Volume 3, Nova Scotia,* eds. Philip Girard and Jim Phillips, 273-302. Toronto: University of Toronto Press for the Osgoode Society, 1990.

PUBLIC POLICY/SOCIAL SERVICES

3008 ABBOTT, Ruth K. and R.A. Young. "Cynical and Deliberate Manipulation? Child Care and the Reserve Army of Female Labour in Canada." *Journal of Canadian Studies* 24, 2 (Summer 1989): 22-38.

3009 AITKEN, Gail. "Critical Compromises in Ontario's Child Welfare Policy." In *The Canadian Welfare State: Evolution and Transition,* ed. Jacqueline S. Ismael, 274-99. Edmonton: University of Alberta Press, 1987.

3010 ANDREW, Caroline. "Women and the Welfare State." *Canadian Journal of Political Science* 17, 4 (December 1984): 667-83.

3011 BAKER, Maureen. "Family and Population Policy in Quebec: Implications for Women." *Canadian Journal of Women and the Law* 7, 1 (1994): 116-32.

3012 BARNHORST, Richard and Laura C. Johnson, eds. *The State of the Child in Ontario.* Toronto: Oxford University Press, 1991.

3013 BELL-ALTENSTAD, Kristin and Sue Vail. "Developing Public Policy for Women in Sport: A Discourse Analysis." *Canadian Woman Studies* 15, 4 (Fall 1995): 109-12.

3014 BERTON, Pierre. *The Dionne Years: A Thirties Melodrama.* Toronto: McClelland and Stewart, 1977.

3015 BLAKE, Raymond B. "Mackenzie King and the Genesis of Family Allowances in Canada, 1939-1944." In *The Good Fight: Canadians and World War II,* eds. J.L. Granatstein and Peter Neary. Toronto: Copp Clark Limited, 1995. Also in *Social Welfare Policy in Canada: Historical Readings,* eds. Raymond B. Blake and Jeff Keshen. Toronto: Copp Clark, 1995.

3016 BRADBURY, Bettina. "Mourir chrétiennement: La vie et la mort dans les établissements catholiques pour personnes âgées à Montréal au XIXe siècle." *Revue d'histoire de l'Amérique française* 46, 1 (été 1992): 143-75.

3017 BULLEN, John. "Orphans, Idiots, Lunatics and Historians: Recent Approaches to the History of Child Welfare in Canada." *Histoire sociale/Social History* XVIII (May 1985): 133-45.

3018 BUMSTED, J.M. "Home Sweet Suburb: The Great Post-War Migration." *The Beaver* (October-November 1992): 26-34. Reprinted in *Coming of Age: Readings in Canadian History Since World War II,* eds. Donald Avery and Roger Hall, 139-48. Toronto: Harcourt Brace & Company Canada, 1996.

3019 BURT, Sandra. "Legislators, Women, and Public Policy." In *Changing Patterns: Women in Canada,* eds. Sandra Burt, Lorraine Code and Lindsay Dorney, 129-56. Toronto: McClelland & Stewart, 1988. Revised and retitled as "The Changing Patterns of Public Policy" in 2nd edition, 212-42, 1993.

3020 CAMPBELL, Robert A. "Ladies and Escorts: Gender Segregation and Public Policy in British Columbia Beer Parlours, 1925-1945." *BC Studies* 105/106 (Spring/Summer 1995): 119-38.

3021 CHUNN, Dorothy E. "Rehabilitating Deviant Families Through Family Courts: The Birth of 'Socialized' Justice in Ontario, 1920-1940." *International Journal of the Sociology of Law* 16 (1988): 137-58.

3022 CHUNN, Dorothy, E. "Boys Will Be Men, Girls Will Be Mothers: The Legal Regulation of Childhood in Toronto and Vancouver." *Sociological Studies of Child Development* 3 (1990): 87-110.

3023 CHUNN, Dorothy. *From Punishment to Doing Good: Family Courts and Socialized Justice in Ontario, 1880-1940.* Toronto: University of Toronto Press, 1992.

3024 CHUNN, Dorothy. "Regulating the Poor in Ontario: From Police Courts to Family Courts." In Historical *Perspectives on Law and Society in Canada* eds. Tina Loo and Lorna R. McLean. Mississauga: Copp Clark Longman, 1994.

3025 COHEN, Marjorie Griffin. "Social Policy and Social Services" In *Canadian Women's Issues, Volume I: Strong Voices,* Ruth Roach Pierson, Marjorie Griffin Cohen, Paula Bourne and Philanda Masters, 264-320. Toronto: James Lorimer and Company, 1994.

3026 COHEN, Marjorie Griffin. "Feminism's Effect on Economic Policy." In *Canadian Women's Issues, Volume II: Bold Visions,* Ruth Roach Pierson and Marjorie Griffin Cohen, 263-359. Toronto: James Lorimer and Company, 1995.

3027 COOK, Sharon Anne. "'A Quiet Place...to Die': Ottawa's First Protestant Old Age Homes for Women and Men." *Ontario History* 81, 1 (1989): 25-40.

3028 CÔTÉ, Denyse and Marie-Paule Maurice. "Certain impacts du régime fédéral des allocations familiales sur les femmes francophones du Québec." *Canadian Social Work Review* 10, 2 (Summer 1993): 157-82.

3029 CÔTÉ, Denyse and Marie-Paule Maurice. "Les allocations familiales fédérales et les femmes francophones du Québec." *Bulletin de l'Association québécoise d'histoire politique* 2, 4 (printemps 1994): 26-30.

3030 CÔTÉ, Sylvie. "Les orphelinats catholiques au Québec de 1900 à 1945." *Canadian Woman Studies* 7, 4 (Winter 1986): 36-38.

3031 COULTER, Rebecca. "'Not to Punish but to Reform': Juvenile Delinquency and the Children's Protection Act in Alberta, 1909-1929." In *Social Welfare Policy in Canada: Historical Readings,* eds. Raymond B. Blake and Jeff Keshen. Toronto: Copp Clark, 1995.

3032 CREESE, Gillian. "Sexual Equality and the Minimum Wage in British Columbia." *Journal of Canadian Studies* 26, 4 (Winter 1991/92): 120-40.

3033 DAIGLE, Johanne. "Une révolution dans la tradition: Les Réformes dans le champ de la santé au cours des années 1960 et l'organisation du travail hospitalier." In *Jean Lesage et l'éveil d'une nation: les débuts de la révolution tranquille,* ed. Robert Campeau, 148-54. Sillery, QC: Presses de l'Université du Québec, 1989.

3034 DAVIES, Megan J. "'Services Rendered, Rearing Children for the State': Mothers' Pensions in British Columbia, 1919-1931." In *Not Just Pin Money: Selected Essays on the History of Women's Work in British Columbia,* eds. Barbara K. Latham and Roberta J. Pazdro, 249-63. Victoria: Camosun College, 1984.

3035 DE LA COUR, Lykke, Cecilia Morgan and Mariana Valverde. "Gender Regulation and State Formation in Nineteenth-Century Canada." In *Colonial Leviathan: State Formation in Mid-Nineteenth-Century Canada,* eds. Allan Greer and Ian Radforth, 163-91. Toronto: University of Toronto Press, 1992.

3036 DICKSON, James and Bob Russell. *Family, Economy and State: The Social Reproduction Process Under Capitalism* Toronto: Garamond Press, 1986.

3037 DODD, Dianne and Catherine Bailey. "Strengthening the Canadian Family: The Blue Books and Family Allowance." *The Archivist* 107 (1994): 14-16.

3038 DOHERTY, Gillian. *Child Care Policy in Canada: An Annotated Bibliography.* Toronto: Childcare Resource and Research Unit, 1994.

3039 DONNELLY, Maureen. "The Disparate Impact of Pension Reform on Women." *Canadian Journal of Women and the Law* 6, 2 (1993): 419-54.

3040 DUFFY, Ann *et al*, eds. "Women in Poverty." A special issue of *Canadian Woman Studies* 12, 4 (Summer 1992).

3041 DUMONT, Micheline. "Des garderies au XIXe siècle: les salles d'asile des Soeurs Grises à Montréal." *Revue d'histoire de l'Amérique française* 34, 1 (juin 1980): 27-55. Reprinted in *Maîtresses de maison, maîtresses d'école: Femmes, famille et éducation dans l'histoire du Québec,* eds. Nadia Fahmy-Eid and Micheline Dumont, 261-85. Montréal: Boréal Express, 1983.

3042 DUMONT, Micheline. "Des religieuses, des murs et des enfants." *L'Action nationale* 84, 4 (avril 1994): 483-508. [l'affaire des enfants de Duplessis]

3043 EICHLER, Margrit. "Family Change and Social Policies." In *Family Matters: Sociology and Contemporary Canadian Families,* Karen Anderson, *et al*, 63-86. Scarborough: Nelson Canada, 1988.

3044 EICHLER, Margrit. *Families in Canada Today: Recent Changes and Their Policy Consequences.* Toronto: Gage Educational Publishing Company, 1988.

3045 EVANS, Patricia M. "Targeting Single Mothers for Employment: Comparisons from the United States, Britain, and Canada." *Social Service Review* 66, 3 (September 1992): 378-98.

3046 EVANS, Patricia M. and Eilene L. McIntyre. "Welfare, Work Incentives, and the Single Mother: An Interprovincial Comparison." In *The Canadian Welfare State: Evolution and Transition,* ed. Jacqueline S. Ismael, 101-25. Edmonton: University of Alberta Press, 1987.

3047 FINKEL, Alvin. "Even the Little Children Cooperated: Family Strategies, Childcare Discourse, and Social Welfare Debates, 1945-1975." *Labour/Le Travail* 36 (Fall 1995): 91-118.

3048 GEE, Ellen M. and Susan A. McDaniel. "Social Policy for an Aging Society." *Journal of Canadian Studies* 28, 1 (Spring 1993): 139-52.

3049 GILL, Pauline. *Les enfants de Duplessis.* Montréal: Éditions Libre Expression, 1991.

3050 GÖLZ, Annalee. "Family Matters: The Canadian Family and the State in the Postwar Period." *left history* 1, 2 (Fall 1993): 9-49.

3051 GRAHAM, John R. "The Haven, 1878-1930: A Toronto Charity's Transition from a Religious to a Professional Ethos." *Histoire sociale/Social History* XXV, 50 (November 1992): 283-306.

3052 GRAYSON, Linda M. and Michael Bliss, eds. *The Wretched of Canada: Letters to R.B. Bennett, 1930-1935.* Toronto: University of Toronto Press, 1971.

3053 GUBERMAN, Nancy, J. LeBlanc, F. David and J. Belleau. *Un mal invisible: L'isolement social des femmes.* Montréal: Les Éditions du remue-ménage, 1993.

3054 HADDAD, Jane and Stephen Milton. "The Construction of Gender Roles in Social Policy: Mothers' Allowances and Day Care in Ontario Before World War II." *Canadian Woman Studies* 7, 4 (Winter 1986): 68-70.

3055 HARRISON, Phyllis. "In the Beginning Was Charlotte..." *Canadian Welfare* 51, 2 (March/April 1975): 14-15. [Charlotte Whitton]

3056 HERON, Craig. "Saving the Children." *Acadiensis* 13, 1 (1983): 168-75.

3057 HOBBS, Margaret and Ruth Roach Pierson. "When is a Kitchen Not a Kitchen?" *Canadian Woman Studies* 7, 4 (Winter 1986): 71-76.

3058 HOBBS, Margaret and Ruth Roach Pierson. "'A Kitchen That Wastes No Steps...': Gender, Class and the Home Improvement Plan, 1936-40." *Histoire sociale/Social History* XXI (May 1988): 9-37.

3059 HORNICK, Joseph, Nicholas Bala and Robin Vogl, eds. *Canadian Child Welfare Law: Children, Families and the State.* Toronto: Thompson Educational Publishing, Inc., 1991.

3060 HUDSON, Joe and Burt Galaway, eds. *Single Parent Families: Canadian Research and Policy Implications.* Toronto: Thompson Educational Publishing, 1993.

3061 ISMAEL, Jacqueline S., ed. *The Canadian Welfare State: Evolution and Transition.* Edmonton: University of Alberta Press, 1987.

3062 JEAN, Dominique. "Les parents québécois et l'état canadien au début du programme des allocations familiales, 1944-1945." *Revue d'histoire de l'Amérique française* 40, 1 (été 1986): 73-95.

3063 JEAN, Dominique. "Le recul du travail des enfants au Québec entre 1940 et 1960: une explication des conflits entre les familles pauvres et l'Etat providence." *Labour/Le Travail* 24 (1989): 91-129.

3064 JEAN, Dominique. "Family Allowances and Family Autonomy: Quebec Families Encounter the Welfare State, 1945-1955." In *Canadian Family History: Selected Readings,* ed. Bettina Bradbury, 401-37. Toronto: Copp Clark Pitman, 1992. Reprinted in *Constructing Modern Canada: Readings in Post-Confederation History,* ed. Chad Gaffield, 396-432. Toronto: Copp Clark Longman Ltd., 1994.

3065 JOHNSON, Andrew F. "Restructuring Family Allowances: 'Good Politics at No Cost?'" In *Social Welfare Policy in Canada: Historical Readings*, eds. Raymond B. Blake and Jeff Keshen. Toronto: Copp Clark, 1995.

3066 JOHNSON, Laura Climenko. "Women and Children Last: A Decade of Day Care in Canada." *Canadian Women's Studies* 2, 2 (1980): 51-52.

3067 JOHNSON, Laura and Dick Barnhorst, eds. *Children, Families and Public Policy in the 90s.* Toronto: Thompson Educational Publishing, Inc., 1991.

3068 JONES, Andrew and Leonard Rutman. *In the Children's Aid: J.J. Kelso and Child Welfare in Ontario.* Toronto: University of Toronto Press, 1981.

3069 JOYAL, Renée. "L'évolution des modes [législatifs] de contrôle de l'autorité parentale et son impact [depuis 1869] sur les relations entre parents et enfants dans la société québécoise." *International Journal of Canadian Studies*, Numéro hors série (hiver 1993): 73-84.

3070 JOYAL, Renée. "La Loi québécoise de protection de l'enfance de 1944: genèse et avortement d'une réforme." *Histoire sociale/Social History* XXVII, 53 (May 1994): 33-64.

3071 JOYAL, Renée. "Les familles et l'état: une histoire à suivre." *Cap-aux-Diamants* 39 (automne 1994): 18-21.

3072 KITCHEN, Brigitte. "Women and the Social Security System in Canada" *Atlantis* 5, 2 (1980): 88-99.

3073 KITCHEN, Brigitte. "Wartime Social Reform: The Introduction of Family Allowances." *Canadian Journal of Social Work Education* 7, 1 (1981): 29-54.

3074 KITCHEN, Brigitte. "The Family and Social Policy." In *The Family: Changing Trends in Canada*, ed. Maureen Baker. Toronto: McGraw-Hill Ryerson, 1984.

3075 KITCHEN, Brigitte. "The Patriarchal Bias of the Income Tax in Canada." *Atlantis* 11, 2 (Spring 1986): 35-46.

3076 KITCHEN, Brigitte. "The Marsh Report Revisited." *Journal of Canadian Studies* 21, 2 (Summer 1986): 38-48. Reprinted in *Coming of Age: Readings in Canadian History Since World War II*, eds. Donald Avery and Roger Hall, 128-39. Toronto: Harcourt Brace & Company Canada, 1996.

3077 KITCHEN, Brigitte. "The Introduction of Family Allowances in Canada." In *The 'Benevolent' State: The Growth of Welfare in Canada*, eds. Allan Moscovitch and Jim Albert, 222-41. Toronto: Garamond Press, 1987.

3078 KITCHEN, Brigitte. "Family Policy." In *Families: Changing Trends in Canada*, Maureen Baker, *et al.* 306-29. Toronto: McGraw-Hill Ryerson, 1990.

3079 LACOMBE, Dany. *Ideology and Public Policy: The Case of Pornography.* Toronto: Garamond Press, 1988.

3080 LAPOINTE-ROY, Huguette. *Charité bien ordonnée: Le premier réseau de lutte contre la pauvreté à Montréal au 19e siècle.* Montréal: Boréal Express, 1987.

3081 LEAH, Ronnie. "Women's Labour Force Participation and Day Care Cutbacks in Ontario." *Atlantis* 7, 1 (Fall 1981): 36-44.

3082 LEGAULT, Gisèle and Ann Paquet-Deehy, comps. *Condition féminine et service social.* Montréal: Librairie de l'Université de Montréal, 1990.

3083 LÉPINE, Sylvie. "L'État et les allocations familiales, une politique qui n'a jamais vraiment démarré." *Recherches féministes* 3, 1 (1990): 65-81.

3084 LIND, Loren and Susan Prentice. *Their Rightful Place: An Essay on Children, Families and Childcare in Canada.* Toronto: James Lorimer & Company, 1995.

3085 LITTLE, Margaret. "The Blurring of Boundaries: Private and Public Welfare for Single Mothers in Ontario." *Studies in Political Economy* 47 (Summer 1995): 89-109.

3086 LITTLE, Margaret Hillyard. "Claiming a Unique Place: The Introduction of Mothers' Pensions in BC." *BC Studies* 105/106 (Spring/Summer 1995): 80-102.

3087 LUPTON, Nora. "Notes on the British Columbia Protestant Orphans' Home." In *In Her Own Right: Selected Essays on Women's History in BC*, eds. Barbara Latham and Cathy Kess, 43-54. Victoria: Camosun College, 1980.

3088 MacKENZIE, S. and M. Truelove. "Changing Access to Public and Private Services: Non-Family Childcare." In *The Changing Social Geography of Canadian Cities*, eds. Larry S. Bourne and David F. Ley, 326-42. Montreal and Kingston: McGill-Queen's University Press, 1993.

3089 MARONEY, Heather Jon. "'Who has the baby?' Nationalism, Pronatalism and the Construction of a 'Demographic Crisis' in Quebec, 1960-1988." *Studies in Political Economy* 39 (Autumn 1992): 7-36. Reprinted in *Feminism in Action: Studies in Political Economy*, eds. M. Patricia Connelly and Pat Armstrong. Toronto: Canadian Scholars' Press, 1993.

3090 MARKS, Lynne. "Indigent Committees and Ladies Benevolent Societies: Intersections of Public and Private Poor Relief in Late Nineteenth Century Small Town Ontario." *Studies in Political Economy* 47 (Summer 1995): 61-87.

3091 MARSHALL, Dominique Jean. "The Decline of Child Labour in Quebec, 1940-1960: Conflict Between Poor Families and the Welfare State." In *Historical Perspectives on Law and Society in Canada*, eds. Tina Loo and Lorna R. McLean. Mississauga: Copp Clark Longman, 1994.

3092 MARSHALL, Dominique. "Nationalisme et politiques sociales au Québec depuis 1867: un siècle de rendez-vous manqués entre l'État, l''Église et les familles." *British Journal of Canadian Studies* 9, 2 (1994): 301-47.

3093 MATTERS, Diane L. "Public Welfare Vancouver Style, 1910-1920." *Journal of Canadian Studies* 14, 1 (Spring 1979): 3-15.

3094 McCALLUM, Margaret. "Keeping Women in Their Place: The Minimum Wage in Canada, 1910-1925." *Labour/Le Travail* 17 (Spring 1986): 29-56. Reprinted in *Canadian Working Class History: Selected Readings*, eds. Laurel Sefton-MacDowell and Ian Radforth. Toronto: Canadian Scholars Press, 1992.

3095 McCANNELL, Kathryn, Claire McCarthy and Barbara Herringer. "Images of Women in Canadian Social Policy: Em-bodying Patriarchy." In *The Anatomy of Gender: Women's Struggle for the Body*, eds. Dawn H. Currie and Valerie Raoul, 175-87. Ottawa: Carleton University Press, 1992.

3096 McCLAIN, Janet with C. Doyle. *Women and Housing: Changing Needs and the Failure of Policy*. Ottawa: Canadian Council on Social Development, 1984.

3097 McCORMACK, Thelma. *Politics and the Hidden Injuries of Gender: Feminism and the Making of the Welfare State*. The CRIAW Papers No. 28. Ottawa: Canadian Research Institute for the Advancement of Women, 1991.

3098 McDANIEL, Susan A. *Towards Family Policies in Canada with Women in Mind*. Feminist Perspectives, No. 17. Ottawa: Canadian Research Institute for the Advancement of Women, 1990.

3099 MENZIES, June. *The Canada Pension Plan and Women*. Ottawa: Canadian Advisory Council on the Status of Women, 1974.

3100 MIRON, John R., *et al*, eds. *House, Home, and Community: Progress in Housing Canadians, 1945-1986*. Montreal and Kingston: McGill-Queen's University Press, 1993.

3101 NATIONAL COUNCIL ON WELFARE. *Women and Poverty Revisited: A Report*. Ottawa: National Council on Welfare, 1990.

3102 NIHMEY, John and Stuart Foxman. *Time of Their Lives: The Dionne Tragedy*. Toronto: Macmillan of Canada, 1986.

3103 NOBLE, Joey. "'Classifying' the Poor: Toronto Charities, 1850-1880." *Studies in Political Economy* 2 (Autumn 1979): 109-28. [YWCA]

3104 NOEL, Jan. "Women and Social Welfare in the Montreal Region, 1800-1833: Preliminary Findings." In *Changing Roles of Women within the Christian Church in Canada*, eds. Elizabeth Gillan Muir and Marilyn Färdig Whiteley, 261-83. Toronto: University of Toronto Press, 1995; reprinted and retitled as "'Femmes Fortes' and the Montreal Poor in the Early Nineteenth Century." In *Canadian Women: A Reader*, eds. Wendy Mitchinson, *et al*, 68-85. Toronto: Harcourt Brace Canada, 1996.

3105 PELLETIER, Guy. "La garderie québécoise en milieux urbain et rural: une analyse socio-historique." In *Éducation en milieu urbain*, eds. Manuel Crespo and Claude Lessard, 433-52. Montreal: Presses de l'Université de Montréal, 1985.

3106 PIERSON, Ruth Roach. "Gender and the Unemployment Insurance Debates in Canada, 1934-1940." *Labour/Le Travail* 25 (Spring 1990): 77-103. Reprinted in *Reappraisals in Canadian History: Post-Confederation*, eds. D. Gilbert, C.M. Wallace and R.M. Bray, 336-67. Scarborough: Prentice Hall Canada Inc., 1992.

3107 PORTER, Ann. "Women and Income Security in the Post-War Period: The Case of Unemployment Insurance, 1945-1962." *Labour/Le Travail* 31 (Spring 1993): 111-44. Reprinted in *Canadian Women: A Reader*, eds. Wendy Mitchinson, *et al*, 322-52. Toronto: Harcourt Brace Canada, 1996.

3108 PRENTICE, Susan. "Workers, Mothers, Reds: Toronto's Postwar Daycare Fight." *Studies in Political Economy* 30 (Autumn 1989): 115-41. Reprinted in *Feminism in Action: Studies in Political Economy*, eds. M. Patricia Connelly and Pat Armstrong. Toronto: Canadian Scholars' Press, 1993; and in *Social Welfare Policy in Canada: Historical Readings*, eds. Raymond B. Blake and Jeff Keshen. Toronto: Copp Clark, 1995.

3109 PURDY, Sean. "'This is Not a Company; It is a Cause': Class, Gender and the Toronto Housing Company, 1912-1920." *Urban History Review* 21, 2 (March 1993): 75-91.

3110 PURVEY, Diane. "Alexandra Orphanage and Families in Crisis in Vancouver, 1892-1938." In *Dimensions of Childhood: Essays in the History of Children and Youth in Canada*, eds. Russell Smandych, Gordon Dodds and Alvin Esau, 107-33. Winnipeg: University of Manitoba, Legal Research Institute, 1991.

3111 ROOKE, Patricia T. and R.L. Schnell. "Charlotte Whitton meets 'the Last Best West': The Politics of Child Welfare in Alberta, 1929-1949." *Prairie Forum* 6, 2 (Fall 1981): 143-62.

3112 ROOKE, Patricia T. and R.L. Schnell. "Child Welfare in English Canada, 1920-1948." *Social Service Review* 55, 3 (1981): 484-506.

3113 ROOKE, Patricia T. and R. L. Schnell. "Childhood and Charity in Nineteenth-Century British North America." *Histoire sociale/Social History* XV, 29 (May 1982): 157-79. Reprinted in *Reappraisals in Canadian History: Pre-Confederation*, eds. A.D. Gilbert, C.M. Wallace and R.M. Bray, 506-29. Scarborough: Prentice Hall Canada Inc., 1993.

3114 ROOKE, Patricia T. and R.L. Schnell. "The Rise and Decline of British North American Protestant Orphans' Homes as Woman's Domain, 1850-1930." *Atlantis* 7, 2 (Spring 1982): 21-35.

3115 ROOKE, Patricia T. and R.L. Schnell. "Charlotte Whitton and the 'Babies for Export' Controversy, 1947-48." *Alberta History* 30, 1 (1982): 11-16.

3116 ROOKE, Patricia T. and R.L. Schnell. "Guttersnipes and Charity Children: Nineteenth Century Child Rescue in the Atlantic Provinces." In *Studies in Childhood History: A Canadian Perspective,* eds. Patricia T. Rooke and R.L. Schnell, 82-104. Calgary: Detselig Enterprises, 1982.

3117 ROOKE, Patricia T. and R.L. Schnell. "'Making the Way More Comfortable': Charlotte Whitton's Child Welfare Career, 1920-1948." *Journal of Canadian Studies* 17 (Winter 1982/1983): 33-45.

3118 ROOKE, Patricia T. and R.L. Schnell. *Discarding the Asylum: From Child Rescue to the Welfare State in English Canada, 1800-1950.* New York: University Press of America, 1983.

3119 ROSE, Ruth. "Les femmes et la pauvreté au Québec." In *Encrages féministes: Un moment de reflexion dans la recherche féministe,* ed. Isabelle Lasvergnas, 127-38. Montréal: Université du Québec à Montréal, Centre de recherche féministe, Group interdisciplinaire d'enseignement et de recherche féministes, 1989.

3120 RUSSELL, Bob. "A Fair or a Minimum Wage? Women Workers, the State, and the Origins of Wage Regulation in Western Canada." *Labour/Le Travail* 28 (Fall 1991): 59-88.

3121 RUTMAN, Leonard. "J.J. Kelso and the Development of Child Welfare." In *The 'Benevolent' State: The Growth of Welfare in Canada,* eds. Allan Moscovitch and Jim Albert, 68-76. Toronto: Garamond Press, 1987.

3122 SANGSTER, Joan. "Women Workers, Employment Policy and the State: The Establishment of the Ontario Women's Bureau, 1963-1970." *Labour/Le Travail* 36 (Fall 1995): 119-46.

3123 SARRASIN, Richard. "L'évolution de la politique familiale québécoise [de 1950 à aujourd'hui]." *Intervention* 99 (octobre 1994): 7-16.

3124 SCHNELL, R.L. "'A Children's Bureau for Canada': The Origins of the Canadian Council on Child Welfare, 1913-1921." In *The 'Benevolent' State: The Growth of Welfare in Canada,* eds. Allan Moscovitch and Jim Albert, 95-110. Toronto: Garamond Press, 1987.

3125 SCHNELL, R.L. "Female Separatism and Institution-Building: Continuities and Discontinuities in Canadian Child Welfare, 1913-1935." *International Review of History and Political Science* 25, 2 (1988): 14-40.

3126 SCHULZ, Patricia Vandebelt. "Day Care in Canada: 1850-1962." In *Good Day Care: Fighting For It, Getting It, Keeping It,* ed. Kathleen Gallagher Ross, 137-58. Toronto: The Women's Press, 1978.

3127 "Social Welfare of Women." A special issue of *Canadian Journal of Social Work Education* 6, 2/3 (1980).

3128 SPEISMAN, Stephen A. "Munificent Parsons and Municipal Parsimony: Voluntary vs. Public Poor Relief in Nineteenth Century Toronto." *Ontario History* 65, 1 (March 1973): 32-49.

3129 STRONG-BOAG, Veronica. "Canada's Early Experiments with Income Supplements: The Introduction of Mothers' Allowances." *Atlantis* 4, 2, Part 2, (Spring 1979): 35-43.

3130 STRONG-BOAG, Veronica. "'Wages for Housework': Mothers' Allowances and the Beginnings of Social Security in Canada." *Journal of Canadian Studies* 14, 1 (Spring 1979): 24-34. Reprinted in *Social Welfare Policy in Canada: Historical Readings,* eds. Raymond B. Blake and Jeff Keshen. Toronto: Copp Clark, 1995.

3131 STRONG-BOAG, Veronica. "Working Women and the State: the case of Canada, 1889-1945." *Atlantis* 6, 2 (1981): 1-9. Reprinted in *Women and the Canadian Labour Force,* eds. Naomi Hersom and Dorothy E. Smith, 439-61. Ottawa: Social Sciences and Humanities Research Council of Canada, 1983.

3132 STRONG-BOAG, Veronica. "Home Dreams: Women and the Suburban Experiment in Canada, 1945-60." *Canadian Historical Review* 72, 4 (December 1991): 471-504. Reprinted in *Constructing Modern Canada: Readings in Post-Confederation History,* ed. Chad Gaffield, 477-505. Toronto: Copp Clark Longman Ltd., 1994.

3133 STRUTHERS, James. *The Limits of Affluence: Welfare in Ontario, 1920-1970.* Toronto: University of Toronto Press, 1994.

3134 SUTHERLAND, Neil. "Social Policy, Deviant Children, and the Public Health Apparatus in British Columbia between the Wars." *Journal of Educational Thought* 14, 2 (August 1980): 80-91.

3135 URSEL, Jane. "The State and the Maintenance of Patriarchy: A Case Study of Family, Labour and Welfare Legislation in Canada." In *Family, Economy and State: The Social Reproduction Process Under Capitalism,* eds. James Dickinson and Bob Russell, 150-91. Toronto: Garamond, 1986. Reprinted in *Gender and Society: Creating a Canadian Woman's Sociology,* ed. Arlene Tigar McLaren, 108-45. Toronto: Copp Clark Pitman, 1988.

3136 URSEL, Jane. *Private Lives, Public Policy: 100 Years of State Intervention in the Family.* Toronto: Women's Press, 1992.

3137 VALVERDE, Mariana. "Representing Childhood: The Multiple Fathers of the Dionne Quintuplets." In *Regulating Womanhood: Historical Essays on Marriage, Motherhood and Sexuality,* ed. Carol Smart, 119-46. London and New York: Routledge, 1992.

3138 VALVERDE, Mariana. "Families, Private Property, and the State: The Dionnes and the Toronto Stork Derby." *Journal of Canadian Studies* 29, 4 (Winter 1994/95): 15-35.

3139 VALVERDE, Mariana. "Building Anti-Delinquent Communities: Morality, Gender, and Generation in the City." In *A Diversity of Women: Ontario, 1945-1980,* ed. Joy Parr, 19-45. Toronto: University of Toronto Press, 1995.

3140 VICKERS, Jill McCalla, ed. *Taking Sex Into Account: The Policy Consequences of Sexist Research.* Ottawa: Carleton University Press, 1984.

3141 WATTS, Rob. "Family Allowances in Canada and Australia, 1940-1945: A Comparative Critical Case Study." *Journal of Social Policy* 16, 1 (1987).

3142 WILLS, Gale. *A Marriage of Convenience: Business and Social Work in Toronto, 1918-1957.* Toronto: University of Toronto Press, 1995.

MASS CULTURE/MEDIA

THE HISTORICAL STUDY of images of Canadian women in the media, and especially in print advertising, enjoyed a vogue in the 1970s that reflected contemporary feminist concerns about the issue of sexism in the media and its implications for the status of women. Mass circulation magazines such as *Maclean's* were surveyed in these initial studies but the bulk of scholars' attention was devoted to women's magazines, particularly the English and French versions of *Chatelaine*. Little attention was devoted to portrayals of women in non-print media, with the exception of some interesting studies of images of women in films, especially those produced by the National Film Board of Canada. After a lull of some years, as historians turned away from images to study the lived experiences of women, the linguistic turn in the discipline has stimulated interest in the subject of media discourses and their historical role in the construction of gender and femininity in Canada. This interest, combined with historians' recent discovery of the topic of consumption, suggests that the study of advertising and shopping is likely to become a growth area in Canadian women's history in the near future. As Cynthia Wright has recently noted, the rise of consumer culture in the twentieth century and the appearance of the department store as an institution to disseminate a class-based culture had profound implications for Canadian women, and for the reorganization of class and gender relations, that are just beginning to be examined by historians.

Directly related to this scholarly interest in the history of consumption is the recent attention to leisure and tourism, particularly as related to the rise of a mass consumer culture. In several promising new studies, Douglas Baldwin and Diane Tye have examined the mass appeal of Lucy Maud Montgomery's fictional offspring, Anne of Green Gables, who has provided such a stimulus to the tourist industry in Prince Edward Island in recent decades. A similar function was performed during the Great Depression by the Dionne Quintuplets, according to Cynthia Wright, who has documented the importance of the Quints as tourist attractions to the Ontario government and the economy of Northern Ontario. Karen Dubinsky has explored the "imaginary geography" of Niagara Falls using the concepts of gender and sexualized space in a study that provides a model for future work on the history of leisure and tourism in Canada.

The potential for future scholarship along these lines is suggested by the many surviving memoirs of intrepid women adventurers, such as Agnes Deans Cameron, Mina Hubbard, and even Lady Ishbel Aberdeen, published at a time when reading travellers' accounts still constituted a form of exotic escapist entertainment. Many of these accounts were written by journalists who belonged to a new breed of woman professional appearing in the late nineteenth century to challenge the association of journalism with hard-drinking, cigar-smoking men. Often writing under pseudonyms and usually confined to the women's pages, these pioneers wrote influential columns in the daily press of many Canadian cities, and a few, like Kit Coleman and Flora Shaw, were posted as correspondents to cover the Spanish-American War and the Klondike Gold Rush. Female journalists and their associations have attracted considerable attention from Canadian women's historians because of their pioneering status as female professionals, because, as highly literate women, many left substantial records of their lives, and because of the critical roles they played in both the first and second waves of organized feminism in Canada. In the early twentieth century, women journalists played a vital role in the suffrage movement, particularly on the Prairies, and in the 1960s they helped to launch both Voice of Women and the Royal Commission on the Status of Women. The Commission was headed by Florence Bird, widely known to Canadians as journalist, Anne Francis.

CONSUMPTION/ADVERTISING

3143 BLAND, Sue. "Henrietta the Homemaker and Rosie the Riveter: Images of Women in Advertising in *Maclean's* Magazine, 1939-1950." *Atlantis* 8(2) Spring 1983: 61-86. Reprinted in *Canadian Working Class History: Selected Readings,* eds. Laurel Sefton-MacDowell and Ian Radforth, Toronto: Canadian Scholars Press, 1992.

3144 DODD, Dianne. "Women in Advertising: The Role of Canadian Women in the Promotion of Domestic Electrical Technology in the Interwar Period." In *Despite the Odds: Essays on Canadian Women and Science,* ed. Marianne Gosztonyi Ainley, 134-51. Montreal: Véhicule Press, 1990.

3145 FRADET, Louise. "Femmes, cuisines, et consommation de masse au Québec, 1945-60." *Bulletin du Regroupement des chercheurs-chercheures en histoire des travailleurs et travailleuses du Québec* 17, 2 (été 1991): 23-35.

3146 LAMBERT, Anne. "Images for Sale: How Eaton's Saw Us." *Branching Out* 4 (March-April 1977): 30-33.

3147 MACGREGOR, R.M. "The Distorted Mirror: Images of Visible Minority Women in Canadian Print Advertising." *Atlantis* 14 (Spring 1989): 137-43.

3148 PARR, Joy. "Shopping for a Good Stove: A Parable About Gender, Design, and the Market." In *A Diversity of Women: Ontario, 1945-1980,* ed. Joy Parr, 75-97. Toronto: University of Toronto Press, 1995.

3149 RAYMOND, Sylvie. "Entre mode et modestie: sexe et pudeur chez Dupuis Frères." *Cap-aux-Diamants* 40 (hiver 1995): 45-47.

3150 STEPHENSON, Harold E. and Carlton McNaught. *The Story of Advertising in Canada.* Toronto: Ryerson Press, 1940. [Ch. 9 and 15 on female consumers]

3151 WRIGHT, Cynthia. "'Feminine Trifles of Vast Importance': Writing Gender into the History of Consumption." In *Gender Conflicts: New Essays in Women's History,* eds. Franca Iacovetta and Mariana Valverde, 229-60. Toronto: University of Toronto Press, 1992. Reprinted in *Constructing Modern Canada: Readings in Post-Confederation History,* ed. Chad Gaffield, 288-310. Toronto: Copp Clark Longman Ltd., 1994.

MEDIA/COMMUNICATIONS

3152 AITKEN, Kate. *Making Your Living is Fun.* Toronto: Longmans, Green, 1959.

3153 ANDERSON, Doris. "Women's Magazines in the 1970s." *Canadian Women's Studies* 2, 2 (1980): 15-16.

3154 BARRETT, Caroline and Marie-Josée des Rivières. "La femme dans la littérature populaire québécoise (1945-1960)." *Revue de l'université d'Ottawa* 50 (janvier/mars 1980): 99-108.

3155 BELL E. Moberly. *Flora Shaw.* London: Constable, 1947. [correspondent for the *Times* of London, 1890s]

3156 BETTINNOTTI, J. and J. Coulon. *Que c'est bête, ma belle: études sur la presse féminine au Québec.* Montréal: Soudeyns-Donzé, 1983.

3157 BIRD, Florence. *Anne Francis: An Autobiography.* Toronto: Clarke, Irwin, 1974.

3158 BOIVIN, Aurelien and Kenneth Landry. "Françoise et Madeleine: Pionnières du journalisme féminin au Québec." *Atlantis* 4, 1 (Fall 1978): 63-74.

3159 BREDEN, Marian. "Feminist Cultural Politics: Women in Community Radio in Canada." *Resources for Feminist Research* 20, 1/2 (1991): 36-41.

3160 BRUCE, Jean. "Women in CBC Radio Talks and Public Affairs." Canadian Oral History Association. *Journal* 5 (1981/82).

3161 BUENTE, Gail. "The Intrepid Miss Cameron and the Kid." *Herizons* 4, 7 (October/November 1986): 32-33. [Agnes Deans Cameron]

3162 BURKHOLDER, Mabel. *"Kit" Kathleen Blake Coleman: Pioneer Canadian Newspaperwoman.* Niagara Falls, ON: Canadian Women's Press Club of Hamilton, 1934.

3163 CASH, Gwen. *I Like British Columbia.* Toronto: Macmillan Co. of Canada, 1938.

3164 CASH, Gwen. *Off the Record: The Personal Reminiscences of Canada's First Woman Reporter.* Langley, BC: Stagecoach Press, 1977.

3165 CERCLE DES FEMMES JOURNALISTES. *Vingt-Cinq à la une.* Montréal: Les Éditions la Presse, 1976.

3166 CREAN, Susan. *Newsworthy: The Lives of Media Women.* Toronto: Stoddart Publishing, 1985.

3167 CREAN, Susan, ed. *Twist and Shout: A Decade of Feminist Writing in **This Magazine**.* Toronto: Second Story Feminist Press, 1992.

3168 CURRIE, Margaret. *Margaret Currie, Her Book.* Toronto: Hunter-Rose Co., 1924. [based on her women's column in the *Montreal Star*, 1920s]

3169 DAVIS, Angela E. "'Country Homemakers': The Daily Lives of Prairie Women as Seen through the Woman's Page of the *Grain Growers' Guide*, 1908-1928." In *Canadian Papers in Rural History, Vol. VIII,* ed. Donald H. Akenson, 163-74. Gananoque, ON: Langdale Press, 1992.

3170 DAVIS, Mrs. May. "A Pinafored Printer." *Saskatchewan History* 11, 2 (Spring 1956): 63-69.

3171 DAY, Moira. "Elsie Park Gowan's (re)-Building of Canada, 1937-1938: Revisioning the Historical Radio Series through Feminist Eyes." *Theatre History in Canada* 14, 1 (Spring 1993): 3-19.

3172 DEMPSEY, Lotta. *No Life for a Lady.* Markham, ON: Paperjacks, 1977.

3173 DENAULT, Jocelyne. "Cinquante ans de cinéma des femmes au Québec: une recherche difficile." *Canadian Woman Studies* 7, 3 (Fall 1986): 35-38.

3174 DES ORMES, Renée. *Robertine Barry en littérature: Françoise, pionnière du journalisme féminin au Canada, 1863-1910.* Quebec: L'Action sociale, 1949.

3175 DES RIVIÈRES, Marie-Josée. "*Châtelaine* et la littérature, 1960-1975." *Recherches féministes* 2, 2 (1989): 121-33.

3176 DES RIVIÈRES, Marie-Josée. *Châtelaine et la littérature, 1960-1975: essai.* Montréal: Éditions de l'Hexagone, 1992.

3177 DES RIVIÈRES, Marie-Josée. "Les nouvelles de *Châtelaine,* 1976-1980." In *La nouvelle: écriture(s) et lecture(s),* eds. Agnes Whitfield and Jacques Cotnam, 137-46. Montreal/Toronto: XYZ éditeur/GREF, 1993.

3178 DUMONT-JOHNSON, Micheline. "La parole des femmes: les revues féminines, 1938-1968." In *Idéologies au Canada français, 1940-1976, tome 2,* eds. Fernand Dumont, Jean Hamelin and Jean-Paul Montminy, 5-45. Quebec: Les presses de l'Université Laval, 1981.

3179 ERIN RESEARCH. *The Portrayal of Gender in Canadian Broadcasting: Summary Report, 1984-1988.* Ottawa: Canadian Radio-Television and Telecommunications Commission, 1988.

3180 FAHMY-EID, Nadia. "La presse féminine au Québec (1890-1920): Une pratique culturelle et politique ambivalente." In *Femmes et politique,* ed. Yolande Cohen, 101-15. Montréal: Éditions du Jour, 1981.

3181 FAHMY-EID, Nadia and Micheline Dumont. "Recettes pour la femme idéale: Femmes/Famille et éducation dans deux journaux libéraux: *Le Canada* et *la Patrie* (1900-1920)." *Atlantis* 10, 1 (Fall 1984): 46-59.

3182 FAITH, Kathleen. "Media, Myths and Masculinization: Images of Women in Prison." In *Too Few to Count: Canadian Women in Conflict with the Law,* eds. Ellen Adelberg and Claudia Currie, 181-219. Vancouver: Press Gang Publishers, 1987.

3183 FERGUSON, Ted. *Kit Coleman: Queen of Hearts.* Toronto: Doubleday Canada, 1978.

3184 FREEMAN, Barbara. "'Every Stroke Upward': Women Journalists in Canada, 1880-1906." *Canadian Woman Studies* 7, 3 (Fall 1986): 43-46.

3185 FREEMAN, Barbara M. "'An Impertinent Fly': Canadian Journalist Kathleen Blake Watkins Covers the Spanish-American War." *Journalism History* 15, 4 (Winter 1988): 132-40.

3186 FREEMAN, Barbara M. *Kit's Kingdom: The Journalism of Kathleen Blake Coleman.* Ottawa: Carleton University Press, 1989.

3187 FREEMAN, Barbara M. "Kathleen Blake Coleman: An Irishwoman Becomes a Canadian Pioneer Journalist, 1889-1915." *Journal of Newspaper and Periodical History* 6, 2 (1990): 27-30.

3188 FREEMAN, Barbara M. "The Media and the Royal Commission on the Status of Women in Canada, 1966-72: Research in Progress." *Resources for Feminist Research* 23, 3 (1994): 3-9.

3189 FREEMAN, Barabara M. "'CBC Matinee', the 'Press Girls' and the Royal Commission on the Status of Women, 1968." *Fréquence/Frequency: Journal of the Association for the Study of Canadian Radio and Television* 3/4 (1995): 5-25.

3190 FREEMAN, Barbara M. "Framing Feminine/Feminist: English-language Press Coverage of the Hearings of the Royal Commission on the Status of Women in Canada, 1968." *International Journal of Canadian Studies* 11 (Spring 1995): 11-32.

3191 GABRIEL, Chris and Katherine Scott. "Women's Press at Twenty: The Politics of Feminist Publishing." In *And Still We Rise: Feminist Political Mobilizing in Contemporary Canada,* ed. Linda Carty, 25-52. Toronto: Women's Press, 1993.

3192 GORHAM, Deborah. "Pen and Buckskin: Women Journalists in the West Who Knew Wheat and Justice." *Content: Canada's National Newsmagazine* 85 (May 1978): 22-23.

3193 GOTTLIEB, Lois C. and Wendy Keitner. "Images of Canadian Women in Literature and Society in the 1970s." *International Journal of Women's Studies* 2 (November/December 1979): 513-27.

3194 HAIG, Kennethe M. *Brave Harvest: The Life of E. Cora Hind.* Toronto: Thomas Allen, 1945.

3195 HAMEL, Reginald. *Gaëtane de Montreuil, journaliste québécoise 1867-1951.* Montréal: L'Aurore, 1976.

3196 HARRIS, Debbie Wise. "Colonizing Mohawk Women: Representation of Women in the Mainstream Media." *Resources for Feminist Research* 20, 1/2 (Spring/Summer 1991): 15-20.

3197 HENRY, Ann. *Laugh, Baby, Laugh.* Toronto: McClelland and Stewart, 1970.

3198 HIND, E. Cora. *Seeing For Myself: Agricultural Conditions around the World.* Toronto: Macmillan, 1937.

3199 JOSIE, Edith. *Here Are the News.* Toronto and Vancouver: Clarke Irwin, 1966. [Indian reporter for the *Whitehorse Star*]

3200 KENDALL, Georgina. *The Newspapering Murrays.* Toronto: McClelland and Stewart, 1967; revised edition, Lillooet BC: Lillooet Publishers, 1974. [Margaret Murray]

3201 KERNAGHAN, Lois. "'M.J.K.L.'–A Victorian Contradiction." *Nova Scotia Historical Quarterly* 5, 3 (September 1975): 231-41. [Mary Jane (Katzman) Lawson, author and editor]

3202 KIRKWOOD, Hilda. "Women in the *Forum:* 1945-1946." *Canadian Forum* 55 (September 1975): 29-30.

3203 LABONTÉ, René. "Gabrielle Roy, journaliste, au fil de ses reportages (1939-1945)." *Studies in Canadian Literature* 7, 1 (1982): 90-109.

3204 LAKE, Robert, Judith Scrimger and Marie Riley. "Pursuing Order: Ten Years of Editorial Coverage of the Abortion Issue in the *Globe and Mail.*" *Atlantis* 17, 1 (Fall/Winter 1991): 20-27.

3205 LANG, Marjorie. "Separate Entrances: The First Generation of Canadian Women Journalists." In *Re(Dis)covering Our Foremothers: Nineteenth Century Canadian Women Writers,* ed. Lorraine McMullen, 77-90. Ottawa: University of Ottawa Press, 1989.

3206 LANG, Marjorie. "Women About Town: Chroniclers of the Canadian Social Scene at the Turn of the Century." *Journal of Newspaper and Periodical History* 6, 2 (1990): 3-14.

3207 LANG, Marjorie and Linda Hale. "Women of *The World* and Other Dailies: The Life and Times of Vancouver Newspaper Women in the First Quarter of the Twentieth Century." *BC Studies* 85 (Spring 1990): 3-23.

3208 LAPOINTE, Germaine. *Une journaliste intemporelle, Germaine Bernier.* Montréal: Bellarmin, 1978.

3209 LESTER, Tanya. "Panning Out Tales on the Gold Rush Trails." *Herizons* (March 1984): 35-36. [Faith Fenton, journalist]

3210 LÉVESQUE, Andrée. "Journaliste au masculin: Eva Circé-Côté (1871-1940)." *Les Bâtisseuses de la Cité,* 87-96. Montréal: ACFAS, 1993.

3211 MacBETH, Madge. *Over My Shoulder.* Toronto: Ryerson Press, 1953.

3212 MacBETH, Madge. *Boulevard Career.* Toronto: Kingswood House, 1957.

3213 MacDONALD, Cheryl. "Our Intrepid Reporter." *The Beaver* 68, 2 (April/May 1988): 29-33. [Sara Jeannette Duncan]

3214 MARTIN, Michele. "Changing the Picture: Women and Media in Quebec." In *Changing Patterns: Women in Canada,* eds. Sandra Burt, Lorraine Code and Lindsay Dorney, 177-211. Toronto: McClelland & Stewart, 2nd ed., 1993.

3215 MASTERS, Philanda. "Women, Culture and Communications." In *Canadian Women's Issues, Volume I: Strong Voices,* Ruth Roach Pierson, Marjorie Griffin Cohen, Paula Bourne and Philanda Masters, 394-449. Toronto: James Lorimer and Company, 1994.

3216 MATHEWS,-KLEIN, Yvonne. "How They Saw Us: Images of Women in National Film Board Films of the 1940s and 1950s." *Atlantis* 4, 2 (Spring 1979): 20-33.

3217 MEDIAWATCH. "Two Years of Sexism in Canadian Newspapers: A Study of 15 Newspapers." *Resources for Feminist Research* 20, 1/2 (Spring/Summer 1991): 21-22.

3218 MICHON, Jacques. "Mme B.D. Simpson, éditrice 1945-1948." *Éditeurs transatlantiques,* 161-83. Sherbrooke: Ex-libris, 1991.

3219 NUGENT, Andrea. "Canada's Silenced Communicators: A Report on Women in Journalism and Public Relations." *Atlantis* 7 (1982): 123-35.

3220 PAZDRO, Roberta J. "Agnes Deans Cameron: Against the Current." In *In Her Own Right: Selected Essays on Women's History in BC,* eds. Barbara Latham and Cathy Kess, 101-23. Victoria: Camosun College, 1980.

3221 PELLETIER, Francine, *et al.* "Les femmes journalistes: le pouvoir? quel pouvoir?" *Canadian Journal of Communication* 14, 3 (Fall 1989): 82-96.

3222 ROBINSON, Gertrude J. "The Media and Social Change: 30 Years of Magazine Coverage of Women and Work (1950-1977)." *Atlantis* 8, 2 (Spring 1983): 87-112.

3223 ROBINSON, Gertrude J. "Women and the Media in Canada: A Progress Report." In *Seeing Ourselves: Media Power and Policy in Canada,* eds. Helen Holmes and David Taras, 260-69. Toronto: Harcourt Brace Jovanovich Canada, 1992.

3224 ROWLAND, Robin. "Kit Watkins: The Journalist Who Opened the Way for Canadian Newspaper Women." *Content: Canada's National News Media Magazine* 85 (May 1978): 12-21. Reprinted in *The News: Inside the Canadian Media,* eds. B. Zwicker and D. Macdonald. Ottawa: Deneau Publishers, 1982.

3225 ROWLAND, Robin. "Kit's Secret." *Content: Canada's National News Media Magazine* November 1978.

3226 RYMELL, Heather. "Images of Women in the Magazines of the '30s and '40s." *Canadian Woman Studies* 3 (Summer 1981): 96-99.

3227 SEIFERT, Carol. "An Inventory of Articles Concerning Women in *MacLeans,* 1905-1920." *Resources for Feminist Research* 8, 2 (July 1979): 60-67.

3228 SEIFERT, Carol. "An Inventory of Articles Concerning Women in the *Canadian Magazine,* 1883-1919." *Resources for Feminist Research* 8, 2 (July 1979): 56-59.

3229 STEVEN, Peter. *Brink of Reality: New Canadian Documentary Film and Video.* Toronto: Between the Lines, 1993. [includes interviews with Sara Diamond, Judith Doyle, Brenda Longfellow and Alanis Obomsawin]

3230 TAUSKY, Thomas E., ed. *Sara Jeannette Duncan: Selected Journalism.* Ottawa: Tecumseh Press, 1978.

3231 TAYLOR, Anita. "Implementing Feminist Principles in a Bureaucracy: Studio D and the National Film Board of Canada." In *Women Communicating: Studies of Women's Talk,* eds. Barbara Bate and Anita Taylor. Norwood, NJ: Ablex Publishing Corp., 1988.

3232 TROTTIER, Madeleine and Rober Mayer. "Images de la femme au Canada français." Faculté de Droit, Université Laval. *Les cahiers de Droit,* 7(2) 1965/66: 343-352. [*Le Devoir,* 1935 and 1965]

3233 TURCOTTE, Dorothy. "Kit Coleman—A Gutsy Female—Pioneer Journalist." *Early Canadian Life* 3, 4 (May 1979).

3234 USHERWOOD, Stephen. "From Our Own Correspondent: Flora Shaw on the Klondike, 1898." *History Today* 27, 7 (July 1977): 445-51.

3235 VALOIS, Jocelyne. "La presse féminine et le rôle social de la femme." *Recherches sociographiques* 7, 3 (sept.-déc. 1967): 351-75.

3236 VIPOND, Mary. "The Image of Women in Canadian Mass Circulation Magazines in the 1920s." *Modernist Studies* 1 (1974/75): 9-13. Reprinted in *The Neglected Majority: Essays in Canadian Women's History*, eds. Susan Mann Trofimenkoff and Alison Prentice, 116-24. Toronto: McClelland and Stewart, 1977.

3237 WHYARD, Flo. "The Yukon's Edith Josie." *Alaska* 39, 1 (January 1973): 12-13, 53-54. [Loucheux columnist for the *Whitehorse Star*]

3238 WILSON, Susannah J. "The changing image of women in Canadian mass circulating magazines, 1930-1970." *Atlantis* 2, 2 Part 2 (Spring 1977): 33-44.

3239 WOLFE, Margie. "Feminist Publishing in Canada." *Canadian Women's Studies* 2, 2 (1980): 11-14.

3240 WOLLOCK, Jeffrey. "Did Stinson Jarvis Hypnotize 'Kit of the Mail'?" *Ontario History* 67, 4 (December 1975): 241-46.

3241 WYMAN, Georgina. "The Day Women Took Over the Toronto *Globe*." *Branching Out*, (March/April 1974): 22-23, 39-40.

3242 YARDLEY, M. Jeanne and Linda J. Kenyon. "Dead and Buried: Murder and Writing Women's Lives." *International Journal of Canadian Studies* 11 (Spring 1995): 195-206.

TOURISM/LEISURE

3243 ABERDEEN, Countess of. *Through Canada with a Kodak* (1893). With an introduction by Marjory Harper. Reprints in Canadian History. Toronto: University of Toronto Press, 1994.

3244 BALDWIN, Douglas. "L.M. Montgomery's *Anne of Green Gables*: The Japanese Connection." *Journal of Canadian Studies* 28, 3 (Fall 1993): 123-33.

3245 BOSANQUET, Mary. *Saddlebags for Suitcases*. Toronto: McClelland and Stewart, 1942.

3246 CAMERON, Agnes Deans. *The New North: An Account of a Woman's 1908 Journey Through Canada to the Arctic*. Edited by David Richeson. Saskatoon: Western Producer Prairie Books, 1986.

3247 COLLIS, Septima M. (Levy). *A Woman's Trip to Alaska*. New York: Cassell Publishing Co., 1890.

3248 COOKE, Alan. "A Woman's Way." *The Beaver* (Summer 1960): 40-45. [Mina Hubbard]

3249 DUBINSKY, Karen. "'The Pleasure is Exquisite but Violent': The Imaginary Geography of Niagara Falls in the Nineteenth Century." *Journal of Canadian Studies* 29, 2 (Summer 1994): 64-88.

3250 EDGELLER, Evelyn. *Mary Belle Barclay: Founder of Canadian Hostelling*. Calgary: Detselig, 1988.

3251 GOTSCH-TREVELYAN, Katherine. *Unharboured Heaths*. Toronto: McClelland and Stewart, 1933. [travels across Canada, 1929]

3252 GOWAN, Elsie Park. "A Quaker in Buckskin." *Alberta Historical Review* 5, 3 (Summer 1957): 1-6. [Mary Schäffer]

3253 HARDING, Les. *The Journeys of Remarkable Women: Their Travels on the Canadian Frontier*. Waterloo: Escart Press, 1995.

3254 HUBBARD, Mrs. Leonidas. *A Woman's Way Through Unknown Labrador*. London: John Murray, 1908; St. John's: Breakwater Books, 1981.

3255 HUNTER, Patricia L. and David J. Whitson. "Women, Leisure and Familism: Relationships and Isolation in Small Town Canada." *Leisure Studies* 10, 3 (September 1991): 219-33.

3256 HUTCHINS, Ozzie. "The Weaker Sex." *Canada West Magazine* 7, 3 (Fall 1977): 4-7. [a 1932 trek along the Yukon Telegraph Trail]

3257 JASEN, Patricia. *Wild Things: Nature, Culture, and Tourism in Ontario, 1790-1914*. Toronto: University of Toronto Press, 1995.

3258 NIEMI, J. and B. Weiser, eds. *Rivers Running Free: Canoeing Stories by Adventurous Women*. Seattle: Seal Press, 1992.

3259 REICHWEIN, Pearlann. "Guardians of the Rockies." *The Beaver* 74, 4 (Aug./Sept. 1994): 4-14. [Elizabeth Parker and Mary Schäffer, conservationists]

3260 ROTH, Mark. "The Photographs and Travels of Mary Schäffer Warren." *The Beaver* (Winter 1978): 28-33.

3261 SMITH, Cyndi. *Off the Beaten Track: Women Adventurers and Mountaineers in Western Canada*. Lake Louise, AB: Coyote Books, 1989.

3262 TYE, Diane. "Multiple Meanings Called Cavendish: The Interaction of Tourism with Traditional Culture." *Journal of Canadian Studies* 29, 1 (Spring 1994): 122-34. [Lucy Maud Montgomery]

3263 VYVYAN, Lady Clara. *Arctic Adventure*. London: P. Owen, 1961. [1926 journey in the Canadian Arctic]

3264 WHALEN, Dwight. "Daredevil in a Petticoat." *Canada West* 9, 2 (Summer 1979): 9-11. [1901 plunge over Niagara Falls in a barrel]

3265 WRIGHT, Cynthia. "They Were Five: The Dionne Quintuplets Revisited." *Journal of Canadian Studies* 29, 4 (Winter 1994/95): 5-14.

MATERIAL CULTURE/POPULAR CULTURE

BECAUSE OF THE paucity of written records left by the majority of women in the past, academic women's historians have learned over the past two decades to broaden their definition of the documentary source to include images and physical objects of human manufacture, or artifacts. In so doing, they have drawn extensively on the experience of researchers and curators in the museum field, who have long appreciated the artifact as a primary source and who have developed an extensive expertise in material history or the study of material culture--the design, production, use and meaning of objects of daily life such as clothing and bedding, tools and utensils, food, furniture, and domestic architecture. Particularly in the field of domestic history, museum collections of objects such as stoves, photographs and quilts are now being recognized as significant and underutilized resources for research on Canadian women's history. Folklorists, who study expressions of traditional or popular culture, are also contributing to the field of women's history their expertise in the use of oral history as a research methodology and their familiarity with the analysis of non-textual sources such as folk tales and songs, and popular rituals such as charivaris and public processions, as well as the material objects of daily life.

The growing scholarly interest in women's roles as makers of history and preservers of culture has recently revealed the important contributions of Canadian women such as Janet Carnochan and Janet Powell as pioneer museum workers and local historians. Yet until recently the scholarship produced by museum professionals was of little interest to women's historians working in the academy. The publication of several Canadian articles on women and museums in a recent special issue of *Gender and History*, suggests, however, that attitudes on this front are changing rapidly and that such scholarship will no longer be confined to museum periodicals such as *Muse and Musées*. To date, most scholarship has focussed on particular aspects of women's material culture such as clothing and food preparation. Costume collections tend to be heavily biased in favour of items worn for special occasions by the middle and upper classes rather than reflecting the daily wear of the majority of the population. Nevertheless sources such as photographs, paintings and catalogues have contributed to the growth of a substantial literature on women's costume and fashions. Quilts, bedding, needlework and hooked rugs have been studied extensively not only as functional items in the domestic environment but also as forms of women's artistic expression and shared cultural values. Surviving cookbooks, cooking utensils and appliances have facilitated research into the history of diet and cooking techniques in a variety of contexts, and a new appreciation of domestic architecture is contributing to insights about the history of family life and of the home and kitchen as women's workplaces. Publications that deal analytically with questions of the collection, interpretation and display of objects pertaining to the history of women are now appearing on a regular basis.

Despite the national and international prominence of a few Canadian women like Edith Fowke, Madeleine Doyon-Ferland and especially Helen Creighton, whose activities as a folklorist have become the subject of some controversy in recent years, academic folklore studies, much more so than museology, has been almost entirely a male-dominated field. The result, as noted by Pauline Greenhill and Diane Tye in a recent discussion of women and traditional culture, has been a disciplinary bias in favour of "high-performance, public, male genres" and against "the more communal, collaborative forms associated with the domestic sphere." A few Canadian scholars, such as Bonnie Huskins in a recent study of public processions in the Maritime region, have made promising beginnings exploring the ways in which folklore has served to display and recreate images of women and understandings of gender, while revealing a good deal about notions of women's place in public and private spheres of activity. Because of the neglect of this area by scholars, our knowledge of women's folklore remains fragmentary.

MATERIAL CULTURE/MUSEUMS

3266 ABRAHAMSON, Una. *God Bless Our Home: Domestic Life in Nineteenth Century Canada.* Don Mills: Burns and MacEachern, 1966.

3267 ADAMSON, Anthony and Marion MacRae. *The Ancestral Roof: Domestic Architecture of Upper Canada.* Toronto: Clarke, Irwin, 1963.

3268 ARCHER, P. Colleen. "Colours of History: Artists of the Quilting Bee." *The Beaver* 71, 6 (December 1991/January 1992): 47-51.

3269 ARMSTRONG, Audrey. *Harness in the Parlour: A Book of Early Canadian Fact and Fiction.* Toronto: Musson Book Co., 1974.

3270 BARA, Jana. "Fashion Plates and Muffins." *Horizon Canada* 5, 53 (1986): 1256-61.

3271 BARA, Jana. "Cradled in Furs: Winter Fashions in Montreal in the 1860s." *Dress: Journal of the Costume Society of America* 16 (1990): 38-47.

3272 BARRETT, Lois (Pete). "Clothes Had to Be Tidy and Clean." *Them Days: Stories of Early Labrador* 9, 3 (March 1984): 33-35.

3273 BARRETT, Lois (Pete). "Things We Had, We Made." *Them Days: Stories of Early Labrador* 10, 3 (March 1985): 41-43.

3274 BARSS, Beulah, M. *The Pioneer Cook: A Historical View of Canadian Prairie Food.* Calgary: Detselig Enterprises, 1980.

3275 BATES, Christina. *Out of Old Ontario Kitchens.* Toronto: Pagurian Press, 1978.

3276 BATES, Christina. *"Beauty Unadorned": Dressing Children in Late Nineteenth-Century Ontario.* Microfiche Report Series, no. 382. Ottawa: Environment Canada, Canadian Parks Service, 1984.

3277 BATES, Christina. "'Beauty Unadorned': Dressing Children in Late Nineteenth-Century Ontario." *Material History Bulletin* 21 (Spring 1985): 25-34.

3278 BATES, Christina. "Blue Monday: A Day in the Life of a Washerwoman, 1840..." *Canadian Collector* (July/August 1985): 44-48.

3279 BEAUDOIN-ROSS, Jacqueline. *Form and Fashion: Nineteenth-Century Montreal Dress.* Kingston and Montreal: McGill-Queen's University Press in collaboration with the McCord Museum of Canadian History, 1992.

3280 BEAUDOIN-ROSS, Jacqueline and Pamela Blackstock. "Costume in Canada: The Sequel." *Material History Review* 34 (Fall 1991): 42-67. [annotated bibliography]

3281 BEESON, Patricia. *Macdonald Was Late for Dinner: A Slice of Culinary Life in Early Canada.* Peterborough: Broadview Press, 1993.

3282 BIRD, Michael. "Ontario Fraktur Art, a Decorative Tradition in Three Germanic Settlements." *Ontario History* 68, 4 (December 1976): 247-72.

3283 BLACKSTOCK, Pamela. "Nineteenth Century Fur Trade Costume." *Canadian Folklore* 10, 1/2 (1988): 183-208.

3284 BOORMAN, Sylvia. *Wild Plums in Brandy: A Cookery of Wild Foods in Canada.* New York: McGraw-Hill, 1962.

3285 BOUCHARD, Lorraine. "La mariée des années' 40." *Cap-aux-Diamants* 4, 2 (Summer 1988): 21-23.

3286 BOUCHARD, Lorraine. "Le costume de la mariée, reflet de la vie quotidienne?" *Canadian Folklore* 10, 1/2 (1988): 53-78.

3287 BRENT, Martha Eckmann. "A Stitch in Time: Sewing Machine Industry of Ontario, 1860-1897." *Material History Bulletin* 10 (Spring 1980).

3288 BRETT, Katherine B. *Women's Costume in Early Ontario.* Toronto: Royal Ontario Museum, 1965.

3289 BRETT, Katherine B. *Women's Costume in Ontario, 1867-1907.* Toronto: Royal Ontario Museum, 1966.

3290 BURNHAM, Dorothy K. *The Comfortable Arts: Traditional Spinning and Weaving in Canada.* Ottawa: National Gallery of Canada, 1981.

3291 BURNHAM, Eva. "Textiles in Canada." *CCI: Journal of the Canadian Conservation Institute* 3 (1978): 35-39.

3292 BURNHAM, Harold B. and Dorothy K. Burnham. *"Keep Me Warm One Night": Early Handweaving in Eastern Canada.* Toronto: University of Toronto Press, 1972.

3293 CALLIHOO, Victoria. "Early Life in Lac Ste. Anne and St. Albert in the 1870's." *Alberta Historical Review* 1 (Autumn 1953): 21-26.

3294 CANADIAN HOME ECONOMICS ASSOCIATION. *The Laura Secord Canadian Cook Book.* Toronto: McClelland and Stewart 1966.

3295 CARELESS, Virginia. *Bibliography for the Study of British Columbia's Domestic Material History.* Mercury Series. History Division Paper, no. 20. Ottawa: National Museum of Man, 1976.

3296 CARELESS, Virginia A.S. *Clue to a Culture: Food Preparation of the O'Reilly Family.* Victoria: Royal British Columbia Museum, 1993.

3297 CARELESS, Virginia A.S. *Responding to Fashion: The Clothing of the O'Reilly Family.* Victoria: Royal British Columbia Museum, 1993.

3298 CLEAVER, Katherine. "Victorian Looking Glass." *Costume Society of Ontario Newsletter* 18, 3 (Fall/Winter 1988): 11-12.

3299 COLLARD, Eileen. *Women's Dress in the 1920's: An Outline of Women's Clothing in Canada During the Roaring Twenties.* Burlington: E. Collard, 1981.

3300 CONROY, Mary. *300 Years of Canada's Quilts.* Toronto: Griffin House, 1976.

3301 COOK, Jenny. "Bringing the Outside In: Women and the Transformation of the Middle-class Maritime Interior, 1830-1860." *Material History Review* 38 (Fall 1993): 36-49.

3302 DALE, Linda. "A Woman's Touch: Domestic Arrangements in the Rural Newfoundland Home." *Material History Bulletin* 15 (Summer 1982): 19-22

3303 DAWSON, Joyce Taylor. "A Note on Research in Progress: The Needlework of the Ursulines of Early Quebec." *Material History Bulletin* 5 (Spring 1978): 73-80.

3304 DENHEZ, Marc. *The Canadian Home: From Cave to Electronic Cocoon.* Toronto: Dundurn Press, 1994.

3305 DENNIS, Thelma. "Eaton's Catalogue: Furnishings for Rural Alberta, 1886-1930." *Alberta History* 37, 2 (Spring 1989): 21-31.

3306 DEVEAU, Mme. William D. "Vêtements acadiens d'autrefois." La société historique acadienne. *Les cahiers* 7 (mars 1965): 26-28.

3307 DUBUC, Elise and Luce Vermette. "Dossier: Place aux femmes," a special issue of *Musées* 14, 1 (avril 1992). [women and museums]

3308 DUNCAN, Dorothy. "Victuals and Viands in the New Province of Upper Canada." In *The Capital Years: Niagara-on-the-Lake, 1792-1796,* eds. Richard Merritt, Nancy Butler and Michael Power, 143-64. Toronto and Oxford: Dundurn Press, 1991.

3309 DUNTON, Hope. *From the Hearth: Recipes from the World of 18th Century Louisbourg.* Sydney, NS: University College of Cape Breton Press, 1986.

3310 DURAND, Marie. "La courtepointe québécoise: création ou emprunt?" *Material History Review* 34 (Fall 1991): 20-31.

3311 EVANS, Valerie. "In Mourning." *Material History Bulletin* 23 (Spring 1986): 49-52.

3312 FERGUSON, Carol and Margaret Fraser. *A Century of Canadian Home Cooking.* Scarborough: Prentice-Hall, 1992.

3313 FIELD, John L. *Janet Carnochan.* Markham, ON: Fitzhenry and Whiteside, 1985. [pioneer museum worker]

3314 FINLAY, Camille Sobrian. "The Tragedy of Inge-Va." *Rotunda* 26, 4 (Spring 1994): 34-39. [excavation of the privy of a wealthy 19th-century family in Perth, Ontario]

3315 FORD, Judy and Ellen McDonald "The crafts of Labrador women." *Canadian Women's Studies* 1 (Spring 1979): 96.

3316 FORTIER, Yvan. "Le festin de Lady Cartier: la table et l'étiquette au Québec, vers 1865." *Continuité* 52 (hiver 1992): 7-14.

3317 FRANKS, Patricia. *Grandma Was A Pioneer.* Cobalt, ON: Highway Book Shop, 1977.

3318 FYSON, Donald. "Du pain au madère: l'alimentation à Montréal au début du XIXe siècle." *Revue d'histoire de l'Amérique française* 46, 1 (été 1992): 67-90.

3319 GAGNON, Louise. *L'apparition des modes enfantines au Québec.* Québec: Institut québécois de recherche sur la culture, 1992.

3320 GIBBONS, Lillian. "Early Red River Homes." *Historical and Scientific Society of Manitoba* (1945/46): 26-42.

3321 GRANT, Gail Paton. "Getting Started: Outfitting the Bride in Seaside." *Canadian Folklore* 15, 2 (1993): 69-82.

3322 GRANT, Laurence. "'Her Stories': Working with a Community Advisory Committee on a Women's History Exhibit at a Canadian Municipal Museum." *Gender and History* 6, 3 (November 1994): 410-18.

3323 GRENIER, Nicole. *Courtepointes québécoises.* Montréal: Musée du Québec, Ministère des Affaires culturelles, 1977.

3324 GUILLET, Edwin C. *Pioneer Arts and Crafts.* Toronto: University of Toronto Press, 1940, 1968; reprint edition, 1973.

3325 HAMEL, Nathalie. "Rencontre de la tradition et du modernisme: les vêtements dans la Beauce du XXe siècle." *Canadian Folklore* 15, 2 (1993): 83-94.

3326 HARVEY, Kerridwen. "Looking for Women in the Museum: Has Women's Studies Really 'Come a Long Way'?" *Muse* 11, 4 (Winter 1994): 24-31.

3327 HEAMAN, Ken. "No Place Like Home: Photographs of Domestic Interiors in Ontario, 1880-1920." *Museum Quarterly* 14 (1986): 16-22.

3328 HOLMES, Janet. "Economic Choices and Popular Toys." *Material History Bulletin* 21 (Spring 1985).

3329 HOOD, Adrienne. "Early Canadian Quilts: Marriage of Art and Utility." *Rotunda* 17, 3 (1984/85): 28-35.

3330 HOOD, Adrienne D. and David-Thiery Ruddel. "Artifacts and Documents in the History of Quebec Textiles." In *Living in the Material World: Canadian and American Approaches to Material Culture,* ed. Gerald Pocius. St. John's: ISER Books, Memorial University of Newfoundland, 1990.

3331 JOB, Marilyn. "From Inconspicuous to Proud: A Look at the Design and Marketing of Maternity Clothes in the Twentieth Century." *Costume Society of Ontario Newsletter* 15, 1/2 (Autumn 1985): 6-10.

3332 KERKHOVEN, Marijke. "Prairie Panache." *Glenbow* 6, 4 (July/August 1986): 10.

3333 KERKHOVEN, Marijke. "Bloomers, Books and Belles: School Costume in Alberta." *Glenbow* 6 (November/December 1986): 9-10.

3334 KNIBB, Helen. "'Present but Not Visible': Searching for Women's History in Museum Collections." *Gender and History* 6, 3 (November 1994): 352-69.

3335 LANGDON, E. *Pioneer Gardens.* Toronto: Holt, Rinehart and Winston of Canada, 1972.

3336 LASSITER, Collette and Jill Oakes. "Ranchwomen, Rodeo Queens and Nightclub Cowgirls: The Evolution of Cowgirl Dress." In *Standing on New Ground: Women in Alberta,* eds. Catherine A. Cavanaugh and Randi R. Warne, 55-69. Edmonton: University of Alberta Press, 1993.

3337 LEWIS, D.B. "Samplers." *York Pioneer* (1961): 12-14.

3338 LOWER, Thelma Reid. "The Fashionable Woman's Hat." *British Columbia Historical News* 28, 3 (Summer 1995): 20-21.

3339 LUSSIER, Suzanne. "La tradition du secret." *Canadian Folklore* 15, 2 (1993): 13-30.

3340 MacDONALD, Ann C. "Historic Costume on the Island: An Analysis of Family Photographs/PEI Women's Fashions of the 1870s and 1880s." *Canadian Home Economics Journal* 39, 1 (Winter 1989): 22-24.

3341 MacLAREN, George. "The Arts of the Micmac of Nova Scotia." *Nova Scotia Historical Quarterly* 4, 2 (June 1974): 167-77.

3342 MAY, Margaret. "Janet Carnochan Pioneer Museum Worker, 1839-1926." *Museum Quarterly* 12 (1983): 17-20.

3343 McGRATH, Judy, *et al.* "Waste Not, Want Not (Flour Bags and Other Handy Material)." *Them Days: Stories of Early Labrador* 10, 2 (December 1984): 57-63.

3344 McKENDRY, Ruth. *Quilts and Other Bed Coverings in the Canadian Tradition.* Toronto: Van Nostrand Reinhold, 1979.

3345 MINHINNICK, Jeanne. *At Home in Upper Canada.* Toronto: Clarke, Irwin, 1970.

3346 MOOGK, Peter. "At Home in Early Niagara Township." In *The Capital Years: Niagara-on-the-Lake, 1792-1796,* eds. Richard Merritt, Nancy Butler and Michael Power, 165-85. Toronto and Oxford: Dundurn Press, 1991.

3347 MORTON, Sandra. "History of Alberta Quilts." *Material History Bulletin* 18 (Fall 1983).

3348 NORRIS, J.A., comp. *The Book of Giving: A History of the Ontario Handweavers and Spinners, 1956-1979.* Toronto: Ontario Handweavers and Spinners, 1979.

3349 NOWELL-SMITH, Felicity. "Feeding the Nineteenth-Century Baby: Implications for Museum Collections." *Material History Bulletin* 21 (Spring 1985).

3350 O'DEA, Shane. "The Development of Cooking and Heating Technology." *Material History Bulletin* 15 (1982).

3351 PATTERSON, Nancy-Lou. "Mennonite Folk Art of Waterloo County." *Ontario History* 60, 3 (September 1968): 81-104.

3352 PATTERSON, Nancy-Lou. "The Traditional Arts of Mennonite Women." *Artmagazine* 7 (December 1975): 34-37.

3353 PATTERSON, Nancy-Lou. "Anna Weber Hat Das Gemacht: Anna Weber (1814-1888)—A Fraktur Painter of Waterloo County, Ontario." *Mennonite Life* (December 1975): 15-19.

3354 PHELPS, Marion L. "An Ojibwa Chieftan's Granddaughter Once Lived in Potton." *Québec-Histoire* 2, 2 (Winter 1973): 90-91. [Charlotte Mono-nonco Katawebeday, creator of an Ojibwa maiden's costume]

3355 POCIUS, Gerald L. "Hooked Rugs in Newfoundland: The Representation of Social Structure in Design." *Journal of American Folklore* 92 (1979): 273-84.

3356 REILLY, Sharon. "Material History and the History of Women." In *First Days, Fighting Days: Women in Manitoba History*, ed. Mary Kinnear, 1-17. Regina: Canadian Plains Research Center, University of Regina, 1987.

3357 RILEY, Barbara. "Domestic Food Preparation in British Columbia, 1895-1935." *Material History Bulletin* 14 (Spring 1982).

3358 RILEY, Barbara. "Domestic Work: Oral History and Material Culture." Canadian Oral History Association. *Journal* 8 (1985): 9-14.

3359 RILEY, Barbara. "Research and the Development of a Domestic History Collection." *Material History Bulletin* 22 (Fall 1985): 58-62.

3360 ROBSON, Scott and Sharon MacDonald. *Old Nova Scotia Quilts.* Halifax: Formac Publishing, 1994.

3361 ROUTH, Caroline. *In Style: 100 Years of Canadian Women's Fashion.* Toronto: Stoddart Publishing, 1993.

3362 ROWAT, Theresa. "Photographic Archival Sources for Costume Research." *Material History Review* 34 (Fall 1991): 32-41.

3363 ROWLES-SIMPSON, Edith. "Bannock, Beans and Bacon: An Investigation of Pioneer Diet." *Saskatchewan History* (Winter 1952): 1-15. Reprinted in *Pages from the Past,* ed. D.M. Bocking, 102-19. Saskatoon: Western Producer Prairie Books, 1979.

3364 RUDDEL, David-Thiery. "The Domestic Textile Industry in the Region and City of Quebec, 1792-1835." *Material History Bulletin* 17 (Spring 1983): 95-125.

3365 RUDDEL, David-Thiery. "Domestic Textile Production in Colonial Quebec, 1608-1840." *Material History Bulletin* 31 (Spring 1990): 39-49.

3366 RUDDEL, David-Thiery. "Consumer Trends, Clothing, Textiles and Equipment in the Montreal Area, 1792-1835." *Material History Bulletin* 32 (Fall 1990): 45-64.

3367 RUSH, Anita. "Changing Women's Fashion and Its Social Context, 1870-1905." *Material History Bulletin* 14 (Spring 1982): 37-46.

3368 RUSSELL, Hilary. "'Canadian Ways': An Introduction to Comparative Studies of Housework, Stoves and Diet in Great Britain and Canada." *Material History Bulletin* 19 (Spring 1984): 1-12.

3369 RUSSELL, Hilary. "Reflections of an Image Finder: Some Problems and Suggestions for Picture Researchers." *Material History Bulletin* (Fall 1984): 79-83.

3370 RUSSELL, Hilary. "Training, Restraining and Sustaining: Infant and Child Care in the Late Nineteenth Century." *Material History Bulletin* 21 (Spring 1985).

3371 RUSSELL, Loris S. "The First Canadian Cooking Stove." *Canada: An Historical Magazine* 3, 2 (December 1972): 34-35.

3372 SAINT-PIERRE, Angeline. *Émilie Charmand, tisserande.* Québec: Éditions Garneau, 1976. [domestic weaving]

3373 SANDS, Gwen. "From Pioneer to Professional: Women in Crafts." *Communiqué* 8 (May 1975): 24-26.

3374 SCHECHTER, Rebecca. "Canadian Pioneer Cookery—A Structural Analysis." *Journal of Canadian Studies* 12, 4 (1977): 3-11.

3375 SCOTT, Elizabeth M. "A Feminist Approach to Historical Archaeology: Eighteenth-Century Fur Trade Society at Michilimackinac." *Historical Archaeology* 25, 4 (1991): 42-53.

3376 SÉGUIN, Robert-Lionel. "Nos anciens utensiles à confire." *Revue d'histoire de l'Amérique française* 24, 3 (décembre 1970): 403-6.

3377 SÉGUIN, Robert-Lionel. *Les jouets anciens du Québec.* Montréal: Leméac, 1976.

3378 SEVERIN, Elizabeth. "Muslin Gowns and Moccasins." In *The Capital Years: Niagara-on-the-Lake, 1792-1796,* eds. Richard Merritt, Nancy Butler and Michael Power, 131-41. Toronto and Oxford: Dundurn Press, 1991.

3379 STRAHLENDORF, Evelyn Robson. *Dolls of Canada: A Reference Guide.* Toronto: University of Toronto Press, 1989.

3380 SUMMERS, John. "Beyond Brown Bread and Oatmeal Cookies: New Directions for Historical Kitchens." *Material History Bulletin* 27 (Spring 1988): 1-13.

3381 TAYLOR, Margaret and Frances McNaught. *The Early Canadian Galt Cook Book.* Toronto: William Briggs, 1898; Toronto: Coles Canadiana Collection, 1974.

3382 TIVY, Mary. "Nineteenth-Century Canadian Children's Games." *Material History Bulletin* 21 (Spring 1985).

3383 WALLACE-CASEY, Cynthia. "Into the Kitchens of Kings Landing: Interpreting the Private Sphere of Women's Work." In *Studies in History and Museums,* ed. Peter E. Rider, 121-27. Hull: Canadian Museum of Civilization, 1994.

3384 WILLIAMS, Alice. "The Spirit of My Quilts." *Canadian Woman Studies* 10, 2/3 (Summer/Fall 1989): 49-55.

3385 *Women's Hats Yesterday and Today.* Montreal: Château Ramezay, 1989.

POPULAR CULTURE/FOLKLORE

3386 BUCK, Ruth Matheson. "Wives and Daughters." *Folklore* 9, 4 (Autumn 1988): 14-15.

3387 COLE, Douglas and Christine Mullins. "'Haida Ida': The Musical World of Ida Halpern." *BC Studies* 97 (Spring 1993): 3-37.

3388 COSBEY, Robert C. *All in Together Girls: Skipping Songs from Regina, Saskatchewan.* Regina: Canadian Plains Research Center, University of Regina, 1980.

3389 CREIGHTON, Helen. *A Life in Folklore.* Toronto: McGraw-Hill Ryerson, 1975.

3390 DRAKE, Earl G. "Regina in 1898: The Fair and the Fair Sex." *Saskatchewan History* 7 (Spring 1955): 56-63.

3391 "Early Entertainment." *Urban Reader* 5, 1 (1977): 4-9. [turn-of-the-century Vancouver]

3392 GIBBONS, Lillian and D. McDowell. "On With the Dance...Historic Balls in Manitoba." *Manitoba Pageant* 21, 4 (Summer 1976): 1-3.

3393 GODIN, Christine. "L'oeuvre pionnière de Madeleine Doyon-Ferland." *Canadian Folklore* 10, 1/2 (1988): 13-33. [Laval University professor of "arts et traditions populaires," 1944-1977]

3394 GREENHILL, Pauline and Diane Tye. "Women and Traditional Culture." In *Changing Patterns: Women in Canada,* eds. Sandra Burt, Lorraine Code and Lindsay Dorney, 309-37. Toronto: McClelland & Stewart, 1993.

3395 HUSKINS, Bonnie. "The Ceremonial Space of Women: Public Processions in Victorian Saint John and Halifax." In *Separate Spheres: Women's Worlds in the 19th Century Maritimes,* eds. Janet Guildford and Suzanne Morton, 145-59. Fredericton: Acadiensis Press, 1994.

3396 LAFORGE, Valerie. "Madeleine Doyon-Ferland." *Culture et tradition* 9 (1985): 13-31.

3397 LANGLOIS, Janet. "Smuggling Across the Windsor-Detroit Border: Folk Art, Sexual Difference and Cultural Identity." *Canadian Folklore* 13, 1 (1991): 23-34.

3398 MARSHALL, Vera G. "Great Grandmother Isabel: A Story of the Turn of the Century." *Nova Scotia Historical Quarterly* 6, 1 (March 1976): 57-66.

3399 McKAY, Ian. "'He is more picturesque in his oilskins': Helen Creighton and the Art of Being Nova Scotian." *New Maritimes* 12, 1 (Sept./Oct. 1993): 12-22.

3400 McKAY, Ian. "Helen Creighton and the Politics of Antimodernism." In *Myth and Milieu: Atlantic Literature and Culture, 1918-1939,* ed. Gwendolyn Davies, 1-16. Fredericton: Acadiensis Press, 1993.

3401 McKAY, Ian. *The Quest of the Folk: Antimodernism and Cultural Selection in Twentieth-Century Nova Scotia.* Montreal and Kingston: McGill-Queen's University Press, 1994. [Helen Creighton, Mary Black]

3402 MOOGK, Peter N. "'Thieving Buggers' and 'Stupid Sluts': Insults and Popular Culture in New France." *William and Mary Quarterly,* 3rd series 36 (1979). Reprinted in *Interpreting Canada's Past: Volume I, Before Confederation,* ed. J.M. Bumsted, 63-83. Toronto: Oxford University Press, 1986.

3403 MOORE, Christopher. "Fowke on Folk." *The Beaver* 72, 1 (February/March 1992): 60-62. [interview with folklorist Edith Fowke]

3404 MORGAN, E.C. "Pioneer Recreation and Social Life." *Saskatchewan History* 18, 2 (1965): 41-54.

3405 POCIUS, G.L. "First Day That I Thought of It, Since I Got Wed." *Western Folklore* 35 (April 1976): 109-22. [sex roles and the role of singer in a Newfoundland outport]

3406 POWELL, Jean. *The Life and Work of R. Janet Powell.* Grimsby, ON: Grimsby Historical Society, 1974. [local historian]

3407 SKIDMORE, P. "Sex and Song: Roles and images of women in popular music at the turn of the century." *Atlantis* 2, 2 (1977): 22-32.

3408 TREMBLAY-MATTE, Cécile. *Chansons écrites au féminin, de Madeleine de Verchères à Mitsou.* Montréal: Éditions Trois, 1991.

3409 TRUDEL, Jean. "La danse traditionnelle au Québec." *Forces* 32 (1975): 33-43.

3410 TYE, Diane. "Local Character Anecdotes: A Nova Scotia Case Study." *Western Folklore* 48 (July 1989).

3411 TYE, Diane. "'A Very Lone Worker': Woman-Centred Thoughts on Helen Creighton's Career as a Folklorist." *Canadian Folklore* 15, 2 (1993): 107-18.

3412 WEBB, Jeff A. "Cultural Intervention: Helen Creighton's Folksong Broadcasts, 1938-1939." *Canadian Folklore* 14, 2 (1992): 159-70.

MILITARY/WAR

UNTIL THE 1970s and the advent of women's history, as a distinct field of study, Canadian women were almost entirely absent from the accounts of military historians, and war was presented as an enterprise in which only men participated. In fact, as recent scholarship has shown, Canadian women often did much more than weep on the sidelines, playing a variety of roles as active participants in military conflicts. In addition, women's daily lives, definitions of femininity, and traditional gender roles have all been dramatically affected by wars throughout Canadian history.

No Canadian historian has done more to demolish the notion that the study of war has nothing to do with women than Ruth Roach Pierson whose landmark studies of Canadian women and World War II challenged the popular perception that the war had liberated women, and documented the extensive efforts of political and military authorities to ensure that female war workers and members of the armed forces would remain "feminine" at the end of the conflict. World War II has received the bulk of attention from Canadian historians studying women and war, particularly in view of the recent fiftieth anniversary which has triggered the publication of a torrent of memoirs and popular histories.

The First World War has been much less well served by Canadian women's historians. It has been recognized as a turning point in the struggle for women's political rights and as a critical stimulus to the mobilization of women's organizations in support of causes such as Prohibition. There are, however, no studies of women's labour force participation, especially in the war industries, or of government and military policies comparable to those undertaken on the Second World War. A weakness of the scholarship on both world wars, which tends to take a pan-Canadian perspective, is that we know little about how various local, regional, and cultural contexts shaped the ways in which women experienced war and their responses to it. Aside from a few accounts of Black women and Japanese Canadian women during the Second World War, our knowledge is confined largely to the experiences of white women.

Scholarship on Canadian women's involvement in pre-twentieth-century military conflicts is patchy at best. Recent years have seen a flurry of activity on Loyalist women, notably by Janice Potter-Mackinnon, who has challenged the invisibility of women in traditional accounts of Loyalist suffering and heroism. New studies of Molly Brant remind us that First Nations women frequently played important diplomatic roles in early military conflicts. Women who have embodied traditional definitions of female military heroism, such as Laura Secord and Madeleine de Verchères, are now being reinterpreted in exciting ways by cultural historians exploring the construction of national symbols.

GENERAL

3413   AMBROSE, Linda M. "'Working Day and Night Helping Dick': Women in Post-War Planning on the Canadian Youth Commission, 1942-43." *Historical Studies in Education* 3, 1 (Spring 1991): 75-92.

√ – 3414   ARNEY, Ada. *Here Come the Khaki Skirts...the women volunteers: A pictorial review of the Canadian Women's Army Corps during the Second World War.* Cobalt, ON: Highway Book Shop, 1988.

3415   ARNOLD, Gladys. *One Woman's War: A Canadian Reporter with the Free French.* Toronto: Lorimer, 1987.

3416   AUGER, Geneviève and Raymond Lamothe. *De la poêle à frire à la ligne de feu: la vie quotidienne des Québécoises pendant la guerre '39-'45.* Montréal: Boréal Express, 1981.

3417   BAILLAIRGÉ, Frédéric-Alexandre. *Marie-Madeleine de Verchères et les siens.* Saint-Jacques: Éditions du Pot de fer, 1991.

3418   BOWMAN, Phylis. *We Skirted the War!* Prince Rupert, BC: P. Bowman, 1975.

3419   BOWMAN, Phylis. "A CWAC in Victoria, 1942 1945." *British Columbia Historical News* 27, 4 (Fall 1994): 25-27.

3420   BRAND, Dionne. "'We weren't allowed to go into factory work until Hitler started the war': The 1920s to the 1940s." In *'We're Rooted Here and They Can't Pull Us Up': Essays in African Canadian Women's History,* Peggy Bristow, *et al.* 171-91. Toronto: University of Toronto Press, 1994.

3421   BRANDT, Gail Cuthbert. "'Pigeon-Holed and Forgotten': The Work of the Subcommittee on the Post-War Problems of Women, 1943." *Histoire sociale/Social History* XV, 29 (May 1982): 239-59.

3422   BROADFOOT, Barry. *Six War Years: 1939-1945: Memories of Canadians at Home and Abroad.* Toronto: Doubleday, 1973.

3423   BRUCE, Jean. *After the War.* Don Mills: Fitzhenry and Whiteside, 1982.

√ – 3424   BRUCE, Jean. "Canadian Women in the Second World War." Canadian Oral History Association. *Journal* 6 (1983).

√ – 3425   BRUCE, Jean. *Back the Attack! Canadian Women During the Second World War—At Home and Abroad.* Toronto: Macmillan, 1985.

3426   BURGESS, Marilyn. "Proudly She Marches: Wartime Propaganda and the Lesbian Spectator." *Cinéaction* (Winter 1990/91): 22-27.

3427   BURLEIGH, H.C. "A Tale of Loyalist Heroism." *Ontario History* 42, 2 (1950): 91-99. [Sarah Kast McGinnis]

3428   BUZEK, Beatrice Ross. "'By fortune wounded': Loyalist Women in Nova Scotia." *Nova Scotia Historical Review* 7, 2 (1987): 45-62.

3429   CASH, Gwen. *A Million Miles from Ottawa.* Toronto: Macmillan of Canada, 1942. [life on Vancouver Island awaiting a possible Japanese invasion]

3430   CLINT, Mabel Brown. *Our Bit.* Montreal: Alumnae Association of the Royal Victoria Hospital, 1934. [nursing in World War I]

3431   COLLIER, Dianne. *Hurry Up and Wait: An Inside Look at Life as a Canadian Military Wife.* Carp, ON: Creative Bound, 1994.

3432   CONRAD, W. Hugh. *Athene, Goddess of War: The Canadian Women's Army Corps: Their Story.* Dartmouth, NS: Writing and Editorial Services, 1983.

3433   CÔTÉ, Jean. *Madeleine de Verchères, l'intrépide "Magdelon."* Outremont: Québecor, coll. "Récit historique," no. 1, 1995.

3434   COUILLARD, Danielle. "Le travail des femmes québécoises durant la deuxième guerre mondiale." *Cahiers d'histoire* 3, 2 (printemps 1983): 3-24.

3435   DENAULT, Jocelyne. "Des femmes devant et derrière la caméra: le cas de l'Office national du film du Canada, 1941-1945." *Recherches féministes* 6, 1 (1993): 113-18.

3436   DENNEY, C.D. "In Memory of Mary Rose (Pritchard) Sayers: The Last Witness." *Saskatchewan History* 24, 2 (Spring 1971): 63-72. [Frog Lake Massacre, 1884]

3437   DOUGHTY, A.G. *Daughter of New France.* Ottawa: Mortimer Press, 1916. [Madeleine de Verchères]

3438   EPP, Marlene. "Alternative Service and Alternative Gender Roles: Conscientious Objectors in BC During World War II." *BC Studies* 105/106 (Spring/Summer 1995): 139-58.

3439   FALLIS, Donna. "World War I Knitting." *Alberta Museums Review* (Fall 1984): 8-10.

3440   FORESTELL, Diane G. "The Necessity of Sacrifice for the Nation at War: Women's Labour Force Participation, 1939-1946." *Histoire sociale/Social History* XXII, 44 (November 1989): 333-47.

3441   FREEMAN, Barbara M. "Her Amplified Voice: Gender, War Propaganda and Canadian Motherhood, 1939-1943." Simone de Beauvoir Institute. *Newsletter* 12, 2 (1992): 43-54.

3442   FREEMAN, Barbara M. "Mother and Son: Gender, Class, and War Propaganda in Canada, 1939-1945." *American Journalism* 12, 3 (Summer 1995): 260-75.

3443   FRYER, Mary Beacock. "Sarah Sherwood: Wife and Mother, an 'Invisible' Loyalist." In *Eleven Exiles: Accounts of Loyalists and the American Revolution,* eds. Phyllis R. Blakely and John N. Grant, 245-62. Toronto: Dundurn Press, 1982.

3444   GOSSAGE, Carolyn. *Greatcoats and Glamour Boots: Canadian Women at War, 1939-1945.* Toronto: Dundurn Press, 1991.

3445   GOULD, Florence E. "A War Bride's Journey in 1917." *Okanagan Historical Society Report* 37 (1974): 48-51.

3446 GUNDY, H. Pearson. "Molly Brant—Loyalist." *Ontario History* 45, 3 (1953): 97-108.

3447 GWYN, Sandra. *Tapestry of War: A Private View of Canadians in the Great War.* Toronto: Harper Collins, 1992.

3448 HARRISON, Deborah and Lucie Laliberté. *No Life Like It: Military Wives in Canada.* Toronto: James Lorimer, 1994.

3449 HIBBERT, Joyce. *The War Brides.* With an introduction by Mavis Gallant. Toronto: Peter Martin Associates, 1978.

3450 *History of Shipbuilding in British Columbia as Told by Shipyard Workers.* Vancouver: Marine Retirees Association, 1977. [Ch. 14, women in shipbuilding during World War II.]

√ –3451 JACOBSEN, Carl G. "Women in the Canadian Forces: past, present and future: a critique." *Atlantis* 4, 2 Part 2 (Spring 1979): 284-86.

3452 JOHNSTON, A.J.B. "Into the Great War: Katharine McLennan goes overseas, 1915-1919." In *The Island: New Perspectives on Cape Breton History, 1713-1990,* ed. Kenneth Donovan, 129-44. Fredericton/Sydney: Acadiensis Press/University College of Cape Breton Press, 1990.

3453 JOHNSTON, Elizabeth Lichtenstein. "Recollections of a Georgia Loyalist, Part II." *Atlantis* 5, 1 (Fall 1979): 154-82.

3454 KIEFER, Nancy and Ruth Roach Pierson. "The War Effort and Women Students at the University of Toronto, 1939-45." In *Youth, University and Canadian Society: Essays in the Social History of Higher Education,* eds. Paul Axelrod and John G. Reid, 161-83. Montreal and Kingston: McGill-Queen's University Press, 1989.

3455 LATTA, Ruth. *The Memory of All That: Canadian Women Remember World War II.* Burnstown, ON: General Store Publishing House, 1992.

3456 LE ROUGETEL, Katy. "Cats, Mothers, Nut Tappers." *Branching Out* (July/August 1977): 38-41. [women workers in World War II]

3457 LENNON, Mary Jane and Syd Charendoff. *On the Homefront: A Scrapbook of Canadian World War II Memorabilia.* Erin, ON: The Boston Mills Press, 1981.

3458 LEWIS, Norah. "'Isn't this a terrible war?': The Attitudes of Children to Two World Wars." *Historical Studies in Education* 7, 2 (Fall 1995): 193-215.

3459 MARTINEAU, Barbara Halpern. "Before the Guerillières: Women's Films at the NFB During World War II." In *Canadian Film Reader,* eds. Seth Feldman and Joyce Nelson, 58-67. Toronto: Peter Martin, 1977.

3460 McKENZIE, Ruth. *Laura Secord, The Legend and the Lady.* Toronto: McClelland and Stewart, 1971.

3461 McNEIL, Bill. *Voices of a War Remembered: An Oral History of Canadians in World War Two.* Toronto: Doubleday Canada Limited, 1991.

3462 MOIR, John S. "An Early Record of Laura Secord's Walk." *Ontario History* 51, 2 (1959): 105-8.

3463 MORGAN, Cecilia. "'Of Slender Frame and Delicate Appearance': The Placing of Laura Secord in the Narratives of Canadian Loyalist History." *Journal of the Canadian Historical Association* NS 5 (1994): 195-212.

3464 MORTON, Desmond and Cheryl Smith. "Fuel for the Home Fires: The Patriotic Fund, 1914-1918." *The Beaver* 75, 4 (Aug./Sept. 1995): 12-19.

3465 NEARY, Peter and Shaun Brown. "The Veterans Charter and Canadian Women Veterans of World War II." *Papers in Political Economy* 35 (1994). Reprinted in *The Good Fight: Canadians and World War II,* eds. J.L. Granatstein and Peter Neary. Toronto: Copp Clark Limited, 1995.

3466 NICHOLSON, G.W.L. *Canada's Nursing Sisters.* Toronto: Samuel Stevens Hakkert, 1975.

3467 NORTON, Mary Beth. "Eighteenth-Century American Women in Peace and War: The Case of the Loyalists." *William and Mary Quarterly* 3rd Series, 33 (July 1976): 386-409. Reprinted in *Interpreting Canada's Past: Volume One, Pre-Confederation,* ed. J.M. Bumsted, 231-55. Toronto: Oxford University Press, 1993.

3468 OIWA, Keibo, ed. *Stone Voices: Wartime Writings of Japanese Canadian Issei.* Montreal: Véhicule Press, 1992.

3469 OMATSU, Maryka. *Bittersweet Passage: Redress and the Japanese Canadian Experience.* Toronto: Between the Lines, 1992.

3470 PARSON, Edna Tyson. *A Houseful of Canada.* Nepean, ON: Abacus Print Services, 1992. [Ottawa boarding house in World War II]

3471 PEATE, Mary. *Girl in a Sloppy Joe Sweater: Life on the Canadian Home Front During World War Two.* Montreal: Optimum Pub. International, 1989.

3472 PEPPER, Paul E. "War of 1812 lists of orphans, pensioners and widows: as published in the *Kingston Gazette,* Kingston, Upper Canada, Saturday, January 4, 1817." *Families* 31, 3 (August 1992).

3473 PIERSON, Ruth Roach. "Women's Emancipation and the Recruitment of Women into the Labour Force in World War II." Canadian Historical Association. *Historical Papers* (1976): 141-73. Reprinted in *The Neglected Majority: Essays in Canadian Women's History,* eds. Susan Mann Trofimenkoff and Alison Prentice, 125-45. Toronto: McClelland and Stewart, 1977; and in *Interpreting Canada's Past: Volume II, After Confederation,* ed. J.M. Bumsted, 333-62. Toronto: Oxford University Press, 1986; 2nd edition, 558-93, 1993.

3474 PIERSON, Ruth Roach. "'Home aide': A Solution to Women's Unemployment after World War II." *Atlantis* 2, 2 Part 2 (Spring 1977): 85-97.

3475 PIERSON, Ruth Roach. "'Jill Canuck': CWAC of All Trades, But No 'Pistol Packing Momma.'" Canadian Historical Association. *Historical Papers* (1978): 106-33.

3476 PIERSON, Ruth Roach. "Ladies or Loose Women: The Canadian Women's Army Corps in World War II." *Atlantis* 4, 2 Part 2 (Spring 1979): 245-66.

3477 PIERSON, Ruth Roach. "The Double Bind of the Double Standard: VD Control and the CWAC in World War II." *Canadian Historical Review* 62, 1 (March 1981): 31-58.

3478 PIERSON, Ruth Roach. "Canadian Women and Canadian Mobilization During the Second World War." *International Review of Military History* 51 (1982): 181-207.

3479 PIERSON, Ruth Roach. *Canadian Women and the Second World War*. Historical Booklet No. 37. Ottawa: Canadian Historical Association, 1983. Abridged in *Readings in Canadian History: Post Confederation*, eds. R. Douglas Francis and Donald B. Smith, 488-507. Toronto: Holt, Rinehart and Winston Canada, 1986.

3480 PIERSON, Ruth Roach. *"They're Still Women After All": The Second World War and Canadian Womanhood*. Toronto: McClelland and Stewart, 1986.

3481 PIERSON, Ruth Roach. "'They're Still Women After All': Wartime Jitters Over Femininity." In *The Challenge of Modernity: A Reader on Post-Confederation Canada*, ed. Ian McKay, 407-20. Toronto: McGraw-Hill Ryerson, 1992. Reprinted in *The Good Fight: Canadians and World War II*, eds. J.L. Granatstein and Peter Neary. Toronto: Copp Clark Limited, 1995. [excerpted from *They're Still Women After All*]

3482 PIERSON, Ruth Roach. "'They're Still Women After All': The Second World War and Canadian Womanhood." In *Coming of Age: Readings in Canadian History Since World War II*, eds. Donald Avery and Roger Hall, 103-23. Toronto: Harcourt Brace & Company Canada, 1996. [excerpted from *They're Still Women After All*]

3483 PIERSON, Ruth Roach and Marjorie Cohen. "Educating Women for Work: Government Training Programs for Women before, during, and after World War II." In *Modern Canada: 1930-1980s*, eds. Michael S. Cross and Gregory S. Kealey, 208-43. Toronto: McClelland and Stewart, 1984.

3484 PILKINGTON, Gwendoline Evans. *Time Remembered: A Woman's Story of World War II*. Burnstown, ON: General Store Publishing House, 1993.

3485 POTTER, Janice. "Patriarchy and Paternalism: The Case of the Eastern Ontario Loyalist Women." *Ontario History* 81, 1 (March 1989): 3-24. Abridged in *Rethinking Canada: The Promise of Women's History*, 2nd edition, eds. Veronica Strong-Boag and Anita Clair Fellman, 59-72. Toronto: Copp Clark Pitman Ltd., 1991. Reprinted in *Reappraisals in Canadian History: Pre-Confederation*, eds. A.D. Gilbert, C.M. Wallace and R.M. Bray, 250-70. Scarborough: Prentice Hall Canada Inc., 1993.

3486 POTTER-MACKINNON, Janice. *While the Women Only Wept: Loyalist Refugee Women in Eastern Ontario*. Montreal and Kingston: McGill-Queen's University Press, 1993.

3487 PRENTICE, Alison, *et al*. "The 'Bren Gun Girl' and the Housewife Heroine." In *Readings in Canadian History: Post Confederation*, 3rd edition, eds. R. Douglas Francis and Donald B. Smith, 440-62. Toronto: Holt, Rinehart and Winston of Canada, 1990; 4th edition, 436-58, 1994. [excerpted from *Canadian Women: A History*]

3488 RAMKHALAWANSINGH, Ceta. "Women During the Great War." In *Women at Work: Ontario, 1850-1930*, eds. Janice Acton, *et al*. Toronto: Canadian Women's Educational Press, 1974.

3489 READ, Daphne, ed. *The Great War and Canadian Society: An Oral History*. With an introduction by Russell Hann. Toronto: New Hogtown Press, 1978.

3490 RICHARDSON, Evelyn B. *B... Was for Butter and Enemy Craft*. Halifax: Pethric Press, 1976. [memoir of a lighthouse-keeping family, Nova Scotia, World War II]

3491 ROBINSON, Helen Caister. "Molly Brant: Mohawk Heroine." In *Eleven Exiles: Accounts of Loyalists and the American Revolution*, eds. Phyllis R. Blakely and John N. Grant, 116-42. Toronto: Dundurn Press, 1982.

3492 ROE, Kathleen Robson. *War Letters from the CWAC*. Toronto: Kakabeka Publishing Co. Ltd., 1975.

3493 SCHEINBERG, Ellen. "The Tale of Tessie the Textile Worker: Female Textile Workers in Cornwall During World War II." *Labour/Le Travail* 33 (Spring 1994): 153-86.

3494 SIMPSON, Suzanne, Doris Toole and Cindy Player. "Women in the Canadian forces: past, present and future." *Atlantis* 4, 2 Part 2 (Spring 1979): 266-83.

3495 SYMONS, Ellen. "Under Fire—Canadian Women in Combat." *Canadian Journal of Women and the Law* 4, 2 (1991): 477-511.

3496 SZYCHTER, Gwen. "The War Work of Women in Rural British Columbia: 1914-1919." *British Columbia Historical News* 27, 4 (Fall 1994): 5-9.

3497 THOMPSON, John Herd. "'The Beginnings of Our Regeneration': The Great War and Western Canadian Reform Movements." Canadian Historical Association. *Historical Papers,* (1972): 227-45. Reprinted in *The Prairie West: Historical Readings,* eds. R. Douglas Francis and Howard Palmer, 450-65. Edmonton: Pica Pica Press, 1985; and in *An Introduction to Canadian History,* ed. A.I. Silver. Toronto: Canadian Scholars' Press, 1991.

3498 TURNBULL, Elsie G. "Women at Cominco During the Second World War." In *Not Just Pin Money: Selected Essays on the History of Women's Work in British Columbia,* eds. Barbara K. Latham and Roberta J. Pazdro, 429-34. Victoria: Camosun College, 1984.

3499 "Two Months in the Camp of Big Bear: The Life and Adventures of Theresa Gowanlock and Theresa Delany." In *The Frog Lake "Massacre,"* ed. Stuart Hughes, 168-242. Carleton Library Series No. 97. Toronto: McClelland and Stewart, 1976.

3500 WHITTON, Charlotte. *Canadian Women in the War Effort.* Toronto: Macmillan of Canada, 1942.

3501 WICKS, Ben. *When the Boys Came Marching Home: True Stories of the Men Who Went to War, and the Women Who Took Them Back.* Don Mills: Stoddart Publishing, 1991.

3502 WICKS, Ben. *Promise You'll Take Care of My Daughter: The Remarkable War Brides of World War II.* Don Mills: Stoddart Publishing, 1992.

3503 WILSON, Barbara M., ed. *Ontario and the First World War 1914-1918: A Collection of Documents.* Toronto: Champlain Society, University of Toronto Press, 1977.

3504 ZIEGLER, Mary. *We Serve That Men May Fly: The Story of the Women's Division Royal Canadian Air Force.* Hamilton: RCAF (W. D.) Association, 1973.

POLITICS

SINCE 1978, when Jill McCalla Vickers first posed the question, "Where are the women in Canadian politics?", historians and political scientists have made considerable progress in chronicling the political participation of women in Canada's past. Contrary to popular belief, that participation did not begin with the achievement of the federal franchise in 1920. Despite their lack of direct access to political power, women in the British North American colonies made their influence felt in a variety of ways, as documented by historians in recent studies of New Brunswick temperance crusades, the Family Compact in Upper Canada, the Lower Canadian Rebellions of 1837-38, the Escheat Movement on Prince Edward Island, and the Métis Resistance of 1870. The influence exerted by the wives and mistresses of Prime Ministers and Governors General, some of whom, like Lady Ishbel Aberdeen, have been active public figures in their own right, is also receiving scholarly attention.

When Canadian women received the franchise in the early twentieth century, there was widespread concern among political party elites that women would disrupt traditional voting patterns by voting as a block. These fears were dismissed in the 1920s, leaving both political strategists and political scientists free to ignore women altogether. Not until the 1970s did feminist scholars raise the possibility that women constituted a "second electorate" whose distinctive political behaviour merited serious consideration. Since then, studies of the "gender gap" in Canadian politics have proliferated. Canadian women have been studied extensively not only as voters but also as political candidates, politicians, and members of party elites. Women's presence in third parties, especially socialist parties, has been much more thoroughly documented than their relationship with traditional parties, but, for women politicians, the tension between "independence" and "partisanship" noted by Sylvia Bashevkin appears to have transcended party lines. Happily for historians, many of these educated and highly articulate women, including Thérèse Casgrain, Ellen Louks Fairclough, Judy LaMarsh, and Rosemary Brown, have left published memoirs, providing us with first-hand accounts of their difficult struggles to gain acceptance and legitimacy.

Women's achievement of legal personhood in the 1929 Persons Case, which led directly to the appointment of Cairine Wilson as Canada's first woman senator, has been described as a significant milestone in the history of Canadian women's struggle for political rights. More momentous, however, was the powerful and effective lobby by Canadian women's organizations in the early 1980s to ensure that the provisions of the Charter of Rights and Freedoms would apply equally to male and female persons. Women's participation in constitutional debates, and the complex relationship between nationalism and feminism in Quebec, have been major preoccupations of feminist political scientists and historians for nearly two decades, with the "Yvettes" episode of the 1980 referendum campaign attracting particular notice. Recent scholarship is also examining the implications of self-government for First Nations women and the role of women in reserve politics.

BIOGRAPHIES/MEMOIRS

3505 AITKEN, Kate and Byrne Hope Sanders. *Hey Ma! I Did It.* Toronto: Clarke Irwin, 1953.

3506 ARMSTRONG, Sally. *Mila.* Toronto: Macmillan, 1992. [Mila Pivnicki Mulroney]

3507 BÉIQUE, Mme F.L. *Quatre-vingts ans de souvenirs.* Montréal: Éditions Bernard Valiquette, 1939. [memoirs of a Senator's wife]

3508 BLACK, Martha Louise. *My Ninety Years.* Anchorage, AS: Northern History Library, Alaska Publishing Co., 1976.

3509 BROWN, Rosemary. *Being Brown: A Very Public Life.* Toronto: Random House, 1989.

3510 BRUN, Josette. "Marie de Saint-Étienne de La Tour." *Les Cahiers de la Société historique acadienne* 25, 4 (oct./déc. 1994): 244-62.

3511 BUECKERT, Dennis. *Above the Shoulders: A Critical Look at Kim Campbell.* Hull: Voyageur Publishing, 1993.

3512 BYNG, Viscountess Marie Evelyn (Moreton). *Up the Stream of Time.* Toronto: Macmillan of Canada, 1945.

3513 CARELESS, J.M.S. "George Brown and the Mother of Confederation." Canadian Historical Association. *Annual Report* (1960): 57-73.

3514 CARON, Anita and Lorraine Archambault, eds. *Thérèse Casgrain, une femme tenace et engagée.* Québec: Presses de l'Université Laval, 1993.

3515 CARSTAIRS, Sharon. *Not One of the Boys: A Woman, a Fighter, a Liberal with a Cause.* Toronto: Macmillan Canada, 1993.

3516 CASGRAIN, Thérèse. *Une femme chez les hommes.* Montréal: Éditions du Jour, 1971.

3517 CASGRAIN, Thérèse. *A Woman in a Man's World.* Translated by Joyce Marshall. Toronto: McClelland and Stewart, 1972.

3518 COPPS, Sheila. *Nobody's Baby: A Survival Guide to Politics.* Toronto: Deneau, 1986.

3519 CORMACK, Barbara Villy. *Perennials and Politics: The Life Story of the Hon. Irene Parlby.* Sherwood Park, AB: Professional Printing, 1968.

3520 CROWLEY, Terry. *Agnes Macphail and the Politics of Equality.* Toronto: James Lorimer & Company, 1990.

3521 CROWLEY, Terry. "Agnes Macphail and Canadian Working Women." *Labour/Le Travail* 28 (Fall 1991): 129-48.

3522 DAVIDSON, True. *The Golden Strings.* Toronto: Griffin House, 1973.

3523 DESBARATS, Lilian Scott. *Recollections.* Ottawa: n.p., 1957.

3524 DOBBIN, Murray. *The Politics of Kim Campbell: From School Trustee to Prime Minister.* Toronto: James Lorimer, 1993.

3525 DOYLE, James. "Barbara M. Hanley: First Woman Mayor in Canada." *Ontario History* 84, 2 (June 1992): 133-40.

3526 DUFFERIN, Marchioness of. *My Canadian Journal, 1872-1878* (1891). Toronto: Coles Publishing, 1971.

3527 FAIRCLOUGH, Ellen Louks. *Saturday's Child: Memoirs of Canada's First Female Cabinet Minister.* Edited and with an introduction by Margaret Conrad. Toronto: University of Toronto Press, 1995.

3528 FARRELL, Ann. *Grace MacInnis: A Story of Love and Integrity.* Toronto: Fitzhenry and Whiteside, 1994.

3529 FEAVER, George. "The Webbs in Canada: Fabian Pilgrims on the Canadian Frontier." *Canadian Historical Review* 58, 3 (September 1977): 263-76.

3530 FERGUSON, C. Bruce. *Alderman Abbie Lane of Halifax.* Halifax: Lancelot Press, 1976.

3531 FIFE, Robert. *Kim Campbell: The Making of a Politician.* Scarborough: HarperCollins, 1993.

3532 FONTAINE, Marie-Blanche. *Une femme face à la Confédération.* Montréal: Les éditions de l'homme, 1965.

3533 FORSYTH, Carolyn June. "'Whatever My Sex, I'm No Lady': Charlotte Whitton—Politician, Welfare Pioneer." *Makara* 2, 4 (1977): 27-31.

3534 FOWLER, Marian. "Portrait of Elizabeth Simcoe." *Ontario History* 69, 2 (1977): 79-100.

3535 FRYER, Mary Beacock. *Elizabeth Postuma Simcoe 1762-1850: A Biography.* Toronto: Dundurn Press, 1989.

3536 FRYER, Mary Beacock. "Mrs. Simcoe from Neglected Sources." *Ontario History* 82, 4 (December 1990): 305-15.

3537 GILLEN, Mollie. *The Prince and His Lady: The Love Story of the Duke of Kent and Madame de St Laurent.* Toronto: Grosvenor House 1970; Halifax: Goodread Biographies, 1985.

3538 GODSELL, Patricia, ed. *The Diary of Jane Ellice.* Canada: Oberon Press, 1975. [wife of Private Secretary of Lord Durham, 1838]

3539 HOLT, Simma. *The Other Mrs. Diefenbaker: A Biography of Edna May Brower.* Markham, ON: PaperJacks, 1982.

3540 IACOVETTA, Franca. "'A Respectable Feminist': The Political Career of Senator Cairine Wilson, 1921-1962." *Atlantis* 11 (Fall 1985): 108-23. Reprinted in *Beyond the Vote: Canadian Women and Politics,* eds. Linda Kealey and Joan Sangster, 63-85. Toronto: University of Toronto Press, 1989.

3541 INNIS, Mary Quayle, ed. *Mrs. Simcoe's Diary.* Toronto: Macmillan Co., 1965.

3542 JACKSON, R. "First Woman Speaker." *Atlantic Advocate* 63, 8 (April 1973: 17-18). [Muriel McQueen Fergusson]

3543 KIMMEL, David. "The Spirit of Canadian Democracy: Margaret Fairley and the Communist Cultural Worker's Responsibility to the People." *left history* 1, 1 (Spring 1993): 34-55.

3544 KIMMEL, David and Gregory S. Kealey. "With Our Own Hands: Margaret Fairley and the 'Real Makers' of Canada." *Labour/Le Travail* 31 (Spring 1993): 253-85.

3545 KNOWLES, Valerie. *First Person: A Biography of Cairine Wilson, Canada's First Woman Senator.* Toronto and Oxford: Dundurn Press, 1988.

3546 KNOWLES, Valerie. "First Lady of the Red Chamber." *The Beaver* 72, 5 (Oct.-Nov. 1992): 16-19. [Senator Cairine Wilson]

3547 LAMARSH, Judy. *Memoirs of a Bird in a Gilded Cage.* Toronto: McClelland and Stewart, 1969.

3548 LAMARSH, Judy. *A Very Political Lady.* Toronto: McClelland and Stewart, 1979.

3549 LAURIER, Wilfrid. *Dearest Emilie: The Love Letters of Sir Wilfrid Laurier to Madame Emilie Lavergne.* With a preface by Paul Gérin-Lajoie and introduction by Charles Fisher. Toronto: NC Press, 1989.

3550 LÉVESQUE, Andrée. "Les Québécoises et leur citoyenneté: la citoyenneté selon Éva Circé-Côté." In *La politique des droits: Citoyenneté et construction des genres aux 19e et 20e siècles,* eds. Hans Ulrich Jost, Monique Pavillon and François Valloton, 89-104. Paris: Éditions Kimé, 1994.

3551 LEWIS, S.P. *Grace: The Authorized Biography of Grace Woodsworth MacInnis, 1905-1991.* Madeira Park, BC: Harbour Publishing, 1993.

3552 LINDSTRÖM, Varpu. "Martta Laitinen's Story: Her Work for Socialism in Finland, Canada and the Soviet Karleia." *Canadian Woman Studies* 10, 4 (Winter 1989): 68-71.

3553 LOWE, Mick. *One Woman Army: The Life of Claire Culhane.* Toronto: Macmillan, 1992. [Communist labour/anti-war activist and "prison abolitionist"]

3554 MacDONALD, Agnes. "By Car and by Cow-Catcher." *Canada: An Historical Magazine* 2, 2 (December 1974): 41-63. [reprinted from *Murray's Magazine,* 1887]

3555 MacLEAN, Una. "The Honourable Irene Parlby." *Alberta Historical Review* 7, 2 (Spring 1959): 1-6.

3556 McDOWELL, Linda. "Harriet Dick—A Lady Ahead of Her Time?" *Manitoba Pageant* 20, 4 (Summer 1975): 11-13.

3557 McKENNA, Katherine M.J. "Anne Powell and the Early York Elite." In *"None was ever better...": The Loyalist Settlement of Ontario,* eds. S.F. Wise, D. Carter-Edwards and J. Witham, 31-43. Cornwall, ON: Ontario Historical Society, 1984.

3558 McLAUGHLIN, Audrey. *A Woman's Place: My Life and Politics.* Toronto: Mcfarlane Walter & Ross, 1992.

3559 McLAUGHLIN, Florence. *First Lady of Upper Canada.* Toronto: Burns and MacEachern, 1968, 1973. [Elizabeth Simcoe]

3560 McSHERRY, James. "The Invisible Lady: Sir John A. MacDonald's First Wife." *Canadian Bulletin of Medical History* 1, 1 (Summer 1984): 91-97.

3561 MIDDLETON, R.M., ed. *The Journal of Lady Aberdeen: The Okanagan Valley, 1890-1916.* Victoria: Sono Nis Press, 1986.

3562 MONCK, Frances Elizabeth Owen. *My Canadian Leaves.* London: Richard Bentley and Son, 1891. [wife of Governor General, 1864-65]

3563 NORCROSS, Elizabeth. "Mary Ellen Smith: The Right Woman in the Right Place at the Right Time." In *Not Just Pin Money: Selected Essays on the History of Women's Work in British Columbia,* eds. Barbara K. Latham and Roberta J. Pazdro, 357-64. Victoria: Camosun College, 1984.

3564 PENNINGTON, Doris, ed. *A Brave and Glorious Adventure: The Letters and Speeches of Agnes Macphail.* Toronto: Simon & Pierre, 1989.

3565 PENNINGTON, Doris. *Agnes Macphail, Reformer: Canada's First Female MP.* Toronto: Simon & Pierre, 1989.

3566 PROOM, Juliette. "Tilly Jean Rolston: She Knew How to Throw a Party." In *Not Just Pin Money: Selected Essays on the History of Women's Work in British Columbia,* eds. Barbara K. Latham and Roberta J. Pazdro, 381-88. Victoria: Camosun College, 1984.

3567 REYNOLDS, Louise. "'A Great Premier's Wife': Baroness Macdonald of Earnscliffe." *Canada: An Historical Magazine* 2, 2 (December 1974): 22-40.

3568 REYNOLDS, Louise. *Agnes: The Biography of Lady Macdonald.* Ottawa: Carleton University Press, 1990.

3569 RILEY, Susan. *Political Wives: The Lives of the Saints.* Toronto: Deneau, 1987.

3570 ROBERTS, Barbara. "'They Drove Him to Drink': Donald Creighton's Macdonald and His Wives." *Canada: An Historical Magazine* 3, 2 (Dec. 1975): 51-64.

3571 ROBERTSON, Heather. *More Than a Rose: Prime Ministers, Wives and Other Women.* Toronto: Seal Books, 1991.

3572 ROOME, Patricia. "Alberta Socialist: Amelia Turner." In *Citymakers: Calgarians After the Frontier,* eds. M. Foran and S.S. Jamieson, 225-46. Calgary: Historical Society of Alberta, 1987.

3573 ROOME, Patricia. "Amelia Turner and Calgary Labour Women, 1919-1935." In *Beyond the Vote: Canadian Women and Politics,* eds. Linda Kealey and Joan Sangster, 89-117. Toronto: University of Toronto Press, 1989. Reprinted in *The Prairie West: Historical Readings,* eds. R. Douglas Francis and Howard Palmer, 424-49. Edmonton: Pica Pica Press, 1992.

3574 SANGSTER, Joan. "The Making of a Socialist-Feminist: The Early Career of Beatrice Brigden, 1888-1941." *Atlantis* 13, 1 (Fall 1987): 13-28.

3575 SAYWELL, John T., ed. *The Canadian Journal of Lady Aberdeen, 1893-1898.* Toronto: University of Toronto Press, 1960.

3576 SMITH, M.B. "The Lady Nobody Knows." In *British Columbia: A Centennial Anthology*, ed. R.E. Watters, 472-81. Toronto, McClelland and Stewart, 1958. [Lady Amelia Douglas]

3577 STAMP, Robert M. *Royal Rebels: Princess Louise and the Marquis of Lorne*. Toronto and Oxford: Dundurn Press, 1988.

3578 STEWART, Margaret and Doris French. *Ask No Quarter: A Biography of Agnes Macphail*. Toronto: Longmans, Green, 1959.

3579 TAYLOR, Georgina M. "Gladys Strum: Farm Woman, Teacher and Politician." *Canadian Woman Studies* 7, 4 (Winter 1986): 89-93.

3580 TEMAIR, Ishbel Maria. Countess of Aberdeen and Lord Aberdeen. *We Twa: Reminiscences of Lord and Lady Aberdeen*, 2 vols. London: W. Collins, 1925.

3581 TROFIMENKOFF, Susan Mann. "Thérèse Casgrain and the CCF in Quebec." *Canadian Historical Review* 66 (June 1985): 125-53. Reprinted in *Beyond the Vote: Canadian Women and Politics*, eds. Linda Kealey and Joan Sangster, 139-68. Toronto: University of Toronto Press, 1989.

3582 VANCE, Catherine. *Not By Gods But By People...The Story of Bella Hall Gould*. Toronto: Progress Books, 1968.

3583 VAN STEEN, Marcus. *Governor Simcoe and His Lady*. Toronto: Hodder and Stoughton, 1968.

3584 VILLIERS, Hon. Katherine. *Memoirs of a Maid of Honour*. London: Ivor Nicholson and Watson, 1931. [Lady-in-Waiting to wife of the Governor General, 1914]

3585 WAITE, P.B. "Annie and the Bishop: John S.D. Thompson Goes To Ottawa, 1885." *Dalhousie Review* 57, 4 (Winter 1977/78): 605-18.

3586 WALSH, Susan. "The Peacock and the Guinea Hen: Political Profiles of Dorothy Gretchen Steeves and Grace McInnis." In *Not Just Pin Money: Selected Essays on the History of Women's Work in British Columbia*, eds. Barbara K. Latham and Roberta J. Pazdro, 365-79. Victoria: Camosun College, 1984. Reprinted in *The Neglected Majority: Essays in Canadian Women's History, Vol. 2*, eds. Alison Prentice and Susan Mann Trofimenkoff, 144-59. Toronto: McClelland and Stewart, 1985; and in *British Columbia Reconsidered: Essays on Women*, eds. Gillian Creese and Veronica Strong-Boag, 73-89. Vancouver: Press Gang Publishers, 1992.

3587 WRIGHT, J.F.C. *The Louise Lucas Story*. Montreal: Harvest House, 1965. [CCF activist, Saskatchewan, 1930s and 1940s]

POLITICAL PARTICIPATION

3588 ANDREW, Caroline. "Voluntarism and Women's Lobbying in Ottawa." In *Women and Counter-Power*, ed. Yolande Cohen, 118-23. Montreal: Black Rose Books, 1989. [Ottawa-Carleton Social Planning Council]

3589 AZOULAY, Dan. "Winning Women for Socialism: The Ontario CCF and Women, 1947-1961." *Labour/Le Travail* 36 (Fall 1995): 59-90.

3590 BASHEVKIN, Sylvia. "Women's Participation in Ontario Political Parties, 1971-1981." *Journal of Canadian Studies* 17 (Summer 1982): 44-54.

3591 BASHEVKIN, Sylvia. "Social Change and Political Partisanship: The Development of Women's Attitudes in Quebec, 1965-1979." *Comparative Political Studies* 16, 2 (July 1983): 147-72.

3592 BASHEVKIN, Sylvia. *Toeing the Lines: Women and Party Politics in English Canada*. Toronto: University of Toronto Press, 1985; Oxford University Press, 2nd edition, 1993.

3593 BASHEVKIN, Sylvia. "Independence Versus Partisanship: Dilemmas in the Political History of Women in English Canada." In *Rethinking Canada: The Promise of Women's History*, eds. Veronica Strong-Boag and Anita Clair Fellman, 246-75. Toronto: Copp Clark Pitman Ltd., 1986; 2nd edition, 415-45, 1991. [excerpted from *Toeing the Lines*]

3594 BASHEVKIN, Sylvia B. "Political Participation, Ambition and Feminism: Women in the Ontario Party Elites." *American Review of Canadian Studies* 23, 4 (November 1986): 457-80.

3595 BASHEVKIN, Sylvia B. "Political Parties and the Representation of Women." In *Canadian Parties in Transition: Discourse, Organization and Representation*, eds. Alain G. Gagnon and A. Brian Tanguay, 446-60. Scarborough: Nelson Canada, 1989.

3596 BEEBY, Dean. "Women in the Ontario CCF 1940-1950." *Ontario History* 74, 4 (Dec. 1982): 258-83.

3597 BITTERMANN, Rusty. "Women and the Escheat Movement: The Politics of Everyday Life on Prince Edward Island." In *Separate Spheres: Women's Worlds in the 19th Century Maritimes*, eds. Janet Guildford and Suzanne Morton, 23-38. Fredericton: Acadiensis Press, 1994.

3598 BLACK, Jerome H. and Nancy E. McGlen. "Male-Female Political Involvement Differentials in Canada, 1965-1974." *Canadian Journal of Political Science* 12, 3 (September 1979): 471-97.

3599 BOUCHARD, Pierrette. "Féminisme et marxisme: un dilemme pour la Ligue communiste canadienne." *Canadian Journal of Political Science* 20, 1 (March 1987): 57-78.

3600 BOYD, Rosamonde Ramsay. "Women and Politics in the United States and Canada." *Annals of the American Academy of Political and Social Sciences* 375 (January 1968): 52-57.

3601 BRODIE, M. Janine. "The Recruitment of Canadian Women Provincial Legislators, 1950-1975." *Atlantis* 2, 2, Part 1 (Spring 1977): 6-17.

3602 BRODIE, M. Janine. *Women and Politics in Canada*. Toronto: McGraw-Hill Ryerson, Ltd., 1984.

3603 BRODIE, M. Janine. "The Gender Factor and Leadership Conventions in Canada." In *Party Democracy in Canada*, ed. George Perlin, 172-87. Scarborough: Prentice-Hall, 1987.

3604 BRODIE, M. Janine. "Women and Politics: Many Participate but Few are Selected." In *Politics: Canada*, eds. P.W. Fox and G. White, 18-25. Toronto: McGraw-Hill Ryerson, 1987.

3605 BURNONVILLE, Francine. *Les femmes sont-elles allées trop loin? De la citoyenneté au pouvoir politique.* Montréal: Éditions Le Jour, 1992.

3606 BURSTYN, Varda. "The Waffle and the Women's Movement." *Studies in Political Economy* 33 (Autumn 1990): 175-84.

3607 BURT, Sandra. "Different Democracies? A Preliminary Examination of the Political Worlds of Canadian Men and Women." *Women and Politics* 6, 4 (Winter 1988): 57-79.

3608 BURT, Sandra. "Rethinking Canadian Politics: The Impact of Gender." In *Canadian Politics in the 1990s,* 3rd edition, eds. Michael Whittingham and Glen Williams, 208-20. Scarborough: Nelson Canada, 1990.

3609 BUSH, Patricia, Jocelyne Praud and Nadine Jubb. *Women and Politics, 1980-1990: A Selected Bibliography.* Toronto: Department of Political Science, York University, 1991.

3610 CAMPBELL, Gail G. "Disfranchised but not Quiescent: Women Petitioners in New Brunswick in the Mid-19th Century." *Acadiensis* 18, 2 (Spring 1989): 22-54. Reprinted in *Atlantic Canada Before Confederation: The Acadiensis Reader, Volume One,* 2nd edition, eds. P.A. Buckner and David Frank, 261-93. Fredericton: Acadiensis Press,1990; and in *Separate Spheres: Women's Worlds in the 19th Century Maritimes,* eds. Janet Guildford and Suzanne Morton, 39-66. Fredericton: Acadiensis Press, 1994. Abridged in *Rethinking Canada: The Promise of Women's History,* 2nd edition, eds. Veronica Strong-Boag and Anita Clair Fellman, 81-96. Toronto: Copp Clark Pitman Ltd., 1991.

3611 CANADIAN ADVISORY COUNCIL ON THE STATUS OF WOMEN. *Women in Politics: Becoming Full Partners.* Ottawa: Canadian Advisory Council on the Status of Women, 1988.

3612 CARBERT, Louise, B. Crow and D. Steinstra. "Voices from the Hinterland: The Study of Women's Political Participation in English Canada." In *Women in Politics: A Reader,* ed. L. Duke. Toronto: Prentice-Hall, 1991.

3613 CARTER, Connie and Eileen Daoust. "From Home to House: Women in the BC Legislature." In *Not Just Pin Money: Selected Essays on the History of Women's Work in British Columbia,* eds. Barbara K. Latham and Roberta J. Pazdro, 389-405. Victoria: Camosun College, 1984.

3614 CHISTE, Katherine Beaty. "Aboriginal Women and Self-Government: Challenging Leviathan." *American Indian Culture and Research Journal* 18, 3 (1994): 19-44.

3615 CLARKE, Harold D. and Allan Kornberg. "Moving Up the Political Escalator: Women Party Officials in the United States and Canada." *Journal of Politics* 41, 2 (May 1979): 442-77.

3616 COCHRANE, Jean. *Politics.* Women in Canadian Life Series. Toronto: Fitzhenry and Whiteside, 1977.

3617 COHEN, Yolande. "The Role of Associations in Democracy." In *Women and Counter-Power,* ed. Yolande Cohen, 220-30. Montreal: Black Rose Books, 1989.

3618 CROSSLEY, Diane. "The BC Liberal Party and Women's Reforms, 1916-1928." In *In Her Own Right: Selected Essays on Women's History in BC,* eds. Barbara Latham and Cathy Kess, 229-53. Victoria: Camosun College, 1980.

3619 DANDURAND, R. and E. Tardy. "Le phénomène des Yvettes à travers quelques quotidiens." In *Femmes et politique,* ed. Yolande Cohen, Montreal: Le Jour, 1981.

3620 DE SÈVE, Micheline. "Women, Political Action and Identity." In *Culture and Social Change: Social Movements in Québec and Ontario,* eds. Colin Leys and Marguerite Mendell, 128-39. Montreal: Black Rose Books, 1992.

3621 DESROCHERS, Lucie. *L'Accès des femmes au pouvoir politique: où en sont-elles?* Montreal: Conseil du statut de la femme, 1988.

3622 DROUILLY, Pierre. *Répertoire du personnel politique féminin, 1921-1989.* Québec: Bibliothèque de l'Assemblée Nationale, 1990.

3623 DROUILLY, Pierre and Jacques Dorion. *Candidates, députées et ministres: les femmes et les élections: suivi d'un Répertoire du personnel politique québécois féminin, 1921-1987.* Québec: Bibliothèque de l'Assemblée nationale, 1988.

3624 DUMONT, Micheline. "L'expérience historique des femmes face à l'avenir politique et constitutionnel du Québec." *L'Action Nationale* 81, 5 (mai 1991): 610-22.

3625 DUMONT, Micheline. "Les Québécoises dans la crise constitutionnelle canadienne." *Zeitschrift für Kanada-Studien* 12, 1 (1992): 25-34.

3626 ERICKSON, Lynda. "Political Women in a Partisan World: Women Party Activists in British Columbia in the 1980s." In *British Columbia Reconsidered: Essays on Women,* eds. Gillian Creese and Veronica Strong-Boag, 96-116. Vancouver: Press Gang Publishers, 1992.

3627 FINKEL, Alvin. "Populism and Gender: The UFA and Social Credit Experiences." *Journal of Canadian Studies* 27, 4 (Winter 1992/93): 76-97. Reprinted in *Canadian Women: A Reader,* eds. Wendy Mitchinson, *et al,* 299-319. Toronto: Harcourt Brace Canada, 1996.

3628 FISKE, Jo-Anne. "Native Women in Reserve Politics: Strategies and Struggles." In *Community Organization and the Canadian State,* eds. Roxana Ng, Gillian Walker and Jacob Muller, 131-46. Toronto: Garamond Press, 1990.

3629 FORTIN, J. *Women in the National Assembly: From the Right to Vote to the Sharing of Power.* Québec: Secrétariat à la condition féminine, 1990.

3630 FOURNIER, Francine. "Les femmes et la vie politique au Québec." In *Les femmes dans la société québécoise: Aspects historiques,* eds. Marie Lavigne and Yolande Pinard, 169-90. Montréal: Boréal Express, 1977. Reprinted in *Travailleuses et féministes: Les femmes dans la société québécoise,* eds. Marie Lavigne et Yolande Pinard, 337-58. Montréal: Boréal Express, 1983.

3631 FRAGER, Ruth A. "Politicized Housewives in the Jewish Communist Movement of Toronto, 1923-1933." In *Beyond the Vote: Canadian Women and Politics,* eds. Linda Kealey and Joan Sangster, 258-75. Toronto: University of Toronto Press, 1989.

3632 GALLANT, Cécile. *Women and the Acadian Renaissance.* Moncton, NB: Les Éditions d'Acadie, 1992.

3633 GARNER, John. *The Franchise and Politics in British North America.* Toronto: University of Toronto Press, 1969. [Ch. 12, "Minors, Women and Indians"]

3634 GIDENGIL, Elisabeth. "Economic Man—Social Woman? The Case of the Gender Gap in Support for the Canada-US Free Trade Agreement." *Comparative Political Studies* 28 (October 1995): 384-408.

3635 GILBERT, Marianne, *et al.* "Herstory." *Herstory and Policy,* 11-42. Vancouver: British Columbia New Democratic Party, 1977. [Women's Rights Committee of the British Columbia New Democratic Party, 1962-1977]

3636 GINGRAS, Anne-Marie. *Les Femmes et la politique: une relation très tumultueuse.* Montréal: Fédération des femmes du Québec, 1988.

3637 GREER, Allan. "La république des hommes: les Patriotes de 1837 face aux femmes." *Revue d'histoire de l'Amérique française* 44, 4 (printemps 1991): 507-28.

3638 HESKETH, Bob. "From Crusaders to Missionaries to Wives: Alberta Social Credit Women, 1932-1955." *Prairie Forum* 18, 1 (Spring 1993): 53-75.

3639 HOSEK, Chaviva. "Women and the Constitutional Process." In *And No One Cheered: Federalism, Democracy, and the Constitution Act,* eds. Keith Banting and Richard Simeon, 280-300. Toronto: Methuen, 1983.

3640 JEAN, Michèle and Marie Lavigne. "Quarante ans de vote...et après." *La gazette des femmes* 2, 1 (avril 1980): 8-10.

3641 JEAN, Michèle and Marie Lavigne. "Le phénomène des Yvettes." *Atlantis* 6 (1981): 17-23.

3642 JEAN, Michèle, Jacqueline Lamothe, Marie Lavigne and Jennifer Stoddart. "Nationalism and Feminism in Quebec: The 'Yvettes' Phenomenon." In *The Politics of Diversity: Feminism, Marxism and Nationalism,* eds. Roberta Hamilton and Michèle Barrett, 322-38. Montreal: Book Center, 1986.

3643 JEFFRIES, Theresa M. "Sechelt Women and Self-Government." *BC Studies* 89 (1991): 81-88. Reprinted in *In Celebration of Our Survival: The First Nations of British Columbia,* eds. Doreen Jensen and Cheryl Brooks, 81-86. Vancouver: University of British Columbia Press, 1991; and in *British Columbia Reconsidered: Essays on Women,* eds. Gillian Creese and Veronica Strong-Boag, 90-95. Vancouver: Press Gang Publishers, 1992.

3644 KAY, Barry J., Ronald D. Lambert, Steven D. Brown and James E. Curtis. "Gender and Political Activity in Canada, 1965-1984." *Canadian Journal of Political Science* 20, 4 (December 1987): 851-63.

3645 KAY, Barry J., *et al.* "Feminist Consciousness and the Canadian Electorate: A Review of National Election Studies 1965-1984." *Women and Politics* 8, 2 (1988): 1-22.

3646 KAY, Barry, Ronald Lambert, Steven Brown and James Curtis. "Single-Issue Interest Groups and the Canadian Electorate: The Case of Abortion in 1988." *Journal of Canadian Studies* 26, 2 (Summer 1991): 142-54.

3647 KEALEY, Linda. "Canadian Socialism and the Woman Question, 1900-1914." *Labour/Le Travail* 13 (1984): 77-100.

3648 KEALEY, Linda. "Women in the Canadian Socialist Movement, 1904-1914." In *Beyond the Vote: Canadian Women and Politics,* eds. Linda Kealey and Joan Sangster, 171-95. Toronto: University of Toronto Press, 1989.

3649 KEALEY, Linda and Joan Sangster, eds. *Beyond the Vote: Canadian Women and Politics.* Toronto: University of Toronto Press, 1989.

3650 KERMOAL, Nathalie. "Les rôles et les souffrances des femmes métisses lors de la Résistance de 1870 et de la Rébellion de 1885." *Prairie Forum* 19, 2 (Fall 1994): 153-68.

3651 KINNEAR, Mary. "Post-Suffrage Prairie Politics: Women Candidates in Winnipeg Municipal Elections, 1918-1938." *Prairie Forum* 16, 1 (Spring 1991): 41-58.

3652 KOHN, Walter S.G. "Women in the Canadian House of Commons." *American Review of Canadian Studies* 14, 3 (November 1984): 298-311.

3653 KOME, Penny. *The Taking of Twenty-eight: Women Challenge the Constitution.* Toronto: The Women's Press, 1983.

3654 KOPINAK, Kathryn M. "Women in Canadian Municipal Politics: Two Steps Forward, One Step Back." *Canadian Review of Sociology and Anthropology* 22, 3 (1985): 394-410. Reprinted in *Gender and Society: Creating a Canadian Women's Sociology*, ed. Arlene Tigar McLaren, 372-89. Toronto: Copp Clark Pitman, 1988.

3655 KOPINAK, Kathryn. "Gender Differences in Political Ideology in Canada." *Canadian Review of Sociology and Anthropology* 24, 1 (February 1987): 23-38.

3656 LALONDE, Michèle. "La femme de 1837-1838: Complice ou contre-révolutionnaire?" *Liberté* 7 (1965): 146-73.

3657 LAMOTHE, Jacqueline and Jennifer Stoddart. "Les Yvettes ou: Comment un parti politique traditionnel se sert encore une fois des femmes." *Atlantis* 6 (1981): 10-16.

3658 LAMOUREUX, Diane. *Citoyennes? Femmes, droit de vote et démocratie*. Montréal: Les Éditions du remue-ménage, 1989.

3659 LANGEVIN, Liane. *Missing Persons: Women in Canadian Federal Politics*. Ottawa: Canadian Advisory Council on the Status of Women, 1977.

3660 LANGFORD, Nanci. "'All That Glitters': The Political Apprenticeship of Alberta Women, 1916-1930." In *Standing on New Ground: Women in Alberta*, eds. Catherine A. Cavanaugh and Randi R. Warne, 71-85. Edmonton: University of Alberta Press, 1993.

3661 LATERREUR, Marc. "Correspondance Laurier— Mme Joseph Lavergne, 1891-1893." Canadian Historical Association. *Annual Report* (1964): 37-41.

3662 LINDSTRÖM-BEST, Varpu. "Finnish Socialist Women in Canada, 1890-1930." In *Beyond the Vote: Canadian Women and Politics*, eds. Linda Kealey and Joan Sangster, 196-216. Toronto: University of Toronto Press, 1989.

3663 MAILLÉ, Chantal. "Le vote des Québécoises aux élections fédérales et provinciales depuis 1921: une assiduité insoupçonnée." *Recherches féministes* 3, 1 (1990): 83-95.

3664 MAILLÉ, Chantal. *Les Québécoises à la conquête du pouvoir politique: Enquête sur l'émergence d'une élite féminine au Québec*. Montréal: Éditions Saint Martin, 1990.

3665 MAILLÉ, Chantal with Valentina Pollon. *Primed for Power: Women in Canadian Politics*. Ottawa: Canadian Advisory Council on the Status of Women, 1990.

3666 MANLEY, John. "Women and the Left in the 1930s: The Case of the Toronto CCF Women's Joint Committee." *Atlantis* 5 (Spring 1980): 100-17.

3667 MAPPIN, Patricia. *Canadian Women in Politics: From Victims to Victors*. Edmonton: Legislative Assembly of Alberta, 1991.

3668 MARCHILDON, Rudy G. "The 'Persons' Controversy: The Legal Aspects of the Fight for Women Senators." *Atlantis* 6, 2 (Spring 1981): 99-113.

3669 MATHEWS, Robin. "Susanna Moodie, Pink Toryism and Nineteenth Century Ideas of Canadian Identity." *Journal of Canadian Studies* 10, 3 (August 1975): 3-15.

3670 McCALLUM, Sandra K. and Anne A. McLellan. "The Person's Case: A Beginning Not the End." *Women as Persons*, Special Publication No. 8. *Resources for Feminist Research* (Fall 1980): 76-79.

3671 McDOWELL, Linda. "Some Women Candidates for the Manitoba Legislature." *Transactions of the Historical and Scientific Society of Manitoba* 3, 32 (1975/76): 5-20.

3672 McKEE-ALLAIN, Isabelle. "Les Acadiennes d'aujourd'hui: des gardiennes de la race et/ou de la main-d'oeuvre à bon marché." In *Les Acadiens: État de la recherche*, eds. Jacques Lapointe and André Leclerc, 178-86. Québec: Conseil de la vie française en Amérique, 1987.

3673 McKENNA, Katherine M.J. "The Role of Women in the Establishment of Social Status in Early Upper Canada." *Ontario History* 83, 3 (September 1990): 179-206. Reprinted in *The Invention of Canada: Readings in Pre-Confederation History*, ed. Chad Gaffield, 312-33. Toronto: Copp Clark Longman Ltd., 1994.

3674 MEGYERY, Kathy, ed. *Women in Canadian Politics: Toward Equity in Representation*. Research Studies, Vol. 6, Royal Commission on Electoral Reform and Party Financing. Toronto and Oxford: Dundurn Press, 1991.

3675 MYERS, Patricia A. "'A Noble Effort': The National Federation of Liberal Women of Canada, 1928-1973." In *Beyond the Vote: Canadian Women and Politics*, eds. Linda Kealey and Joan Sangster, 39-62. Toronto: University of Toronto Press, 1989.

3676 NATIVE WOMEN'S ASSOCIATION OF CANADA. *Native Women and Self-Government: A Discussion Paper*. Ottawa: Native Women's Association of Canada, 1992.

3677 NEWTON, Janice. "Women and *Cotton's Weekly*: A Study of Women and Socialism in Canada, 1909." *Resources for Feminist Research* 8 (Fall 1980): 58-60.

3678 NEWTON, Janice. "From Wage Slave to White Slave: The Prostitution Controversy and the Early Canadian Left." In *Beyond the Vote: Canadian Women and Politics*, eds. Linda Kealey and Joan Sangster, 217-36. Toronto: University of Toronto Press, 1989.

3679 NEWTON, Janice. "The Alchemy of Politicization: Socialist Women and the Early Canadian Left." In *Gender Conflicts: New Essays in Women's History*, eds. Franca Iacovetta and Mariana Valverde, 118-48. Toronto: University of Toronto Press, 1992.

3680 NEWTON, Janice. *The Feminist Challenge to the Canadian Left, 1900-1918*. Montreal and Kingston: McGill-Queen's University Press, 1995.

3681 PAYNE-O'CONNOR, Josephine. *Sharing Power: Women in Politics, Vancouver Island Profiles*. Victoria: Kachine Press, 1986.

3682 PELLETIER, Réjean and Manon Tremblay. "Les femmes sont-elles candidates dans des circonscriptions perdues d'avance: de l'examen d'une croyance." *Canadian Journal of Political Science* 25, 2 (1992): 249-67.

3683 PRÉVOST, Nicole, *et al. Les femmes sur le chemin du pouvoir*. Québec: Conseil du statut de la femme, 1988.

3684 REEVES-MORACHE, Marcelle. "La Canadienne pendant les troubles de 1837-38." *Revue d'histoire de l'Amérique française* 5, 1 (juin 1951).

3685 REEVES-MORACHE, Marcelle. "Doux visage de la Canadienne d'autrefois." *Québec-Histoire* 1, 3/4 (juillet/décembre 1971): 88-95. [Rebellions of 1837-38]

3686 REEVES-MORACHE, Marcelle. *Les Québécoises de 1837-1838*. Montréal: Éditions Albert St-Martin, Société nationale populaire du Québec, 1975.

3687 ROBINSON, Gertrude, J. and Armande Saint-Jean. *Women Politicians and their Media Coverage: A Generational Analysis*. Ottawa: Royal Commission on Electoral Reform and Party Financing, 1991.

3688 SANGSTER, Joan. "The Communist Party and the Woman Question, 1922-1929." *Labour/Le Travail* 15 (Spring 1985): 25-56.

3689 SANGSTER, Joan. "The Role of Women in the Early CCF, 1933-1940." In *Beyond the Vote: Canadian Women and Politics,* eds. Linda Kealey and Joan Sangster, 118-38. Toronto: University of Toronto Press, 1989.

3690 SANGSTER, Joan. *Dreams of Equality: Women on the Canadian Left, 1920-1950*. Toronto: McClelland and Stewart, 1989.

3691 SHARPE, Sydney. *The Gilded Ghetto: Women and Political Power in Canada*. Toronto: Harper Collins, 1994.

3692 SIMARD, Carolle. "Changement et insertion des femmes dans le système politique." *Politique* 5 (hiver 1984): 27-50.

3693 SIMARD, Carolle. "Les femmes dans l'État." In *L'ère des Libéraux: le pouvoir fédéral de 1963 à 1984,* eds. Yves Bélanger and Dorval Brunelle, 357-81. Sillery: Presses de l'Université du Québec, 1988.

3694 SPENCER, Samia I. "Women in Government: A View from Quebec." *Québec Studies* 4 (1986): 90-117.

3695 SPENCER, Samia I. and William A. Spencer. "Female Deputies and Cabinet Members in Quebec: Past and Present." *American Review of Canadian Studies* 22, 3 (Autumn 1992): 329-50.

3696 STONE, Olive M. "Canadian Women as Legal Persons: How Alberta Combined Judicial, Executive and Legislative Powers to Win Full Legal Personality for All Canadian Women." *Alberta Law Review* 17, 3 (1979): 331-71.

3697 STUDLAR, Donley T. and Richard E. Matland. "The Growth of Women's Representation in the Canadian House of Commons and the Election of 1984: A Reappraisal." *Canadian Journal of Political Science* 27, 1 (March 1994): 53-80.

3698 TARDY, Évelyne. "Les femmes et la campagne référendaire." In *Québec: Un pays incertain,* 184-203. Montréal: Québec-Amérique, 1980.

3699 TAYLOR, Georgina M. "'The Women...Shall Help to Lead the Way': Saskatchewan CCF-NDP Women Candidates in Provincial and Federal Elections, 1934-1965." In *"Building the Co-operative Commonwealth": Essays on the Democratic Socialist Tradition in Canada,* ed. J. William Brennan, 141-60. Regina: Canadian Plains Research Centre, University of Regina, 1984.

3700 TAYLOR, Georgina M. "Oral Sources for Women's History: Saskatchewan Co-operative Commonwealth Women." Canadian Oral History Association. *Journal* 7 (1984): 28-36.

3701 TAYLOR, Georgina M. "'Should I Drown Myself Now or Later?' The Isolation of Rural Women in Saskatchewan and Their Participation in the Homemakers' Clubs, the Farm Movement and the Co-operative Commonwealth Federation, 1910-1967." In *Women, Isolation and Bonding: The Ecology of Gender,* ed. Kathleen Storrie, 79-100. Toronto: Methuen, 1987.

3702 TREMBLAY, Manon. "Les femmes, des candidates moins performantes que les hommes? Une analyse des votes obtenus par les candidates et candidats du Québec à une élection fédérale canadienne, 1945-1993." *International Journal of Canadian Studies* 11 (Spring 1995): 59-82.

3703 TRIMBLE, Linda. "A Few Good Women: Female Legislators in Alberta, 1972-1991." In *Standing on New Ground: Women in Alberta,* eds. Catherine A. Cavanaugh and Randi R. Warne, 87-118. Edmonton: University of Alberta Press, 1993.

3704 UHLANER, Carole J. "La participation politique des femmes au Québec: 1965-1977." In *Comportement électoral au Québec,* ed. Jean Crête, 201-42. Chicoutimi, QC: G. Morin, 1984.

3705 VICKERS, Jill McCalla. "Where are the Women in Canadian Politics?" *Atlantis* 3 (Spring 1978): 40-51.

3706 VICKERS, Jill McCalla. "Feminist Approaches to Women in Politics." In *Beyond the Vote: Canadian Women and Politics,* eds. Linda Kealey and Joan Sangster, 16-36. Toronto: University of Toronto Press, 1989.

3707 VICKERS, Jill McCalla and M. Janine Brodie. "Canada." In *The Politics of the Second Electorate: Women and Public Participation,* eds. Joni Lovenduski and Jill Hills, 52-82. London/Boston: Routledge & Kegan Paul, 1981.

3708 **WEIR**, Lorna. "Social Movement Activism in the Formation of Ontario New Democratic Party Policy on Abortion, 1982-1984." *Labour/Le Travail* 35 (Spring 1995): 163-93.

3709 **WILSON**, Marion C., ed. *Women in Federal Politics: A Bio-Bibliography.* Ottawa: National Library of Canada, 1975.

3710 **ZABORSKY**, D. "Feminist Politics: the Feminist Party of Canada." *Women's Studies International Forum* 10, 6 (1987): 613-21.

RELIGION

THE LAST FIVE years have seen extraordinary growth in the scholarship on women and religion in Canadian history. In marked contrast to the 1970s when both students and scholars in secular Canadian universities were uncomfortable with the subject of religion, the power of religious beliefs and institutions in Canada's past has now become a respectable subject of study for historians of politics, social services and social reform movements, moral regulation, education, and even family life. While feminist historians in the 1970s tended to approach religion as ideology and as inherently oppressive to women, a more ambivalent, and frequently sympathetic approach predominates in the scholarship of the past decade.

For the past twenty-five years, the role of Roman Catholic French-speaking female religious orders in Quebec society has attracted considerable attention from feminist scholars. Of particular interest has been the prominent place of women religious in New France, where they established and administered a network of social services that had no counterpart among English-speaking North American colonies, and their crucial role in the educational and healthcare systems in Quebec, often operating under the auspices of the Catholic Church, from the flowering of religious communities in the 1840s, until the 1960s and the Quiet Revolution. Canadian women's historians have been especially interested in the question of the relationship of Quebec women religious to turn-of-the-century feminism and to the possibility of their detrimental impact on the organization and mobilization of laywomen. Much energy has also been expended investigating the appeal of membership in a female religious community to francophone Quebec women, and in examining convent life as an alternative to marriage and motherhood. Recent scholarship on race and the nature of cross-cultural contacts in colonial contexts has sparked renewed interest in Catholic missions to the First Nations in New France, with special attention to the figures of Marie de l'Incarnation and Kateri Tekakwitha.

By comparison, English-speaking Roman Catholic communities are only beginning to receive serious scholarly attention from historians in other parts of the country. As recently as 1992, Ruth Compton Brouwer described the topic of women and religion in English-speaking Canada as languishing in a state of "unacknowledged quarantine" due to the disinterest of feminist scholars. That a significant shift is occurring is suggested by the outpouring of scholarly studies of Protestant churchwomen's organizations and their role in the provision of social services, of evangelical Protestantism and its implications for individual women and for turn-of-the-century feminism, and of the careers of early women preachers and later struggles for the ordination of women. Of particular note are the many studies of female missionaries both as representatives of a new career alternative for middle-class women and as agents of cross-cultural contacts both within Canada and overseas.

Recently, there are indications of a growing interest in the history of Anabaptist women in Canada, especially Mennonites. As yet, there is only a small body of historical scholarship on Jewish women in Canada, and no historical work at all on women of other religious traditions such as Islam or Hinduism. Some passing attention has been paid by women's historians to spiritualism and witchcraft in Canadian history but the New Age Movement of the past several decades has received no serious study.

GENERAL

3711   ALLEN, Christine. "Women in Colonial French America." In *Women and Religion in America, vol. 2, The Colonial and Revolutionary Period*, eds. Rosemary Radford Ruether and Rosemary Skinner Keller, 79-131. San Francisco: Harper and Row, 1983.

3712   ANDERSON, Grace and Joanne Clark. *God Calls, Man Chooses: An Analysis of Women's Experience in Canadian Church History*. Burlington: Trinity Press, 1990.

3713   BROUWER, Ruth Compton. "Transcending the 'unacknowledged quarantine': Putting Religion into English-Canadian Women's History." *Journal of Canadian Studies* 27, 3 (Fall 1992): 47-61.

3714   DUMAIS, Monique. "Présence des discours féministes en sciences religieuses au Canada." *Journal of Canadian Studies* 27, 3 (Fall 1992): 62-74.

3715   HIGGINS, Michael W. and Douglas R. Letson, eds. *Women and the Church: A Sourcebook*. Toronto: Griffin House, 1986.

3716   LEGGE, Marilyn J. "Colourful differences: 'Otherness' and image of God for Canadian feminist theologies." *Studies in Religion* 21, 1 (1992): 67-80.

3717   LEONARD, Ellen. "Experience as a source for theology: A Canadian and Feminist Perspective." *Studies in Religion* 19, 2 (Spring 1990): 143-62.

3718   MUIR, Elizabeth Gillan and Marilyn Färdig Whiteley, eds. *Changing Roles of Women within the Christian Church in Canada*. Toronto: University of Toronto Press, 1995.

3719   MUIR, Elizabeth Gillan and Marilyn Färdig Whiteley. "Putting Together the Puzzle of Canadian Women's Christian Work." In *Changing Roles of Women within the Christian Church in Canada*, eds. Elizabeth Gillan Muir and Marilyn Färdig Whiteley, 3-16. Toronto: University of Toronto Press, 1995.

3720   POLLOCK, Gordon. "'Tin hat' on the disciples of Brigham Young': Nova Scotians, Mormons and Polygamy, 1920-1928." *Nova Scotia Historical Review* 14, 1 (1994): 41-68.

JUDAISM

3721   COSSMAN, Brenda, *et al*, eds. "Jewish Women." A special issue of *Fireweed* 35 (Spring 1992).

3722   DRAPER, Paula J. "The Role of Canadian Jewish Women in Historical Perspective." In *Canadian Jewish Women of Today: Who's Who of Canadian Jewish Women*, ed. Edmond Y. Lipsitz, 3-10. Downsview: J.E.S.L. Educational Products, 1983.

3723   DRAPER, Paula J. and Janice B. Karlinsky. "Abraham's Daughters: Women, Charity and Power in the Canadian Jewish Community." In *Looking into My Sister's Eyes: An Exploration in Women's History*, ed. Jean Burnet, 75-90. Toronto: Multicultural History Society of Ontario, 1986.

3724   FISHBANE, Simcha. "A Female Rite of Passage in a Montreal Modern Orthodox Synagogue: the Bat Mitzvah Ceremony." In *Renewing Our Days: Montreal Jews in the Twentieth Century*, eds. Ira Robinson and Mervin Butovsky. Montreal: Véhicule Press, 1995.

3725   MEDJUCK, Sheva. "If I Cannot Dance to It, It's Not My Revolution: Jewish Feminism in Canada Today." In *The Jews in Canada*, eds. Robert Brym, William Shaffir and Morton Weinfeld, Toronto: Oxford University Press, 1993.

3726   ZUCKERMAN, Francine, ed. *Half the Kingdom: Seven Jewish Feminists*. Montreal: Véhicule Press, 1990.

PROTESTANTISM

3727   ANDERSON, Cora. "Shall Women Preach? Principles and Practices in the Salvation Army and in the Methodist Church in Ontario, 1882-1900." *Conrad Grebel Review* 8, 3 (Fall 1990): 275-88.

3728   ARCHER, S.A., comp. *A Heroine of the North: Memories of Charlotte Selina Bompas (1830-1917), Wife of the First Bishop of Selkirk (Yukon)*. Toronto: Macmillan Co., 1929.

3729   AUSTIN, Alvyn. *Aimee Semple McPherson*. Toronto: Fitzhenry and Whiteside, 1980.

3730   BARBER, Marilyn. "The Motor Caravan Mission: Anglican Women Workers on the Canadian Frontier in the New Era." In *Changing Roles of Women within the Christian Church in Canada*, eds. Elizabeth Gillan Muir and Marilyn Färdig Whiteley, 219-37. Toronto: University of Toronto Press, 1995.

3731   BARNETT-COWAN, Alyson. "The Bishop's Messengers: Harbingers of the Ordination of Women." *Journal of the Canadian Church Historical Society* 28, 2 (October 1986): 75-91.

3732   BARNETT-COWAN, Alyson. "The Bishop's Messengers: Women in Ministry in Northwestern Manitoba, 1928-1979." In *The Anglican Church and the World of Western Canada, 1820-1970*, ed. Barry Ferguson, 176-87. Regina: Canadian Plains Research Center, University of Regina, 1991.

3733   BAYS, Patricia, ed. *Partners in the Dance: Stories of Canadian Women in Ministry*. Toronto: Anglican Book Center, 1994.

3734   BENTALL, Shirley. "Lucy Lowe Bagnall—Missionary Pioneer and Distinguished Educator." In *Costly Vision: The Baptist Pilgrimage in Canada*, ed. Jarold Knox Zeman, 59-67. Burlington: Welch, 1988.

3735   BRADBROOK, Pauline. "A brief account of the Church of England Women's Association in Newfoundland." Canadian Church Historical Society. *Journal* 28, 2 (October 1986): 92-105.

3736   BROUWER, Ruth Compton. "The Canadian Methodist Church and Ecclesiastical Suffrage for Women, 1902-1914." Canadian Methodist Historical Society. *Papers* 2 (1977): 1-27.

3737 BROUWER, Ruth Compton. "The 'Between-Age' Christianity of Agnes Machar." *Canadian Historical Review* 65, 3 (September 1984): 347-70.

3738 BROUWER, Ruth Compton. "'New Women' for God: Marion Fairweather and the Founding of the Canadian Presbyterian Mission in Central India, 1873-80." Canadian Historical Association. *Historical Papers* (1984).

3739 BROUWER, Ruth Compton. "Presbyterian Women and the Foreign Missionary Movement, 1876-1914: The Context of a Calling." Canadian Society of Presbyterian History. *Papers* (1984/85): 1-24.

3740 BROUWER, Ruth Compton. "Wooing 'the Heathen' and the Raj: Aspects of Women's Work in the Canadian Presbyterian Mission in Central India, 1877-1914." *Proceedings of the Canadian Society of Church History* (1987): 17-32.

3741 BROUWER, Ruth Compton. "'Far Indeed from the Meekest of Women': Marion Fairweather and the Canadian Presbyterian Mission in Central India, 1873-1880." In *Canadian Protestant and Catholic Missions, 1820s-1960s: Historical Essays in Honour of John Webster Grant,* eds. John S. Moir and C.T. McIntire. New York: Peter Lang, 1988.

3742 BROUWER, Ruth Compton. "Opening Doors Through Social Service: Aspects of Women's Work in the Canadian Presbyterian Mission in Central India, 1877-1914." In Leslie A. Flemming, ed. *Women's Work for Women: Missionaries and Social Change in Asia.* Boulder: Westview Press, 1989, 11-34. Reprinted in *Prophets, Priests, and Prodigals: Readings in Canadian Religious History, 1608 to Present,* eds. Mark G. McGowan and David B. Marshall, 241-61. Toronto: McGraw-Hill Ryerson, 1992.

3743 BROUWER, Ruth Compton. *New Women for God: Canadian Presbyterian Women and India Missions, 1876-1914.* Toronto: University of Toronto Press, 1990.

3744 BUCK, Ruth Matheson, ed. "Documents of Western History: The Journal of Eleanor Shepphird Matheson, 1920." *Saskatchewan History* 22, 2 (Spring 1969): 66-73 and 22, 3 (Autumn 1969): 109-17. [wife of a missionary to Indian reserves]

3745 CADDELL, G.L. *Barbara Heck: Pioneer Methodist.* Cleveland, TN: Pathway Press, 1966.

3746 CLARKE, F.E., ed. *My Mother's Journal.* Boston and Chicago: United Society of Christian Endeavour, c. 1911. [Ottawa and Aylmer, 1850s]

3747 COLLINS, Michael. "Sister Aimee." *The Beaver* 69, 3 (June/July 1989): 28-32. [Aimee Semple McPherson]

3748 COLWELL, Judith. "The Role of Women in the Nineteenth Century Baptist Church of Ontario." Canadian Society of Church History. *Papers* 15 (1985): 31-57.

3749 COLWELL, Judith. "The Fitch Twins: Poets and Social Workers." In *Costly Vision: The Baptist Pilgrimage in Canada,* ed. Jarold Knox Zeman, 43-58. Burlington: Welch, 1988.

3750 COOK, Ramsay. "Francis Marion Beynon and the Crisis of Christian Reformism." In *The West and the Nation: Essays in Honour of W.L. Morton,* eds. Carl Berger and Ramsay Cook, 187-208. Toronto: McClelland and Stewart, 1976.

3751 COOK, Sharon Anne. "The Ontario Young Woman's Christian Temperance Union: A Study in Female Evangelicalism, 1874-1930." In *Changing Roles of Women within the Christian Church in Canada,* eds. Elizabeth Gillan Muir and Marilyn Färdig Whiteley, 299-320. Toronto: University of Toronto Press, 1995.

3752 COOK, Sharon Anne. "'A Gallant Little Band': Bertha Wright and the Late Nineteenth-Century Evangelical Woman." *Journal of the Canadian Church Historical Society* 37, 1 (April 1995): 3-22.

3753 COOK, Sharon Anne. *"Through Sunshine and Shadow": The Woman's Christian Temperance Union, Evangelicalism, and Reform in Ontario, 1874-1930.* Montreal and Kingston: McGill-Queen's University Press, 1995.

3754 CORBETT, Beatrice. "Susan Moulton Fraser McMaster." *Inland Seas* 31, 3 (Fall 1975): 192-200. [Baptist church and founding of McMaster University]

3755 CUMMINGS, Emily W. *Our Story... Woman's Auxiliary of the Missionary Society Of the Church of England in Canada, 1885-1928.* Toronto: Garden City Press, c. 1928.

3756 DAVIES, Gwendolyn. "'In the Garden of Christ': Methodist Literary Women in Nineteenth-Century Canada." In *The Contribution of Methodism to Atlantic Canada,* eds. Charles H.H. Scobie and John Webster Grant. Montreal and Kingston: McGill-Queen's University Press, 1992.

3757 DAVY, Shirley, ed. *Women, Work and Worship in the United Church of Canada.* Toronto: United Church of Canada, 1983.

3758 DAVY, Shirley. "Why Church Women's Organizations Thrived." *Canadian Woman Studies* 2 (Winter 1983): 50-61.

3759 DEKAR, Paul R. "Envoys of Peace: Canadian Baptist Women Missionaries as Peacemakers." In *Costly Vision: The Baptist Pilgrimage in Canada,* ed. Jarold Knox Zeman, 85-99. Burlington: Welch, 1988.

3760 DOBBIN, L.L. "Mrs. Catherine Gillespie Motherwell, Pioneer Teacher and Missionary." *Saskatchewan History* 14, 1 (Winter 1961): 7-26.

3761 DONNELLY, Mary Rose and Heather Dau. *Katherine.* Winfield, BC: Wood Lake Books, 1992. [a Canadian missionary in China]

3762 EPP, Frank H. and Marlene G. Epp. "The Diverse Roles of Ontario Mennonite Women." In *Looking into My Sister's Eyes: An Exploration in Women's History*, ed. Jean Burnet, 223-42. Toronto: Multicultural History Society of Ontario, 1986.

3763 EPP, Marlene. "Women in Canadian Mennonite History: Uncovering the 'Underside.'" *Journal of Mennonite Studies* 5 (1987): 90-107.

3764 EPP, Marlene. "The Mennonite Girls' Homes of Winnipeg: A Home Away from Home." *Journal of Mennonite Studies* 6 (1988): 100-14.

3765 EPP, Marlene. "Women's History and Mennonite Archives." *Archivaria* 30 (Summer 1990): 167-70.

3766 EPP, Marlene. "Carrying the Banner of Nonconformity: Ontario Mennonite Women and the Dress Question." *Conrad Grebel Review* 8, 3 (Fall 1990): 237-57.

3767 EPP, Marlene. "Nonconformity and Nonresistance: What Did It Mean to Mennonite Women?" In *Changing Roles of Women within the Christian Church in Canada*, eds. Elizabeth Gillan Muir and Marilyn Färdig Whiteley, 55-74. Toronto: University of Toronto Press, 1995.

3768 FAST, Vera. *Missionary on Wheels: Eva Hasell and the Sunday School Caravan Mission.* Toronto: Anglican Book Centre, 1979.

3769 FAST, Vera K. "Eva Hasell and the Caravan Mission." In *The Anglican Church and the World of Western Canada, 1820-1970*, ed. Barry Ferguson, 167-75. Regina: Canadian Plains Research Center, University of Regina, 1991.

3770 FLETCHER-MARSH, Wendy L. "The Limitations and Opportunity of Gender: Women and Ecclesiastical Structures in Canadian Anglicanism, 1920-55." *Journal of the Canadian Church Historical Society* 37, 1 (April 1995): 41-54.

3771 FRIESEN, John W. "Pacifism and Anastasia's Doukhobor Village." *Alberta History* 41, 1 (Winter 1993): 14-19.

3772 GAGAN, Rosemary. "'More Than 'A Lure to the Gilded Bower of Matrimony': The Education of Methodist Women Missionaries, 1881-1925." *Historical Studies in Education* 1, 2 (Fall 1989): 239-59.

3773 GAGAN, Rosemary. "The Methodist Background of Canadian WMS Missionaries." Canadian Methodist Historical Society. *Papers* (1989): 115-36.

3774 GAGAN, Rosemary. *A Sensitive Independence: Canadian Methodist Women Missionaries in Canada and the Orient, 1881-1925.* Montreal and Kingston: McGill-Queen's University Press, 1992.

3775 GAGAN, Rosemary R. "Two Sexes Warring in the Bosom of a Single Mission Station: Feminism in the Canadian Methodist Japan Mission, 1881-1895." In *Changing Roles of Women within the Christian Church in Canada*, eds. Elizabeth Gillan Muir and Marilyn Färdig Whiteley, 136-57. Toronto: University of Toronto Press, 1995.

3776 GOFORTH, Rosalind. *Climbing.* Toronto: Evangelical Publishers, 1940. [memoirs of a missionary]

3777 GRAHAM, Ferne. "Katharine Hockin: A Woman in Mission." *Touchstone* 10, 2 (May 1992): 11-19.

3778 GRANT, John Webster. "Presbyterian Women and the Indians." Canadian Society of Presbyterian History. *Papers* (1978): 21-36.

3779 GRANT, John Webster. "Two-thirds of the Revenue: Presbyterian Women and Native Indian Missions." In *Changing Roles of Women within the Christian Church in Canada*, eds. Elizabeth Gillan Muir and Marilyn Färdig Whiteley, 99-116. Toronto: University of Toronto Press, 1995.

3780 GRAY, Leslie R., ed. "Phoebe Roberts' Diary of a Quaker Missionary Journey to Upper Canada." *Ontario History* 42, 1 (1950): 7-46.

3781 HAGLUND, Diane. "Side Road on the Journey to Autonomy: The Diaconate Prior to Church Union." In *Women, Work and Worship in the United Church of Canada*, ed. Shirley Davy, 206-27. Toronto: United Church of Canada, 1983.

3782 HALL, Alfreda. *A Baptist Minister, A Woman: The Story of the Reverend Mae Benedict Field, Canadian Baptist Missionary and Minister.* Toronto: Published privately by Alfreda Hall, Yorkminster Park Baptist Church, 1983.

3783 HALL, Nancy. "The Professionalisation of Women Workers in the Methodist, Presbyterian, and United Churches of Canada." In *First Days, Fighting Days: Women in Manitoba History*, ed. Mary Kinnear, 120-33. Regina: Canadian Plains Research Center, University of Regina, 1987.

3784 HALLETT, Mary E. "Nellie McClung and the Fight for the Ordination of Women in the United Church of Canada." *Atlantis* 4, 2 (Spring 1979): 2-16.

3785 HALLETT, Mary. "Ladies—We Give You the Pulpit!" *Touchstone* 4, 1 (January 1986): 6-17.

3786 HALLETT, Mary. "Lydia Gruchy—The First Woman Ordained in the United Church of Canada." *Touchstone* 4, 1 (January 1986): 18-23.

3787 HAMILTON, Sylvia. "The Women at the Well: African Baptist Women Organize." In *And Still We Rise: Feminist Political Mobilizing in Contemporary Canada*, ed. Linda Carty, 189-203. Toronto: Women's Press, 1993.

3788 HANCOCK, Carol L. "Nellie L. McClung." *Touchstone* 1, 1 (January 1983): 31-35.

3789 HANCOCK, Carol L. "Nellie L. McClung: A part of a pattern." In *Prairie Spirit: Perspectives on the Heritage of the United Church of Canada in the West*, eds. Dennis L. Butcher *et al*, 203-15. Winnipeg: University of Manitoba Press, 1985.

3790 HEADON, Christopher. "Women and Organized Religion in Mid and Late Nineteenth Century Canada." *Journal of the Canadian Church Historical Society* 20, 1/2 (March-June 1978): 3-18.

3791 HENDERSON, Mary Gillespie. *Memories of My Early Years.* Montreal: Charters and Charters, 1937. [minister's wife]

3792 HILL, Meredith. "The Women Workers of the Diocese of Athabasca, 1930-1970." *Journal of the Canadian Church Historical Society* 28, 2 (1986): 63-74.

3793 HOBBS, Helen G. "'What She Could': Women in the Gospel Workers Church, 1902-1955." In *Changing Roles of Women within the Christian Church in Canada,* eds. Elizabeth Gillan Muir and Marilyn Färdig Whiteley, 201-18. Toronto: University of Toronto Press, 1995.

3794 HODDER, Morley F. "Stella Anna Burry: Dedicated Deaconess and Pioneer Community Worker." *Touchstone* 3, 3 (October 1985): 24-33.

3795 HOLMES, Mrs. Robert. "Experiences of a Missionary's Wife." *Alberta Historical Review* 12, 2 (Spring 1964): 18-25. [Lesser Slave Lake, 1902-1914]

3796 HOOKE, Katharine N. "Women's Teaching and Service: An Anglican Perspective in Ontario, 1867-1930." *Journal of the Canadian Church Historical Society* 33, 2 (October 1990): 3-23.

3797 HUME, Blanche. *Barbara Heck.* Toronto: Ryerson Press, 1930.

3798 IVISON, Stuart. "The Activities of Margaret Edwards Cole (1853-1929) as a Baptist Church Member, Journalist, Temperance Worker and Advocate of Women's Suffrage in Canada." *Canadian Society of Church History Papers* (1984): 140-55.

3799 JOHNSON, Geoffrey. "The Road to Winsome Womanhood: The Canadian Presbyterian Mission among East Indian Women and Girls in Trinidad, 1868-1939." In *Canadian Protestant and Catholic Missions, 1820s-1960s: Historical Essays in Honour of John Webster Grant,* eds. John S. Moir and C.T. McIntire. New York: Peter Lang, 1988.

3800 KEMPER, Alison. "Deaconess as Urban Missionary and Ideal Woman: Church of England Initiatives in Toronto, 1890-1895." In *Canadian Protestant and Catholic Missions, 1820s-1960s: Historical Essays in Honour of John Webster Grant,* eds. John S. Moir and C.T. McIntire. New York: Peter Lang, 1988.

3801 KLASSEN, Pamela E. *Going by the Moon and the Stars: Stories of Two Russian Mennonite Women.* Waterloo: Wilfrid Laurier University Press, 1994.

3802 KORINEK, Valerie J. "No Women Need Apply: The Ordination of Women in the United Church, 1918-65." *Canadian Historical Review* 74, 4 (December 1993): 473-509.

3803 LANE, Hannah M. "'Wife, Mother, Sister, Friend': Methodist Women in St. Stephen, New Brunswick, 1861-1880." In *Separate Spheres: Women's Worlds in the 19th Century Maritimes,* eds. Janet Guildford and Suzanne Morton, 93-117. Fredericton: Acadiensis Press, 1994.

3804 MacDONALD, Heidi. "A Century of Anglican Women Religious in Two Nova Scotian Hospitals." *Journal of the Canadian Church Historical Society* 37, 1 (April 1995): 23-40.

3805 MacEWAN, Grant. "Elizabeth Boyd McDougall: First in the Southwest." In *And Mighty Women Too,* ed. Grant MacEwan, 42-50. Saskatoon: Western Producer Prairie Books, 1975.

3806 MacFARLANE, Mary Anne. "Faithful and Courageous Handmaidens: Deaconesses in the United Church of Canada, 1925-1945." In *Changing Roles of Women within the Christian Church in Canada,* eds. Elizabeth Gillan Muir and Marilyn Färdig Whiteley, 238-58. Toronto: University of Toronto Press, 1995.

3807 MacLEOD, G. Enid and Irene M.J. Szuler. "Medical Missionaries of the Early Female Medical Graduates, 1894-1929." *Nova Scotia Medical Journal* 69, 1 (February 1990): 7-14, 30.

3808 MARKS, Lynne. "The 'Hallelujah Lasses': Working-Class Women in the Salvation Army in English Canada, 1882-92." In *Gender Conflicts: New Essays in Women's History,* eds. Franca Iacovetta and Mariana Valverde, 67-117. Toronto: University of Toronto Press, 1992. Abridged in *Rethinking Canada: The Promise of Women's History,* 2nd edition, eds. Veronica Strong-Boag and Anita Clair Fellman, 182-205. Toronto: Copp Clark Pitman Ltd., 1991.

3809 MARR, Lucille. "Anabaptist Women of the North: Peers in the Faith, Subordinates in Marriage." *Mennonite Quarterly Review* 61 (October 1987): 347-62.

3810 MARR, Lucille. "Hierarchy, Gender and the Goals of the Religious Educators in the Canadian Presbyterian, Methodist and United Churches, 1919-39." *Studies in Religion* 20, 1 (1991): 65-74.

3811 MARR, M. Lucille. "Church Teen Clubs, Feminized Organizations? Tuxis Boys, Trail Rangers, and Canadian Girls in Training, 1919-1939." *Historical Studies in Education* 3, 2 (Fall 1991): 249-67.

3812 MARR, Lucille. "Sunday School Teaching: A Women's Enterprise: A Case Study from the Canadian Methodist, Presbyterian and United Church Tradition, 1919-1939." *Histoire sociale/Social History* XXVI, 52 (November 1993): 329-44.

3813 McDOUGALL, Mrs. John. "Incidents of Mission Life, 1874." *Alberta Historical Review* 14, 1 (Winter 1966): 26-29.

3814 McFARLANE, John. "Dr. Jessie Saulteaux: The Faith Goes On." *Touchstone* 9, 1 (January 1991): 41-46.

3815 McKEEN, R. Catherine. "Harriet Christie: The People-Maker Lady." *Touchstone* 8, 2 (May 1990): 20-34.

3816 McKENNA, Katherine M.J. "'The Union between Faith and Good Works': The Life of Harriet Dobbs Cartwright, 1808-1887." In *Changing Roles of Women within the Christian Church in Canada*, eds. Elizabeth Gillan Muir and Marilyn Färdig Whiteley, 284-98. Toronto: University of Toronto Press, 1995.

3817 McMULLEN, Lorraine. "Lily Dougall: The Religious Vision of a Canadian Novelist." *Studies in Religion* 16, 1 (Winter 1987): 79-90. [Baptist]

3818 McPHERSON, Margaret E. "Head, heart and purse: The Presbyterian Women's Missionary Society in Canada, 1876-1925." In *Prairie Spirit: Perspectives on the Heritage of the United Church of Canada in the West*, eds. Dennis L. Butcher *et al*, 147-70. Winnipeg: University of Manitoba Press, 1985.

3819 McPHERSON, Margaret E. "'From Caretakers to Participants': Amanda Norris MacKay and the Presbyterian Women's Missionary Society, 1876-1925." *Touchstone* 9, 3 (September 1991): 32-44.

3820 MERRICK, Eerl C. *These Impossible Women—100 Years—The Story of the Union Baptist Women's Missionary Union of the Maritime Provinces.* Fredericton: Brunswick Press, 1970.

3821 MILLER, Naomi. "Sunday School Vans and Their Drivers." *British Columbia Historical News* 27, 4 (Fall 1994): 10-14.

3822 MITCHINSON, Wendy. "Canadian Women and Church Missionary Societies in the Nineteenth Century: A Step Towards Independence." *Atlantis* 2, 2, Part II (Spring 1977): 57-75.

3823 MORGAN, Cecilia. "Gender, Religion and Rural Society: Quaker Women in Norwich, Ontario, 1820-1880." *Ontario History* 82, 4 (Dec. 1990): 273-87.

3824 MORRISON, George M. "Emma Douse Crosby, 'Mother of the Tsimpsheans.'" *Touchstone* 4, 3 (October 1986): 38-45.

3825 MORTON, W.L. with Vera Fast, ed. *God's Galloping Girl: The Peace River Diaries of Monica Storrs, 1929-1931.* Vancouver: University of British Columbia Press, 1979.

3826 MUIR, Elizabeth. "Petticoats in the Pulpit: Three Early Canadian Methodist Women." Canadian Society of Church History. *Papers* (1984): 26-49.

3827 MUIR, Elizabeth. "Woman as Preacher: Early 19th Century Canadians." In *Women: Images, Role-Models*, 195-201. Ottawa: Canadian Research Institute for the Advancement of Women, 1984.

3828 MUIR, Elizabeth. "Methodist Women Preachers: An Overview." Canadian Methodist Historical Society. *Papers* (1987): 46-57.

3829 MUIR, Elizabeth. "The Bark Schoolhouse: Methodist Episcopal Missionary Women in Upper Canada, 1827-1833." In *Canadian Protestant and Catholic Missions, 1820s-1960s: Historical Essays in Honour of John Webster Grant*, eds. John S. Moir and C.T. McIntire, 23-47. New York: Peter Lang, 1988.

3830 MUIR, Elizabeth Gillan. *Petticoats in the Pulpit: The Story of Early Nineteenth-Century Methodist Women Preachers in Upper Canada.* Toronto: United Church Publishing House, 1991.

3831 MUIR, Elizabeth Gillan. "Beyond the Bounds of Acceptable Behaviour: Methodist Women Preachers in the Early Nineteenth Century." In *Changing Roles of Women within the Christian Church in Canada*, eds. Elizabeth Gillan Muir and Marilyn Färdig Whiteley, 161-82. Toronto: University of Toronto Press, 1995.

3832 OWEN, Michael. "'Keeping Canada God's Country': Presbyterian School-homes for Ruthenian Children." In *Prairie Spirit: Perspectives on the Heritage of the United Church of Canada in the West*, eds. Dennis L. Butcher, *et al*, 184-201. Winnipeg: University of Manitoba Press, 1985.

3833 OWEN, Michael. "'Lighting the Pathways for New Canadians': Methodist and United Church WMS Missions in Eastern Alberta, 1904-1940." In *Standing on New Ground: Women in Alberta*, eds. Catherine A. Cavanaugh and Randi R. Warne, 1-18. Edmonton: University of Alberta Press, 1993.

3834 PARSONS, Shelagh. "Women and Power in the United Church of Canada." In *Women, Work and Worship in the United Church of Canada*, ed. S. Davy, 172-88. Toronto: United Church of Canada, 1983.

3835 PEDERSEN, Diana. "'The Power of True Christian Women': The YWCA and Evangelical Womanhood in the Late Nineteenth Century." In *Changing Roles of Women within the Christian Church in Canada*, eds. Elizabeth Gillan Muir and Marilyn Färdig Whiteley, 321-37. Toronto: University of Toronto Press, 1995.

3836 PEDERSEN, Diana. "Providing a Woman's Conscience: The YWCA, Female Evangelicalism, and the Girl in the City, 1870-1930." In *Canadian Women: A Reader*, eds. Wendy Mitchinson, *et al*, 194-210. Toronto: Harcourt Brace Canada, 1996.

3837 PETER, Karl and Ian Whitaker. "The Changing Roles of Hutterite Women." *Prairie Forum* 7, 2 (Fall 1982): 267-77.

3838 PETERS, Victor. *All Things Common: The Hutterian Way of Life.* Minneapolis: University of Minnesota Press, 1965.

3839 PRANG, Margaret. "'The Girl God Would Have Me Be': The Canadian Girls in Training, 1915-1939." *Canadian Historical Review* 66, 2 (1985): 154-84.

3840 PRANG, Margaret. "Caroline Macdonald and Prison Work in Japan." University of Toronto—York University Joint Centre for Asia Pacific Studies. *Working Paper Series* (March 1988): 1-34.

3841 PRANG, Margaret. "Caroline Macdonald of Japan." *Touchstone* 6, 1 (January 1988): 33-42.

3842 PRANG, Margaret. *A Heart at Leisure from Itself: Caroline Macdonald of Japan.* Vancouver: University of British Columbia Press, 1995.

3843 REID, Elspeth M. "Women's Missionary Records in the Presbyterian Archives." *Archivaria* 30 (Summer 1990): 171-79.

3844 RICH, Elain Sommers. *Mennonite Women: A Story of God's Faithfulness, 1683-1983.* Kitchener: Heald Press, 1985.

3845 RIDOUT, Katherine. "A Woman of Mission: The Religious and Cultural Odyssey of Agnes Wintemute Coates." *Canadian Historical Review* 71, 2 (June 1990): 208-44.

3846 ROBERTSON, Allen and E.B. Carolene, eds. *Memoir of Mrs Eliza Ann Chipman: Wife of the Rev. William Chipman, of Pleasant Valley, Cornwallis.* Hantsport, NS: Lancelot Press, 1989.

3847 ROSS, H. Miriam. "Shaping a vision of mission: Early influences on the United Baptist Woman's Missionary Union." In *An Abiding Conviction: Maritime Baptists and Their World,* ed. Robert S. Wilson, 83-107. Hantsport, NS: Lancelot Press, 1988.

3848 ROSS, H. Miriam. "Women's Strategies for Mission: Hannah Maria Norris Blazes the Trail in 1870." Canadian Society of Church History. *Papers* (1992): 5-23.

3849 ROSS, H. Miriam. "Sharing a Vision: Maritime Baptist Women Educate for Mission, 1870-1920." In *Changing Roles of Women within the Christian Church in Canada,* eds. Elizabeth Gillan Muir and Marilyn Färdig Whiteley, 77-98. Toronto: University of Toronto Press, 1995.

3850 ROSS, H. Miriam. "'Sisters' in the Homeland: Vision for Mission among Maritime Baptist Women, 1867-1920." In *A Fragile Stability: Definition and Redefinition of Maritime Baptist Identity,* ed. David T. Priestly. Hantsport, NS: Lancelot Press, 1995.

3851 ROTH, Lorraine. *Willing Service: Stories of Ontario Mennonite Women.* Waterloo: Mennonite Historical Society of Ontario, 1992.

3852 RUTHERDALE, Myra. "Models of G/race and Boundaries of Gender: Anglican Women Missionaries in Canada's North, 1860-1945." *Canadian Woman Studies* 14, 4 (Fall 1994): 44-47.

3853 RUTHERDALE, Myra. "Revisiting Colonization Through Gender: Anglican Missionary Women in the Pacific Northwest and the Arctic, 1860-1945." *BC Studies* 104 (Winter 1994/95): 3-24.

3854 SHIPLEY, Nan. *Anna and the Indians.* Toronto: Ryerson Press, 1955. [Anna Jane Young Gaudin, Northwest Territories]

3855 SHIPLEY, Nan. *Frances and the Crees.* Toronto: Ryerson Press 1957. [Frances Pickell Stevens, Northwest Territories]

3856 SINCLAIR, Donna. *Crossing Worlds: The Story of the Woman's Missionary Society of the United Church of Canada.* Toronto: United Church Publishing House, 1992.

3857 SINCLAIR, Donna. "Victoria Cheung." *Touchstone* 11, 3 (September 1993): 37-43.

3858 SISSONS, C.B., ed. "Letters of Mary Lewis Ryerson from 1832 to 1842." *Victoria University Occasional Papers,* 1 (April 1948): 5-18. [wife of a Methodist preacher]

3859 STACKHOUSE, John G., Jr. "Women in Public Ministry in 20th-century Canadian and American Evangelicalism: Five Models." *Studies in Religion* 17, 3 (Fall 1988): 471-85.

3860 STIMPSON, Geoffrey. *A Century of Service: A History of the Women's Auxiliary and Anglican Church Women in Canada and the Diocese of Qu'Appelle.* Regina: Qu'Appelle Diocesan Anglican Church Women, 1986.

3861 THOMAS, John. "Servants of the Church: Canadian Methodist Deaconess Work, 1890-1926." *Canadian Historical Review* 65, 3 (September 1984): 371-95.

3862 THOMAS, Mrs. P.A. "Kindly Dispatch Miss Gadsby." *North* 17, 1 (January/February 1970): 6-19. [missionary in Great Slave Lake area, 1879-1903]

3863 THOMPSON, Arthur N. "The Wife of the Missionary." *Journal of the Canadian Church Historical Society* 15, 2 (June 1973): 35-44.

3864 VAN DIE Marguerite. "'A Woman's Awakening': Evangelical Belief and Female Spirituality in Mid-Nineteenth-Century Canada." In *Canadian Women: A Reader,* eds. Wendy Mitchinson, *et al,* 49-68. Toronto: Harcourt Brace Canada, 1996.

3865 VAN DIEREN, Karen. "The Response of the WMS to the Immigration of Asian Women, 1888-1942." In *Not Just Pin Money: Selected Essays on the History of Women's Work in British Columbia,* eds. Barbara K. Latham and Roberta J. Pazdro, 79-97. Victoria: Camosun College, 1984. [Women's Missionary Society]

3866 WARNE, Randi R. "Christian Feminism in the United Church of Canada: Resources in Culture and Tradition." In *Women, Work, and Worship in the United Church of Canada,* ed. Shirley Davy, 189-205. Toronto: United Church of Canada, 1983.

3867 WARNE, Randi R. "Nellie McClung's Social Gospel." In *Changing Roles of Women within the Christian Church in Canada,* eds. Elizabeth Gillan Muir and Marilyn Färdig Whiteley, 338-54. Toronto: University of Toronto Press, 1995.

3868 WHELEN, Gloria. "Maria Grant, 1854-1937: The Life and Times of an Early Twentieth Century Christian." In *In Her Own Right: Selected Essays on Women's History in BC,* eds. Barbara Latham and Cathy Kess, 125-46. Victoria: Camosun College, 1980.

3869 WHITEHEAD, Margaret. "'Women Were Made for Such Things': Women Missionaries in British Columbia, 1850s-1940s." *Atlantis* 14, 1 (1988): 141-50.

3870 WHITEHEAD, Margaret. "'A Useful Christian Woman': First Nations' Women and Protestant Missionary Work in British Columbia." *Atlantis* 18, 1/2 (Fall/Winter 1992–Spring/Summer 1993): 142-66.

3871 WHITEHEAD, Margaret. "'Let the Women Keep Silence': Women Missionary Preaching in British Columbia, 1860s-1940s." In *Changing Roles of Women within the Christian Church in Canada*, eds. Elizabeth Gillan Muir and Marilyn Färdig Whiteley, 117-135. Toronto: University of Toronto Press, 1995.

3872 WHITELEY, Marilyn. "Modest, Unaffected and Fully Consecrated: Lady Evangelists in Canadian Methodism, 1884-1900." Canadian Methodist Historical Society. *Papers* (1987): 18-31. Reprinted in *Changing Roles of Women within the Christian Church in Canada*, eds. Elizabeth Gillan Muir and Marilyn Färdig Whiteley, 183-200. Toronto: University of Toronto Press, 1995.

3873 WHITELEY, Marilyn Färdig. "Women Learning to Work for Women: The Chinese Rescue Home in Victoria, BC." Canadian Society of Church History. *Papers* (1988): 87-96.

3874 WHITELEY, Marilyn Färdig. "Called to a More Suitable Mission: Conversion in the Life of Annie Leake Tuttle." Canadian Methodist Historical Society. *Papers* (1988): 34-47.

3875 WHITELEY, Marilyn Färdig. "Elizabeth Dimsdale Aikenhead: 'Lady Evangelist.'" *Touchstone* 7, 1 (January 1989): 35-41.

3876 WHITELEY, Marilyn Färdig. "'Doing Just About What They Please': Ladies' Aids in Ontario Methodism." *Ontario History* 82, 4 (Dec. 1990): 289-304.

3877 WHITELEY, Marilyn Färdig. "Conversion and Corrective Domesticity: The Mission of the Chinese Rescue Home." Canadian Methodist Historical Society. *Papers* (1990): 158-73.

3878 WHITELEY, Marilyn Färdig. "'My Highest Motive in Writing': Evangelical Empowerment in the Autobiography of Annie Leake Tuttle." Canadian Society of Church History. *Papers* (1992): 25-38.

3879 WHITELEY, Marilyn Färdig. "'Allee Samee Melican Lady': Imperialism and Negotiation at the Chinese Rescue Home." *Resources for Feminist Research* 22 (1993): 45-50.

3880 WILSON, Lois. *Turning the World Upside Down: A Memoir.* Toronto: Doubleday Canada, 1989.

3881 WITHROW, William Henry. *Barbara Heck: A Tale of Methodism.* Toronto: William Briggs, 1895.

3882 YORK, Eva Rose. *Why My Dream Comes True.* Toronto: n.p., 1935. [memoir of a Toronto evangelist and founder of home for unwed mothers]

ROMAN CATHOLICISM

3883 AGNES, Sister Mary. *The Congregation of the Sisters of St. Joseph.* Toronto: St. Joseph's Convent, 1951.

3884 AINSLEY, Claire. "Les communautés religieuses féminines du diocèse de Montréal de 1650 à 1986." In *L'Eglise de Montréal, aperçus d'hier et d'aujourd'hui, 1836-1986*, 198-235. Montréal: Fides, 1986.

3885 ALLEN, Prudence, RSM. "Six Canadian Women: Their Call, Their Witness, Their Legacy." *Canadian Catholic Review* 5, 7 (July/Aug. 1987): 246-58.

3886 ARCAND, R. "Expansion et déclin d'une communauté religieuse au Québec, les Soeurs de Sainte Anne (1928-1969)." *Cahiers d'histoire* 9, 3 (printemps 1989): 41-64.

3887 ARSENAULT, Laurette. "Les Fondatrices." *Revue d'histoire et de traditions populaires de la Gaspésie* 54/55 (avril/septembre 1976): 88-96. [Hôtel-Dieu de Gaspé]

3888 BARABÉ, Paul-Henri. *Un Siècle de Miséricorde.* Montréal: Les Soeurs de Miséricorde, 1948.

3889 BARCLAY, Robert George. "Grey Nuns Voyage to Red River (1844)." *The Beaver* (Winter 1966): 15-23.

3890 BAUDOIN, Marthe. "The Religious of the Sacred Heart in Canada, 1842-1980." Canadian Catholic Historical Association. *Study Sessions* (1981): 43-60.

3891 BAUDOIN, Marthe. *Les religieuses du Sacré-Coeur au Canada.* Montréal: Religieuses du Sacré-Coeur, 1992.

3892 BEAUPRÉ, Marie. *Jeanne Le Ber, première recluse du Canada français, 1662-1714.* Montréal: Éditions ACF, 1939.

3893 BEGNAL, Reverend Sister Calista. "The Sisters of the Congregation of Notre-Dame, Nineteenth Century Kingston." Canadian Catholic Historical Association. *Study Sessions* 40 (1973): 27-33.

3894 BEGNAL, Calista. "The Daughters of Marguerite Bourgeoys in Toronto, 1932-1982." Canadian Catholic Historical Association. *Study Sessions* 49 (1982): 73-86.

3895 BÉLANGER, Anne. "Une éducatrice d'hier pour aujourd'hui: Marie Guyart de l'Incarnation." La Société canadienne d'histoire de l'Église catholique. *Sessions d'étude* 39 (1972): 55-64.

3896 BÉLANGER, Diane and Lucie Rozon. *Les religieuses au Québec.* Montréal: Éditions Libre Expression, 1982.

3897 BERGERON, Angèle. "Les Augustines en terre québécoise." *Eglise canadienne* 23, 3 (février 1990): 82-84.

3898 BERNIER, Hélène, ed. *Marguerite Bourgeoys.* Montréal and Paris: Fides, 1958.

3899 BÉRUBÉ, Véronique F.J. "Les Filles de Jésus." *Revue d'histoire du Bas-Saint-Laurent* 9, 2 (mai/août 1983): 32-40.

3900 BOCKING, D.H. "The First Mission of the Sisters Faithful Companions of Jesus in the North-West Territories, 1883." *Saskatchewan History* 36, 2 (Spring 1983): 70-77.

3901 BONIN, Sr. Marie. "The Grey Nuns and the Red River Settlement." *Manitoba History* 11 (Spring 1986): 12-14.

3902 BOUCHARD, Gérard. "Familles à prêtres? Familles à soeurs? Parenté et recrutement religieux au Saguenay (1882-1947)." *Revue d'histoire de l'Amérique française* 48, 4 (printemps 1995): 483-508.

3903 BOUCHARD, Mary Alban, CSJ. "Pioneers Forever: The Community of St. Joseph in Toronto and Their Ventures in Social Welfare and Health Care." In *Catholics at the 'Gathering Place': Historical Essays in the Archdiocese of Toronto, 1841-1991,* eds. Mark McGowan and Brian Clarke, 105-18. Hamilton: Dundurn Press, 1993.

3904 BOUCHER, Ghislaine. *Du Centre à la Croix: Marie de l'Incarnation, 1599-1692: Symbolique Spirituelle.* Sillery: Les Religieuses de Jésus-Marie, 1976.

3905 BOUCHER, Ghislaine. *Dieu et Satan dans la vie de Catherine de Saint-Augustin 1632-1668.* Montréal: Bellarmin, 1979.

3906 BURSTIN, H.V. *Blessed Kateri Tekakwitha: Iroquois Virgin, 1656-1680.* Québec: Éditions Magnificat, 1981.

3907 CARON, Anita, ed. *Femmes et pouvoir dans l'Église.* Montréal: VLB éditeur, 1991.

3908 CARON, Anita, *et al.* "Femmes dans l'Église catholique: Statut et pouvoir (1945-1985)." *Annales de L'ACFAS* 58 (1990): 399.

3909 CASGRAIN, Henri-Raymond. *Histoire de la Mère Marie de l'Incarnation, première Superiéure des Ursulines.* Montréal: [n.p.], 1964.

3910 CHABOT, Marie-Emmanuelle. "Marie Guyart de l'Incarnation." In *The Clear Spirit: Twenty Canadian Women and Their Times,* ed. Mary Quayle Innis, 25-41. Toronto: University of Toronto Press, 1966.

3911 CHABOT, Marie-Emmanuelle. "Les Ursulines de Québec en 1850." La société d'histoire de l'Église catholique. *Sessions d'étude* (1969): 75-92.

3912 CHABOT, Emmanuelle. *Elles ont tout donné: Les Ursulines de Stanstead de 1884 à 1934.* Québec: Anne Sigier, 1983.

3913 CHALMERS, J.W. "Marguerite Bourgeoys, Preceptress of New France." In *Profiles of Canadian Educators,* eds. Robert S. Patterson, *et al*, 4-20. Toronto: D.C. Heath Canada, 1974.

3914 CHARBONNEAU, Fernande. *Marguerite Bourgeoys: Traits Spirituels et Mystiques.* Montréal: Éditions Paulines, 1983.

3915 CHICOINE, Emilia. *La Métaire de Marguerite Bourgeoys à la Pointe-Saint-Charles.* Montréal: Fides, 1986.

3916 CIMICHELLA, André-M. *Marguerite Bourgeoys, lumière sur notre ville.* Montréal: Éditions Jésus-Marie et notre temps, 1974.

3917 CLARKE, Brian. "The Parish and the Hearth: Women's Confraternities and the Devotional Revolution among the Irish Catholics of Toronto, 1850-85." In *Creed and Culture: The Place of English-Speaking Catholics in Canadian Society,* eds. Terrence Murphy and Gerald Stortz, 185-203. Montreal and Kingston: McGill-Queen's University Press, 1993.

3918 CLERMONT, Norman. "Catherine Tekakwitha: 1656-1680." *Culture* 7, 1 (1987): 47-53.

3919 COATES, Colin. "Authority and Illegitimacy in New France: The Burial of Bishop Saint-Vallier and Madeleine de Verchères vs. the Priest of Batiscan." *Histoire sociale/Social History* XXII, 43 (May 1989): 65-90.

3920 COMBY, Jean, ed. *L'itinéraire mystique d'une femme: rencontre avec Marie de l'Incarnation, ursuline.* Paris/Montréal: Éditions du Cerf et Bellarmin, 1993.

3921 COOPER, Barbara J. "The Convent: An Option for Québécoises, 1930-1950." *Canadian Woman Studies* 7, 4 (Winter 1986): 31-35.

3922 COOPER, Barbara J. "A Re-examination of the Early Years of the Institute of the Blessed Virgin Mary (Loretto Sisters) in Toronto." In *Catholics at the 'Gathering Place': Historical Essays in the Archdiocese of Toronto, 1841-1991,* eds. Mark McGowan and Brian Clarke, 89-104. Hamilton: Dundurn Press, 1993.

3923 CÔTÉ, Pauline. "Socialisations sacrales, acteurs féminins, post-modernité: les femmes dans le Renouveau charismatique canadien francophone." *Studies in Religion* 17, 3 (Summer 1988): 329-46.

3924 CUNEO, Michael W. *Catholics Against the Church: Anti-Abortion Protest in Toronto, 1969-1985.* Toronto: University of Toronto Press, 1989.

3925 D'ALLAIRE, Micheline. "Les prétentions des religieuses de l'hôpital-général de Québec sur le palais épiscopal de Québec." *Revue d'histoire de l'Amérique française* 23, 1 (juin 1969): 53-67.

3926 D'ALLAIRE, Micheline. "Origine sociale des religieuses de l'Hôpital-Général de Québec." *Revue d'histoire de l'Amérique française* 23, 4 (mars 1970): 559-82.

3927 D'ALLAIRE, Micheline. *L'Hôpital-Général de Québec, 1692-1764.* Montréal: Fides, 1971.

3928 D'ALLAIRE, Micheline. "Conditions matérielles requises pour devenir religieuse au XVIIIe siècle." In *L'Hôtel-Dieu de Montréal, 1642-1973,* ed. Michel Allard, 183-208. Montréal: Les Cahiers de Québec, 1973.

3929 D'ALLAIRE, Micheline. "Jeanne Mance à Montréal en 1642: Une femme d'action qui force les événements." *Forces* 23 (1973): 39-46.

3930 D'ALLAIRE, Micheline. *Vingt ans de crise chez les religieuses du Québec, 1960-1980.* Montréal Éditions Bergeron, 1984.

3931 D'ALLAIRE, Micheline. *Les dots des religieuses au Canada français, 1639-1800: étude économique et sociale.* Montréal: Hurtubise HMH, 1986.

3932 D'ALLAIRE, Micheline. "Mon approche de l'histoire des communautés religieuses." La société canadienne d'histoire de l'Église catholique. *Études d'histoire religieuse* 57 (1990): 37-43.

3933 D'AMOUR, Soeur Cécile. "L'Oeuvre des Missionaires Oblats de Sacré-Coeur et de la Marie Immaculée dans l'Église." La Société canadienne d'histoire de l'Église catholique. *Sessions d'étude* (1970): 247-58.

3934 DANYLEWYCZ, Marta. "Changing Relationships: Nuns and Feminists in Montreal, 1890-1925." *Histoire sociale/Social History* 28 (November 1981). Reprinted in *The Neglected Majority: Essays in Canadian Women's History, Vol. 2*, eds. Alison Prentice and Susan Mann Trofimenkoff, 122-43. Toronto: McClelland and Stewart, 1985; and in *Prophets, Priests, and Prodigals: Readings in Canadian Religious History, 1608 to Present*, eds. Mark G. McGowan and David B. Marshall, 191-213. Toronto: McGraw-Hill Ryerson, 1992.

3935 DANYLEWYCZ, Marta. *Taking the Veil: An Alternative to Marriage, Motherhood and Spinsterhood in Quebec, 1840-1920*. Toronto: McClelland and Stewart, 1987.

3936 DANYLEWYCZ, Marta. "In Their Own Right: Convents, An Organized Expression of Women's Aspirations." In *Rethinking Canada: The Promise of Women's History*, 2nd edition, eds. Veronica Strong-Boag and Anita Clair Fellman, 161-81. Toronto: Copp Clark Pitman Ltd., 1991. [excerpted from *Taking the Veil*]

3937 DAVELUY, Marie-Claire. *Dix fondatrices canadiennes-francaise: Profils mystiques*. Québec: L'Imprimerie Françiscaine Missionaire, 1947.

3938 DAVELUY, Marie-Claire. *Jeanne Mance 1606-1673*. Montréal: Fides, 1962.

3939 DAVELUY, Marie-Claire, ed. *La Société de Notre-Dame-de-Montréal, 1639-1663: Son histoire, ses membres, son manifeste*. Montreal: Fides, 1965.

3940 DAVIS, Natalie Zemon. *Women on the Margins: Three Seventeenth-Century Lives*. Cambridge: Harvard University Press, 1995. [Marie de l'Incarnation]

3941 DEFAIN, Dominique Régis. "La place des femmes dans les *Relations* du R.P. Le Jeune." *Études canadiennes/Canadian Studies* 30 (1991): 57-72.

3942 DE MOISSAC, Élisabeth. "Les Soeurs Grises et les événements de 1869-1870." La société canadienne d'histoire de l'Église catholique. *Sessions d'étude*, 37 (1970): 215-28.

3943 DENAULT, Bernard and Benoit Lévesque, eds. *Éléments pour une sociologie des communautés religieuses au Québec*. Montréal: Presses de l'université de Montréal, 1975.

3944 DEROY-PINEAU, Françoise. *Marie de l'Incarnation: Marie Guyart, femme d'affaires, mystique, mère de la Nouvelle France, 1599-1672*. Paris: Éditions Robert Laffont, 1989.

3945 DESJARDINS, Soeur Jeanne. "Le Couvent de Douglastown—77 ans de service." *Revue d'histoire et de traditions populaires de la Gaspésie* 15, 1 (janvier/mars 1977): 7-22.

3946 DESLANDRES, Dominique. "Un projet éducatif au XVIIe siècle: Marie de l'Incarnation et la femme amérindienne." *Recherches amérindiennes au Québec* 13, 4 (1983): 277-85.

3947 DESLANDRES, Dominique. "L'éducation des Amérindiennes d'après la correspondance de Marie Guyart de l'Incarnation." *Studies in Religion* 16, 1 (Winter 1987): 91-110.

3948 DEVALK, Alphonse. "Understandable But Mistaken: Law, Morality and the Canadian Catholic Church, 1966-1969." Canadian Catholic Historical Association. *Study Sessions* 49 (1982): 87-109.

3949 DOWN, Sister Mary Margaret. *A Century Of Service: A History Of The Sisters Of Saint Ann And Their Contribution To Education In British Columbia, the Yukon and Alaska*. Victoria: Sisters Of Saint Ann, 1966.

3950 DRUMMOND, Margaret Mary. *The Life and Times of Margaret Bourgeoys*. Boston: Angel Guardian Press, 1907.

3951 DUCHARUSSOIS, Rev. Father P. *The Grey Nuns in the Far North*. Toronto: McClelland and Stewart, 1919.

3952 DUCHESNE, Lorraine, Danielle Juteau and Nicole Laurin. "La longevité des religieuses au Québec de 1901 à 1971." *Sociologie et sociétés* 19, 1 (avril 1987): 145-52.

3953 DUCHESNE, Lorraine and Nicole Laurin. "Les trajectoires professionnelles des religieuses au Québec de 1922 à 1971." *Population* 50, 2 (mars/avril 1995): 385-414.

3954 DUMAIS, Monique. "Les femmes dans l'Église du Québec." *Relations* 37 (septembre 1977): 244-50.

3955 DUMAIS, Monique. "Perspectives pour les femmes telles que proposées par un évêque entre 1928-1950." *Revue d'histoire du Bas Saint-Laurent* 5 (décembre 1978): 33-36.

3956 DUMAIS, Monique. "Les religieuses, leur contribution à la société québécoise." *Canadian Women's Studies* 3, 1 (1981): 18-20.

3957 DUMAIS, Monique. "Religion catholique et valeurs morales des femmes au Québec au XXe siècle." *Canadian Issues* 7 (1985): 164-80.

3958 DUMAIS, Monique. "Générations de femmes religieuses." *Canadian Woman Studies* 7, 4 (Winter 1986): 29-30.

3959 DUMAIS, Monique. "Témoignage d'un groupe de femmes: De l'émergence d'une autre parole chez les femmes chrétiennes et féministes." In *Encrages féministes: Un moment de réflexion dans la recherche féministe*, ed. Isabelle Lasvergnas, 145-52. Montréal: Université du Québec à Montréal, Centre de recherche féministe, Group interdisciplinaire d'enseignement et de recherche féministes, 1989.

3960 DUMAIS, Monique. "L'autre salut: femmes et religions." *Recherches féministes* 3, 2 (1990): 1-11.

3961 DUMAIS, Monique. "L'originalité de l'oeuvre sociale des congrégations religieuses de Montréal aux XIXe et XXe siècles." *Études d'histoire religieuse* 59 (1993): 25-41.

3962 DUMAIS, Monique. "Synergie: Femmes et religion au Québec depuis 1970." *Religiologiques* 11 (printemps 1995): 51-64.

3963 DUMONT, Micheline. "Les communautés religieuses et la condition féminine." *Recherches sociographiques* 19, 1 (1978): 79-102. Revised and retitled as "Vocation religieuse et condition féminine." In *Travailleuses et féministes: Les femmes dans la société québécoise*, eds. Marie Lavigne and Yolande Pinard, 271-92. Montréal: Boréal Express, 1983.

3964 DUMONT, Micheline. "Le défi des religieuses enseignantes aujourd'hui." *Canadian Woman Studies* 7, 3 (Fall 1986): 51-54.

3965 DUMONT, Micheline. "Les charismes perdus: L'avenir des congrégations religieuses féminines en l'an 2000." *Recherches féministes* 3, 2 (1990): 73-111. [decline within female congregations in Quebec since 1960s]

3966 DUMONT, Micheline. "Une perspective féministe dans l'histoire des congrégations de femmes." La société canadienne d'histoire de l'Eglise catholique. *Études d'histoire religieuse* 57 (1990): 29-35.

3967 DUMONT, Micheline and Nadia Fahmy-Eid, eds. *Les Couventines: L'éducation des filles au Québec dans les congrégations religieuses enseignantes, 1840-1960.* Montréal: Boréal Express, 1986.

3968 DUMONT, Micheline and Marie-Paule Malouin. "Evolution et rôle des congrégations religieuses enseignantes féminines au Québec, 1840-1960." Société canadienne d'histoire de l'Eglise catholique. *Sessions d'étude* 50 (1983): 201-30.

3969 DUPRIEZ, Flora. "Quelques repères historiques concernant la situation des femmes dans l'Église." In *Femmes et pouvoir dans l'Église*, ed. Anita Caron. Montréal: VLB, 1991.

3970 DWYER, June. "Sisters of St. Joseph Health Care Ministry in Toronto, 1851-1991." In *Spiritual Roots: The Roman Catholic Archdiocese of Toronto at 150 Years of Age*, eds. John Duggan and Terry Fay, 73-80. Toronto: Our Lady of Lourdes Sesquicentennial History, 1991.

3971 EVAN, Richard Xavier. "The Literature Relating to Kateri Tekakwitha, the Lily of the Mohawks, 1656-1680." *Bulletin des recherches historiques* 46 (1940): 193-209, 241-45.

3972 FERLAND, Soeur Léonie. *Un Voyage au cercle polaire.* Montréal: Imprimerie de l'Hôpital Général des Soeurs Grises, c. 1937. [a Grey Nun's mission to Aklavik in 1937]

3973 "First Mission of the Sisters Faithful Companions of Jesus in the North-West Territories, 1883." *Saskatchewan History* 36 (Spring 1983): 70-77.

3974 FOLEY, Mary Ann. "Uncloistered Apostolic Life for Women: Marguerite Bourgeoys' Experiment in Ville-Marie." *US Catholic Historian* 10, 1/2 (1992): 37-44.

3975 FORAN, J.K. *Jeanne Mance or "The Angel of the Colony."* Montreal: Herald Press, 1931.

3976 GAGNON, François-Marc. "La France apportant la foi aux Hurons de Nouvelle-France: un tableau conservé chez les Ursulines du Québec." *Journal of Canadian Studies* 18, 3 (Autumn 1983): 5-20.

3977 GAGNON, Serge. *Plaisir d'amour et crainte de Dieu: Sexualité et confession au Bas-Canada.* Sainte Foy: Les Presses de l'Université Laval, 1990.

3978 GALARNEAU, C. "Les communautés religieuses au Québec, 1837-1914." La Société canadienne d'histoire de l'Église catholique. *Sessions d'étude* (1969): 13-19.

3979 GENEVIÈVE, Sister Ste. Mary. *Marguerite Bourgeoys, Pioneer Teacher.* New York: Farrar, Straus and Co, 1963.

3980 GOURDEAU, Claire. *Les délices de nos coeurs: Marie de l'Incarnation et ses pensionnaires amérindiennes, 1639-1672.* Sillery: Les éditions du Septentrion, 1994.

3981 GROULX, Lionel. *Marguerite Bourgeoys.* Montréal: Bureau Marguerite Bourgeoys, 1930.

3982 GROULX, Lionel. *Jeanne Mance.* Montréal: Comité des Fondateurs de l'Église canadienne, 1957.

3983 GROULX, Lionel. *La Grande Dame de Notre Histoire.* Montréal: Fides, 1966. [Marie Guyart de l'Incarnation]

3984 HENNÉGUIN, Jacques. "Marie de l'Incarnation (l'Ursuline canadienne) et la pauvreté." *XVIIe Siècle* 89 (1970): 3-22.

3985 HÉROUX, Liliane. "Des Femmes en gris." La Société canadienne d'histoire de l'Église catholique. *Sessions d'étude* (1969): 49-56.

3986 HOFFMAN, Barbara. "Women of God: The Faithful Companions of Jesus." *Alberta History* 43, 4 (Autumn 1995): 2-12.

3987 HUDON, Christine. "Des dames chrétiennes: la spiritualité des catholiques Québécoises au XIXe siècle." *Revue d'histoire de l'Amérique française* 49, 2 (automne 1995): 169-94.

3988 HUOT, Giselle. *Une femme au séminaire. Marie de la Charité (1852-1920) fondatrice de la première communauté dominicaine du Canada, 1887.* Montréal: Bellarmin, 1987.

3989 HUOT, Giselle. *Un rêve inouï: des milliers de jeunes: Mère Marie-Elizabeth, 1840-1881, fondatrice de la Congrégation des Soeurs de Notre-Dame du Saint-Rosaire de Rimouski.* Sainte-Foy: A Sigier, [1991].

3990 INGLIS, George. "The Grey Nuns of the North." *North* 14, 1 (1967): 12-15.

3991 JEAN, Soeur Marguerite. "L'État et les communautés religieuses féminines au Québec, 1639-1840." *Studia Canonica* 6, 1 (1972): 163-79.

3992 JEAN, Soeur Marguerite. *L'évolution des communautés religieuses de femmes au Canada de 1639 à nos jours.* Montréal: Fides, 1977.

3993 JEAN, Michèle. "Féminisme et religion au Québec, 1900-1978." In *La femme et la religion au Canada français*, ed. Elisabeth J. Lacelle, 33-42. Montréal: Bellarmin, 1979.

3994 JOHNSTON, A.J.B. *Religion and Life at Louisbourg, 1713-1758.* Montreal and Kingston: McGill-Queen's University Press, 1984.

3995 JORDAN, Mary, ed. *To Louis from Your Sister Who Loves You, Sara Riel.* Toronto: Griffin House, 1974. [Grey Nun missionary, 1860-1883]

3996 JUNEAU, Georgianna. *Mother Mary of the Sacred Heart, 1806-1885, Foundress of the Good Shepherd Congregation of Quebec, and Her Collaborators.* Sainte-Foy: Soeurs du Bon-Pasteur de Québec, 1989.

3997 JUTEAU-LEE, Danielle. "Les religieuses du Québec: leurs influences sur la vie professionelle des femmes, 1908-1954." *Atlantis* 5, 2 (Spring 1980): 22-33.

3998 JUTEAU, Danielle. "Les communautés religieuses de femmes au Québec. Une recherche en cours." *Questions de culture* 9, 1986.

3999 JUTEAU, Danielle and Nicole Laurin. "Nuns in the Labour Force: A Neglected Contribution." *Feminist Issues* 6 (Fall 1986): 75-87.

4000 JUTEAU, Danielle and Nicole Laurin. "L'évolution des formes de l'appropriation des femmes: des religieuses au 'mères porteuses'." *Canadian Review of Sociology and Anthropology* 25, 2 (May 1988): 183-207.

4001 JUTEAU, Danielle and Nicole Laurin. "From Nuns to Surrogate Mothers: Evolution of the Forms of the Appropriation of Women." *Feminist Issues* 9, 1 (Spring 1989): 13-40.

4002 JUTRAS, Claude. "Les archives des Filles de Jésus." *Archives* 24, 4 (printemps 1993): 55-62.

4003 KOPPEDRAYER, K.I. "The Making of the First Iroquois Virgin: Early Jesuit Biographies of the Blessed Kateri Tekakwitha." *Ethnohistory* 40, 2 (Spring 1993): 277-306.

4004 LACELLE, Elizabeth J., ed. *La femme et la religion au Canada français.* Montréal: Bellarmin, 1979.

4005 LACOMBE, Guy. *Religieux et religieuses.* Edmonton: Duval, [1993?].

4006 LAMBERT, Thérèse. *Marguerite Bourgeoys, éducatrice, 1620-1700: Mère d'un pays et d'une église.* Montréal: Bellarmin, 1978.

4007 LAMIRANDE, Émilien. *Élisabeth Bruyère: Fondatrice des soeurs de la Charité d'Ottawa.* Montréal: Bellarmin, 1993.

4008 LAPOINTE-ROY, Huguette. "Les religieuses hospital-ières de Saint-Joseph: 329 ans de présence à Montréal." In *L'Histoire des croyants: Mémoire vivante des hommes, Vol. 2*, eds. Brigitte Waché, *et al*, 650-59. Abbéville: Imprimerie F. Paillart, 1959.

4009 LAUER, Bernarda. "Russian Germans and the Ursulines of Prelate, Sask., 1919-1934." Canadian Catholic Historical Association. *Study Sessions* 46 (1979): 83-98.

4010 LAURIN, Nicole, Danielle Juteau and Lorraine Duchesne. *À la recherche d'un monde oublié: Les communautés religieuses de femmes au Québec de 1900 à 1970.* Montréal: Le Jour, 1991.

4011 LAURIN-FRENETTE, Nicole and Nadia Fahmy-Eid. "Femmes et Église du Québec: éléments pour une interprétation socio-historique." In *Femmes et pouvoir dans l'Église*, ed. Anita Caron. Montréal: VLB, 1991.

4012 LEBRUN-LAPIERRE, Odette. "Les Soeurs Grises à Longueuil." Société d'histoire de Longueuil. *Bulletin* 9 (1976): 23-31.

4013 LÉGARÉ, Jacques. "Les religieuses du Canada: leur évolution numérique entre 1965 et 1980." *Recherches sociographiques* 10, 1 (1969): 7-21.

4014 LORTIE, Jeanne D'Arc. *Lettres d'Elisabeth Bruyère, Tome 2: 1850-1856.* Montréal: Éditions Paulines, 1992.

4015 MacLEAN, Judith Flora. "The Woman Speaks Her Mind: The Role of Oral Histories in Documenting Women's Participation in the Antigonish Movement." Canadian Oral History Association. *Journal* 11 (1991): 23-28.

4016 MacPHERSON, Sarah. "Religious Women in Nova Scotia: A Struggle for Autonomy. A Sketch of the Sisters of St. Martha of Antigonish, Nova Scotia, 1900-1960." Canadian Catholic Historical Association. *Study Sessions* 51 (1984): 89-106.

4017 MARSHALL, Joyce, ed. and trans. *Word from New France: The Selected Letters of Marie de l'Incarnation.* Toronto: Oxford University Press, 1967.

4018 MARTEL, Suzanne. *Au temps de Marguerite Bourgeois quand Montréal était un village.* Montréal: Éditions du Méridien, 1982.

4019 MAURA, Sister. *The Sisters of Charity, Halifax.* Toronto: Ryerson Press, 1956.

4020 McGAHAN, Elizabeth W. "Inside the Hallowed Walls: Convent Life Through Material History." *Material History Bulletin* 25 (Spring 1987): 1-9.

4021 McGUIRE, Rita. "The Grey Sisters in the Red River Settlement, 1844-1870." Canadian Catholic Historical Association. *Historical Studies* 53 (1986): 21-37.

4022 McMAHON, Nancy. "Les religieuses hospitalières de Saint Joseph and the Typhus Epidemic, Kingston, 1847-1848." Canadian Catholic Historical Association. *Historical Studies* (1991): 41-55.

4023 MISSION MONTRÉAL. *Les congrégations religieuses dans l'histoire de la ville.* Montréal: Fides, 1992.

4024 MITCHELL, Soeur Estelle. *Elle a beaucoup aimé: Vie de la Bienheureuse Marguerite d'Youville.* Montréal: Fides, 1958.

4025 MITCHELL, Soeur Estelle. *Marguerite d'Youville: Foundress of the Grey Nuns.* Montréal: Palm Publishers, 1965.

4026 MITCHELL, Estelle. *Le soleil brille à minuit: Les Soeurs Grises dans les Territoires du Nord-Ouest.* Montréal: Beauchemin, 1970.

4027 MITCHELL, Estelle. *Les Soeurs Grises de Montréal à la Rivière-Rouge, 1844-1984.* Montréal: Editions du Méridien, 1987.

4028 MURPHY, Sister Mary. "The Grey Nuns Travel West." *Historical and Scientific Society of Manitoba* (1944): 3-13.

4029 O'GALLAGHER, Marianna. "The Sisters of Charity of Halifax—the Early and Middle Years." Canadian Catholic Historical Association. *Study Sessions* 47 (1980): 57-68.

4030 OURY, Dom Guy. *Marie de l'Incarnation, 1599-1672,* 2 vols. Québec: Presses de l'Université Laval, 1973.

4031 PAUL-ÉMILE, Sister. "Les débuts d'une congrégation: Les Soeurs Grises de la Croix à Bytown, 1845-1850." La Société canadienne d'histoire de l'Église catholique. *Rapport* 10 (1942/43): 47-76.

4032 PAUL-ÉMILE, Sister. *The Grey Nuns of the Cross: Sisters of Charity, Ottawa, Ontario, Vol. II, The Evolution of the Institute, 1876-1967.* Ottawa: Grey Nuns of the Cross, 1988.

4033 PELLETIER-BAILLARGEON, Hélène. "La Québécoise d'hier." *Canadian Woman Studies* 5, 2 (Winter 1983): 42-44.

4034 PICHETTE, Robert. *Les Religieuses, pionniers en Acadie.* Montmagny, QC: Marquis, 1990.

4035 PLANTE, Lucienne. "Marguerite Bourgeoys, fille de France, missionnaire en Nouvelle-France." In *L'Histoire des croyants: Mémoire vivante des hommes, Vol. 2,* eds. Brigitte Waché, *et al,* 643-50. Abbeville: Imprimerie F. Paillart, 1959.

4036 POISSANT, Simone. *Marguerite Bourgeoys, 1620-1700.* Montréal: Bellarmin, 1993.

4037 POULOT, A. "Les Ursulines de Québec." Canadian Historical Association. *Annual Report* (1952): 66-70.

4038 RAPLEY, Elizabeth. *The Dévotes: Women and Church in Seventeenth-Century France.* Montreal and Kingston: McGill-Queen's University Press, 1990.

4039 ROBILLARD, Denise. *Émilie Tavernier-Gamelin.* Montréal: Méridien, 1988.

4040 ROUSSEAU, François. *La Croix et le scalpel: Histoire des Augustines et de l'Hôtel-Dieu de Québec, I. 1639-1892.* Québec: Septentrion, 1989.

4041 ROY, Louise. "Les pensionnats des Soeurs de Sainte-Anne dans la région métropolitaine 1850-1988." *Cahiers de la Société historique de Montréal* 7, 1 (décembre 1988): 364-72.

4042 ROY, Louise. *Les Soeurs de Sainte-Anne: Un siècle d'histoire, Tome 2: 1900-1950.* Montréal: Éditions Paulines et Soeurs de Sainte-Anne, 1992.

4043 ST. PAUL, Mother M. *From Desenzano to "the Pines": A Sketch of the History of the Ursulines of Ontario.* Toronto: Macmillan, 1941.

4044 SAVARD-BONIN, Jeanne. *Une Stigmatisée: Marie-Rose Ferron, 1902-1936.* Montréal: Éditions Paulines, 1987.

4045 SINCLAIR-FAULKNER, Tom. "One Size Fits All: Marie de l'Incarnation." *Touchstone* 10, 1 (January 1992): 40-45.

4046 SISTERS OF MERCY. *Sisters of Mercy of Newfoundland 150th Anniversary 1842-1992.* St. John's: Sisters of Mercy of Newfoundland, 1992.

4047 SMYTH, Elizabeth. "*Congregavit nos in unum Christi amor.* The Congregation of the Sisters of St. Joseph, in the Archdiocese of Toronto, 1851-1920." *Ontario History* 84, 3 (September 1992): 225-40.

4048 SMYTH, Elizabeth. "'Much exertion of the voice and great application of the mind': Teacher Education Within the Congregation of the Sisters of St. Joseph of Toronto, Canada, 1851-1920." *Historical Studies in Education* 6, 3 (1994): 97-113.

4049 SMYTH, Elizabeth. "Christian Perfection and Service to Neighbours: The Congregation of the Sisters of St Joseph, Toronto, 1851-1920." In *Changing Roles of Women within the Christian Church in Canada,* eds. Elizabeth Gillan Muir and Marilyn Färdig Whiteley, 38-54. Toronto: University of Toronto Press, 1995.

4050 SOEURS DE LA CHARITE DE QUÉBEC. *Mère Mallet et l'Institut des Soeurs de la Charité de Québec.* Québec: Les Soeurs de la Charité de Quebéc, 1939.

4051 STANLEY, Laurie C.C. "'So Many Crosses to Bear': The Religious Hospitallers of St Joseph and the Tracadie Leper Hospital, 1868-1910." In *Changing Roles of Women within the Christian Church in Canada,* eds. Elizabeth Gillan Muir and Marilyn Färdig Whiteley, 19-37. Toronto: University of Toronto Press, 1995.

4052 SYLVESTRE, Paul-François. *Les communautés religieuses en Ontario français: Sur les traces de Joseph Le Caron.* Montréal: Éditions Bellarmin, 1984.

4053 TREMBLAY, Fleurette. *Voici que je viens ...: biographie de Soeur Rose-Yvonne Tremblay, a.s.a., 1916-1985.* Montréal: Éditions Paulines, 1989.

4054 "Les Ursulines de Gaspé: Un demi-siècle de présence, 1924-1974." *Revue d'histoire de la Gaspesie* (avril/juin 1974): 76-189. [special issue marking fifty years of Ursuline service in the Gaspé]

4055 *Les Ursulines de Québec, 1639-1989.* Québec: Le Comité des Fêtes du 350e anniversaire du fondation de l'École des Ursulines de Québec, 1989.

4056 VERDUYN, Christl. "La religion dans le journal d'Henriette Fadette." *Atlantis* 8, 2 (Spring 1983): 45-50.

4057 WEAVER, Emily P. *Sisters of St. Boniface.* Toronto: Ryerson Press, 1930.

4058 ZINK, Sister Ella. "Immigrants and the Church: The Sisters of Service, 1920-1930." Canadian Catholic Historical Association. *Study Sessions* 43 (1976): 23-38.

WITCHCRAFT/SUPERNATURAL

4059 BALLSTADT, Carl, Michael Peterman and Elizabeth Hopkins. "'A Glorious Madness': Susanna Moodie and the Spiritualist Movement." *Journal of Canadian Studies* 17, 4 (Winter 1982/83): 88-101.

4060 BRAULT, Louis. *Vie Extraordinaire de Madame Brault, 1856-1910.* Montréal: Librairie Beauchemin, 1941. [Marie-Louise Brault, mystic]

4061 DUCAS, Marie-Claude. "Oyez, oyez, les sorcières sont parmi nous." *Châtelaine* 33, 11 (novembre 1992): 107-12.

4062 FRIGON, Sylvie. "Femmes, hérésies et contrôle social: des sorcières aux sages-femmes et au-delà." *Canadian Journal of Women and the Law* 7, 1 (1994): 133-55.

4063 GLENN, Eleanor Margaret. "Superstition and the Supernatural in Nineteenth Century Upper Canada" *Families* 32, 3 (August 1993): 131-50.

4064 GREENLAND, Cyril. "Mary Edwards Merrill, 1858-1880, 'The Psychic.'" *Ontario History* 68, 2 (June 1976): 80-92.

4065 PEARL, Jonathan L. "Witchcraft in New France in the Seventeenth Century: The Social Aspects." *Historical Reflections* 4, 2 (Winter 1977): 191-206.

4066 SÉGUIN, Robert-Lionel. *La sorcellerie au Québec du XVIIe au XIXe siècle.* Montréal: Leméac, 1978.

SCIENCE/TECHNOLOGY

THE STUDY OF women's relationship to science and technology is a relative latecomer to Canadian women's history, but women's historians have not been alone in their neglect of this field. For many years, the widespread popular convictions that there was no indigenous Canadian scientific tradition, and that technological innovation occurred elsewhere in the world, impeded the growth of the history of Canadian science and technology as a distinct field of study. In the 1980s, the growing public recognition of the importance of science and technology to economic development coincided with much consternation in educational circles over the continuing absence of women from the fields of science and engineering at all levels of the education system. Feminist scholars in a variety of disciplines, including history, turned their attention to science as a gendered enterprise which presented systemic barriers to women's participation, and to the relationship of gender to technological change.

According to Marianne Gosztonyi Ainley, who has made the most significant contribution to our knowledge of women's role in the development of Canadian science, women have been active for more than two hundred years, although few of these women are known to us. Most were relegated to subordinate positions doing low-paid routine work or were encouraged to specialize in fields closely associated with "wome"'s work," where they would not compete directly with men. Their relative invisibility in the profession, compounded by short-sighted archival policies, has made their activities and even their presence difficult to document. Several scholars have undertaken the challenging tasks of identifying women's scientific publications, research grants, and membership in scientific associations in ways that are beginning to shed light on the discriminatory practices that helped to exclude women from the profession. Progress has been evident in uncovering the contribution of early amateur natural scientists, including Catharine Parr Traill, and a few biographical studies of prominent women scientists, such as the nuclear physicist Harriet Brooks, have also been produced.

Questions about the relationship of gender to technology have prompted women's historians to explore the differential impact of technology on women and, more recently, to examine women's responses to technology and their contribution to technological innovation. The computer revolution of the 1980s, with its devastating implications for women's occupations in the clerical sector, helped to generate interest in the effects of new workplace technologies, such as the typewriter, on women workers in the past. Recent studies by scholars like Bettina Bradbury have raised questions about the impact technological changes and the reorganization of labour processes that accompanied industrialization, for factory workers, domestic servants, and housewives. Until recently, the study of domestic technology was the province of historians employed by museums and historic sites who have undertaken extensive research on cooking technology, the technology of infant feeding, and domestic architecture, among other topics (*see Material Culture/Popular Culture*). They have recently been joined by academic historians studying consumerism and advertising, who are investigating the introduction and promotion of domestic electrical appliances in the twentieth century (*see Mass Culture/Media*). Little attention has yet been paid to regional variations in the impact and timing of technological change, although a recent study by Angela Davis draws our attention to the importance of urban/rural divisions. Women's work and technology in preindustrial settings remain woefully understudied topics but a significant new contribution by Heather Menzies suggests that understanding women's technological practices as Ontario cheesemakers may lead us to rethink long-standing assumptions about technological dependency.

GENERAL

4067   AINLEY, Marianne Gosztonyi. "A Family of Women Scientists." Simone de Beauvoir Institute. *Bulletin* 7, 1 (1986): 5-10.

4068   AINLEY, Marianne Gosztonyi. "D'assistantes anonymes à chercheures scientifiques: une rétrospective sur la place des femmes en science." *Cahiers de recherche sociologique* (UQAM) 4, 1 (avril 1986): 55-71.

4069   AINLEY, Marianne Gosztonyi. "Des femmes dans les sciences et des sciences sur les femmes." *Cahiers de recherche sociologique* (UQAM) 4, 1 1986.

4070   AINLEY, Marianne Gosztonyi. "Women Scientists in Canada: The Need for Documentation." *Resources for Feminist Research* 15, 3 (November 1986): 7-8.

4071   AINLEY, Marianne Gosztonyi. "Field Work and Family: North American Women Ornithologists, 1900-1950." In *Uneasy Careers and Intimate Lives: Women in Science, 1789-1979,* eds. Prina G. Abir-Am and Dorinda Outram, 60-76. New Brunswick and London: Rutgers University Press, 1987.

4072   AINLEY, Marianne Gosztonyi, ed. *Despite the Odds: Essays on Canadian Women and Science.* Montreal: Véhicule Press, 1990.

4073   AINLEY, Marianne Gosztonyi. "Last in the Field? Canadian Women Natural Scientists, 1815-1965." In *Despite the Odds: Essays on Canadian Women and Science,* ed. Marianne Gosztonyi Ainley, 25-62. Montreal: Véhicule Press, 1990.

4074   AINLEY, Marianne Gosztonyi. "In Memoriam: Margaret Howell Mitchell, 1901-1988." *Auk* 107 (1990): 601-2.

4075   AINLEY, Marianne Gosztonyi. "One Hundred Years of Women and Science in Ontario." *Crucible* 21 (1990): 14-15.

4076   AINLEY, Marianne Gosztonyi. "In Memoriam: Louise de Kiriline Lawrence, 1894-1992." *Auk* 109 (1992): 909-10.

4077   AINLEY, Marianne Gosztonyi. "'Women's Work' in Canadian Chemistry." *Canadian Woman Studies* 13, 2 (Winter 1993): 43-46.

4078   AINLEY, Marianne Gosztonyi. "Margaret H. Mitchell (1901-1988)." In *Ornithology in Ontario,* eds. Martin McNicholl and J. Cranmer-Byng, 185-88. Whitby, ON: Hawk Owl Publishing, 1994.

4079   AINLEY, Marianne Gosztonyi. "Louise De Kiriline Lawrence (1894-1992) and the World of Nature: A Tribute." *Canadian Field Naturalist* 108, 1 (1994): 111-18.

4080   AINLEY, Marianne Gosztonyi and Tina Crossfield. "Canadian Women's Contributions to Chemistry, 1900-1970." *Canadian Chemical News* 46, 4 (April 1994): 16-18.

4081   AINLEY, Marianne Gosztonyi and Catherine Millar. "A Select Few: Women and the National Research Council of Canada, 1916-1991." *Scientia Canadensis* 15, 2 (1991): 105-16.

4082   ANAND, Kailash K. assisted by Anita K. Anand. "Cypra Cecilia Krieger and the Human Side of Mathematics." In *Despite the Odds: Essays on Canadian Women and Science,* ed. Marianne Gosztonyi Ainley, 248-51. Montreal: Véhicule Press, 1990.

4083   BEAUCHAMP, Rachelle Sender and Lisa Avedon, eds. "Women in Science: Options and Intolerance." A special issue of *Women's Education des femmes* 9, 2 (Fall 1991).

4084   BENSTON, Margaret Lowe. "The Myth of Computer Literacy." *Canadian Woman Studies* 5, 4 (1984): 20-22.

4085   BERNARD, Elaine. "Science, Technology and Progress: Lessons from the History of the Typewriter." *Canadian Woman Studies* 5, 4 (1984): 12-14.

4086   BRADBURY, Bettina. "Women's Workplaces: The Impact of Technological Change on Working-class Women in the Home and in the Workplace in Nineteenth-Century Montreal." In *Women, Work and Place,* ed. Audrey Kobayashi, 27-44. Montreal and Kingston: McGill-Queen's University Press, 1994.

4087   CHU, Clara M. and Bertrum H. MacDonald. "Women in Canadian Science and Technology Before World War I: Their Publication Record." *Scientia Canadensis* XII, 2 (Fall/Winter 1988): 75-96. Revised and retitled as "The Public Record: An Analysis of Women's Contribution to Canadian Science and Technology Before the First World War." In *Despite the Odds: Essays on Canadian Women and Science,* ed. Marianne Gosztonyi Ainley, 63-73. Montreal: Véhicule Press, 1990.

4088   COLE, Jean. "Catharine Parr Traill—Botanist." In *Portraits: Peterborough Area Women Past and Present,* ed. Gail Corbett, 73-79. Woodview, ON: Portraits' Group, 1975.

4089   COLLARD, Elizabeth. "Flowers to heal and comfort: Mrs. Traill's Books for Collectors." *Canadian Collector* 13 (May/June 1978): 32-36.

4090   CROSSFIELD, Tina. "Experience and Perception: A Comparison of the Environmental Outlooks of Catharine Parr Traill and Susanna Moodie in 19th Century Canada." Simone de Beauvoir Institute. *Bulletin* 15 (1995): 20-30.

4091 DAGG, Anne I. "The Status of Some Canadian Women Ph.D. Scientists." *Atlantis* 11 (Fall 1985): 66-78.

4092 DAVIS, Angela E. "'Valiant Servants': Women and Technology on the Canadian Prairies, 1910-1940." *Manitoba History* 25 (Spring 1993): 33-42.

4093 ESTEY, Ralph H. "Margaret Newton: Distinguished Canadian Scientist." In *Despite the Odds: Essays on Canadian Women and Science,* ed. Marianne Gosztonyi Ainley, 236-47. Montreal: Véhicule Press, 1990.

4094 MacCALLUM, Elizabeth. "Catharine Parr Traill, A Nineteenth Century Ontario Naturalist." *The Beaver* 306 (Autumn 1975): 39-45.

4095 MARCHAND, Suzanne. "L'impact des innovations technologiques sur la vie quotidienne des Québécoises du début du XXe siècle (1910-1940)." *Material History Bulletin* 28 (Fall 1988): 1-14.

4096 MEADOWCROFT, Barbara. "Alice Wilson, 1881-1964: Explorer of the Earth Beneath Her Feet." In *Despite the Odds: Essays on Canadian Women and Science,* ed. Marianne Gosztonyi Ainley, 204-19. Montreal: Véhicule Press, 1990.

4097 MENZIES, Heather. "Re-thinking the Social Contract: Women, Work, and Technology in the Post-Industrial Era." *Canadian Journal of Women and the Law* 4, 1 (1990): 205-16.

4098 MENZIES, Heather. "Technology in the Craft of Ontario Cheesemaking: Women in Oxford County circa 1860." *Ontario History* 87, 3 (September 1995): 293-304.

4099 MESSING, Karen, Maria de Koninck and Lesley Lee, eds. "Women and Sciences." A special issue of *Resources for Feminist Research* 15, 3 (1986).

4100 MORRELL, C. "Uncommon Knowledge: Women in Science and Women's Studies." In *Hitting the Books: The Politics of Educational Retrenchment,* ed. Terry Wotherspoon. Toronto: Garamond Press, 1990.

4101 PETERMAN, Michael A. "'Splendid Anachronism': The Record of Catharine Parr Traill's Struggles as an Amateur Botanist." In *Re(Dis)covering Our Foremothers: Nineteenth Century Canadian Women Writers,* ed. Lorraine McMullen, 173-85. Ottawa: University of Ottawa Press, 1989.

4102 RAYNER-CANHAM, M.F. and G.W. Rayner-Canham. "Canada's First Woman Nuclear Physicist, Harriet Brooks, 1876-1933." In *Despite the Odds: Essays on Canadian Women and Science,* ed. Marianne Gosztonyi Ainley, 195-203. Montreal: Véhicule Press, 1990.

4103 RAYNER-CANHAM, M.F. and G.W. Rayner Canham. *Harriet Brooks: Pioneer Nuclear Scientist.* Montreal and Kingston: McGill-Queen's University Press, 1992.

4104 RENDER, Shirley. *No Place for a Lady: The Story of Canadian Women Pilots, 1928-1992.* Winnipeg: Portage and Main Press, 1992.

4105 SCHERMAN, Katharine. *Spring on an Arctic Island.* Boston: Little, Brown and Co., 1956. [scientific expedition in 1954]

4106 SPRING, Joyce. *Daring Lady Flyers: Canadian Women in the Early Years of Aviation.* Porters Lake, NS: Pottersfield Press, 1994.

4107 STANWELL-FLETCHER, Theodora Cope. *Driftwood Valley.* Boston: Little Brown and Co., 1948. [naturalist in north-central British Columbia, 1937-1941]

4108 STANWELL-FLETCHER, Theodora Cope. *The Tundra World.* Boston: Little, Brown and Co., 1952. [naturalist in Churchill, Manitoba, 1930-1949]

4109 STANWELL-FLETCHER, Theodora Cope. *Clear Lands and Icy Seas.* New York: Dodd, Mead, 1958. [northern voyages of a naturalist, 1950s]

4110 THURE, Karen. "Martha Harper Pioneered in the Air Business." *Smithsonian* 7, 6 (1976): 94-100.

4111 TRAILL, C.P. *Canadian Wild Flowers.* Painted and lithographed by Agnes Fitzgibbon. Montreal: John Lovell, 1868; Toronto: Coles Publishing Co., 1972.

4112 VON BAEYER, Edwinna. "Isabella Preston (1881-1964): Explorer of the Horticultural Frontier." In *Despite the Odds: Essays on Canadian Women and Science,* ed. Marianne Gosztonyi Ainley, 220-35. Montreal: Véhicule Press, 1990.

SEXUALITY/SEXUAL ORIENTATION

JUDGING THE NUMBER of graduate students now engaged in research in this field, and the recent inauguration of the Canadian Committee on the History of Sexuality under the auspices of the Canadian Historical Association, it is likely that the history of sexuality will emerge as one of the major growth areas in Canadian history over the next decade. Yet this success did not come easily, and the field still lacks credibility in the eyes of many members of the profession. Michael Bliss's pioneering 1970 article on pre-Freudian sexual ideas in Canada had few successors until recently, and Gary Kinsman's *The Regulation of Desire* remains, after a decade, the only overview of the history of sexuality in Canada. This slow progress indicates a deep-seated adherence to the notion that sexuality is biological and natural, is therefore unchanging, and is not the province of historians. Historical scholarship on sexuality is based on the premise that sexuality and sexual identity, like gender, are socially constructed and change over time. Sexual behaviours and ideologies, popular attitudes toward sex, forms of sexual regulation, and constructions of sexual identity all have histories that are finally being explored. Scholarship on both homosexuality and heterosexuality has begun to appear in mainstream Canadian historical journals, and the work of Canadian scholars has also been published in the new international *Journal of the History of Sexuality*.

Scholars working on the history of sexuality in Canada confront particular problems, not the least of which is the location of archival sources. The relegation of sexuality to the private sphere has resulted in a scarcity of public records, and archival collections policies have not emphasized acquisitions in this area. This is particularly the case in the field of gay and lesbian history, which has been much slower than women's history to gain legitimacy among professional archivists and historians, a lag that has prompted community activists to establish their own archives. Steven Maynard dates the beginning of the search for a gay and lesbian past in Canada to the establishment of the Canadian Gay Archives in

1973; this collection has proved critical for documenting the history of the gay liberation movement and gay and lesbian subcultures. Oral history and discourse analysis are important methodological tools for studying the history of sexuality. While medical discourses on sexuality have been fruitfully examined by Wendy Mitchinson, Angus McLaren, and others *(see also Health/Medicine)*, the majority of scholars have been drawn to the rich, if highly problematic, records produced by the criminal justice system *(see also Law/Public Policy)*. As Maynard has recently observed: "Court records are to the history of sexuality what the census was to social history in the 1970s."

Since the 1970s, prostitution and campaigns to regulate or suppress prostitution in Canada's past have generated much interest among women's historians, resulting in new insights into working-class women's lives, the motivations of police and purity reformers, and the treatment of women who did not conform to the prevailing code of respectability *(see also Law/Public Policy)*. In the 1980s, the prominence of violence against women as a contemporary feminist issue prompted scholarly investigations into the topics of sexual violence and wife assault in the past, revealing that violence against women is by no means a new phenomen and that, historically, both middle-class and working-class women have employed a variety of strategies to resist it *(see also Feminism/Women's Movements and Law/Public Policy)*. The small but growing scholarship on lesbian history in Canada has focussed on the bar culture of the 1940s to the 1960s, lesbian feminist organizing since the 1970s, lesbian motherhood, and sexual orientation and human rights legislation *(see also Feminism/Women's Movements, Families/Life Stages and Law/Public Policy)*. Recent work by a small number of scholars has begun to examine the social construction of heterosexuality, as in the case of Karen Dubinsky's important study of rape and heterosexual relations, and Mary Louise Adams's "search for sexual discourse" in public discussions of immorality, delinquency, and indecency.

GENERAL

4113 ADAMS, Mary Louise. "Almost Anything Can Happen: A Search for Sexual Discourse in the Urban Spaces of 1940s Toronto." *Canadian Journal of Sociology* 19, 2 (1994): 217-32.

4114 ADAMS, Mary Louise. "Youth, Corruptibility, and English-Canadian Postwar Campaigns against Indecency, 1948-1955." *Journal of the History of Sexuality* 6, 1 (July 1995): 89-117.

4115 AKENSON, Don. *At Face Value: The Life and Times of Eliza McCormack/John White.* Kingston and Montreal: McGill-Queen's University Press, 1990. [A "hoax" publicly acknowledged by the author, this work suggests that 19th-century politician John White was a lesbian cross-dresser.]

4116 ARNUP, Katherine, *et al*, eds. "The Lesbian Issue." A special issue of *Resources for Feminist Research* 12, 1 (March 1983).

4117 ARNUP, Katherine and Amy Gottlieb. "Annotated Bibliography." *Resources for Feminist Research* 12, 1 (March 1983): 90-100. [lesbian sources]

4118 AVERILL, Harold. "The Church, Gays, and Archives." *Archivaria* 30 (Summer 1990): 85-90.

4119 AVERILL, Harold and J.A. Fraser *Organizing an Archives: The Canadian Gay Archives Experience.* Toronto: Canadian Gay Archives, 1983.

4120 BALL, Christine. "Female Sexual Ideologies in Mid to Late Nineteenth-Century Canada." *Canadian Journal of Women and the Law* 1, 2 (1986): 324-38.

4121 BALL, Christine. "Female Sexual Ideologies in Mid-to Late-Nineteenth Century Canada." *Resources for Feminist Research* 15, 3 (November 1986): 24-27.

4122 BEARCHELL, Chris. "Why I am a Gay Liberationist: Thoughts on Sex, Freedom, the Family and the State." *Resources for Feminist Research* 12, 1 (March 1983): 57-60.

4123 BERTRAND, Luce. "La violence faite à la femme lesbienne." *Canadian Woman Studies* 4, 4 (1983). Reprinted in 11, 3 (1991): 31-33.

4124 BLISS, Michael. "Pure Books on Avoided Subjects: Pre-Freudian Sexual Ideas in Canada." Canadian Historical Association. *Historical Papers* (1970): 89-108. Reprinted in *Studies in Canadian Social History,* eds. M. Horn and R. Sabourin, 326-46. Toronto: McClelland and Stewart, 1974; and in *Medicine in Canadian Society: Historical Perspectives,* ed. S.E.D. Shortt, 207-35. Montreal and Kingston: McGill-Queen's University Press, 1981.

4125 BOLUS, Malvina. "The Son of I. Gunn." *The Beaver* (Winter 1971): 23-26. [1807 birth of a child to a female cross-dresser]

4126 BUCHBINDER, Howard, *et al*. *Who's on Top? The Politics of Heterosexuality.* Toronto: Garamond Press, 1987.

4127 CAMPER, Carol, *et al*, eds. "Sex and Sexuality." A two-part special issue of *Fireweed* 37 (Winter 1993) and 38 (Spring 1993).

4128 CANADIAN GAY ARCHIVES. *Lesbian and Gay Heritage of Toronto.* Toronto: Canadian Gay Archives, 1982.

4129 CANADIAN WOMEN'S MOVEMENT ARCHIVES. *Lesbian and Gay Holdings at the Canadian Women's Movement Archives.* Toronto: Canadian Women's Movement Archives, 1987.

4130 CHAMBERLAND, Line. "Le lesbianisme: continuum féminin ou marronage? Réflexions pour une théorisation de l'expérience lesbienne." *Recherches féministes* 2, 2 (1989): 135-45.

4131 CHAMBERLAND, Line. "Remembering Lesbian Bars: Montreal, 1955-1975." *Journal of Homosexuality* 25, 3 (1993): 231-69. Co-published in *Gay Studies from the French Cultures: Voices from France, Belgium, Brazil, Canada and The Netherlands,* eds. Rommel Mendès-Leite and Pierre-Olivier de Busscher, 231-69. New York: The Haworth Press, 1993. Reprinted in *Canadian Women: A Reader,* eds. Wendy Mitchinson, *et al*, 352-79. Toronto: Harcourt Brace Canada, 1996.

4132 DESJARDINS, Gaston. "La pédagogie du sexe: un aspect du discours catholique sur la sexualité au Québec (1930-1960)." *Revue d'histoire de l'Amérique française* 43, 3 (hiver 1990): 381-401.

4133 DUPRAS, André and Hélène Dionne. "L'émergence de la sexologie au Québec." *Scientia Canadensis* 11, 2 (Fall/Winter 1987): 90-108.

4134 DUROCHER, Constance. "Heterosexuality: Sexuality or Social System?" *Resources for Feminist Research* 19, 3/4 (December 1990): 13-18.

4135 FINDLAY, Deborah. "Discovering Sex: Medical Science, Feminism and Intersexuality." *Canadian Review of Sociology and Anthropology* 32, 1 (February 1995). [1950s]

4136 HART, Fiona. "The Construction of Masculinity in Men's Friendships: Misogyny, Heterosexism and Homophobia." *Resources for Feminist Research* 19, 3/4 (December 1990): 60-67.

4137 HIGGINS, Ross and Line Chamberland. "Mixed Messages: Gays and Lesbians in Montreal Yellow Papers in the 1950s." In *The Challenge of Modernity: A Reader on Post-Confederation Canada,* ed. Ian McKay, 422-31. Toronto: McGraw-Hill Ryerson, 1992.

4138 KHAYATT, Didi. "Personal Politics and Sexuality." *Resources for Feminist Research* 19, 3/4 (December 1990): 8-13.

4139 KINSMAN, Gary. *The Regulation of Desire: Sexuality in Canada.* Montreal: Black Rose Books, 1987, revised 2nd edition, 1996.

4140 LAROUCHE, Jean-Marc. "L'émergence de la sexologie au Québec: De la militance éthique à la sexosophie." *Studies in Religion* 18, 1 (Winter 1989): 5-24.

4141 LUMSDEN, Ian. "Sexuality and the State: The Politics of 'Normal' Sexuality." *Atkinson Review of Canadian Studies* 1, 2 (Spring 1984): 3-9.

4142 MAYNARD, Steven. "'The Burning Wilful Evidence': Lesbian/Gay History and Archival Research." *Archivaria* 33 (Winter 1991-92): 195-201.

4143 MAYNARD, Steven. "Making Waves: Gender and Sex in the History of Seafaring." *Acadiensis* 22, 2 (Spring 1993): 144-53.

4144 MAYNARD, Steven. "Sex, Court Records, and Labour History." *Labour/Le Travail* 33 (Spring 1994): 187-93.

4145 MAYNARD, Steven. "In Search of 'Sodom North': The Writing of Lesbian and Gay History in English Canada, 1970-1990." *Canadian Review of Comparative Literature* 21, 1/2 (March/June 1994): 117-32.

4146 McKAY, Ian. "Debating Sexuality in Halifax, 1920: Mrs. Donald Shaw and Others." In *The Challenge of Modernity: A Reader on Post-Confederation Canada*, ed. Ian McKay, 331-45. Toronto: McGraw-Hill Ryerson, 1992.

4147 McLAREN, Angus. "Sex Radicalism in the Canadian Pacific Northwest, 1890-1920." *Journal of the History of Sexuality* 2, 4 (April 1992): 527-46. Reprinted in *American Sexual Politics: Sex, Gender, and Race since the Civil War*, eds. John C. Fout and Maura Shaw Tantillo, 141-60. Chicago and London: University of Chicago Press, 1993.

4148 MILLER, Alan V. *Lesbian Periodical Holdings in the Canadian Gay Archives*. Toronto: Canadian Gay Archives, 1981.

4149 MILLER, Alan V. "Canadian Gay Archives: Holdings of Lesbian Periodicals." *Resources for Feminist Research* 12, 1 (March 1983): 85-86.

4150 O'LEARY, D., ed. *A Crisis of Understanding: Homosexuality and the Canadian Church*. Toronto: Welch, 1986.

4151 PLEAU, Marcel. "Les gais et lesbiennes du Québec: une histoire politique à écrire." *Bulletin de l'Association québécoise d'histoire politique* 2, 4 (printemps 1994): 20-23.

4152 RIORDON, Michael. *The First Stone: Homosexuality and the United Church*. Toronto: McClelland and Stewart, 1990.

4153 ROSS, Becki. "Heterosexuals Only Need Apply: The Secretary of State's Regulation of Lesbian Existence." *Resources for Feminist Research* 17, 3 (1988): 35-38.

4154 RUMSCHEIDT, Barbara. "Institutionalizing Christian Heterosexism in the Maritime Conference of the United Church of Canada." *Resources for Feminist Research* 19, 3/4 (December 1990): 75-80.

4155 RYLEY, Bay. "From Regulated to Celebrated Sexuality: Can-Can Girls and Gold Diggers of the Klondike." *Canadian Woman Studies* 14, 4 (Fall 1994): 58-61.

4156 SAUNDERS, Martha. "Sexuality, Justice and Feminist Ethics." *Resources for Feminist Research* 19, 3/4 (December 1990): 33-39.

4157 SCHLESINGER, Benjamin, ed. *Sexual Behaviour in Canada: Patterns and Problems*. Toronto: University of Toronto Press, 1977.

4158 SQUIRE, Anne M. "Homosexuality, Ordination and the United Church of Canada." *Queen's Quarterly* 92, 2 (Summer 1991): 338-52.

4159 ROTENBERG, Lori. "Impact of Homophobia, Heterosexism and Closetedness on Intimacy Dynamics in Lesbian Relationships." *Resources for Feminist Research* 18, 2 (1989): 3-9.

4160 SÉGUIN, Robert-Lionel. *La Vie libertine en Nouvelle-France au XVIIe siècle*. Montréal: Lémeac, 1972.

4161 STONE, Sharon Dale, ed. *Lesbians in Canada*. Toronto: Between the Lines, 1990.

4162 STRANGE, Carolyn. "From Modern Babylon to a City Upon a Hill: The Toronto Social Survey Commission of 1915 and the Search for Sexual Order in the City." In *Patterns of the Past: Interpreting Ontario's History*, eds. Roger Hall, William Westfall and Laurel Sefton MacDowell, 255-77. Toronto and Oxford: Dundurn Press, 1988.

4163 STRANGE, Carolyn. *Toronto's Girl Problem: The Perils and Pleasures of the City, 1880-1930*. Toronto: University of Toronto Press, 1995.

4164 VALVERDE, Mariana. *Sex, Power and Pleasure*. Toronto: The Women's Press, 1985.

4165 WINTER, Bronwyn. "La 'communauté lesbienne' et l'idéologie hétéropatriarchale: les pièges du libéralisme." *Resources for Feminist Research* 19, 3/4 (December 1990): 49-53.

4166 ZAREMBA, Eve. "Shades of Lavender: Lesbian Sex and Sexuality." In *Still Ain't Satisfied: Canadian Feminism Today*, eds. M. Fitzgerald, C. Guberman and M. Wolfe, 85-92. Toronto: Canadian Women's Educational Press, 1982.

SPORT/PHYSICAL EDUCATION

COMPARED WITH TOPICS such as education or work, which have preoccupied feminist scholars from the early 1970s, Canadian women's historians came late to the study of sport and physical education, and the literature remains undeveloped. During the 1970s, a small number of studies were produced by former athletes like Abby Hoffman, who looked to their pioneering counterparts in the past for inspiration. Early investigations by physical education graduates Ann Hall and Marian Pitters-Caswell documented nineteenth-century opposition to women's participation in sports and athletics, proclaimed the 1920s and 1930s as the "golden age" of women's sport in Canada, and explored the links between women's participation in sports and the emergence of organized feminism.

Sport history has had great difficulty gaining acceptance in Canadian historical writing, and only in the past decade has it to come into its own as a legitimate field for scholarly investigation. Women's sport history has been further disadvantaged by the indifference of feminist scholars to sport issues. Regarding sport as a hopelessly male institution contaminated by its associations with violence and competition, grass-roots feminist organizations were reluctant to mobilize on sport issues during the 1970s. It was not until 1981 that the Canadian Association for the Advancement of Women and Sport was organized, its newsletter providing an important outlet for articles on the history and sociology of women's sport. In the 1980s, public discussions concerning the low participation rate of girls in organized physical activity, the underfunding of women's athletics, media portrayals of female athletes, homophobia in sports organizations, and legal challenges to the exclusion of girls from boys' sports teams, have helped to increase awareness of the links between feminism and women's sports.

At present there are few scholarly treatments of women's sport history in Canada, and most of these have been published in sport history journals and in two international anthologies on the history of women's sports. Some solid work has been produced on outstanding athletes such as Ethel Catherwood and Barbara Ann Scott and, of course, on Canada's internationally renowned championship basketball team of the interwar decades, the Edmonton Grads. The participation of Canadian women in the Olympic and Commonwealth Games has also received attention, and interesting new work has appeared on the history of women in professional rodeo. Recent studies by sociologists adopting a labour perspective explore the widespread discrimination against women in coaching and sports administration.

The only book-length treatment of Canadian women's sport history remains Helen Lenskyj's *Out of Bounds*. Lenskyj was the first scholar to apply a radical feminist perspective to women's sport in Canadian history, tracing links between sport, sexuality, femininity, and heterosexism, and arguing that the institution of sport has enforced male control over female sexuality and the female reproductive function. Her book and many articles examine the place of physical education in girls' schooling, and the impact of the medical profession, the media, modern psychiatry and psychology on Canadian women's participation in, and experience of, sport. Recent interest in post-structuralist approaches and discourse analysis suggests the potential for future work by scholars interested in examining medical and media constructions of gender, female athleticism, femininity and the female body.

GENERAL

4167 AGGER, Ellen. "Out of the Kitchen and Into the Streets." *Canadian Women's Studies* 2, 2 (1980): 90-91. [women's running and races in the 1970s]

✓ 4168 BLACKWOOD, Faye, *et al*, eds. "Women and Girls in Sport and Physical Activity." A special issue of *Canadian Woman Studies* 15, 4 (Fall 1995).

4169 BRAND, Johanna. "The Girls of Summer." *Herizons* 6, 2 (Summer 1992): 21-23. [Canadian women playing in American baseball league, 1940s-50s]

4170 BRAY, C. "YWCA Physical Education Departments During World War Two." *Proceedings. 5th Canadian Symposium on the History of Sport and Physical Education,* 402-11. Toronto: University of Toronto Press, 1982.

4171 CHALUS, Elaine. "The Edmonton Commercial Graduates: Women's History, An Integrationist Approach." In *Winter Sports in the West,* eds. Elise A. Corbet and Anthony W. Rasporich, 69-86. Calgary: Historical Society of Alberta, 1990.

4172 COCHRANE, Jean, Abby Hoffman and Pat Kincaid. *Sports.* Women in Canadian Life Series. Toronto: Fitzhenry & Whiteside, 1977.

4173 DEWAR, J. "The Edmonton Grads: The Team and Its Social Significance, 1915-1940." In *Her Story in Sport: A Historical Anthology of Women in Sports,* ed. Reet Howell, 541-47. West Point, NY: Leisure Press, 1982.

4174 GEORGE, Judith Jenkins. "The Fad of North American Women's Endurance Swimming During the Post World War I Era." *Canadian Journal of History of Sport* 26, 1 (May 1995): 52-72.

4175 GURNEY, Helen. *Girls' Sports: A Century of Progress in Ontario High Schools.* Don Mills: Federation of School Athletic Associations, 1979.

4176 GURNEY, Helen. "Major Influences on the Development of High School Girls' Sports in Ontario." In *Her Story in Sports: A Historical Anthology of Women in Sports,* ed. Reet Howell, 472-91. West Point, NY: Leisure Press, 1982.

4177 HALL, M. Ann. "Sport and Physical Activity in the Lives of Canadian Women." In *Canadian Sport: Sociological Perspectives,* eds. R.S. Gruneau and J.G. Albinson. Don Mills: Addison-Wesley, 1976.

✓ 4178 HALL, M. Ann. "Rarely Have We Asked Why: Reflections on Canadian Women's Experience in Sport." *Atlantis* 6, 1 (Fall 1980): 51-60.

4179 HALL, M. Ann, ed. "Special Issue: The Gendering of Sport, Leisure, and Physical Education." *Women's Studies International Forum* 10, 4 (1987).

✓ 4180 HALL, M. Ann and Dorothy A. Richardson. *Fair Ball: Towards Sex Equality in Canadian Sport.* Ottawa: Canadian Advisory Council on the Status of Women, 1982.

4181 HALL, Ann, *et al. Sport in Canadian Society: An Introduction.* Toronto: McClelland and Stewart, 1991.

4182 HANSON, Christilot. *Canadian Entry.* Toronto: Clarke Irwin, 1966. [equestrian dressage competition at the Tokyo Olympics]

4183 HOFFMAN, Abby. "1923-1935: the golden age of women's sport." *Branching Out* 7, 1 (1980): 23-5, 52.

4184 HOTCHKISS, Ron. "'The Matchless Six': Canadian Women at the Olympics, 1928." *The Beaver* 73, 5 (Oct./Nov. 1993): 23-42.

4185 HOWELL, Nancy. *Sports and Games in Canadian Life, 1700 to the Present.* Toronto: Macmillan, 1969.

4186 HOWELL, Reet, ed. *Her Story in Sport: A Historical Anthology of Women in Sports.* West Point, NY: Leisure Press, 1982.

4187 HOWELL, Reet. "Women in the Sports Halls of Fame." In *Her Story in Sports: A Historical Anthology of Women in Sports,* ed. Reet Howell, 343-50. West Point, NY: Leisure Press, 1982.

4188 KEYES, Mary. "Woman and Sport." In *A Concise History of Sport in Canada,* eds. Don Morrow *et al,* 230-55. Toronto: Oxford University Press, 1989.

4189 LAMONT, Kate. *We Can Achieve: A History of Women in Sport at the University of Alberta.* Edmonton: Academic Print and Publishing, 1988.

4190 LE CLAIR, Jill. *Winners and Losers: Sport and Physical Activity in the 90s.* Toronto: Thompson Educational Publishing, 1993.

4191 LECOMPTE, Mary Lou. "Cowgirls at the Crossroads: Women in Professional Rodeo, 1885-1922." *Canadian Journal of History of Sport* 20, 2 (December 1989): 27-48.

4192 LECOMPTE, Mary Lou. "Home on the Range: Women in Professional Rodeo, 1929-1947." *Journal of Sport History* 17, 3 (Winter 1990): 318-46.

4193 LENSKYJ, Helen. "Femininity First: Sport and Physical Education for Ontario Girls, 1890-1930." *Canadian Journal of History of Sport* 13, 2 (December 1982): 4-17.

4194 LENSKYJ, Helen. "Moral Physiology in Physical Education and Sport for Girls in Ontario, 1890-1930." *Proceedings. 5th Canadian Symposium on the History of Sport and Physical Education,* 139-50. Toronto: University of Toronto Press, 1982.

4195 LENSKYJ, Helen. "We Want to Play...We'll Play: Women and Sport in the Twenties and Thirties." *Canadian Woman Studies* 4, 3 (Spring 1983): 15-18.

4196 LENSKYJ, Helen. "A Kind of Precipitate Waddle: Early Opposition to Women Running." In *Sport and the Sociological Imagination*, eds. N. Theberge and P. Donnelly, 153-61. Fort Worth: Texas Christian University Press, 1984.

4197 LENSKYJ, Helen. *Out of Bounds: Women, Sport and Sexuality.* Toronto: The Women's Press, 1986.

4198 LENSKYJ, Helen. "Physical Activity for Canadian Women, 1890-1930: Media Views." In *From Fair Sex to Feminism: Sport and the Socialization of Women in the Industrial and Post-Industrial Eras*, eds. J.A. Mangan and Roberta J. Park, 208-31. London: Frank Cass and Co. Ltd., 1987.

4199 LENSKYJ, Helen. *Women, Sport and Physical Activity: Research and Bibliography.* Ottawa: Fitness and Amateur Sport Canada, 1988; 2nd edition, 1991.

4200 LENSKYJ, Helen. "Common sense and physiology: North American medical views on women and sport, 1890-1930." *Canadian Journal of History of Sport* 21, 1 (May 1990): 49-64.

4201 LENSKYJ, Helen. "Putting the Physical into Education: The Politics of Teaching Women's Sport History in High School." *History and Social Science Teacher* 25, 3 (Spring 1990): 138-43.

4202 LENSKYJ, Helen. "Training for 'True Womanhood': Physical Education for Girls in Ontario Schools, 1890-1920." *Historical Studies in Education* 2, 2 (Fall 1990): 205-23.

4203 LENSKYJ, Helen Jefferson. "Good Sports: Feminists Organizing on Sport Issues in the 1970s and 1980s." *Resources for Feminist Research* 20, 3/4 (Fall/Winter 1991): 130-35.

4204 LENSKYJ, Helen. "Whose Sport? Whose Traditions? Canadian Women and Sport in the Twentieth Century." *International Journal of the History of Sport* 9, 1 (1992): 141-50.

4205 LEWIS, Pamela. "Myrtle Cook McGowan: a special tribute." *CAAWS Newsletter* 4, 1 (Spring 1985): 6-8.

4206 LINDSAY, Peter. "Woman's Place in Nineteenth Century Canadian Sport." *Canadian Association of Health, Physical Education and Recreation Journal* 37, 1 (Sept./Oct. 1970): 25-28. Reprinted in *Canadian Woman Studies* 1, 4 (1979): 22-24; in *Physical Activity and the Social Sciences*, 5th edition, ed. W.N. Widmeyer, 91-96. Ann Arbor, MI: Mouvement Pub., 1983; and in *Her Story in Sport: A Historical Anthology of Women in Sports*, ed. Reet Howell, 80-86. West Point, NY: Leisure Press, 1982.

4207 MANN, Brenda and Peat O'Neil. "Corsets unlaced: the beginning of women in sport." *Branching Out* 3 (July/August 1976): 32-35.

4208 McDONALD, David. "The Golden Age of Women and Sport in Canada." *Champion Magazine* 5, 1 (March 1981). Reprinted in *Canadian Woman Studies* 15, 4 (Fall 1995): 12-15.

4209 McDONALD, David and Lauren Drewery. *For the Record: Canada's Greatest Women Athletes.* Rexdale, ON: John Wiley and Sons Canada Limited, 1981.

4210 McFADDEN, Fred. *Abby Hoffman.* Don Mills: Fitzhenry and Whiteside, 1977.

4211 McFARLANE, Brian. *Proud Past, Bright Future: One Hundred Years of Canadian Women's Hockey.* Don Mills: Stoddart Publishing, 1994.

4212 MITCHELL, S. "The Development of Women's Organized Sport in the 1920s: A Study of the Canadian Ladies' Golf Union." In *Her Story in Sport: A Historical Anthology of Women in Sports*, ed. Reet Howell, 564-71. West Point, NY: Leisure Press, 1982.

4213 MORROW, Don. "Sweetheart Sport: Barbara Ann Scott and the Post World War II Image of the Female Athlete in Canada." *Canadian Journal of History of Sport* 8, 1 (May 1987): 36-54.

4214 PALMASON, Diane. "In memory of Myrtle." *CAAWS Newsletter* 4, 1 (Spring 1985): 9-10.

4215 PARASCHAK, Victoria. "Organized Sport for Native Females on the Six Nations Reserve, Ontario from 1968 to 1980: A Comparison of Dominant and Emergent Sport Systems." *Canadian Journal of History of Sport* 21, 2 (December 1990): 70-80.

4216 PARKS, A.E. Marie. *The Development of Women's Athletics at the University of Toronto.* Toronto: Women's Athletic Association, 1961.

4217 PITTERS, Marian. "Women's Participation in Sporting Activities as an Indicator of a Feminist Movement in Canada Between 1867-1914." In *Her Story in Sport: A Historical Anthology of Women in Sports*, ed. Reet Howell, 141-53. West Point, NY: Leisure Press, 1982.

4218 PITTERS, Marian. "An Analysis of Humour Pertaining to Sportswomen in Canadian Newspapers from 1910-1920." In *Her Story in Sports: A Historical Anthology of Women in Sports*, ed. Reet Howell, 223-33. West Point, NY: Leisure Press, 1982.

4219 RANDALL, Nora Delahunt. "Ladies of the court: the Edmonton grads, 1915-1940." *Makara* 1 (August-September 1976): 12-17.

4220 RANSOM, Diane. "The 'Saskatoon Lily': A Biography of Ethel Catherwood." *Saskatchewan History* 41, 3 (Autumn 1988): 81-98.

4221 REILLY, Heather. "Attitudes to Women in Sport in Eastern Ontario, 1867-1885." *Proceedings. 5th Canadian Symposium on the History of Sport and Physical Education,* 380-86. Toronto: University of Toronto Press, 1982.

4222 ROXBOROUGH, Henry. *One Hundred - Not Out: The Story of Nineteenth Century Canadian Sport.* Toronto: Ryerson Press, 1966.

4223 SCHRODT, Barbara. "Canadian Women at the Olympics, 1924-1972." *Canadian Association of Health, Physical Education and Recreation Journal* 42, 4 (March/April 1976): 34-42. Revised and reprinted in *Her Story in Sport: A Historical Anthology of Women in Sports,* ed. Reet Howell, 273-83. West Point, NY: Leisure Press, 1982.

4224 SCHRODT, Barbara. "Canadian Women at the Commonwealth Games: 1930-1974." *Canadian Association of Health, Physical Education and Recreation Journal* 44, 4 (March/April 1978): 30-37. Revised and reprinted in *Her Story in Sport: A Historical Anthology of Women in Sports,* ed. Reet Howell, 284-93. West Point, NY: Leisure Press, 1982.

4225 SMITH, Michael J. "Graceful Athleticism or Robust Womanhood: The Sporting Culture of Women in Victorian Nova Scotia, 1870-1914." *Journal of Canadian Studies* 23, 1/2 (Spring/Summer 1988): 120-37.

4226 SPEARS, Betty. "Mary, Mary, Quite Contrary, Why Do Women Play?" *Canadian Journal of History of Sport* 18, 1 (May 1987): 67-75.

4227 "A Sporting Life." *Alberta History* 26, 2 (Spring 1978): 13-20.

4228 SWAIN, Sue. "History of the Ontario Women's Intercollegiate Athletic Association (OWIAA)." *Canadian Association of Health, Physical Education and Recreation Journal* 49 (Nov./Dec. 1982): 26-28.

4229 SWAIN, Susan. "Barbara Ann, are you still happy, Happy?" *Chatelaine* 48 (November 1975): 51, 74+.

4230 THÉBÈRGE, Nancy. "Gender, Work and Power: The Case of Women in Coaching." *Canadian Journal of Sociology* 15, 1 (Winter 1990): 59-75.

4231 THÉBÈRGE, Nancy. "Managing Domestic Work and Careers: The Experience of Women in Coaching." *Atlantis* 17, 2 (1992): 11-21.

4232 VERTINSKY, Patricia A. "Gender Relations, Women's History and Sport History: A Decade of Changing Enquiry, 1983-1993." *Journal of Sport History* 21, 1 (Spring 1994): 1-24.

4233 VERTINSKY, Patricia A. "Sport History and Gender Relations, 1983-1993, Bibliography." *Journal of Sport History* 21, 1 (Spring 1994): 25-58.

4234 WENN, Stephen R. "Give Me the Keys Please: Avery Brundage, Canadian Journalists, and the Barbara Ann Scott Phaeton Affair." *Journal of Sport History* 18, 2 (Summer 1991): 241-54.

4235 WISE, S.F. and D. Fisher. *Canada's Sporting Heroes.* Don Mills: General Publishing Co., 1974.

4236 YOUNG, Alexander. "Maritime Attitudes to Women in Sport, 1920-1939." *Proceedings. 5th Canadian Symposium on the History of Sport and Physical Education,* 227-31. Toronto: University of Toronto Press, 1982.

4237 ZEIGLER, Earl. "A Brief Chronicle of Sport and Physical Activity for Women." *Proceedings of the Second Canadian Symposium on the History of Sport and Physical Education,* 377-95. Ottawa: Dept. of Health and Welfare, 1972. Reprinted in *A History of Physical Education and Sport in the United States and Canada,* ed. E.F. Zeigler, 139-54. Illinois: Stipes Publishing Co., 1975.

4238 ZERBE, Louisa. "The 1930 UBC Women's Basketball Team: Those Other World Champions." In *Her Story in Sports: A Historical Anthology of Women in Sports,* ed. Reet Howell, 548-51. West Point, NY: Leisure Press, 1982.

UNIONS/LABOUR ACTIVISM

THE STRONG INFLUENCE of socialist feminism on Canadian women's historians in the 1970s ensured that the question of women's historical relationship to the labour movement in Canada would be one of the first issues addressed by "second-wave" feminist scholars. Committed to "learning from yesterday," labour historians sought the historical origins of Canadian women's low rate of participation in unions, by hoping to discredit the prevailing view that women workers were passive, uninterested in labour issues and difficult to organize. Many studies of the nineteenth and early twentieth centuries have identified the distinctive characteristics of the female labour force and the systemic barriers within the labour movement that mitigated against the organization of women workers. Women who were young and single, and whose jobs were classified as unskilled by virtue of their association with women's traditional work, confronted unions dedicated to protecting the interests of their skilled male membership, and a masculine union culture that made few concessions to the particular needs of women. The attempts of marginalized women workers to improve conditions sometimes made them more visible to their contemporaries and hence to historians. Women's participation in strikes and union drives has been an ongoing topic of investigation for labour historians who have found in such efforts, successful or not, inspiring examples of women's agency and resistance to oppressive working conditions.

Class divisions between women discouraged close ties between the labour movement and the women's movement at the turn of the century. Exceptional women such as Helena Gutteridge and others whose lives embodied a commitment to both feminism and the cause of working women have not surprisingly attracted the notice of historians. Some social reformers and labour activists came to support state intervention, rather than unions, as a solution to the exploitation of women workers, and early campaigns for the introduction of a minimum wage law and other forms of protective legislation have also been the subject of ongoing investigation (see also Law/Public Policy). The socialist sympathies of many feminist labour historians have stimulated enquiries about the roles of socialist and Communist women in the labour movement, and a vigorous debate is in progress about their class and gender loyalties, their attempts to reconcile socialism and feminism, and the socialist position on labour and "the woman question" (see also Politics). While the relationship between class and gender has been central to historical studies of Canadian women's labour activism, little attention has been paid as yet to the importance of religious and ethnic/racial identities. In Quebec, several scholars have examined the role of women in Catholic unions, while the importance of ethnicity and race has been highlighted in recent studies of the Jewish labour movement in Toronto and the unionization of shoreworkers in British Columbia.

The recent movement of Canadian women's historians into the interwar and post-World War II eras, as well as a growing commitment to the use of oral history, has spawned new studies of women's labour activism in a more contemporary context. While women workers' participation in landmark strikes continues to engage the interest of historians, some are also investigating the increasingly militant role of working-class housewives in strikes involving male workers. The role of employers in thwarting the organization of women workers is finally receiving attention in recent studies of the introduction of recreation programs and other welfare schemes in the workplace. The dramatic increase in the percentage of organized women workers since the 1970s, has been attributed to the growth of public sector unionism, and to attempts by industrial unions to recoup their recent losses in the male-dominated manufacturing sector by organizing women workers in the clerical and service sectors. Some of these unions have been the focus of major studies by historians and sociologists examining the compatibility of class consciousness and female gender consciousnessness in Canadian unions since the 1950s. A major preoccupation has been the relationship of trade union feminism to the wider women's movement and the coming together, since the 1970s, of a broad spectrum of women on issues such as pay equity and sexual harrassment (see Feminism/Women's Movements). Labour leaders like Grace Hartman and Madeleine Parent, both of whom served on the National Action Committee on the Status of Women, embody the links between these two movements. Parent also symbolizes the particular links between unionism and feminism documented in the growing scholarship on the role of women within the militant nationalist trade union movement in Quebec.

GENERAL

4239 BAKER, Patricia. "Reflections on Life Stories: Women's Bank Union Activism." In *Women Challenging Unions: Feminism, Democracy, and Militancy*, eds. Linda Briskin and Patricia McDermott, 62-86. Toronto: University of Toronto Press, 1993.

4240 BALKAN, Donna. "Practicing What We Preach...Women, Unions and Affirmative Action." *Canadian Woman Studies* 6, 4 (Winter 1985): 49-51.

4241 BANNERMAN, Josie, Kathy Chopik and Ann Zurbrigg. "Cheap at Half the Price: The History of the Fight for Equal Pay in BC." In *Not Just Pin Money: Selected Essays on the History of Women's Work in British Columbia*, eds. Barbara K. Latham and Roberta J. Pazdro, 297-313. Victoria: Camosun College, 1984.

4242 BERNARD, Elaine. *The Long Distance Feeling: A History of the Telecommunications Workers Union*. Vancouver: New Star Books, 1982.

4243 BERNARD, Elaine. "Last Back: Folklore and the Telephone Operators in the 1919 Vancouver General Strike." In *Not Just Pin Money: Selected Essays on the History of Women's Work in British Columbia*, eds. Barbara K. Latham and Roberta J. Pazdro, 279-86. Victoria: Camosun College, 1984.

4244 BLACK, Errol. "25¢ an Hour; 48 Hours a Week; More Toilets; Less Cats: The Labour Struggles of the 'Girls' at the A.E. McKenzie Company in Brandon." *Prairie Forum* 17, 1 (Spring 1992): 33-59.

4245 BOEHM, Marina C. *Who Makes the Decisions?: Women's Participation in Canadian Unions*. Kingston: Industrial Relations Centre, Queen's University, 1991.

4246 BRISKIN, Linda. "Women, Unions and Leadership." *Canadian Dimension* (January/February 1990): 38-41. Reprinted in *Work in Canada: Readings in the Sociology of Work and Industry*, eds. Graham S. Lowe and Harvey J. Krahn, 284-91. Scarborough: Nelson Canada, 1993.

4247 BRISKIN, Linda and Patricia McDermott, eds. *Women Challenging Unions: Feminism, Democracy, and Militancy*. Toronto: University of Toronto Press, 1993.

4248 BRISKIN, Linda and Lynda Yanz, eds. *Union Sisters: Women in the Labour Movement*. Toronto: The Women's Press, 1983.

4249 BURR, Christina. "Defending 'The Art Preservative': Class and Gender Relations in the Printing Trades Unions, 1850-1914." *Labour/Le Travail* 31 (Spring 1993): 47-73.

4250 BURR, Christina. "'That Coming Curse—The Incompetent Compositress': Class and Gender Relations in the Toronto Typographical Union during the Late Nineteenth Century." *Canadian Historical Review* 74, 3 (Sept. 1993): 344-66.

4251 CAMPBELL, Marie. "Sexism in British Columbia Trade Unions, 1900-1920." In *In Her Own Right: Selected Essays on Women's History in BC*, eds. Barbara Latham and Cathy Kess, 167-86. Victoria: Camosun College, 1980.

4252 CONDE, Carole and Karl Beveridge. *First Contract: Women and the Fight to Unionize*. Toronto: Between the Lines, 1986.

4253 CORNISH, Mary and Laurell Ritchie. *Getting Organized: Building a Union*. Toronto: Women's Press, 1980.

4254 COULTER, Rebecca Priegert. "Alberta Nurses and the 'Illegal' Strike of 1988." In *Women Challenging Unions: Feminism, Democracy, and Militancy*, eds. Linda Briskin and Patricia McDermott, 44-61. Toronto: University of Toronto Press, 1993.

4255 CREESE, Gillian. "The Politics of Dependence: Women, Work and Unemployment in the Vancouver Labour Movement Before World War II." *Canadian Journal of Sociology* 13, 1/2 (Winter/Spring 1988): 121-42. Reprinted in *Class, Gender and Region: Essays in Canadian Historical Sociology*, ed. Gregory S. Kealey. St. John's: Committee on Canadian Labour History, 1988; and in *British Columbia Reconsidered: Essays on Women*, eds. Gillian Creese and Veronica Strong-Boag, 364-90. Vancouver: Press Gang Publishers, 1992.

4256 CREESE, Gillian. "Power and Pay: The Union and Equal Pay at BC Electric/Hydro." *Labour/Le Travail* 32 (Fall 1993): 225-45.

4257 CUNEO, Carl J. *Pay Equity: The Labour-Feminist Challenge*. Toronto: Oxford University Press, 1990.

4258 DAIGLE, Johanne. "L'évolution des revendications des travailleuses salariées québécoises depuis la crise." *Relations* 41 (juillet/août 1981).

4259 DEN HERTOG, Johanna. "Helena Gutteridge, 1880-1960" BC Teachers' Federation. *Labour History* 1 (Fall 1978): 37.

4260 DIAMOND, Sara. "You Can't Scare Me. I'm Sticking to the Union," *Kinesis* (June 1979): 13-17.

4261 DIAMOND, Sara. "Women in the British Columbia Labour Movement." Canadian Oral History Association. *Journal* 6 (1983).

4262 DIAMOND, Sara. "A Union Man's Wife: The Ladies' Auxiliary Movement in the IWA, The Lake Cowichan Experience." In *Not Just Pin Money: Selected Essays on the History of Women's Work in British Columbia*, eds. Barbara K. Latham and Roberta J. Pazdro, 287-96. Victoria: Camosun College, 1984.

4263 DIONNE, Danielle S. "Syndicalisme au féminin." *Canadian Women's Studies* 2, 4 (1980): 28-31.

4264 DORION, Jacques. "Laure Gaudreault, cinquante ans de syndicalisme enseignant au Québec." *Education Québec* 5 (juillet/août 1975): 21-30.

4265 DUMAS, Evelyn. "The Shmata Strikes." In *The Bitter Thirties in Quebec*, ed. and trans. Arnold Bennett, 43-69. Montreal: Black Rose Books, 1975.

4266 DUMAS, Marie-Claire and Francine Mayer, eds. *Les femmes et l'équité salariale, un pouvoir à gagner!* Montréal: Les Éditions du remue ménage, 1989.

4267 EDELSON, Miriam. *Challenging Unions: Feminist Process and Democracy in the Labour Movement.* Ottawa: Canadian Research Institute for the Advancement of Women, 1987.

4268 FAHMY-EID, Nadia and Lucie Piché. *Si le travail m'était conté autrement: Les travailleuses de la CTCC-CSN. Quelques fragments d'histoire, 1921-1976.* Montréal: Confédération des syndicats nationaux, 1987.

4269 FERLAND, Jacques. "Syndicalisme 'parcellaire' et syndicalism 'collectif': une interprétation socio-technique des conflits ouvriers dans deux industries québécoises, 1880-1914." *Labour/Le Travail* 19 (Spring 1987): 49-88.

4270 FERLAND, Jacques. "'In Search of the Unbound Prometheia': A Comparative View of Women's Activism in Two Quebec Industries, 1869-1908." *Labour/Le Travail* 24 (Fall 1989): 11-44.

4271 FRAGER, Ruth. "No Proper Deal: Women Workers and the Canadian Labour Movement, 1870-1940." In *Union Sisters: Women in the Labour Movement,* eds. Linda Briskin and Lynda Yanz, 44-64. Toronto: The Women's Press, 1983.

4272 FRAGER, Ruth. "Sewing Solidarity: The Eaton's Strike of 1912." *Canadian Woman Studies* 7, 3 (Fall 1986): 96-98.

4273 FRAGER, Ruth. "Class and Ethnic Barriers to Feminist Perspectives in Toronto's Jewish Labour Movement, 1919-1939." *Studies in Political Economy* 30 (Autumn 1989): 143-65. Reprinted in *Canadian Working Class History: Selected Readings,* eds. Laurel Sefton-MacDowell and Ian Radforth. Toronto: Canadian Scholars' Press, 1992; and in *Feminism in Action: Studies in Political Economy,* eds. M. Patricia Connelly and Pat Armstrong. Toronto: Canadian Scholars' Press, 1993.

4274 FRAGER, Ruth. "Class, Ethnicity, and Gender in the Eaton Strikes of 1912 and 1934." In *Gender Conflicts: New Essays in Women's History,* eds. Franca Iacovetta and Mariana Valverde, 189-228. Toronto: University of Toronto Press, 1992.

4275 FRAGER, Ruth. *Sweatshop Strife: Class, Ethnicity, and Gender in the Jewish Labour Movement of Toronto, 1900-1939.* Toronto: University of Toronto Press, 1992.

4276 FUDGE, Judy. "Community Unionism: Coalition Fights to Clean up the Garment Industry." *Canadian Dimension* 28, 2 (March/April 1994): 27-29. [organizing homeworkers]

4277 GAGNON, D. "L'impact de la féminisation du marché du travail sur les développements récents de la structure industrielle québécoise." *Cahiers de l'AC-FAS* 41 (1986): 37-59.

4278 GAGNON, Mona-Josée. "Les femmes dans le mouvement syndical québécois." *Sociologie et Sociétés* 6, 1 (mai 1974): 17-36.

4279 GAGNON, Mona-Josée. "Les comités syndicaux de condition féminine." In *Travailleuses et féministes: Les femmes dans la société québécoise,* eds. Marie Lavigne and Yolande Pinard, 161-76. Montréal: Boréal Express, 1983.

4280 GAGNON, Mona-Josée. "Women in the Trade-Union Movement in Quebec." In *Quebec Since 1945: Selected Readings,* ed. Michael D. Behiels, 157-74. Toronto: Copp Clark Pitman, 1987.

4281 GANNAGÉ, Charlene. "Changing Dimensions of Control and Resistance: The Toronto Garment Industry." *Journal of Canadian Studies* 24, 4 (Winter 1989/90): 41-60.

4282 GAUVIN-CHOUINARD, Monique and Michèle Caron. "Les femmes et le syndicalisme au Nouveau-Brunswick." *Égalité* 10 (automne 1983): 95-108.

4283 GÉRIN-LAJOIE, Soeur Marie. "Le syndicalisme féminin." In *Québécoises au XXe siècle,* ed. Michèle Jean, Montréal: Éditions du Jour, 1974.

4284 GERVAIS, Solange Fernet. "Regroupement des femmes au Québec." *Resources for Feminist Research* 11, 1 (March 1982): 64-65. [organization of Quebec agricultural workers since 1920]

4285 GINGRAS, Anne-Marie, Chantal Maillé and Evelyne Tardy. *Sexes et militantisme.* Montréal: CIDIHCA, 1989.

4286 HOGUE, Jacqueline. "Madeleine Parent: une militante chevronnée." *Canadian Woman Studies* 7, 3 (Fall 1986): 103-04.

4287 HORODYSKI, Mary. "Women and the Winnipeg General Strike of 1919." *Manitoba History* 11 (Spring 1986): 28-37.

4288 HORODYSKI, Mary. "The Eaton's Strike." *Fireweed* 25 (Fall 1987): 68-71.

4289 HORODYSKI, Mary. "'That was quite a strike alright...': Women and the Winnipeg General Strike of 1919." *Fireweed* 26 (Winter/Spring 1988): 12-31.

4290 HOWARD, Irene. "The Mothers' Council of Vancouver: Holding the Fort for the Unemployed, 1935-38." *BC Studies* 69/70 (Spring/Summer 1986): 249-87.

4291 KATES, Christine J.N. "'Identical or Substantially Identical': Bell Canada and the Struggle for Equal Pay, 1967-1976." *Canadian Journal of Women and the Law* 4, 1 (1990): 133-65.

4292 KEALEY, Linda. "Women and Labour during World War I: Women Workers and the Minimum Wage in Manitoba." In *First Days, Fighting Days: Women in Manitoba History,* ed. Mary Kinnear, 76-99. Regina: Canadian Plains Research Center, University of Regina, 1987.

4293 KEALEY, Linda. "No Special Protection, No Sympathy: Women's Activism in the Canadian Labour Revolt of 1919." In *Class, Community and the Labour Market: Wales and Canada, 1850-1930*, eds. Deian R. Hopkin and Gregory S. Kealey, 134-59. St. John's: Society for Welsh Labour History and the Canadian Committee on Labour History, 1989.

4294 KIDD, Dorothy. "Women's Organization: Learning from Yesterday." In *Women at Work: Ontario, 1850-1930*, eds. Janice Acton, *et al*, 331-61. Toronto: Canadian Women's Educational Press, 1974.

4295 KNIGHT, Phyllis and Rolf Knight. *A Very Ordinary Life*. Vancouver: New Star Books, 1974.

4296 KUMAR, Pradeep. "Collective Bargaining and Women's Workplace Concerns." In *Women Challenging Unions: Feminism, Democracy, and Militancy*, eds. Linda Briskin and Patricia McDermott, 207-30. Toronto: University of Toronto Press, 1993.

4297 KUMAR, Pradeep and Lynn Acri. *Unions' Collective Bargaining Agenda on Women's Issues: The Ontario Experience*. Kingston: Industrial Relations Centre, Queen's University, 1993.

4298 LACELLE, Nicole. *Madeleine Parent, Léa Roback, Entretiens avec Nicole Lacelle*. Montréal: Les Éditions du remue-ménage, 1988.

4299 LAPOINTE, Michelle. "Le syndicat catholique des allumetières de Hull, 1919-1924." *Revue d'histoire de l'Amérique française* 32, 4 (mars 1979): 603-28.

4300 LEAH, Ronnie. "Linking the Struggle: Racism, Feminism and the Union Movement." In *Race, Class and Gender: Bonds and Barriers*, ed. Jessie Vorst, 166-95. Toronto: Between the Lines, 1989.

4301 LEMAIRE, Christine. "Les femmes dans *Le Monde Ouvrier*, 1929-1937." *Cahiers d'histoire* 6, 1 (automne 1985): 63-81.

4302 LEROUX, Eric. "Les revendications syndicales concernant le salaire minimum des femmes au Québec, 1919-1937." *Bulletin du Regroupement des chercheurs-chercheures en histoire des travailleurs et travailleuses du Québec* 20, 3 (automne 1994): 5-18.

4303 LIPSIG-MUMME, Carla. "Organizing Women in the Clothing Trades: Homework and the 1983 Garment Strike in Canada." *Studies in Political Economy* 22 (Spring 1987): 41-71.

4304 LUCE, Sally R. and Kristen Ostling. "Women and White Collar Unions: An Annotated Bibliography." *Resources for Feminist Research* 10, 2 (July 1981): 95-106.

4305 LUXTON, Meg. "From Ladies' Auxiliaries to Wives' Committees: Housewives and the Unions." In *Through the Kitchen Window: The Politics of Home and Family*, eds. Meg Luxton and Harriet Rosenberg, 63-81. Toronto: Garamond Press, 1986.

4306 LUXTON, Meg and June Corman. "Getting to Work: The Challenge of the 'Women Back Into Stelco' Campaign." *Labour/Le Travail* 28 (Fall 1991): 149-85.

4307 MacLEOD, Catherine. "Women in Production: The Toronto Dressmaker's Strike of 1931." In *Women at Work: Ontario, 1850-1930*, eds. Janice Acton, *et al*, 309-29. Toronto: Canadian Women's Educational Press, 1974.

4308 MAKI, D.R. "Unions as 'Gatekeepers' of Occupational Sex Discrimination: Canadian Evidence." *Applied Economics* 15, 4 (August 1983): 469-78.

4309 MARCHAK, Patricia. "Women, Work and Unions in Canada." *International Journal of Sociology* (Winter 1975/76).

4310 McDERMOTT, Patricia. "The Eaton's Strike: We Wouldn't Have Missed It for the World!" In *Women Challenging Unions: Feminism, Democracy, and Militancy*, eds. Linda Briskin and Patricia McDermott, 23-43. Toronto: University of Toronto Press, 1993.

4311 MITCHELL, Tom. "Documents and Archives." *Manitoba History* 19 (Spring 1990): 35-37. [Beatrice Brigden, 1919 correspondence re labour church]

4312 MORIN, Albanie. "Les Femmes dans la lutte syndicale au Québec." *L'Égale* 1, 1 (1976).

4313 MURRAY, Sylvie. *A la jonction du mouvement ouvrier et du mouvement des femmes: la ligue auxiliaire de l'Association internationale des machinistes, Canada, 1903-1980*. Montréal: Regroupement des chercheurs-chercheures en histoire des travailleurs et travailleuses du Québec, Collection "Etudes et documents" No 3, 1990.

4314 MURRAY, Sylvie. "Quand les ménagères se font militantes: La Ligue auxiliaire de l'Association internationale des machinistes, 1905-1980." *Labour/Le Travail* 29 (Spring 1992): 157-86.

4315 MUSZYNSKI, Alicja. "The Organization of Women and Ethnic Minorities in a Resource Industry: A Case Study of the Unionization of Shoreworkers in the BC Fishing Industry, 1937-1949." *Journal of Canadian Studies* 19, 1 (Spring 1984): 89-107.

4316 PARENT, Madeleine. "Interview with Madeleine Parent." *Studies in Political Economy* 30 (1989): 13-36. Reprinted in *Feminism in Action: Studies in Political Economy*, eds. M. Patricia Connelly and Pat Armstrong, Toronto: Canadian Scholars' Press, 1993.

4317 PARR, Joy. "Womanly Militance, Neighbourly Wrath: New Scripts for Old Roles in a Small-Town Textile Strike." In *Women, Work and Place*, ed. Audrey Kobayashi, 73-97. Montreal and Kingston: McGill-Queen's University Press, 1994.

4318 PENFOLD, Steven. "'Have You No Manhood in You?': Gender and Class in the Cape Breton Coal Towns, 1920-1926." *Acadiensis* 23, 2 (Spring 1994): 21-44.

4319 PENNEY, Jennifer, ed. *Hard Earned Wages: Women Fighting for Better Work*. Toronto: Women's Press, 1983.

4320 PICHÉ, Lucie. "Entre l'accès à l'égalité et la préserva-tion des modèles: ambivalence du discours et des revendications du Comité féminin de la CTCC-CSN, 1952-1966." *Labour/Le Travail* 29 (Spring 1992): 187-209.

4321 REITER, Ester. "The Interchangeable Worker and Fighting Back: Identifying Some Strategic Issues." *Labour/Le Travail* 21 (Spring 1988): 173-89.

4322 REITER, Ester. "First-Class Workers Don't Want Second-Class Wages: The Lanark Strike in Dunnville." In *A Diversity of Women: Ontario, 1945-1980*, ed. Joy Parr, 168-99. Toronto: University of Toronto Press, 1995.

4323 ROSENTHAL, Star. "Union Maids: Organized Women Workers in Vancouver, 1900-1915." *BC Studies* 41 (Spring 1979): 36-55. Reprinted in *Reappraisals in Canadian History: Post-Confederation*, eds. A.D. Gilbert, C.M. Wallace and R.M. Bray, 172-89. Scarborough: Prentice Hall Canada Inc., 1992.

4324 SAINT-PIERRE, Céline. "Recognizing the Working Mother: The Quebec Labour Movement and the Feminization of the Labour Force." In *The Challenging of Restructuring: North American Labor Movements Respond*, eds. Jane Jenson and Rianne Mahon, 269-84. Philadelphia: Temple University Press, 1993.

4325 SANGSTER, Joan. "Women and Unions in Canada: A Review of Historical Research." *Resources for Feminist Research* 10, 2 (July 1981): 2-6.

4326 SANGSTER, Joan. "The 1907 Bell Telephone Strike: Organizing Women Workers." *Labour/Le Travailleur* III (1978): 109-30. Reprinted in *Rethinking Canada: The Promise of Women's History*, eds. Veronica Strong-Boag and Anita Clair Fellman, 137-56 Toronto: Copp Clark Pitman Ltd., 1986; 2nd edition, 249-68, 1991; and in *Canadian Labour History: Selected Readings*, ed. David J. Bercuson, 43-61. Toronto: Copp Clark Pitman, 1987.

4327 SANGSTER, Joan. "The Softball Solution: Female Workers, Male Managers and the Operation of Paternalism at Westclox, 1923-60." *Labour/Le Travail* 32 (Fall 1993): 167-99.

4328 STAINSBY, Jill, *et al. AUCE and TSSU: Memoirs of a Feminist Union, 1972-1993*. Burnaby, BC: Teaching Support Staff Union Publishing, 1994.

4329 STARR, Christina. "Interview: Madeleine Parent." *Women's Education des femmes* 6, 3 (Summer 1988): 7-12.

4330 STEEDMAN, Mercedes. "The Promise: Communist Organizing in the Needle Trades, The Dressmakers' Campaign, 1928-1937." *Labour/Le Travail* 34 (Fall 1994): 37-74.

4331 SUFRIN, Eileen. *The Eaton Drive: The Campaign to Organize Canada's Largest Department Store, 1948 to 1952*. Toronto: Fitzhenry & Whiteside, 1982.

4332 SUGIMAN, Pamela. "The Sales Clerks: Alienation and Obstacles to the Collective Expression of Discontent." *Atlantis* 8, 1 (Fall 1982): 13-33.

4333 SUGIMAN, Pamela. "'That wall's comin' down': Gendered Strategies of Worker Resistance in the UAW Canadian region (1963-1970)." *Canadian Journal of Sociology* 17, 1 (Winter 1992): 1-28.

4334 SUGIMAN, Pamela. "Unionism and Feminism in the Canadian Auto Workers' Union, 1961-1992." In *Women Challenging Unions: Feminism, Democracy, and Militancy*, eds. Linda Briskin and Patricia McDermott, 172-88. Toronto: University of Toronto Press, 1993.

4335 SUGIMAN, Pamela. *Labour's Dilemma: The Gender Politics of Auto Workers in Canada, 1937-1979*. Toronto: University of Toronto Press, 1994.

4336 WADE, Susan. "Helena Gutteridge: Votes for Women and Trade Unions." In *In Her Own Right: Selected Essays on Women's History in BC*, eds. Barbara Latham and Cathy Kess, 187-203. Victoria: Camosun College, 1980.

4337 WARSKETT, Rosemary. "Can a Disappearing Pie Be Shared Equally? Unions, Women, and Wage 'Fairness'." In *Women Challenging Unions: Feminism, Democracy, and Militancy*, eds. Linda Briskin and Patricia McDermott, 249-65. Toronto: University of Toronto Press, 1993.

4338 WATSON, Louise. *She Never Was Afraid: The Biography of Annie Buller*. Toronto: Progress Books, 1976.

4339 WHITE, Jerry. *Hospital Strike: Women, Unions and Public Sector Conflict*. Toronto: Thompson Educational Publishing, 1990.

4340 WHITE, Julie. *Women and Unions*. Ottawa: Canadian Advisory Council on the Status of Women, 1980.

4341 WHITE, Julie. *Mail and Female: Women and the Canadian Union of Postal Workers*. Toronto: Thompson Educational Publishing, 1990.

4342 WHITE, Julie. *Sisters and Solidarity: Women in Unions in Canada*. Toronto: Thompson Educational Publishing, 1993.

4343 WHITTAKER, Jo Ann. "The Comox Nurses Strike of 1939." *British Columbia Historical News* 22, 4 (Fall 1989): 18-20.

4344 WOYWITKA, Anne B. "A Pioneer Woman in the Labour Movement." *Alberta History* 26, 1 (Winter 1978): 10-16. Reprinted in *Rethinking Canada: The Promise of Women's History*, eds. Veronica Strong-Boag and Anita Clair Fellman, 191-99. Toronto: Copp Clark Pitman Ltd., 1986.

4345 YANZ, Lynda. "Women and Unions—A Bibliography." *Resources for Feminist Research* 10, 2 (July 1981): 85-87.

4346 YANZ, Lynda and Linda Briskin, eds. "Women and Trade Unions." A special issue of *Resources for Feminist Research* 10, 2 (July 1981).

4347   YANZ, Lynda and David Smith. "Annotated List of
       Women's Strikes." *Resources for Feminist Research* 10,
       2 (July 1981): 77-83.

4348   YANZ, Lynda and David Smith. "Women and Trade
       Unions: A Guide to Primary Source Material."
       Resources for Feminist Research 10, 2 (July 1981):
       89-94.

WORK/ECONOMY

THE LARGEST BODY of scholarship on the history of Canadian women, produced by sociologists and political economists, as well as by historians, pertains to the topic of women and work. Because most aspects of women's lives are related in some way to work, further references to this subject will be found in every section of this bibliography. In the 1970s, feminist scholars sought the origins of occupational gender segregation and wage disparities that confined the majority of women in the paid labour force to low-paid, deadend jobs in fields dominated by women. Historians initially focussed their attention on the critical decades of urbanization and industrialization from the 1880s to the 1920s, a focus that has recently broadened to include women's work in the preindustrial period and especially in the post-World War II era. A sizable scholarship now exists documenting twentieth-century Canadian women's changing labour force participation rates, wage differentials, occupational gender segregation, the concentration of women in part-time work, the relationship of women's paid and unpaid work to the family, the origins of the double day, and changing conceptions of skill in women's work.

During the 1980s, the pioneering work of sociologist Graham Lowe on the feminization of clerical work helped to explain the process by which women had come to dominate this sector of the economy by the 1970s. That process was linked to the introduction of the typewriter and the reorganization of office work. An equally dramatic transformation of clerical work linked to the microchip revolution of the 1980s has stimulated an intense scholarly interest in the relationship of gender and technology in the clerical and communications sectors, evident in recent studies of telephone and telegraph operators. Some exploratory studies of the history of women in banking indicate the importance of a topic that requires further investigation. Historians of business and finance in Canada have generally ignored women, while labour historians have neglected this sector in favour of industrial work and domestic service. The growing interest in Canadian business history, combined with recent media attention to female entrepreneurship, has stimulated the growth of a small body of scholarship revealing the historical prominence of women in family business enterprises and in self-employed female occupations, such as millinery and dressmaking. Also receiving considerable attention are the admission of women to male-dominated professional occupations, such as medicine and law; the emergence of female-dominated professions

and paraprofessions, such as social work, nursing and dietetics; and the feminization of professions such as pharmacy and teaching (see also Education and Health/Medicine).

While some attention has been paid to Maritime and Ontario women in industrial occupations (see also Unions/Labour Activism), the majority of historical studies of women in the manufacturing sector in Canada have focussed on the textile and garment industries in Quebec, reflecting both the latter's importance as the industrial heartland of Canada at the turn of the century and the importance of women's cheap "unskilled" labour in subsidizing the development of these industries. Given the increasing prominence of women workers in the service sector over the course of the twentieth century, the relative neglect of this area by Canadian historians is noteworthy, particularly the subject of women's work in retail sales. In addition to the studies of the clerical and communications sectors noted above, there has been some notice paid to women workers in food processing and fast food outlets, and scholarship on immigrant domestic workers is flourishing. (see also Ethnicity/Immigration). Despite Veronica Strong-Boag's development of a suggestive framework for studying the history of housework in Canada, the subject of women's work in the home has been relatively neglected except by sociologists and by historians working in the museum field (see also Material Culture/Popular Culture).

While early scholarship on the subject of women's work was dominated by studies of urban women in industrial settings or in domestic service, a burgeoning scholarship on farm women's work reflects contemporary debates over the "triple day" of farm women and the value of their labour in the context of the disappearing family farm. While Prairie historians have long been attracted to the study of the rural pioneer experience, the recent growth of scholarship on farm women in Ontario and Quebec reflects the belated recognition by Central Canadian historians of the critical importance of the agricultural sector in Canada's past. While traditional histories of the fur trade, mining and lumber economies have overlooked the presence of women on resource frontiers, recent studies are directing our attention to women's activities in mining and lumber camps, in the Klondike Gold Rush, and in the fur trade (see also First Nations). Thanks largely to the work of sociologists and political economists, a substantial scholarship also exists on the role of women in fishing economies in Atlantic Canada and British Columbia.

AGRICULTURE

4349 ANDERSON, Allan. *Remembering the Farm: Memories of Farming, Ranching and Rural Life in Canada, Past and Present.* Toronto: Macmillan, 1977.

4350 BAILEY, Mrs. A.W. "Recollections and Reminiscences: The Year We Moved." *Saskatchewan History* 20, 1 (Winter 1967): 19-31. Reprinted in *Pages from the Past: Essays on Saskatchewan History,* ed. D.H. Bocking, 225-38. Saskatoon: Western Producer Prairie Books, 1979. [1930s]

4351 BALL, Rosemary R. "'A Perfect Farmer's Wife': Women in 19th Century Rural Ontario." *Canada: An Historical Magazine* 3, 2 (December 1975): 3-21.

4352 BARBER, Marilyn. "Help for Farm Homes: The Campaign to End Housework Drudgery in Rural Saskatchewan in the 1920s." *Scientia Canadensis* 9, 1 (June 1985): 3-26. Reprinted in *Science, Technology and Medicine in Canada's Past: Selections from Scientia Canadensis,* eds. Richard A. Jarrell and James P. Hull, 223-46. Thornhill: The Scientia Press, 1991.

4353 BINNIE-CLARK, Georgina. *A Summer on the Canadian Prairie.* London: Edward Arnold, 1910.

4354 BINNIE-CLARK, Georgina. *Wheat and Woman.* With an introduction by Susan Jackel. Toronto: University of Toronto Press, 1979.

4355 BLACKBURN, J.H. "A Woman's Work is Never Done." *Land of Promise,* 169-75. Toronto: Macmillan of Canada, 1970. [early 20th century Alberta]

4356 BLISS, Jacqueline. "Seamless Lives: Pioneer Women of Saskatoon, 1883-1903." *Saskatchewan History* 43, 3 (Autumn 1991): 84-100.

4357 BOLLMAN, Ray D. and Pamela Smith. "Integration of Canadian Farm and Off-Farm Markets and the Off-Farm Work of Farm Women, Men, and Children." In *The Political Economy of Agriculture in Western Canada,* eds. G.S. Basran and David A. Hay, 185-202. Toronto: Garamond Press, 1988.

4358 BROOKES, Alan A. and Catherine Wilson. "'Working Away' from the Farm: The Young Women of North Huron, 1910-1930." *Ontario History* 77, 4 (1985): 281-300.

4359 BRUCE, Anna. "By Covered Wagon to Canada." *Alberta History* 42, 1 (Winter 1994): 8-13.

4360 BUCK, Ruth M. "In the Midst of Life: Letters to a Friend." *The Beaver* 71, 6 (Dec. 1991/Jan. 1992): 33-46. [Prince Albert and Fort Macleod, 1883-84]

4361 CANTLON, Mrs. F.M. "Breaking the Prairie Sod." *Alberta Historical Review* 13 (Summer 1965): 22-24.

4362 CAREY, Patricia. "Farm Wives, the Forgotten Women." *Canadian Women's Studies* 1, 2 (1978): 4-5.

4363 CAYFORD, Alice Carey. "Homesteading on the Bow." *Alberta History* 41, 3 (Summer 1993): 8-13.

4364 CEBOTAREV, E.A. and Frances M. Shaver, eds. "Women and Agricultural Production." A special issue of *Resources for Feminist Research* 11, 1 (March 1982).

4365 CEBOTAREV, E.A., F.M. Shaver, J.L. Newton, G.A. Jaffee, C. Zavitz and Adele Mueller. "An Annotated Bibliography on Women in Agricultural and Rural Societies: Canada." *Resources for Feminist Research* 11, 1 (March 1982): 93-100.

4366 CEBOTAREV, N., W.M. Blacklock and L. McIsaac. "Farm Women's Work Patterns." *Atlantis* 11, 2 (Spring 1986): 1-22.

4367 COHEN, Marjorie Griffin. "The Decline of Women in Canadian Dairying." *Histoire sociale/Social History* XVII, 34 (November 1984): 307-34. Reprinted in *The Neglected Majority: Essays in Canadian Women's History, Vol. 2,* eds. Alison Prentice and Susan Mann Trofimenkoff, 61-83. Toronto: McClelland and Stewart, 1985; and in *Rethinking Canada: The Promise of Women's History,* 2nd edition, eds. Veronica Strong-Boag and Anita Clair Fellman, 134-60. Toronto: Copp Clark Pitman Ltd., 1991.

4368 COHEN, Marjorie Griffin. *Women's Work, Markets, and Economic Development in Nineteenth-Century Ontario.* Toronto: University of Toronto Press, 1988.

4369 COOPER, Barbara. "Farm Women: Some Contemporary Themes." *Labour/Le Travail* 24 (1989): 167-80.

4370 CÔTÉ, Elizabeth, ed. *La recherche du "Matrimoine" Témoignages.* Sutton: Elizabeth Côté Communications, 1991. [sur la condition des femmes en milieu agricole]

4371 DION, Marcelle and Steve Welsh. "Participation of Women in the Labour Force: A Comparison of Farm Women and All Women in Canada." In *Rural and Small Town Canada,* ed. Ray D. Bollman. Toronto: Thompson Educational Publishing Co., 1992.

4372 DION, Suzanne. *Les femmes dans l'agriculture au Québec.* Longueuil: Éditions La Terre de Chez-Nous, 1983.

4373 DION, Suzanne and Gisele Painchaud. "La participation des femmes dans la vie syndicale agricole." *Resources for Feminist Research* 11 (March 1982): 7-8.

4374 DRYDEN, Jean E. and Sandra L. Myers. "The Letters of Barbara Alice Slater: Homesteading on the Canadian Prairies, 1909-1918." *Montana* 37, 1 (Winter 1987): 14-33.

4375 DUERKOP, John D. "A Remarkable Pioneer Family: The Widow Clark and Her Children." *Saskatoon History Review* 5 (1990): 35-41.

4376 EVANS, Barbara. "'We Just Lived It As It Came Along': Stories from Jessie's Albums." In *Standing on New Ground: Women in Alberta,* eds. Catherine A. Cavanaugh and Randi R. Warne, 33-54. Edmonton: University of Alberta Press, 1993.

4377 FAIRBANKS, Carol. "Lives of Girls and Women on the Canadian and American Prairies." *International Journal of Women's Studies* 2 (Sept./Oct. 1979): 452-72.

4378 FAIRBANKS, Carol and Sara Brooks Sundberg, eds. *Farm Women on the Prairie Frontier: A Sourcebook for Canada and the United States.* Metuchen, NJ: The Scarecrow Press, 1983.

4379 FAIRWEATHER, Joan. "Farm Families: The Voices of Experience." *The Archivist* 107 (1994): 17-18.

4380 FORTIN, Gerald. "Le rôle de la femme dans l'évolution de l'agriculture du Québec." *La Famille dans l'évolution de l'agriculture.* Ottawa: Vanier Institute of the Family, 1968.

4381 FORTIN, Gerald. "Women's Role in the Evolution of Agriculture in Quebec." *The Family in the Evolution of Agriculture,* 25-31. Ottawa: Vanier Institute of the Family, 1968.

4382 GAGAN, David. "Land, Population and Social Change: The 'Critical Years' in Rural Canada West." *Canadian Historical Review* 59, 3 (September 1978): 293-318.

4383 GHORAYSHI, Parvin. "The Indispensable Nature of Wives' Work for the Farm Family Enterprise." *Canadian Review of Sociology and Anthropology* 26, 4 (August 1989): 571-95.

4384 GIROUARD-DÉCARIE, Jeanne. "La fermière canadienne-française." *Québec-Histoire* 2, 2 (hiver 1973): 32-36.

4385 GRAFF, Linda. "Industrialization of Agriculture: Implications for the Position of Farm Women." *Resources for Feminist Research* 11 (March 1982): 10-11.

4386 GRESKO, Jacqueline. "'Roughing It in the Bush' in British Columbia: Mary Moody's Pioneer Life in New Westminster, 1859-1863." In *Not Just Pin Money: Selected Essays on the History of Women's Work in British Columbia,* eds. Barbara K. Latham and Roberta J. Pazdro, 105-17. Victoria: Camosun College, 1984. Reprinted in *British Columbia Reconsidered: Essays on Women,* eds. Gillian Creese and Veronica Strong-Boag, 38-51. Vancouver: Press Gang Publishers, 1992.

4387 GROUPE DE RECHERCHE EN ÉCONOMIE ET POLITIQUE AGRICOLE. *Changer l'agriculture ou s'intégrer. Rapport du colloque sur les femmes en agriculture.* Québec: Université Laval, 1988.

4388 HALL, Mrs. Mary Georgina Caroline. *A Lady's Life on a Farm in Manitoba.* London: W.H. Allen and Co., 1884.

4389 HOPKINS, Monica. *Letters from a Lady Rancher.* Calgary: Glenbow Museum, 1982.

4390 INDERWICK, Mary E. "A Lady and Her Ranch." *Alberta Historical Review* 15, 4 (Autumn 1967): 1-9. Reprinted in *The Best from Alberta History,* ed. Hugh Dempsey, 65-77. Saskatoon: Western Producer Prairie Books, 1981.

4391 JAMESON, Sheilagh S. "Women in the Southern Alberta Ranch Community, 1881-1914." In *The Canadian West: Social Change and Economic Development,* ed. Henry Klassen, 63-78. Calgary: Comprint Publishing, 1977.

4392 JONES, David C. "'From Babies to Buttonholes': Women's Work at Agricultural Fairs." *Alberta History* 29, 4 (1981): 26-32.

4393 KEMPTHORNE, Roberta. "Behind Every Hero." *Manitoba History* 23 (Spring 1992): 23-24. [Gussie Boulton]

4394 KINNEAR, Mary. "'Do you want your daughter to marry a farmer?': Women's Work on the Farm, 1922." In *Canadian Papers in Rural History, Vol. VI,* ed. Donald H. Akenson, 137-53. Gananoque, ON: Langdale Press, 1988.

4395 KOHL, Seena B. *Working Together: Women and Family in Southwestern Saskatchewan.* Toronto: Holt, Rinehart and Winston, 1976.

4396 KOHL, Seena B. "Women's Participation in the North American Family Farm." *Women's Studies International Quarterly* 1 (1977): 47-54.

4397 L'ARCHEVÊQUE-DUGUAY, Jeanne, ed. *Lettres d'une paysanne à son fils.* Montréal: Léméac, 1977. [rural life, 1908-1927]

4398 LATZER, Beth Good. *Myrtleville: A Canadian Farm and Family, 1837-1967.* Carbondale and Edwardsville, IL: Southern Illinois University Press, 1976.

4399 LECKIE, Gloria J. "Female Farmers in Canada, 1971-1986." *Professional Geographer* 45, 2 (May 1993): 180-93.

4400 LOEWEN, Royden, K. "'The Children, the Cows, My Dear Man and My Sister': The Transplanted Lives of Mennonite Farm Women, 1874-1900." *Canadian Historical Review* 73, 3 (September 1992): 344-73. Reprinted in *Perspectives on Canadian Economic History,* 2nd edition, eds. Douglas McCalla and Michael Huberman. Mississauga: Copp Clark Longman, 1994; and in *Canadian Women: A Reader,* eds. Wendy Mitchinson, *et al,* 119-42. Toronto: Harcourt Brace Canada, 1996.

4401 MacNAB-DE VRIES, Georgina and Pieter J. De Vries. "Subsistence Agriculture, Wage Labour and the Definition of Women's Roles: A Cape Breton Example." *Resources for Feminist Research* 11, 1 (March 1982): 8-10.

4402 McGEE, Molly. *Women in Rural Life: The Changing Scene.* Toronto: Ontario Ministry of Agriculture and Food, 1985.

4403 McNELLIS, Anna. "A Woman's View of Pioneer Life." *Alberta History* 42, 3 (Summer 1994): 11-14. [reprinted from *Lethbridge Herald,* 1931]

4404 MITCHELL, Zara. "Two Pioneer Women." *British Columbia Historical News* 27, 1 (Winter 1993/94): 23-26.

4405 [MORISETTE, Diane, ed.] *Growing Strong: Women in Agriculture.* Ottawa: Canadian Advisory Council on the Status of Women, 1987.

4406 NEIL, Catherine. "Recollections of a Sheep Herder's Bride, Part One." *Alberta History* 35, 2 (Spring 1987): 18-24.

4407 NEIL, Catherine. "Recollections of a Sheep Herder's Bride, Part Two." *Alberta History* 35, 3 (Summer 1987): 20-28.

4408 NEIL, Catherine. "Recollections of a Sheep Herder's Bride, Part Three." *Alberta History* 35, 4 (Autumn 1987): 22-29.

4409 NEIL, Catherine. "Recollections of a Sheep Herder's Bride, Part Four." *Alberta History* 36, 1 (Winter 1988): 19-26.

4410 ODDIE, Emmie. "Western Women in Agriculture." In *Development of Agriculture on the Prairies: Proceedings of Seminar*, ed. J.H. Archer, 30-34. Regina: University of Regina, 1975.

4411 PARSLOE, Muriel Jardine. *A Parson's Daughter.* London: Farber and Farber, 1935. [farming in Manitoba]

4412 PIEROTH, Doris H. "Peace River Journey, 1916." *The Beaver* 71, 1 (Feb./Mar. 1991): 35-38. [young bride joins the homesteaders]

4413 REIMER, Bill. "Women as Farm Labour." *Rural Sociology* 51, 2 (1986): 143-55.

4414 REIMER, Bill and Frances M. Shaver. "Modernisation, rapports de production et division sexuelle du travail à la ferme dans le comté de Montmagny, 1951-1981." *Recherches sociographiques* 29, 2/3 (1988): 329-48.

4415 ROBERTS, Sara Ellen. *Alberta Homestead: Chronicle of a Pioneer Family.* Edited by Lathrop E. Roberts. Austin: University of Texas Press, 1971. [1906-1912]

4416 ROGER, Gertrude Minor. *Lady Rancher.* Surrey, BC: Hancock House Publishers, 1979.

4417 ROSE, Hilda. *The Stump Farm: A Chronicle of Pioneering.* Boston: Little, Brown and Company, 1928. [Alberta, 1920s]

4418 ROSS, Lois L. *Harvest of Opportunity: New Horizons for Farm Women.* Saskatoon: Western Producer Prairie Books, 1990.

4419 RUTHIG, Elizabeth. "Homestead Days in the McCord District." *Saskatchewan History* 7 (Winter 1954): 22-27.

4420 SHORTALL, Sally. "Canadian and Irish Farm Women: Some similarities, differences and comments." *Canadian Review of Sociology and Anthropology* 30, 2 (1993): 172-90.

4421 SILVERMAN, Eliane Leslau. "Preliminaries to a Study of Women in Alberta, 1890-1929." Canadian Oral History Association. *Journal* 3, 1 (1978): 22-26.

4422 SILVERMAN, Eliane Leslau. "Women and the Victorian Work Ethic on the Alberta Frontier: Prescription and Description." In *The New Provinces: Alberta and Saskatchewan, 1905-1980,* eds. Howard Palmer and Donald Smith, 91-99. Vancouver: Tantalus Research Limited, 1980.

4423 SILVERMAN, Eliane Leslau. *The Last Best West: Women on the Alberta Frontier 1880-1930.* Montreal: Eden Press, 1984.

4424 SIMARD, Pierrette. *Recherche sur la femme et le travail en milieu rural.* Ottawa: Canadian Research Institute for the Advancement of Women, 1979.

4425 SIME, Jessie Georgina. *In a Canadian Shack.* Toronto: Macmillan of Canada, 1937. [memoir of a town-bred Englishwoman on an early 20th century farm in Quebec]

4426 SMITH, Pamela. "'Not Enough Hours, Our Accountant Tells Me': Trends in Children's, Women's and Men's Involvement in Canadian Agriculture." *Canadian Journal of Agricultural Economics* 33 (1985): 161-95.

4427 SMITH, Pamela. "Murdoch's, Becker's and Sorochan's Challenge: Thinking Again About the Roles of Women in Primary Agriculture." In *The Political Economy of Agriculture in Western Canada,* eds. G.S. Basran and David A. Hay, 157-74. Toronto: Garamond Press, 1988.

4428 SMITH, Pamela. "Beyond 'Add Women and Stir' in Canadian Rural Society." In *Rural Sociology in Canada,* eds. David A. Hay and Gurcharn S. Basran. Toronto: Oxford University Press, 1992.

4429 SPRINGETT, Evelyn Cartier. *For My Children's Children.* Montreal: Unity Press, 1937. [memoir of an Alberta rancher's wife]

4430 STOBIE, Margaret. "Nine Days and Nights on the Trail, 1904." *The Beaver* 70, 3 (June/July 1990): 6-13. [pioneer bride in Alberta's land rush of 1904]

4431 STRANGE, Kathleen. *With the West in Her Eyes.* Toronto: Macmillan of Canada, 1945. [memoir of farming in Alberta by World War I British war bride]

4432 SUNDBERG, Sara Brooks. "Farm Women on the Canadian Prairie Frontier: The Helpmate Image." In *Farm Women on the Prairie Frontier: A Sourcebook for Canada and the United States,* eds. Carol Fairbanks and Sara Brooks Sundberg, 71-90. Metuchen, NJ: The Scarecrow Press, 1983. Reprinted in *Rethinking Canada: The Promise of Women's History,* eds. Veronica Strong-Boag and Anita Clair Fellman, 95-106. Toronto: Copp Clark Pitman Ltd., 1986; and in *Reappraisals in Canadian History: Post-Confederation,* eds. A.D. Gilbert, C.M. Wallace and R.M. Bray, 159-71. Scarborough: Prentice Hall Canada Inc., 1992.

4433 SUNDBERG, Sara Brooks. "A Female Frontier: Manitoba Farm Women in 1922." *Prairie Forum* 16, 2 (Fall 1991): 185-204.

4434 SZYCHTER, Gwen. "Women's Role in Early Farming in British Columbia." *British Columbia Historical News* 24, 1 (Winter 1990/91): 22-5. [title page incorrectly identifies issue as vol. 23, no. 4]

4435 THOMPSON, M.J. "A Whey with Cheese." *This Country Canada* 6 (Summer 1994): 68-72. [Bertha Pope, Ontario cheesemaker]

4436 TREMBLAY, Martine. "La division sexuelle du travail et la modernisation de l'agriculture à travers la presse agricole, 1840-1900." *Revue d'histoire de l'Amérique française* 47, 2 (automne 1993): 221-44.

4437 VAN DE VORST, Charlotte. *Making Ends Meet: A History of Women's Economic Contribution to the Family Farm in Manitoba.* Winnipeg: University of Manitoba Press, 1992.

4438 WATSON, Mrs. Edward. "Reminiscences of Mrs. Edward Watson." *Saskatchewan History* 5 (Spring 1952): 66-67. [homesteading in Craik, Saskatchewan, in 1905]

4439 WAXMAN, Sydell. "The Mothers of Confederation." *The Beaver* 72, 5 (Oct./Nov. 1992): 20-25. [unending toil of 19th-century pioneer women]

4440 WILLICK, Liz. "Farm Women Cultivate a Living." *Herizons*, 1(3) May 1983: 26-28.

BUSINESS/FINANCE

4441 BANDEEN, Mona, *et al*, eds. "Women Entrepreneurs." A special issue of *Canadian Woman Studies* 15, 1 (Winter 1994).

4442 BARNES, Michael. *Gold Camp Pioneer: Roza Brown of Kirkland Lake.* Cobalt, ON: Highway Book Shop, 1973.

4443 BASKERVILLE, Peter A. "She Has Already Hinted at 'Board': Enterprising Urban Women in British Columbia, 1836-1896." *Histoire sociale/Social History* XXVI, 52 (November 1993): 205-27.

4444 DAGENAIS, Michèle. "Itinéraires professionnels masculins et féminins en milieu bancaire: Le cas de la Banque d'Hochelaga, 1900-1929." *Labour/Le Travail* 24 (1989): 45-68.

4445 GARLING, Carol. "Millinery: A Dying Art." *Costume Society of Ontario Newsletter* 18, 2 (Summer 1988): 10-11. [women's hatmaking in Toronto, 1890-1988]

4446 GIROUX, Jacqueline. *Femme de cœur et femme de têtes.* Montréal: La société historique du marigot de Longueuil, 1989. [Montreal milliner Yvette Brillon, 1930s-1960s]

4447 HANSEN, Barbara. "An Historical Study of Women in Canadian Banking, 1900-1975." *Canadian Woman Studies* 1, 2 (Winter 1978/79): 17-22.

4448 KENNEDY, Else M. "The Pioneer Bride of Chemainus." *British Columbia Historical News* 28, 4 (Fall 1995): 15-17. [Isabel Julia Askew ran her husband's sawmill after his death]

4449 McDOWELL, John E. "Madame la Framboise." *Michigan History* 56 (Winter 1972): 271-86. [owner of 18th-century fur-trading business at Michilimackinac]

4450 PLAMONDON, Lilianne. "Une femme d'affaires en Nouvelle-France: Marie-Anne Barbel, veuve Fornel." *Revue d'histoire de l'Amérique française* 31, 2 (septembre 1977): 165-86.

4451 PLAMONDON, Lilianne. "A Businesswoman in New France: Marie-Anne Barbel, The Widow Fornel." In *Rethinking Canada: The Promise of Women's History,* eds. Veronica Strong-Boag and Anita Clair Fellman, 45-58. Toronto: Copp Clark Pitman Ltd., 1986.

4452 RUDIN, Ronald. "Bankers' Hours: Life Behind the Wicket at the *Banque d'Hochelaga,* 1901-21." *Labour/Le Travail* 18 (Fall 1986): 63-76.

4453 SYMONS, Gladys L. "Ethnicity, Career and Gender: Managerial Women in France and Canada." *Études canadiennes/Canadian Studies* 21, 2 (December 1986): 137-46.

4454 THORNHILL, Mary Elizabeth. *Between Friends.* Toronto: Reginald Saunders, 1935. [memoir of the owner of a wholesale lace business]

4455 YOUNG, Brian. "Getting Around Legal Incapacity: The Legal Status of Married Women in Trade in Mid-Nineteenth Century Lower Canada." In *Canadian Papers in Business History, Vol. I,* ed. Peter Baskerville, 1-16. Victoria: Public History Group, University of Victoria, 1989.

CLERICAL/COMMUNICATIONS

4456 BOWMAN, Phylis. "The Cedarvale Postmistress." *British Columbia Historical News* 28, 4 (Fall 1995): 2-4.

4457 DEMPSEY, Hugh. "Confessions of a Calgary Stenographer." *Alberta History* 36, 2 (Spring 1988): 1-15.

4458 GREGORY, Judith. "The Electronic Sweatshop." In *Perspectives on Women in the 1980s,* eds. Joan Turner and Lois Emery, 99-112. Winnipeg: University of Manitoba Press, 1983.

4459 HESSING, Melody. "Talking on the Job: Office Conversations and Women's Dual Labour." In *British Columbia Reconsidered: Essays on Women,* eds. Gillian Creese and Veronica Strong-Boag, 391-415. Vancouver: Press Gang Publishers, 1992.

4460 KUYEK, Joan Newman. *The Phone Book: Working at the Bell.* Toronto: Between the Lines, 1981.

4461 LOWE, Graham S. "Women, Work and the Office: The Feminization of Clerical Occupations in Canada, 1901-1931." *Canadian Journal of Sociology* 5, 4 (1980): 361-81. Reprinted in *Rethinking Canada: The Promise of Women's History,* eds. Veronica Strong-Boag and Anita Clair Fellman, 107-22. Toronto: Copp Clark Pitman Ltd., 1986; abridged in 2nd edition, 269-85, 1991; also in *Interpreting Canada's Past: Volume Two, Post-Confederation,* 2nd edition, ed. J.M. Bumsted, 395-420. Toronto: Oxford University Press, 1993.

4462 LOWE, Graham S. "The Administrative Revolution in the Canadian Office: An Overview." In *Work in the Canadian Context,* eds. Katherine L.P. Lundy and Barbara D. Warme, 153-73. Toronto: Butterworths, 1981.

4463 LOWE, Graham S. "Class, Job and Gender in the Canadian Office." *Labour/Le Travail* 10 (Autumn 1982): 11-37. Reprinted in *Canadian Working Class History: Selected Readings,* eds. Laurel Sefton-MacDowell and Ian Radforth. Toronto: Canadian Scholars' Press, 1992.

4464 LOWE, Graham S. "Mechanization, Feminization and Managerial Control in the Early Twentieth Century Canadian Office." In *On the Job: Confronting the Labour Process in Canada,* eds. Craig Heron and Robert Storey, 177-209. Montreal and Kingston: McGill-Queen's University Press, 1986.

4465 LOWE, Graham S. *Women in the Administrative Revolution: The Feminization of Clerical Work.* Toronto and Buffalo: University of Toronto Press, 1987.

4466 MARTIN, Michèle. "Feminisation of the Labour Process in the Communication Industry: The Case of the Telephone Operators, 1876-1904." *Labour/Le Travail* 22 (Fall 1988): 139-62. Reprinted in *Reappraisals in Canadian History: Post-Confederation,* eds. A.D. Gilbert, C.M. Wallace and R.M. Bray, 189-210. Scarborough: Prentice Hall Canada Inc., 1992.

4467 MARTIN, Michèle. *"Hello, Central?": Gender, Technology and Culture in the Formation of Telephone Systems.* Montreal and Kingston: McGill-Queen's University Press, 1991.

4468 McLEOD, Kelsey. "Pioneer Postmistress." *British Columbia Historical News* 27, 4 (Fall 1994): 28-30.

4469 MENZIES, Heather. *Women and the Chip: Case Studies of the Effects of Informatics on Employment in Canada.* Montreal: Institute for Research on Public Policy, 1981.

4470 MENZIES, Heather. *Computers on the Job: Surviving Canada's Microcomputer Revolution.* Toronto: Lorimer, 1982.

4471 PRENTICE, Alison, *et al.* "Work in the Electronic Era." In *Canadian Working Class History: Selected Readings,* eds. Laurel Sefton-MacDowell and Ian Radforth. Toronto: Canadian Scholars' Press, 1992. [excerpted from *Canadian Women: A History*]

4472 TILLOTSON, Shirley. "The Operators Along the Coast: A Case Study of the Link Between Gender, Skilled Labour and Social Power, 1900-1930." *Acadiensis* 20, 1 (Autumn 1990): 72-88.

4473 TILLOTSON, Shirley. "'We may all soon be 'first-class men': Gender and Skill in Canada's early twentieth century urban telegraph industry." *Labour/Le Travail* 27 (Spring 1991): 97-125.

GENERAL

4474 ABELLA, Irving and David Millar, eds. *The Canadian Worker in the Twentieth Century.* Toronto: Oxford University Press, 1978.

4475 ACTON, Janice, *et al. Women at Work: Ontario, 1850-1930.* Toronto: Canadian Women's Educational Press, 1974.

4476 AMATO, Sheila and Pat Staton. *Making Choices! Women in Non-Traditional Jobs.* Toronto: Green Dragon Press, 1987.

4477 ANDREW, Caroline and Beth Moore Milroy, eds. *Life Spaces: Gender, Household, Employment.* Vancouver: University of British Columbia Press, 1988.

4478 ANGER, Dorothy, Carmelita McGrath and Sandy Pottle. *Women and Work in Newfoundland.* St. John's: Royal Commission on Employment and Unemployment, Newfoundland and Labrador, 1986.

4479 ARMSTRONG, Hugh and Pat Armstrong. "The segregated participation of women in the Canadian labour force, 1941-1971." *Canadian Review of Sociology and Anthropology* 12, 4 (November 1975): 370-84.

4480 ARMSTRONG, Hugh and Pat Armstrong. *A Working Majority: What Women Must Do For Pay.* Ottawa: Canadian Advisory Council on the Status of Women, 1983.

4481 ARMSTRONG, Hugh and Pat Armstrong. *The Double Ghetto: Canadian Women and Their Segregated Work.* Toronto: McClelland and Stewart, 1978; 2nd edition, 1984; 3rd edition, 1994.

4482 ARMSTRONG, Hugh and Pat Armstrong. "Looking Ahead: The Future of Women's Work." *Australian-Canadian Studies* 3 (1985): 1-11.

4483 ARMSTRONG, Hugh and Pat Armstrong. "Taking Women into Account: Redefining and intensifying employment in Canada." In *Feminization of the Labor Force: Paradoxes and Promises,* eds. Jane Jenson, Elisabeth Hagen and Ceallaigh Reddy, 65-84. New York: Oxford University Press, 1988.

4484 ARMSTRONG, Hugh and Pat Armstrong. "Women's Work in the Labour Force" In *Gender and Society: Creating a Canadian Women's Sociology,* ed. Arlene Tigar McLaren, 275-315. Toronto: Copp Clark Pitman, 1988. [excerpted from *The Double Ghetto,* 1984]

4485 ARMSTRONG, Hugh and Pat Armstrong. *Theorizing Women's Work: English-Canadian Perspectives.* Toronto: Garamond Press, 1988.

4486 ARMSTRONG, Pat. *Labour Pains: Women's Work in Crisis.* Toronto: Women's Press, 1984.

4487 BACKHOUSE, Constance and Leah Cohen. *The Secret Oppression: Sexual Harassment of Working Women.* Toronto: Macmillan of Canada, 1978.

4488 BARRY, Francine. *Le Travail de la femme au Québec: l'évolution de 1940 à 1970.* Montréal: Presses de l'Université du Québec, 1977.

4489 BEAUREGARD, Micheline. *Le maintien des femmes dans les secteurs "non-traditionnels."* Québec: Université Laval, Chaire d'étude sur la condition des femmes, 1994.

4490 BÉLAND, François and Micheline de Sève. "La distribution des emplois entre les sexes et les groupes linguistiques au Québec." In *La morphologie sociale en mutation au Québec,* eds. S. Langlois and François Trudel, 61-88. Montréal: Association canadienne-française pour l'avancement des sciences, 1986.

4491 BÉLISLE, Diane and Yolande Pinard. "De l'ouvrage des femmes québécoises." In *Du travail et de l'amour: Les dessous de la production domestique*, Louise Vandelac, *et al*, 99-133. Montréal: Albert Saint-Martin, 1985.

4492 BARRY, Francine. *Le travail de la femme au Québec: L'évolution de 1940-1970*. Montréal: Presses de l'Université du Québec, 1977.

4493 BIRD, Patricia. "Hamilton Working Women in the Period of the Great Depression." *Atlantis* 8, 2 (Spring 1983): 125-36.

4494 BOULET, J.-A. and Laval Lavalée. *The Changing Economic Status of Women*. Ottawa: Economic Council of Canada, 1984.

4495 BOURNE, Paula, ed. *Women's Paid and Unpaid Work: Historical and Contemporary Perspectives*. Toronto: New Hogtown Press, 1985.

4496 BOYD, Monica. "Sex Difference in the Canadian Occupational Attainment Process." *Canadian Review of Sociology and Anthropology* 19 (February 1982): 1-28.

4497 BOYD, Monica. "Socio-Economic Indices and Sexual Inequality: A Tale of Scales." *Canadian Review of Sociology and Anthropology* 23 (1986): 457-80.

4498 BOYD, Monica, Mary Ann Mulvihill and John Myles. "Gender, Power and Postindustrialism." *Canadian Review of Sociology and Anthropology* 28, 4 (November 1991): 407-36.

4499 BRADBURY, Bettina. "Women and Wage Labour in a Period of Transition: Montreal, 1861-1881." *Histoire sociale/Social History* XVII, 33 (May 1984): 115-31. Reprinted in *Canadian Labour History: Selected Readings*, ed. David J. Bercuson, 27-42. Toronto: Copp Clark, 1987; 2nd edition, 1994.

4500 BRADBURY, Bettina. "Women's History and Working-Class History." *Labour/Le Travail* 19 (Spring 1987): 23-43.

4501 BRADBURY, Bettina. "Women and the History of Their Work in Canada: Some Recent Books." *Journal of Canadian Studies* 28, 3 (Fall 1993): 159-78.

4502 BRETON, Albert. *Marriage, Population and the Labour Force Participation of Women*. Ottawa: Economic Council of Canada, 1984.

4503 BURGESS, Joanne. "Separate Histories No Longer: Women and the Writing of Canadian Labour History." In *Canada ieri e oggi 3: atti dell'80 Convegno internazionale di studi canadesi, Torre Canne (Brindisi), 25-28 aprile 1990*. Vol. 2, eds. Luigi Bruti Liberati and Fabrizio Ghilardi, 179-90. Fasano (Br-Italia): Schena Editore, 1992.

4504 BURGESS, Joanne, Louis Fournier, Nicole Thivièrge and Jean-Paul Bernand. "Table-ronde: Histoire des travailleurs/histoire des femmes: points de rencontre et points du rupture." *Bulletin du Regroupement des chercheurs en histoire des travailleurs du Québec* 11, 2/3 (été/automne 1985): 101-14.

4505 CALZAVARA, L. "Trends in the Employment Opportunities of Women in Canada." *Research Studies of the Commission on Equality in Employment*, 515-36. Ottawa: Supply and Services Canada, 1985.

4506 CANADA. LABOUR CANADA, WOMEN'S BUREAU. *Sexual Equality in the Workplace: Proceedings of a Conference Sponsored by the Women's Bureau, Labour Canada, March 17-19, Toronto*. Ottawa: Labour Canada, 1983.

4507 CANADIAN RESEARCH INSTITUTE FOR THE ADVANCEMENT OF WOMEN. *Women and Work: An Inventory of Research*. Ottawa: Canadian Research Institute for the Advancement of Women, 1978.

4508 CARROLL, William K. "Which Women are More Proletarianized? Gender, Class and Occupation in Canada." *Canadian Review of Sociology and Anthropology* 24, 4 (November 1987): 571-85.

4509 CARTER, Donald, ed. *Women and Industrial Relations: Proceedings of the 28th Conference of the Canadian Industrial Relations Association, June 2, 3, 4, 1991, Queen's University, Kingston, Ontario*. Ottawa: National Library of Canada, 1991.

4510 CHADWICK, Jean, Dell Texmo and Karin Hughes. *This is Our Work: Some Newfoundland Women Talk about Their Careers*. St. John's: Newfoundland Status of Women Council, 1975.

4511 CLERMONT, L. *Les femmes et l'aménagement du temps de travail salarié, Québec*. Québec: Conseil du statut de la femme, 1983.

4512 COHEN, Marjorie. "Changing Perceptions of the Impact of the Industrial Revolution on Female Labour." *International Journal of Women's Studies* 7, 4 (1984): 291-305.

4513 COHEN, Marjorie. *Free Trade and the Future of Women's Work: Manufacturing and Service Industries*. Toronto: Garamond Press, 1987.

4514 COHEN, Marjorie. "Capitalist Development, Industrialization, and Women's Work." In *Perspectives on Canadian Economic Development: Class, Staples, Gender, and Elites*, ed. Gordon Laxer, 311-32. Toronto: Oxford University Press, 1991. Reprinted in *Work in Canada: Readings in the Sociology of Work and Industry*, eds. Graham S. Lowe and Harvey J. Krahn, 14-24. Scarborough: Nelson Canada, 1993.

4515 COHEN, Marjorie Griffin. "Paid Work." In *Canadian Women's Issues, Volume II: Bold Visions*, Ruth Roach Pierson and Marjorie Griffin Cohen, 83-161. Toronto: James Lorimer and Company, 1995.

4516 COHEN, Yolande, *et al*. "Les métiers féminins: une conquête? Histoire comparée des fermières et infirmières dans l'entre-deux-guerres." *Resources for Feminist Research* 15, 4 (Dec. 1986/Jan. 1987): 54-55.

4517 CONNELLY, Patricia. "Female Labour Force Participation: Choice or Necessity?" *Atlantis* 3, 2, Part 1 (Spring 1978): 40-53.

4518 CONNELLY, Patricia. *Last Hired, First Fired: Women and the Canadian Work Force.* Toronto: The Women's Press, 1978.

4519 CONNELLY, Patricia. "Women Workers and the Family Wage in Canada." In *Women and the World of Work,* ed. Anne Hoiberg, 223-37. New York: Plenum Press, 1982.

4520 CONNELLY, Patricia, and Marcia MacDonald. "The Canadian Economy and Women's Work: An Historical Overview." *Studies in Political Economy* (Winter 1983): 47-50.

4521 COPP, Terry. *The Anatomy of Poverty: The Condition of the Working Class in Montreal, 1897-1929.* Toronto: McClelland and Stewart, 1974.

4522 CORRECTIVE COLLECTIVE. *Never Done: Three Centuries of Women's Work in Canada.* Toronto: Canadian Women's Educational Press, 1974.

4523 CREESE, Gillian. "The British Columbia Working Class: New Perspectives on Ethnicity/Race and Gender." *Labour/Le Travail* 27 (Spring 1991): 192-95.

4524 CROSS, D. Suzanne. "The Neglected Majority: The Changing Role of Women in 19th Century Montreal." *Histoire sociale/Social History* VI, 12 (November 1973): 202-23. Reprinted in *The Neglected Majority: Essays in Canadian Women's History,* eds. Susan Mann Trofimenkoff and Alison Prentice, 66-86. Toronto: McClelland and Stewart, 1977; and in *The Canadian City: Essays in Urban History,* eds. Gilbert A. Stelter and Alan F.J. Artibise, 255-81 Toronto: McClelland and Stewart, 1977; 2nd edition, 304-27, 1984.

4525 CROSS, Michael, S. *The Workingman in the Nineteenth Century.* Toronto: Oxford University Press, 1974.

4526 DANDURAND, Renée B. and Francine Descarries, eds. *Mères et travailleuses: de l'exception à la règle.* Québec: Institut québécois de recherche sur la culture, 1992.

4527 DAVID, Hélène. *Femmes et emploi: le défi de l'égalité.* Québec: Presses de l'Université du Québec, 1986.

4528 DELLAVALLE, P.A. and B. Meyer. "Changes in Relative Female-Male Unemployment: Canadian-United States Comparison." *Industrial Relations* 31, 3 (1976): 417-33.

4529 DIAMOND, Sara. *Women's Labour History in British Columbia: A Bibliography, 1930-1948.* Vancouver: Press Gang, 1980.

4530 DIAMOND, Sara. *Chambermaids and Whistlepunks: An Oral History of Women in BC Labour, 1930-1955.* Vancouver: Press Gang, 1983.

4531 DIAMOND, Sara. "Union Maid History." *Women's Education des femmes* 5, 2 (Winter 1986): 24-28. [teaching women's labour history]

4532 DUBINSKY, Karen. "Who is Listening? Teaching Labour History to People Who Don't Want to Learn It (or, Cry me a River, White Boy)." *Labour/Le Travail* 31 (Spring 1993): 287-92.

4533 DUFFY, Ann, Nancy Mandell and Norene Pupo. *Few Choices: Women, Work and Family.* Toronto: Garamond Press, 1989.

4534 DUFFY, Ann and Norene Pupo. *The Part-Time Paradox: Connecting Gender, Work and Family.* Toronto: McClelland and Stewart, 1992.

4535 DUFFY, Ann and Norene Pupo. "Part-time Paradox: Connecting Gender, Work, and Family." In *Work in Canada: Readings in the Sociology of Work and Industry,* eds. Graham S. Lowe and Harvey J. Krahn, 53-59. Scarborough: Nelson Canada, 1993.

4536 EICHLER, Margrit. "The Connection Between Paid and Unpaid Work." In *Women's Paid and Unpaid Work: Historical and Contemporary Perspectives,* ed. Paula Bourne, 61-78. Toronto: New Hogtown Press, 1985.

4537 ERRINGTON, Jane. "School Mistresses and Scullery Maids: A Survey of Women and their Work in Early Upper Canada." In *A Collection of Talks of Historical Interest,* 4-28. Kingston: Pittsburg Historical Society, 1990.

4538 ERRINGTON, Elizabeth Jane. *Wives and Mothers, School Mistresses and Scullery Maids: Working Women in Upper Canada, 1790-1840.* Montreal and Kingston: McGill-Queen's University Press, 1995.

4539 FORESTELL, Nancy. "Working Women in St. John's, the 1920s." In *Newfoundland History 1986: Proceedings of the First Newfoundland Historical Society Conference,* ed. Shannon Ryan, 219-29. St. John's: Newfoundland Historical Society, 1986.

4540 FORESTELL, Nancy. "Times Were Hard: The Pattern of Women's Paid Labour in St. John's Between the Two World Wars." *Labour/Le Travail* 24 (Fall 1989): 147-66.

4541 FORESTELL, Nancy and Jessie Chisholm. "Working-Class Women as Wage Earners in St. John's, Newfoundland, 1890-1921." In *Feminist Research: Prospect and Retrospect,* ed. Peta Tancred-Sheriff, 141-55. Montreal and Kingston: McGill-Queen's University Press for the Canadian Research Institute for the Advancement of Women, 1988.

4542 FOX, Bonnie. "The Female Reserve Army of Labour." *Atlantis* 7, 1 (Fall 1981): 45-56.

4543 FOX, Bonnie. "Women's Role in Development." In *Perspectives on Canadian Economic Development: Class, Staples, Gender, and Elites,* ed. Gordon Laxer, 333-52. Toronto: Oxford University Press, 1991.

4544 FOX, Bonnie J. and John Fox. "Women in the Labour Market 1931-81: Exclusion and Competition." *Canadian Review of Sociology and Anthropology* 23, 1 (February 1986): 22-46.

4545 FOX, Bonnie J. and John Fox. "Occupational Gender Segregation of the Canadian Labour Force, 1931-1981." *Canadian Review of Sociology and Anthropology* 24, 3 (August 1987): 374-97.

4546 FOX, Bonnie J. and John Fox. *Occupational Gender Segregation of the Canadian Labour Force, 1931-1981.* Toronto: Institute for Social Research, York University, 1987.

4547 GASKELL, Jane S. "Conceptions of Skill and the Work of Women: Some Historical and Political Issues." *Atlantis* 8, 2 (1983): 11-25. Reprinted in *The Politics of Diversity: Feminism, Marxism and Nationalism,* eds. Roberta Hamilton and Michèle Barrett. Montreal: Book Centre Inc., 1986.

4548 GESCHWENDER, James A. "Married Women's Waged Labor and Racial/Ethnic Stratification in Canada." *Canadian Ethnic Studies* 26, 3 (1994): 53-73.

4549 GILBERT, Anne. "Emploi féminin et milieu géographique: tendances hors Québec." *Canadian Journal of Regional Science* 16, 2 (Summer 1993): 213-35.

4550 GOLD, Sylvia. "Women, Work, and Place: The Canadian Context" In *Women, Work and Place,* ed. Audrey Kobayashi, 98-111. Montreal and Kingston: McGill-Queen's University Press, 1994.

4551 GRENIER, Gilles. "Participation au marché du travail, revenus et langues au Québec: le cas des femmes mariées." *L'actualité économique* 64, 1 (mars 1988): 5-22.

4552 GUNDERSON, Morley. "Time Pattern of Male-Female Wage Differentials—Ontario 1946-1971." *Relations Industrielles* 31, 1 (1976): 57-71.

4553 HERON, Craig, Shea Hoffmitz, Wayne Roberts and Robert Storey. *All That Our Hands Have Done: A Pictorial History of the Hamilton Workers.* Oakville: Mosaic Press, 1981.

4554 HERSON, Naomi and Dorothy E. Smith, eds. *Women and the Canadian Labour Force.* Ottawa: Social Sciences and Humanities Research Council, 1982.

4555 HILL, Christina Maria. "Women in the Canadian Economy." In *Canada (Ltd.),* ed. R.M. Laxer, 84-106. Toronto: McClelland and Stewart, 1973.

4556 JAIN, Harish C. "Race and Sex Discrimination in Employment in Canada: Theories, Evidence and Policies." *Industrial Relations* 37, 2 (1982): 344-66.

4557 JOHNSON, Leo. "The Political Economy of Ontario Women in the Nineteenth Century." In *Women at Work: Ontario, 1850-1930,* Janice Acton, *et al,* 13-31. Toronto: Canadian Women's Educational Press, 1974.

4558 JONES, Charles, Lorna Marsden and Lorne Tepperman. *Lives of Their Own: The Individualization of Women's Lives.* Toronto: Oxford University Press, 1990.

4559 KATZ, Michael. "Women and Early Industrialization." *York Social History Project First Research Report. Working Paper no. 2.* Downsview: York University, 1975.

4560 KEALEY, Greg. *Working Class Toronto at the Turn of the Century.* Toronto: New Hogtown Press, 1973.

4561 KEMPENEERS, Marianne. "Questions sur les femmes et travail: une lecture de la crise." *Sociologie et sociétés* 19, 1 (avril 1987): 57-71.

4562 KITCHEN, Brigitte. *Employment Strategies for Women and the Sexual Division of Labour.* Toronto: School of Social Work, York University, 1988.

4563 KITCHEN, Brigitte. "Employment Strategies for Women and the Sexual Division of Labour." In *Unemployment and Welfare: Social Policy and the Work of Social Work,* eds. Graham Riches and Gordon Terrowetsky, 141-60. Toronto: Garamond Press, 1990.

4564 KLEIN, Alice and Wayne Roberts. "Besieged Innocence: The 'Problem' and Problems of Working Women—Toronto, 1896-1914." In *Women at Work: Ontario, 1850-1930,* Janice Acton, *et al.* 211-59. Toronto: Canadian Women's Educational Press, 1974.

4565 KOBAYASHI, Audrey, ed. *Women, Work and Place.* Montreal and Kingston: McGill-Queen's University Press, 1994.

4566 LAVIGNE, Marie and Yolande Pinard. "Travail et mouvement des femmes: une histoire visible. Bilan Historiographique." In *Travailleuses et féministes: Les femmes dans la société québécoise,* eds. Marie Lavigne and Yolande Pinard, 7-60. Montréal: Boréal Express, 1983.

4567 LAVIGNE, Marie and Jennifer Stoddart. "Les travailleuses Montréalaises entre les deux guerres." *Labour/Le Travailleur* 2 (1977): 170-83.

4568 LAVIGNE, Marie and Jennifer Stoddart. "Ouvrières et travailleuses montréalaises, 1900-1940." In *Les femmes dans la société québécoise: Aspects historiques,* eds. Marie Lavigne and Yolande Pinard, 125-44. Montréal: Boréal Express, 1977. Reprinted in *Travailleuses et féministes: Les femmes dans la société québécoise,* eds. Marie Lavigne and Yolande Pinard, 99-113. Montréal: Boréal Express, 1983.

4569 LAVIGNE, Marie and Jennifer Stoddart. "Women's Work in Montreal at the beginning of the century." In *Women in Canada,* 2nd edition, ed. Marylee Stephenson, 129-47. Don Mills: General Publishing Co. Ltd., 1977.

4570 LE BOURDAIS, Céline and Hélène Desrosiers. "Les femmes et l'emploi: une analyse de la discontinuité des trajectoires féminines." *Recherches féministes* 3, 1 (1990): 119-34.

4571 LEGAULT, Ginette. *Repenser le travail: Quand les femmes accèdent à l'égalité.* Montréal: Liber, 1991.

4572 LENTON, Rhonda L. "Home Versus Career: Attitudes Towards Women's Work Among Canadian Women and Men, 1988." *Canadian Journal of Sociology* 17, 1 (Winter 1992): 89-98.

4573 LOWE, Graham S. *Women, Paid/Unpaid Work, and Stress: New Directions for Research.* Ottawa: Canadian Advisory Council on the Status of Women, 1989.

4574 LUXTON, Meg. "Taking on the Double Day." *Atlantis* 7, 1 (Fall 1981): 12-22.

4575 MacDONALD, Martha. "Studying Maritime Women's Work: Underpaid, Unpaid, Invisible, Invaluable." In *Teaching Maritime Studies,* ed. Phillip Buckner, 119-29. Fredericton: Acadiensis Press, 1986.

4576 MacLEAN, Annie. "Factory Legislation for Women in Canada." *American Journal of Sociology* 5 (September 1899): 172-81.

4577 MARSDEN, Lorna. "Some Problems of Research on Women in the Canadian Labour Force." *Atlantis* 2, 2 (1977): 116-24.

4578 MARSDEN, Lorna. "'The Labour Force' is an Ideological Construct: A Guiding Note to the Labour Economists." *Atlantis* 7, 1 (1981): 57-64.

4579 MARSDEN, Lorna R. "The Relationship Between the Labor Force Employment of Women and the Changing Social Organization in Canada." In *Women and the World of Work,* ed. Anne Hoiberg, 65-76. New York: Plenum Press, 1982.

4580 McPHERSON, Kathryn. "Feminist Reflections on the Writing of Canadian Working Class History in the 1980s." *Labour/Le Travail* 27 (Spring 1991): 185-89.

4581 MILLER, Paul W. "Gender Differences in Observed and Offered Wages in Canada, 1980." *Canadian Journal of Economics* 20, 2 (1987): 225-44.

4582 MUISE, D.A. "The Industrial Context of Inequality: Female Participation in Nova Scotia's Paid Labour Force, 1871-1921." *Acadiensis* 20, 2 (Spring 1991): 3-31. Reprinted in *Farm, Factory and Fortune: New Studies in the Economic History of the Maritime Provinces,* ed. Kris Inwood, 121-48. Fredericton: Acadiensis Press, 1993.

4583 NAKHAIE, M. Reza. "Class, Gender and Ethnic Income Inequalities in 1973 and 1984: Findings from the Canadian National Surveys." *Review of Radical Political Economics* 26, 1 (March 1994): 26-55.

4584 PARR, Joy. "Women Workers in the Twentieth Century." In *Lectures in Canadian Labour and Working-Class History,* eds. W.J.C. Cherwinski and Gregory S. Kealey, 79-88. St. John's: Committee on Canadian Labour History and New Hogtown Press, 1985.

4585 PEITCHINIS, Stephen G. *Women at Work: Discrimination and Response.* Toronto: McClelland & Stewart, Inc., 1989.

4586 PHILLIPS, Paul with Greg Mason. "Women in the Manitoba Labour Market: A Study of their Changing Economic Role." In *The Canadian West: Social Change and Economic Development,* ed. Henry Klassen. Calgary: Comprint Publishing, 1977.

4587 PHILLIPS, Paul and Erin Phillips. *Women and Work: Inequality in the Canadian Labour Market,* Toronto: James Lorimer & Company, 1983; rev. 2nd edition, 1993.

4588 PIERSON, Ruth Roach. "The History of Women and Paid Work." In *Women's Paid and Unpaid Work: Historical and Contemporary Perspectives,* ed. Paula Bourne, 17-34. Toronto: New Hogtown Press, 1985.

4589 PIVA, Michael J. *The Condition of the Working Class in Toronto, 1900-1921.* Ottawa: University of Ottawa Press, 1979.

4590 PRENTICE, Alison. "Writing Women Into History: The History of Women's Work in Canada." *Atlantis* 3, 2, Part II (Spring 1978): 72-83.

4591 RENAUD, Jean and Paul Bernard. "Places et agents: les divisions ethnique et sexuelle du travail au Québec de 1931 à 1981." *Cahiers québécois de démographie* 13, 1 (avril 1984): 87-100.

4592 ROBERTS, Barbara. "Trends in the Production and Enforcement of Female 'Dependence.'" *Canadian Journal of Women and the Law* 4, 1 (1990): 217-34.

4593 ROBERTS, Wayne. *Honest Womanhood: Feminism, Femininity and Class Consciousness Among Toronto Working Women, 1893-1914.* Toronto: New Hogtown Press, 1977. Reprinted in *Readings in Canadian History: Post Confederation,* 2nd edition, eds. R. Douglas Francis and Donald B. Smith. Toronto: Holt, Rinehart and Winston Canada, 1986.

4594 ROSE, Damaris and Paul Villeneuve. "Gender and Occupational Restructuring in Montreal in the 1970s." In *Women, Work and Place,* ed. Audrey Kobayashi, 130-61. Montreal and Kingston: McGill-Queen's University Press, 1994.

4595 ROSE, Damaris and Paul Villeneuve wirh Fiona Colgan. "Women Workers and the Inner City: Some Implications of Labour Force Restructuring in Montreal, 1971-81." In *Life Spaces: Gender, Household, Employment,* eds. Caroline Andrew and Beth Moore Milroy, 31-64. Vancouver: University of British Columbia Press, 1988.

4596 SANGSTER, Joan. "Canadian Working Women in the Twentieth Century." In *Lectures in Canadian Labour and Working-Class History,* eds. W.J.C. Cherwinski and Gregory S. Kealey, 58-78. St. John's: Committee on Canadian Labour History and New Hogtown Press, 1985.

4597 SANGSTER, Joan. *Earning Respect: The Lives of Working Women in Small-Town Ontario, 1920-1960.* Toronto: University of Toronto Press, 1995.

4598 SANGSTER, Joan. "Doing Two Jobs: The Wage-Earning Mother, 1945-70." In *A Diversity of Women: Ontario, 1945-1980,* ed. Joy Parr, 98-134. Toronto: University of Toronto Press, 1995.

4599 SMILLIE, Christine. "The Invisible Workforce Strikes for Recognition." *Briarpatch* 14, 5 (June 1985): 26-29.

4600 SMILLIE, Christine. "The Invisible Workforce: Women Workers in Saskatchewan from 1905 to World War II." *Saskatchewan History* 34, 2 (Summer 1986): 62-78.

4601   SMITH, J. Barry and Morton Stelcner. "Labour Supply of Married Women in Canada, 1980." *Canadian Journal of Economics* 21, 4 (November 1988): 857-70.

4602   SOROKA, Lewis A. "Male/Female Income Distributions, City Size and Urban Characteristics: Canada, 1970-1980." *Urban Studies* 24, 5 (October 1987): 417-26.

4603   STATON, Pat. "Validating Women's Work Through 'Grass-Roots' History: Bertha Adkins—A Case Study." *Canadian Woman Studies* 7, 4 (Winter 1986): 82-85.

4604   STRONG-BOAG, Veronica. "The Girl of the New Day: Canadian Working Women in the 1920s." *Labour/Le Travailleur* 4 (1979): 131-64. Reprinted in *The Consolidation of Capitalism, 1896-1929*, eds. Michael S. Cross and Gregory S. Kealey, 169-210. Toronto: McClelland and Stewart, 1983.

4605   STRONG-BOAG, Veronica. "Canada's Wage-Earning Wives and the Construction of the Middle Class, 1945-60." *Journal of Canadian Studies* 29, 3 (Fall 1994): 5-25.

4606   TREMBLAY, Diane-Gabrielle. "Labour Market Activity and Forms of Employment: The Evolution of the Sexual Division of Labour in Canada and the United States." In *Women and Industrial Relations: Proceedings of the 28th Conference of the Canadian Industrial Relations Association, June 2, 3, 4, 1991, Queen's University, Kingston, Ontario*, ed. Donald Carter. Ottawa: National Library of Canada, 1991.

4607   VAISEY, G. Douglas, comp. *The Labour Companion: A Bibliography of Canadian Labour History from 1950 to 1975*. Halifax: Committee on Canadian Labour History, 1980.

4608   VILLENEUVE, Paul and Damaris Rose. "Gender and the Separation of Employment from Home in Metropolitan Montreal, 1971-1981." *Urban Geography* 9, 2 (March/April 1988): 155-79.

4609   WEEKS, Wendy. "Part-time Work: The Business View on Second-Class Jobs for Housewives and Mothers." In *Working Canadians: Readings in the Sociology of Work and Industry*, eds. Graham S. Lowe and Harvey J. Krahn, 137-46. Toronto: Methuen, 1984.

4610   WHITE, Julie. *Women and Part-Time Work*. Ottawa: Advisory Council on the Status of Women, 1983.

4611   WILSON, Susannah Jane. *Women, the Family and the Economy*. Toronto: McGraw-Hill Ryerson, 1982.

4612   "Women's Employment in Canada: A Look at the Past." *Canada Manpower and Immigration Review* 8, 1 (1975): 1-8.

4613   WORKING LIVES COLLECTIVE. *Working Lives: Vancouver, 1886-1986*. Vancouver: New Star Books, 1985.

HOUSEWORK

4614   ANTLER, Ellen. "The Economics of 'Home Economics': A Newfoundland Example." *Resources for Feminist Research* 11, 1 (March 1982): 19-20.

4615   BÉLISLE, Diane and Yolande Pinard. "Un peu d'histoire." In *Du travail et de l'amour, les dessous de la production domestique*, ed. Louise Vandelac, 69-133. Montréal, 1985.

4616   BELLA, Leslie. *The Christmas Imperative: Leisure, Family and Women's Work*. Halifax: Fernwood Publishing, 1992.

4617   DAY, Tanis. "Capital-Labour Substitution in the Home." *Technology and Culture* 33, 2 (April 1992): 302-27. Reprinted in *Perspectives on Canadian Economic History*, eds. Douglas McCalla and Michael Huberman. Mississauga: Copp Clark Longman, 1994.

4618   DYCK, Isabel. "Integrating Home and Wage Workplace: Women's Daily Lives in a Canadian Suburb." *Canadian Geographer* 33, 4 (1989): 329-41. Reprinted in *British Columbia Reconsidered: Essays on Women*, eds. Gillian Creese and Veronica Strong-Boag, 172-97. Vancouver: Press Gang Publishers, 1992.

4619   FAIRLEY, Margaret. "Domestic Discontent." *Canadian Forum* 55 (September 1975): 31. [reprinted from 1920]

4620   FOX, Bonnie, ed. *Hidden in the Household: Women's Domestic Labour Under Capitalism*. Toronto: The Women's Press, 1980.

4621   KOME, Penny. *Somebody Has to Do It: Whose Work is Housework?* Toronto: McClelland & Stewart, 1982.

4622   LUXTON, Meg. *More Than a Labour of Love: Three Generations of Women's Work in the Home*. Toronto: Women's Press, 1980.

4623   LUXTON, Meg. "Two Hands for the Clock: Changing Patterns in the Gendered Division of Labour in the Home." *Studies in Political Economy* 12 (Fall 1983): 27-44. Reprinted in *The Challenge of Modernity: A Reader on Post-Confederation Canada*, ed. Ian McKay, 439-55. Toronto: McGraw-Hill Ryerson, 1992; and in *Canadian Family History: Selected Readings*, ed. Bettina Bradbury, 304-18. Toronto: Copp Clark Pitman, 1992.

4624   MARCHAND, Azilda. "Les femmes au foyer: hier et demain." *Canadian Women's Studies* 2, 4 (1980): 46-48.

4625   McPHERSON, Kathryn. *A 'Round the Clock Job: A Selected Bibliography on Women's Work at Home in Canada*. Ottawa: Social Sciences and Humanities Research Council, 1983.

4626   MEISSNER, Martin, E.W. Humpreys, S.M. Meis and W.J. Scheu. "No Exit for Wives: Sexual Division of Labour and the Cumulation of Household Demands." *Canadian Review of Sociology and Anthropology* 12 (1975): 424-39.

4627 MERCIER, Lucie. "Quotidienneté et activités domestiques. Un univers en mutation," *Questions de Culture* 9 (1986).

4628 PIERSON, Ruth Roach. "The Politics of the Domestic Sphere." In *Canadian Women's Issues, Volume II: Bold Visions*, Ruth Roach Pierson and Marjorie Griffin Cohen, 1-82. Toronto: James Lorimer and Company, 1995.

4629 PROULX, Monique. *Five Million Women: A Study of the Canadian Housewife*. Ottawa: Advisory Council on the Status of Women, 1978.

4630 SINCLAIR, Peter R. and Lawrence Felt. "Separate World: Gender and Domestic Labour in an Isolated Fishing Region." *Canadian Review of Sociology and Anthropology* 29, 1 (February 1992): 55-71.

4631 STAEBLER, Edna, ed. *Haven't Any News: Ruby's Letters from the Fifties*. Waterloo: Wilfrid Laurier University Press, 1995. [daily life of a housewife in small-town Ontario]

4632 STRONG-BOAG, Veronica. "Discovering the Home: The Last 150 Years of Domestic Work in Canada." In *Women's Paid and Unpaid Work: Historical and Contemporary Perspectives*, ed. Paula Bourne, 35-60. Toronto: New Hogtown Press, 1985.

4633 STRONG-BOAG, Veronica. "Keeping House in God's Country: Canadian Women at Work in the Home." In *On the Job: Confronting the Labour Process in Canada*, eds. Craig Heron and Robert Storey, 124-51. Montreal and Kingston: McGill-Queen's University Press, 1986.

4634 VANDELAC, Louise, Diane Bélisle, Anne Gauthier and Yolande Pinard. *Du travail et de l'amour: Les dessous de la production domestique*. Montréal: Saint-Martin, 1985.

MANUFACTURING/BLUE COLLAR

4635 BEATTIE, Betsy. "Dutiful Daughters: Maritime-Born Women in New England in the Late Nineteenth Century." *Retrospection* 2, 1 (1989): 16-31.

4636 BEATTIE, Betsy. "'Going Up to Lynn': Single, Maritime-Born Women in Lynn, Massachusetts, 1879-1930." *Acadiensis* 22, 1 (Autumn 1992): 65-86.

4637 BLOOMFIELD, Elizabeth and G.T. Bloomfield. *Canadian Women in Workshops, Mills and Factories: The Evidence of the 1871 Census Manuscripts*. Guelph: Department of Geography, University of Guelph, 1991.

4638 BRANDT, Gail Cuthbert. "'Weaving It Together': Life Cycle and the Industrial Experience of Female Cotton Workers in Quebec, 1910-1950." *Labour/Le Travail* VII (1981): 113-26. Reprinted in *The Neglected Majority: Essays in Canadian Women's History, Vol. 2*, eds. Alison Prentice and Susan Mann Trofimenkoff, 160-73. Toronto: McClelland and Stewart, 1985.

4639 BRANDT, Gail Cuthbert. "Industry's Handmaidens: Women in the Quebec Cotton Industry." *Canadian Women's Studies* 3 (1981): 79-82.

4640 BRANDT, Gail Cuthbert. "The Transformation of Women's Work in the Quebec Cotton Industry, 1920-1950." In *The Character of Class Struggle: Essays in Canadian Working-Class History*, ed. Bryan D. Palmer. Toronto: McClelland & Stewart, 1986.

4641 BRANDT, Gail Cuthbert. "Women in the Quebec Cotton Industry, 1890-1950." *Material History Bulletin* 31 (Spring 1990): 99-105.

4642 DAGG, Alexandra and Judy Fudge. "Sewing Pains: Homeworkers in the Garment Trade." *Our Times* (June 1992): 22-25. Reprinted in *Work in Canada: Readings in the Sociology of Work and Industry*, eds. Graham S. Lowe and Harvey J. Krahn, 190-94. Scarborough: Nelson Canada, 1993.

4643 DU BERGER, Jean and Jacques Mathieu, eds. *Les ouvrières de Dominion Corset à Québec, 1886-1988*. Sainte-Foy: Presses de l'Université Laval, 1993.

4644 GANNAGÉ, Charlene. *Double Day, Double Bind: Women Garment Workers*. Toronto: The Women's Press, 1986.

4645 GÖLZ, Annalee, David Millar and Barbara Roberts with Lois Kunkel and Astrid Mendelsohn Zimmer. *A Decent Living: Women Workers in the Winnipeg Garment Industry*. Toronto: New Hogtown Press, 1991.

4646 GRANT, Janine and Kris Inwood. "Gender and Organization in the Canadian Cloth Industry, 1870." In *Canadian Papers in Business History, Vol. I*, ed. Peter Baskerville, 17-31. Victoria: Public History Group, University of Victoria, 1989.

4647 GRANT, Michel and Ruth Rose. "L'encadrement du travail à domicile dans l'industrie du vêtement au Québec." *Relations industrielles/Industrial Relation* 40 (1985): 473-92.

4648 JOHNSON, Laura C. and Robert E. Johnson. *The Seam Allowance: Industrial Home Sewing in Canada*. Toronto: Women's Press, 1982.

4649 KEALEY, Greg, ed. *Canada Investigates Industrialism*. Toronto: University of Toronto Press, 1973.

4650 LAFLEUR, Ginette. "L'industrialisation et le travail rémunéré des femmes, Moncton, 1881-91." In *Feminist Research: Prospect and Retrospect*, ed. Peta Tancred-Sheriff, 127-40. Montreal and Kingston: McGill-Queen's University Press for the Canadian Research Institute for the Advancement of Women, 1988,

4651 LEACH, Belinda. "'Flexible' work, precarious future: Some lessons from the Canadian clothing industry." *Canadian Review of Sociology and Anthropology* 30, 1 (1993): 64-82.

4652 LEPP, Annalee, David Millar and Barbara Roberts. "Women in the Winnipeg Garment Industry, 1950s-1970s." In *First Days, Fighting Days: Women in Manitoba History,* ed. Mary Kinnear, 149-72. Regina: Canadian Plains Research Center, University of Regina, 1987.

4653 McCALLUM, Margaret. "Separate Spheres: The Organisation of Work in a Confectionery Factory, Ganong Bros., St. Stephen, New Brunswick." *Labour/Le Travail* 24 (Fall 1989): 69-90.

4654 McINTOSH, Robert. "Sweated Labour: Female Needleworkers in Industrializing Canada." *Labour/Le Travail* 32 (Fall 1993): 105-38. Reprinted in *Canadian Women: A Reader,* eds. Wendy Mitchinson, *et al,* 142-72. Toronto: Harcourt Brace Canada, 1996.

4655 MOCHORUK, James D. and Donna Webber. "Women in the Winnipeg Garment Trade, 1929-45." In *First Days, Fighting Days: Women in Manitoba History,* ed. Mary Kinnear, 134-48. Regina: Canadian Plains Research Center, University of Regina, 1987.

4656 MYERS, Sharon. "'Not to Be Ranked as Women': Female Industrial Workers in Turn-of-the-Century Halifax." In *Separate Spheres: Women's Worlds in the 19th Century Maritimes,* eds. Janet Guildford and Suzanne Morton, 161-83. Fredericton: Acadiensis Press, 1994.

4657 PARR, Joy. "Rethinking Work and Kinship in a Canadian Hosiery Town, 1910-1950." *Feminist Studies* 13, 1 (Spring 1987): 137-62. Reprinted in *Canadian Family History: Selected Readings,* ed. Bettina Bradbury, 220-40. Toronto: Copp Clark Pitman, 1992.

4658 PARR, Joy. "Disaggregating the Sexual Division of Labour: A Transatlantic Case Study." *Comparative Studies in Society and History* 30, 3 (July 1988): 511-33.

4659 PARR, Joy. *The Gender of Breadwinners: Women, Men and Change in Two Industrial Towns, 1880-1950.* Toronto: University of Toronto Press, 1990.

4660 PORTER, Ann and Barbara Cameron. *The Impact of Free Trade on Women in Manufacturing.* Ottawa: Canadian Advisory Council on the Status of Women, 1987.

4661 ROUILLARD, Jacques. *Les travailleurs du coton au Québec, 1900-1915.* Montréal: Presses de l'Université du Québec, 1974.

4662 SARNY, Dominique. "Apprivoiser la ville: le cas des ouvrières de Dominion Corset." *Canadian Folklore* 16, 1 (1994): 74-83.

4663 STEEDMAN, Mercedes. "Skill and Gender in the Canadian Clothing Industry, 1890-1940." In *On the Job: Confronting the Labour Process in Canada,* eds. Craig Heron and Robert Storey, 152-72. Montreal and Kingston: McGill-Queen's University Press, 1986.

4664 TROFIMENKOFF, Susan. "One Hundred and Two Muffled Voices: Canada's Industrial Women in the 1880s." *Atlantis* 3, 1 (Fall 1977): 66-82. Reprinted in *Canada's Age of Industry, 1849-1896,* eds. Michael S. Cross and Gregory S. Kealey, 212-29. Toronto: McClelland and Stewart, 1982; in *Rethinking Canada: The Promise of Women's History,* eds. Veronica Strong-Boag and Anita Clair Fellman, 82-94. Toronto: Copp Clark Pitman Ltd., 1986; and in *Canadian Working Class History: Selected Readings,* eds. Laurel Sefton-MacDowell and Ian Radforth, Toronto: Canadian Scholars Press, 1992.

PROFESSIONS/PUBLIC SECTOR

4665 ARCHIBALD, Kathleen. *Sex and the Public Service.* Ottawa: Queen's Printer, 1970.

4666 ARMSTRONG, Pat and Hugh Armstrong. "Sex and the Professions in Canada." *Journal of Canadian Studies* 27, 1 (Spring 1992): 118-35.

4667 BEAVERIDGE, Janice. "Getting a Job Done and Doing It Well: Dr. Blossom Wigdor, Psychologist and Gerontologist." In *Despite the Odds: Essays on Canadian Women and Science,* ed. Marianne Gosztonyi Ainley, 252-62. Montreal: Véhicule Press, 1990.

4668 *Beneath the Veneer: Report of the Task Force on Barriers to Women in the Public Service.* Ottawa: Canadian Government Publishing Centre, 1990.

4669 CHARLES, Aline and Nadia Fahmy-Eid. "La diététique et la physiothérapie face au problème des frontières interprofessionnelles (1950-1980)." *Revue d'histoire de l'Amérique française* 47, 3 (hiver 1994): 377-408.

4670 COBURN, David. "Professionalization and Proletarianization: Medicine, Nursing, and Chiropractic in Historical Perspective." *Labour/Le Travail* 34 (Fall 1994): 139-62.

4671 COLLIN, Johanne. "Les femmes dans la profession pharmaceutique au Québec: rupture ou continuité?" *Recherches féministes* 5, 2 (1992): 31-56.

4672 COLLIN, Johanne. "Féminisation, mutations professionnelles et transformation de l'image identitaire d'un groupe: le cas de la pharmacie au Québec." *Genèse et dynamique des groupes professionnels,* 171-81. Lille: Presses universitaires de Lille, 1994.

4673 COLLIN, Johanne. *Changement d'ordonnance: mutations professionnelles, identité sociale et féminisation de la profession pharmaceutique au Québec, 1940-1980.* Montréal: Boréal, 1995.

4674 DE LA COUR, Lykke. "The 'Other' Side of Psychology: Women Psychologists in Toronto from 1920 to 1945." *Canadian Woman Studies* 8, 4 (Winter 1987): 44-46.

4675 EWAN, Gail. "Agnes Higgins, nutritionist, 1911-1985, and the Montreal Diet Dispensary." *Resources for Feminist Research* 15, 3 (November 1986): 48-49.

4676 FAHMY-EID, Nadia and Aline Charles. "Raison d'État ou du plus fort? La diététique et la physiothérapie en quête d'une pratique exclusive au Québec, 1950-1980." *Histoire sociale/Social History* XXVI, 51 (May 1993): 95-113.

4677 FAHMY-EID, Nadia and Lucie Piché. "Le savoir négocié: les stratégies des associations de technologie médicale, de physiothérapie et de diététique pour l'accès à une meilleure formation professionnelle (1930-1970)." *Revue d'histoire de l'Amérique française* 43, 4 (printemps 1990): 509-34.

4678 GAUCHER, Dominique. "La formation des Hygiénistes à l'Université de Montréal, 1910-1975: De la santé publique à la médecine préventive." *Recherches Sociographiques* 20, 1 (janvier/avril 1979).

4679 GILROY, Marion, ed. *As We Remember It: Interviews with Pioneering Librarians of British Columbia.* Vancouver: School of Librarianship, University of British Columbia, 1970.

4680 HARDY, Allison Taylor. "Women: Always Diplomatic and More Recently Diplomats." *International Perspectives* (July/August 1976): 26-32.

4681 HEAP, Ruby. "Physiotherapy's Quest for Professional Status in Ontario, 1950-80." *Canadian Bulletin of Medical History* 12, 1 (1995): 69-99.

4682 KEMPENEERS, Marianne. *Le travail au féminin: analyse démographique de la discontinuité professionnelle des femmes au Canada.* Montréal: Les Presses de l'Université de Montréal, 1992.

4683 KEMPENEERS, Marianne and Marie-Hélène Saint-Pierre. "Discontinuité professionnelle et charges familiales: Regards sur les données canadiennes." *Cahiers québécois de démographie* 18, 1 (1989): 63-85.

4684 KINNEAR, Mary. *In Subordination: Professional Women, 1870-1970.* Montreal and Kingston: McGill-Queen's University Press, 1995.

4685 MARSHALL, Katherine. "Women in Male-Dominated Professions." *Canadian Social Trends* (Winter 1987): 7-11.

4686 MARSHALL, Katherine. "Women in Professional Occupations: Progress in the 1980s." *Canadian Social Trends* (Spring 1989): 13-16.

4687 McCORMACK, Thelma. "Post Mortem—Lépine: Women in Engineering." *Atlantis* 16, 2 (Spring 1991): 85-90. Reprinted in *Work in Canada: Readings in the Sociology of Work and Industry,* eds. Graham S. Lowe and Harvey J. Krahn, 195-202. Scarborough: Nelson Canada, 1993.

4688 MORGAN, Nicole. *The Equality Game: Women in the Federal Public Service, 1908-1987.* Ottawa: Canadian Advisory Council on the Status of Women, 1988.

4689 MUZZIN, Linda, Greg Brown and Roy Hornosty. "Consequences of feminization of a profession: The case of Canadian pharmacy." *Women and Health* 21, 2/3 (1994): 39-56.

4690 MUZZIN, Linda, Greg Brown and Roy Hornosty. "Gender, Educational Credentials, Contributions and Career Advancement: Results of a Follow-up Study in Hospital Pharmacy." *Canadian Review of Sociology and Anthropology* 32, 2 (1995).

4691 NADEAU, France. "La femme acadienne dans la fonction publique du Nouveau-Brunswick." In *Les Acadiens: Etat de la recherche,* eds. Jacques Lapointe and André Leclerc, 229-33. Québec: Conseil de la vie française en Amérique, 1987.

4692 PICHÉ, Lucie and Nadia Fahmy-Eid. "À la recherche d'un statut professionnel dans le champ paramédical: le cas de la diététique, de la physiothérapie et de la technologie médicale (1940-1973)." *Revue d'histoire de l'Amérique française* 45, 3 (hiver 1992): 375-401.

4693 STIEB, Ernest, *et al.* "Women in Ontario Pharmacy, 1867-1927." In *Despite the Odds: Essays on Canadian Women and Science,* ed. Marianne Gosztonyi Ainley, 121-33. Montreal: Véhicule Press, 1990.

4694 STRUTHERS, James. "A Profession in Crisis: Charlotte Whitton and Canadian Social Work in the 1930s." *Canadian Historical Review* 62, 2 (June 1981): 169-85. Reprinted in *The 'Benevolent' State: The Growth of Welfare in Canada,* eds. Allan Moscovitch and Jim Albert, 111-25. Toronto: Garamond Press, 1987.

4695 STRUTHERS, James. "'Lord Give Us Men': Women and Social Work in English Canada, 1918 to 1953." Canadian Historical Association. *Historical Papers* (1983). Reprinted in *The 'Benevolent' State: The Growth of Welfare in Canada.* eds. Allan Moscovitch and Jim Albert, 126-43. Toronto: Garamond Press, 1987.

RESOURCE ECONOMIES

4696 ALBERTS, Laurie. "Petticoats and Pickaxes." *Alaska Journal* 7, 3 (Summer 1977): 146-59.

4697 ANDERSON, Mary W. "The Miner's Angel." *Canadian West Magazine* 7, 4 (October/December 1991): 152-59. [Nellie Cashman]

4698 ANTLER, Ellen. "Women's Work in Newfoundland Fishing Families." *Atlantis* 2, 2, Part II (Spring 1977): 106-13.

4699 BACKHOUSE, Frances H. "Women of the Klondike." *The Beaver* 68, 6 (Dec. 1988/Jan. 1989): 30-36.

4700 BACKHOUSE, Frances. *Women of the Klondike.* Vancouver/Toronto: Whitecap Books, 1995.

4701 BERTON, Laura B. *I Married the Klondike.* Toronto: McClelland and Stewart, 1954.

4702 BINKLEY, Marian and Victor Thiessen. "'Ten Days a Grass Widow—Forty-eight Hours a Wife': Sexual Division of Labour in Trawlermen's Households." *Culture* 8, 2 (1988): 39-51.

4703 BOBILLIER, R.P. *Une Pionnière du Yukon.* Chicoutimi, QC: Publications de la Société Historique du Saguenay, no. 13, 1948.

4704 BRENNAN, T. Ann. *The Real Klondike Kate.* Fredericton: Goose Lane Editions, 1990.

4705 CAMPBELL, Catherine. "Bessie Hall, Master Mariner." *Nova Scotia Historical Review* 7, 2 (1987): 8-12.

4706 CARMICHAEL, Jack. "Lady Miners, Lemon Extract and Fried Rattlesnake." *BC Outdoors* 21, 1 (January/February 1976): 10-11, 13-14.

4707 CONNELLY, Patricia and Martha MacDonald. "Women's Work: Domestic and Wage Labour in a Nova Scotia Community." *Studies in Political Economy* 10 (Winter 1983): 45-72. Reprinted in *The Politics of Diversity: Feminism, Marxism and Nationalism,* eds. Roberta Hamilton and Michèle Barrett. Montreal: Book Centre Inc., 1986.

4708 CONNELLY, M. Patricia and Martha MacDonald. "State Policy, the Household and Women's Work in the Atlantic Fishery." *Journal of Canadian Studies* 26, 4 (Winter 1991/92): 18-32.

4709 COTTON, H. Barry. "Piebiter Creek: a personal reminiscence of Delina C. Noel." *British Columbia Historical News* 27, 4 (Fall 1994): 2-4.

4710 DAVIS, Mary Lee. *Sourdough Gold.* Boston: Wilde Co., 1933.

4711 DODGE, Helen Carmichael. *My Childhood in the Canadian Wilderness.* New York: Vantage Press, 1961. [New Brunswick lumber camps]

4712 DUNCAN, Helen. *Kate Rice, Prospector.* Toronto: Simon and Pierre, 1983.

4713 EBER, Dorothy Harley. "A Feminine Focus on the Last Frontier." *Arctic Circle* (Spring 1994): 16-21.

4714 ELLIS, Lucia. *Klondike Kate: The Life and Legend of Kitty Rockwell.* New York: Hastings House, 1962.

4715 FERRY, Eudora Bundy. *Yukon Gold: Pioneering Days in the Canadian North.* New York: Exposition Press, 1971.

4716 FRANK, David. "The Miner's Financier: Women in the Cape Breton Coal Towns, 1917." *Atlantis* 8, 2 (Spring 1983): 137-43.

4717 GODSELL, Jean W. *I Was No Lady ... I Followed the Call of the Wild: The Autobiography of a Fur Trader's Wife.* Toronto: Ryerson Press, 1959.

4718 GOUDIE, Elizabeth. *Woman of Labrador.* Edited and with an introduction by David Zimmerly. Toronto: Peter Martin Associates, 1973. [autobiography of a trapper's wife]

4719 ILCAN, Suzan. "Women and Casual Work in the Nova Scotia Fish Processing Industry." *Atlantis* 11, 2 (Spring 1986): 23-34.

4720 KELCEY, Barbara. "Not All Goddesses of Liberty: Women in the Klondike Goldrush." *Musk-Ox* 37 (Winter 1989): 184-88.

4721 KELCEY, Barbara E. "What to Wear to the Klondike: Outfitting Women for the Gold Rush." *Material History Review* 37 (Spring 1993): 20-29.

4722 LEWIS, Jane, Marilyn Porter and Mark Shrimpton, eds. *Women, Work and Family in the British, Canadian and Norwegian Offshore Oil Fields.* New York: St. Martin's Press, 1988.

4723 MacDONALD, Martha and M. Patricia Connelly. "Class and Gender in Fishing Communities in Nova Scotia." *Studies in Political Economy* 30 (Autumn 1989): 61-85. Reprinted in *Feminism in Action: Studies in Political Economy,* eds. M. Patricia Connelly and Pat Armstrong. Toronto: Canadian Scholars' Press, 1993.

4724 MacDONALD, Martha and Patricia Connelly. "Class and Gender in Nova Scotia Fishing Communities." In *Restructuring and Resistance from Atlantic Canada,* eds. Bryant Fairley, Colin Leys and James Sacouman, 151-70. Toronto: Garamond Press, 1990.

4725 MANDY, E. Madge. *Our Trail Led Northwest.* Surrey: BC: Heritage House, 1992.

4726 MAYER, Melanie J. *Klondike Women: True Tales of the 1897-98 Gold Rush.* Athens: Swallow Press, 1989.

4727 McCAY, Bonnie J. "Fish Guts, Hair Nets and Unemployment Stamps: Women and Work in Co-operative Fish Plants." In *A Question of Survival: The Fisheries and Newfoundland Society,* ed. P.R. Sinclair, 105-31. St. John's: Institute for Social and Economic Research, Memorial University of Newfoundland, 1988.

4728 MITCHELL, Dorothea. *Lady Lumberjack.* Vancouver: Mitchell Press, 1967.

4729 MOORE, Carolyn. "Crisis and Opportunity: Three White Women's Experience of the Klondike." *Canadian Woman Studies* 14, 4 (Fall 1994): 51-54.

4730 MUSZYNSKI, Alicja. "Race and Gender: Structural Determinants in the Formation of British Columbia's Salmon Cannery Labour Force." In *Class, Gender and Region: Essays in Canadian Historical Sociology,* ed. Gregory S. Kealey. St. John's: Committee on Canadian Labour History, 1988.

4731 NADEL-KLEIN, Jane and Dona Lee Davis, eds. *To Work and To Weep: Women in Fishing Economies.* St. John's: Institute of Social and Economic Research, Memorial University of Newfoundland, 1988.

4732 NEIS, Barbara. "From 'Shipped Girls' to 'Brides of the State': The Transition from Familial to Social Patriarchy in the Newfoundland Fishing Industry." *Canadian Journal of Regional Science* 16, 2 (Summer 1993): 185-211.

4733 NEWELL, Dianne. "The Industrial Archaeology of the Organization of Work: A Half Century of Women and Racial Minorities in British Columbia Fish Plants." *Material History Review* 33 (Spring 1991): 25-36.

4734 PARRISH, Maud. *Nine Pounds of Luggage.* London: n.p., 1940. [Klondike gold rush]

4735 PORTER, Marilyn. "'Women and Old Boats': The Sexual Division of Labour in a Newfoundland Outport." In *The Public and the Private*, eds. Eva Gamarnikow, *et al*, 91-105. London: Heinemann, 1983. Reprinted in *Gender and Society: Creating a Canadian Woman's Sociology*, ed. Arlene Tigar McLaren, 169-83. Toronto: Copp Clark Pitman, 1988.

4736 PORTER, Marilyn. "'She Was Skipper of the Shore-Crew': Notes on the History of the Sexual Division of Labour in Newfoundland." *Labour/Le Travail* 15 (Spring 1985): 105-23. Reprinted in *Canadian Family History: Selected Readings*, ed. Bettina Bradbury, 158-75. Toronto: Copp Clark Pitman, 1992.

4737 PORTER, Marilyn. "Mothers and Daughters: Linking Women's Life Histories in Grand Bank, Newfoundland, Canada." *Women's Studies International Forum* 11, 6 (1988): 545-58. Reprinted in *Rethinking Canada: The Promise of Women's History*, 2nd edition, eds. Veronica Strong-Boag and Anita Clair Fellman, 396-414. Toronto: Copp Clark Pitman Ltd., 1991.

4738 PORTER, Marilyn. "Time, the Life Course and Work in Women's Lives: Reflections from Newfoundland." *Women's Studies International Forum* 14, 1/2 (1991): 1-13.

4739 REDDIN, J. Estelle. "Making Ends Meet: The Way of the Prince Edward Island Fisherman's Wife." *Canadian Folklore* 13, 2 (1991): 85-98.

4740 ROMIG, Elsie Craig. *A Pioneer Woman in Alaska*. Caldwell, Idaho: Claxton Printers, 1948. [Klondike gold rush]

4741 SHAND, Margaret Clark and Ora M. Shand. *The Summit and Beyond*. Caldwell, ID: Claxton Printers, 1959. [Klondike gold rush]

4742 STAINSBY, Jill. "It's the Smell of Money: Women Shoreworkers of British Columbia." *BC Studies* 103 (Autumn 1994): 59-82.

4743 STEVENSON, John. "Queen of the Klondike." *Canadian West* (May, August and October 1986).

4744 THIERRY, Joyce. "Northern Bride, 1947." *The Beaver* 69, 4 (Aug./Sept. 1989): 27-33. [wife of a Hudson's Bay Company post manager]

4745 THOMPSON, Ruby Trench. *Pioneers of Athabaska: Autobiography of a Trader-Trapper's Wife*. Alderwood Minor, WA: Raymond Thompson Co., 1967. [Northern Alberta, 1920]

4746 TOLBOOM, Wanda Neill. *Arctic Bride*. Toronto: Ryerson Press, 1956. [wife of a Hudson's Bay post manager, 20th century Northern Quebec]

4747 TYRRELL, Mary Edith. *I Was There*. Toronto: Ryerson Press, 1938. [Klondike gold rush]

4748 VAN KIRK, Sylvia. "A Vital Presence: Women in the Cariboo Gold Rush, 1862-1875." In *British Columbia Reconsidered: Essays on Women*, eds. Gillian Creese and Veronica Strong-Boag, 21-37. Vancouver: Press Gang Publishers, 1992.

4749 WILLIAMSON, Eileen. "Bush Wife." *The Beaver* (Winter 1975): 40-45. [Casummit Lake, Ontario, 1930s]

SERVICE OCCUPATIONS

4750 ANDERSON, Robin John. "Domestic Service: The YWCA and Women's Employment Agencies in Vancouver, 1898-1915." *Histoire sociale/Social History* XXV, 50 (November 1992): 307-33.

4751 BARBER, Marilyn J. "Below Stairs: The Domestic Servant." *Material History Bulletin* 19 (Spring 1984): 37-46.

4752 BARBER, Marilyn. "The Servant Problem in Manitoba, 1896-1930." In *First Days, Fighting Days: Women in Manitoba History*, ed. Mary Kinnear, 100-19. Regina: Canadian Plains Research Center, University of Regina, 1987.

4753 COULTER, Rebecca. "Young Women and Unemployment in the 1930s: The Home Service Solution." *Canadian Woman Studies* 7, 4 (Winter 1986): 77-80.

4754 FOLKES, Patrick. "Cooks and Ladies' Maids: Women in Sail and Steam on the Great Lakes in the Nineteenth Century." *Fresh Water: A Journal of Great Lakes Marine History* 1, 1 (Spring 1986): 24-30.

4755 KLIPPENSTEIN, Frieda Esau. "'Doing What We Could': Mennonite Domestic Servants in Winnipeg, 1920s to 1950s." *Journal of Mennonite Studies* 7 (1989): 145-66.

4756 LACELLE, Claudette. "Les domestiques dans les villes canadiennes au XIXe siècle: effectifs et conditions de vie." *Histoire sociale/Social History* XV, 29 (May 1982): 181-207.

4757 LACELLE, Claudette. *Urban Domestic Servants in 19th-Century Canada*. Ottawa: Environment Canada, 1987.

4758 LENSKYJ, Helen. "A 'Servant Problem' or a 'Servant-Mistress Problem'? Domestic Service in Canada, 1890-1930." *Atlantis* 7, 1 (Fall 1981): 3-11.

4759 LESLIE, Genevieve. "Domestic Service in Canada, 1880-1920." In *Women at Work: Ontario, 1850-1930*, eds. Janice Acton, *et al*, 71-125. Toronto: Canadian Women's Educational Press, 1974.

4760 REITER, Ester. *Making Fast Food: From the Frying Pan into the Fryer*. Montreal and Kingston: McGill-Queen's University Press, 1991; 2nd edition 1996.

4761 STODDART, Jennifer and Veronica Strong-Boag. "...And Things Were Going Wrong at Home." *Atlantis* 1, 1 (Fall 1975): 38-44. [turn-of-the-century servant problem]

AUTHOR INDEX

Gilroy, Joan, 1593
Gilroy, Marion, 4679
Giltrow, Janet, 766
Gingras, Anne-Marie, 3636, 4285
Gingras, Marcelle, 96
Girard, Philip, 2883, 2884, 2978, 2979
Girouard, Guylaine, 424
Girouard-Décarie, Jeanne, 384
Giroux, Jacqueline, 4446
Giroux, Nicole, 1594
Giroux, Suzanne, 2680, 2681
Givner, Joan, 97
Gleason, Mona, 425
Glenn, Eleanor Margaret, 767, 4063
Glennie, Judy, 2696
Glogowska, Barbara, 904
Glynn, Alexandra K.R., 889
Go, Amy, 850
Godard, Barbara, 98-102
Godard, Beatrice, 2453
Godfrey, C.M., 426
Godin, Christine, 3393
Godsell, Jean W., 4717
Godsell, Patricia, 3538
Goforth, Rosalind, 3776
Gogan, Tanya, 1803
Gold, Muriel, 259
Gold, Sylvia, 4550
Gölz, Annalee, 2134, 2210, 3050, 4645
Gonzales, Ellice B., 1992, 1993
Goodman, Jacqueline, 2015
Goodson, Ivor, F., 501
Goodwin, Theresa, 633
Gordon, Loraine, 2942
Gorham, Deborah, 1410, 1411, 1595-1597, 1763, 1804, 2537, 2565, 3192
Gossage, Carolyn A., 311, 535, 3444
Gossage, Peter, 1297, 1348, 1349, 2454, 2780, 2966
Gotell, Lise, 1598, 2885
Gotsch-Trevelyan, Katherine, 3251
Gottfriedson, Mary, 1576
Gottlieb, Amy, 4117
Gottlieb, Lois C., 103, 3193
Goudie, Elizabeth, 4718
Gough, Lyn, 1805
Gould, Florence E., 3445
Gould, Jan, 2318
Gould, K., 1599
Gould, Karen, 107
Gourdeau, Claire, 3980
Gowan, Elsie Park, 3252
Goy, Joseph, 1143
Goyder, John, 427
Graff, Linda, 4385

Graham, Elizabeth, 634
Graham, Ferne, 3777
Graham, Frank W., 1412
Graham, John R., 3051
Grant, Agnes, 104, 105
Grant, Dorothy Metie, 2589, 2781
Grant, Francis W., 2319
Grant, Gail Paton, 3321
Grant, Gail, 2211
Grant, Janine, 4646
Grant, John Webster, 3778, 3779
Grant, Laurence, 3322
Grant, Michel, 4647
Gratton, P., 635
Gravel, Pauline, 1806
Graveline, M. Jean, 1600
Gray, James H., 1239, 2782
Gray, Leslie R., 3780
Gray, Rachel, 636
Grayson, Linda M., 3052
Greaves, Lorraine, 1807
Green, Gretchen, 1994
Green, H. Gordon, 2639
Green, J., 2886
Green, Mary Jean, 106, 107
Green, R., 1928
Greene, Alma, 1906
Greenglass, Esther, 2135
Greenhill, Pauline, 768, 3394
Greenland, Cyril, 4064
Greenwood, Donna, 1482
Greer, Allan, 536, 3637
Gregory, Judith, 4458
Grenier, Gilles, 4551
Grenier, Nicole, 3323
Gresko, Jacqueline, 769, 4386
Griffis, Edith May, 637
Griffiths, Linda, 260
Griffiths, N.E.S., 1808, 2395, 2396
Grindstaff, Carl F., 978, 1004, 1085,1298
Gross, Wendy L., 2980
Grosskurth, Phyllis, 108
Groulx, Lionel, 3981-3983
Groupe de recherche en économie et politique agricole, 4387
Growe, Sarah Jane, 2686
Guay, Hélène, 537
Guberman, Connie, 1584, 1601
Guberman, Nancy, 3053
Guemple, Lee, 1995
Guérin, Yvonne, 1996
Guettel, Charnie, 1602
Guildford, Janet, 638, 2136
Guillemette, E. Andre, 881
Guillet, Edwin Clarence, 639, 3324
Gulbinowicz, Eva, 979

Gunderson, Morley, 1603, 4552
Gundy, H. Pearson, 3446
Gunnars, Kristjana, 109
Guppy, N., 428
Gupta, Nila, 1023
Gurney, Helen, 4175, 4176
Guyon, Louise, 2569
Gwyn, Sandra, 2, 2103, 3447

H

Hacker, Carlotta, 1413, 2538, 2539
Haddad, Jane, 3054
Haffey, Helen, 2498
Hagan, John, 2815, 2902
Haggerty, Joan, 1164
Haglund, Diane, 3781
Haig, Kennethe M., 3194
Haig-Brown, Celia, 1997
Hale, Linda Louise, 1271, 1272, 1604, 2072, 2212, 3207
Haley, Ella, 1809
Haliburton, Gordon M., 1165
Hall, Alfreda, 3782
Hall, Constance, 312
Hall, M. Ann, 4177-4181
Hall, Mrs. Mary Georgina Caroline, 4388
Hall, Nancy, 3783
Hallett, Mary E., 1414, 1415, 3784-3786
Hallli, Shiva S., 1060, 1086
Hallman, Dianne M., 640, 2213
Halpenny, Frances G., 110
Halpern, Sylvie, 2455
Ham, Mary C., 1416
Hambleton, Ronald, 111
Hamel, Martine, 1087
Hamel, Nathalie, 3325
Hamel, Réginald, 112, 3195
Hamel, Thérèse, 641
Hamilton, Gordon, 2257
Hamilton, Marie, 716
Hamilton, Roberta, 1605-1607
Hamilton, Sylvia, 713-716, 3787
Hammerton, A. James, 770
Hancock, Carol L., 1417, 3788, 3789
Hansen, Barbara, 4447
Hanson, Christilot, 4182
Harding, Les, 3253
Hardy, Allison Taylor, 4680
Harkin, D., 1810
Harney, Robert F., 880
Harrigan, Patrick J., 538, 539, 642
Harris, Debbie Wise, 3196
Harris R. Cole, 771

Harrison, Deborah, 3448
Harrison, Marjorie, 772
Harrison, Phyllis, 773, 3055
Harshaw, Josephine P., 1811
Hart, Anne, 2540
Hart, Christopher , 2687
Hart, Fiona, 4136
Hart, Julia Catherine Beckwith, 113
Hart, Margaret J., 2320
Harvey, Cameron, 2943
Harvey, Dr. Robert, 1418
Harvey, Kathryn, 2783, 2784
Harvey, Kerridwen, 3326
Harvey, Robert Paton, 2321
Hathaway, Ann, 774
Hathaway, Debbie, 1812
Hauck, Philomena, 2104
Hawke, Liedewy, 1240
Hawley, Donna Lea, 1050, 2785
Hayden, Michael, 429, 540
Hayes, Brigid, 2749
Hayman, Sasha McInnes, 313
Hayward, Victoria, 314
Headon, Christopher, 3790
Heald, Susan, 393
Healey, Theresa, 2105
Healy, W.J., 2322
Heaman, Ken, 3327
Heap, Ruby, 383, 430, 541, 542, 643, 4681
Heath, T.C., 1608
Heath, Terrence, 1265
Hébert, Monique, 644
Hembroff-Schleicher, Edythe, 315, 316
Henderson, Mary Gillespie, 3791
Hénneguin, Jacques, 3984
Henripin, Jacques, 1088-1093
Henry, Ann, 3197
Herbert, Jacinth, 717
Heriot, Joan, 2323
Herman, Didi, 2887, 2888
Hernandez, Carmencita R., 1609
Hernandy, C., 1041
Heron, Craig,, 3056, 4553
Héroux, Liliane, 3985
Herring, D.A., 1094
Herringer, Barbara, 3095
Herrington, Walter S., 2324
Herson, Naomi, 4554
Hesketh, Bob, 3638
Hesse, M.G., 114
Hessing, Melody, 4459
Hett, Francis P., 775
Heward, S.A., 776
Hewitt, Molly, 1813
Hibbert, Joyce, 3449
Hicks, Anne, 1419
Hicks, Myrtle, 2325

P

Paramedical education, 411-412

Parent, Madeleine, 4286, 4298, 4316, 4329

Paris, ON 4657-4659

Parker, Elizabeth, 3259

Parlby, Irene, 1425, 3519, 3555

Parlow, Kathleen, 258, 271

Parr, Joy, 2228

Patterson, Dr. Margaret Norris, 2939, 2942

Patterson, Emily Susan, 2720

Pay equity, 1585, 1587, 1603, 1837, 2878, 2902, 4241, 4256-4257, 4266, 4291, 4337 (see also Affirmative action and Employment equity)

Peace activism, 502, 1429, 1455, 1441, 1572, 1653, 1676, 1682, 1688, 1703, 1727, 1737, 1763, 1830-1832, 1850

Peace River, 2284, 2328, 2543, 3824, 4412

Pension reform, 3039, 3099

Pensionnat Assomption, 532

Perry, Helen Sophia, 2367

Persons Case, 1425, 1448, 1652, 3668, 3670, 3696

Peterborough, 2302, 2836, 4327, 4597

Pharmacy, 2599, 4671-4673, 4689-4690, 4693

Photography, 299, 308, 322-324, 346-351, 373-374, 1163, 1856, 3327

Physiotherapy, 4669, 4676-4677, 4681, 4692

Pickthall, Marjorie, 171

Picture Brides
    Armenian, 899
    Japanese, 839, 856

Piercey, Rhoda Maude, 2647

Pinaud, Dame, 621

Pinkham, Mrs. W.C., 815

Pinzer, Maimie, 2358

Playwrights' Studio Group, 159

Polish women, 903-904

Political Equality League of Manitoba, 1812

Pornography, 1511, 1531, 1545, 1552, 1623, 1631, 1657, 3079

Port Coquitlam, BC, 1798

Postal workers, 4456, 4468

Poverty, 1485-1486, 3040, 3101, 3119

Powell, Anne Murray, 1171-1172, 3557, 3673

Powell, Anne, 1171, 1319

Powell, R. Janet, 3406

Prairie women, 2108, 2421 (see also Alberta, Manitoba, and Saskatchewan)
    and agriculture, 4377-4387, 4432
    and technology, 4092
    and the Grain Growers' Guide, 3169
    home remedies of, 2596
    in dance, 255
    in fiction, 12, 70, 172, 242
    pioneer cooking of, 3274
    work and feminism, 1736
    writers, 228

Prelate, SK, 4009

Presbyterian Church, 3738-3743, 3778-3779, 3783, 3810, 3818-3819, 3832, 3843

Press
    agricultural, in Quebec, 4436
    and abortion coverage, 3204
    and physical activity for women, 4198
    and R.E.A.L. Women, 1390
    and suffrage activism, 1615
    and violence against women, 1734, 2811
    and women's sports, 4218
    architectural, 287-288
    coverage of women's murders, 3242
    ethnicity and the, 1024
    image of women in *Le Devoir*, 3232
    labour, 918, 4301
    Miss Rye's children and the, 836
    sexism in newspapers, 3217

Preston, Isabella, 4112

Primrose, Olive Clare, 1282

Prince Edward Island, 2098 (see also Atlantic women; Charlottetown; Maritime women; and Montgomery, Lucy Maud)
    divorce on, 2993-2994
    Escheat Movement on, 3597
    feminist organizing on, 1699

Hospital School of Nursing, 2661
    Jarvis family of, 1150
    Scottish ancestry women on, 1496
    tourism on, 3244, 3262
    women's fashions on, 3340
    women's writings, 1482
    work of fisherman's wife on, 4739

Prison system, 2737-2738, 2749, 2765, 2772, 2793, 2800, 2839-2840, 3182

Prohibition (see Temperance)

Property rights
    and the Charter of Rights and Freedoms, 2852
    of farm women, 2983-2984
    of married women, 2959, 2966-2967

Prostitution
    and criminal justice, 2742, 2744, 2803, 2816-2820, 2829-2830, 2833
    and feminists, 1492, 1722
    and suicide, 2790
    and the Canadian Left, 3678
    and the filles du roi, 877, 882-883, 906
    and the North-West Mounted Police, 2786
    bibliography on, 2785
    in Calgary, 2747, 2779
    in Halifax, 2773
    in Hull, 2822
    in Montreal, 2358, 2795, 2830
    in Toronto, 2834
    in Vancouver, 2826
    in Winnipeg, 2764
    letters of Maimie Pinzer, 2358
    on the Prairies, 2782

Protestant
    Academies in Quebec, 622
    Homes for the Aged, 3027
    Orphans' Homes, 3087, 3114

Provincial Council of Women of Ontario, 1822

Psychiatry, 2575, 2585, 2617, 2623

Psychologists, 4667, 4674

Public service, 4688, 4691

Quakers, 579, 1301, 3252, 3780, 3823

Quebec 2139, 2142, 2145-2146, 2355, 2374, 2379, 2385, 2389-2390, 2403, 2405-2408, 2412-2413, 2430, 4004-4005 (see also Montreal, New France, and Quebec City)
    abortion struggle in, 2456-2458
    agricultural press and women's work, 4436
    and World War Two, 3416, 3434
    anti-pornography campaigns in, 1531
    archival holdings on women in, 2061, 2074, 2076, 2084
    attitudes toward women in, 1503
    bibliography on women in, 2099-2100, 2106-2107, 2109, 2122
    Catholic sex education in, 4132
    child welfare in, 2486-2487, 3030, 3041, 3069-3071, 3091, 3105
    childbirth in, 2515, 2524
    childhood in, 1251
    Children of Duplessis, 3042, 3049
    clothing industry in, 4647
    contraception in, 2459
    costume and fashion in, 3271, 3279, 3285-3286, 3319
    cotton workers in, 4638-4641, 4661
    dietetics in, 4676-4677
    divorce in, 2972, 2974
    doctors in, 2528
    domestic technology in, 4095
    Family Allowances in, 3028-3029, 3062-3064, 3083
    family incomes in, 1372
    family law in, 2986
    family life in, 1153, 1162, 1190, 1201
    female criminality in, 2774, 2794
    female religious communities in, 3884, 3896, 3930-3932, 3943, 3952-3969, 3978, 3991-3992, 3997-4001, 4010-4011